S0-ASJ-416

₱ 22.50

Jennet Walker Doernberg

The
Current History
Encyclopedia
of
Developing
Nations

Jennet Walker Doernberg

EDITED BY

Carol L. Thompson

Mary M. Anderberg

Joan B. Antell

CONSULTING EDITORS

Marvin Alisky *Professor of Political Science,*
Arizona State University, Tempe, Arizona

Dwight B. Heath *Professor of Anthropology,*
Brown University, Providence, Rhode Island

Richard W. Hull *Professor of History,*
New York University, New York, New York

Virginia Curtin Knight *Associate Editor,*
Current History, Furlong, Pennsylvania

Jon Kraus *Professor of Political Science,*
State University of New York, Fredonia, New York

William H. Lewis *Professor of Political Science,*
George Washington University, and Senior Associate of the Carnegie Endowment
for International Peace, Washington, D.C.

Jan S. Prybyla *Professor of Economics,*
Pennsylvania State University, University Park, Pennsylvania

Aaron Segal *Division of International Programs,*
National Science Foundation, Washington, D.C.

Elbert P. Thompson *Vice President,*
Current History Inc., Furlong, Pennsylvania

Arthur Campbell Turner *Professor of Political Science,*
University of California, Riverside, California

Brian Weinstein *Professor of Political Science,*
Howard University, Washington, D.C.

Warren Weinstein *Country Director, U.S. Peace Corps, Ivory Coast*

The
Current History
Encyclopedia
of
Developing
Nations

McGraw-Hill Book Company

New York St. Louis San Francisco Auckland
Bogotá Hamburg Johannesburg London
Madrid Mexico Montreal New Delhi
Panama São Paulo Singapore
Sydney Tokyo Toronto

Library of Congress Cataloging in Publication Data

Main entry under title:

The Current History encyclopedia of developing nations.
    Includes index.
    1. Underdeveloped areas.   I. Thompson, Carol L.
II. Anderberg, Mary M.   III. Antell, Joan B.
HC59.7.C83   909'.0972'4   80-21623

ISBN 0-07-064387-3

Copyright © 1982 by McGraw-Hill, Inc. All rights reserved.
Printed in the United States of America. No part of this
publication may be reproduced, stored in a retrieval system,
or transmitted, in any form or by any means, electronic,
mechanical, photocopying, recording, or otherwise, without
the prior written permission of the publisher.

1 2 3 4 5 6 7 8 9 0   HDHD   8 9 8 7 6 5 4 3 2 1

The editors for this book were Robert Rosenbaum, Dorothy Young, and Ann Gray;
the designer was Naomi Auerbach; and the production supervisor
was Sally Fliess. It was set in Trump Mediaeval
by Waldman Graphics.

It was printed and bound by Halliday Lithograph.

Contents

Central America and the Caribbean 283

South America 329

Contributors

Kenneth L. Adelman
Senior Political Scientist
Strategic Studies Center
SRI International
Washington, D.C.

Marvin Alisky
Professor of Political Science
Arizona State University
Tempe, Arizona

Rolando A. Alum, Jr.
Professor of Anthropology
Center for Labor Studies
Empire State College
State University of New York
New York, New York

Robin L. Anderson
Assistant Professor of Latin
    American History
Arkansas State University
State University, Arkansas

Belinda A. Aquino
Professor of Political Science and
    Director of Philippine Studies
University of Hawaii
Honolulu, Hawaii

Peter Bechtold
Chairman, Near East and North
    African Studies
Foreign Service Institute
Rosslyn, Virginia

Salvatore Bizzarro
Associate Professor of Spanish and
    Latin American Studies
The Colorado College
Colorado Springs, Colorado

W. A. Bladen
Associate Professor of Geography
University of Kentucky
Lexington, Kentucky

Richard Butwell
Vice President for Academic
    Programs and Professor of
    Political Science
Murray State University
Murray, Kentucky

Louis J. Cantori
Associate Professor of Political
    Science
University of Maryland
Baltimore, Maryland

Rita Cassidy
Associate Professor of History
Saint Mary's College
Notre Dame, Indiana

Joseph S. Chung
Professor of Economics and
    Chairman of the Department of
    Economics and Finance
Illinois Institute of Technology
Chicago, Illinois

John L. Collier
Chairman of African Studies
Foreign Service Institute
Rosslyn, Virginia

Frank C. Darling
Professor of Political Science
De Pauw University
Greencastle, Indiana

Arthur J. Dommen
Department of State
Washington, D.C.

Stephen A. Douglas
Associate Professor of Political
    Science
University of Illinois
Urbana-Champaign, Illinois

Alasdair Drysdale
Assistant Professor of Geography
University of New Hampshire
Durham, New Hampshire

Tissa Fernando
Associate Professor of Sociology
University of British Columbia
Vancouver, B.C.

William J. Fleming
Assistant Professor of History
Indiana University—Purdue
    University
Indianapolis, Indiana

John E. Frazer
Writer on India
Philadelphia, Pennsylvania

Kenneth W. Grundy
Professor of Political Science
Case Western Reserve University
Cleveland, Ohio

Raymond Hames
Assistant Professor of Anthropology
Pennsylvania State University
University Park, Pennsylvania

Dwight B. Heath
Professor of Anthropology
Brown University
Providence, Rhode Island

James D. Henderson
Associate Professor of History
Grambling State University
Grambling, Louisiana

Thomas H. Henriksen
National Fellow of the Hoover
    Institution
Stanford University
Stanford, California

Geoffrey S. Howard
Visiting Lecturer
Fordham University
Bronx, New York

Russell Warren Howe
Writer on Africa
Washington, D.C.

List of Contributors

Richard W. Hull
Professor of History
New York University
New York, New York

Hans H. Indorf
Legislative Staff Director for
Senator Robert Morgan
Washington, D.C.

Nake M. Kamrany
Professor of Economics
University of Southern California
Los Angeles, California

P. P. Karan
Professor of Geography
University of Kentucky
Lexington, Kentucky

Ramon Knauerhase
Professor of Economics
University of Connecticut
Storrs, Connecticut

Jon Kraus
Professor of Political Science
State University of New York
Fredonia, New York

René Lemarchand
Professor of Political Science
University of Florida
Gainesville, Florida

Victor T. Le Vine
Professor of Political Science
Washington University
St. Louis, Missouri

William H. Lewis
Professor of Political Science
Sino-Soviet Institute
George Washington University
Washington, D.C.

R. Doss Mabe
Lecturer in Anthropology
Yale University
New Haven, Connecticut

John D. Martz
Professor and Chairman of the
Department of Political Science
Pennsylvania State University
University Park, Pennsylvania

Ronald H. McDonald
Professor and Chairperson of the
Department of Political Science
The Maxwell School
Syracuse University
Syracuse, New York

Riall W. Nolan
Planning and Development
Collaborative International
Washington, D.C.

J. Norman Parmer
Professor of History and Vice
President for Academic Affairs
Trinity University
San Antonio, Texas

B. Marie Perinbam
Associate Professor of African
History
University of Maryland
College Park, Maryland

James J. Phillips
Assistant Professor of Anthropology
Franklin Pierce College
Rindge, New Hampshire

Peter A. Poole
Director of the Center for
International Studies
Old Dominion University
Norfolk, Virginia

Jan S. Prybyla
Professor of Economics
Pennsylvania State University
University Park, Pennsylvania

M. Rashiduzzaman
Associate Professor of Political
Science
Glassboro State College
Glassboro, New Jersey

Robert A. Rupen
Professor of Political Science
University of North Carolina
Chapel Hill, North Carolina

John T. Scholz
Assistant Professor of Political
Science
State University of New York
Stony Brook, New York

Ann T. Schultz
Associate Professor of Government
and International Relations
Clark University
Worcester, Massachusetts

Peter Schwab
Associate Professor of Political
Science
State University of New York
Purchase, New York

Aaron Segal
Division of International Programs
National Science Foundation
Washington, D.C.

Elman R. Service
Professor of Anthropology
University of California
Santa Barbara, California

Feraidoon Shams B.
Assistant Professor of Social Science
Howard University
Washington, D.C.

L. Edward Shuck, Jr.
Director of International Programs
Bowling Green State University
Bowling Green, Ohio

Dwight James Simpson
Professor of International Relations
San Francisco State University
San Francisco, California

Shirin Tahir-Kheli
Assistant Professor of Political
Science
Temple University
Philadelphia, Pennsylvania

Arthur Campbell Turner
Professor of Political Science
University of California
Riverside, California

Victor C. Uchendu
Director of the African Studies
Center and Professor of
Anthropology
University of Illinois
Urbana-Champaign, Illinois

George Volsky
Research Associate
Center for Advanced International
Studies
University of Miami
Miami, Florida

Brian Weinstein
Professor of Political Science
Howard University
Washington, D.C.

Warren Weinstein
Country Director
U.S. Peace Corps
Ivory Coast

David P. Werlich
Associate Professor of History and
Chairman of the Latin American
Studies Program
Southern Illinois University
Carbondale, Illinois

Norman E. Whitten, Jr.
Professor of Anthropology
University of Illinois
Urbana-Champaign, Illinois

Preface

This book evaluates the developing nations in terms of the ways in which they satisfy the basic human needs of their citizens. The focus is on people under pressure of economic development. Ninety-three developing countries with populations of more than 1 million are included; specifically excluded are the centrally planned Eastern European countries and the world's industrial nations. The culture, politics, and history of each country are discussed briefly, along with each country's potential for development.

The articles are arranged regionally and within each region alphabetically; an area map introduces each section.

In the statistical boxes that introduce each article, the editors have selected population totals and growth rates and gross national product figures from the *World Bank Atlas.*

Some statistical material has been furnished by the authors; other statistics are drawn from reports of the World Bank, the State Department, the United Nations, and other reliable sources. Unfortunately, accurate statistical material is not available in every instance; the authors have evaluated whatever data they have been able to acquire.

Valuable assistance for this project was provided by our staff of consulting editors and by officials at the World Bank, the U.S. Departments of State and Commerce, and the United Nations.

C. L. T.

The *Current History* Encyclopedia of Developing Nations

Africa
South
of
the
Sahara

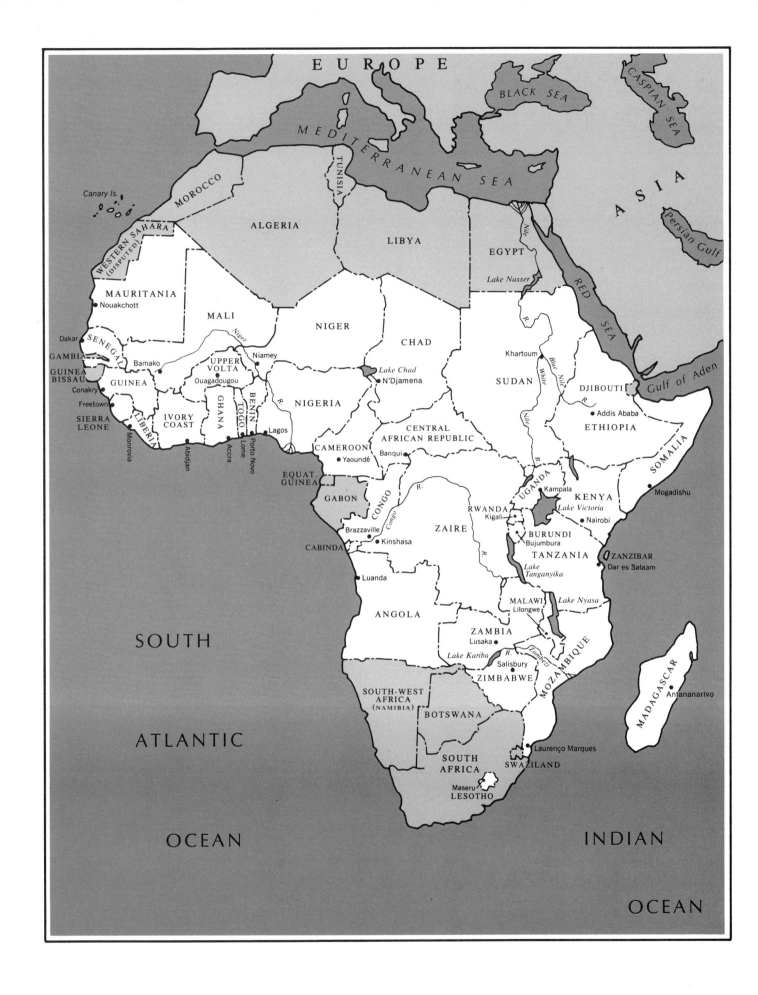

Angola

(People's Republic of Angola)

Area: 481,351 sq mi (1,246,699 sq km)
Population: 6.7 million
  Density: 14 per sq mi (5 per sq km)
  Growth rate: 2.3% (1970–1977)
Percent of population under 14 years of age: 42%
Infant deaths per 1,000 live births: 86 (1960)
Life expectancy at birth: 41.8 years
Leading causes of death: not available
Ethnic composition: Ovimbundu 33%; Mbundu 25%;
  Kongo 15%
Languages: African languages, Portuguese
Literacy: 10%
Religions: animist (majority); Roman Catholic
Percent population urban: 20–30%
Percent population rural: 70–80%
Gross national product: $2 billion
  Per capita GNP: $300 (est.)
  Per capital GNP growth rate: −3.4% (1970–1977)
Inflation rate: not available

Angola is a large nation, comprising some 481,351 square miles (about 1.25 million sq km) in southwest Africa. Bordered by Zaire, Zambia, and Namibia, it occupies a key location and serves as a transportation link to the Atlantic Ocean. In 1975–1976, Angola captured the world's spotlight with its brutal civil war, triggered by Portuguese decolonization. Three large ethnic-political factions went into full battle, and Soviet-Cuban intervention occurred on a scale never before seen in Africa. The scars of that civil war are evident in the continuing Cuban presence, the United States refusal to extend diplomatic recognition, and the delay in improving the living standards of the people. Angola needs food, a basic infrastructure, roads, railroads, and health and medical facilities; fulfillment of all these needs has been postponed by the continuing struggles within the nation.

Angola's terrain varies from heavily wooded hills and patches of forest in the north to flat, dry brushland and barren desert in the south. It holds vast mineral wealth, although much of Angola remains unexplored and unexploited.

Angola contains approximately 7 million people; its average population density is 14 persons per square mile (5 persons per square kilometer). Most of the population lives along the coast; there are fewer than 3 people per square mile (1.2 per sq km) in the eastern two-thirds of the country. Angola's immense size and sparse population make for an underpopulation problem, one which is unlikely to be remedied soon. Between 1960 and 1970, Angola's average annual growth rate was a mere 1.6 percent, small by African standards. The population today is almost entirely black and mulatto; 90 percent are illiterate. Although before independence Roman Catholicism was the official religion, most Angolans today follow traditional African religions.

Before independence in November 1975, the white population of Angola was considerable, the second largest (after South Africa) on the entire continent. This population grew rapidly in the decade and a half before independence. Though Portugal administered the territory on paper for over 5 centuries, it left it relatively untouched until modern times. Indeed, Angola's white population was miniscule until the regime of Antônio de Oliveira Salazar first encouraged settlement during the 1930s and 1940s. The flow of whites into Angola speeded up after World War II and eventually reached over 305,000. During Angola's devastating civil war (1975–1976), all but a handful of whites were airlifted out.

Angola's current population consists of three large ethnic groups. The largest, the Ovimbundu, constitute perhaps one-third of the entire population and live in the central highlands and the south. The Mbundu (or Kimbundu), nearly one-fourth of the population, live in the capital city of Luanda and eastward, and have most readily adopted Portuguese ways. The Kongo (or Bakongo) make up 15 percent of the population and live in the north.

The ethnic identity of these three groups took on a political coloration during and after the civil war. Most of the Kongos belonged to the Angolan National Liberation Front (FNLA), the victorious Angolan Popular Liberation Movement (MPLA) was made up of Mbundu, and the Ovimbundu generally support the still-battling National Union for Total Angolan Independence (UNITA) faction. Ethnic and political affiliations remain strong; mutual antagonisms remain fierce.

Angola's internal conflict is accompanied by an appalling lack of education and skilled labor. Angola's literacy rate is estimated at between 10 and 15 percent, but even this estimate may be an exaggeration. The Portuguese did virtually nothing to help educate the indigenous population until after the 1960 uprising. Colonial authorities claimed that primary school enrollment eventually reached one-third of those eligible, and secondary school enrollment, one-tenth, but these figures (probably exaggerated) included large numbers of whites. Angola's only university was built and run primarily for whites.

The tiny number of educated and skilled Angolans came from the assimilado (literally, "assimilated") population. To qualify as an assimilado, according to Portuguese standards, an individual had to be considered "cultured," i.e., literate, comfortable in Portuguese habits and customs. Assimilados comprised 1 percent or less of the entire Angolan black population in 1960 and only slightly more in 1970. Most Angolans categorized as assimilados were in fact mulattos. This condition endures; the MPLA, a Marxist clique which forms today's ruling Angolan elite, is predominantly composed of mulattos once considered assimilados.

In December 1977 the MPLA was formally transformed into a Marxist-Leninist party. President Agostinho Neto, who had won the civil war in 1976 with Soviet and Cuban help, ended the first MPLA party congress by announcing that membership on the ruling central committee would be restricted to those with at least "eight years of faithful militancy" behind them. When Neto died in a plane crash in September 1979, he was succeeded by José Eduardo dos Santos.

President Neto restricted political involvement in Angola exclusively to MPLA members and categorically refused to permit any type of coalition with members of the other liberation movements, even though the MPLA is said to enjoy the support of less than 20 percent of all Angolans.Other liberation movements, particularly UNITA, continue to cause problems. With an estimated 20,000 guerrillas (compared with 3,000 in 1974), UNITA claims to control over one-third of Angola—the southern and southeastern regions inhabited by 2.5 million people. While this claim may be disputed, UNITA's effectiveness is evident. It has disrupted the opening of the Benguela railroad and has broken other transportation links into major cities as well.

Political and security problems have thus far prevented Angola from becoming the wealthy nation it could be. Because of its vast natural resources and well-developed transportation network, Angola was a fairly prosperous Portuguese colony. In the early 1970s, Angola's rate of economic growth was an impressive 6 percent annually. The nation attained a per capita gross national product of slightly over $500— respectable among sub-Saharan African states—and had a total GNP estimated at $3 billion in 1974.

The civil war fundamentally altered the picture. The violent battles are said to have resulted in from 100,000 to 300,000 fatalities and considerable eco-

Newly harvested coffee beans are being dried at a government coffee plantation in the small town of Gabela. (Photo: United Nations/ J. P. Laffont.)

nomic damage. Angola's foreign minister estimated total war damage at between $600 million and $700 million (roughly four times the total 1976 receipts of the Angolan government.) Such estimates are clearly inflated, but the war was ravaging. Of even greater long-term significance, the war prompted the flight of skilled white manpower. Many of the whites were born in Angola and intended to remain if stability came with independence. Their departure caused shortages of skilled labor in agriculture, industry, the services, and government administration.

In addition, the war accentuated deep and bitter tribal antagonisms. Kongo, supporting the FNLA, and Ovimbundu, supporting UNITA, became more bitterly opposed to the Mbundu-based MPLA government. Many FNLA and UNITA members subsequently retreated into the rural areas (often to avoid any Cuban or Mbundu retaliation) and thus withdrew themselves from the money economy, to which they had been contributing. Finally, the new Angolan government assumed office without political experience, in part because of the lack of political participation in Portugal (for decades under tough dictatorship) and in its colonies.

These factors contributed to Angola's economic decline. The few reports which have leaked out of Angola since the civil war paint a dismal economic picture of food riots, epidemics, and general hardship in the urban areas. Most crops, including the once lucrative coffee, are no longer being planted in significant quantities. Medical services are scarce; malnutrition is said to be widespread. The school system is crippled; only 1 percent of the secondary school instructors are currently teaching.

The Angolan government is intent on boosting the nation's economy. At present, however, the government has more pressing priorities: increasing its political stability (avoiding another coup attempt) and improving its military situation by gaining territory now under UNITA control.

Under colonialism, agricultural production was split into a European sector of large-scale and relatively capital-intensive units employing 200,000 to 300,000 blacks and an African sector of small-scale and relatively undeveloped units. Today, because the European sector has disappeared, virtually all agriculture in Angola consists of subsistence farming, engaged in by between three-fourths and four-fifths of the population. There are few means of transportation into the cities and little excess production for the city dwellers. Urban Angolans are existing day to day, enduring the hardships and bracing themselves for a long period of adjustment. Much of the best agricultural land remains under UNITA control. Few agricultural products can be exported. Some estimates indicate that the 1976 coffee crop was down some 85 percent from the previous year; the figures for 1977 were reportedly even worse. Angola's prosperous cattle ranches—an estimated 3 million to 4.5 million herd existed in 1973—and timber from the small en-

*Far Left:
On the pavement in
front of the Bank of
Angola building in
Luanda, women sell
fish and other farm
products. (Photo:
United Nations/
J. P. Laffont.)*

colony. Unlike the territories administered by the British, French, and Belgians, Portuguese colonies were left relatively undeveloped. Because Portugal was the least developed West European country and had few resources of its own, it did not invest resources for basic development efforts, particularly in the countryside. Lacking the means of exploitation, Portugal wished to exclude all foreign activities in its territories. This policy was somewhat altered in the 1960s when Angola's vast potential was first realized. By the time of independence, natural resources constituted the bulk of Angola's export earnings: oil led the way as the primary earner, diamonds were in third place after coffee, and iron followed in fourth.

The Gulf Oil Company of the United States exploited the oil resources offshore Cabinda, which became the backbone of Angola's foreign trade. Revenue from oil grew from nothing to more than 40 percent of Angola's export revenue during the final 8 years of colonialism, accounting for two-thirds of the growth in Angola's export earnings during that period. Estimates place preindependence oil production at 150,000 barrels per day (7.5 million tons or 6.75 million metric tons, per year); there are plans to increase production to around 200,000 barrels per day over the coming years.

Oil production is currently up to preindependence levels, but this is true of no other segment of Angola's

clave of Cabinda have, for the most part, been left unattended.

Rural Angolans continue to work their subsistence farms, relatively unaffected by the decline in the money economy. Because transportation for the small surpluses they previously sold in local markets is lacking, little commerce is taking place in the interior.

Because of its limited resources and authority, the Angolan government has concentrated on improving economic conditions in the urban areas. Soon after independence in 1975, the government nationalized Portuguese holdings: banks, insurance companies, stores, factories, and plantations. This was a relatively painless move since most of the Portuguese managers and owners had already departed. At the time, the government exempted non-Portuguese concerns like Cabinda Gulf Oil, the major U.S. investor in Angola, and DIAMANG, the major foreign-owned mining consortium.

In August 1976, the new government revealed its list of top economic priorities. These included: controlling the labor situation, particularly in the ports; repairing the highway bridges and highways destroyed during the war; and encouraging the migration of workers into regions producing coffee, cotton, sisal, and other agricultural products in order to increase production.

Angola was settled as an agricultural and mining

*Off the coast of oil-
rich Cabinda, oil
exploration
continues. Oil
provides valuable
export earnings for
the nation's
economy. (Photo:
United Nations/
J. P. Laffont.)*

economy. Cabinda Gulf, a subsidiary of Gulf Oil, provides some $600 million per year to the Angolan government.

Iron ore has been mined in Angola's central highlands, reputed to contain one of the world's richest deposits of high-grade ore. Diamonds have been mined by DIAMANG, an international consortium that includes South African, Belgian, British, and American firms. Previously, the company had virtual sovereignty over its mines, located near the Zairian border. It maintained its own army guards at the boundaries, operated on a time zone different from the rest of the country, and imported equipment and exported diamonds under a special agreement that exempted its transactions from normal Angolan duties.

Angola represents one of Africa's last frontiers. Because of its huge size and relatively small population, its location in rich southern Africa, and its limited preindependence development, Angola has vast stretches of unexplored and undeveloped lands. Along with Nigeria and South Africa, Angola could well emerge as one of the richest of all African states in the coming decades.

Furthermore, Angola will be a—if not the—key country in Central Africa. It sits astride vital shipping lanes; has excellent ports, airfields, and a developed inland transportation network; and is rich in natural minerals. It is rather self-sufficient and has neighbors, Zaire and Zambia, that depend heavily on its railroads and ports for their own economic prosperity.

For the time being, however, Angola's political, economic, and security problems do not offer much

hope for rapid development or prosperity. The country is in a state of internal disarray and instability. Increasingly under attack because of its ideological rigidity and inability to compromise with opponents, the MPLA leadership—and the party itself—has fallen prey to increasing factionalization.

Were its political and military troubles solved, Angola's prospects would become exceptionally bright almost overnight. Despite the devastation of the civil war, Angola retains a basic infrastructure on which real economic gains can be realized. It has a well-developed transportation system: ports at Luanda and Lobito are among the finest on the continent; the highway system is one of Africa's best; and three railroad systems, terminating at Luanda, Benguela/Lobito, and Mocamedes, link these cities to the interior and to neighboring Zaire and Zambia. Angola also has substantial facilities for the production of hydroelectric power and potential for much greater production, rich agricultural and cattle-grazing lands, staggering mineral wealth, and a low population density.

The country could easily become not only self-sufficient in foodstuffs, but a breadbasket for Africa, exporting sugar cane, rice, wheat, peanuts, tobacco, cashews, olives, and many other products. Its fishing industry could provide essential protein to large areas of the continent. Its mineral potential seems exceptional. But for the moment at least, Angola's vast potential wealth and promise are overshadowed by the even vaster problems and difficulties facing the new nation.

Kenneth L. Adelman

Benin
(People's Republic of Benin)

Area: 43,483 sq mi (112,620 sq km)
Population: 3.3 million
  Density: 76 per sq mi (29 per sq km)
  Growth rate: 2.9% (1970–1977)
Percent of population under 14 years of age: 45%
Infant deaths per 1,000 live births: 40% die before age of 5
Life expectancy at birth: 41 years
Leading causes of death: malaria or malaria-related diseases
Ethnic composition: Fon, Yoruba, Bariba, 40 others
Languages: French (official), Kirundi
Literacy: 20%
Religions: animist, Vodun 65%; Christian 15%; Muslim 13%
Percent population urban: 10% (est.)
Percent population rural: 90% (est.)
Gross national product: $770 million
  Per capita GNP: $230
  Per capita GNP growth rate: 0.5% (1970–1977)
Inflation rate: not available

Benin, known in colonial and post-independence times as Dahomey, has suffered many coups d'etat and changes of government in the past two decades, and is relatively isolated from its neighbors, Togo and Nigeria. Its fractious present reflects a turbulent past, when the country was wracked by slaving and tribal wars and was governed, at least in the south, by traditional regimes of extraordinary harshness and cruelty. Benin has a history of fratricidal and patricidal intrigues. Today, like Haiti, its ethnic descendant, it is a country of intense poverty, even by regional standards, set in a landscape of haunting beauty.

In a curious break with the country's famous past, in 1975, the ancient name Dahomey was dropped in favor of People's Republic of Benin, a name taken from the Bight of Benin, which in turn takes its name from the ancient kingdom of Benin, now a central-southern state in the federation of Nigeria.

A narrow sliver of territory about 400 miles (640 km) long from north to south and about 75 miles (120 km) wide at the coast, Benin was carved out of West Africa at the Berlin Congress of 1884–1885 as a French possession, bounded by Germany's Togo to the west and Britain's Nigeria to the east. To the north, Benin borders Upper Volta and Niger, which are also French-speaking.

Behind Benin's swampy coast, peppered with lagoons, lie a thinly forested interior and a hilly north. Benin's principal southern peoples are the Fon and the Yoruba. There are over forty other ethnic groups: the most numerous in the north is the Bariba.

Before independence, Dahomey had the highest level of literacy in French-speaking Africa, and today over 20 percent of the population understands French, the official language. The population numbers over 3 million, concentrated in a country about the size of Pennsylvania. Life expectancy is 41 years, and about 40 percent of the population dies before the age of five.

Known on old maps as the Slave Coast, Benin's south was formerly a Portuguese trading center. The inland kingdom of Dahomey, with its capital at Abomey, was of continual interest to eighteenth and nineteenth century explorers and traders. Its economy was based on the slave trade, and so numerous were Dahomey's exports of slaves that today there are considerably more persons of Dahomeyan origin outside the country than inside: most of the population of Haiti is thought to be of Dahomeyan extraction, and hundreds of thousands of people of Dahomeyan descent live in Brazil.

The French brought considerable Christianization, and about 15 percent of the population—mostly in the south—is Roman Catholic. Muslims, nearly all in the poor northern region, about equal Christians in number. Most Dahomeyans, including many Christians and Muslims, are also devoted to the traditional faiths, some of surpassing complexity, the best known being *vodun* (known as voodoo in Haiti, Brazil, and elsewhere). Traditional West African family patterns prevail, and most land is vested in the tribe.

All Beninese official statistics have been declared secret since 1975, but it is known that over 90 percent of the Beninese are subsistence farmers. Per capita yearly income is estimated to be about $150. The economy has been virtually stagnant for many years, and the imbalance of trade is about 33 percent. The attempted communalization of tribal land—in effect, the attempt to transform family holdings into collective farms—has, by and large, failed because of lack of popular support. There are shortages of many essential and semiessential goods, and trade with Nigeria in smuggled goods thrives. But for an authoritarian state, repression is modest. It is believed that there are fewer than 100 political prisoners, most of them connected with the abortive coup in 1977.

Exports, totaling about $100 million in 1978, consist of oil palm products, cotton, kapok, copra, peanuts, and some low-grade coffee. Cotton production has fallen by about 66 percent since 1972, and palm oil production has fallen recently because of diminished rainfalls. Benin's principal trading partners are France, other members of the European Economic Community, Nigeria, and Ivory Coast. The port of Cotonou has benefited from the bottlenecks at Nigeria's Lagos harbor, which led many European, Japanese, and American exporters of goods to Nigeria to unload at Cotonou for transshipment. The government is far and away the principal employer of wage earners, although about half a million people are modest independent traders. The most important light industries produce textiles, shoes, beer, and cement. The largest industrial operation is the 2,000-employee cotton-cloth plant at Parakou. A second cement plant, financed by the Saudis, is to be constructed near Cotonou.

French trade and influence began to supplant that of Brazil and Portugal in the late nineteenth century. After the Berlin Congress (1884–1885), France began the conquest of the country, finally subjugating it in 1892. Dahomey was one of the territories of French West Africa, ruled by a governor general whose office was in Dakar, Senegal.

Two young boys stand beside a dry-store hut that they built for a farmer's club project. (Photo: FAO/Caracciolo/Banoun.)

Dahomey achieved independence in 1960, at the same time as most of the other French territories in Africa. The first President, Hubert Maga, was overthrown by a military coup in 1963, inspired by the coup in neighboring Togo. Three more coups, partly inspired by similar developments in Nigeria and Ghana, followed in the next 4 years.

Civilian government was restored under Emile-Dersin Zinsou, a physician and former foreign minister, in 1968, but the following year another military coup drove Zinsou into exile. A popular figure, Zinsou was condemned to death in absentia in order to ensure his continued absence.

Some civilian leaders, including Maga, were invited to participate in the government, in the hope of attracting French support for the junta. But in 1972 this semimilitary government was overthrown by a sixth coup, led by Major Mathieu Kerekou, who has remained in power ever since. In 1977, Dahomeyan exiles aided by European private legionnaires landed at Cotonou airport and attempted to seize the capital, but they were driven off.

Kerekou introduced a radical, revolutionary regime, claiming to follow Marxist-Leninist doctrines. The nationalization of all foreign enterprises was announced, and most of the small European and Lebanese population left the country; in fact, many of their enterprises were placed in private—albeit native—hands. Later an ostensibly liberal foreign-investment code was introduced with little success.

Under the Kerekou regime, Benin is ruled by decrees issued by President (and party chairman) Kerekou himself, advised by a council of ministers chosen by the President and by a party central committee headed by a six-member politburo. The National Revolutionary Council serves as a rubber-stamp legislature. The judicial system, patterned on the French, is being revised. The country's former chief justice, Louis Ignacio-Pinto, was for many years a familiar figure at the International Court of Justice at The Hague.

Benin maintains limited political ties with France and with other former French colonies and belongs, on a largely inactive basis, to regional associations, but it has also broadened its relations with Communist states. Benin's armed forces are supplied by the Soviet Union, North Korea, and France. The country continues to receive limited aid from the United States ($600,000 in 1979, plus $400,000 of Public Law 480 food aid because of semidrought), but its relations with Washington are limited.

Planning for the development of Benin's infrastructure has focused on the nation's geographical advantage as a maritime access for Nigeria and Niger. A $41-million project that would double the capacity of Cotonou's port is under consideration by a consortium of international donors headed by the World Bank. The road from Cotonou to the Niger border is being resurfaced with the aid of French, American, and World Bank financing. Nigeria is helping to widen and resurface the Lagos-Cotonou road, and transcoastal transport, including transport to the west (to Togo, Ghana), will be facilitated by a new bridge now being constructed across the Cotonou lagoon with international assistance, including help from the United States. In the long run, the influence of neighboring Nigeria seems sure to be a decisive factor in Benin's economic and political development.

Benin has excellent tourist potential—superb beaches, lagoon villages built on stilts, and the fascinating old capital at Abomey, in addition to wild boar and antelope hunting—but the present regime is cautious about encouraging visitors, and this attitude seems likely to continue unless there is a change of government. A new airport hotel is, however, under construction at Cotonou, and a new tourist lodge is being built in the Pendjari game reserve in the north. A new beach hotel in Cotonou and another at Grand Popo, on the Togolese border, are planned. The People's Republic of China is building a sports and convention complex.

Despite its poor economic performance and a decline in administrative efficiency, caused in part by the departure of members of the old Dahomeyan elite, Benin's traditional acceptance of rigid rule, dating from precolonial times, gives support to the Cuba-type system that the junta is trying to create. On the other hand, the now well-established tradition of (largely bloodless) coups makes the future unpredictable.

President Kerekou's ideal is a stimulated, indoctrinated society patterned on Cuba that can shake off the inhibitions of tradition and religion to build a proud, modern nation with appropriate technology. But lethargy and corruption, fear and resignation have so far proved insuperable, and the kind of risk on questionable regimes investors were sometimes prepared to take in the 1960s is no longer in fashion. Today, a disproportionately large crop of intellectuals dream and plot in Benin, and each new wave of discontent leads to still another junta. But every successive junta finds that without money, natural resources, or a vigorous and hardworking "revolutionary" population, Benin cannot prosper.

Russell Warren Howe

Burundi

(Republic of Burundi)

Area: **10,747 sq mi (27,834 sq km)**
Population: **4.3 million**
  Density: **400 per sq mi (154 per sq km)**
  Growth rate: **1.9% (1970–1977)**
Percent of population under 14 years of age: **51%**
Infant deaths per 1,000 live births: **160**
Life expectancy at birth: **males 40 years; females 43 years**
Leading causes of death: **Infectious and parasitic diseases**
Ethnic composition: **Hutu 80%; Tutsi 19%; Twa 1%**
Languages: **Kirundi, French, Swahili**
Literacy: **10%**
Religions: **Christian 50%; Muslim 15%; traditional**
Percent population urban: **not available**
Percent population rural: **not available**
Gross national product: **$610 million**
  Per capita GNP: **$140**
  Per capita GNP growth rate: **0.6% (1970–1977)**
Inflation rate: **15% (1974–1978)**

The remote landlocked state of Burundi in central Africa may face a crisis of survival before the end of the century. Burundi is one of the world's poorest countries, and the quality of life there is one of the world's lowest. Less than half the population are able-bodied adults; this ratio explains the very low per capita income, $90 a year, with as little as $40 to $50 a year in rural areas. The population continues to grow at a rate of between 2.1 and 2.8 percent, although a 1 percent emigration rate means that net growth may be only 1.2 to 1.8 percent a year. Nevertheless, Burundi's population—4 million—will have doubled by the year 2005.

Emigrants from Burundi seek economic opportunities in the larger, neighboring states of Tanzania, Uganda, and Zaire. Emigration is also partly the result of continuing ethnic tensions between the dominant Tutsi, a numerical minority of about 20 percent, and the Hutu majority, who are more or less excluded from power. In 1972–1973, almost a quarter of a million Hutu were killed or forced into exile by the Tutsi after an aborted Hutu uprising. Since then, Hutu refugees have continued to try to escape the harshness of ethnic discrimination.

Burundi is a breathtakingly beautiful country that straddles the Congo (Zaire)-Nile watershed, with seemingly unending hills dotted with indigenous homesteads known as *rugos*. Most hills are topped with a small wood, the result of efforts at reforestation. Between the hills are marshlands and streams, which wind their way to Africa's mighty Nile to the north and Zaire River to the west. In the early morning mist, the hills are foreboding as they rise abruptly from the shores of Lake Tanganyika. In the past, the hills formed a natural fortress and protected Burundi against marauding Arab slavers during the nineteenth century.

Burundi's physical quality of life index (PQLI) is 23, one of the world's lowest. This index is based on an average of ratings for life expectancy (40 years for a boy, 43 for a girl), infant mortality (in the range of 160 per 1,000) and literacy (estimated at 10 percent, with functional literacy probably even lower). About 6 percent of the population is familiar with French; the others speak Kirundi, the national language. There is a significant community of Swahili speakers in the capital, and Swahili is understood along the coast of Lake Tanganyika and in some administrative centers.

Agricultural production is declining as a result of overcropping and lack of adequate fertilizers. As supplies of firewood dwindle and because alternate fuels are too expensive for the rural population, even crop residues are being used as an energy source. Demographic pressures are forcing new households to move to increasingly marginal lands. The average population density is 400 per square mile (154 per sq km) on agricultural land, and cash crops are grown on 37 percent of the land under use. Pasture accounts for 23 percent and forests for another 3 percent. Pasture is increasingly being diverted to crops, but pasture lands tend to be of poor quality. Existing arable land is not well managed.

Rural Burundians have three main sources of cash income: food crops, cash crops, and herding. (The Twa, a pygmoid ethnic group numbering at most 1 percent of the population, engage in artisanry.) Coffee is the major cash crop, and approximately 400,000 small producers grow coffee in northern and central Burundi. In Ngozi Province, where most coffee is grown, the average farm family is estimated to have an annual cash income of $390, of which 36 percent comes from coffee. By means of controlled prices and heavy taxation, the government siphons off most of the coffee proceeds, although producer prices have been increased in recent years in order to reduce smuggling.

As a result of rises in world coffee prices, Burundi is registering a current account balance surplus, and reserves by late 1977 amounted to about $86 million, equivalent to ten months of imports. Government investment in agriculture is lopsided in favor of coffee, tea, and other export crops. The country's heavy dependence on coffee earnings for foreign exchange makes the economy vulnerable to market fluctuations, weather conditions, and the biological cycle of the coffee trees. A recent upward trend in coffee prices will help Burundi, but the negative impact of the continuing transport difficulties caused by the war between Uganda and Tanzania augur poorly for Burundi's immediate economic future.

Land in Burundi is owned on an individual basis;

in 1977, the government put an end to the last vestiges of land clientship known as *ubugererwa*. Client farmers who once cropped a patron's lands in return for a share of the yield and services are entitled to the land or to compensation. However, this land-reform program is still in progress, and it has been difficult to enforce. At the same time, access to productive inputs is skewed in favor of the dominant Tutsi group.

Cattle herding in Burundi is also predominantly a Tutsi endeavor, although there are some Hutu cattle owners. The national herd was estimated at 760,000 in 1973. Cattle ownership fulfills an economic function and is a source of prestige, but productivity is low because of shortages of feed, poor health conditions, inadequate facilities (e.g., most of the existing 130 dipping tanks have deteriorated because of insufficient supervision), and too many old cattle. As many as 90 percent of the animals have beef measles, and because brucellosis is rife, the fertility of the herd is low. Unlike neighboring Rwanda, Burundi exports few cattle.

Burundi's educational system is undergoing a fundamental reform, but educational facilities are skewed in favor of the Tutsi-inhabited regions. Thus, there are 377 school classrooms in the President's home province but only 80 in a region mostly Hutu in ethnic composition. Educational reforms began in 1973 with the decision to use Kirundi for primary school instruction. Despite some difficulties, this appears to have been a success. For teachers, most of

whom lack adequate competence in French, "Kirundization" has proved very helpful. The primary school curriculum has been given a greater agricultural content and orientation: schoolchildren work two hours a week cultivating food and cash crops. In the upper primary grades, agricultural subjects are supplemented by training in related skills. In addition, primary schools are being transformed into community centers where nonformal adult-education programs are provided. Programs for out-of-school youth are also offered. When classes are not in session, the facilities are to be used to provide in-service training for lower-level ministerial staff.

A two-track system has been introduced; at the end of the fourth year, students are sent either into an academic program, which follows the prereform model, or to practical schools, which have self-contained programs so that students can be trained for agriculture. Unfortunately, 50 percent of the students drop out within the first 2 years.

The educational reforms face several serious obstacles. There are not enough teachers for the primary schools, and teacher training still follows unsatisfactory prereform methods. The Rural Education Bureau, responsible for teacher training, lacks trained personnel and clearly defined functions. In addition, there are shortages of educational resources and difficulties caused by the gnawing ethnic issue. Because there are not enough schools, teachers, or funds, only 20 to 25 percent of the children of primary school age attend classes. The urban population and the children of better-educated Burundians account for a relatively larger part of this small school-going population; most of them are Tutsi, reinforcing the castelike social situation.

Agricultural training facilities are underutilized, and the quality of education offered at these institutions is questionable. Some graduates of the Technical Agricultural Institute have good technical backgrounds but cannot communicate with extension agents or rural leaders and have little empathy for the problems that face rural Burundians. At the secondary level, there is some attempt to train agricultural field assistants, but graduates tend to fail to adapt their learning to local agricultural realities. One recent report concluded that as of 1978 practical agricultural training was almost nonexistent.

The rural population's training needs are not being met because few adults are literate; without schools they will remain illiterate. The World Bank has agreed to build 100 multipurpose educational centers in order to reach the country's poorest people and provide places for 27,000 new students. The centers will provide basic instruction in reading, writing, and mathematics as well as training in improved agricultural skills. However, the educational system's bias toward politically favored groups leaves doubt as to whose needs will be served.

Partly because of educational constraints, Burundi lacks the trained manpower needed to make its econ-

Workers load a shipment of hides. A lake steamer will take the hides from the port of Bujumbura to Kigoma in Tanzania, from where they will be shipped by rail to Dar es Salaam. (Photo: United Nations.)

omy grow and prosper. Political uncertainties and upheavals block the institutions that would accommodate such trained manpower. Opportunities for wage employment are extremely limited for the unskilled, and only 6 percent of the population are wage earners (121,000 out of the total labor force of 1.9 million). Even if all new projects outlined in the latest national development plan were to reach fruition, only 6,800 new jobs would be created in the years between 1978 and 1982. Yet there are an estimated 40,000 15-year-olds entering the job market each year.

After a decade of economic stagnation because of social strife and inherent poverty, the 5-year plan for 1978–1982 outlines a number of goals to engender a more active economy: (1) a substantial increase in the rate of economic growth in order to provide greater employment opportunities and more income for the poorest segments of the population; (2) a significant rise in investments; (3) a more active role for the government in mobilizing financial and human resources and participating in mixed enterprises in the commercial and productive sectors; (4) increased decentralization of economic and social activity; (5) settlement of the peasant population in villages and migration from densely to less densely populated areas; and (6) greater emphasis on agricultural production, especially production of food crops, and integrated rural development.

The 5-year plan's quantitative targets are practical only if serious manpower shortages and the low absorptive capacity of the economy can be overcome. At best, the maximum annual rate of growth of the gross domestic product is targeted at 4.7 percent in real terms. The performance of Burundi's 5-year plans has been very poor, and there is little reason to expect significant change. Government supervision of development projects is weak, and often the workers are inadequately trained. Coordination among the different national institutions responsible for the determination of economic and financial policy is not yet sufficient.

Burundi's development problems are further complicated by the government's investment priorities. The current allocation of government revenue has benefited primarily the administrative, justice, and defense functions to the detriment of funds required to operate and maintain roads, schools, irrigation works, health facilities, and agricultural extension services. There are no extension services or government supports for subsistence farming or the production of food crops, and it is almost impossible to obtain credit in rural areas despite the fact that more than half the population is engaged in agricultural pursuits. On the other hand, extension services are available to producers of the cash crops that are the chief source of government revenue, and social services are skewed to benefit the ruling Tutsi elite.

It was not until the end of the nineteenth century that Europeans penetrated Burundi and not until 1903 that Germany established its sovereignty there. Even

after they established themselves, the Germans fought a protracted war against guerrillas led by Burundi's monarch (*mwami*) and dissident chiefs. By 1908, German rule had extended to all but the southern part of the country, but World War II interrupted German plans for the territory, which passed into Belgian hands until its independence in 1962. During the years between initial colonization and independence, Burundi's stratified society was polarized: there were two opposing ethnic groups, the Hutu and the Tutsi. The Belgians favored the Tutsi and provided them with educational and job opportunities denied most Hutu. As a result, at independence many fewer Hutu had been trained or prepared to play a central role in state affairs. In addition, precolonial Tutsi supremacy and the years of colonial preference for Tutsi put the Hutu at a psychological disadvantage: they were unable to defend their own interests. As a result, at independence, the army and the government bureaucracies were overwhelmingly Tutsi and the dominant political party was controlled by Tutsi.

When Belgium surrendered authority in 1962, Burundi reverted to monarchy. But colonialism and the advent of European ideas and institutions had created internal strains that the monarchy was unable to contain. Within 3 years, the Hutu launched an unsuccessful revolt against the mwami and Tutsi. In a barbarous act of revenge, all key educated Hutu were executed, and a pogrom was launched against the Hutu inhabitants of Burundi's central province, the traditional seat of the kingdom. Eighteen months later, the monarchy was swept away by a Tutsi-inspired military coup. A new regime established a caste society where Hutu had few, if any, rights and suffered open discrimination. In 1969, those Hutu intellectuals and army officers who had escaped death in 1965 were executed on trumped-up charges. Ethnic tensions continued to mount.

In April 1972, Hutu irregulars launched a revolt in southern Burundi and attacked Tutsi in and around the capital city. Although the revolt caught the authorities off guard, they soon regained control. In its aftermath, the stunned Tutsi unleashed selective genocide; all Hutu with any education, including primary schoolchildren, were murdered. Many died after being tortured; others were starved to death or buried alive. For 2 horrifying years, sporadic pogroms were launched against Hutu, while Hutu guerrillas hit back at Tutsi. In the final count, at least 250,000 Hutu died or fled, and Tutsi rule became a mirror image of South African apartheid.

In 1976, a second military coup brought younger Tutsi officers to power. The new leadership committed itself in word and (though to a lesser extent) in deed to social reform. The underlying problems remain, and the country is still a prisoner of its gory past. Burundi's potential for development must be considered in the context of its recent history, which is why most international funding agencies consider Burundi a most difficult country in which to work.

Students from the agricultural school at Gitega learn how to use a theodite in surveying. The school is part of the government's effort to introduce modern farming techniques. (Photo: United Nations/FAO/ Defever.)

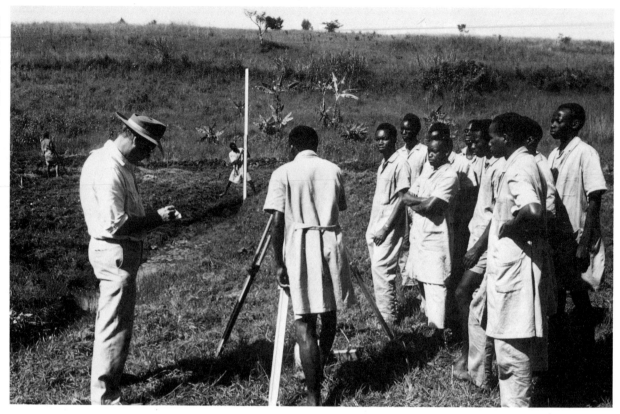

The future for Burundi's population, dispersed in nearly a million tiny farm units in hilly terrain, is bleak. By 1982, there may be only 0.8 acres (0.33 hectares) available to support every 4.2 persons and death rates will probably increase because of malnutrition. The government spends much of its energy making sure that the Hutu majority cannot revolt again; to this end, the Soviet Union has recently provided sophisticated weapons to the Tutsi army, and the People's Republic of China has constructed military camps throughout the country. The new President, Colonel Jean-Baptiste Bagaza, who deposed his first cousin Michel Micombero in 1976, was apparently committed to furthering development in Burundi, but by 1979 there were indications that he might allow ethnic considerations to distort his plans. The infusion of military hardware is only one such indication.

The single positive sign for Burundi's future is the presence of nickel. Vast nickel deposits were discovered during the 1970s, but their exploitation will require the investment of over a billion dollars in Burundi's physical infrastructure and manpower. Unfortunately, because of the size of the needed investment, the social fabric of Burundi's tense society may be convulsed more than once more before nickel is actually mined. Although Burundi is voicing populist and socialist rhetoric and proclaiming a commitment to social justice, it remains a backward land, gripped by fear, ethnic tension, and looming economic disaster.

Warren Weinstein

Cameroon
(United Republic of Cameroon)

Area: 183,568 sq mi (475,442 sq km)
Population: 8.1 million
  Density: 44 per sq mi (17 per sq km)
  Growth rate: 2.2% (1970–1977)
Percent of population under 14 years of age: 40% (1975)
Infant deaths per 1,000 live births: 142
Life expectancy at birth: 44 years
Leading causes of death: insect-borne diseases, parasite infestation, infantile diseases
Ethnic composition: over 150 groups, including Bamiléké, Fulani, Bamoun, Douala, Fang, Beti
Languages: French (official), English (official), various African languages
Literacy: adult 65%
Religions: Christian 49%; Muslim 15%; traditional
Percent population urban: 28% (1978)
Percent population rural: 72% (1978)
Gross national product: $3.7 billion
  Per capita GNP: $460
  Per capita GNP growth rate: 1.0% (1970–1977)
Inflation rate: 10–14% (1979)

Cameroon was born to the sound of gunfire. When the country became independent on Janaury 1, 1960, it was still in the grip of a rebellion. The government faced such serious social and economic problems that few knowledgeable observers thought it could survive.

The pessimists were wrong. The government of President Ahmadou Ahidjo is still in office today, some 20 years later. It overcame the rebellion, enlarged the country by integrating it with the former British Cameroons, and made considerable progress toward self-sustaining economic growth and national integration. Today, Cameroon presents a picture of orderly and balanced development, and it enjoys a high measure of political and social stability. Compared to some of its neighbors, Cameroon is doing well.

Located at the crook of West Africa, where the coastline takes a north-south direction from its previous east-west axis, Cameroon has been called an Africa in miniature. Its climatic, geographic, social, and political features reflect the diversity of the continent, and its history has been almost a microcosm of the African experience.

The country extends some 700 miles (1,127 km) between 2 and 13°N latitude and its 183,568 square miles (475,239 sq km) encompass almost the entire range of African climates and vegetation, from a semidesert sub-Saharan zone in the north to the equatorial rain forest in the south.

From the 8th parallel north to the shores of Lake Chad, grassy savanna dotted with scrub bushes and trees gradually gives way to desert rock and dry pan. Here, there are important game preserves, complete with elephants, antelope, lions, giraffes, and innumerable birds. Between the 6th and 8th parallels, the Adamawa plateau extends in a series of hills toward the western range of mountains, anchored on the south coast by Mount Cameroon (13,350 ft, 4,069 m), and in the extreme north by the Mandara hills. In the center of the country, the Adamawa plateau inclines toward the dense southern equatorial forests, thinly populated by a bewildering variety of ethnic groups and gorged with swift rivers and streams. The Adamawa plateau is also Cameroon's main water source. It feeds the country's principal interior river basin and its main outlet, the Sanaga (the falls of which provide hydroelectric power for most of the southern part of the country), and all the neighboring river basins.

Over the centuries, migrating peoples moved north and west from the Congo basin, east from Nigeria and the sub-Saharan savannas, and southwest from the area of the Sudan, and washed like waves onto and sometimes across the line of mountains and hills running north-south from Mount Cameroon to Lake Chad. The result was a gradual accumulation of more than 150 culturally diverse ethnic groups in what is today the United Republic of Cameroon, with an estimated 8.1 million people.

In the northern Cameroon, mainly in the savanna and semidesert zones, the dominant peoples are the Muslim Fulani, who became the rulers of the north as a result of a holy war (jihad) launched from Nigeria during the nineteenth century. Even though the great northern Fulani rulers (lamidos) no longer enjoy undisputed authority, they remain politically important because many of their followers still regard them with fear and awe. President Ahmadou Ahidjo, himself a Fulani from the northern town of Garoua, has gone to great lengths to reduce the powers of the lamidos and bring them and their people into the modern economic and political arena. The north also contains many Kirdi, non-Muslim animist peoples living in the western hills and the "duckbill" area west of the Logone River.

Most of Cameroon's peoples, however, live in the south and southwest, where Cameroon's great ethnic diversity is most evident. In the Cameroon highlands, there are Bamiléké, Tikar, Bassa, Bulu, Ewondo-speaking peoples, as well as the Bamoun, an Islamized people related to the Bamiléké, plus a variety of peoples speaking several Nigerian languages. The Bamiléké are the most numerous of these peoples, and are known for their industriousness, commercial talents, and eagerness to move ahead. The Bamoun are among the few Muslim hill peoples; their great sultan, Njoya, invented a wholly original alphabet and fostered the arts and literature around the turn of the nineteenth centry.

Along the southwest coast live the Douala (who gave their name to the country's main port), and a number of different groups live on the slopes of Mount Cameroon. The southeastern forests are inhabited by a variety of peoples, including the dominant Fang (Pangwe), a few Pygmies, and several groups related to peoples in neighboring Equatorial Guinea, Gabon, Congo, and the Central African Empire.

The southern peoples are also diverse in their religious affiliations, and include most of Cameroon's Christians, both Roman Catholic and Protestant. Because of the Christian missions that have operated in the country since the middle of the nineteenth century, some 49 percent of all Cameroonians call themselves Christians; another 15 percent are Muslims, and the rest (around 36 percent) adhere to some form of traditional African religion.

The south and southwest contain the country's largest cities: Douala (population 460,000), the principal port, located at the mouth of the Sanaga River; Yaoundé (310,000), the capital, located inland and the seat of the country's only Catholic archdiocese; Nkongsamba (75,000), the main town of the Bamiléké area. Douala and Yaoundé are Cameroon's principal commercial centers. A relatively smaller southern town, Edéa (26,000), is important because of its large aluminum works (which processes Guinean bauxite with power from the nearby Edéa Falls).

Cameroon is a country with extraordinary social and cultural diversity and a range of lifestyles from modern urban living to simple seminomadism. The north's largest ethnic group, the Fulani, have little solidarity and tend to think of themselves as members of the several large and small chiefdoms whose centers are the main towns of Garoua, Yagoua, Ngaoundéré, and Maroua. Many Fulani have become involved in national political and economic life, but most still live as they have in the past, herding cattle, cultivating small plots, and trading. The government

has had great success in persuading many northerners—both Fulani and Kirdi—to take up cotton farming (cotton is the country's fourth most important agricultural export crop), and the Transcameroon Railway now links northern and southern towns. But the Cameroon north still is far less developed than the south, and its people are considerably poorer. The south's most prolific and active people, the Bamiléké, have adapted to the country's economy and society without too much friction.

To be sure, there is still some leftover anti-Bamiléké resentment, which sometimes causes violence, but by and large the Bamiléké do well in commerce, education, industry, and the country's civil service. Further, they and their immediate neighbors in the southwest (the Bulu, Bassa, and Ewondo) are Cameroon's principal growers of coffee and cocoa, which are the country's most important agricultural exports. Once areas where people lived in fear, the picturesque villages and towns of the Bamiléké region now reflect the satisfaction of active and prosperous citizens.

Another group that is important to Cameroon is the Douala. The Douala were the first to experience contact with Europeans—and to witness both the brutal and beneficent sides of colonialism. They were Cameroon's first Christians, and became the first people to adopt European ways and habits. Highly urbanized, the Douala form a key part of the country's growing and enterprising middle class.

Cameroon's very diversity has probably helped to maintain its political and social peace. Since no one group or combination of groups has been able effectively to dominate the system, Cameroonians have managed to reconcile many of their differences through compromise or arbitration. Prosperity has made the job of social reconciliation that much easier. Cameroonians realize that they are much better off than their neighbors in west and equatorial Africa.

Economic planning began after 1970, when the rebellion finally ended. The secret of Cameroon's economic success is the decision to keep agriculture as the mainstay of the economy. Over three-fourths of the population live off the land, producing one-third of the value of everything produced in the country. This accounts for almost half the country's earnings from selling its goods abroad. The deliberate policy of promoting agricultural growth was launched in 1972 with President Ahidjo's "green revolution," a plan designed to make Cameroon self-sufficient, produce surpluses for export, and increase the production of such key cash crops as cocoa, coffee, sugar, and cotton. Despite natural disasters like drought and pests and despite unpredictable changes in the world market for cocoa and coffee, Cameroon earns substantial profits on what it sells abroad. In addition, the country now grows increased amounts of cereals like sorghum, maize, wheat, millet, and rice.

Although industrial goods account for less than one-fourth of Cameroon's exports, the government is still interested in boosting industry, particularly the

Nomadic herdsmen from Sangmélima bring cattle from the Niger River to Yaoundé; over three-fourths of the people still live off the land. (Photo: United Nations.)

aluminum industry. Opened in 1957, the Edéa aluminum plant is now the second largest in Africa, producing over 55,000 tons (44,885 mt) of aluminum ingots a year from bauxite imported from nearby Guinea on the West African coast. The government hopes that the Edéa plant will eventually process Cameroon's own immense deposits of bauxite located some 500 miles north, near the town of Garoua. The Edéa plant runs on electricity generated by a large hydroelectric plant on the nearby Sanaga River; this source of power, together with the power to be produced by another hydroelectric plant and dam upriver, will make the country virtually self-sufficient in the production of electricity. It may even be able to sell electricity to its neighbors.

In addition to aluminum ingots, which it sells abroad, Cameroon also has other useful industrial enterprises. It makes most of its own cloth, and the plantations of the Cameroon Development Corporation (CDC) on the slopes of Mount Cameroon produce bananas, rubber latex, palm oil, and tea, most of which are sold abroad. The CDC, with over 20,000 people on its payroll, is the country's largest employer and one of its most profitable enterprises.

Cameroon also produces enough petroleum for its own needs, and in 1978 managed to export some 600,000 tons (544,200 t) of crude oil. The oil deposits, located off Victoria in the Bight of Biafra, are considered rich enough to warrant the construction of a refinery, which will begin to operate in late 1980 and will process about 1.5 million tons (1.36 t) of crude a year. Other factories produce goods for local consumption. There are also a good banking system and a large and active local business community providing goods and services.

Cameroon's modern history begins with the coming of the first Europeans to the Fernando Po Island and the mouth of the Sanaga River in 1472. These Portuguese mariners caught some small crayfish, which they mistook for shrimp. As a result, they named the river Rio dos Camaroēs, or River of Shrimp. The name came to be used not only for the river, but also for the country as a whole. Cameroon is the English-language version of the name.

From the seventeenth to the late nineteenth centuries French, English, German, Dutch, Portuguese, and Spanish traders operated along the Cameroon coast. The French, English, and Germans established semipermanent stations at Douala and Kribi. The English also founded a Protestant mission on Fernando Po (and soon after moved the mission to Victoria, at the foot of Mount Cameroon).

In 1884, the Germans bested the British in a struggle to see who would be the first to sign a treaty of protection with the Douala chiefs. During their period of rule, the Germans laid the groundwork of the country's basic road and rail network and of part of its modern economy; they also extended their control north to Lake Chad and defined the territory's basic frontiers. The German protectorate (called Kamerun)

Cocoa beans are drying in the sun. Cocoa and coffee are Cameroon's most important agricultural exports. (Photo: United Nations/Carolyn Redenius.)

lasted from 1884 to 1916, when Germany lost its colonies as a result of its defeat in World War I. In 1922, Britain and France were each given a portion of the Kamerun protectorate under the mandate system of the League of Nations. The British were given two separate mountainous pieces along the Nigerian border amounting to one-fifth of the territory. This became the British Cameroons. The French took over the rest, which became the French Cameroun.

After World War II, the two Cameroon mandates were converted into United Nations trusteeships, arrangements that obligated Britain and France to move the territories toward self-government and independence. Then, in 1960, France granted its Cameroun trusteeship complete independence. In 1961, following a special referendum in the British Cameroons supervised by the United Nations, the southern portion of the British Cameroons joined the Cameroun Republic in a new federal republic. The northern part joined Nigeria when that country became independent that same year.

The Cameroon Federal Republic was a very unusual new country: it was Africa's first—and thus far, the only—bilingual (French and English) federation. The federation came to an end in 1972, and the two states were merged to form a single unified nation, the United Republic of Cameroon.

Cameroon also experienced a period of internal political and ethnic turmoil. In 1955, a radical nationalist party, the Union of Cameroonian Peoples (UPC) attempted to ignite a nationwide revolt against the government of the French Cameroun. The UPC revolt, which involved the Bassa and Bamiléké areas of the country in guerrilla warfare, finally ended in 1970 when its last leaders were captured, tried, and executed.

Cameroon owes much of its good fortune to the fact that it has been led by the same group of intelligent, practical people for more than 20 years. President Ahidjo became Prime Minister of Cameroon in 1958, 2 years before the country gained its independence; he has been its leader ever since. Now in his late fifties, Ahidjo combines toughness with pragmatism and quiet reserve. He tries to balance north and south, east and west, major and minor ethnic groups in his Cabinet. Though Ahidjo can be very tough, even brutal, he has pursued policies of forgiveness and reconciliation with his enemies when it suited him or the country. While he put down the UPC revolt (with French help) and imprisoned or executed its leaders, he also persuaded many guerrilla chiefs to support the government and even to run for office. In 1962, he forced all the country's political parties into a single national party, the Cameroon National Union, arresting and imprisoning opposition leaders (later released) who balked at the move.

While there are probably still some political prisoners in Cameroonian jails, their number is small, and even though the government operates one of Africa's most efficient police forces, students and other critics of the regime express themselves relatively openly. There is a national legislature, and elections are held periodically, but the President has the last word on all important matters. Some Cameroonians resent President Ahidjo's high-handedness (his most vehement critics, all of them abroad, call him a fascist and a dictator), but almost all agree that he is a unifying and centralizing force.

Ahidjo is still comparatively young, and he will probably remain at the top for some years to come. However, he has not groomed anyone to succeed him; his sudden departure would send damaging shock waves throughout the country and make it more difficult for his successors to grapple with the country's problems.

Cameroon is altogether too dependent on trade with France (which takes 26 percent of Cameroon's exports and sells it 43 percent of its imports); it has accumulated large debts to foreign creditors; more people are flocking to the cities than can find jobs; and gaps in the standard of living between the poorer and richer parts of the country remain too wide for comfort. All things considered, however, Cameroon's economy is strong, and it has become one of the most attractive places in Africa for foreign investment. Most important, the country's general prosperity has helped smooth over the rough edges of old antagonisms between ethnic groups and between the Muslim north and the Christian south.

Thus far, Cameroon has been able to confront and deal realistically with its problems, and has prospered in the process. Barring unforeseen difficulties, Cameroon should continue to prosper and to remain an object lesson for a continent too often beset by policital, economic, and social failures.

Victor T. Le Vine

Central African Republic

Area: 242,000 sq mi (626,777 sq km)
Population: 1.9 million
  Density: 8 per sq mi (3 per sq km)
  Growth rate: 2.2% (1970–1977)
Percent of population under 15 years of age: 40%
Infant deaths per 1,000 live births: 200 (1960)
Life expectancy at birth: 41 years
Leading causes of death: not available
Ethnic composition: more than 30 groups, including Banda, Baya, Mandjia, Sara, Nzakara, Zande
Languages: French (official), Sango (national)
Literacy: 18%
Religions: Protestant 40%; Catholic 28%; animist 24%; Muslim 8%
Percent population urban: 20%
Percent population rural: 80%
Gross national product: $480 million
  Per capita GNP: $250
  Per capita GNP growth rate: 0.9% (1970–1977)
Inflation rate: not available

The Central African Republic (CAR) is landlocked at the center of the huge African continent. By river, CAR is 1,000 miles (1,600 km) from the sea; the country must therefore maintain special relationships with its eastern and southern neighbors, Cameroon, Congo, and Zaire, which can block all trade with the outside world. (To CAR's north, Chad is equally dependent on the goodwill of coastal states.) Fortunately, internal trade is easier, because CAR is largely flat savanna with an extensive road system. With a total land area of 242,000 square miles (626,777 sq km), CAR is larger than France, although the population is barely 4 percent of that of France, once its colonial master. Location, underpopulation, lack of resources, and unpredictable leadership are the critical problems of this impoverished state.

Most of the 1.9 million Africans live in the moderate climate of the central and southern CAR, where the Oubangui, Mbomou, Lobaye, and Nana rivers flow toward the Congo. With the exception of the Nzakara and the Zande, who live in the southeast along the frontier with Sudan and Zaire, none of the Central African peoples boasted unified kingdoms in the recent past. Lineages, extended families, and regions claim their loyalties.

About 80 percent of the population live in rural areas. Since the colonial era, villages have been grouped for the most part along the roads. Climate and soil permit the cultivation of food and crops like cotton and coffee destined for export. Although the government and Christian missionaries have established some medical facilities, health care and schools in rural areas are woefully inadequate.

Bangui, the capital, has about 350,000 inhabitants and most health, educational, economic, and political activities are concentrated there. Berberati has a population of about 60,000; other important towns are Bouar, Bangassou, and Bambari. Like most other African states, CAR has a very young population; about 40 percent are less than 15 years old. Observers estimate that 200,000 students are enrolled in primary schools, 19,000 in secondary schools; the university boasts an enrollment of 500.

There are more than thirty ethnic groups, none of which are highly organized as political entities. Thus interethnic relationships are usually peaceful. The Banda, probably the largest single ethnic group, are spread through the center of the country. Without a capital and without a leader, they identify with their regions, and their customs are similar to those of their immediate neighbors.

The Baya and the Mandjia, who live in the west, are famous because of their violent revolts against French rule. In the far north live the Sara, related to the peoples of southern Chad. The Nzakara and Zande live in Bangassou and Zemio in the southeast.

Very small ethnic groups, along the rivers and in the region of Bangui, have played the most important role in the recent development of the country. Because they live along the southern rivers, they met the French before any of their neighbors and served them as guides, canoe paddlers, and interpreters. They attended the first rudimentary schools that taught French and arithmetic. With this education, they filled the first openings for African clerks, priests, traders, and, later, professionals. The first politicians came from the riverine peoples. The Mgbaka, Banziri, Sango, and Yakoma peoples have played key roles in the history of the CAR, even though they are far outnumbered by the Banda and Baya.

The Sango language forms the basis of a lingua franca, also called Sango, used almost all over CAR much the way Swahili is used in Tanzania. Because the Sango ethnic group is small, no one fears that the use of a language based on their speech will permit them to control the country. All three of CAR's first political leaders, said to be closely related, came from the Mgbaka group.

Although the people of CAR are among the poorest in Africa, mineral resources and agriculture promise a better future. Diamonds are the most important export; about 50,000 people are involved in mining and searching for these precious stones. Many diamonds are shipped to Belgium and Israel to be cut. The French estimate that there are also about 20,000 tons (18,000 t) of uranium in the area of Bakouma. (France is particularly interested in uranium for its nuclear program). An American satellite has discovered a huge deposit of iron ore beneath the country's grasslands, but it will be several years before the deposit can be exploited.

Since the 1920s, CAR has been a major exporter of cotton, introduced by the French to reduce their dependence on American cotton. The country also exports coffee and wood. Small factories produce cement, cloth, shoes, cigarettes, and beer for local consumption, but the Central Africans believe that imported products are superior. High prices and low prestige inhibit the development of local industries. A development program (once called "operation Bokassa") begun in 1966, is supposed to raise levels of agricultural output.

Like other former French colonies, CAR has very close ties with Paris in terms of trade, finances, and investments. France backs the money of CAR; the unit of currency is the franc of the African Financial Community (CFA). The country cannot easily trade with states outside the CFA franc zone without the involvement of the French Treasury. About half of CAR's imports come from France, including manufactured goods, beverages, and even some food products. One-third of CAR's exports go to France, which means that the former colonial power maintains a favorable balance of trade with CAR as it does with most of its former colonies. (In the last few years,

In a primitive area, a young woman from Yimbi washes her clothes at a new cement well equipped with a pump. More than two-thirds of the people live in rural areas with inadequate medical facilities, schools, and health care. (Photo: United Nations/Caracciolo-Banoun.)

CAR erroneously claimed to have had no deficits in foreign trade.)

At first glance, there appears to be room for optimism in the economic realm, but deeper investigation reveals a more gloomy picture. Despite a commitment to rational allocation of resources through planning, considerable funds were wasted on the military and the personal expenses of the former head of state. Jean-Bedel Bokassa, who ruled the country from 1966 to 1979, considered government revenue his own and traveled widely, purchasing homes and other properties in Europe. His coronation as Africa's only emperor reportedly cost $22 million, which CAR could ill afford to spend.

No matter who is head of state, CAR tries to maintain close relations with its coastal neighbors. For example, it belongs to the Customs Union of the States of Central Africa (UDEAC), and the francophone Common African and Mauritian Organization (OCAM). The leader of CAR meets regularly on an individual basis with French President Valéry Giscard d'Estaing and officially within the framework of the new heads-of-state organization the French have promoted with the French-speaking countries of Africa.

Two of CAR's three political leaders have been innovative. Barthélemy Boganda, a priest, founded a political party, Movement of Social Evolution in Black Africa (MESAN), in 1952. His party's influence spread throughout the country, and after he became Prime Minister he changed the name of the country from Oubangui-Chari to Central African Republic, a name change which reflected his long-term plan for central Africa. He proposed the unification of Congo with his country as the nucleus of a large state, the United States of Latin Africa, stretching from Chad to, and including, Angola. Because at that time neither Angola nor Spanish Guinea (which would also have been included) were on the path to independence, Boganda appeared to be a dangerous radical to many Europeans. Boganda proposed strict controls in economic matters and promised to transform his country and region with outside assistance from the French, in particular. A tragic airplane crash in March 1959 put an end to Boganda's life.

Boganda's young cousin, David Dacko, who had already worked in MESAN, took on the mantle of leadership and led the country to independence on August 13, 1960. On the last day of December 1965, the army under the leadership of Jean-Bedel Bokassa, reportedly a cousin of Dacko, overthrew the civilian government and seized power for itself.

Jean-Bedel Bokassa began his career in the French army, fighting in Indochina against the nationalist movement there. He raised himself quickly in rank to general, then to marshal. As head of state, he was an unpredictable and flamboyant figure, some of whose activities embarrassed and angered his countrymen. All radio messages issued in his name began with a list of his titles, and pink postage stamps portrayed him with medals down to his knees.

On December 4, 1977, Bokassa proclaimed himself Emperor Bokassa I and changed the name of the country to Central African Empire. The crowning, complete with gilded carriage, gold throne, ermine gowns, and white horses, was extensively reported by newspapers around the world, to the amusement of most non-Africans (and the chagrin of most Africans).

Popular dissatisfaction with Bokassa grew gradually, and several opposition movements were formed outside the country. One of the most important was the Patriotic Front of Oubangui (FPO), headed by Abel Goumba; another was the Movement for the Liberation of the Central African People (MLPC), founded in 1978 by Ange Patassé, a former Prime Minister.

Within the country, demonstrating students posed a more serious threat to the continued existence of the government in 1977 and 1978. Soldiers, some of whom reportedly were sent by General Mobutu from Zaire, suppressed the demonstrations. There were many deaths, particularly in early 1979, when schoolchildren were murdered by the emperor himself. Several attempts were made to assassinate the emperor, but he escaped unharmed.

On September 21, 1979, former President David Dacko took over the government and, with the help of French troops, reestablished the republic, while Bokassa fled into exile in the Ivory Coast. After a few weeks of happy relief, Central Africans began to reevaluate Dacko. He encouraged a French military presence, banned all strikes, delayed promised elec-

A rural craftsman displays his metal wares. Handicraft industries are being encouraged in rural areas. (Photo: United Nations/Caracciolo-Banoun.)

tions, and arrested Ange Patassé, who had criticized his leadership. In early 1980, the other opposition leaders called the Dacko regime illegal and demanded the withdrawal of the French soldiers. Students demonstrated and further upheavals were predicted.

On December 24, 1980, a CAR court sentenced deposed Emperor Jean-Bedel Bokassa to death in absentia and ordered the seizure of all his property.

The people of the Central African Republic can compare the Bokassa era with the worst period of their history. Before the arrival of the French, Arab slave traders raided this area, carrying off Central Africans to what is today northern Sudan, where a slave market was regularly held. The very earliest days of French rule were also characterized by authoritarianism and brutal rule, although later colonial rule was increasingly democratic and constructive.

In 1903 the French chose the name of the southern river, the Oubangui, and of the northern river, the Chari, for the land they were claiming as their own. Thus, Oubangui-Chari was born. However, the French were less interested in the country for its own sake than in crossing it to get to Chad. French military columns traversed Oubangui-Chari, recruiting porters and gathering provisions along the way. Because the French government had no intention of spending money for development, concessionary companies won control of huge areas.

In 1919, Governor Auguste Henri Lamblin began a program to structure this backwater. He transformed the administration and set the colony on the road to genuine development. Roads were built, schools were opened, and new crops were introduced. Félix Eboué, a black colonial administrator from French Guyana, initiated cotton production at Bangassou in 1924 and 1925. It proved to be a great success and spread elsewhere in the colony. Cotton cultivation was arranged in such a way that families could work in the fields near their villages, and cotton became the mainstay of the economy. A little gold was also mined near Bambari.

With the arrival of World War II, Eboué, who had become governor of Chad, led a movement to support General Charles de Gaulle's Free French, and Oubangui-Chari followed. The people endured many hardships to supply cotton, rubber, and some gold for the French effort in World War II.

After World War II, the French began a series of reforms designed to provide more opportunities for Africans. They extended citizenship and voting rights to all, raised the salaries of African civil servants, opened more schools, and began development programs. Although Ghana's independence in 1957 signaled political change for all of Africa, the people of Central Africa rejected the Ghanaian model in 1958. They approved a new French constitution providing

for new links between France and Africa, despite the growing trend for independence throughout the continent, because they feared the loss of French aid. In addition, many Central Africans, like Jean-Bedel Bokassa, had considerable loyalty and love for France.

For their part, the French encouraged and continue to encourage close association, warning that an abrupt break would mean the end of aid. They subsidized the Central African school system with new teachers and books, and they constructed new facilities. Later, they encouraged Central Africa to join associations of former French colonies, like the African and Malagasy Union (UAM) and the Common African and Mauritian Organization (OCAM). CAR has never wavered in its support for French-sponsored organizations even though English-speaking countries have characterized these organizations as neocolonialist.

Culture, leadership, and the building of viable institutions are key issues for the future of CAR. CAR is still identified primarily by the use of French, but some primary schools are experimenting with Sango as a medium of instruction. A complete Sango dictionary has been published, and linguists continue their research. The widespread use of the Sango language could permit an important, possibly a revolutionary, change in the sense of identity in the country.

Those who would like to see Sango the official language of CAR claim the people would gain new pride in their traditions and a new confidence in their destiny. But many Central Africans are worried that if they do not get a good French education, they will never obtain good jobs in the civil service or the professions. There is evidence, however, that wherever the local languages are made official, ordinary people have greater access to jobs.

The second issue is leadership. Jean-Bedel Bokassa treated the country as if it were his own backyard, and David Dacko seems weak and beholden to the French. The Central Africans look for ways to shield themselves from the regime. Thus, they avoid paying taxes, fail to meet production quotas, refuse to listen to speeches, and make jokes about the government and the country.

Capricious and oppressive leadership followed by weak leadership has undermined the process of institution building and nation building. Institutions have been manipulated for the benefit of individuals and small elites, and as a result Central Africans see no reason to respect or protect their institutions.

The Central African Republic holds no promise of wealth or prominence. On the other hand, because of the unifying factor of language, the absence of ethnic strife, and shared values, the country could become a stable nation. Restrained, self-sacrificing, and intelligent leadership is the key to its future.

Brian Weinstein

Chad
(Republic of Chad)

Area: 496,000 sq mi (1,284,634 sq km)
Population: 4.3 million
  Density: 9 per sq mi (3 per sq km)
  Growth Rate: 2.2% (1970–1977)
Percent of population under 14 years of age: 40% (1975)
Infant deaths per 1,000 live births: 160 (1960)
Life expectancy at birth: 39 years
Leading causes of death: ethnic violence
Ethnic composition: Sara (including Mbaye, Madjingaye, Ngambaye, Kaba), Maba, Dadju, Barma, Buduma, Toubou
Languages: Chadian Arabic, French
Literacy: 7%
Religions: Muslim, animist, Christian
Percent population urban: not available
Percent population rural: not available
Gross national product: $620 million
  Per capita GNP: $140
  Per capita GNP growth rate: −1.0% (1970–1977)
Inflation rate: not available

Twice the size of Texas, and stretching a thousand miles from the Libyan desert in the north to the tropical grasslands of the Logone Valley in the south, landlocked Chad has experienced one of the longest (14 years) and most devastating civil wars recorded in the annals of independent black Africa. As in the Sudan, its neighbor to the east, where Christian southerners rose in rebellion against Muslim northerners, the civil war in Chad involves a complex mixture of regional, ethnic, and religious issues, pitting the Sudanic-Nilotic Muslims of the north against the Bantu-animist-Christian populations of the south.

Unlike the war in the Sudan, however, the Chadian rebellion is a northern phenomenon. France's 10-year military involvement (1969–1979) on the side of the N'Djamena (formerly Fort Lamy) authorities failed utterly to quell the insurgency. Libyan support of the rebels, on the other hand, proved decisive in assuring the victory of north over south and one faction over the other. The fall of N'Djamena to the pro-Libyan faction in December 1980, coinciding with the announcement of a union between Chad and Libya, signaled a totally new phase in the tormented history of Chad.

The civil war cannot be explained simply as a conflict between north and south, Arab and Negro. Yet, regional and ecological cleavages have contributed to the social identities of the Chadian people.

Northern Chad, representing about four-fifths of the country, is a compact bloc of arid and semiarid desert land, bounded on the south by the Chari River and in the north and east by the spectacular escarpments of the Tibesti, Waddai, and Sila mountain ranges. Much of the area is a huge, rocky plateau dotted by occasional date and palm oases (Fada, Largeau, Zouar), rising to heights of 11,000 feet (3,300 m) in the Tibesti massif, and gradually giving way to the savanna that stretches from Lake Chad to the Sudan.

The most notable exception to this uniformly barren savanna landscape is found in the vicinity of Lake Chad. Despite the drying-up process that has been going on almost continuously since the drought that lasted from 1967 to 1973, the lacustrine zone is a distinctive subregion, in which relatively rich alluvial soils make possible the cultivation of a variety of food crops, including millet, sorghum, and wheat.

Although animal husbandry is the main occupation of the northern population, the growing scarcity of grassland and water has imposed tremendous hardships on men and cattle. As a result, nomads and herders have closed in on the more prosperous, settled areas of the south, creating social conflict in recent years. Subsoil resources are said to include substantial deposits of oil and uranium, the former in the Kanem region and the latter in the Bornou-Ennedi-Tibesti (BET) prefecture. Unconfirmed reports of uranium deposits in the Aouzou strip—covering some 25,000 square miles (64,750 sq km) in an area adjacent to the Libyan border—were presumably the chief reason that Libya tried to claim and occupy this area in 1973.

Southern Chad covers the area south and southwest of the Chari River and accounts for more than half the country's population of approximately 4 million. This is what the French called "useful Chad." The north has clearly the worst of the bargain in terms of rainfall and soil fertility; the south, in contrast, enjoys anywhere from 35 to 45 inches (90 to 115 cm) of rain annually (as against 1 inch in Largeau). Here soil and climatic conditions are ideally suited to the cultivation of cotton, Chad's main export crop.

Small industries located in the south, including cotton ginning and meat processing, account for less than 10 percent of the gross domestic product. Mineral production is nonexistent. What little economic development has taken place in the country is very heavily concentrated in the south, around the capital city, N'Djamena. Although per capita income is estimated at $50, there are significant disparities between the relatively higher income area south of the Chari, where cotton and food crops are grown, and the lower income area of the north. The striking unevenness of development between north and south is a critical element of the northern insurgency.

Ecological and development differences between north and south are both the cause and the symptom of basic cultural divisions. The main line of cleavage is between the Christianized sedentaries of the south, mostly of Sara origins, and the predominantly Islamized pastoral groups of the north, for the most part seminomadic Arabic-speaking cattle herders. Yet the distinction between Christianized sedentaries and Islamized nomads must be qualified. For one thing, nomadic pressure upon sedentary life has led to a considerable intermingling of populations. A major consequence of the severe drought of 1973 has been an accelerated influx of nomadic elements into the urban centers of the south, where they have become more or less permanently settled. Further, of a total of roughly 1.2 million Sara, only one-fourth at the most are Christian; the rest are either animist—the vast majority—or Muslim.

Neither language nor religion is an accurate index of ethnic homogeneity. Although Chadian Arabic is widely used as a lingua franca throughout the north, at least twelve linguistic groups can be identified, of which the principal are Moundang-Toubouri, in southwestern Chad, Kanembu-Zaghawa in the central and northern regions, Maba in the Waddai, and Sara-Baguirmi in the south. Even within the same language group, further distinctions are in order.

From the perspective of their traditional mode of sociopolitical organization, the populations of Chad fall roughly into three major groups. Among the Islamized populations of the north (collectively referred to as Arabs by most commentators, even though a great many are of Berber origins and dark-skinned), the clan is the basic sociopolitical unit. The extended, agnatic family system acts as a major source of social fragmentation within the clan, causing endless splits. In this extraordinarily fluid, fissiparous social system lies the key to the factional divisions that have pla-

gued the leadership of the northern rebellion. Though most leading personalities are of Toubou origin, including Hissene Habre and Oueddei Goukouni, their Toubou identity has proved of little help in promoting and maintaining internal cohesion.

In contrast to this fluid, amorphous social organization, the populations of Baguirmi, Waddai, and Kanem-Bornou share a long tradition of centralized authority, associated with the archaic kingdoms of the same name. Their early history is closely related to the penetration of Islam in the Sahel and the subsequent expansion of trans-Saharan trade networks in the eighteenth and nineteenth centuries. In the late eighteenth century, they acquired the broad territorial base and centralized bureaucratic and military structures that enabled them to become major participants in the slave trade. Slave raiding was their main source of power and prosperity and the key element behind their expansionist policies.

Of all the factors that have contributed to the emergence of a consciousness of Sara identity, few have had a more powerful psychological impact than their historic subjugation to the rulers of Baguirmi. To this day in the minds of most Sara, the concept of Islam is inextricably bound up with the periodic razzias (raids) they suffered at the hands of their imperialist neighbor to the north.

Social organization among the Sara centers on the village community. No consolidation of power has ever occurred on any substantial territorial scale. Au-

Farmers plant drought-resistent millet. Sorghum and wheat are also grown wherever the soil is relatively rich and water is available. (Photo: United Nations/ Carl Purcell.)

thority is vested in the village chief (*mbang*), usually assisted by a council of elders. Traditionally, the authority of the chiefs was far from absolute; only in the 1920s and 1930s, with the increasing reliance of the colonial authorities on local chiefs for the collection of taxes and the compulsory cultivation of cotton, was their rule transformed into a starkly oppressive system designed to enforce the directives of the colonial state. Nor is there much evidence of a strong sense of "Saraness" among Sara-speaking elements before the advent of colonial rule. Until the arrival of the French, only the Madjingaye referred to themselves as Sara, a term of Arabic origin used by the people of Baguirmi to designate their captives. Ultimately the term Sara came to be used by the Sara themselves as a symbol of their common cultural heritage and as a means of ordering their political universe.

Although precolonial history offers a major clue to the north-south conflict, the tremendous social dislocations and human sufferings caused by French colonial rule played a crucial role in awakening a collective class consciousness among the Sara. Incessant French demands to meet the labor requirements of the colonial administration led to human exploitation on a scale unprecedented even during the worst of the razzias conducted by slave traders.

The construction of the Congo-Océan railway in the late 1920s and early 1930s was made possible only through massive recruitment of Sara laborers. In subsequent years thousands of Sara were mobilized for the compulsory cultivation of cotton, and it was

Women use long poles to make holes for planting seeds. Agricultural development is very important in Chad, where the scarcity of grassland and water imposes tremendous hardship on people and cattle. (Photo: FAO/World Programme/ B. Szynalski.)

among the Sara that France's nascent colonial army recruited the bulk of its *tirailleurs* (indigenous infantry units). The net effect of all this was to create a rural proletariat of deracinated Sara, whose class consciousness eventually coincided with their own sense of Saraness.

In Chad, as elsewhere in Africa, ethnic violence remains an urban phenomenon. It was in N'Djamena, in August and November 1946, that rioting first broke out between Sara and non-Sara; similar incidents occurred in Sahr in November 1947; and it was in the southern town of Moundou, in the heart of Sara territory, that hundreds of Muslims were massacred in February 1979, in the worst orgy of violence since the beginning of the civil war.

The main catalyst of urban violence in the 1940s came from the introduction of the vote. At the time of the first elections to the French National Assembly in 1946, the Chadian electorate numbered only 22,-000. Though limited in scope, electoral competition unleashed a deadly struggle between the pro-Sara, militantly anticolonial Chadian Progressive Party (PPT), then led by West Indian Gabriel Lisette and the pro-European, northern-dominated, and predominantly Muslim Chadian Democratic Union (UDT). The fusion of class and ethno-religious cleavages within the framework of political parties sharpened mutual hatred between Sara and non-Sara. Only in the mid-1950s, with the outbreak of the Algerian war, did the French authorities begin to sense the threat of another kind of subversion, this time identified with the pro-Islamic and presumably pro-Algerian affinities of the UDT supporters. The trend towards Sara hegemony became even more evident after independence in 1960. The overthrow of Gabriel Lisette on August 24, 1960, and his replacement by François Tombalbaye as President marked the beginning of a new era.

The monopoly of power achieved by the Sara-dominated PPT in the years immediately following independence made the eviction of non-Sara elements inevitable. By 1963, all northerners had been eliminated from Cabinet positions. The sheer arbitrariness of the fiscal measures adopted in 1965 intensified anti-Sara sentiments throughout the central and northern regions.

The spark that ignited the rebellion was the Mangalme incident of October 1965. Infuriated by what they considered to be an intolerable fiscal burden, a group of Moubi villagers from Mangalme sous-préfecture murdered an entire delegation of visiting government officials. By 1967 the rebellion had penetrated large areas of the Guera prefecture and in the fall of 1968 threatened the Chari-Baguirmi. By 1969, the line of demarcation between rebels and loyalists coincided roughly with the predominantly Sara prefectures of the south and the Islamized north.

In 1966, opposition to the Tombalbaye regime was channeled into an organized liberation front, the National Liberation Front (FROLINAT) initially led by

Ibrahim Abatcha. Born of the fusion of two separate opposition movements, Chadian National Union (UNT) and the Chadian National Liberation Movement (MNLT), from the very beginning the FROLINAT was plagued by factional strife.

A major source of dissension stems from the interference of foreign governments. At first, the Sudan acted as a major supplier of arms to guerrillas in the east, until the Chadian authorities threatened to retaliate by throwing their weight behind the Anyanya rebellion in the southern Sudan. In 1971, Libya formally recognized the FROLINAT, and from then on played a decisive role, providing a privileged sanctuary, arbitrating factional strife within the rebellion, and supplying weapons. By 1975, at least three rebel armies were claiming the mantle of revolutionary legitimacy: Hissene Habre's second army in the Bournou-Ennedi-Tibesti prefecture, Abba Siddick's partisans in the extreme northeast along the Sudan border, and Mohammad Baghlani's eastern army in the Waddai region. A year later, Habre's second army suffered a major split when his immediate rival, Goukouni Oueddei, backed by Libya, asserted himself as the main spokesman of the northern faction.

Given the extraordinarily fragmented character of the insurgency, its relatively poor leadership, and the considerable military assistance supplied by the French to the Chadian government, the ultimate collapse of the N'Djamena regime to the rebels seems astonishing. In fact, Tombalbaye's overthrow in 1975 brought to a head the tensions that had been building up within the government and the army ever since 1972, when his policy of Chadization led to the forced imposition of the Yondo initiation ceremony on all civil servants.

Disaffection was further intensified by purges of Cabinet ministers suspected of plotting against the regime. Following the arrest of General Félix Malloum, the army chief of staff, in June 1973, discontent spread to the armed forces, and on April 13, 1975, units of the army and gendarmerie overthrew the government. As head of the Supreme Military Council, the ruling junta, President Malloum inherited a situation bordering on chaos, marked by continued disaffection in the south and spreading insurgency in the north.

But perhaps the greatest handicap faced by the N'Djamena authorities stemmed from their unwillingness to employ any means other than military in dealing with the rebellion. That there was no viable military solution to the conflict was made plain by the utter futility of French efforts at pacification. In the end, the military successes of the FROLINAT made a negotiated settlement unavoidable. Yielding to the pressures from the governments of Niger, Libya, and the Sudan, delegations of the FROLINAT and the Chadian government met at Sebha (Libya) in March 1978, to negotiate a cease-fire. The next step toward reconciliation occurred in August 1978, when a short-lived accord accepted Hissene Habre as Prime Minister and Malloum as President in a government in which north and south were almost evenly represented.

When Habre's rebel army attacked Malloum's regulars in N'Djamena in early 1979, the Sara populace reacted by slaughtering some 800 Muslim civilians in the southern town of Moundou. A precarious peace was restored after the signature of the Kano agreement in March, shortly after France's decision to withdraw its 2,500 soldiers. In August, nine rival groups formed a transitional government of national union with Goukouni Oueddei, a northern rebel leader, as President and Waddal Abdelkadar Kamougue, a southern Christian, as Vice President, and Hissene Habre as Defense Minister. Despite the coalition government agreement of August 1979, fighting continued between the forces of Goukouni and those of Hissene Habre. In December 1980, Libya's Colonel Muammar el-Qaddafi actively intervened in the struggle on the side of Goukouni. Libya's massive military support gave a decisive edge to Goukouni in December 1980. In early January 1981, Qaddafi announced that Chad would merge with Libya despite the objections of other African states and the Organization of African Unity.

To the heavy toll in human lives exacted by civil strife must be added the tremendous costs of a war effort that brought the economy almost to a standstill. Very little has been done to convert Chad's vast

In the Lake Chad area, villagers collect sand and carry it in bowls; they use this sand to raise a barrage to prevent lake water from filtering back to an area under cultivation. Near Lake Chad, rich soils permit the cultivation of millet, sorghum, and wheat. (Photo: FAO/World Food Programme/ F. Nattioli.)

untapped mineral wealth—ranging from petroleum to uranium, and from zinc and copper to wolfram and tungsten—into tangible assets for economic and social development. Its literacy rate (7 percent) is among the lowest in Africa; so is the average life expectancy (39 years). Public health care is nonexistent. Exports cover less than half the value of imports and the external debt is now estimated at $250 million. In early 1980, there were some 30,000 men under arms in Chad, and some sections of the capital were all but deserted. More than 14 years of warfare transformed the country into an economic disaster area and left deep scars on the social system.

Chad's capacity to survive as an independent nation is in doubt; its leaders have given every indication that they cannot work out a viable political compromise among rival factions. Short of a genuine and lasting national reconciliation, there seems little hope of resolving the political, economic, and social problems that make Chad a microcosm of developing Africa.

René Lemarchand

Congo (Brazzaville)
(People's Republic of the Congo)

Area: 132,000 sq mi (342,000 sq km)
Population: 1.5 million
  Density: 11 per sq mi (4 per sq km)
  Growth rate: 2.5% (1970–1977)
Percent of population under 14 years of age: 42%
Infant deaths per 1,000 live births: 180 (1960)
Life expectancy at birth: 43.5 years
Leading causes of death: not available
Ethnic composition: Bakongo, Lari, Mbochi, Batéké, Sangha
Languages: French (official), Lingala (national), Kikongo (national)
Literacy: 30%
Religions: animist 48%; Christian 47%; Muslim 5%
Percent population urban: 40%
Percent population rural: 60%
Gross national product: $780 million
  Per capita GNP: $540
  Per capita GNP growth rate: 0.8% (1970–1977)
Inflation rate: not available

The People's Republic of the Congo experienced serious setbacks, after a good start on the road to development, just before and just after independence. A weakened economy after a decade of scientific socialism, a series of coups and assassinations, and heightened competition between northerners and southerners challenge Congo's leaders. The search for solutions on the left and on the right confuses people already fatigued by show trials, revolutionary rhetoric, and multiple foreign influences.

The land area of 132,000 square miles (342,000 sq km) is rather small by African standards, but the People's Republic of the Congo is almost as large as Japan. Straddling the equator—which means there are about 12 hours of darkness and 12 hours of daylight each day—Congo lies on the Atlantic coast of Africa, wedged in like a comma between Zaire to the south and Gabon, Cameroon, and the Central African Republic to the north. Most of the area is in the heart of the equatorial rain forest. In fact, about 60 percent of Congo is covered with trees and bushes; the rest is savanna. The Congo and Oubangui (Zaire) Rivers

delineate the frontier between Congo and Zaire. These waterways and their numerous tributaries, like the Sangha, are part of a great river system in central Africa that has an enormous potential for hydroelectric power.

Like other countries in this region, Congo's population is small, relative to the land area; it is currently about 1.5 million. Cities are disproportionately large, however. Brazzaville, the capital, has about 300,000 inhabitants, and Pointe-Noire, the major port, has about 200,000 people. Other towns are also significant. About 40 percent of the people live in urban areas, making Congo one of the most urbanized states in Africa. The two major cities were built by the French to service neighboring colonies, Gabon, Oubangui-Chari (now the Central African Republic), and Chad, which were grouped together in what was called French Equatorial Africa. Before 1960, Brazzaville was the capital of the federation.

For these reasons, until recently Congo had the only railroad—the Congo-Océan—in French Equatorial Africa, and the only adequate port. Imported goods unloaded in Pointe-Noire even today move along the railroad to Brazzaville, where they are put on ships to be carried to Bangui, the capital of the Central African Republic. Between 1959 and 1962, a second railroad was built—the Comilog line—to provide a link to southeastern Gabon. The Comilog transports manganese from Gabon through Congo to the coast.

Brazzaville also had the first secondary schools, university, and major religious seminaries in the region. Students from neighboring countries, including Zaire (before 1960), traveled to Brazzaville to pursue secondary and postsecondary studies. Since 1960, Brazzaville has declined in importance. Each country has tried to build its own institutions, and Cameroon has become an important communication link for the landlocked states, Chad and the Central African Republic. However, Congo belongs to the Customs Union of Central African States (UDEAC), formed by these countries after independence to strengthen their economic and political ties. Relations with Zaire have followed a different and at times stormy path. Each country has traded accusations with the other concerning their support, or alleged support, of opposition movements. Relations are more cordial now.

Although almost two-thirds of the population of Congo live in rural areas and are engaged in agriculture, their contribution to the gross national product is slight. They produce industrial crops like cocoa, coffee, and sugar cane, but most income for the national budget comes from the export of natural resources. Congolese resources include oil, copper, lead, zinc, phosphate, and wood; and most of them are exported. An early euphoria about oil has given way to pessimism, because oil production may end in the early 1980s unless more fields are discovered offshore. Because of its early political importance and the presence of a communications infrastructure Congo has more small manufacturing establishments than most of its neighbors. Facilities permit sugar refining and the processing of peanut oil and palm oil for cooking; there are sawmills, a cement factory, a brewery, and a cigarette factory. Some cloth is also produced.

Despite these advantages, the economy of Congo has reached a crisis stage. Since 1968, the country has embarked on a socialist course without the necessary state apparatus. The government has nationalized some businesses and set up 60 state trading, distribution, and agricultural enterprises. These state businesses and a gigantic civil service have proved to be inefficient, corrupt, and hungry for an inordinate proportion of tax revenue and export earnings. With a trade deficit running at about $1 million a year, ineffective aid programs from both Communist and Western countries, problems collecting taxes, and widespread corruption, Congo is in a state of economic crisis.

Fortunately for the Congolese, the French, who are still Congo's major trading partner, are willing to help. France has given loans and grants to repair the railroad, and French business has promised more investments and stepped up a search for oil. (There are now about 8,000 French in the country.) Among Communist countries, East Germany in particular has provided assistance. But despite experiments with socialism, the Congolese have hesitated to set up their own currency. They prefer to remain in the franc zone, using the franc of the African Financial Community (CFA). In this way, France backs the country's money, so that it is freely convertible and stable. This facilitates trade and investment.

Congo's economic problems are serious, but far more intractable are the perennially difficult relationships among ethnic groups. Congo is famous for ethnic conflict. The southern Lari and the related Bakongo account for about 47 percent of the total population; northerners like the Mbochi and Batéké account for another 11 percent and 20 percent respectively. The Vili on the coast and several other scattered groups number another 22 percent. Tension persists most between the Lari and the Mbochi.

As in other African countries, the most politically active ethnic groups were those who had the earliest contacts with European education and administration. The Vili and the Lari were the first African clerks and teachers; later, they were the first African politicians. As early as the 1930s and 1940s, the Lari organized mutual aid societies under André Matswa. Perceiving them as a protonationalist movement, the French suppressed the organizations and arrested Matswa, making him a martyr. A cycle of demonstration and colonial repression that caused the deaths of many Lari led the Lari inevitably to a heightened political consciousness and sense of unity. Even though they had not particularly opposed the French, many of them became more radical because of colonial overreaction. As a result, Lari and Bakongo joined other movements to unite all the Bakongo peoples in the three countries of Congo, Zaire, and Angola. They also supported the efforts of a Lari priest, Abbé Fulbert Youlou, to organize a political party, the Democratic Union for the Defense of African Interests (UDDIA).

In reaction, the Mbochi began organizing their own political party, the African Socialist Movement (MSA), under Jacques Opangault. These ethnic-based parties clashed as early as 1948 in the streets of Pointe-Noire. Eleven years later, Mbochi fought Lari under party banners in Brazzaville. Each confrontation left dead and wounded in its wake, and the bitterness increased.

After independence in 1960 the southerners dominated the government, and their strength increased

A field of corn is sprayed with a pesticide. Efforts are being made to diversify crops in this country that straddles the Equator. (Photo: United Nations/ Caracciolo/Banoun.)

up to 1968. From 1968 to the present, however, the northerners have had the upper hand. During these years, coup, countercoup and political assassination have been intimately linked to complex interethnic relations. Almost all personal relationships in urban areas, appointments to civil service positions, and political changes are affected by ethnic loyalties.

These deep divisions are, however, not immediately visible to the outside observer. The Mbochi, Lari, and Batéké are all Bantu. Probably half of them are Christian. They attend the same school system. Congo, in fact, has a very high rate of school attendance, particularly at the primary level, with 450,000 pupils, practically 100 percent of the school-age population, in attendance. (According to law, all children must attend school between the ages of 6 and 16.)

The roots of contemporary political problems go far back into the colonial and precolonial past. Before the delineation of contemporary political frontiers by the French, the Belgians, and the Portuguese, today's ethnic groups were part of political systems with different, albeit less well-defined, geographical frontiers. For example, the capital of the Bakongo kingdom to which the Lari belonged is in northern Angola. The Batéké were linked with Batéké in Gabon's Upper Ogooué region; the coastal people belong to the Loango kingdom; and the Mbochi's loyalties stretched north.

Competition between French and Belgian interests and explorers like Pierre Savorgnan de Brazza as well as the famous Berlin Congress in 1884–1885 set the

Young men use a 1,500-foot fishing net; the government is encouraging fishing in an effort to diversify the economy. (Photo: United Nations/ Caracciolo/Banoun.)

frontiers of Zaire and Congo, then called the Belgian Congo and the French Congo respectively. These frontiers divided ethnic groups and set members of the same group along different paths of political change.

Because of a sense of ethnicity and a high rate of literacy (30 percent), Congo has had an interesting— if somewhat agitated—political history since World War II. With the extension of citizenship and voting rights in 1946, political parties grew in strength. Under the leadership of the somewhat flamboyant Abbé Fulbert Youlou, UDDIA won the majority of seats in the local assembly by means considered dishonest by opponents.

In 1958, General Charles de Gaulle returned to power in Paris and offered the French people and the Africans a new constitution linking the two peoples in a Franco-African community. Although Congo voted to join the community, the country declared its independence only two years later, on August 15, 1960. Because neighboring Zaire, more distant English-speaking states, and Cameroon and Togo had demanded independence and received it, Congo's leaders could no longer resist the sweep of history. Youlou, the country's first Prime Minister, became President after independence in 1960.

Safely ensconced in the presidential palace, the former home of the Governor General of French Equatorial Africa, Youlou made no secret of his pro-French sympathies. He refused to promote a vigorous Africanization of the civil service, the army's officer corps, and businesses. French business interests maintained their privileges, and a certain amount of antiblack racism persisted. Thus a growing group of unemployed school and university graduates began working against the regime. Railroad, dock, and other workers, who had been organized into vigorous trade unions, also began to criticize a regime they saw as deeply corrupt. In August 1963, workers and students declared a general strike, and they quickly forced President Youlou to resign. Alphonse Massemba-Débat, another southerner who had been president of the National Assembly, replaced Youlou.

In order to reorganize the society and mobilize the people to work for the country—and in order to build a loyal constituency for himself—Massemba-Débat created a single party, the National Revolutionary Movement (MNR). More important, he set up a youth wing, the Youth of the National Revolutionary Movement (JMNR). These organizations and the government established warm relationships with the People's Republic of China and other Communist states. A few enterprises were nationalized. With revolutionary slogans on their lips, the JMNR organized unemployed youth into self-styled vigilante brigades, which harassed those not considered sufficiently loyal to the regime and party. The arrest and expulsion of United States embassy personnel led to the closing of American offices and the cessation of diplomatic relations in 1965.

In 1968, under the leadership of Captain Marien Ngouabi, a Mbochi, the army seized power and further radicalized the regime. Ngouabi suppressed trade unions and created a new single party, the Congolese Worker's Party (PCT). At the same time, he declared that the country would follow the path of scientific socialism or Marxism. The name of the country was changed to the People's Republic of the Congo. More extensive nationalization of private property followed. Quickly, however, other military men organized coups against their colleagues.

President Ngouabi was assassinated on March 18, 1977. Former President Massemba-Débat and other southerners were immediately accused of the crime, hastily tried, and executed. A mass trial in January 1978 set the stage for the execution and imprisonment of other southerners.

A northerner, General Joachim Yhomby-Opango, replaced Ngouabi and approached the United States and other Western countries for aid and the normalization of relations. Under Yhomby-Opango, the country seemed to be moving from the socialist path, although he was abruptly replaced in 1979 by Colonel Denis Sassou-Nguesse, another northerner, who apparently contined to turn toward the West. The highest ranking southerner is the Prime Minister, Colonel Louis Sylvain-Goma, who also served under President Ngouabi.

France continues to be the most important influence in Congo. During the colonial period French was the only language used as a medium of instruction in the schools, and French culture was systematically promoted. The path to higher education led exclusively to France. Today most Congolese believe that the French language and culture are superior to their own as well as to American or Russian culture. With independence and the extension of the school system, even more children than before have learned French (and believe in the superiority of French culture).

On the other hand, increasing numbers of intellectuals and teachers would like to assert a Congolese and an African identity through the promotion of African languages like Lingala and Kikongo, both spoken widely. Increasing calls for the use of African languages in education and government frighten poorer people, however, because they believe that if their children do not receive a French-style education, they will never have access to the best jobs. Because of the ever-present ethnic tension, the elevation to official status of one language over another could lead to intense conflict.

It is also unfortunate that the urban population has become highly politicized over the last 15 years, taking to the streets quickly to support or to oppose governments. As a result institutions lack permanence, and personalities play an overly important role in politics.

New leaders, intellectuals, and the common people are searching for solutions to these problems. Rapid solutions to some of them are needed to prevent complete discouragement with the promises of African independence. Solutions labeled capitalist have failed; solutions labeled socialist have failed. Pessimism is growing and may lead finally to the complete rejection of the processes of modernization and development. If this occurs, Congo's leaders will bear the responsibility for sabotaging the building of their nation.

Brian Weinstein

Ethiopia

Area: 472,000 sq mi (1,222,480 sq km)
Population: 31 million
  Density: 66 per sq mi (25 per sq km)
  Growth rate: 2.5% (1970–1977)
Percent of population under 14 years of age: 44% (1967 est.)
Infant deaths per 1,000 live births: 162 (1970)
Life expectancy at birth: 35 years (1970)
Leading causes of death: malaria, tuberculosis, intestinal parasites
Ethnic composition: Amhara, Oromo, Tigre
Languages: Amharic (official until 1974), Tigrinya, Gallinya, Arabic
Literacy: 7%
Religions: Ethiopian Orthodox Christian 35–40%; Muslim 40–45%; animist 15%
Percent population urban: 7%
Percent population rural: 93%
Gross national product: $3.64 billion
  Per capita GNP: $120
  Per capita GNP growth rate: 0.2 (1970–1977)
Inflation rate: not available

Ethiopia has been a socialist state since 1974, when Emperor Haile Selassie was overthrown by revolutionary left-wing elements of the military. Today, the entire population, estimated at more than 30 million, is caught up in the throes of the revolution, and from the interior to the towns, the lives of Ethiopians have been strikingly altered. Since the revolution, the peasants have been given land that for centuries they worked as serfs; the urban population has been organized into *kebelles* (associations of urban dwellers) that function as local political and judicial organizations; and the once-powerful functionaries of the Haile Selassie regime have been arrested, forced into exile, or killed. The attempt by the military to impose socialism from above has revolutionized life in Ethiopia.

Ethiopia's past and present have been defined in part by its geographical position. Since 1953, Ethiopia has been the object of superpower interest because of its border on the Red Sea, a major waterway through which oil is shipped from the Persian Gulf to West Europe, Israel, and the United States. It has also had to battle domestic insurgents in the troubled province of Eritrea in order to maintain its outlets to the sea. Ethiopia's vast mountain range has also influenced the course of its history; the rugged terrain has formed a natural barrier to foreign invasion. In its 3,000-year history, Ethiopia was never colonized. Except for the years between 1935 and 1941, when it was occupied by Italy, Ethiopia has controlled its own destiny. But perhaps the most important influence on Ethiopia before 1974 was feudalism, which defined the political system, shackled agricultural growth, impeded modernization, and formed the bedrock of all social and political power.

Ethiopia's territory is divided between the highlands of the north and the lowlands of the south. About two-thirds of the land rises high above the lowlands to form part of the East African Rift Plateau. In Ethiopia, its general elevation is 5,000–10,000 feet (1,500–3,000 meters) above sea level, and it is dotted with high mountain ranges and cratered cones. In the north, the Great Rift Valley is marked by the Danakil Depression, a large triangular desert that is one of the hottest places in the world. Above the Danakil is a hot, arid coastal strip of land between 10 and 50 miles (16 and 80 km) wide that leads to the Red Sea coast.

Villagers walk along a partially paved road in Bedelle. Less than 10 percent of the people live near an all-weather road in this country of rugged terrain. (Photo: United Nations/Muldoon, Jr.)

Lake Tana, Ethiopia's largest lake, lies at the center of the highlands.

In contrast, the lowlands, descending from the southwestern slopes of the Great Rift Valley, are less abrupt and are broken by river exits, leading to largely tropical, sparsely populated lowland. The southeast, in the arid Ogaden, is largely desert.

The cool zone in the center of the western and eastern part of the high plateau has temperatures ranging from 32 to 60°F (0 to 15°C). The temperate zone in the high plateau in the northwest has temperatures between 60 and 85°F (5 and 30°C), while the hot zone, which encompasses the Danakil Depression, east Ogaden, the lowlands of Eritrea, and the belts along the Sudan and Kenya border, has temperatures ranging from 80 to 120°F (25 to 50°C).

All the country's rivers originate in the highlands, and the Blue Nile River, which has its source in Lake Tana, flows into Egypt's Nile River. Vegetation ranges from forests to desert scrub to eucalyptus trees to grasslands. There are minor amounts of gold, manganese ore, quarry salt, and platinum. The land area is 54 percent grassland, of which some 8 percent is cultivated; forests occupy about 7 percent; the rest of Ethiopia is desert, water, or nonagricultural land. The many great rivers and streams are not being used to generate hydroelectric power.

Although the country covers 472,000 square miles (1,222,480 sq km), much land is underutilized. The havoc caused by the redistribution of land has not yet brought agricultural development, although there are indications that after distribution is normalized, agricultural growth will accelerate.

Coffee is the major export crop; more than 300,000 tons (27,000 t) are produced yearly. Teff, a grain used domestically, is planted widely. The livestock population is estimated at 50 million, the largest in Africa. Livestock constitutes one-eighth the value of total exports. Industry is basically local and is very small scale. Transportation is largely by road, but roads are poor and often impassable, and only some 8 percent of the population lives near an all-weather road. Since 1917, there has been a railroad between Addis Ababa and Djibouti used for exporting Ethiopian goods, but the line is often closed because of Ethiopia's constant state of war with Somalia.

Ethiopia has only one major city—Addis Ababa, the capital, with a population of 1,046,300 (1975 est.). Because of the influx of refugees from Eritrea province, which has been attempting to secede since 1962, the population of Addis Ababa has grown rapidly. Asmara, the once-beautiful capital of Eritrea, has been destroyed by incessant Ethiopian bombing.

Ethiopia is a lively mix of ethnic groups, but until the revolution of 1974 one group, the Amhara, dominated society and set all the norms and values. Constituting 19 percent of the population, the Amhara have dominated culture and politics since 1270. They have controlled the monarchy, the Ethiopian Orthodox (Coptic) Church, the military, and all other social and political institutions. The Tigre, in the north, make up about 16 percent of the populace and have historically aligned themselves with the Amhara in order to gain power.

The Oromo (Galla)—mostly Muslim—comprise 40 percent of the population and have been dominated by the other two ethnic groups. They were forcibly integrated into the Ethiopian empire in the nineteenth century, though many reject their inclusion. There are also dozens of smaller ethnic groups. Until 1974, the official language was Amharic, and the Amhara controlled all social and political institutions, established the cultural patterns, and oppressed all other ethnic groups. In 1974, their power was torn from them when the old regime was dismantled.

From the fourth century, the Ethiopian Orthodox Church—which adheres to the doctrine of Monophysitism—has been a power in the country. Cooperating with the Amhara, who filled most of its positions, the church established Ethiopia's cultural framework, owning 18 percent of the land and participating fully in the feudal system. After the revolution the church was stripped of its land, its political authority was nullified, and all religions were granted equal status.

Most Ethiopian art is church-related because of the once-dominant role of the church. There are paintings on the walls and ceilings of many churches. But since those in the interior are painted on the mud and wattle walls of the churches, they are fast disintegrating. The deacons and priests make no attempt at restoration because they believe they should not intrude on the work of the past. There are a few modern artists, notably Afewerk Tekle. His mural depicting modern Africa can be found in Africa Hall, Addis Ababa, the site of conferences of the Organization of African Unity. Ethiopian music is also essentially related to the church.

Until the revolution, Ethiopians had little appreciation of the nation, but were oriented toward their ethnic group or the church. There was little integration of non-Amhara into Ethiopia's political or economic life. Whether a new national culture will arise from the revolution is still to be seen; social existence is certainly more nationally oriented than it was before 1974. Some ethnic antagonisms have been eliminated, and the powers of the church and of the Amhara have declined greatly.

For most Ethiopians, life today is still primitive and oppressive. Most rural Ethiopians work very, very hard from early morning until darkness falls, seven days a week. Most farmers do not own oxen, and the men pull their own plows on their small plots of land, aided by their male children. In their mud and wattle huts, village women feed their families, care for their small children, provide all the needs of the household and wait on the male adults and male children. Until the revolution, Ethiopian peasants did not know that there was any other way to live.

Family life is stratified along sex lines. The male head of the household is the primary authority figure. In the cities, male authority has been diminished because of Western influences, and women play a more

powerful family role than they do in rural settings. Religion, too, has been a factor in family existence. Both the Orthodox Church and Islam (practiced by some 40 percent of the people) have reinforced the male authority role. Both prohibit the questioning of the primary family authority.

Until 1974, the ruling class in Ethiopia was made up of Amhara elite, who filled all political and economic positions of any significance. Most of Ethiopia's 30 million people (1977 est.) are peasants, who have traditionally made up the lowest strata in the class system. A middle class of urbanized government bureaucrats is small in both numbers and power. No accurate figures can be given for any of these groups because no census has ever been taken in Ethiopia. In 1974, class roles were altered, but the structure remained. The lifestyle of the peasants improved, while the Amhara ruling class was eliminated and replaced by military rulers.

Education in Ethiopia has been a disaster. According to the government's own figures, in 1965 only 3.2 percent of rural children between the ages of 7 and 14 attended school, although in the urban centers the figure was 69 percent. From 1961 to 1966, 74.3 percent of all students left school between the first and sixth grades, and 72.5 percent dropped out between the seventh and twelfth grades. In 1966, there were only 945 schools served by 11,501 teachers, most of whom were untrained. Literacy is said to be 5 percent.

The educational system was neglected in rural Ethiopia, and only slightly less neglected in urban centers. At present, the university system is only open intermittently because college students, who oppose the ruling elite, use the campus as a staging ground for the opposition. Whether the new leaders will eventually develop an educational system that will function as more than a tool to reinforce their socialist values remains to be seen.

Until his overthrow on September 12, 1974, Haile Selassie ruled Ethiopia with an iron fist. Emperor since 1930 and wielding real power since 1916, Haile Selassie maintained a feudal system that incorporated most of the peasant population. No opposition was

A rural house in the village of Godino shows the government's effort to improve living conditions in rural Ethiopia, where life is still very primitive. (Photo: United Nations/ Ray Witlin.)

permitted, and the emperor's power was viewed as emanating from God. With the help of private landlords and the Ethiopian Orthodox Church, Haile Selassie headed a government that owned 79 percent of the arable land and imposed a regime that allowed no legal, political, or economic rights to the oppressed class of tenant farmers and peasants.

In 1974, the lives of Ethiopians changed dramatically. The Provisional Military Administrative Committee (PMAC—or Dergue, as it is otherwise known), under the leadership of Lieutenant Colonel Mengistu Haile Mariam, a Shankele, took power, espousing a socialist ideology.

Ethiopia was underdeveloped economically because of the feudal land-tenure system. Arable land was not used productively by the ruling class. Tenant farmers who paid usurious rental rates, a tithe, and oppressive taxes had little incentive to farm land productively. A land reform program, which gave each peasant family free use of a 25-acre (10-hectare) plot was proclaimed in 1975. Peasant associations were set up to enforce the decree. The former tenant farmers were jubilant, and gave their full support to the Mengistu regime. At the same time, in Addis Ababa, kebelles were created to impose socialist values on the urban population and to root out supporters of the old regime. Truly revolutionary, both programs generated turmoil and violence. Those opposed to the new government, including the very radical left, were executed or jailed. Clearly, life changed radically for all Ethiopians after 1974, and the peasants who had suffered intolerably under previous governments benefited most from the change.

At the present revolutionary moment, family and social life is disrupted. Via the kebelles and peasant associations, people are admonished to turn in those who oppose (or may oppose) the new government, and this policy has affected the traditional family. It is doubtful that male primacy will ever again flourish as it did before 1974. In addition to the politicizing of the family, women have attained major positions in the revolution and have been armed. Children, too, are armed and are asked to watch their families for signs of counterrevolutionary activity.

The Dergue is intent on creating a new society and eradicating all signs of the past. The once-strong alliance with the United States has ended, and a new military alliance with the Soviet Union has taken its place. Self-proclaimed Marxist Mengistu Haile Mariam and his corulers maintain that Ethiopia was traditionally a feudal and oppressive state; and they are using the Soviet model to generate a new society. They see violence as a legitimate tool. Thus opponents are treated harshly, and new revolutionary institutions have been created to socialize the population.

Ethiopia has moved from feudalism to a socialist society very rapidly and very violently. Indeed, havoc reigns: the government is unable to develop and modernize the society because all its energies and resources are thrown into the war against its enemies. The Dergue is on a revolutionary road; the people of Ethiopia are caught up in events they would have found not only unbelievable but impossible to imagine before the revolution. The Dergue sees the past as cruel and evil, and makes no attempt to link Ethiopia's past with its future. Whatever the future brings, it will have little relationship to the old Ethiopia. A new Ethiopia is being born.

Peter Schwab

Ghana
(Republic of Ghana)

Area: 92,000 sq mi (238,280 sq km)
Population: 10.9 million
  Density: 118 per sq mi (46 per sq km)
  Growth rate: 3.0% (1970–1977)
Percent of population under 15 years of age: 47.5%
Infant deaths per 1,000 live births: 59 (1970)
Life expectancy at birth: 48 years (1978)
Leading causes of death: not available
Ethnic composition: Akan (Fanti, Ashanti, others), Ewe, Ga, Dagomba, Mamprussi, Gonja
Languages: English (official), Akan, Ewe, Ga, Mole-Dagbani
Literacy: adults 30%
Religions: Christian 43%; traditional 38%; Muslim 12%
Percent population urban: 33% (1975)
Percent population rural: 67% (1975)
Gross national product: $4.25 billion
  Per capita GNP: $390
  Per capita GNP growth rate: −2% (1970–1977)
Inflation rate: 145% (from June 1976 to June 1977) and higher

The first sub-Saharan African colony to obtain its independence (in 1957), Ghana was for some years a path-breaking country in politics, economic policies, and the anticolonial and Pan-African movement. Since the early 1960s, however, Ghanaians have experienced a depressed economy and a series of civilian and military regimes. During the most recent military regime (lasting from 1972 to 1979), economic conditions rapidly deteriorated; there were incredible rises in the prices of domestic foods and imports, accompanied by social dislocation and distress, and political conflict. Ghanaians have become desperate, and their political life is angry and harsh. Ghana returned to domestic civilian rule in late 1979 under the most disadvantageous conditions for future political and economic stability and progress.

Ghana is a small West African country of 92,000 square miles (238,280 sq km)—the size of Wyoming—

bordered on the south by the Atlantic Ocean, on the west by the Ivory Coast, on the east by Togo, and on the north by Upper Volta. A former British colony known as the Gold Coast, Ghana had few economic ties to these former French colonies except for the migrant workers from Upper Volta and the Ewe people, who live in both Ghana and Togo. Ghana is a fairly flat land, relieved only by the Togo hills, ranging in altitude from 1,000 to 3,000 feet (305 to 915 m) in the southwest, and some sharp scarps (rock faces) in the south and north. The southern and central portions of the country (except along the coast), with a mean rainfall of between 50 and 83 inches (127 and 210 cm) annually, are heavy rain forests, the source of Ghana's timber and cocoa. In the north and along the southeast Atlantic coast, with rainfall of between 43 and 50 inches (110 and 127 cm), the vegetation is largely savanna and scrub. The north is a large producer of Ghana's staple crops, cotton, and rice.

In the 1960s, a major dam and hydroelectric project was established on the Volta River in the south, at Akosombo, creating Lake Volta, one of the largest man-made lakes in the world. The old railway system, built to handle exports, runs from Sekondi to Takoradi, the seaport in western Ghana, north through the cocoa, timber, and gold regions to Kumasi, and back down to Accra, the coastal capital.

Ghana had a population of 8.6 million in 1970 and about 10.3 million in 1976; the annual rate of population growth is currently 3.1 percent. The Ghanaian people belong to a number of ethnic and linguistic groups. The largest linguistic group is the Akan (44 percent), of which the most important are the southwest coastal Fanti people (11.3 percent), the Ashanti (13.3 percent) in the south-central area, who created Ghana's most powerful traditional kingdom in the eighteenth and nineteenth centuries, and lesser numbers of Akyem; Akwapim, Kwahu (important as merchants), Brong, and Nzima.

The Akan people live in south and central Ghana. The Ga-Adangbe people (8.3 percent) live in the coastal capital, Accra, and in its hinterland. The highly adaptive and well-educated Ewe (13 percent) originate in southeastern Ghana. In the north, there is one major language cluster, the Mole-Dagbani, in which the Dagomba (3.2 percent) and Mamprussi (0.9 percent) are numerically small but of major sociopolitical importance. The same is true of the Gonja (0.9 percent) in the north.

Of the 8.6 million people in Ghana in 1970, some 6.5 percent were foreigners. The expulsion of aliens in 1970 was designed to create more jobs for Ghanaians. Foreign migrant labor has been of enormous importance in Ghana's development, particularly in agriculture, mining of gold and bauxite, trading and wage labor. The expulsion of aliens undoubtedly hurt the economy because foreign migrant workers were willing to take lowly and unpleasant jobs which Ghanaians scorn.

Agricultural production, trade, mission education, and wage labor moved from the south northward;

thus the Fanti, Akim, Ga-Adangbe, and Ewe in the south had greater opportunities and resources (education, labor skills, wealth from agriculture) than the Ashanti in the south-central area and the northerners. For this reason, ethnic origins frequently entered the political calculus of civilian life. A sensitivity to government expenditures and to representation by ethnic areas and regions has continued under civilian and military regimes, flaring up periodically despite the efforts of most governments to play down ethnic origins.

Religion is important in the lives of many Ghanaians. In 1970, about 43 percent identified themselves as Christians, 38 percent traditionalists, 12 percent Muslims, and 7 percent no religion. Many Christians belong to syncretistic Christian sects, combining Christian beliefs and practices with traditional African beliefs. The Christian Council and Catholic Bishops Conference have played important public roles.

Ghanaians are a friendly and outgoing people. Traditional practices of hospitality have endured, but deference to the elderly and to the chiefs has declined as educational skills have become more useful and prestigious and secular government has preempted many of the roles of chiefs. Nonetheless, in many areas of Ghana, and especially in the north and in Ashanti, chiefs, who are frequently well educated, continue to play important social, political, and eco-

A farmer sprays rice plants with pesticide; rice is increasingly grown as a cereal crop to provide food. (Photo: United Nations/FAO/ F. Botts.)

nomic roles. Chiefs and their appointees held two-thirds of the seats in local councils and one-third of the seats in district councils under the recent military regime and had an important institutional impact on local development. Regional houses of chiefs and a National House of Chiefs meet regularly and possess significant advisory influence.

The root of the social system is the extended family, incorporating parents, grandparents, brothers and sisters and their families, and cousins. Despite the rapid growth of the cities, where households tend to include only the nuclear family and visiting relatives, extended family ties are maintained by regular travel and the retention of land rights in rural areas. An unfortunate but understandable side effect of the extended family and village or ethnic loyalties is nepotism.

The movement from rural areas to towns and cities has accelerated. Ghana's urban population (towns over 5,000) has grown from 23 percent of the total in 1960 to 33 percent in 1975. The capital, Accra, grew from 367,343 in 1960 to 639,964 in 1970; greater Accra grew from 491,817 in 1960 to 851,614, at an annual rate of 5.6 percent. At this rate Accra will have a population of 1,468,523 in the 1980s.

The flight to the towns for jobs and a better life has vastly outpaced the capacities of the cities to construct housing and elementary facilities to cope with this population influx. Accurate data are not available, but unemployment is high, around 15 percent or more.

Ghanaians employed in the wage economy included 20.8 percent of the population in 1970, or 24 percent if apprentices and sharecroppers are included, an increase of only 1 percent from 1960. During the years between 1971 and 1974, the military regime increased government employment by 22 percent by spending vast sums, a pattern that continued until the end of the decade, with few results in increased

Jute, imported from Pakistan, is processed at the Fibre Bag Manufacturing Corporation plant in Kumasi. (Photo: United Nations/ PJ/DB.)

productivity. The number of Ghanaians engaged in agriculture declined from 61.8 percent in 1960 to 57.2 percent in 1970, of whom 29.5 percent were peasant farmers. Of these peasant farmers, 12.3 percent were self-employed cocoa farmers, whose exports continue to earn Ghana more than 60 percent of its foreign exchange. Another 13.1 percent in 1970 were unpaid family workers, mostly occupied in agricultural production. The 2 percent decline in peasant farmers during the decade from 1960 to 1970, a decline that continued throughout the 1970s, helps to account for the inability of Ghanaian agriculture to increase staple food production enough to feed the growing urban population. As food prices soared in the rural areas in the 1970s, men were increasingly obliged to abandon the land for urban jobs, leaving women and older people as the major source of agricultural labor.

The proportions of the Ghanaian work force employed in mining (1 percent), construction (2.3 percent), utilities (0.4 percent), and commerce (13.9 percent) in 1970 showed a small decline from 1960. An extremely large percentage of those engaged in commerce are marketwomen, who are particularly important in the wholesale and retail distribution of food and clothing and are an important socioeconomic (and occasionally) political force. As prices for local foods and other commodities soared in the 1970s, with shortages of essential commodities and ineffectual price controls, a flourishing black market developed, and the so-called "market queens" at the major city and town markets were accused of black market activities.

The proportions of Ghanaians employed in manufacturing (12 percent), transportation and communications (2.7 percent), and services (10.5 percent, including many government employees) in 1970 showed a relative increase over 1960. The number of people employed in services and manufacturing continued to increase during the 1970s, but the continuous disruption of shipments of imported components for manufacturing led to the significant underemployment of industrial workers. In the late 1970s, many factories were operating at between 40 and 50 percent of plant capacity; some had to shut down altogether.

The staple Ghanaian foods include such crops as cassava, cocoyam, yam, plantain (large banana) and such cereal crops as maize (Indian corn), guinea-corn, millet, and, increasingly, rice. In addition, fish (local and imported), wheat (bread), as well as indigenous fruits (pineapples and oranges), and peanuts are regular features of the Ghanaian diet. While guinea chicken has traditionally been available, attempts to increase the production of cattle, sheep, and poultry—primarily in the north and on the eastern coastal plains—have failed. Meat and poultry prices soared beyond the means of all but the most well-to-do Ghanaians in the late 1970s, with per pound costs five to six times their costs in the United States.

Indeed, one must define the condition of life of

Ghanaians in the 1970s in terms of food prices, which in the past consumed a little over 50 percent of the income of the average Ghanaian. The prices of local foods rose by 160 percent between 1963 and 1972, while the overall national consumer price index rose by 126 percent. But during the years between 1972 and 1977, local food prices rose by an astronomical 871 percent, while the CPI rose by 712 percent (in official figures; actual market prices were higher). Prices in the rural areas increased even more rapidly than in the cities, as the government and traders diverted supplies to feed urban inhabitants; but the earnings of the rural population kept up with inflation better than urban wages. In 1978, food prices increased another 89 percent over 1977 prices, while the CPI rose by 123 percent.

These cold figures bespeak the general impoverishment of Ghanaians over the last 8 years. A bewildered population watched the prices of basic foods and other commodities rise out of sight. The corrosive effect of inflation, compounded by a drastically inflated exchange rate for the Ghanaian currency (the cedi), has driven people out of productive jobs into trading, has encouraged smuggling of items subject to government price controls, and has induced more and more Ghanaians to engage in illicit activities in order to survive. Only food farmers, traders, smugglers, and corrupt government officials have prospered.

The development strategies pursued by Ghana have varied in some important ways under the different regimes that Ghana has had since independence from Great Britain in 1957. Ghana was ruled from 1957 to early 1966 by Kwame Nkrumah and the Convention People's Party (CPP), which had led the nationalist movement in Ghana. Although the economy grew at a fairly rapid rate during the years between 1955 and 1962, external economic problems and the desire to hasten the pace of development led the regime to adopt a dominant role in investment in agriculture and industry. Enormous state-sector investments were made during the period between 1961 and 1965; these investments were partly financed by excessive foreign borrowing. But mismanagement, state-sector inefficiencies, and corruption resulted in the waste of much of this investment. Very large increases were also made in social service expenditures. When international prices for Ghana's main export, cocoa, declined sharply, Ghana's economy suffered.

The National Liberation Council (NLC) overthrew the Nkrumah government, denounced both its authoritarianism and its economic mismanagement, and held power from 1966 to 1969. In order to reduce inflation and heavy overseas indebtedness, the NLC government reemphasized foreign and domestic capital investment, reintroduced pro-Western foreign policies, reduced both investment spending and the government's involvement in the economy, and fired many government workers. Yet, its deflationary policies and the absence of capital investment led to a generally stagnant economy.

As the NLC promised, democratic elections were held in 1969. A new civilian government came to power under the Progress Party (PP), led by Prime Minister Kofi Busia, which held power from October 1969 to January 1972. Despite its emphasis on private capital, the government still played a substantial economic role through state corporations and spending. It sought during 1970–1971 to increase the rate of economic growth. The rapid fall in cocoa prices during 1971 led to a severe balance of payments crisis, an austerity budget, antitrade union policies, and a sharp devaluation of the Ghanaian currency in 1971. Despite significant economic growth during 1970–1971, public antagonism to the inflationary impact of these policies contributed to another coup.

Under Colonel (later General) I. K. Acheampong, the military seized power in January 1972 and unilaterally repudiated some of Ghana's huge foreign debt and rescheduled other parts, reducing Ghana's immediate repayments but also eliminating sources of external financing. The imposition of economic controls was not effective. By 1978–1979, the economy was in a shambles. The core Acheampong policy to increase agricultural production, Operation Feed Yourself, was the most significant failure, because of poor policies and poor implementation and the severe droughts of 1975–1977. Government budget expenditures on agriculture increased elevenfold between 1971–1972 and 1977–1978, from 3.0 percent to 7.3 percent of the budget. However, production of many staple food crops fell or was stagnant. There were significant production increases only in cotton, palm oil, sugar cane, and rice (until 1977). This accounts for the inflation in food prices.

Ghana's key crop, cocoa, which provides 60 to 70 percent of its foreign exchange earnings, declined: the volume of cocoa beans and products exported declined by 69 percent during the years between 1972 and 1977, 50 percent from the average volume during

In the 1960s, the Volta Dam at Akosombo was constructed to provide hydroelectric power; Lake Volta, one of the world's largest artificial lakes, was created. (Photo: World Bank/Pamela Johnson.

the years between 1967 and 1971. This decline is in part accounted for by the fact that some cocoa was smuggled into surrounding countries that offered much higher prices to farmers; the decline was also due in part to long-term trends (old trees, old farmers). Indeed, all Ghana's major exports have declined in volume—timber, gold, bauxite, diamonds. Smuggling, high prices, inadequate funds for production, and corruption are perennial difficulties.

Many of Ghana's problems stem from its lack of foreign exchange and its policy of overvaluing its currency (including smuggling), reducing its ability to provide needed imports, especially spare parts. The overvaluation of the currency was accelerated by increasing budgetary deficits, and the government sought to stave off economic recession and political disaster by increased spending. Budget deficits were eliminated by simply printing money, increasing the supply of currency. Tax receipts were sufficient to cover only 50 percent of the budget in 1975–1976 and 1976–1977, only 40 percent in 1977–1978. During 1970–1977, Ghana experienced a real increase in gross domestic product of only 0.6 percent per year. This would mean a decline in per capita income of over 2 percent a year, were the population to increase at a rate of only 2.7 percent.

By tightly controlling imports, Ghana achieved trade balance surpluses during the years between 1972 and 1978 (except 1974) but had significant overall balance of payments deficits. It received little foreign assistance until 1978, when it accepted a package of economic reforms proposed by the International Monetary Fund. Control over imports impeded growth. So did mismanagement and corruption.

Ultimately, Acheampong's economic disasters and authoritarianism heightened civilian resistance to his continued rule. In 1976–1977, to save his regime Acheampong proposed a future Union Government (UniGov) whose goal was to provide continued military participation and to exclude political parties from politics. Civilian groups that formed to oppose Union Government were harassed and intimidated, and, after the March 1978 referendum, their leaders were arrested. In the referendum, the opposition mustered 44.5 percent against UniGov and alleged widespread fraud. Students and lawyers went on a 4-month strike until Acheampong was removed from power in July 1978 by Lieutenant General Edward Akuffo, who ultimately acceded to full civilian rule.

The Akuffo government adopted a program of economic reforms, among them a needed but drastic 139 percent devaluation (which raised import prices), an end to price controls and a decline in import controls, an austerity budget, and a (mismanaged) currency exchange to reduce the money supply. The immediate effect of these policies was to increase prices rapidly, causing widespread industrial unrest. Akuffo was ousted from power in June 1979 by low-level officers who insisted on a bloody purge of the senior military officers. Many leading officers, including Generals Acheampong and Akuffo, were quickly executed after closed military trials in June 1979.

Several new political parties were formed in 1979 to contest the June 1979 election held under the pro-

Ghanaian women clean fish caught by local fishermen at Tema. In the background stands the alumina storage dome belonging to the Volta Aluminum Company. (Photo: World Bank/Pamela Johnson.)

visions of the new constitution, which provided for a president and a single-house National Assembly. Only three parties were significant: the People's National Party (PNP), which won the Assembly election with 71 (51 percent) of the 140 seats; the Popular Front Party (PFP), under Victor Owusu, and the United National Convention (UNC), under political veteran William Ofori-Atta. The PFP and UNC won, respectively, 42 (30 percent) and 13 (9 percent) of the 140 Assembly seats and 30 percent and 17 percent of the vote in the first presidential election.

In a run-off election on July 11, 1979, Hilla Limann was elected President, and on September 24 he was sworn into office. Because of popular demands for employment and wage increases to offset inflation, his new civilian government will find it difficult to hold down government spending.

In the last century, Ghana, formerly the Gold Coast, has experienced British colonial rule, British cultural norms, and British political and economic institutions. Ghana's economy expanded to the international market, and Ghana became the world's foremost cocoa producer. Nationalism, independence (1957), and postcolonial attempts to refashion economic institutions created difficult situations for the new nation. In terms of overall economic and social well-being, Ghana is still one of the more prosperous countries in Africa, but in the last decade it has made little or no progress; in many areas it has actually regressed. Its current political and economic problems are overwhelming. A civilian regime must try to elicit public support and cooperation from an urban and rural citizenry that is skeptical of government policies. Unemployment in Ghana has soared and will stay high for some time. In 1960, a larger percentage of children of primary school age were in school (59 percent) in Ghana than in any other African country, but this percentage had hardly changed 15 years later (60 percent in 1975). The government increased the percentage of children attending secondary school during the years between 1960 and 1975 (from 3 percent to 35 percent), but these students have increasingly poor employment prospects. Ghanaians still enjoy a standard of living far higher than that in most African states, but must spend all their income on food and other essentials. With a population increase reaching 3.1 percent annually, 47.5 percent of Ghanaians were less than 15 years old in 1977. A tremendous effort to provide essential services (health, education) and employment is thus required. Ghana's future depends on the stability of its civilian government and on its ability to restore sustained economic growth.

Jon Kraus

Guinea

(People's Revolutionary Republic of Guinea)

Area: 95,000 sq mi (246,048 sq km)
Population: 5.1 million
  Density: 54 per sq mi (21 per sq km)
  Growth rate: 3% (1970–1977)
Percent of population under 18 years of age: 50%
Infant deaths per 1,000 live births: 172
Life expectancy at birth: 42 years
Leading causes of death: not available
Ethnic composition: Fula, Mandingo (Malinke), Susu
Languages: French (official), tribal
Literacy: 10% (1978)
Religions: Muslim, animist, Christian
Percent population urban: 15% (est.)
Percent population rural: 85% (est.)
Gross national product: $1.07 billion
  Per capita GNP: $210
  Per capita GNP growth rate: 2.5% (1970–1977)
Inflation rate: not available

Guinea's emergence as a separate nation derives from artificial borders drawn when this West African country became a colony of France in 1898, after two decades of warfare against the French. It retained these borders when it became a separate independent nation 60 years later. The richest of the French African colonies until the mid-1950s, Guinea holds an estimated one-third of the world's reserves of bauxite and has modest reserves of diamonds, iron, and uranium. But foreign investment has not been attracted to this one-party autocratic state, with an economy patterned after Cuba's, bureaucratic red tape, lack of statistical data, inefficient production methods, and shortages of trained middle-class personnel.

Guinea is bordered by Senegal, Mali, the Ivory Coast, Liberia, Sierra Leone, Guinea-Bissau (formerly Portuguese Guinea), and the Atlantic Ocean. Over half the country consists of the Fouta Djallon mountain range, which cradles the headwaters of the Niger, Senegal, and Gambia Rivers. The coastal area and the foothills behind it are pastoral and agricultural; the mountain ridge area is essentially pastoral, while the rain forest of the southeast produces oil palm and export fruit crops, along with typical African forest subsistence agriculture. Rainfall is heavy on the coast and in the forest area. The principal natural resource is bauxite.

Guinea has a population of about 5.1 million, growing at a rate of about 3 percent a year (1970–1977). Life expectancy is 42 years and approximately half the population is under 18 years of age. About 40 percent of the children die between the ages of 6 months and 5 years, directly or indirectly from malaria.

Over three-fourths of the population is Muslim; the rest follow native religions or Catholicism. The largest single ethnic/linguistic group, the Fula (better known as the Fulani of Nigeria), number over 1 million and occupy the high northern area. Mandingo (also known locally as Malinke, or "people of the king") number about 750,000 and are spread throughout most of the interior. About 500,000 Susu form the largest group in the coastal area.

Education is free but not compulsory. Elementary education, which reaches about 3 children out of every 4 in that age group, is in the local vernacular. French, the official language of Guinea, is understood by an estimated 10 percent of the population.

Guinea's predominantly Islamic culture has absorbed traditional patterns, including the placating of ancestors, seen as saintly or mischievous intermediaries with a spirit god. Life is perceived in concentric rings—the family, the clan, the ethnic group, the nation. Islam and the governing Democratic Party require loyalties that—in varying degrees according to ethnic group and level of education—can cut across these rings. Most land in Guinea belongs to the ethnic groups, and is distributed by the leadership according to family need.

Guinea was the coastal French colony in Africa most attracted to its traditional past; it has been most reluctant to embrace the Europeanization that so greatly influenced the coastal elites of similar French possessions. Native dress remained and remains common in the capital, even for middle-class men, in an age when it has largely disappeared from other French-speaking African cities.

Occupying an area about the size of Oregon, the country is almost exclusively rural. Conakry, the capital, has a population of about 600,000. The other large towns—Labé (450,000), Nzérékoré (300,000), and Kankan (275,000)—are essentially sprawling villages. Most Guineans remain rather inefficient subsistence farmers or government employees, with a few employed in the bauxite-alumina industries, and a few in raising export crops like pineapples and bananas, both of high quality.

Guinea keeps virtually no accurate national statistics of any sort, but international economic bodies believe Guinea has a gross domestic product (GDP) of about $1.2 billion, with a per capita GDP of about $200. Guinea exploits about 1 million tons a month of its bauxite resources and has a transformation industry producing 700,000 tons a year of alumina from bauxite. In addition, Guinea hopes to expand its modest diamond-mining industry (now hard-hit by smuggling to harder-currency neighbors). Diamond mining on an industrial scale began at Kouroussa in 1979 and 600 million tons of iron ore have been identified in the Nimba Mountains. A Franco-Italo-Japanese firm is extracting modest quantities of uranium.

Guinea is a well-watered country. It already makes use of hydroelectric power (partly for alumina production) and hopes to expand further in this area if substantial international funding becomes available. Agricultural export plans call for the increased development of pineapples, bananas, palm oil, low-quality robusta coffee (mostly for the instant coffee industry), and fishing, including shrimping.

Oil prospecting by East European countries in the 1960s proved negative, but new offshore drilling methods have revived hopes of oil, and a United States–led prospecting group is now at work. Guinea imports all its petroleum products and a wide range of finished goods; but by severely restricting consumption, it manages to preserve a small favorable trade balance.

Although Guinea's economy is organized along a localized version of Marxism-Leninism, bauxite and alumina have always been joint projects, managed by the government and three international consortia, two of them 51 percent Western-owned and the other, 51 percent Soviet-owned. Since legislation to attract foreign investment was passed in 1972, international capital has been sought for iron mining and other equity-intensive sectors of the economy: a Swiss-Arab consortium is considering investment in bauxite mining at Ayekoye, while a Euro-American group is considering a smaller bauxite project at Dabola, in the Fouta Djallon.

Total foreign investment in Guinea is estimated at $600 million, about a quarter of it American; but most of this is preindependence investment swollen by inflation. The development of new foreign investment has been sluggish, partly because of poor living conditions for expatriates, bureaucratic deficiencies, and endless red tape. However, if a Nimba iron-mining project is launched, this will add a further $800 million of foreign investment.

Fula rest in the entrance to their primitive dwelling; Guinea is essentially a nation of sprawling villages. (Photo: United Nations/ JGB.)

The Guinean currency, the sili ("elephant"), is not exchangeable on world markets. The sili is officially worth U.S. $.05 but changes on the black market for 1 cent. International trading is conducted in French francs and other strong currencies. Telephone and other technical services, including sanitation, are poor. The total outstanding foreign debt is over $1 billion, about half owed to Communist countries, and is rising by about $100 million a year—about the equivalent of all foreign-exchange income. Guinea's infrastructural developments, mostly funded by Communist-bloc loans, have not been paid for by increased production.

In 1958, after a UN–sponsored election that obliged France to set a date for the independence of Togo (a UN territory administered by France), President Charles de Gaulle felt obliged to offer a choice between nationhood and subsidized partial autonomy to French West African and French Equatorial African colonies. Guinea, led by a feisty socialist, Ahmed Sekou Touré, was the only colony that chose to break its colonial links. De Gaulle ordered the colony abandoned by all French civil servants and stopped all aid. The United States hesitated to recognize Guinean independence immediately for fear of offending France. Thus the Soviet Union and other Soviet-bloc countries established a firm foothold—a foothold that has persisted, with some ups and downs, to this day.

At the time of independence, Touré, a labor leader, was Prime Minister, mayor of Conakry, and a member of the French National Assembly. He created a one-party state and imprisoned or exiled thousands of political critics. Much of the country's middle-class elite fled, creating a dearth of professional, entrepreneurial, and administrative personnel like that created in the early 1960s in Cuba by Fidel Castro, whose policies and regime Touré greatly admires. Today, there are nearly 500,000 Guinean refugees in neighboring Senegal, where they make up one-eighth of the population. About 20,000 Guineans had returned from Senegal by late 1978.

Beginning in 1977, as part of a program to satisfy international human rights advocates, the Touré regime began to release political prisoners and to extend amnesty to exiles condemned for their political opinions. At the same time Touré tried to improve relations with France, the United States, and other Western powers, to expand trading links, and to attract investment.

Claiming descent from Samori, a nineteenth-century up-country warlord and slave dealer who has become a hero to Guineans because of his armed opposition to French colonization, Touré isolated Guinea from the mainstream of West African politics. He rules through a few aging ministers, along with 33 provincial governors, and a more widely spread party hierarchy that directly administers 170 districts and thousands of localized authorities called "powers." There is a rubber-stamp National Assembly with 150 members.

President Touré has moderated the harshness of his regime to satisfy international human rights concerns. He has also liberalized the higher levels of the economy somewhat to try to attract investment. In 1978, he resumed diplomatic relations with neighboring Senegal and ordered the Soviet air force to cease conducting Atlantic reconnaissance flights out of Conakry. During 1979, Touré reduced still further his links with Moscow, obliging the Soviet air force to move its Atlantic reconnaissance base from Conakry to Luanda, Angola, and reducing the Soviet military mission to a handful. The Guinean leader then began to cooperate with his neighbors in development plans for the Gambia River basin.

In 1978, President Valéry Giscard d'Estaing of France accepted an invitation to visit Guinea, the first visit from a French head of government in two decades of independence. Giscard promised increased French aid.

France and the United States remain Guinea's principal Western trading partners, and Guinea, self-sufficient in food before independence, remains a net importer of food from the West. This is largely due to inefficient working methods and a tendency to smuggle large quantities of food to neighboring countries in exchange for hard currency. The hard currency, in turn, can buy scarce but essential items like bicycle parts, imported cloth, and pharmaceuticals. Thus food supplies have diminished as the population has increased.

Like many similar third world regimes, Guinea seems to be seeking transformation slowly, afraid that major changes will be seen as an admission of failure

Soussou women carry their wares to the local market; colorful native dress is still the rule. (Photo: United Nations/JGB.)

by the regime, and might therefore be regarded as an invitation to overthrow. Touré and his colleagues are moving gingerly toward some accommodation with the West, partly to satisfy a growing popular demand for living standards closer to the living standards of neighboring coastal countries like Senegal and the Ivory Coast. But no rapid or major changes are anticipated. In this area, Touré is expected to mimic the cautious approach of Fidel Castro in Cuba. Touré is also an admirer of China. A strict Muslim, he hopes to attract economic assistance from wealthy countries in the Middle East; in 1978, he visited several oil-rich countries of that area. The Arab Bank for African Development and the Islamic Development Bank have financed a $12 million cement plant near Conakry.

Although U.S. and other Western aid is slightly on the increase, Guinea has difficulty qualifying for multilateral aid because of its poor statistical data and inefficient administration. However, Guinea belongs to the African Development Bank (ADB) and to the Economic Community of West African States (ECOWAS), a nascent free-trade-zone project. One urgently needed program is the improvement of the Conakry-Kankan railroad, which has only been patched up in the past 20 years.

Any change in government is likely to be military. Although a coup d'état has been freely predicted by observers for 20 years, Touré has so far succeeded in avoiding this disaster by keeping his armed forces small, playing its senior officers off against each other, and maintaining a relatively strong security network of informers, including East European instructors, in the military. Most of Guinea's bourgeois opposition leaders live in France, Senegal, and the Ivory Coast, and time has eroded their zeal to overturn the regime.

Russell Warren Howe

Ivory Coast
(Republic of Ivory Coast)

Area: 124,000 sq mi (322,500 sq km)
Population: 7.8 million
  Density: 63 per sq mi (24 per sq km)
  Growth rate: 6% (1970–1977)
Percent of population under 14 years of age: 40%
Infant deaths per 1,000 live births: 170 (1978)
Life expectancy at birth: 43.5 years
Leading causes of death: not available
Ethnic composition: 60 ethnic groups, including Baoule, Agni, Malinke, Bambara, Dioula, Lobi, Bobo, Koulango, Senoufu
Languages: French (official), Dioula, various African languages
Literacy: 20% (1978)
Religions: traditional 64%; Muslim 22%; Christian 14%
Percent population urban: 35%
Percent population rural: 65%
Gross national product: $6.58 billion
  Per capita GNP: $840
  Per capita GNP growth rate: 1.1% (1970–1977)
Inflation rate: average 18% last 5 years (1978)

Since independence in 1960, the Ivory Coast has achieved an unparalleled increase in economic growth compared with other African and third world countries, averaging annual increases of over 7 percent in the GNP. The "Ivorian miracle" in this small, coastal West African state the size of New Mexico has taken place under the stable and authoritarian single-party rule of the diminutive President Felix Houphouet-Boigny and his Democratic Party of the Ivory Coast (PDCI). Sustained economic progress has been largely the result of several key policies: continuing intimate economic and political ties with France, the ex-colonial power; the ardent advocacy of capitalism and an unrestricted entry for foreign capital; a growth strategy that focused on increased agricultural production and diversification of crops for export by African farmers; and import-substitution industrialization.

Houphouet-Boigny's choice of capitalist policies and his close ties with France have not been popular in Africa and have marked the Ivory Coast as a conservative state. However, while most African states have encountered repeated military intervention and intermittent economic growth or stagnation, the Ivory Coast has compelled its critics to acknowledge its success. Nonetheless, the Ivorian miracle has not been without problems and tensions. Rapid economic growth has led to quickened urbanization, which was about 35 percent in the late 1970s, and urban unemployment is widespread. Educated Ivorians increasingly demand the many middle- and upper-level jobs still held by French, Lebanese, and other Africans, in a country where 25 percent of the population is foreign-born. Income distribution is highly uneven, both regionally and individually. Private investment has slowed in recent years, and outflows of capital (profits, salaries) have hurt the balance of payments. The government has increased its direct participation in the economy to offset this decline, which has led to heavy foreign borrowing and indebtedness.

A small country bordering the Atlantic Ocean, the Ivory Coast is surrounded by Ghana to the east, Upper Volta and Mali to the north, both of which provide migrant labor, and Guinea and Liberia to the west. The southern 40 percent of the country is forest, with heavy rainfall, and is the source of the Ivory Coast's three major exports—coffee, cocoa, and timber. The northern part of the country edges into drier savanna, where maize, cotton, tobacco, and sugar are cultivated. In the northwest are the picturesque Man Mountains. None of the several small rivers are navigable as they meet the Atlantic, but the opening of the Vridi Canal in 1950, cutting through the lagoons around Abidjan, the coastal capital, created a major seaport. The country has good all-weather roads, and a railroad runs from Abidjan north to Upper Volta.

The Ivory Coast had an estimated (1975) population of 6.7 million people, with an estimated growth of about 4 percent per year, 2.4 percent through births and 1.6 percent through immigration. Of the 6.7 million, about 75 percent are Ivorians, divided into some 60 ethnic groups. Of crucial economic importance in agriculture and urban labor are the over 1 million immigrant workers from Upper Volta, Mali, and Guinea, the 50,000 to 60,000 French citizens, many of whom are active in government, state corporations, industry, and large and small commerce, and the 100,000 Lebanese, also in retail trade. Given many indigenous languages, French is the official national language; Dioula is the lingua franca of African commerce. In religion, 64 percent of the people practice traditional religions, 22 percent are Muslim, and 14 percent are Christian.

The urban population almost tripled from 1955 (13 percent) to 1975 (35 percent). Abidjan, the coastal capital, had a population of over 900,000 in the late 1970s and is the center of Ivorian development. Bouaké, in the center of Baoulé country, had a population of 120,000, and Gagnoa and Daloa had almost 50,000 and 65,000, respectively. The exodus to the towns has left agricultural work to women and to migrant workers from the north who seek wage employment in the Ivory Coast. Migration to the towns has also created increasing unemployment and underemployment in the cities, especially in Abidjan, where riots by the unemployed caused a major political shock in 1969.

Abidjan, with close to 15 percent of the Ivory Coast's population, is the focal point of development, commerce, industry, and political life. Built on four peninsulas that converge on the lagoons near the ocean, it has been inundated by immigration. The Plateau is the center of Abidjan, combining the open colonial structures with the postindependence ministerial office buildings and the more recent skyscrapers. Abidjan is the site of business and government offices, the major French trading establishments, the National Assembly, and the grand and remote Presidential Palace. Of the 50,000 French in the Ivory Coast, 20,000 are employed or self-employed in the private sector, and about 6,000 are in government—mostly in Abidjan.

Across the lagoon is Cocody, the residential area of the French and the prosperous Ivorian middle class. Also in Cocody are the University of Abidjan and the Hotel Ivoire, one of the most architecturally striking hotels in the world. Under construction is an "African

Riviera," a cluster of hotels and resort facilities financed by government and foreign capital to draw in tourists.

Treichville, also across the lagoon, is the largest African area, neatly laid out French-style, with many ethnically homogeneous quarters, including Baoulé, Beté, Malinke, Yoruba, Hausa, Dioula, and Senoufu neighborhoods. These are working-class quarters, with thousands of African and Lebanese shops, a great market, and a boisterous nightlife. Beyond Treichville are the industrial zones, with new industries in food processing, chemicals, and textiles. Then there are the poorer African townships of Adjamé and Koumassi.

Rapid population increases have created *bidonvilles*, or slum quarters, on the outskirts of the city. Within the city, rigid government housing codes permit only expensive buildings, and so there is little housing for new migrants. Even low-cost housing is usually controlled by the small Ivorian political and administrative elite; a 1977 inquiry showed that 7,000 of 21,000 low-cost houses had been sublet by high-salaried Ivorians for high prices.

The French presence is significant not only in government, finance, commerce, and education but also in the culinary arts and in the dress of educated Ivorians.

In the mid-1970s it was estimated that 86 percent of the population were engaged in agriculture; this percentage had declined by the late 1970s. In 1970, only 11.7 percent of the laboring population were in the modern wage sector, but another 15.3 percent were also paid wages, employed in small-scale artisan activities, domestic service, and agriculture.

In the private sector, in 1974, 82 percent of the wage-employed in agriculture were non-Ivorian African migrant workers, while 17 percent were Ivorians. This reflects the pronounced Ivorian aversion to en-

Workers are checking loads of logs to be shipped from the port of Abidjan; timber, an important commodity in the economy, is shipped to France, Germany, Great Britain, and other West European nations. (Photo: United Nations/H. Bijur/ PAS.)

gage in agriculture as paid workers and the fact that many Ivorians are self-employed farmers who hire labor. Indeed, the early Ivorian nationalists included many prosperous coffee and cocoa farmers, including Houphouet-Boigny, who established an enormous plantation in his home town of Yamousskro with foreign technical assistance. The number of those working in industry increased from 20,780 in 1966 to 43,243 in 1974, of whom Ivorians represented 62 percent, other Africans 34.4 percent, and non-Africans 3.6 percent. In the private service sector, in 1974, Ivorians represented a majority of 53.6 percent, other Africans 35 percent, and non-Africans 11.2 percent.

The data on wage employment in the private sector (excluding the self-employed) indicate the enormous inequality in incomes between Ivorians, other Africans, and non-Africans. The lowest 40 percent of income earners received about 19.7 percent and the top 20 percent earned 51.6 percent of all income in 1974. In 1970 the Ivory Coast ranked among those countries where the poorest 40 percent received the least income. By 1974, Ivorian farmers were receiving substantial government price increases for agricultural products. Nonagricultural workers received about four times as much as predominantly non-Ivorian African agricultural workers received.

The government's economic development policy has been incredibly successful in terms of economic growth rates and increases in production and exports though markedly less successful in increasing the living standards of the 80 percent of the population making 42 to 48 percent of all income. During the 15 years, 1960–1975, the GNP in the Ivory Coast increased by 7.4 percent in real terms. With an average annual population increase of about 3.8 percent during these years, real per capita income increased by 3.6 percent a year, though less during 1971–1975. Growth continued in the late 1970s, with GNP in-

creases of 12 percent in 1976 and 8 percent in 1977 and 1978, though it will be much slower in 1979 and 1980. In 1950, per capita income was estimated at $70; it had risen to $145 in 1960 and $450 in 1974 (or $190 at 1950 prices). In part because of the phenomenal increase in coffee, cocoa, and timber prices in the late 1970s, per capita income was estimated at almost $1,000 at the end of 1978.

The development strategy of the Ivory Coast has had several features, including close relations with France with assurances of a protected market in France for its exports, a stable currency linked to the French franc, and an open door to foreign capital, especially French. The last has led to a fairly rapid increase in light industry and commerce. While some of the investment has gone into import-substitution industrialization of elite consumer goods, a significant amount of money has wisely been invested in agro-industries, processing coffee, cocoa, timber, pineapples, and cotton (into textiles) for export. The agro-industries have been growing much more rapidly than industries requiring imported components.

The major industrial products, in terms of production and workers employed, are grain and flour, canned and preserved food, animal fat products, textiles (much of them exported), woods, chemicals, construction materials, electrical materials, and electric and water energy. In January 1975, 67.6 percent of manufacturing capital was foreign (primarily French), 24 percent Ivorian government, and 8.5 percent Ivorian private. Ivorian government ownership has increased significantly since then and includes the single refinery and the state shipping line.

The Ivory Coast has also focused on increased production of agriculture for export and crop diversification, reducing dependence on a single crop. Thus, while the volume of coffee exports increased by 72 percent between 1960 and 1975, as a total of all exports it declined from 48.5 to 25.2 percent. The volume of cocoa exports increased by 169 percent during the period 1960–1975 but held steady at 22 to 23 percent of total exports. Timber increased from 16 to 20 percent of exports, while the volume of timber exports increased by 183 percent. During the period 1960–1975 pineapples increased from 1.5 percent of exports to 3.7 percent, cotton from 0.5 to 3.8 percent, palm oil from 0 to 3.9 percent, petroleum products from 0 to 5.4 percent, and other products from 5.2 to 11.8 percent.

In support of increased agricultural production and diversification, the government devoted 12 percent of public investment to agriculture in the period 1961–1975. Large portions of these funds were invested in state plantations, which showed substantial production increases despite great cost overruns. Specialized semiautonomous institutes were established to oversee the development of many of these crops. Much less attention and public money have been devoted to the increased production of staple food crops (except rice). Thus, there have been much smaller in-

The hydroelectric dam at Kossou on the Bandama River has an installed capacity of 174 megawatts and has reduced the country's dependence on imported oil. (Photo: United Nations/Wolff/JMcG.)

creases in the production of Ivorian staple foods, which include tropical root crops like yams, cassava, and plantain (large banana) and cereals like maize (Indian corn) and millet. Paddy rice has been the exception, increasing from 250,000 tons (226,750 t) in 1965 to over 400,000 tons (362,800 t) in the mid- and late 1970s. Increased food imports have stimulated new government encouragement for food production.

The Ivory Coast has successfully undertaken audacious and controversial development projects. The Koussou hydroelectric complex on the Bandama River, south of Bouaké, with an installed capacity of 174 megawatts, was considered by the World Bank as excessive in terms of Ivory Coast needs. It was completed in 1972, and its relatively cheap supply of energy has decreased Ivorian dependence on imported oil since the spiraling oil price increases. Large plantations of oil palm and coconut palm were considered too ambitious but were carried out successfully, with production reaching markets as oil prices boomed. The creation of the port of San Pedro, in the undeveloped, underpopulated rain forest of the southwest coast, was very expensive, but when it was completed in 1972 it permitted a large increase in timber exports.

More recently, however, the government has not been able to find the external investment for an iron-ore complex nor for a timber plantation and paper pulp plant with an annual capacity of 400,000 tons (362,800 t). The government has decided to undertake the pulp plant itself, but found it difficult to secure loans for the necessary foreign exchange ($500 million at 1975 prices).

The Ivory Coast has been able to diversify its major trading partners. While in 1960 France bought 51 percent of its exports and supplied 65 percent of its imports, in 1976 France took only 25.4 percent of its exports and provided only 38.4 percent of its imports. Other Common Market countries have increased their share of Ivory Coast exports from 15 to 36 percent between 1960 and 1974, and Ivorian imports from the Common Market increased from 10 to 18 percent between 1960 and 1974. Exports to the United States have doubled from 7 to 14 percent (between 1960 and 1974) as have imports, from 3 to 6 percent during the same period.

Despite the Ivory Coast's economic success in its first 19 years of independence, it confronts significant development problems. Although the rapid increase in its exports has given it a healthy balance of trade, for many years it has had an overall balance of payments deficit. This is due to a declining inflow of foreign private capital, large service payments (insurance, freight, commissions), and a heavy outflow of profits and salaries (some 60 percent of the latter, or about $200 million annually, from French inhabitants).

As foreign capital inflow declined, the government increased its share in investment from 40 percent (in the 1960s) to 60 percent of the total. To maintain this investment, the Ivory Coast started to borrow heavily abroad. By 1978, it had an external debt of $4 billion (though only half of it had been drawn on by mid-1979). This meant that an increasingly large percentage of its exports would have to be used to repay past debts, from 12.4 percent in 1978 to a potential 25 to 30 percent in 1981. In 1978–1979, the Ivory Coast adopted an austerity program, reducing government investment spending and eliminating prestige projects. With declining cocoa and coffee prices in 1978–1979 and timber exports unlikely to increase, its balance of payments may worsen.

The Ivory Coast has made impressive strides in education, but problems remain. Primary school students as a percentage of school-age children (between 5 and 14) rose from 9 percent in 1955 to 31 percent in 1960 to 47 percent in 1971. The number of primary school students increased by another 40 percent by 1978. Secondary school students as a percentage of school-age children (between 15 and 19) rose from 1 percent in 1955 to 18 percent in 1971 and the percentage has continued to increase. The only university, in Abidjan, had over 7,000 students in 1978, with some 2,000 more Ivorians studying abroad.

The problems are cost and employment. The share of education in the country's recurrent budget (i.e., apart from investment) increased from 22 percent in 1960 to 33 percent in 1973, the highest percentage in the world, and it has continued to rise. The costs reflect the fact that education is virtually free through college, that 75 percent of secondary school teachers are highly paid expatriates, and that an expensive system of television education has been introduced, with the object of improving instruction in French and reforming the curriculum.

In the mid-1970s, it was optimistically estimated that the modern salary sector could absorb 30,000 new employees a year, but more than 50,000 people were seeking salaried jobs. For the middle-level (high school education) and high-level (university) work force, it was estimated that during 1975–1980 the Ivory Coast would have 3 to 5 times more applicants than jobs. One solution, for which there is great support among the educated Ivorians, is to replace the French workers with Ivorians (Ivorianization). In the mid-1970s, there were over 12,000 French in public and private employment; they held 80 percent of the jobs requiring a university education, 60 percent of those needing upper secondary education, and 30 percent of those requiring lower secondary education. Ivorianization of many of these French-held positions would save a great deal of money, open up jobs for the newly educated, and reduce sharply the outflow of salary remittances that hurts the balance of payments. The government has resisted rapid Ivorianization for years, and several thousand technical assistants cannot easily be replaced as industry rapidly expands. Over 9,500 of the French are in private-sector management. A plan for Ivorianization of the private-sector management posts has been implemented slowly.

The government is also seeking to reform the educational system, to alter the largely French curriculum to meet Ivorian needs. Emphasis is to be placed on vocational education, specialized work force needs, and agricultural skills. Such a reform will be difficult to implement in a society and culture where an elite education based on French standards gives access to elite employment, income, and status.

Since 1944, the dominant figure in Ivory Coast political life has been Felix Houphouet-Boigny (he added Boigny, meaning "irresistible force," in 1946), who took the Ivory Coast to independence in 1960. His Democratic Party of the Ivory Coast (PDCI) established a single-party state very quickly, and Houphouet was elected President four times for 5-year terms, most recently 1975.

Houphouet, 75 years old in 1980, has maintained vigorous control over Ivorian political life, employing both patronage and repression. Ivorian economic prosperity has generally helped to keep the government popular, as has Houphouet's status as a nationalist leader. When discontent erupted among the unemployed in Abidjan in 1969, Houphouet started a series of "dialogues," meeting with many Ivorian and expatriate groups, hearing their grievances and acting on them, a method to which he periodically resorts. Young French-educated Ivorians demanding change have been mollified with jobs in public enterprises or civil service; the latter has grown from 19,904 employees in 1965 to 42,969 in 1975, and its salaries in 1976 absorbed 52 percent of the ordinary budget. The PDCI is no longer a mass party but the network of an old elite, firmly guided by one of Houphouet's oldest lieutenants, Philippe Yacé. A net of party secretaries covers the country, in tandem with the centralized structure of administration, overseen locally by prefects and subprefects.

The political system faces challenging problems, including the succession to Houphouet. A constitutional change in 1976 made Yacé, Speaker of the National Assembly, heir apparent. But when he organized too much publicity for himself in 1979, he was sent to Europe for a rest, and Houphouet announced that he would seek reelection again in 1980.

A second major problem is the vast inequality, both between the regions and between the elite and non-elite. Responding to discontent because of the undoubted corruption among the entrenched Ivorian elite, Houphouet took drastic action in 1977 and fired nine of his ministers, including the four most powerful, who had served in the government almost since independence. However, this does little to relieve the lack of opportunity for political participation in the regime.

Without any opposition, the party has grown flabby with age. The National Assembly is a rubber stamp for government policies. But although the trade unions have no power and are relatively inactive, the government increased urban wages in the 1970s enough to increase real wages. The Chamber of Commerce and other French interest groups are influential.

In foreign policy, Houphouet has acted as the conservative statesman, intent on maintaining close ties with France and acting as spokesman for many of the former French colonies in West Africa in opposing the actions of more radically nationalist African states. The presence of a 600-man French troop contingent is a measure of French support for Houphouet, France's most valuable African ally, a guarantee against any coup d'état from within. Like many conservative leaders, Houphouet is leery of change. He has chided the Western countries openly about failing to look after Western interests in Africa. The Ivory Coast is one of the few African countries that maintains friendly ties with Israel. Houphouet has also pursued the extremely unpopular policy of attempting to open a "dialogue" with South Africa in the hope that it will change its apartheid policies without violence.

Social, economic and politican conditions of life have changed dramatically for Ivorians in the last 40 years. Until after World War II, the Ivory Coast was a colonial backwater, greatly overshadowed by Senegal. Its traditional political institutions, fashioned and controlled by the French since the late nineteenth century, had withered. Some change had occurred in Abidjan, while up-country towns were stagnant. Since 1945, the Ivory Coast has changed dramatically in terms of political life, urbanization, health standards, educational opportunities, social habits, and economic prosperity. The Ivorian economic miracle is world famous. The government policy of paying high prices to farmers for produce has increased rural incomes. The Ivory Coast has continued to defy the predictions of those who said its economic model led not to the genuine development of a national economy but simply to high growth figures, with the profits siphoned off to France.

However, the next few years pose serious questions. An authoritarian and rusty political system will have to handle the succession without unleashing drastic change. Will it do so with repression, or will it permit political participation? In 1979–1980 the government cut back on expenditures in order to hold down inflation and foreign indebtedness. It is not clear whether the economy will be able to return to the growth rates of the 1970s, especially with the slowdown in foreign private investment and the increasingly dominant government role in investment.

Jon Kraus

Kenya

(Republic of Kenya)

Area: 224,960 sq mi (582,646 sq km)
Population: 15.2 million
  Density: 68 per sq mi (26 per sq km)
  Growth rate: 3.8% (1970–1977)
Percent of population under 14 years of age: 46% (1973)
Infant deaths per 1,000 live births: 129 (1975)
Life expectancy at birth: 50 years (1975)
Leading causes of death: not available
Ethnic composition: Luo, Luhya, Kikuyu, Kamba, Meru, Giriama, Kalenjin
Languages: English, Swahili
Literacy: not available
Religions: Christian, Muslim, animist
Percent population urban: 15%
Percent population rural: 85%
Gross national product: $4.8 billion
  Per capita GNP: $320
  Per capita GNP growth rate: 0.9% (1970–1977)
Inflation rate: not available

Kenya is one of the most scenic countries in the world. Its physical beauty is matched by an extraordinary diversity of races and peoples. The ability of this multiethnic and multiracial society to harness human energies is the key to its destiny. A population of more than 15 million is already pressing on the limited resources of arable land and water. For political reasons, resources must be allocated to promote economic growth while satisfying major ethnic and even racial claimants.

Kenya borders the Indian Ocean for 250 miles (400 km) of gracious tropical coast, thrusts 500 miles (800 km) inward to the shores of Lake Victoria, and stretches into the arid north to encompass Lake Rudolf and to border Ethiopia and Somalia. Its surface is carved midway by the Great Rift Valley that originates in the Arabian Peninsula and slices southwestward across Ethiopia, Kenya, and Tanzania. The heartland of Kenya consists of green, temperate valleys and highlands on both sides of the Rift Valley, rising to 5,000 feet (1,500 m) at Nairobi, to 9,000 feet (2,700 m) in the nearby Aberdare Mountains, and to majestic snow-clad Mount Kenya at 17,000 feet (5,100 m).

Geographically and culturally, there are several Kenyas. The coast is wet, warm, and humid, cooled by evening breezes, and inhabitated by 15 percent of the total population, the easygoing farmers and fishermen of the Bajan, Giriama, and other related (mostly Muslim) Swahili-speaking peoples. Mombasa, with a cosmopolitan population of over 300,000, is the principal port for all of East Africa. It is a historic city with Arab, Persian, Portuguese, and African roots and a style and nightlife all its own.

Two-thirds of Kenya is desert—arid, pastoral country, with the moonlike landscapes of Lakes Rudolf and Baringo. Known once as the Northern Frontier Districts, this region shelters less than 5 percent of the total population, consisting mostly of Karamajong, Tugen, and Somali pastoralists with their colorful herds of cattle, camels, and goats. Subject to troubled border clashes with Uganda, Ethiopia, and Somalia, where irredentist claims are loud and clear, this region preoccupies the government, which can neither accept its loss nor contribute to its livelihood and welfare.

Western Kenya is a tropical land bordering one tip of massive Lake Victoria, offering its inhabitants arable, occasionally flooded, plains and steep rugged hills and plateaus. The Luo, comprising 20 percent of the population of Kenya, live along the lake in Nyanza, engaged in fishing, raising livestock, and cotton and rice cultivation. A tall, slender Nilotic people who migrated down the Nile to Kenya several centuries ago, the Luo, and their Bantu neighbors, the Luhya, have been quick to seek Western education for their children. They have also sought resources from the central government to promote their relatively backward home areas.

Kenya's temperate Central Highlands enjoy fertile, volcanic soils, temperatures normally between 60 and 80°F (15 and 25°C) throughout the year, perennial rivers and streams, and two rainy seasons each year, March to May and mid-October to mid-December. It was the highlands that first attracted European settlers to Kenya in 1900; more than a century earlier, the pastoral Masai and the agricultural Kikuyu fought

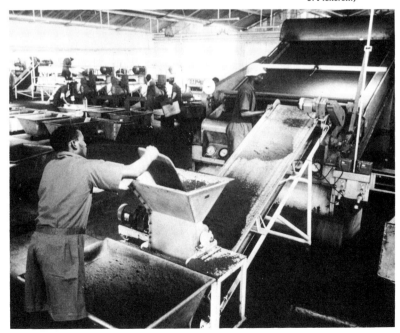

In this tea factory, workers are making instant tea; coffee, sisal, cotton, and tea are major export crops. (Photo: United Nations/ J. Pickerell.)

46

Africa South of the Sahara

over the highlands inconclusively, and the highlands remain the political and economic center of Kenya. Nairobi, a new town in the eastern highlands created by the railway line to Uganda, is perhaps the most cosmopolitan and modern city in black Africa, with a population close to 600,000 and growing 6 percent a year.

Since independence, the Kikuyu, comprising 25 percent of the population, and the culturally related Kamba and Meru peoples, have controlled the central government and much of the resources of Nairobi and the surrounding fertile highlands. Approximately 50,000 Europeans and 150,000 descendants of immigrants from India and Pakistan play a dominant role in modern commerce and industry, giving Nairobi and, to a lesser extent, Mombasa their distinctly multiracial character.

Kenya's fragile economy is nonetheless one of the strongest and most dynamic in Africa. Principal export crops are coffee (including high-quality and high-priced Arabica), tea, sisal, cotton, and, in recent years, flowers, strawberries, and other exports for the winter European market. Industry is concentrated in Nairobi and Mombasa, where consumer goods factories produce for the Kenyan and neighboring markets. Tourism has grown steadily since independence in 1962; coastal and national parks attract more than 200,000 annual visitors from West Europe, North America, and Japan.

The per capita income was estimated at $270 in 1977, appreciably higher than Tanzania's or Uganda's. However, this income is badly skewed. Racially, it

Children, who often work in the fields, are harvesting pyrethrum flowers used in the making of an insecticide. Flowers and fruits are also grown for export to West European markets. (Photo: United Nations/ Y. Lehmann.)

favors Asians and Europeans; ethnically, it favors the Kikuyu, who live in and around Nairobi; and, in terms of social classes, it favors better-educated Africans in government and business. Contrasts of wealth and poverty in Nairobi and elsewhere in Kenya are stark and are aggravated by the opulence that comes with international tourism.

Kenya's principal economic problems are open and disguised unemployment, the drastic reduction of unused arable land, the uncertain markets and prices for agricultural exports, and the lags in domestic food production. Kenyans are primarily maize eaters, and the introduction of high-yielding varieties of maize seed has helped, but the country is at best precariously self-sufficient in foodstuffs.

The disruption of trade ties with Tanzania and Uganda because of the breakup of the East African Community has also hurt Kenyan industries, which rely on a national market whose total gross national product is more than $4.5 billion, including subsistence production.

Population has been growing at more than 3 percent annually as infant mortality has fallen from an estimated 159 deaths per 1,000 live births in 1960 to 129 per 1,000 in 1975. The government first supported family planning in 1965 and has launched a national campaign to reduce fertility. However, less than 10 percent of fertile women, mostly in cities, have accepted the concept of family planning, and in 1975 birth rates were estimated at 48.7 per 1,000. Life expectancy has risen from 42.5 years in 1960 to 50 years in 1975, another reflection of lower infant mortality and improved rural social services.

Income, educational, and other disparities promote a prodigious urbanization, focused on Nairobi and Mombasa. Secondary cities such as Kisumu, Nakuru, Thika, and Nyeri are also growing, but at less than half the 6 percent rate of Nairobi. Primary and secondary school graduates or dropouts, with only a 1 in 3 chance of finding employment in Nairobi, are still better off than their peers who stay at home, so much greater are the opportunities in the capital. Nairobi's teeming shantytowns, crime waves, and social unrest have defied effective response.

Rail and road networks strengthen the domination of Nairobi, a transport hub for Kenya and East Africa. Literally, almost all roads lead to Nairobi. Nairobi and Mombasa provide the vital lifeline for landlocked Uganda's exports and imports and handle traffic from landlocked Rwanda. The closing of the Kenyan-Tanzanian border has inconvenienced travelers and traders, since the productive areas of Northern Tanzania are most closely linked to Nairobi and Mombasa. Movement to Ethiopia and Somalia is mostly by air or camel, although the Nairobi to Addis Ababa Trans-African highway remains open.

Kenya's social and cultural life operates at several levels. Many Kenyans still turn to their racial and ethnic groups for cultural and social activities, with the exception of athletics. Athletics is a national pastime and Olympic champions, such as Kipchoge Keino, are national heroes. English and Swahili are coequal national languages used in all the media, but English remains the language of prestige, higher education, and large-scale business. Swahili is spoken melodiously as a first language along the coast and, less grammatically, as a second language by many people up-country.

Little has emerged in Kenya in the way of Swahili literature. Kenya has produced a handful of talented artists and writers, most notably the novelist Ngugi Wa Thiono (*Weep Not Child*, *Petals of Blood*). Ngugi's arbitrary imprisonment in 1978 prompted international protests which contributed to his release. Kenya enjoys a relatively vigorous press and considerable freedom of expression.

Kenya's Asians live mostly in Nairobi and Mombasa and are themselves subdivided into the Gujerati, Sikh, Patel, Ismaili, and other communities, each with its own social centers, mosques, and temples. The European community is more transient and multinational than it was in the 1900 to 1960 British white settler epoch. The community supports cinemas, motor rallies, a theater, and polo, among other activities.

Africans tend to socialize on ethnic and class lines, from nightclubs and bars catering to the senior civil service elite down to the meanest Nairobi brothels and bars. Vernacular languages still predominate, with English the preferred second language. Ethnic intermarriage is still rare, and extended family ties prevail. Many Nairobi residents provide shelter for young rural relatives, and many farmwives, especially among the Kikuyu, have husbands working and living in Nairobi.

Some 85 percent of all Kenyans still live in villages, but village life has been fundamentally disrupted in the last 20 years. Even the basic Kikuyu staple diet of maize meal cooked as a "porridge" known as *ugali*, bananas, and goat or chicken stew has been altered by the addition of locally grown rice and even fresh vegetables. Most important is the spread of individual landholding under a program of land consolidation begun by the colonial government in the 1950s. Initially mandatory but now voluntary, consolidation has proved enormously popular except among the pastoral peoples. The fencing of land, bestowal of title deeds, and changes in inheritance were the prerequisites for modern commercial farming, especially among the Kikuyu. Consolidated land can be mortgaged, used for credit, deeded to a single heir instead of the customary fragmentation, and farmed aggressively.

Consolidation has changed the physical face of much of the central region and parts of the rest of the country. Fences, pastures, farm homes, and terraces have taken the place of what were common land and communal villages 20 years ago. Rich and poor and landless farmers have emerged; they employ relatives and neighbors as tenants or day laborers. Tractors and artificial insemination, breed livestock, and hybrid seeds have all come to some of the new owners. Others have little or no land and swell the ranks of a new rural proletariat.

Consolidation is almost completed among the Kikuyu, Kamba, and Meru and is well advanced among the Luo and Luhya. Coastal residents cling to communal village life and communal agriculture, especially for coconut and copra farming. The pastoral peoples (Masai) have mostly rejected consolidation as invidious to their ways of life, and efforts have been made to encourage the Masai and others to try group ranches.

Some of the village life that has been lost is splendidly preserved in Nairobi's Museum of Natural History, a world-renowned center for research on the origins of man.

Modern Kenyan history begins in the sixth century A.D., with the establishment along the coast of a series of city-states—Lamu Island, Gedi, Malindi, and Mombasa—with a unique blend of African, Asian,

Buyers and sellers crowd an outdoor grain market in a town near Nairobi. (Photo: United Nations/ Y. Lehmann.)

and Persian influences. The Portuguese briefly held Mombasa during the sixteenth and seventeenth centuries and built the imposing coral Fort Jesus. Along the coast, a casual Swahili language, culture, and society evolved, nominally subject to the sultan of Zanzibar Island; inland, Bantu cultivators and Nilotic pastoralists competed for land and space.

Coastal Arab merchants and slavers were the first to penetrate the Kenyan interior, followed in the mid-nineteenth century by European explorers and missionaries. The construction of the Mombasa-to-Uganda railway was the decisive event in Kenyan history, revealing the extent of fertile land in the highlands and making European settlement possible.

While Kenya remained a British Crown Colony from 1900 to 1962, the white settlers, never exceeding 70,000, gained extensive economic and political power. Much of the highlands was reserved for white settlement, mainly at the expense of the Kikuyu, who became farm laborers. A modern cash economy, based on exports and subsidies in the Kenyan market, benefited the settlers and the Asian merchants. Africans experienced economic and social discrimination, as did Asians to a lesser extent, especially in the segregated capital of Nairobi. African protests were voiced from the outset by chiefs and elders and, in the 1920s by the first stirrings of trade unions and nationalist movements. African ex-soldiers who had been conscripted to serve in World Wars I and II were another protest group.

Kenya turned to the politics of confrontation after World War II. The white settlers clung to their privileges, and the colonial government was slow to redress real African grievances. An underground protest movement known as Mau Mau fought a war of protest from 1952 to 1957. The British crushed Mau Mau militarily while making a series of political and economic concessions that ended the domination of the white settlers.

During the turbulent 1950s, African nationalism found its voice in Kenya through the formation of trade unions and political parties, especially the Kenya African National Union (KANU). As African majority rule neared, younger leaders turned to Jomo Kenyatta as a symbol of national unity. Sent abroad by the Kikuyu people to study in the 1920s, *Mzee* (Swahili for "elder") Kenyatta had returned to Kenya in 1946 as a moderate political organizer. He was subsequently detained for 7 years for instigating Mau Mau, a charge he always denied, and was released in 1959 to lead KANU to an electoral victory. In 1962, 3 years later, he led Kenya to independence.

Postindependence history was dominated by President Kenyatta, whose death in 1978 marked the end of an era. Kenyatta's political motto of *harambee*, Swahili for "let us pull together," was the key to his administration. Europeans and Asians were reassured about their businesses and farms, except for those settler estates that were bought for transfer under a land-reform program. Foreign investment was sought, tourism was encouraged, and a Western development strategy was pursued.

Kenyatta, his large family, and his entourage headed the new and highly visible wa-Benzi people—African owners of Mercedes-Benz cars. Africanization of the civil service and of some retail and small-scale wholesale trade produced a new elite and various middle classes. There was much discontent caused by the predominant role of the Kikuyu in the acquisition of new wealth, but there was also recognition of their thirst for education and achievement.

As Kenya's politics acquired more of a have versus have-not character, detention and other measures were used against actual and potential opposition leaders. Tom Mboya, brilliant trade unionist and Finance Minister, was murdered in 1969. Another assassination in 1974 took the life of the populist politician Joseph Kariuki. Because of Kenyatta's advanced age and the strong social and ethnic unrest, the presidential succession was viewed with foreboding.

Instead, the succession of former Vice President Daniel Arap Moi, a low-key leader from the Western Region, was smoothly managed in August 1978. President Moi released a number of detainees, including novelist Ngugi, and promised to crack down on corruption and to distribute resources more equitably.

Kenya's future depends on its ability to combine political stability with more balanced economic growth. A multiethnic coalition is needed to run the country and to reduce the predominance of the Kikuyu elite. The Luo, in particular, have been shut out and must be included in such a coalition.

At the same time, social and class stratification is becoming a serious problem. The enormous expansion of primary and secondary education (primary enrollment has increased from 30 percent in 1960 to 100 percent in 1975, and enrollment in secondary schools is up from 2 percent to over 10 percent in the same period) has far outstripped the job market. Urbanization centered on Nairobi and not balanced geographically is adding to the burden of unemployment. Meanwhile the ostentatious lifestyles of a small, privileged African elite have strained the social fabric.

Kenya's resource base is also threatened by a population expected to double by the year 2000. There are no significant fossil fuels or other valuable minerals; energy imports, even if they come from nearby Arab states, are a serious liability. The lack of export markets in neighboring countries has hampered industrialization, which has only begun to produce a few capital goods. Foreign investment has emphasized capital-intensive industries that do little to generate employment for the unskilled.

Kenya faces a crisis of expectations, generated by real economic growth, which may threaten a too narrowly based political stability. Yet there is a real African rural middle class, owning its own land, growing coffee, tea, maize, and other cash crops, and paying school fees to educate its sons and daughters. Much will depend on emerging land tenure and inheritance patterns, opportunities to increase agricultural yields through small-scale, appropriate technologies, and the ability of the national leadership to instill a sense of national identity. The extended family ties that continue to mitigate the gap between the haves and the have-nots are likely to wither over time, and individuals will turn to the government as a substitute for the extended family.

Aaron Segal

Lesotho

Area: 11,716 sq mi (30,344 sq km)
Population: 1.3 million
  Density: 111 per sq mi (43 per sq km)
  Growth rate: 2.4% (1970–1977)
Percent of population under 14 years of age: 38% (1975)
Infant deaths per 1,000 live births: 146
Life expectancy at birth: 46 years
Leading causes of death: not available
Ethnic composition: Sotho 85%; Nguni 15%; Caucasian and Asian, less than 1%
Languages: English (official), Sesotho (official), Xhosa, Zulu
Literacy: 60%
Religions: Christian 80%; traditional
Percent population urban: not available
Percent population rural: not available
Gross national product: $360 million
  Per capita GNP: $280
  Per capita GNP growth rate: 9.9% (1970–1977)
Inflation rate: 19% (1974–1979)

Modern Lesotho, a compact, roughly oblong tract of country somewhat larger than the state of Maryland, is enclosed on all sides by the Republic of South Africa. Any traveler to Lesotho must obtain a South African transit visa; overseas visitors without such a visa cannot leave the passenger lounge of Johannesburg's airport, Lesotho's air link with the outside world. Called by its National Tourist Corporation the "kingdom in the sky," Lesotho is the only country in the world completely surrounded by a single neighboring state. In its historical evolution lies the explanation of many of its current strengths and weaknesses.

Topographically, the country is sharply divided. The mountain region formed by the largely inaccessible Maluti and Drakensberg ranges absorbs almost three-fourths of the total land area and is a major watershed, extending from northeast to southwest. A narrow strip of comparatively level ground slopes away from the base of the Maluti to the Caledon River and the plains of the Orange Free State. Only this rolling lowland [5,000–6,000 feet (1,525–1,830 m)] lends itself to plow cultivation.

Lesotho has three major natural resources: diamonds, water and hydroelectric power potential, and a majestic scenic beauty. One large diamond mine is already being developed by De Beers Corporation. Several other developments are planned in areas where labor-intensive techniques can be economi-

cally utilized. There is talk of a hydroelectric project whereby Lesotho would sell power and water to South Africa.

With a population estimated at 1.3 million, the average density is approximately 111 persons per square mile (43 per sq km). However, much of the Maluti is uninhabitable and less than 12 percent of all the land is suitable for cultivation. Thus the bulk of the population is concentrated in the lowland strip, giving the region one of the highest rural population densities in Africa. Few families can maintain themselves through subsistence agriculture; most depend on the remittances of migrant workers. Patterns of migratory labor developed during the century of colonial experience because the imperial power did little to develop an economic infrastructure. It is estimated that, at any given time, some 200,000 Basotho—principally men in the 18- to 40-year age bracket—are employed in South Africa, the majority in mining and farming.

Cattle, sheep, and goats are important elements of the agricultural sector. The country is a net importer of sorghum, maize, and wheat, and it exports livestock, wool, and mohair. Herdboys form an identifi-

Women with their babies on their backs plant trees as part of the government's effort to control soil erosion in this landlocked, largely agricultural country. (Photo: FAO/World Food Programme/ T. Fincher.)

able group in the society; many of them are unable to begin their schooling until they reach the age of 14 or 15, when younger brothers can take over the responsibilities of herding.

A widely respected National Teacher Training College (NTTC) now trains Lesotho's primary school teachers; courses for secondary school teachers are offered at both NTTC and the National University of Lesotho (originally established as Pius XII University College by the Roman Catholic hierarchy). Strong emphasis is placed on science and mathematics as basic skills needed for development work and for the technical training of much-needed middle-level manpower.

Since all land in Lesotho is held in trust for the Basotho people by the king and is allocated for use by local chiefs, incentive for individual improvement is often lacking. However, this land-tenure system has prevented the development of the landed/landless situation, so common in many third world countries.

Despite Lesotho's genuine national community, the country is not immune to ideological and power struggles. A major source of political conflict is Lesotho's relationship with the Republic of South Africa. Prime Minister Leabua Jonathan [Basutoland National Party (BNP)] followed a very pragmatic (if not overly subservient) policy from 1966 through the mid-1970s. More recently, he has been openly critical of South Africa and, in some cases, has adopted a position of confrontation. In the summer of 1978, the Lesotho government hosted a United Nations–sponsored symposium on human rights in South Africa with delegates from several African countries, the major Western powers, and organizations like Amnesty International. The government also supported the efforts of the National University of Lesotho to establish an international center for southern African studies. Jonathan's new stance reflects Lesotho's success in drawing world attention to the peculiar difficulties of its geographical and historical situation and in attracting wide support for its development projects.

Leabua Jonathan's government is not without opposition. In 1970, during the first elections held after independence, it appeared that the BNP might not retain its majority in the National Assembly. The Prime Minister consequently cited election irregularities as a justification for nullifying the returns. Declaring a state of emergency, he suspended the constitution and the Parliament and forced the constitutional monarch, Moshoeshoe II, into temporary exile. An appointive National Assembly has existed since 1973, and there are sporadic discussions on the preparation of a new constitution. A period of relative political calm (probably explained by the observable achievements of the government's economic planning as much as by the confinement or dispersal of opposition leaders after riots in 1974) ended early in 1979 when the main post office in Maseru, the capital, was blown up.

The major emphases of the government's 5-year plans (1970–1975, 1975–1980) have been increased agricultural productivity and improvement in livestock farming; promotion of nonagricultural development, particularly small-scale industries; the creation of 30,000 new jobs in Lesotho; and government-directed development in education and training related to the needs of the nation.

Having identified Lesotho as one of the 25 poorest countries in the world, the United Nations selected it for a concentrated development effort. The activities of the UN development program have been supplemented by those of a number of other international organizations, including the European Economic Community and the African Development Bank. Aid for capital development and technical assistance has come from Canada, Denmark, Sweden, West Germany, Taiwan, and the United States. The estimated U.S. assistance for fiscal 1976 was $2.2 million through the Agency for International Development (AID) and the Food for Peace Program, and the services of 160 Peace Corps volunteers. The Thaba-Bosiu Rural Development Project, jointly funded by the World Bank, the United States, and the Lesotho government, has already resulted in measurable improvement in yields of traditional crops and is paving the way for more remunerative cash crops and livestock farming. This is one of three such projects covering much of the lowlands.

The first 5-year plan found new employment opportunities for only 6,000 people, making it clear that, for some time to come, migratory labor would be essential to Lesotho's economy. On the other hand, the increasingly difficult position of the migrant in South Africa, the political implications of dependence on the Republic, the serious disruption of family life involved, and the loss to Lesotho of a majority of its men in their most productive years are issues of major concern.

A worker operates a weaving machine; small-scale industry is being encouraged to stimulate the largely agricultural economy. (Photo: United Nations/ Kay Muldoon.)

Tourism has become an important source of revenue; the number of tourists increased from approximately 4,000 in the late 1960s to over 80,000 in the mid-1970s. Maseru now boasts a large Holiday Inn, complete with gambling casino; the Victoria Hotel, financed by the recently established Lesotho Bank; and the Maseru Hilton, opened in 1979, also with a gambling casino. New hotels and resort facilities have been opened throughout the country, particularly in the mountain areas. The local travel organizations, the restaurant industry, local handicrafts (and marketing outlets) and road and repair services have benefited from the growth of tourism. Some critics, however, question the heavy emphasis on tourism and its impact on Basotho lifestyles and values.

Industrial development is the primary concern of the National Development Corporation, which offers substantial advantages (e.g., a 6-year tax holiday) to outside investors. The Basotho Enterprises Development Corporation offers local businessmen similar advantages for small-scale enterprises. Factory estates are already operating in Maseru and in the northern town of Maputsoe and are manufacturing a wide range of products, most of which are absorbed by the local market. Maseru has in fact attracted so many job seekers that it is confronted with all the evils of urban sprawl in an area that can hardly be considered urban, despite the recent 100 percent increase in the city's population, now estimated at around 60,000.

But important as it is in reaching employment goals, industrial development cannot be pursued at the expense of agricultural development; it is in the fields that the majority of Basotho find their subsistence. Lesotho is primarily and predominantly a rural country. Most Basotho identify themselves in terms of their roles in family life in the villages. There, too, the women and children keep the nation alive.

Unlike most other African states, Lesotho is a nation-state, with a strong sense of nationhood rooted in its origins, its struggles for survival, and its effort to achieve an economic viability that will give some substance to the political independence it gained in 1966.

In the early days of the nineteenth century, population pressures resulting from the expansion of the Zulu kingdom made much of the area north of the Orange River and west of the Caledon a battleground of Sotho-speaking peoples, themselves harassed by Nguni clans fleeing the Zulu warriors. Leading a small group of his own people, a young Sotho chief, Moshoeshoe, established himself on one of the great natural fortresses of southern Africa, an isolated flat-topped mountain called Thaba Bosiu. By skillful courage and shrewd politics, by diplomacy, by negotiation, and by a humaneness that became legendary, Moshoeshoe began to gather together the remnants of politically and culturally fragmented peoples. Bringing order out of chaos, he won allegiance based on respect and trust and began to build a nation.

Thus, in essence, the original Basotho nation was a political, rather than an ethnic, entity. However, linguistic and cultural assimilation proceeded rapidly, and unity grew out of a shared concern for security. The common historical experiences of the past century and a half have consolidated this sense of unity, giving Lesotho a population proud of being the "children of Moshoeshoe," with a national vernacular language, Sesotho. English is the second official language and is a major medium of instruction beyond the level of fourth-year primary education.

Lesotho met a challenge to its survival in the northward migration of the Boer farmers from Cape Colony in the mid-nineteenth century; in a series of Boer-Basotho wars, it lost a substantial part of its agricultural land to the Orange Free State on its western frontier. Realizing that he could not hold out indefinitely against European weaponry, Moshoeshoe sought the protection of the British, a protection very reluctantly given in 1868 when the Crown annexed what was then called Basutoland. Moshoeshoe had again proved the savior of his people, and in fact had ensured their existence as a nation, although the nation was deprived of its agricultural base and was forced to adopt an increasingly widespread pattern of migratory labor.

British Basutoland was unique in African colonial history. The British were not interested in colonization; they were not looking for mineral wealth or industrial potential in Basutoland because there seemed little of either. Nor did pure philanthropy nor classical humanitarianism explain the British presence. The British were involved in Basutoland because the pressures of South Africa (and the traditions of the British presence in South Africa) had pushed them in. Their respect for Basotho determination to remain in-

People travel on a primitive road to Mokhotlong in the mountainous northern area of this landlocked country called "the kingdom in the sky." (Photo: FAO/World Food Programme/ T. Fincher.)

This road-building crew is made up entirely of women, reflecting the fact that many men must leave Lesotho to find steady work. (Photo: United Nations/Muddou.)

dependent of South Africa was supported by a British administration that remained in the territory until the Basotho resumed control over their own land.

The future? For a long time to come, Lesotho will be dependent on external aid for development and improvement, and the vagaries of external aid are well known. Any changes in South Africa or in its relations with the rest of the world will affect Lesotho; population pressures are increasing, and a reduction in the number of Basotho workers admitted into South Africa or any large-scale repatriation of current workers would be disastrous.

What of the other side of the coin? In its own people Lesotho has an asset that should not be underestimated. Friendly, inured to difficulties, fiercely proud of their heritage, known throughout southern Africa as capable workers and eager for education, the people give solidity to the struggle for self-sufficiency. Their high degree of literacy, estimated by the government at roughly 60 percent, is a major legacy of the missionaries who made widespread primary education a focus of their activities. Historical religious rivalries between Catholics and Protestants (over 80 percent of the people are Christian) are giving way to strong ecumenical activities; although religious rivalries remain evident in government circles, they may be simply a cover for other rivalries.

Plans are in progress that would end Lesotho's absolute dependence on its air links through South Africa. A link with Maputo, Mozambique, would make it possible for international travel to bypass Johannesburg. A new airport outside Maseru capable of servicing international flights is also planned.

If the government can maintain order and stability, if there are no major upheavals in South Africa, if world inflation and the oil crisis do not cause serious reductions in aid programs in the near future, Lesotho should be able to maintain its existence at a level of simple human dignity.

Rita Cassidy

Liberia
(Republic of Liberia)

Area: 43,000 sq mi (111,369 sq km)
Population: 1.7 million
  Density: 39 per sq mi (15 per sq km)
  Growth rate: 3.4% (1970–1977)
Percent of population under 14 years of age: 41%
Infant deaths per 1,000 live births: 137 (1970)
Life expectancy at birth: 46 years
Leading causes of death: malaria, cholera, leprosy, smallpox
Ethnic composition: 16 ethnic groups 90%; descendants of American slaves 5%
Languages: English, 20 dialects
Literacy: 24%
Religions: traditional 75%; Muslim 15%; Christian 10%
Percent population urban: 28%
Percent population rural: 72%
Gross national product: $820 million
  Per capita GNP: $460
  Per capita GNP growth rate: 1.1% (1970–1977)
Inflation rate: not available

Africa's oldest independent republic, Liberia has enjoyed political stability for several decades. This has allowed the country to attract private investment and to attain an annual growth rate of over 4 percent. Major assets include an excellent deep-water port at Monrovia, the capital, and rich natural resources, such as timber, iron ore, and other minerals. Much of the country's economic development has been concentrated in the area of Monrovia and at several major plantations and mining concessions. The country has more unskilled labor than it can employ, and internal migration is adding to the problem of urban unemployment. Yet Liberia also has an urgent need for skilled workers and managers; a related problem is the lack of manufacturing enterprises.

Liberia lies at the southwestern extremity of the western bulge of Africa, with a 355-mile (571-km) coastline on the Atlantic Ocean. Bordered by Sierra

Leone, Guinea, and the Ivory Coast, it is roughly equal in size to Ohio, with 43,000 square miles (111,369 sq km) of territory.

The country's narrow coastal plain gives way to interior hills and plateaus. The highest mountain ranges are the Nimba and Wologizi, which exceed 4,500 feet (1,372 m). The Saint John's Falls and other waterfalls in the Guinea highlands may some day become tourist attractions and important sources of hydroelectric power. The national forests contain several species of rare animals, such as the pygmy hippopotamus, the zebra duiker, the dwarf buffalo, and the potto, which may also serve as a lure for tourists. Liberia lies within the tropical rain forest belt and has distinct wet and dry seasons. Rainfall may exceed 200 inches (508 cm) along the coast between April and May (although Harper in the far south has two rainy seasons). Average rainfall for the country as a whole is about 160 inches (406 cm) a year. Temperatures on the coast average a pleasant 79°F (20°C), but they can vary seasonally from 111 to 48°F (44 to 9°C) in the interior. Fifteen major rivers flow into the Atlantic Ocean; of these, the Saint Paul and the Cavalla are the largest.

With the opening of the Bomi Hills Iron Ore Mine by the Liberia Mining Company in 1951, Liberia became Africa's leading producer of iron ore. In 1961, iron ore replaced rubber as the number one extraction industry, and in 1976 it accounted for 72 percent of total exports. Diamond exports in 1975 exceeded $18.4 million, and related royalties and licenses are an important source of revenue for the government. Other minerals include bauxite, copper, corundum, lead, manganese, tin, and zinc. The richness of its mineral wealth has enabled Liberia to attract foreign investors, such as the Liberian-American-Swedish Minerals Company. This company has undertaken one of the largest private enterprises in Africa, with $300 million invested for the construction of a pelletizing plant, a new port, and a 170-mile (274-km) railway. Management rests largely in foreign hands, however, as there are relatively few Liberian entrepreneurs.

In spite of its mineral wealth, Liberia remains agricultural. In the world market, 77.6 percent of Liberia's exports are minerals, but 72 percent of its working population are employed on the land. The principal crops are rice, cassava, and tropical fruits. Traditional methods of land rotation yield low crops of rice and allow the destruction of valuable timber, which is worth over $1,500 per acre ($607 per hectare). Aided by specialists from Taiwan, the United States, and the United Nations, the Liberian government is trying to overcome these problems.

Liberia's population is estimated at 1.7 million, growing at an annual rate of 3.4 percent (1970–1977). With a density of 39 people per square mile (15 per sq km), the country is underpopulated. Most Liberians (over 90 percent) belong to one of sixteen African ethnic groups; most numerous are the Kpelle (211,000) and the Bassa (166,000). These subsistence farmers use a process of rotating culture in which valuable

timber is burned away to fertilize the soil. Other well-known groups include the seafaring Kru and the Vai, who invented the Vai script about 1815.

The dominant group in Liberia, although comprising less than 5 percent of the population, is descended from some 22,000 freed slaves who migrated to Liberia from the United States and Britain in the nineteenth century. These people founded the Republic of Liberia in 1847, but they had limited contact of any sort with the peoples of the interior until the early twentieth century. The constitution was amended in 1907 to limit Liberian citizenship to blacks. Local Africans were finally given full legal rights of citizenship, including the right to vote, in 1947. Only citizens may own land in Liberia.

President William V. S. Tubman, who served from 1944 to 1971, instituted a policy of unification that has been sucessful in assimilating the peoples of the interior into the mainstream of Liberian society. Increasing opportunities for education and social and political advancement have been opened in recent decades, and intermarriage between the various ethnic groups and settlers has erased many of the distinctions that once prevailed. The unification policy was pursued vigorously by President William R. Tolbert, Jr., Tubman's successor. As a result of the steady migration into the urban centers, ethnic ties and the authority of ethnic leaders were substantially weakened. The main urban centers (with their 1977 population figures) are Monrovia, the capital (204,000), Harbel and Harbel Plantation (60,000), Buchanan (25,000), Yekepa (16,000), Harper (14,000), and Greenville (10,000).

As is true in most developing nations, Liberia's public health facilties are largely concentrated in the urban centers. In 1975, there were 145 physicians and 36 hospitals with 2,522 beds. Although this represented a substantial improvement over the past two

This newly mined iron ore will be moved to the deep-sea port of Monrovia for export. Liberia is a leading exporter of iron ore. (Photo: United Nations/B. Wolff.)

decades, the ratio of 1 doctor per 11,000 inhabitants was still far from adequate. The John F. Kennedy Memorial Medical Center, a teaching institution with modern equipment and 300 beds, is the leading hospital in the country. Located in Monrovia, it is partly responsible for the increasing number of Liberian doctors (52 in 1975).

Over half the doctors and hospital beds are located in or near Monrovia. However, there are important hospitals at the large mining concessions and plantations, notably the Firestone Hospital at Marbel. Dental care facilities are very inadequate, with only 1 dentist for every 62,000 inhabitants. Despite medical advances, tropical diseases—including leprosy, malaria, cholera, smallpox, and yaws—are still found in Liberia.

In the field of education, although a great deal has been accomplished in recent decades, much remains to be done. The school-age population is large—about 650,000 people—and only 190,000 were attending school in 1975. There were only 5,500 teachers (many of them underqualified) to staff 1,054 elementary and 272 secondary schools. The percentage of children between the ages of 6 and 16 who attend school is far lower in rural than in urban areas; it is also generally far lower for girls than for boys. The country needs more and better vocational and technical training; there were only 1,087 students in such institutions in 1974. In that year, however, the government completed 98 new schools as part of its work-oriented

community education project. This was an important step, but the Liberian government is aware that upgrading the skills of its work force is one of its largest and most difficult tasks.

The country's two institutions of higher education are the University of Liberia at Monrovia and Cuttington College near Suakoko. The former is a public institution; the latter is privately operated. Between them, they enroll more than 2,000 students. An average of 400 Liberian students were studying abroad in any given year during the 1970s, many in the United States. The number of Liberians receiving higher education at home and abroad more nearly matched the country's work force needs than the number enrolled in elementary, secondary, and vocational schools. However, as in many developing nations, too many students were trained in high-prestige subjects such as law, for which there was limited demand, and too few were trained in badly needed technical and scientific skills.

Christian (mainly Protestant) missionaries have made intensive efforts in Liberia, and Christianity is widely practiced, particularly in urban areas. Traditional African religious beliefs are still prevalent in rural communities, and Islam has been making progress in recent years.

The process of colonizing the coastal areas with freed black slaves began in 1822. Over the next 70 years, 16,400 settlers arrived from the southern United States, along with 5,700 Africans who were

Shanties of rural migrants line the beachfront in Monrovia. (Photo: United Nations/ B. Wolff.)

freed from slaving vessels by the American and British navies. The settlers were unprepared for the harsh and dangerous conditions, and more than half the original number perished or returned to the United States. The American Colonization Society and other philanthropic organizations provided most of the funds for the settlers' coastal enclaves during the first few decades—an average of about $100,000 per year. Most settlements joined in declaring the Liberian Republic's independence in 1847. This marked the beginning of a roughly 75-year European period. American financial support declined, and the United States did not officially recognize Liberia until 1862, more than a decade after Britain and France. European trade and investment in Liberia increased in this period, and the country faced serious problems of interference in its internal affairs from European colonial powers in the early years of the twentieth century. As late as 1925, about 90 percent of Liberia's foreign trade was with Europe.

In 1926, the long period of American disinterest ended when the Firestone Plantation began to produce natural rubber at Harbel (named for Harvey and Idabelle Firestone). For the next 50 years, Firestone was the country's principal employer. In 1977, Harbel was the world's largest continuous plantation, with 77,000 acres (31,174 hectares) of rubber trees.

The Firestone operation had a far-reaching economic, social, and political impact. A major loan agreement with Firestone in 1926 placed the country under U.S. financial supervision. Between 5 and 10 percent of the population began to receive regular income and learned to function in a money economy. However, Firestone's exploitative labor practices (though approved by the Liberian government) were severely criticized by the League of Nations, and the subsequent scandal led the United States to sever relations with Liberia for 5 years in the 1930s.

During World War II, Liberia's strategic significance to the United States was underlined by President Franklin D. Roosevelt's visit in 1943 and by the building of Robertsfield air base. President Tubman's accession to power in 1944 marked the beginning of very close economic and political ties with the United States that have continued to the present day.

Although Liberia's constitution is modeled on that of the United States, in practice, government power has been highly centralized in the hands of a small political elite, who monopolized most positions in the bureaucracy and undoubtedly enriched themselves at public expense. High priority is given to for-eign investment. Besides Firestone, significant U.S. investors include Goodrich, Uniroyal, Bethlehem Steel, Getty Enterprises, First National City Bank, Chase Manhattan Bank, Chemical Bank, and the International Bank of Washington. With U.S. assistance, projects like the Robertsfield International Airport, Monrovia's water supply and sewage disposal systems, and a hydroelectric dam at Mount Coffee have assisted development.

Liberia's development plan for 1976–1980 called for the investment of $415 million. The Liberian government provided 39.5 percent of these funds, while foreign loans and grants accounted for 60.5 percent. Under this plan, the improvement of road transport received one-third of the total, the largest share of any sector. Education received only 8.4 percent, and all other social services combined (health, housing, and so on) received a like amount. Agriculture received 17.3 percent, indicating a fairly high priority for this sector.

Significantly, manufacturing received only 4.1 percent of available public investment funds. This reflected the government's strong commitment to private enterprise. Despite the development of its extractive industries, Liberia has not reduced its dependence on imported manufactured goods. It has only just begun to transform its own raw materials into the finished goods that its people need.

In summary, the sustained growth of Liberia's GNP appears to depend heavily on continued development of its extractive industries. This in turn depends on maintaining an open-door policy toward foreign investment. However, the development of local industry and import substitution must soon play a much larger role in the country's economic development planning.

Real improvement in the livelihood of the Liberian people involves a far more complex range of factors and programs. These include an active commitment to education and manpower training programs by the government and by foreign and domestic employers. Continued high investment in agriculture and in rural transportation and social services is also necessary.

In April 1980, a coup d'état led by Master Sergeant Samuel K. Doe overthrew the Tolbert government. It is premature to predict the effects of the military government's anti-elite policies or how long the military will maintain control, but the Doe government does not seem either more honest or more efficient than its predecessor.

Peter A. Poole

Madagascar
(Democratic Republic of Madagascar)

Area: 226,658 sq mi (587,044 sq km)
Population: 8.3 million
  Density: 37 per sq mi (14 per sq km)
  Growth rate: 2.5% (1970–1977)
Percent of population under 15 years of age: 45%
Infant deaths per 1,000 live births: 102 (1970)
Life expectancy at birth: 38 years (1975)
Leading causes of death: not available
Ethnic composition: Malagasy tribes, Comoran islanders,
  French, Indians, Chinese
Languages: Malagasy (official), French
Literacy: 40%
Religions: animist, Christian
Percent population urban: 16%
Percent population rural: 84%
Gross national product: $2.05 billion
  Per capita GNP: $250
  Per capita GNP growth rate: −2.7% (1970–1977)
Inflation rate: not available

The island state of Madagascar, which includes five small island dependencies, lies across the Mozambique Channel off Africa's southeast shore. Once known as the Red Island and portrayed by Westerners as an exotic paradise, it is slightly larger than France, with a total area of 226,658 square miles (587,044 sq km). Madagascar has suffered social and political upheaval over the last decade, but its more fundamental problem is the fact that population growth is outstripping food production. Madagascar was once a major exporter of rice and beef, but it now imports grain. Its beef production is consumed locally, with less and less available for shipment abroad.

The population is unevenly distributed, with an average density of 37 people per square mile (14 per sq km). Its 8.3 million people are composed of eighteen ethnic groups of mixed Asian and African descent. All speak a variant of the national language, Malagasy, a derivative of Indonesian. The dialects coincide with regional and ethnic differences.

The dominant ethnic people are the Imerina, who inhabit the verdant and economically advanced central highlands, and related groups (the Vakinankaratra and Sihanaka). These highland people are economically and culturally more advanced than the côtiers (coastal groups), and their educated class has governed the country, albeit with increasing competition from coastal groups. Although the coastal peoples have asserted themselves increasingly since France established its control in 1896, they lack the cohesion or family linkages found among plateau peoples. Sociopolitical rivalries and tensions between highland and coastal Malagasy have been a major element in the island's development, and will continue to be for years to come, despite government efforts to replace ethnic and regional consideration with the rhetoric and commitment of a populist socialism.

Madagascar's economy is predominantly agricultural and rural, dominated by rice cultivation and cattle rearing. A wide variety of other products are grown; production systems range from those of traditional subsistence small-scale farmers and herders (slash-and-burn cultivation and seminomadic herding) to large-scale mechanized and sophisticated systems (cotton estates in the northwest) and elaborate terracing and partial water control. The variety of agricultural products has long protected Madagascar's economy against the vagaries of international commodity prices and the ever-present hazards of drought and cyclones.

Agriculture varies widely from region to region because of variations in climate, topography, soil, and natural vegetation and poor communications or transport links. There is a wide disparity of wealth and levels of development among regions, in particular between the central plateau and the coastal areas to the west and south.

Traditional, largely subsistence farming is the dominant agricultural mode; most of Madagascar's 1.5 million farm families are smallholders (owners or operators of a small holding), and some own cattle. Traditional land rights prevail in most areas, recognizing individual rights to cultivated land that can be passed on to heirs and collective fokonolona (community) rights to pasture. Plantations, most of which were foreign-owned and -managed, have been nationalized since 1975 and have been replaced by state farms, organized along socialist lines and run by ministries or parastatals (government-owned corporations). Implementing a policy of socialism, the government emphasizes socialist cooperatives for farmers.

Rice, a staple, is produced throughout Madagascar, but production is concentrated in the high central plateau and the northwest. Almost half of all cultivated land is devoted to rice and 75 percent of the rice fields are family farms. In 1977, there were an estimated 2.776 billion planted acres (1.124 billion hectares) under crop, which yielded 2.2 million tons (2.0 million t) of rice. The family rice fields rely on partial water control, and yields are subject to climatic vicissitudes. Of the remaining rice fields 23 percent are irrigated with systems developed or supported by the government, and 2 percent are devoted to the production of hilltop rain-fed rice.

In 1978, poor rains resulted in a production decline estimated at 15 percent [i.e., a drop to 1.9 million tons (1.7 million t)]. Overall rice production is increasing at a slower pace than the population growth rate, while marketed production has declined in the past 8 to 11 years. As a result, Madagascar has begun to rely heavily on imports.

In 1976, the government assumed responsibility for

marketing rice production, implementing the Charter of the Malagasy Socialist Revolution of October 1975. The government intervenes at four stages of marketing and pricing: producer prices are fixed each year by the government, with the final decision taken by the Cabinet or by the President; there is a state monopoly on all domestic marketing arrangements; the government controls the quantity and distribution of all imported rice; and the government fixes consumer prices, including a subsidy of almost 40 percent for locally produced rice. A flourishing black market in rice sells at well above official levels.

Government rice marketing has not been very efficient. Not all rice is collected, and regional shortages occur frequently while marketing costs are high. Responsibility for marketing is divided among twelve state companies, working in support of local communities (fokonolonas) that have primary responsibility for marketing rice in their territorial jurisdiction. There was some improvement during 1977 because of better extension services, a rise in producer prices in the spring of 1977, an increase in the area under production, and an improvement in local transportation in the form of additional trucks. However, substantial amounts of rice were imported and will be needed again in the coming years. The rice importing will continue until basic extension services are better organized, pricing policies are revised, transportation improves, and the government rationalizes the multiplicity of authorities responsible for rice marketing.

Similar problems beset Madagascar's cattle industry. Cattle are central to the economy and are a traditional symbol of wealth and status. The livestock sector accounts for about one-third of Madagascar's total agricultural production. As of 1977, there were 6.3 million head of cattle registered; the island has an abundance of pasture and animal diseases are relatively controlled. However, the national herd, estimated to be 7 to 11 million head (1978), has a low productivity, and only 3 to 4 percent of the cattle enter commercial channels every year. Virtually all cattle are owned by traditional herders, who invest very little cash in their livestock and practice no modern livestock techniques.

Livestock production will continue to decline because there is no program to help traditional livestock producers. In recent years, animal collection has also been a problem. Cattle marketing has been handled by two private companies, but under the 1975 charter fokonolonas will increasingly play a key role. The government is moving to nationalize cattle marketing and to control producer prices. State agencies have been assigned responsibility for marketing and are assuming the responsibility for meat exports.

A crucial problem has been the lack of adequate slaughterhouse and deep-freeze facilities. There are now three large modern meat plants in operation (at Antananarivo, Morondava, and Mahajanga). Another problem has been the government pricing policy.

Controlled prices have been well below the market price, and a high proportion of the beef is reportedly sold at higher prices on the unofficial market. For this reason, beef consumption has increased domestically while there has been a decrease in exports.

Madagascar also produces coffee, a major export crop. Production is increasing as the result of a tree rejuvenation program and better cultivation techniques. Cloves are the second most important cash crop, and are produced mainly in the northeast. Madagascar is the world's leading producer of vanilla, which has made a comeback since synthetic vanilla has proved inadequate. Most of the estimated 38,000 vanilla growers are smallholders concentrated in the northeast. Pepper, sugarcane, and cotton are also produced, although sugar and cotton production has been in decline.

Madagascar is also rich in natural forests, which cover 30 million acres (12.12 million hectares), one-fifth of the island's territory. Firewood is extracted regularly from two-thirds of the forests. Because timber cutting has become excessive, the government is obtaining foreign assistance to promote reforestation. Fishing may become important, but the potential is not exploited at the present. Manufacturing is limited to food processing and mainly serves the domestic market. As a result of political changes since 1972,

A worker is making bricks for home building near Antananarivo, the capital of this island state. (Photo: United Nations/ Rajaonina.)

including the official policy of nationalization and government control of marketing, there has been a steady decline in the manufacturing sector. Transportation bottlenecks have compounded the problem, especially because few roads are passable all year long.

Until 1975–1976, the government favored family increases with a system of family allowances. A National Population Council has been created and it has cooperated closely with the Family Planning Association of Madagascar, founded in 1967. The association receives funds from the United Nations and elsewhere to operate clinics in eight cities and rural areas. Abortions are forbidden, and the population continues to grow at a 2.5 percent annual rate. More than 45 percent of the Malagasy are less than 15 years old. The population explosion has strained the country's limited economic and manpower resources, and unemployment is growing, especially in cities like Antananarivo (Tananarive), the capital, Mahajanga, Toamasina, Fianarantsoa, Toliara, and Antsiranana (formerly Diégo-Suarez). On the other hand, there is ample land to sustain double the current population, and the government is encouraging internal migration to underpopulated rural areas. Thus far, this effort has been unsuccessful, and youths migrating to the cities present a serious problem. These youngsters form gangs known as *zoams*, and they have rampaged in the capital city on a few occasions in the last 5 years. Their presence has contributed to growing urban crime.

Education is the sector that most clearly reflects Madagascar's problems. Madagascar inherited a highly centralized educational system from France. Schools and curricula emphasized French and literary course work, rather than scientific and practical studies geared to Madagascar's rural realities. The system prepared primary school students for secondary school entry examinations and produced white-collar workers for the modern sector of the economy and

government. A rigid examination system resulted in a high repetition and dropout rate: less than 3 out of 5 primary school pupils were promoted to the next class at the end of an academic year.

The pupil-teacher ratio in public primary schools was 74 to 1 (compared with 41 to 1 in private primary schools). Twenty-five percent of the government budget was spent on education, but an inordinately high proportion was earmarked for teachers' salaries.

The educational system is contributing to an impending crisis of the educated unemployed: by the end of 1975 there were at least 50,000 unemployed lower secondary school leavers. By 1985, there will be about 170,000 school leavers with only 85,000 jobs to fill. In 1972, student unrest toppled the Tsiranana government that came to power at independence. Student riots in 1978 almost toppled the current military government. The educated unemployed will present the single most important political issue in Madagascar for some time to come.

To address the inadequacies of the educational system, reforms were launched in 1974 to introduce a radical change. Control is being decentralized and Malagasized. The official goals are the enrollment of all children aged 6 to 14 by 1987, the transformation of primary education into a basic 5-year course in Malagasy, greater involvement of local communities in school construction and payment of teachers' salaries, and a greater emphasis on scientific and technical education.

Both educational planning and the new reforms suffer because of an inadequate information base. There are few reliable statistics on the current student population or on the number, type, and location of school buildings. The regime has so far failed to implement decentralization, and existing cadres have no experience in managing the new institutions, in particular the teaching materials production center. The government has not yet published reliable statistics even for the university-level student population, which was estimated at 13,000 in 1978.

After Portugal "discovered" the beautiful island of Madagascar in 1500, the Portuguese, British, Dutch, and French all tried unsuccessfully to establish colonies there. Following three centuries of turbulence, the Merina kingdom extended its rule and welcomed the help of Europeans to maintain order. After a war with France (1883), the French gained control of Madagascar's foreign policy in 1885, and in 1896 France annexed the island. Madagascar became a French Overseas Territory after World War II, and the Malagasy were given French citizenship. Madagascar became an autonomous republic in the French Community in 1958, and was declared a sovereign independent state on June 26, 1960, under President Philibert Tsiranana, who had been helped to power by the French.

In 1972, workers and students rioted in Tananarive and other cities, and on May 18, Tsiranana was forced out of power. A referendum brought the armed forces, under Gabriel Ramanantsoa, to center stage. The mil-

A very primitive ferry transports people and cars across a river in northern Madagascar; men with long poles move the ferry. (Photo: United Nations/ L. Rajaonina.)

itary tried to free Madagascar's economy and foreign policy from strong French influence. Within 18 months, they had nationalized the energy, mining, banking, insurance, and import–export sectors of the country's dual economy. Popular unrest continued, and disturbances in 1973 led to the arrest of several members of the former Tsiranana government. In 1973, France withdrew its military and naval forces from Madagascar.

Ramanantsoa then launched further reforms to socialize the economy. Disruptions caused by rapid political and economic changes generated opposition, because prices rose sharply and there were shortages in basic foodstuffs. Tensions continued to mount. In 1975, General Richard Ratsimandrava assumed power, only to be assassinated 6 days later. A military directorate subsequently gave power to General Didier Ratsiraka, who has continued to transform the country into a socialist state. In 1975, former President Tsiranana and his followers were arrested and tried for plotting Ratsimandrava's murder, but most of them were released. A new constitution was approved in a national referendum on December 21, 1975, and Madagascar became the Democratic Republic of Madagascar, under President Ratsiraka, in January 1976.

On June 30, 1977, elections were held for a National Assembly. President Ratsiraka's national front, including almost all former political parties and their successors, won the elections, and some stability may eventually result. Despite the elections of 1977, decision making is still controlled largely by the army, and it remains to be seen how far the military will transfer that power to the elected institutions.

The government's long-term development strategy is contained in a series of 3-year plans extending to the year 2000. The goals are to be achieved through the promotion of a more efficient use of the existing labor force; an improvement in the standard of living of the less-advantaged population; and the establishment of basic conditions for the expansion of production and consumption. Government interventions envisaged to achieve this include the provision of general education and technical training; the intensification and reorientation of research on the choice of appropriate technology; the development of light industries and labor-intensive activities in urban areas; the extension of credit to smallholders and development of productive infrastructure as well as land reform in rural areas; the promotion of voluntary internal migration between rural areas; and the development of the cooperative movement.

The plans fail to specify how needed agricultural services are to be developed. Despite the government's intentions, the very rapid reform of Madagascar's administrative and economic structures has hampered the achievement of socialist goals. As a result, the economy remains weak. In 1977 and 1978, there were shortages of essential foodstuffs, spare parts, and raw materials for local industry.

There is still large and growing unemployment, it is difficult to persuade farmers and herders to use new techniques, and there is maladministration and a paralysis of the various bureaucracies because government workers are afraid to take the initiative in a climate of political uncertainty. In addition, the authority for various economic and administrative functions is fragmented, and this has been exacerbated by the rapid decentralization of local government and administration through a four-tiered fokonolona system, whose rhetoric emphasizes development from the grass roots up. There are also the problems of corruption, ethnic and regional disparities and antagonisms, and, more crucial in the short term, a dearth of reliable information on which to base concrete economic action.   *Warren Weinstein*

Malawi

(Republic of Malawi)

Area: 45,483 sq mi (117,801 sq km)
Population: 5.8 million
  Density: 127 per sq mi (49 per sq km)
  Growth rate: 3.1% (1970–1977)
Percent of population under 14 years of age: 42% (1970)
Infant deaths per 1,000 live births: 142 (1975)
Life expectancy at birth: 41 years (1975)
Leading causes of death: not available
Ethnic composition: Chewa, Nyanja, Yao, Tumbuku
Languages: English, Chewa
Literacy: 20–25% (est.)
Religions: Catholic, Protestant, Muslim
Percent population urban: 15% (est.)
Percent population rural: 85% (est.)
Gross national product: $1.01 billion
  Per capita GNP: $180
  Per capita GNP growth rate: 3.1% (1970–1977)
Inflation rate: not available

The landlocked republic of Malawi (formerly Nyasaland) in southern Africa is strong in human resources. Its assets include its 5.8 million dedicated, hardworking, resourceful, and culturally closely related people. Its liabilities include high rural-population densities of 300 to 500 persons per square mile (116 to 193 per sq km), meager valuable mineral resources, limited arable land, physical and geographical isolation, and dependence on often unstable neighbors and distant ports and railways. Because of this imbalance between human and natural resources, Malawi has traditionally exported skilled and unskilled workers to its neighbors—Zimbabwe, Zambia, Mozambique, and South Africa. The coming of independence to these four countries and racial strife in South Africa forced Malawi to try to reabsorb nearly 250,000 of its people once employed outside its borders.

Physically, Malawi is a green and verdant land about the size of Pennsylvania. It hangs like a green raindrop alongside the deep, clear blue waters of sliverlike Lake Malawi (formerly Lake Nyasa), Africa's third largest and the world's tenth largest lake. Much of Malawi's 45,483 square miles (117,801 sq km), one-fifth of which is Lake Malawi, consists of highland plateaus 4,000 feet (1,200 meters) and higher. Although the southern lowland country below Lake Malawi and near the Mozambique border is hot and humid, the rest of Malawi enjoys moderate 65 to 85°F (18 to 29°C) temperatures and a rainy season from November to March.

Well-watered Malawi is also well populated. Its three principal ethnic groups (the Nyanja of the central plateau, the Tumbuku of the northern Nyika Plateau, and the Chewa of the southern lowlands) speak closely related and mutually intelligible languages. Since Malawi became independent in 1964, English and Chewa have been the official languages, a hardship only for some smaller northern groups like the Yao, whose language is closer to the Swahili spoken in East Africa. Malawians can and do intermarry freely and share a clear sense of national and cultural unity, enhanced by the common experience of having so many of their men working abroad.

Malawi's economy is predominantly rural and agricultural. The principal cash export crops are coffee, tea, tobacco, and tung oil, augmented in recent years by cotton, sisal, sugar, rice, and tropical fruit. Although Malawi was never a "white-settler" country, before independence its major export crops were grown primarily on European-owned and -managed estates, especially the tea estates on the slopes of

A man dries a catch of fish before it is smoke-cured in a village near Lake Malawi. Fish contributes protein to the home diet. (Photo: United Nations/YN/PAS.)

10,000-foot (3,000-m) Mount Mulanje. Since independence, the government has encouraged the growth of producer and distributor cooperatives for export crops and joint ventures associating Malawian small-scale farmers with foreign-owned processing factories. Output has grown impressively, and the continued high quality and reputation of Malawian exports have been valuable assets in highly competitive markets.

Producing food for domestic consumption is primarily women's work, especially because so many Malawian men are working in the South African mines or in the Zambian copper belt. Women cultivate home vegetable gardens and grow basic foodstuffs like cassava, maize, yams, and other roots and tubers. They supplement their home diets by trading in lively local roadside and lakeside markets. Favorite trade goods include the chambo (similar to perch), rainbow trout, and catfish taken by fishermen from Lake Malawi. Cattle are scarce and used mostly for dairying, especially near Mount Mulanje. Fish from the lake and local streams and locally raised chickens and goats are the principal sources of animal protein in a country where there is generally enough for everyone to eat but not enough protein.

The government's development strategy has been to concentrate on increasing the agricultural output of export and food crops. It has relied on generous credit schemes administered through agricultural development banks, major hydroelectric and irrigation projects on the Shire River funded by the World Bank and other donors to increase the acreage under cultivation, and price and other incentives to encourage cooperatives and small farmers. It is estimated that between 1960 and 1976, gross national product per capita in real terms grew by 3 percent annually, with the population increasing during the same period at 2.7 percent.

Industry, mining, and services have contributed less than 30 percent of the gross domestic product in recent years. Industry consists almost entirely of small factories that either process export crops (sugar refineries and cotton gins) or produce consumer goods for the local market (breweries, textile mills, and assembly plants for transistor radios). A per capita income of $130 in 1976 and a gross national product for that year of $720 million (including an estimate of subsistence output) do not allow much import substitution.

The extension of geological survey work is a major development priority, although Malawi's geology has not yet revealed any valuable mineral deposits. There is some low-grade noncoking coal in the south and a major bauxite deposit near Mount Mulanje. Extensive working of the bauxite deposit may require imported hydroelectric power from the giant Cabora Bassa hydroelectric project in Mozambique. Hydroelectric potential is considerable, and the damming of the Shire River, once completed, should make the country self-sufficient in electricity. However, all other energy sources must be imported over considerable distances and at high cost.

Urbanization is still incipient. It has developed more slowly in Malawi than it has in many African states because Malawians tend to seek work abroad rather than at home. The twin cities of Blantyre and Limbe, once the colonial capital, have a population of about 150,000 and contain much of the national industry, communications, transport, and administrative structure. Some 50 miles (80 km) to the east, the lovely university town of Zomba, with a population of 25,000, nestles at the foot of Mount Mulanje. In 1970, relying on South African financial and technical aid, President Hastings Kamuzu Banda made his centrally located hometown of Lilongwe, 200 miles (320 km) north of Blantyre, the new national capital. Lilongwe still has something of a barracks-and-frontier quality, but its population of 20,000, mostly government workers, is growing rapidly, and this takes some of the pressure off Blantyre.

Malawi's landlocked location is perhaps its most intractable development problem. Although steamers cruise regularly on Lake Malawi, most goods enter and leave the country by road or rail.

To the north, the republic of Tanzania has poor roads and no rail connections, and trade with this country is confined largely to minor items in border areas. In recent years, political hostility between the two governments, mostly over Malawi's close relations with South Africa, have worsened already poor communications. To the west, Zambia is friendly and richer than Tanzania and provides a market for some Malawian goods, especially a refreshing beer made from maize and called Chibuku. However, Zambia is also landlocked and is bedeviled by political and security problems.

Malawi relies primarily on the Mozambican ports of Nacala and Beira and on road and rail connections to Mozambican railways. The Zimbabwe war and the Mozambican involvement in that war have placed a heavy burden on the transport structure of Mozambique. The port of Beira, once closed to Zimbabwe traffic by UN sanctions, has fallen into decay, like Nacala farther north.

Little and poor, Malawi has had to scramble at considerable cost and effort to find a way to the sea. Since 1973 and the energy crisis, import costs and export bottlenecks have further impeded Malawian development. Although South Africa has continued to provide some financial and technical assistance (Malawi is one of the few African states which maintain diplomatic relations with Pretoria), the price has been the forfeiture of possible aid from the Arab oil-exporting states.

The ongoing and apparently worsening crisis throughout southern Africa has also posed a severe dilemma for Malawi. President Hastings Kamuzu Banda has taken a pragmatic stance toward his neighbors. He collaborated openly with the Portuguese before Mozambican independence in 1975; maintained cordial, if informal, relations with the regime of Ian Smith in Rhodesia, and solicited South African aid while spurning Pan-Africanism. These policies have provoked extensive opposition at home and abroad. They may well have contributed to Malawian economic growth and political stability, but as violence increases in neighboring states Malawi may become even more isolated and may even be identified with the losing side.

Reliable figures are hard to come by, but since independence perhaps one-fourth of all Malawian men have been employed outside the country at one time or another. Remittances from this Malawian migration have played an important part in the economy of the country, especially helping to maintain high levels of education. There is evidence that in recent years the money sent home by Malawian migrants has also been used to open small businesses and to engage in commercial agriculture. Malawians enjoy an enviable reputation as reliable and efficient workers and are eagerly sought by neighboring countries. The effects of the diaspora on the wives and families left behind, however, are detrimental.

While the Malawian economy has expanded since independence, the situation of the Malawian migrant has drastically altered. In independent Mozambique and Zambia, for example, preference in employment is often given to nationals, and many Malawians have been forced to return home or to relinquish their Malawian citizenship. After 1975, the Rhodesian war se-

Workers operate a road grader to cut a new road; most goods enter and leave this landlocked country by road or rail. (Photo: United Nations/Pickerell.)

verely disrupted the African economy and forced thousands of Malawians to leave their second homes. South Africa sought to reduce its dependence on imported African labor, and President Banda cracked down on the recruiting of Malawians for South African mines. As a result, the hard-pressed Malawian economy, already hurt by the high costs of imported energy and foreign-trade bottlenecks, was forced to absorb returning migrants while their remittances declined. Hence, the government put even more emphasis on expanding its arable land and increasing its agricultural output.

Education and religion remain the pillars of Malawian life and society and its strongest development assets. With the exception of a few Islamic strongholds in the far north, Malawi was profoundly Christianized in the late nineteenth century, and church and state have long been closely associated. While government control of and support for education has predominated since 1965, Catholic and Protestant church groups continue to play an important role in school administration. The University of Malawi, with an enrollment near 1,000 and several campuses, has a modest reputation, especially in agriculture. More highly regarded is the Soche Hills Teacher Training College and other teacher-training schools, whose graduates were once prominent Malawian exports. Recent figures indicate that 61 percent of Malawi's boys and 48 percent of its girls are receiving primary education. These figures compare favorably with other African countries at similar levels of development. Secondary schools are government- and church-operated, mostly residential, and have high standards and low enrollments. Commercial and

technical education has been encouraged in recent years, and training schemes by the banks, trading firms, and other enterprises have rapidly improved the skills of working Malawians.

On any Sunday in Malawi, much of the population attends church. Church groups are active in organizing scores of communal activities in this quiet, pleasant, and profoundly conservative rural society. Catholics, Protestants, and Muslims peacefully and proudly coexist in a society that is entirely black African except for fewer than 10,000 expatriate white technicians and businessmen and several thousand Indian and Pakistani traders. Since independence, race relations have been generally good, and thousands of white Rhodesian and South African visitors come as tourists to Malawi every year.

Village life is profoundly influenced by the exodus of adult males. Government attempts to organize community–development schemes and Young Pioneer youth groups have had mixed results. Rural training centers and a few agricultural-settlement schemes have tried to involve village women and youths, again with mixed results. The villagers continue to produce a wide range of crafts, including wood and soapstone carvings, woven and embroidered baskets, fishnets and traps for lake dwellers, beadwork, pottery, and traditional musical instruments. Traditional garments—wraparound cloaks known as *chikwembas* for men and long, flowing, wraparound print dresses or skirts known as *chirundu* for women—are still the standard rural attire.

Eighty-year-old President Banda personifies Malawi as much as any developing-country leader reflects his state and society. Since independence, Banda has governed in a no-nonsense, one-party, authoritarian manner, brooking no opposition. Frustrated intellectuals and party dissidents have gone into exile, and Banda has replaced them with loyal followers. Always elegantly dressed, scornful of the foreign press and other, more militant African leaders, Banda has worked hard to retain the support of the villagers, especially women. Stressing the conservative values of Malawian society, he has banned miniskirts, opposition parties and presses, long hair, and other signs of dissent. Airport signs warn visitors that "according to Malawi custom, it is not regarded as proper for a woman to publicly expose any part of her leg above the knee, except when the wearer is engaged in a form of sport for which such clothing is customary."

Banda's outspoken views on South Africa remain extremely controversial among Malawians, although no public criticism is permitted. His administration is often described as rigid, inflexible, unimaginative, and composed mostly of corrupt sycophants. However, his agricultural and irrigation programs and hydroelectric schemes have been productive.

Malawi's present is the direct product of its rich and varied past. Archaeological excavations are beginning to put together a picture of several thousand years of continuous habitation in what is today Ma-

Fishermen pull in their seine net along the Shire River near Lake Malawi. (Photo: United Nations/ YN/PAS.)

lawi. The Chencherere Stone Age rock paintings were found near the mountain town of Dedza, and other sites are being opened up. The shores of Lake Malawi are particularly rich in archaeological finds. There is more and more evidence pointing to the existence of centuries-old permanent trade routes between the grassland societies of East Africa and medieval African settlements like Zimbabwe. Trade extended to the Indian Ocean ports and to the Arab and Portuguese coastal settlements at Mombasa, Manica, Sofala, and elsewhere. A Malawi kingdom sought to control the plateau and lake trade routes and to deal with Arabs, Portuguese, and other Africans.

During the nineteenth century, Arab traders operating out of Zanzibar, together with their local allies, extended slave raiding into Malawi. The effects were devastating; when David Livingstone reached the Shire River in the 1850s he found a war-stricken, underpopulated, and famished land. Subsequently, British missionaries introduced Western education, medicine, and religion, and campaigned for British intervention to end the slave trade. In 1891, Britain established a protectorate over most of present-day Malawi (called Nyasaland from 1907 until 1964), and a relatively benign 75-year period of colonial rule followed.

British efforts to recruit African troops during World War I and the first African nativist religious movements fused to produce the first major African uprising in 1914. However, during the 1920s and 1930s Malawi was quiet again, as hundreds of thousands of missionary-educated young men, like Banda, left for the mines in South Africa or for Rhodesian farms.

The Malawian national movement, its name derived from the sixteenth-century trading kingdom, was galvanized when, in 1953, the British forced the protectorate they called Nyasaland to enter the Central African Federation with white-settler-ruled Southern Rhodesia (now Zimbabwe) and Northern Rhodesia (now Zambia). Placed for the first time under direct settler rather than colonial rule, the Malawians organized and demonstrated in protest and recalled Banda, their legendary hero and leader, from abroad. Briefly imprisoned as an agitator and released when a British Royal Commission found his arrest (and that of hundreds of others) unjustified, Banda swept the first national elections and swiftly took his country out of the Central African Federation and into independence in July 1964. A year later, Malawi became a republic and Banda became its first President for life.

Malawi's future is clouded. Its most serious short-term problem is that of political succession. President Banda has failed to provide for an heir. The military is a minor force, and the party's paramilitary groups may have more weapons and numbers. The party itself is in considerable disarray and lacks coherence. Malawian exile groups are small and dispersed and have little apparent influence. Therefore, it is difficult to predict which political leadership and institutions will survive. Conceivably one or another group of Banda's often unstable supporters may coalesce to govern at least temporarily.

Whatever form the succession takes, Malawi must alter its relations with its neighbors and begin to cooperate with the rest of Africa. The first imperative is to improve its relations with Mozambique and to take steps to strengthen rail, road, and port connections as well as steamer service on shared Lake Malawi. Mozambique's militantly socialist government lacks the financial and technical resources to improve its own northern transport infrastructure. Presumably an understanding between the Malawian and Mozambican governments will be needed to solicit external aid jointly. Similarly, any major bauxite or other mineral projects in Malawi require agreement on improved transport links to Mozambique.

Banda's personal animosities have hurt Malawi's relations with Tanzania and Zambia. No doubt a political succession in Malawi which resulted in a younger and more Pan-African leadership would help to restore friendly relations with these two countries. All three governments could improve their modest trade and transport ties, share certain educational and technical services, and assist one another generally. Malawi might also take part in less intensive programs with Botswana, Lesotho, and Swaziland, like the regional management training center at Blantyre.

Its relations with South Africa will continue to plague Malawi. As a market and as a source of public and private investment, tourists, technical assistance, and employment for migrant labor, South Africa is important, although not vital, to the Malawian economy. Britain remains the major source of aid for Malawi; West Germany, the United States, several Scandinavian countries, and others also help. Banda's controversial opening of diplomatic relations with South Africa generated an estimated $50 million or more from South Africa toward the new capital at Lilongwe (itself a controversial project), but Banda defended his move on political rather than economic grounds, claiming that it contributed toward a nonviolent process of change in South Africa. It is not clear whether Malawi would have any standing in a dialogue on race relations in southern Africa.

Assuming that violence escalates in and around South Africa, a post-Banda Malawi government may change its policies. Breaking or downgrading diplomatic relations with South Africa, phasing out South African aid, terminating migrant-labor contracts, and other measures might be part of such a shift. The political and economic costs to Malawi are hard to predict.

Malawi's fundamental long-term problems concern population density and a viable development strategy. The total population was estimated at 5.047 million in 1970, of which 42 percent were under 14 years of age. One projection estimates a population in the year

2000 of 11.257 million, with 5.102 million less than 14 years old. How is Malawi to feed, clothe, shelter, educate, and provide employment for these people, given its meager natural resources and its external liabilities? Both rural and urban population densities are high, but Banda frowns on family planning and opposes any program of population control which would reduce fertility. The crude birth rate was estimated at 47.7 per 1,000 in 1970–1975 and was projected to fall to 39.5 per 1,000 by the year 2000. To be acceptable to the people, however, any deliberate effort to lower fertility must be combined with a national program to reduce infant mortality (estimated at 142 per 1,000 live births in 1975). The government has concentrated on improving rural health and nutrition services, and life expectancy at birth edged up from an estimated 35 years in 1960 to 41 years in 1975. The consequent size of the projected population for 2000 and its extreme youth mean that Malawi will be hard pressed to meet the basic needs of its people.

It is difficult to plan a viable development strategy in the face of limited resources and high population densities. For almost a century, Malawi exported labor to its neighbors and used the remittances to develop agriculture and social services at home. This strategy is about to come to an end because of circumstances beyond the control of Malawi and Malawians. An alternative strategy, one which emphasizes labor-intensive exports and food-crop, smallholder agriculture, has been formulated and partially implemented. It has provided jobs and increased output, but not on the scale needed if Malawi is to reabsorb its migrants and support its own growing population. No other strategy of export industries, estate agriculture, or tourism seems viable, especially given the uncertainties of external transport. Malawi's cultural homogeneity, its cooperative and communal traditions, its educational heritage and institutions, and the goodwill and resourcefulness of its people are its outstanding assets. These must be harnessed to a new leadership and a viable development strategy.

Aaron Segal

Mali
(Republic of Mali)

Area: 464,873 sq mi (1,204,015 sq km)
Population: 6.3 million
  Density: 13 per sq mi (5 per sq km)
  Growth rate: 2.5% (1970–1977)
Percent of population under 15 years of age: 50%
Infant deaths per 1,000 live births: 200
Life expectancy at birth: 38 years
Leading causes of death: not available
Ethnic composition: Mande (Bambara, Malinke, Sarakolle) 50%; Peul 17%; Voltaic linquistic group 12%; Songhai 6%; Tuareg and Moors 5%
Languages: French (official), Bambara
Literacy: under 5%
Religions: Muslim 90%; indigenous 9%; Christian 1%
Percent population urban: 10%
Percent population rural: 90%
Gross national product: $760 million
  Per capita GNP: $120
  Per capita GNP growth rate: 1.9% (1970–1977)
Inflation rate: 13% for 1978–1979

Situated in the West African savanna astride the Niger River and the south-central Sahara, Mali occupies the area once traversed by Africa's most ancient north-south and east-west trade routes. Although it is landlocked, Mali's location favored its development as a contact zone, which is still reflected in its commercially dominated economy and its social and cultural syntheses. After a brief colonial experience (1885–1960), most of contemporary Mali's 6.3 million people are still grappling with poverty and the aftermath of recent droughts (1968–1975). Even without drought, Mali's poor soil and the inaccessiblity of its mineral deposits limit attempts to modernize its economy.

Located between approximately 11 and 25° north latitude, Mali covers an area of 464,873 square miles (1,204,015 sq km), the size of Texas and California combined. Much of the scenery is spectacular, especially in the southern sandstone highlands, which rise to about 1,739 feet (521 m), on the 3,000-foot (900-m) Bandiagara Plateau in the Hombori Mountains in the east, and in the northern mountains of Adrar des Iforas. Rain, when it falls, averages between 30 and 40 inches (77 to 101 cm) a year, permitting the cultivation of Mali's staple crops, millet and sorghum. Groundnuts, rice, sugarcane, cotton, corn, and oil plants are also grown. In the south, where the bulk of the population lives, temperatures range from 75 to 95°F (24 to 35°C). In the middle and northern zones, where the annual rainfall is approximately 20 and 7 inches (50 and 17 cm), respectively, with temperatures ranging from 80 to 140°F (27 to 60°C), the population is dependent on livestock and trade. The poor Malian soils, combined with traditional practices, keep agricultural productivity low. Productivity and the quality of life are higher in the Niger Delta's 40,000 square miles (103,600 sq km) and in the river's upper course, where populations have been fishing and mining gold along the neighboring tributaries of the upper Senegal River since before the Christian era.

Because of high costs and inadequate transportation and power facilities, this gold ore—together with marble and limestone at Bafoulabé and Diamon, respectively—is among the few minerals mined, although Mali is relatively rich in ores. The estimated 700 million tons (635 million t) of bauxite ore in the west in Kayes, 20 million tons (18 million t) of phosphate in Ansongo in the east, and 35 million tons (132 million t) of known manganese deposits, not to mention scattered deposits of iron ore, copper, zinc, lead, and tungsten, have not been exploited on an industrial scale. Although the National Society of Mineral Resources (SONAREM) has also found lithium in the west and uranium in the Adrar des Iforas, industrial mining has yet to begin.

Throughout the centuries, Mali's development has owed more to its rich cultural and linguistic heritage as one of Africa's busiest contact zones than to its more recent socioeconomic and political changes. In effect, Mali's richest resource is still its people, who, despite some 20 different identities, are striving toward "one people, one aim and one faith." Notable among its peoples are the dominant Mande (Bambara, Malinke, Sarakolle), who represent about 50 percent of the population; the Peul (17 percent), people of the Voltaic linguistic group (12 percent), the Songhai (6 percent), and, in the north, the Tuareg and Moors (5 percent).

The majority of the population (approximately 90 percent) is Muslim, and, indeed, the country has been subject to Islamic influences since the eighth century. Only 1 percent is Christian, both Roman Catholic and Protestant, and approximately 9 percent follow indigenous religions. French is the official language, while Bambara, the language of the Bambara, is spoken by about 80 percent of the population. Dominant social organizations include the extended family, with the clan still playing an important role among the Tuareg of the northern savanna and the desert.

About 90 percent of Mali's population is rural-based, and farmers, herders, and fishermen form 90 percent of the working population. About 27 percent of the working population is engaged in crafts or in home-based industries like textiles and wood carving, and some 3 percent is involved in local trade. Professional itinerant traders (*dyulas*), who have engaged in long-distance trade since at least the fourteenth century, usually incorporate small rural markets into their larger trade networks.

Family units work together, and a division of labor follows sexual lines. Among farmers, domestic household work and crop maintenance is almost exclusively female work. Among pastoralists, men as a rule do not milk animals or make dairy products. Craft industries are usually dominated by men. The exception is the textile industry, where women play a role.

Agricultural technology is, for the most part, rudimentary. The iron-tipped hoe, the machete, and the pick that may have been in use shortly after the beginning of the Christian era are still the main agri-cultural implements. Appropriate or small-scale agricultural technology is being introduced through bilateral and multilateral aid and technical-assistance programs. In most rural areas, land is still owned by the entire lineage, with individual usufruct assigned according to family size and need.

Poor rural health care, unsanitary conditions, and a scarcity of clean drinking water are serious problems. At least 90 percent of the population has practically no access to modern health care, and the doctor to patient ratio is 1 to 32,000.

Exact statistics are not available, but the infant-mortality rate is believed to be high. It is estimated that 50 percent of all children die before their fifth birthdays, and that the infant-mortality rate for the first year of life is 200 per 1,000 live births. (The figure for the United States is 17 per 1,000.) The birthrate itself may reach 50 per 1,000 while the population growth rate probably approaches 2.5 percent. Despite a gross life expectancy of only about 38 years, the population may double by the early part of the twenty-first century. In the absence of precise statistics, estimates suggest that about 50 percent of the population is under 15 years of age.

The large school-age population notwithstanding, there are few modern schools in Mali's 11,000 villages. In the mid 1970s, only 15 percent of Malian children under 15 years of age attended school. Of rural children, 276,000 were in grades 1 to 9; only 16,722 children, urban and rural, were enrolled in sec-

Sitting in front of his very primitive hut, a fisherman mends his net. The people of Mali have engaged in fishing in the Niger River for at least 2,000 years. (Photo: United Nations/ AP/AB.)

ondary schools. In recent years, commercial and technical education has been encouraged.

Mali's communication and transportation systems are limited, although the Niger River is a major transportation artery. Mali's railway link to Dakar and its major roads to the coast through Senegal and the Ivory Coast were built by the French primarily for the shipment of cash crops and other raw materials. Consequently, in areas where raw-material production was too small to warrant the expenditure for communication infrastructures, some communities still suffer from poor communication.

Only 10 percent of Mali's population is urban. About 400,000 Malians live in Bamako, the capital; approximately 32,500 live in Mopti, an old river town famous for its dried fish industry; and a mere 28,500 and 28,000 live in Kayes and Ségou, respectively. Ancient Malian towns like the fabled Timbuktu and Djenné are known more for their historical and cultural resources than for any modern urban development. As in rural communities, life in urban areas is focused on the extended family, buttressed, for the most part, by the Islamic institution of polygynous marriage. Within recent years, however, double-digit inflation (13 percent in 1978 and 1979) in the towns, and changing social attitudes toward the role of women, have begun to have their effect on urban polygyny. But many urban families still retain their ties with rural relatives, and so (depending on how the data are assessed) one can appropriately speak of an urban-rural continuum.

Dominant occupations in urban areas include white-collar jobs, primarily with the government, the largest employer. Less than 1 percent of the work force is employed in Mali's varied light industries, including food processing, the production of textiles, a cement factory, peanut-oil extraction, soap manufacture, ceramics, the production of matches and cigarettes, a brewery, a sugar refinery, and a rice-processing plant. Most urban enterprises are owned and managed by the state, and, with the small private commercial sector, they possess the greatest potential for economic growth. Foreign investors, mainly the French, are represented in the Chamber of Commerce.

Small-scale, Western-style development notwithstanding, Mali is a very African country; its principal social and economic institutions, even those in the process of fairly rapid change, are governed more by African than by non-African values. The social theory that expresses this concept of changing while maintaining continuity is known as L'Option Socialiste. Within this framework, Malians expect that innovations will be integrated into—not simply grafted onto—the indigenous institutions best suited for the purpose.

L'Option Socialiste was chosen partly in response to modern socialist ideologies and partly in relation

In primitive villages, where land is usually owned by the entire lineage and not by individuals, women balance goods on their heads as they trudge down rocky pathways. (Photo: United Nations/ Rozberg.)

to the Malian past. Proud of their heritage, Malians hope that their strong cultural identity will not be irresponsibly sacrificed for rapid economic gains, although it is sometimes difficult to distinguish their desire for a "strong cultural identity" from simple obscurantism and resistance to change. While it is true that modern socialist ideologies originated in Western industrialized societies, the notion of state ownership and the allocation of resources according to need are also embedded in precolonial Malian social theory, as is a belief in the right of the whole to prosper, even at the risk of sacrificing individual rights. The synthesis of doctrinaire Western socialism and Malian precolonial social theory is not so strange as it first seems.

Similarly, Malians traditionally believe that public institutions should reflect continuity. Thus their government is authoritarian, with power concentrated in the President, Brigadier General Moussa Traoré. The second President of Mali, he succeeded Modibo Keita after a bloodless coup on November 19, 1968, and is supported by the eleven-man Military Committee of National Liberation (MLN). Although there is talk of a return to constitutional rule, Mali is governed by decree and, according to precolonial traditions, decisions appear to be reached by consensus.

Beyond the MLN, the Malian elite includes the army and a large bureaucracy. The size of the bureaucracy stems from the fact that the government is the largest employer and was, until recently, committed to hiring every high school and college graduate in Mali. This elite core is reinforced by regional military governors, commandants of the cercles, who supervise administrative and economic activities; and chiefs of the arrondissements, which are administrative divisions of the cercles. These chiefs are usually responsible for collecting taxes, registering births and deaths, and settling local disputes. Malian elites also include many from the ranks of the traditional elite (religious dignitaries, rural notables, and some *dyulas*). Industrialists, investors, community and welfare leaders, and a wide range of professionals complete the ranks of the modern elite.

Partly because of its position as a contact zone, Mali's history is one of the richest in Africa. A major focus of north-south and east-west population movements, the Mali region's complex plural societies combined to create the successive empires and kingdoms of Ghana (fourth to twelfth centuries), Mali (twelfth to fifteenth centuries), and Songhai (fourteenth to sixteenth centuries). During this period of more than 1,000 years, political institutions associated with Islam and the so-called Iron Age of centralized state building were slowly forged. Long-distance trade also developed during this period, primarily between the eleventh and thirteenth centuries. Some Malian towns—like the fabled Timbuktu, Djenné, and Gao—still reveal traces of this earlier heritage.

After the defeat of Songhai at the hands of invading Moroccans shortly before 1600, lesser-known polities came into existence, among them the Peul monarchy of Macina and the Bambara kingdoms of Kaarta and Segou. By the nineteenth century, these monarchies had succumbed to the rule of conservative Islamic reformers, who remained in power until the 1890s.

The French colonial era brought radical political and social changes, especially to members of the precolonial elite. Those most affected were the chiefs, the large landowning families, the traders, and the Islamic notables. The impact of French economic policies on Mali, however, was minimal compared to their impact on Senegal and the Ivory Coast.

Once it came under French domination, however, Mali's administrative fortunes varied. Between 1892 and 1899, Mali, known as the French Sudan, was administered from the capital at Kayes. Between 1899 and 1904, it was merged into Senegambia and Niger, a larger administrative unit which included Senegal, parts of Mauritania, Niger, and Upper Volta. As a result of administrative regroupings which took place between 1904 and 1920, Mali became part of the Upper Senegal and Niger administration, along with Niger, Mauritania, and Upper Volta. Between 1920 and 1959, it was again known as the French Sudan and was part of yet another administrative unit, one which included Upper Volta and Mauritania. In 1959, as the Sudanese Republic, Mali joined Senegal to form the Mali Federation, with membership in the French Community. The federation was, however, shortlived; and on September 22, 1960, the Republic of Mali was proclaimed.

Although Mali's national goals include socioeconomic growth and modernization, these goals may not be realizable. Despite some gains and a committed leadership, Mali is still one of the poorest countries in the world. With per capita income of less than $100 per annum (1979) and a gross domestic product (GDP) of $603 million (1977), Mali's future economic prospects are limited, even with an annual economic growth rate of 7.4 percent (1977). Moreover, with the bulk of the population young, poor, and rural, and the average industrial worker's wage $1,010 per annum, prospects for an expanding economy and consumer markets appear small. The 13 percent inflation rate has also taken its toll. Consequently, Malians are likely to be dependent on foreign aid and technical assistance for the foreseeable future.

B. Marie Perinbam

Mauritania
(Islamic Republic of Mauritania)

Area: 419,229 sq mi (1,085,760 sq km)
Population: 1.5 million
  Density: 4 per sq mi (1 per sq km)
  Growth rate: 2.7% (1970–1977)
Percent of population under 14 years of age: 34%
Infant deaths per 1,000 live births: 187
Life expectancy at birth: 39 years (1979)
Leading causes of death: not available
Ethnic composition: Tukolor, Wolof, Fulani, black Moors, white Moors
Languages: Hassani Arabic (official), French (official), Wolof, Pulaar-Fulfulde
Literacy: 12%
Religions: Muslim
Percent population urban: 70%
Percent population rural: 30%
Gross national product: $420 million
  Per capita GNP: $270
  Per capita GNP growth rate: −0.1% (1970–1977)
Inflation rate: 12.5% average 1978–1979

The survival of Mauritania is as precarious as its people's day-to-day struggle for life. While the sands of the Sahara Desert creep over once-adequate grazing lands and dry up the country's ancient wells, neighboring countries and the Polisario movement (the Western Sahara liberation organization backed by Algeria) have denied Mauritania's right to exist as an independent state within its present frontiers. A war on its northern border from 1976 to 1979 drained the economy and shook the people's confidence in their leaders; repercussions are still noticeable.

This land of over 400,000 square miles (1,085,760 sq km), which is twice the size of France, is located on Africa's western bulge, between Senegal and Morocco and bordering on the Atlantic Ocean. At least 40 percent of its total land area, particularly in the north, is covered with sand; and the droughts of 1973 and 1977 have begun to kill all forms of life in another 25 percent of the land. Even on the coast and in the south, where more than half the people live, there is a bare 10 to 25 inches (25 to 51 cm) of rain in good years.

The sea to the west and the Senegal River to the south are the sources of life and hope. There, Mauritanians produce millet, sorghum, dates, rice, and cattle. Fish is an important source of protein, and so much is caught that Mauritania exports fish. Important deposits of iron, copper, and gypsum have provided most of the government's income, although copper is not now being produced. Iron-ore exports alone now account for 80 percent of all budget receipts. Following the example of several other African states, the government nationalized the French-controlled mines in 1974. The Mining Complex of the North took over the iron mines and the National In-

dustrial and Mining Society (SNIM) took over the copper mines farther south at Akjoujt.

The country's major cities are growing very rapidly. Nouakchott, the capital, had a population estimated at only 5,000 in 1960, the year of independence, and has almost 200,000 today. The port of Nouadhibou in the north now claims to have about 30,000 people, and so does the town of Kaédi. The desire for better jobs and a more interesting life is one motivation for the movement to cities. In addition, the expanding desert is forcing the nomads to stop wandering from well to well. As a result, probably only 30 percent of the population is truly nomadic today, compared with 78 percent just 20 years ago. For the last several years, visitors to Nouakchott have been startled to see nomads setting up their tents on the edge of the city and even within the city, around construction sites or in vacant fields.

The best road in Mauritania extends from Rosso, a town across the Senegal River from Senegal, to Nouakchott. A railroad connects Nouadhibou with Zouerate in the far north, where iron is mined. For most people, camels, along with Peugeot station wagons and trucks (which serve as taxis), are the major means of transportation. Government officials travel by airplane.

The railroad and the mine in the north have been favorite targets of the Polisario movement, which is fighting for the independence of Western Sahara, a former Spanish colony. In 1975, Morocco and Mauritania divided the Sahara, claiming that its 120,000 inhabitants were ethnically related to one or the other and that they favored unification, or reunification. The Polisario movement, supported by Libya and Algeria (which have their own grudges against Morocco), denied this claim and demanded an independent state in Western Sahara. War has raged ever since in this area, and it has even extended into Mauritania, although Mauritania signed an agreement with Polisario in August 1979 giving up its claim. The Mauritanians have paid heavily in money and in lives.

The country's military budget has soared, drawing badly needed funds away from development projects like the Mpourié project on the Senegal River, which is designed to extend rice production. In addition, schools are unable to accommodate more than 20 percent of the school-aged population. Thus, the primary schools have about 58,000 students, and the secondary schools train about 6,500 students. The army takes many who might have gone to school, of course, and has grown from an estimated 1,000 men in 1967 to 15,000 in 1979. In the same period, Polisario forces destroyed Mauritanian property, forced interruptions in mining operations, and encouraged the French to send soldiers into Mauritania to protect French citizens from kidnapping and death. Morocco stationed about 8,000 troops in Mauritania to help fight Polisario, and although most Moroccans have left, Morocco still maintains considerable influence. The presence of foreigners, particularly the Moroccans (who in the past wanted to annex Mauritania), puts the sovereignty of the country in doubt.

As is usual in desert lands with difficult problems, the people are austere, resilient, and proud. They are divided into three major groups: the Tukolor, Wolof, and Fulani (all of whom call themselves black); the black Moors; and the white Moors. The Tukolor, Fulani, and Wolof live in the south along the frontier with Senegal and Mali and account for possibly 30 percent of the population. They have a higher birthrate than other groups and can be expected to increase their percentage of the total population in time. The black Moors look like the Tukolor, Wolof, and Fulani but generally identify themselves with the white Moors, whose language they speak; they may constitute another 20 percent of the population. The white Moors, who are white, tan, or light brown in color, think of themselves as closely linked with the Arab world. Thin and wiry, with straight or only slightly curled hair, narrow noses, and thin lips, they do not fit easily into a racial category and reject the label black. All Moors speak Hassani, a variety of Arabic; other groups have their own languages. Virtually all

the inhabitants are Muslim, and their devotion to Islam led them to name their country the Islamic Republic of Mauritania. Adherence to Islamic law is supported by the state.

Although they face external enemies, the three major groups of Mauritanians are not united; there is considerable hostility among them. During the colonial period, the blacks in the south enthusiastically attended schools (set up by the French) in Mauritania and even in Senegal, where they have many kinspeople. They learned to read and write in French and became clerks and teachers.

The Moors preferred to send their children to Koranic schools and to Islamic secondary schools; they did not learn French and could not find jobs in the colonial administration or in private French-owned businesses when they finished their education. Because French remained the official language of Mauritania when it became independent, the Moors still could not find satisfactory jobs in their own country.

Inevitably, language emerged as an important domestic issue. The Moors claimed that Arabic should be adequate for a job, and because they are the largest single group they forced the government to declare Arabic one of the two official languages. Fearing that the government would require Arabic for government jobs, the blacks protested in 1966. This led to clashes and some deaths. Because it feared continuing vio-

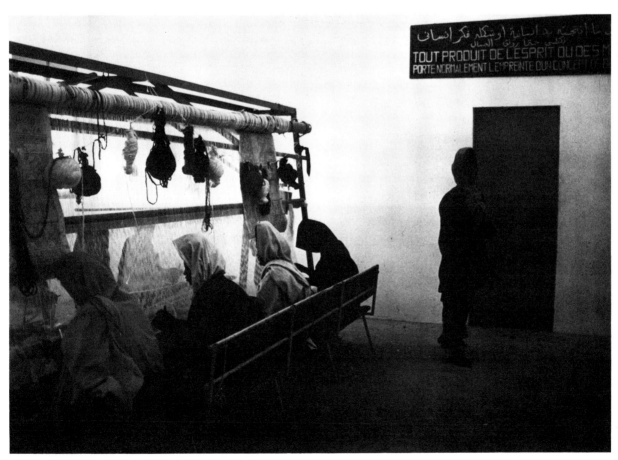

In the nation's capital, robed women workers in a factory weave rugs at a handloom. (Photo: United Nations/J. Laure/ PAS.)

lence, the government has proceeded cautiously. Both French and Arabic arc official today.

The Moors have a lower birthrate than the Tukolor, Fulani, and Wolof, but white and black Moors together outnumber the other groups. The problem for the Moors is that the white Moors generally look down on black Moors, who were once—and in some cases are still—their slaves. For their part, the black Moors, often called Haratins, wish to identify with the high-status white Moors, but other black groups encourage the Haratins to associate with them. All of the black groups accuse the government, controlled by white Moors, of racism and of distorting census data to prolong white political dominance.

In addition to these serious divisions, each major group is divided into castes, lineages, and Islamic brotherhoods. All major groups have noble castes of warriors and religious leaders, who do not usually intermarry with lower castes of artisans, herders, and, of course, slaves. Furthermore, many Mauritanians belong to the Qadirriya or Tijaniya Islamic brotherhoods, headed by marabouts.

The political leaders have tried to overcome these divisions and hold the country together. Moktar Ould Daddah, the country's Prime Minister and then President from 1957 to 1978, came from a noble family of white Moors. Educated in France, he became a lawyer, married a Frenchwoman, and returned to his country to organize a political party and lead all Mauritanians. He and his wife built a single party, the Party of the Mauritanian People (PPM), and worked to diminish ethnic differences.

On July 10, 1978, the military overthrew the President and put him under house arrest until October 1979, when he left for France. Officers set up a Committee for National Recovery (CMRN) and claimed they would solve the country's economic and military problems. The leader of the CMRN was Lieutenant Colonel Mustapha Ould Muhammad Salek, but the key person was the Prime Minister, Ahmed Ould Bouceif, who began negotiations with Polisario to end the war in Western Sahara. The Saharan movement subsequently declared a cease-fire.

This conflict and the various claims and counterclaims to the Sahara are based on a long and complicated history. In the third or fourth century, Berbers moving south pushed the Tukolor, Wolof, and Fulani toward the Senegal River. Three centuries later, the Arabs penetrated into Morocco and toward Mauritania, introducing Islam. With the subsequent collapse of Arab influence and the decline of Islamic scholarship, Mauritania leaned toward black Africa, where new empires absorbed parts of the country.

The Portuguese, the Dutch, and later the French moved south along the coast of West Africa, establishing trading stations. After the 1880s they moved inland, claiming lands as colonies. The French, who had earlier occupied parts of Senegal, began to move into Mauritania in the early 1900s, but Mauritanians fiercely resisted colonization, and the French did not fully control the area until 1930. French attempts to collect taxes, promote the settlement of nomads, and recruit Mauritanian men for their army were met with great hostility.

As a result, the French put very little development money into Mauritania. Until 1958, for example, there was not even a capital; the French ruled Mauritania from the city of Saint-Louis across the border in northern Senegal.

After 1946, citizenship was extended to the Mauritanians, who then elected representatives to the French Parliament. In the economic realm, France began to develop roads and port facilities and to search for mineral resources.

In 1958, General Charles de Gaulle offered France and the colonies a new constitution, which provided

As the dead sands of the desert destroy ancient grazing lands, nomads and their camels seek precious water. (Photo: United Nations/J. Laure/ PAS.)

for a Franco-African community in place of the empire. Mauritania, like all the other French colonies except Guinea, agreed.

But events elsewhere in Africa had already set the independence clock running. Thus in 1960, Mauritania, under the leadership of Ould Daddah, followed other French colonies in declaring independence.

Paradoxically, Mauritania could not have maintained its independence without French help. General de Gaulle agreed to give the country considerable economic assistance, to maintain the local currency, to keep French teachers in the expanding local schools, and most important, to protect the country against Morocco. Morocco claimed that Mauritania was actually part of Morocco and threatened to seize it by force. The French military presence in Port Etienne (now Nouadhibou) and French threats of retaliation protected the new state and permitted it to begin its development programs.

France extended more scholarships to Mauritanian students, promised to develop the iron and copper mines, and built several structures in the new capital. Association with the European Common Market brought more assistance. The personal ties between Ould Daddah and his wife and French citizens were also important.

Mauritania also maintained close ties with other former French colonies. In 1961, just after independence, almost all the former French colonies joined in the African and Malagasy Union (UAM) to coordinate policies.

In 1963, independent African states created the all-African Organization of African Unity (OAU) and the English-speaking countries called on Mauritania and the other French-speaking states to disband the UAM. Under this pressure the UAM dissolved, but in February 1965 Mauritania hosted a meeting of heads of state of French-speaking countries to set up another exclusive organization, the Common African and Malagasy Organization (OCAM), which has its headquarters in Cameroon.

Shortly thereafter, Mauritania broke off its black-African connections and decided to draw closer to the Arab countries. In 1967, the government broke off diplomatic relations with the United States because of its support of Israel in the Arab-Israeli conflict. In 1969 Morocco recognized Mauritania, and visits were exchanged between the two countries. Ould Daddah established personal ties with Algerian and Libyan leaders, and the country joined the Arab League.

Other Arab states began aid programs. The Soviet Union and North Korea also sent aid.

In 1972 and 1973, Mauritania drew further away from both France and its black African neighbors, withdrawing from the franc zone and creating its own currency. The ouguiya replaced the franc. Ould Daddah declared that a cultural revolution would free Mauritania once and for all from dependence on other countries. Moors in particular asserted their Islamic and Arabic identities, while Tukolor, Wolof, and Fulani watched anxiously.

This question of identity remains the most serious issue in Mauritania. Is the country Arab, black African, a Francophone (French-speaking) state, or an Islamic entity? Leaders and people are unable to resolve the question. The French bond is still important. No other country has been so willing to assist Mauritania steadily and consistently. France is Mauritania's primary trading partner, and Mauritania can depend on France for economic assistance with more assurance than it can depend on any other country. (The United States gave Mauritania only about $8 million out of the almost $200 million it received in assistance in 1978.) There are more French in the country—over 1,000—than any other Europeans. And there may be as many as 50,000 Mauritanian workers in France who send home badly needed money.

The steadily encroaching desert, the tensions between Moors and non-Moors, and the continuing war in the Western Sahara are Mauritania's other serious problems. CMRN, the military committee, was replaced in April 1979 by a Military Committee of National Salvation (CMS) because CMRN was unable to resolve current problems. Prime Minister Bouceif died in May, and in June 1979 President Saleu resigned. For a brief period, Lieutenant Colonel Mahmoud Louly became head of state, but in the first week of January 1980 he was overthrown, and Lieutenant Colonel Muhammad Khouna Ould Haidalla became head of state. In a subsequent effort to resolve tensions between Moors and blacks, the new leader increased black representation in the government, giving blacks six Cabinet posts.

Thus, in Mauritania, the struggle for existence never ceases. The life of a Mauritanian, faced with the desert on one side and the sea on the other, is a challenge. A war that is absorbing 60 percent of the annual budget and the increasing divisions between northern Moors and southern blacks threaten the life of the country and challenge its leaders.

Brian Weinstein

Mozambique
(People's Republic of Mozambique)

Area: 303,769 sq mi (786,397 sq km)
Population: 9.94 million
  Density: 33 per sq mi (13 per sq km)
  Growth rate: 2.5% (1970–1977)
Percent of population under 14 years of age: 43%
Infant deaths per 1,000 live births: 93 (1970)
Life expectancy at birth: 43.5 years
Leading causes of death: not available
Ethnic composition: Bantu, Portuguese
Languages: Portuguese, African dialects, English
Literacy: 20%
Religions: animist 69%; Christian 20%; Muslim 11%
Percent population urban: 10%
Percent population rural: 90%
Gross national product: $1.36 billion
  Per capita GNP: $140
  Per capita GNP growth rate: −4.3% (1970–1977)
Inflation rate: not available

Mozambique is undergoing an extensive transformation in life and politics. Since achieving independence from Portugal in 1975, the government has embarked on prodigious programs to rehabilitate and remold the former colony's economy and living patterns. Villagers are being moved from their traditional habitat of scattered huts into collectivized agricultural units, following the Marxist-Leninist principles of the Mozambique Liberation Front (FRELIMO). After centuries of Portuguese rule and a decade of anticolonial guerrilla war in the northern provinces, FRELIMO has embraced a radically socialist vision of development in an African setting.

The southeast-African state of Mozambique, twice the size of California, stretches 1,700 miles (2,735 km) along the Indian Ocean. Some of its ports—Nacala, Beira, and the capital, Maputo (formerly Lourenço Marques)—are among the finest in Africa and enhance the country's gateway location for interior states. Yet its fishing potential has been underexploited. From across the Indian Ocean, the monsoons feed the wet season (October to April) of this mostly tropical land. Even the subtropical position of its southernmost section is moderated by the flow of warm ocean currents along the coastline. Divided almost in half by its principal river, the Zambezi, Mozambique is 44 percent lowland and marshes, the habitat of the tsetse. Only 13 percent is over 3,300 feet (1,006 km) with tropical rain forest; between high and low zones there are pervasive inedible grasslands and savanna. In addition to the Zambezi, there are four other major river basins and many waterways flowing eastward, which have recently been subject to frequent serious flooding with consequent loss of life and destruction of crops and livestock.

Mozambique is well, if not bountifully, endowed, with many natural resources, most of which have nei-

ther been exploited nor even fully explored. Only coal is mined and exported in large quantities, and columbite and tantalite are sold in small but valuable amounts. Copper, bauxite, and beryl are also mined. In the central area, large fields of natural gas have been only partially tapped. Hydroelectric power from the massive Cabora Bassa dam on the Zambezi more than meets domestic demand, and the bulk of the power is transmitted to South Africa in partial repayment for the construction of the project.

Virtually all Mozambique's population belong to Bantu-speaking stock. Before the collapse of Portugal's power, some quarter of a million Portuguese settlers dominated colonial society. There were smaller numbers of Goans, Chinese, Indians and other Europeans in commerce and government. Fewer than 20,000 Portuguese remained after independence. The country still lacks a national social structure, nor is there a coherent social structure within any of the ten major African ethnolinguistic communities. Before the Portuguese military conquest in the nineteenth century, some ethnic groups were organized into polities and even larger confederations. Since their decline, the prevailing social organizations have been small, autonomous clusters consisting of a single village or a group of villages. The Portuguese suppressed any organization representative of ethnic identity or loyalties. This practice has helped the FRELIMO government in its nation-building efforts.

There is no cultural unity among the various groups; instead, the country is divided into two general cultural zones with shared customs. North of the Zambezi Valley, the Makonde, Yao, Makua-Lomwe, and Maravi are predominantly matrilineal and accustomed to the shifting subsistence cultivation of maize, peanuts, and beans. South of the valley, the Shona-Karanga, Tsonga, and Chopi are primarily patrilineal and familiar with sedentary agriculture. The Zambezi Valley itself is a hodgepodge of the two systems. Only 15 to 20 percent of the population speaks Portuguese; the rest converse in local dialects.

Religion, like so much else in Mozambique, mirrors the country's past. Two different seaborne newcomers left their religious imprints on African spiritual life. Hundreds of years before Portuguese ships arrived off the coast in 1498, Arab and Persian merchant sailors brought Islam to the northern seaboard. An estimated 500,000 Muslims lived between the mouth of the Ligonha River and the Tanzanian border in 1970, the last census. Inland, the Yao and Makua-Lomwe were also influenced by the Sunni brand of Islam; but their religious beliefs are syncretistic, with Islam forming a veneer over older, more deeply felt traditional practices.

Christianity came with Portugal's advent in East

Africa. Roman Catholicism, the official religion of the former Portuguese empire, accounts for perhaps 15 to 20 percent of the population; some 5 percent are Protestant. FRELIMO's leadership is explicitly atheistic and hostile to Catholicism in particular, regarding it as a buttress of Portugal's rule.

Traditional Mozambican religions differ in detail, but most have in common the recognition of a remote supreme deity and a desire to propitiate ancestral spirits and gain protection from witchcraft. FRELIMO calls these belief systems obscurantist. To replace them with a secular faith and to build a national consciousness, the government has declared as national holidays the significant dates in the revolution. For example, June 25 is celebrated as both the date of FRELIMO's formation in 1962 and as the day of independence. February 3, the date of the assassination of FRELIMO's first head, Eduardo Mondlane, in 1969 has become a Heroes Day for all dead revolutionaries.

Mozambique is a rural country. Over 90 percent of its populace lives on the land. Much the same can be said of most African countries. What sets Mozambique apart is the government's intent to turn society toward the goals of egalitarianism, the liberation of women, party-guided democracy, and modernization. This has caused uneven dislocations in the old social order. Conventional customs exist side by side with revolutionary institutions, although the sociopolitical slant is still decidedly toward the conventional. Consequently, the government is driven by change and economic development, while the rural masses are still deeply rooted in the past. Extended families and polygynous marriages characterize most familial structures.

Local social organizations have almost always been delineated by kinship. Thus, the way a given ethnic community reckons descent and inheritance has an important effect on political authority, religious practice, economic organization, and a host of social obligations.

North of the Zambezi, for example, where matrilineal communities prevail, young Makua males or their kin escape the obligation of a significant *lobola*, or marriage payment, to the bride's family, while the Makonde, another northern people who also record descent matrilineally, require a gift, usually a rifle and the husband's services, to the maternal uncle. Below the Zambezi, among the Tsonga, a bridewealth payment is made to compensate the parents for the loss of their daughter's services. These differences also regulate a family's choice of home. Once again, the Zambezi River provides a rough demarcation; above it, a married couple usually lives with maternal relatives; below it, the home site is patrilocally resolved.

Under matrilineal law, possessions and land pass from mother to daughter; under the patrilineal system, goods pass from father to son. But because of the dominant position of males in all African societies, the succession to social position through the matrilineal process descends from a man to his sister's sons rather than to his daughters. The impact of Islam on northern peoples has further weakened matrilineal authority and inheritance.

Polygynous marriage has been the rule, although among peoples like the Makonde, monogamy is acceptable. Family stability is fragile because of social and economic patterns. Where polygynous marriage requires the husband to choose each wife from a different village, he is frequently absent from one wife while staying with another. This leads to adultery and divorce. The migration of husbands to faraway cities or across the border for work further destabilizes the family.

There has also been a sexual division of labor in the countryside. In the past, herding, hunting, and wage labor were the provinces of men, while agriculture was the work of women. Men cleared the heavy brush from the fields by the slash-and-burn technique, and women then took over the gardening duties. This left men free to follow masculine pursuits like waging war, hunting, or seeking wage employment on plantations, in the cities, or in South African mines. Returning from the Witwatersrand gold mines, men brought gifts for their women, along with pedal-operated sewing machines, bicycles, and iron plows.

Authority, regardless of the descent chain, has been a male preserve. Traditional chiefs, village headmen, and Portuguese-appointed *regedores* held sway with varying degrees of harshness in the area of taxation. Because these authorities acted, in most instances, as bulwarks of the colonial apparatus, FRELIMO removed them where possible and filled their positions with FRELIMO officials and party committees.

While custom for some years to come will prevail in the vast rural regions, FRELIMO's goals will as-

Near their cluster of primitive huts, village women use long poles to draw water from a shallow open communal well. (Photo: UNICEF/ Revi R. N. Tuluhungwa.)

suredly conflict with it. The fact that more than half of the population is under 20 years of age may facilitate reorientation.

Mozambique is overridingly agricultural. Under colonialism, the largely rural population engaged in subsistence cultivation or worked involuntarily on large-scale commercial plantations which supplied cheap raw materials to Portugal or produced cash crops like cotton, sugar, cashew nuts, tea, sisal, and copra for export. Ninety percent of the preindependence gross national product (GNP) stemmed from agricultural produce, and less than 6 percent of the work force at that time was employed industrially.

Health and medical care pose serious problems. With independence, some 500 Portuguese doctors fled, leaving about 50. Their ranks have been strengthened slightly by the arrival of foreign medical teams, especially from East Europe. Medical care was formerly concentrated in urban areas, but the government has tried to extend the service. Basic innoculations have been given to 95 percent of the population. Assistance for this program came from the World Health Organization.

Since the 1950s, when Portugal emphasized economic development, Mozambicans have been flocking to the cities in search of jobs more lucrative and less arduous than cultivation. Despite colonial and settler restraints on the climb of Mozambicans into the middle and upper strata of the labor force, a tiny minority have become skilled workers, nurses, and even civil servants and businessmen. A slightly larger number hold jobs as carpenters, printers, shoemakers and tailors. Below them, and constituting by far the largest group, are the unskilled and underemployed waiters, domestics, stevedores, construction workers, canners, and fishermen. Nearly all il-

literate, they remain transient and oriented toward the land and family they left behind. While the cities have kept a European core, the suburbs have swelled with migrants. The reed shantytowns surrounding the capital reached an estimated population of 300,000 by 1974.

Like most African countries, decolonized Mozambique faces the urban problems caused by a flood of newcomers who strain the sanitation, security, and health facilities. FRELIMO proposes to meet this challenge by creating green belts around the cities, organizing neighborhoods to tackle their own support services, and reorganizing the countryside into communal villages with their own amenities and educational systems.

Maputo's suburbs have some ethnic character because migrants first tend to settle ethnically. Since most of them come from below the Save River, they have similar languages and cultures. Around Maputo, for example, the lingua franca is Ronga, a southern Tsonga dialect. Individual contact with people outside the home ethnic community helps to loosen but not necessarily replace ancient moorings of allegiance and religion.

The stark stereotype of women as bearers of children and servants of men was only faintly blurred in colonial cities and towns. FRELIMO leaders have criticized male chauvinism, although they are criticized by women for not doing enough to eliminate it. A small but growing minority of articulate and educated women are conscious of their self-worth and aptitude for responsibility.

In the past, voluntary associations partially filled the gap created by weakened customs and institutions. Professional and recreational associations, along with sports, folksinging, and dance groups, af-

Once known as Lourenço Marques, Maputo is a crowded modern port city, the capital of this predominantly rural country. (Photo: United Nations/CIRIC-GENEVA.)

ford opportunities for social interaction. Neighborhood canteens are places to meet, offering food, a telephone, a public clock, and a depository for valuables. During colonial rule, low wages kept most Africans from spending their leisure hours in the white city center. Now, Mozambicans occupy the best apartments and stroll the tree-lined boulevards.

The FRELIMO government has formed separate organizations for women, youths, writers, and workers as mechanisms to attract the support of various segments of the population. As in other socialist societies, these organizations enhance specific programs, incorporate elements of society otherwise left out of the party committees, and moderate popular opposition by giving citizens a voice in their community and work. Workers' production councils have the added objective of boosting factory output.

In the colonial era, nearly half of all industrial activity was centered in Lourenço Marques (now Maputo); the remainder was almost all located in other urban areas. Industrial growth was confined to plants processing sugar, tobacco, beer, and, later, soap, clothing, and small consumer items. The twilight of colonialism saw the beginnings of cement, chemical, glass, and petroleum-refining plants. Overall industrial capacity increased dramatically, although it was still in its infancy when Portugal's sovereignty ended. Chaos followed. Managers and technicians fled from the country, and workers struck for higher wages.

FRELIMO responded by appealing to workers to return to their jobs and by relying on foreign experts to replace the lost Portuguese personnel. Most urban plants do not yet operate smoothly, but a few have surpassed their preindependence production levels. Coal mining, for example, is well ahead of pre-1975 production at the Moatize mines.

Mozambique's past can be divided into three phases: pre-European, European, and post-European. Before the arival of Vasco da Gama, Mozambique had experienced peaceful immigrations and military invasions. Once Portuguese ships arrived, officials and freebooters began to disturb Muslim and African commerce and insert themselves into the hinterland. Although the Portuguese interrupted state formation and trade patterns, their presence was a minor influence until the last years of the nineteenth century. Full-blown colonialism brought only rudimentary development from Portugal, Europe's poorest country. For decades, little attention was paid to African education, health, and well-being. The outbreak of a rural-based revolution in the north, however, gave rise to extensive population resettlement and some last-minute exertions to improve the Mozambican lot. The devastation of the conflict in the north and the resulting flight of European settlers from the country worsened the economic outlook.

Mozambique's future is pointed toward Marxism in an African environment. The party's inner circle, most of whom have been in FRELIMO since its founding, look to socialist models abroad and to revolutionary institutions formed during the war in liberated zones in the north or in sanctuary camps in Tanzania. Development is to be attained by vigorous state intervention and central planning of the economy. Private enterprise will play only a minor role. FRELIMO's slogans call for the "building of heavy industry [as] the decisive factor in the battle to break with misery and imperialist domination" and for the manufacture of its own tractors by the end of the century.

The party's more immediate emphasis is on food production and the collectivization of agriculture into communal villages and cooperative farms. Ideally, each village will consist of 1,250 families (6,000 to 7,000 inhabitants). It is hoped that each village will raise food and produce cash crops and will provide facilities for education, health, and social services. Portugal's resettlement schemes in the north, combined with the worst floods in recent history, have furthered the establishment of these communal villages. Precise data are unobtainable, but it is estimated that several hundred of these communal villages, in varying stages of sophistication, now exist. The highest concentration of them is in the north. Unlike Tanzania, FRELIMO has not resorted to force for resettlement but has relied on persuasion and pre-cooperatives as halfway stages. The Third Congress, held in February 1977, set 1980 as the target date for achievement of preindependence production levels.

Education is an area of special emphasis. FRELIMO focuses on the study of Mozambique's past and geography while teaching children and adults to read and write. It claims to have taught about 2 million people to read Portuguese in the past 3 years. Government-controlled media—radio, newspapers, and wall posters—aim at the eradication of tribalism, male chauvinism, individualism, and capitalism.

Hatched from a largely successful rural insurgency, FRELIMO is the most thoroughgoing Marxist-Leninist party in Africa; Mozambique has thus become an international mecca for young socialists and communists around the world, who act as *cooperantes* in reconstruction and education. Mozambique receives considerable assistance from East Europe and the Scandinavian countries and other non-aligned states. Mozambique enjoys close relations with non-Western Marxist states, particularly Cuba, Vietnam, and North Korea, believing that they have a similar revolutionary heritage and similar development problems. Cuba has furnished much technical assistance to Mozambique.

FRELIMO's blueprints for the future stand in jeopardy not only from natural disasters or party miscalculations but also from the brewing cauldron of racial and political strife that threatens the southern foot of the continent. To the west, the settler-created Zimbabwe-Rhodesia launched deep retaliatory raids into Mozambique's midsection to destroy African nationalist guerrilla camps and to disrupt the country's transportation and production facilities. Maputo's

1976 border closure with Zimbabwe-Rhodesia (now Zimbabwe) cost it between $106 million and $132 million a year and left thousands of transportation workers idle. Internal conflict across Mozambique's southern border in the Republic of South Africa could dwarf current problems because Mozambique is heavily dependent on South Africa for aid and transit fees. Mozambique must rely on its southern neighbor for 15 percent of its imports, and South Africa ships 18 percent of its export goods through Maputo's docks, bringing much-needed foreign exchange to the hard-pressed FRELIMO government, which publicly criticizes South African racial policies.

The uncertainties of Africa are compounded by the looming crises in its austral quarter and make predictions hazardous. Because of its all-embracing commitment to a Marxist future, Mozambique has attracted much continental attention. But the outcome of the conflicts across its borders will affect its development projects and its program to alleviate hunger, disease, and poverty. Whatever the degree of change, the People's Republic of Mozambique will be the African experiment to watch over the next decade.

Thomas H. Henriksen

Niger

(Republic of Niger)

Area: 490,000 sq mi (1,269,100 sq km)
Population: 5 million
  Density: 10 per sq mi (4 per sq km)
  Growth rate: 2.8% (1970–1977)
Percent of population under 14 years of age: 35% (1975)
Infant deaths per 1,000 live births: 162 (1970)
Life expectancy at birth: 38.5 years
Leading causes of death: malnutrition, malaria-related diseases
Ethnic composition: Hausa 50%; Djerma 23%; Fulani 15%; Tuareg 12%
Languages: French (official), Hausa, Djerma
Literacy: 6%
Religions: Muslim 99%
Percent population urban: at most 10%
Percent population rural: at least 90%
Gross national product: $1.11 billion
  Per capita GNP: $220
  Per capita GNP growth rate: −1.8% (1970–1977)
Inflation rate: not available

A poor semidesert associated with many famous empires of the Sahelian past, Niger is a vast, coastless state, highly dependent on assistance from France, its former colonial master. Its chances of modest development, however, have been greatly enhanced by the considerable uranium discoveries that have made it the third largest source of uranium in the non-Communist world.

Covering 490,000 square miles (1,269 million sq km), Niger is larger than California and Texas combined, but it contains only about 6 million mostly nomadic people. Niger is bordered by Libya, Chad, Mali, Upper Volta, Benin (formerly Dahomey), and Nigeria. Its northern borders are mountainous and difficult of passage by any form of transport except camel.

The capital, Niamey, has a population of 80,000, increasing to about 100,000 at the height of the long dry season because of the in-migration of nomads. Rain falls only from June to September. Most of the population is concentrated in the extreme southwest, along the upper reaches of the Niger River.

Niger (meaning "black") takes its name from the European name for the river, which has a score of different names as it flows through literally hundreds of different ethnic and linguistic zones. Niamey, a colonial administrative creation, is the only city. The largest villages are Zinder, Tarwa, and Maradi, with about 20,000 people each.

The main ethnic groups are all Sahelian (from the Arabic word Sahel, meaning "shore", referring to a transitional belt that borders the Sahara as if the Sahara itself were a sea). The Hausa predominate, with 50 percent of the population; the Djerma comprise 23 percent, the Fulani 14 percent and the Tuareg, 12 percent. The Djerma are the heirs of the famed Songhai Empire. The population is over 99 percent Muslim. French is the official language. Life expectancy is put at 37 years, with 60 percent of the population under 16 years of age. Nearly 45 percent of the children die before the age of 5 from malaria or a malaria-related condition.

Life in Niger is typical of life in the Sahelian Islamic countries. Most children have access to a Koranic education, but only 6 percent of them attend schools where instruction is in French. Sahelian Islam has preserved many of the beliefs that existed before the coming of Muhammad, and Muslim piety is mixed with a respect for ancestors and a belief that amulets and tattoos will fend off ill fortune.

Most land is owned according to traditional patterns. Agriculture is largely limited to the southwest; the rest of the population is pastoral and nomadic. Over 90 percent of the population is made up of peasants and herdsmen. The government is by far the main wage-employer. A capitalist society survives from colonial times, notably in the few urban centers. Medical care and transportation facilities are minimal, and camel caravans still cross the desert to sell

*Far left:
In this arid land
where camels
provide most of the
transportation, a
worker is making
rope. (Photo:
United Nations/*

sheep, skins, and salt in North African cities and cattle in the trading centers of Northern Nigeria.

Historically, Niger contains portions of the former empires of Ghana, Songhai, Mali, Gao, Kanem, and Bornu (Bornu is the area around Lake Chad in the country's southeast), but few vestiges of the storied past remain. The trading Hausa, whose main home is Northern Nigeria, now predominate in the area, a reminder of its historical role as a crossroads of camel traffic between the Mediterranean and the gold-producing countries of West Africa. Traders in salt and slaves also passed this way.

Over 50 percent of all exports, until 1977, consisted of peanuts, followed by livestock and skins (20 percent). Outside of the mining sector, completely accurate statistics are largely unobtainable because of the nature of the country, and the government's presence is hardly felt in four-fifths of the nation. Water resources, except in the southwest, are minimal. Two-thirds of the country receives less than 4 inches of rainfall annually, and over the last 5 years rainfall has diminished. This has affected peanut and cotton exports and cut cattle herds by 35 percent. Transportation costs are disproportionately high for such a poor country, and most foreign imports arrive through ports in Nigeria which are 600 to 1,000 miles (965 to 1,609 km) away from market centers in Niger. There is no railroad.

The principal development in Niger in recent times was the discovery of uranium ore at Arlit in the desolate north in 1967. Open-cast production by a French-led consortium of German, Italian, and government interests produces more than 2,000 tons (1,819 t) annually, and production should reach 8,400 tons (7,618 t) in 1984. Production in 1979 was valued at $318 million of which about $220 million was kept in Niger in the form of salaries, taxes, and the government's share in the enterprise. Uranium ore now constitutes nearly 80 percent of the country's export earnings. A second, underground mine at Akuta, operated by a Franco-Japanese-Hispanic consortium, recently began production and is expected to produce 2,000 tons (1,819 t) annually by 1981. Prospecting for more uranium continues at Imuraren (a site reportedly richer than Arlit and Akuta combined), Djado, Intadreft, Amachegh, Tazole, Agadez, Assamaka, Emilulu, West Afasto, and Azelik.

The ore concentrate is sealed in oil drums and shipped over 1,000 miles to Parakou in Benin, whence it is taken by rail to Cotonou, Benin's port-capital, for transport to Europe. A road from Niger through Libya and to the Mediterranean may be built if international financing can be obtained.

Three American companies have looked, so far unsuccessfully, for oil. There are other minerals, like iron, but they are mostly too far from the coast for economic exploitation. Salt and gypsum (for cement) are mined for local consumption.

The French occupation of Niger, agreed to by the European powers at the Berlin Conference of 1884–1885, was not completed until 1922, after prolonged warfare (especially against the blue-veiled Tuareg horsemen). Thereafter, Niger was an essentially peaceful, sleepy colony. Independence was achieved in 1960 without political agitation and with limited enthusiasm.

Discontent with increasing proverty—caused by increased import costs in a stagnant economy and aggravated by a series of Sahelian droughts—led to a

*Outside their
makeshift dwelling,
women are
pounding meal for
the family dinner.
(Photo: United
Nations/
G.A. Patterson.)*

coup d'etat in 1974 in which President Hamani Diori was replaced by Lieutenant Colonel Seyni Kountche. The former single-party system was replaced by a junta, and the leader of the country's original opposition, Bakari Djibo, was permitted to return from exile in Guinea in 1975. His Marxist-oriented Sawaba party remained banned, but acceptance of the junta by the country's most popular civilian political figure greatly increased the junta's acceptance by the population as a whole.

The junta draws on the support of the hardy desert dwellers, who were always the country's best soldiers, rather than on the relatively favored Niger Valley peasants or urban citizens. It intends to try to attract investment to the interior. Western advisers counsel developing the valley area and concentrating on bringing medical, food, and agricultural aid to the interior, but Kountche believes that all political discontent is concentrated in or near Niamey. To give his regime strength, he is intentionally courting the warrior peoples of the Sahelian and Saharan steppe and encouraging university graduates, on their return from Europe, to take government or other employment up-country, away from the conspiratorial atmosphere of the capital.

Thanks largely to uranium, the gross domestic product (GDP) was estimated at $1.7 billion in 1978, up about 350 percent since 1974; but industries are limited to chemicals, cement, peanut shelling, rice processing, a tannery, textiles, and a pasta factory. Generous tax relief, however, is offered to investors. Per capita income is still broadly estimated in the region of $200 a year.

France, the European Economic Community, the United States, Canada, West Germany, and Saudi Arabia give considerable aid to the country, and Libya is beginning to provide assistance; a major program is the development of underground water resources. In 1977, Canada finished a highway from Tillaberi in the west to Lake Chad in the southeast. The United States has given aid in several sectors, including health, partly through a strong Peace Corps contingent.

Niger traditionally imports about twice as much, by value, as it exports, but it has a slightly favorable trade balance. The country will probably remain politically moderate, despite the influence of Libya and Chad, but pressing economic problems remain.

Russell Warren Howe

Nigeria
(Federal Republic of Nigeria)

Area: 357,000 sq mi (924,624 sq km)
Population: over 81 million
  Density: 227 per sq mi (88 per sq km)
  Growth rate: 2.6% (1970–1977)
Percent of population under 14 years of age: 43%
Infant deaths per 1,000 live births: 163
Life expectancy at birth: 41 years
Leading causes of death: not available
Ethnic composition: more than 250 ethnic groups; Hausa-Fulani (29%); Yoruba (20%); Ibo (17%)
Languages: English (official), Hausa, Ibo, Yoruba
Literacy: 25% (1977)
Religions: Muslim 47%; Christian 35%; traditional 18% (1963 Nigerian census)
Percent population urban: more than 20%
Percent population rural: less than 80%
Gross national product: $45.8 billion
  Per capita GNP: $560
  Per capita GNP growth rate: 4.4% (1970–1977)
Inflation rate: 15%

After 13 years of military rule, four military governments, and a civil war, civilian rule was restored in Nigeria in October 1979 under conditions that augured well for its future. In the 1970s Nigeria had a boom economy, awash with oil and the enormous revenues and foreign exchange that oil provides. It will continue to experience rapid economic growth in the 1980s.

However, with its mostly rural and impoverished population growing at a rate of 2.6 percent per year, Nigeria's burst of private and government spending has benefited the few and left the many even poorer. Oil production and exports boomed, providing 75 to 80 percent of government revenues, but cash crops and food agriculture declined sharply in the 1970s, diminishing the incomes of the 70 percent of the population engaged in agriculture. The world's fifth largest oil exporter, Nigeria has become assertively nationalist and has sought an increasingly powerful role in inter-African and international affairs.

Nigeria is both an old and a new land. A thousand years ago, its northern cities formed the terminus of the trans-Saharan trade. Originally the centers of independent Hausa states, in the nineteenth and twentieth centuries they became the centers of important Fulani-dominated Islamic states formed during jihads, or holy wars. Their emirs are still powerful figures. In the south, long a site of urban settlements and Yoruba kingdoms, cities like Ife and Benin date back to the Middle Ages.

Nigeria was formed in 1900, drawing together ancient kingdoms and peoples under British colonial rule. Located in West Africa, it occupies some 357,000 square miles (924,624 sq km), three times the area of the United Kingdom and almost equal in size to Texas and Colorado combined. The south has heavy rainfall and is hot and humid, with great rain forests; in the savanna, the climate is extremely dry and hot. Nigeria is composed of fairly flat lowlands, though the land rises to 6,560 feet (2,000 m) at its eastern border with Cameroon and to over 3,937 feet (1,200 m) on the Jos Plateau, near the country's center, with its impressive scarp face to the south, east, and west. The third longest river in Africa, the Niger, crosses Nigeria for one-third of its 2,604-mile (4,200-km) course, flowing southeasterly and then south until it loses itself in the tributaries of the eastern Nigerian Delta, the site of so much of Nigeria's oil.

Nigeria is Africa's most populous country, but recurring disputes over the census that determines the level of each state's representation and federal allocations have led to different population estimates. The World Bank estimated a population of over 81 million in 1979.

Nigeria has more than 250 ethnic groups, but 10 of these groups account for over 80 percent of the total population. The three regions (Northern, Eastern, and Western) that comprised Nigeria in 1960 were dominated, respectively, by the Hausa-Fulani (about 29 percent of the population), the Ibo (17 percent), and the Yoruba (20 percent). In response to minority demands for more power, the three states became twelve in 1967 and nineteen in 1976.

The Hausa-Fulani (increasingly indistinguishable), Yoruba, and Ibo dominate socioeconomic and political life in Nigeria, despite the strong role of minority groups in the army and during military rule. Living in the densely populated southeast, the Ibo were responsive to change, especially to missionary education (many of them are Christian). Before 1967, well-educated and ambitious Ibo were found throughout Nigeria, employed, in disproportionate numbers, as civil servants, traders, and transporters. Massacres of the Ibo, especially after the Ibo officers' 1966 coup, drove most of them back to the east. The subsequent Ibo secessionist sentiment led to the creation of the independent Republic of Biafra and a 20-month, unsuccessful civil war with Nigeria. Concentrated efforts at reconciliation have made Ibo reintegration possible.

The Yoruba in the west are perhaps the largest cultural group with a common historical tradition. In the eighteenth century, the Yoruba formed a single powerful kingdom, which was later divided. Despite many intra-Yoruba differences (including religious differences between Christians and Muslims), there is a strong Yoruba consciousness, captured by Obafemi Awolowo's Action Party in the 1950s and 1960s and his new Unity Party of Nigeria. In like manner, Nnamdi Azikiwe had strong Ibo support in the National Council of Nigerian Citizens, the principal eastern party, in the 1950s and 1960s and retains it today.

In socioeconomic terms, the north developed less rapidly than the south and resisted strong southern nationalist demands for independence. Through their numerical majority and a party system based on the traditional administrative pattern, the Hausa-Fulani dominated both the north and the federal government from 1960 to 1966. Islam served, and still serves, as a conservative social cement. Women traditionally possessed no significant rights; they finally achieved the right to vote in the 1979 constitution. The division of the north into 10 states (of the 19) has diluted but not destroyed northern power.

Competition for political office and for access to power, status, and government resources and favors has severely exacerbated ethnic and communal conflicts in Nigeria. Ethnic and communal solidarities and fears have been used by politicians to enhance their own power. A high level of ethnic-regional conflict during 1964–1966 set the stage for the 1966 coup and the 1967–1969 civil war.

The 1963 census indicated that about 47 percent of the population were Muslim, living mostly in the north; about 35 percent were Christian, concentrated in the south, and the rest were followers of traditional beliefs, living in the middle belt area of the north.

Well over 20 percent of Nigeria's population is urban, and rural-urban migration has accelerated as job opportunities expand in the towns. Lagos, the capital and largest city, has over 3 million inhabitants (including its suburban population). It is so congested that in the mid-1970s the government decreed odd-even license days for driving. For the great majority of the urban poor, crammed into urban slums, daily travel to work often takes many hours. The military government chose a site for a new federal capital, Abuja, located in a rural area in Nigeria's geographical center. It is hoped that the major organs of government can move there by 1986; it is estimated that its population will be 1.6 million by 2000. Other major cities are Kano, an ancient northern city of white-clay houses with an estimated population of 400,000; Zaria (224,000), also in the north; Kaduna (over 500,000); Ibadan, a Yoruba town with a population of

Improving the nation's railroads is a priority for the Nigerian government. Children watch this worker, who is planing a wooden form for a concrete culvert to run under the tracks. (Photo: World Bank/ John Moss.)

over 1 million; and Port Harcourt (242,000), Nigeria's second major port. Even with Nigeria's oil riches and rapid economic growth, the cities offer few amenities, but for the poor, the overwhelming majority of whom are peasants, they offer more employment opportunities.

Nigeria experienced average increases of over 8 percent in the gross national product (GNP) from 1969 to 1977, a more than 5.5 percent increase in per capita GNP. This growth was fueled by dramatic increases in oil production and, from 1975 on, increases in oil prices. Between 1966 and 1974, oil production increased fivefold; the value of oil exports increased thirtyfold. Oil exports grew from 33 percent of total exports in 1966 to over 80 percent in 1972–1973 and over 90 percent in 1976–1977. Oil has provided over 80 percent of all federal revenue in recent years. The vast increases in oil revenues in 1975 and afterward led to an orgy of government and private spending and importing, which generated increasingly large balance of payments deficits and inflation. When the Organization of Petroleum Exporting Countries (OPEC) forced Nigeria to reduce its oil production and exports sharply in 1975–1978, the revenue from higher oil prices alone could not keep up with increased government spending. With a budget deficit since 1975, Nigeria's balance of payments deficits (in current accounts) have forced the government to borrow heavily abroad ($1.75 billion in 1978).

In 1977–1979, inflation and budgetary balance of payments deficits led the government to reduce its spending and bank credit and increase its import taxes. This came as a jolt to Nigerians. Those who had been benefiting handsomely from government spending protested the government cutbacks vehemently, leading one Nigerian to comment that the country was becoming an increasingly *ajofe* (meaning "freeloader" or "parasite") society. Economic growth declined sharply in 1978–1979.

Mining and quarrying (including oil) constituted over 37 percent of the production of total domestic goods and services (GDP) in 1975 and 45 percent in 1976. Agriculture dropped from 65 percent of GDP in 1966 to 23.4 percent in 1974 to 18.4 percent in 1978. Construction was 5.9 percent of GDP in 1975; distribution, 9.3 percent; government 6.8 percent; and manufacturing, 6.5 percent. All these sectors were stimulated by oil revenues.

With the explosive increase in oil revenues in 1974, both the magnitude and focus of Nigeria's development plan (1975–1980) changed. In an atmosphere of euphoric planning, the 1975–1980 plan set a target of $46.8 billion in gross investments ($31.2 billion by the federal and state governments and $15.6 billion by the private sector). The percentage of total government investment rose from 40 percent under the previous plan to 66 percent under the 1976–1980 plan, indicating a federal government decision to take over majority ownership of major industries in partnership with multinational corporations. These industries include oil (60 percent ownership of all operating companies), refineries, petrochemicals, and electric energy.

The figures tend to mask actual government expenditures. In the 1979–1980 federal recurrent budget, defense consumed 17.9 percent; education, 31.5 percent (including grants to states); police, 6.8 percent; agriculture, only 1.2 percent; health, 3.4 percent; works and housing, 3.6 percent; and public debt charges, 12.4 percent. In the 1979–1980 capital budget, defense involved 9.1 percent of the total; manufacturing and crafts, 20.7 percent; mining (oil), 11 percent; land transport, 14.6 percent; communications, 4.8 percent; education, 5.9 percent; water resources, 5.4 percent; and agriculture, 2.8 percent.

Apart from subsidizing bloated military and police forces, the economic development strategy behind these figures emphasizes two objectives. The government is determined to hold full or majority control of the country's basic industries, frequently in partnership with multinational companies. The government also plans to transfer more and more control of the private sector to Nigerians. Its policy of nativism compels foreign companies to sell 40 percent, 60 percent, or 100 percent of their companies to individual Nigerians. By mid-1979 this involved the transfer of 500 million shares, valued at $736 million, in 1,858 companies. The object of both of these aims has been to encourage import-substitution industrialization.

The state has created a significant capitalist class in Nigeria by extending bank credit to a fortunate few so that they can purchase these shares. The state is thus the creator of domestic capital and an intermediary between domestic and foreign capital. Political

The port of Lagos is being enlarged to carry increasing traffic as Nigeria's economy booms. (Photo: World Bank/ G. Gerster.)

linkages are crucial: senior civil servants and politicians holding office under the military have simultaneously served as senior public officials, board members of local affiliates of multinationals, and investors in local stocks and industries together with cooperative Nigerian businessmen. Enormous opportunities for corruption have thus been created. As one critical observer noted: "The ethics of business penetrated politics; the ethics of politics penetrated business; the ethics of the gangster penetrated both."

Because all agricultural sectors stagnated or grew slowly during the 1970s, the government also tried to stimulate agricultural modernization. The attempt to foster large-scale, capital-intensive agriculture through bank loans and tax concessions, however, did not benefit small peasant producers, who constitute 70 percent of the labor force.

These development policies have tended to generate increasing inequality in Nigeria. To counteract growing inequality among the states, the government tried to devise a system of federal revenue allocation to states based partly on an equal share to all and partly on population figures.

To create greater equality of opportunity, the government launched several public service programs, the most important of them in education. Between 1960 and 1972, little progress was made in education. The percentage of children of primary school age who attended school remained at 26 percent, though the percentage of those of secondary school age who attended increased from 4 percent to 7 percent.

In 1976, after the rise in oil revenues, the federal government launched a program of free, universal primary education (UPE), whose goal was universal primary school attendance by 1980 to reduce the regional inequalities that gave rise to ethnic conflict and civil war. The scale of the program was enormous. Initial projections were that primary school attendance would increase from 4.7 million in 1973 to 11.5 million in 1980, requiring 151,000 new classrooms. In addition, it was projected that secondary school and vocational school enrollments would increase by 347 percent and 786 percent between 1973 and 1980 and that there would be a 500 percent increase in students enrolled in teacher training courses and a 230 percent increase in university students.

All these enrollment projections proved to be underestimates, and the revenues of the federal and state governments have been severely strained by education costs. In 1979–1980 the federal government spent 31.5 percent of its recurrent budget and 6 percent of its capital budget on education, which consumed more than 50 percent of many state budgets.

Universal primary education, the most popular policy in Nigeria, is responsive to popular aspirations, but it has already posed many problems. Although it was supposed to reduce regional inequalities, it has actually increased school-attendance differentials among states and ethnic animosities. Secondary school and university students protest that room and board costs have soared even as tuition has become free. This led, in 1978–1979, to police violence against students, the closing of many schools, and the decision to use military personnel to impose discipline on students. More important, the program has created a new mass of educated unemployed and has encouraged educated rural youth to migrate to the cities in search of employment. In 1975, unemployment was 11.7 percent of the nonagricultural labor force (including the self-employed) and 37.5 percent of the wage labor force. An early estimate indicated that universal primary education school leavers in 1980 would add 1 million persons to the number of unemployed.

The levels of unemployment and inflation are not unrelated to the high levels of crime in Nigeria in recent years, which have not been reduced by the frequent execution of armed robbers. The government's awareness of the causes of crime has not induced it to pursue a development path that emphasizes the creation of jobs and thus greater income equality.

Sacks of cocoa are stored in a warehouse at the port of Lagos. (Photo: World Bank/ G. Gerster.)

Nigeria's first republic (1960–1966) retained democratic forms longer than did most African states. However, as the north extended its power into the south, the country experienced severe regional ethnic conflict and the manipulation of electoral politics. The young and reformist Ibo junior army officers who launched the 1966 coup failed to seize power, and it was seized instead by senior military officers. When the Federal Military Government (FMG) leader, General T.U. Aguiyi-Ironsi, sought to centralize government by decree, junior officers and noncommissioned officers of northern origin mutinied against Ibo and other southern officers in July, 1966 and handed power to middle-ranking northern officers, headed by Yakubu Gowon. Murderous riots against the Ibo in the north and west and the production of oil in the east led to the east's secession as the Republic of Biafra and to civil war. During the war, the Nigerian military grew from 10,000 to 250,000 men. This created a powerful, relatively high-salaried vested interest group, which the military leaders themselves were afraid to demobilize, fearing violent protests because there were no similarly well-paid civilian jobs for them.

Gowon demonstrated effective leadership during the civil war and in the postwar reconciliation period. But in the early 1970s the FMG was increasingly plagued by rampant corruption within the military and civil service, an inability to decrease the military's size, a lack of progress toward the promised restoration of civilian rule, and problems like Lagos's congested port and the disputed 1973 census. In July 1975, junior northern officers removed Gowon and gave power to General Murtala Muhammad.

The swiftness and decisiveness with which Muhammad moved to resolve Nigeria's outstanding problems restored a sense of dignity to the government and made Muhammad Nigeria's first truly popular national leader. His assassination in February 1976 in an unsuccessful coup was the occasion of public mourning. In his few months of rule, Muhammad purged the military of corrupt leaders and initiated a purge of inefficient and corrupt civil servants; involved public advisory committees in the resolution of Nigeria's outstanding problems; and elaborated a program for a return to civilian rule by October 1979, a program which was implemented by his successor, General Olusegun Obasanjo.

Nigeria's new constitution provides for an executive President and a Vice President, both limited to two 4-year terms; a 450-member House of Representatives, with membership based on population; a 95-member Senate with 5 members from each state; and a Cabinet. A broad range of economic, trade regulation, and tax powers are exclusively reserved for the federal government, with some concurrent federal-state powers in agriculture, commerce, commercial development, and education. Federal-state financial relationships are outside the constitution and are largely automatic, with federal disbursements to states made from a distributable pool. A preoccupation with Nigeria's fragile national unity is reflected by provisions requiring successful presidential and state gubernatorial candidates to win not only a majority of all the votes but at least one-fourth of the votes in two-thirds of the states (or the districts) involved. An independent federal electoral commission with strong powers oversees state and federal elections and requires all parties to have nationally representative executives. Before any party can contest an election, it must be recognized by the commission.

On August 16, 1979, Alhaji Shehu Shagari of the National Party defeated Awolowo of the Nigerian Unity Party and Azikiwe of the Nigerian People's party. Shagari's election to the presidency was confirmed by the electoral commission on August 18, and he took office as President on October 11, ushering in the new constitutional government after 13 years of military rule.

In the 1970s, Nigeria launched a vigorous drive for leadership in Africa. While officially nonaligned and actually pro-Western, it has become a powerful proponent of African interests, especially with regard to the liberation conflicts in Angola, Zimbabwe, and South Africa, and to African relations with the European Economic Community. Recognition of its power and stature has induced the world's major powers to court Nigeria. President Carter visited Nigeria in April 1978. The United States is Nigeria's major purchaser of oil; it took 43 percent of its exports in 1976. Nigeria's major sources of imports are the United Kingdom (22 percent in 1976), West Germany (15 percent), the United States (12 percent), Japan (10 percent), and France (8 percent).

Nigeria has come a long way from the poverty of its colonial period. It enters the 1980s as Africa's most populous, powerful, and potentially most prosperous country, but tensions will be quickened, not lessened, by the rapid pace of change made possible by oil wealth. An overwhelming number of Nigerians are poor, and Nigerian prosperity and inflation are leading them into even greater poverty. Unemployment in Nigeria's teeming cities will increase, given Nigeria's pattern of development. Workers will not suffer their declining real wages without protest, nor will the newly educated accept unemployment. Members of the oversized 180,000-man military will not take kindly to further demobilization unless they are guaranteed civilian jobs.

Nigerians are an energetic and ambitious people, but their political economy encourages conflict. Whether civilian politicians will try to use the new political institutions to contain ethnic conflict and foster unity remains to be seen. Having withdrawn to their barracks, the military will watch and wait.

Jon Kraus

Rwanda
(Republic of Rwanda)

Area: 10,169 sq mi (26,338 sq km)
Population: 4.5 million
  Density: 442 per sq mi (171 per sq km)
  Growth rate: 2.9% (1970–1977)
Percent of population under 14 years of age: 38%
Infant deaths per 1,000 live births: 133
Life expectancy at birth: 44 years
Leading causes of death: not available
Ethnic composition: Hutu 89%; Tutsi 10%; Twa 1% (1977)
Languages: Kinyarwanda (official), French (official), Swahili
Literacy: 25% (1977)
Religions: Christian (50%, est.), animist, Muslim
Percent population urban: not available
Percent population rural: not available
Gross national product: $830 million
  Per capita GNP: $180
  Per capita GNP growth rate: 1.3% (1970–1977)
Inflation rate: not available

Landlocked Rwanda sits at the crossroads of central Africa, astride the Zaire (Congo)-Nile divide and some 746 miles (1,200 km) from the nearest ocean port at Mombasa, Kenya. Rwanda is one of the few countries in the world whose commerce must pass through two other countries (Uganda and Kenya) before reaching the sea. It has Africa's highest population density, one of the highest in the world—442 persons per square mile (171 per sq km) and an estimated 1,000 persons per square mile (386 per sq km) of arable land.

The population growth rate is 2.9 percent per annum, a clearly disastrous trend. In 1950, Rwanda had 1.8 million inhabitants; in 1958, the population was estimated to be 2.5 million; in 1970, it rose to 3.7 million; and the August 1978 census indicated that there were some 4.9 million Rwandans. A basically healthy environment and improving systems for health delivery and social service have contributed to rapid population growth. After years of debate and hesitation, the government has decided to address the need for population controls, but this decision may have come too late. The small state's resources are limited and already stretched beyond their capacity to sustain the current population at adequate levels of nutrition.

Rwanda is the land of a thousand hills, whose beauty enchanted the German explorers of the nineteenth century and continues to attract tourists. The hilly topography makes development more challenging because transportation and communication are difficult. Population is a key issue; if current growth continues there will probably be mass starvation. Rwanda's 10,169 square miles (26,338 sq km) are less and less able to yield the food necessary to feed the growing population. Only about half the land area is suitable for agriculture; the rest is made up of lakes, forests, and marshes. Of the total land area, only

about 35 percent is potentially arable; 14 percent is natural pasture. As a result of demographic pressures, pastureland and other marginal lands are being used increasingly for crops. There are only 370,500 acres (150,000 hectares) of forest left because farmers have been clearing forest land for agricultural use. Loss of the natural forests poses a serious problem: if there are no trees left to attract rain clouds, and if the rate of evapotranspiration is upset, there may be attendant climatic changes. In some areas the predictable consequences are already occurring: water tables are declining; springs are drying up; runoff is creating gullies, thereby increasing soil erosion. Disturbance to the natural equilibrium of the Zaire (Congo)-Nile watershed may add to the soil depletion caused by improper and poor soil-management and agricultural practices, and Rwanda may become even less able to feed its population.

Individual caloric intake slipped from 2,500 calories per day in 1973 to 1,900 after 1974. The Food and Agriculture Organization (FAO) estimates that the average Rwandan gets only 80 to 85 percent of his or her minimum daily caloric requirement; and in some regions, the percentage may be lower. The nutritional status of the rural population fell an estimated 16 percent between 1959 and 1975.

In March 1977, the government's Advisory Council for Social and Demographic Matters issued a report on family planning and the need for contraception; and President Juvénal Habyarimana, while recognizing the tradition favoring large families and the large number of Catholics in the population, called publicly for responsible parenthood. In 1978, an Inter-African Seminar on Maternal and Infant Protection and Family Planning led to an official Rwandan request for foreign assistance to train personnel and provide expertise for a national family-planning program. Three pilot family-planning, maternal, and child health centers opened in early 1979. A family-planning secretariat is being organized, and there are plans to design local educational, research, demographic, and media components for the population-planning effort.

Rwanda's 5-year plan (1977–1981) has four goals: (1) to satisfy the food needs of the population, (2) to improve the living conditions of the individual and the collective life of the population, (3) to promote better use of human resources, and (4) to improve the country's position vis-à-vis the outside world. It is uncertain whether there are enough people trained to work in the areas specifically emphasized.

Agriculture remains the backbone of the economy. While higher levels of production have been achieved, agriculture's contribution to the gross domestic product (GDP) decreased from over 53 percent during

1971–1973 to less than 43 percent in 1977–1978. Manufacturing and construction increased in relative importance, accounting for 24 percent of the GDP in 1978. The service sector has also grown, stimulated by higher levels of economic activity, particularly in the developing tourist industry. In 1979, the war between Tanzania and Uganda dealt a severe blow to economic growth. Emergency food and energy shipments were required to enable Rwanda's economy to survive.

Agriculture accounted for 77 percent of Rwanda's exports in 1978, and it employs over 93 percent of the labor force. It is predominantly subsistence; less than 1 percent of total estimated production in 1978 was exported. Because they are made into beer, bananas are the most important local crop, despite government efforts to persuade farmers to curtail their production. In 1978, almost 1.8 million tons (2 million t) of bananas were produced for internal consumption, and 24 percent of the cultivated land was used for bananas. About 90 percent of this production was processed into local beer, which is used widely in social exchange. Sorghum is the next largest crop, and 75 percent of it is also processed into beer.

The major staple crops are sweet potatoes, cassava, Irish potatoes, and beans. Other food crops include peas and maize. These staples are produced on family farms, whose size varies from less than 1 acre to 17.5 acres (0.5 to 7 hectares). Agricultural technology is more advanced for cash crops than for food crops. Traditional methods of growing crops for food prevail, and farmers lack seed varieties, fail to observe proper plant spacing or crop rotation, and use little organic manure, plowing, or forage. Tradition hampers higher production. This is why almost 30 percent of the de-

velopment plan is directly or indirectly committed to the rural sector.

Major problems for agriculture are the lack of storage and transportation facilities and inadequate distribution channels. As a result, despite adequate production, there have been food shortages in some regions in recent years. To correct this, the government and foreign donors have focused on upgrading the country's road network, expanding extension services, and introducing new, labor-intensive farming techniques. The programs are bearing fruit; food-crop production in 1978 was 21 percent higher than in 1974, a year when poor weather conditions created pockets of famine. During the period 1974–1978, food production rose at an average annual rate of 5 percent, well beyond the population growth rate. There was a slowdown in 1977–1978 because of poor weather conditions, and continued high productivity is endangered by increasing demographic pressure on the land.

Cattle are important in the local economy and serve as a measure of wealth and status. However, cattle must compete with people for land, and the cattle herd has thus shrunk from 750,000 in 1971 to 600,000 in 1978. It is estimated that about 25 percent of the population own cattle. Their quality is being improved, as are the pasture and feed. The government is encouraging mixed farming, which integrates livestock and agriculture, and government ranches are being established with external aid. The FAO (UN Food and Agriculture Organization) has a project to emplace adequate veterinary services. Many other farm animals are also raised, including goats, sheep, pigs, and poultry.

The largest source of export earnings and rural incomes is coffee. About half the farm population grows coffee, tea, and pyrethrum, all cash crops. Individual farmers producing coffee numbered half a million at the end of 1977, with the average farmer tending 122 coffee trees on a small holding. The number of coffee growers has been increasing, but production figures have not reflected this increase because of the relatively stable or declining attractiveness of the prices paid to coffee producers. The government siphons off most profits to pay for the country's general development, and because the farmers grow coffee in association with other crops they are able to switch to other crops if the rewards warrant it.

The Office des Cultures Industrielles du Rwanda (OCIR), a state agency, is responsible for coffee processing and marketing. OCIR holds a 51 percent interest in a mixed company, RWANDEX, which markets the coffee and other cash crops. As a result of OCIR-provided extension services, and despite poor weather conditions in recent years, local coffee production grew at a rate of 9.3 percent annually for the period 1974–1978. However, partly because so many trees are old, yields from individual trees are declining. OCIR is helping farmers plant new trees and upgrade the care of those already in production. During 1977–1978, coffee exports earned 55 percent of

In an insecticide plant at Ruhengeri, men are working to extract pyrethrum from a type of chrysanthemum that is one of Rwanda's three cash crops. Pyrethrum is effective, harmless, and nonpolluting. (Photo: United Nations/Unido.)

Rwanda's total export receipts, and in 1978 the government began to ship the crop to Mombasa by chartered cargo plane.

Tea production, mainly in the north and southwest, continues to climb. The government maintains extensive tea plantations, administered by a mixed company in which it has a 49 percent interest. Tea offers a continuous year-round income, which makes it a popular crop for small farmers. While the area of cultivated tea doubled to 19,800 acres (7,900 hectares) between 1974 and 1977, a severe frost in 1978 caused a serious decline in production. Local processing capabilities are being expanded, and tea provided 8 percent of export receipts in 1977 and 7 percent in 1978.

As part of the effort to diversify, mining has been upgraded; in 1980 a plant will open to smelt cassiterite ore. Exports of cassiterite and wolfram accounted for 18 percent of total export receipts in 1977–1978. Manufacturing is quickly expanding (mainly small-scale industries that process agricultural exports and produce import substitutes).

Trained labor is scarce, and the government has launched an educational program to address this problem. It has also instituted salary increments in the public sector, the largest employer. Simultaneously, it has undertaken to curtail public employment, since official salaries eat up too much of the country's meager operating budget.

Rwanda's rugged geography, which makes its development difficult, protected the country from outside invaders for most of the nineteenth century. Rwanda developed in quasi-isolation as a highly stratified society organized as a kingdom under the domination of a minority ethnic group known as the Tutsi. As far back as the fifteenth century, these people moved into the area and slowly extended domination over the agriculturalist Hutu, who were already established there. A small population of pygmoid Twa hunters and gatherers, who were incorporated into the kingdom's social fabric as pariahs, were used by the royalty and chiefs as hired thugs to terrorize the hapless Hutu majority and ensure minority rule.

The original Tutsi-dominated state extended its control over most of present-day Rwanda and over regions now belonging to adjacent states. However, the Hutu to the west retained some local autonomy and were only beginning to experience Tutsi infiltration when Rwanda became a German colony at the end of the 1800s. The Germans decided to reinforce Tutsi rule and administer their new territory through the chiefs and the courts. In the implementation of this indirect-rule formula, European outsiders actually assigned more power and discretion to the chiefs than they had had in the past. The Germans also transformed the basic nature of chieftaincy: tenure no longer depended on the court or local opinion but became a function of German will. As a result, Tutsi rule became increasingly harsh toward the Hutu majority and even toward those Tutsi who lacked wealth or social status. After World War I the Belgians displaced the Germans, but they continued the indirect rule. The Hutu accounted for 85 percent of the population, but Belgian regulations made it nearly impossible for a Hutu to gain an administrative, economic, social, or political position of any note.

The Catholic missions that accompanied German and then Belgian rule introduced the Hutu to avenues for social and economic mobility although the missionaries also favored the Tutsi. The Christian population grew quickly to more than 50 percent, and Christian ethics, including the notions of equality and social justice, were widely disseminated. The Christian teachings inspired a small group of Hutu, helped by missionaries and lay brothers sympathetic to Hutu emancipation, to launch a civil rights movement of sorts in the mid-1950s. Hutu demands outraged the majority of Tutsi chiefs and their allies, and threats and intimidation, often carried out by the Twa, were directed against the nascent Hutu movement's leadership. Belgian administrators and Catholic missionaries began to support Hutu demands, causing a rift between the Belgian administration and the Tutsi that further helped the Hutu cause.

Tensions mounted, and in 1959, after the death of Rwanda's Tutsi monarch, massive violence erupted in the countryside. Thousands of Hutu and Tutsi roamed the hillsides, burning, looting, and attacking each other. By 1960 the violence had toppled Tutsi domination, and the Hutu assumed political control with strong support from the Belgian administration. Fighting continued, however, because the Tutsi refused to accept their changed status and Hutu peasants sought to settle old scores and grab Tutsi lands and wealth.

In July 1962, when Rwanda became independent as a Hutu republic, it was still beset by ethnic violence; tens of thousands of Tutsi fled rather than live under Hutu rule. The economy was in a shambles as a result of the violence that had raged through the countryside for over 2 years. With the mass exodus of Tutsi, the country was left without skilled labor. Few of the Hutu had been educated or trained to assume the reins of power or to run an organization. The armed forces were officered by Belgians, and ministry personnel did not know how to make the ministries function. Tutsi irregulars continued their armed attacks against Hutu officials, almost reconquering the country in 1964.

The new regime and its political arm, the Party for Hutu Emancipation (Parmehutu), remained traumatized by this, and anti-Tutsi feelings marked the lifetime of this government. In 1973, new violence was encouraged against the Tutsi, but the internal context was no longer the same. A Hutu sense of security had been established, and few Hutu believed that Tutsi reconquest was possible. Instead, development problems and income distribution among the Hutu majority had become the population's chief political concerns.

The 1973 violence was climaxed by a military coup that brought Major General Habyarimana to power and began a new phase in national life. The second republic, emphasizing ethnic reconciliation, initiated a quota system whereby the country's Tutsi, which represent 10 percent of the population, would be assured a place commensurate with their numbers. Development needs assumed central importance.

The Tutsi still suffer from discrimination, regional rivalries among the Hutu are still unresolved, and political institutions were only established in 1978, but the new leadership is committed to ethnic reconciliation and is mounting a concerted attack on Rwanda's economic and social problems.

The needs of the economy, coupled with Rwanda's official commitment to development, have made a good impression among many donors, who are prepared to provide grant aid to the country. Nevertheless, serious difficulties remain. In 1978, after the national elections, a new constitution pledged to human rights was adopted. President Habyarimana and his government team will have to translate their program of decentralized development—including local participation—into an effective voluntary system if the country is to solve its grave problems. The need for better coordination at the national level and the establishment of reliable baseline data on the economy are the two most immediate technical tasks that confront the regime.

Warren Weinstein

Senegal
(Republic of Senegal)

Area: 76,124 sq mi (197,160 sq km)
Population: 5.4 million
   Density: 71 per sq mi (27 per sq km)
   Growth rate: 2.6% (1970–1977)
Percent of population under 15 years of age: 41%
Infant deaths per 1,000 live births: 158 (1978)
Life expectancy at birth: 40 years (1975)
Leading causes of death: not available
Ethnic composition: Wolof 33%; Serer 17%; Peul 12%; Diola 8%; Tukolor 8%; Mandingo 8%; European; Lebanese
Languages: Wolof and French (official)
Literacy: 5–10% (1977)
Religions: Muslim 88%; Christian
Percent population urban: 30–35%
Percent population rural: 65–70%
Gross national product: $1.83 billion
   Per capita GNP: $340
   Per capita GNP growth rate: 0.4% (1970–1977)
Inflation rate: 12.1% (1970–1976)

Senegal is one of Africa's most stable and sophisticated nations. A vitally important strategic location, a meager resource endowment, and a legacy of French colonialism and Islamic religious thought will continue to play key roles in determining Senegal's future.

Located at the westernmost point of the African continent, Senegal is the gateway to Africa from the Americas and, to some extent, from Europe. The capital city of Dakar, with its magnificent natural port and its agreeable climate, was the major embarkation point for the slave trade in the eighteenth century, the administrative capital of all of French West Africa in the nineteenth and twentieth centuries, and a critical supply point for the North African Allied campaign in World War II.

Senegal has profited substantially from its strategic location; its crossroads position has meant both eco- nomic activity and educational opportunity. The Senegalese take whatever advantage they can from this asset because the country's geography is otherwise not particularly beneficent. The land itself is poor, lying mainly in the Sahel, a region of semiarid savanna that rings the southern edge of the Sahara Desert. Subject to frequent droughts and plagued by centuries of overgrazing and other improper agricultural practices, Senegal produces only one significant cash crop—peanuts—in addition to subsistence crops of millet, sorghum, and rice.

Water, or the lack of it, is the key problem. The rainy season extends from June through October, but only in the Casamance region is plentiful rainfall assured. Across most of the country—and indeed in all the countries that ring the Sahara—abundant rains are the exception, and each succeeding year of drought sees more and more acreage abandoned and swallowed up by the encroaching desert.

If water is the problem, however, it is also the solution. Senegal has water under the surface and three major river systems—the Senegal River in the north, the Gambia River that originates in eastern Senegal but flows mainly through Gambia, and the Casamance River in the south. If the water resources of the country can be harnessed and if the Senegalese farmers can be retrained to grow new crops on irrigated land, the country will be able to feed itself and even export food.

Toward that end, a major project of integrated resource and human development along the Senegal River has been undertaken by the governments of Senegal, Mali, and Mauritania, supported by foreign aid funds. If successful, the project will lead to a river system designed to capture and use whatever rain falls and to provide water for year-round irrigation of crops like cotton, rice, and vegetables. Whether or not the billions of dollars needed to complete the project will be forthcoming, however, and how successful the retraining of the Senegalese peasants will be are open questions. In any event, the country is trying to forge its own destiny and alleviate one of its most chronic shortages.

With the exception of significant phosphate deposits, Senegal has virtually no natural resources whose exploitation could provide the basis for sustained economic growth. There is some exploration for off-shore oil and mineral deposits, but indications are not favorable. The absence of mineral wealth and the marginal nature of agricultural production have forced Senegal to rely on its human resources, the abilities of its people.

Senegal's 5.4 million people are young—41 percent are less than 15 years old and only 6 percent are over 60—and predominantly rural, although 30 to 35 percent live in urban centers. The population, growing at a rate of 2.7 percent annually, includes some 50,000 non-Africans—primarily Europeans and Lebanese.

Senegal has escaped the strong intertribal rivalries and bloodshed that have plagued so many other African nations. The Wolof, the country's most important ethnic group, constitute approximately one-third of the population, and the Wolof presence and language are dominant in most urban centers, where they work as bureaucrats, teachers, and, especially, traders. The Serer (17 percent of the population) are reputed to be the best farmers in the country and along with the Wolof, comprise most of Senegal's peanut growers. Other important ethnic groups include the pastoral, quasi-nomadic Peul (12 percent), with their prized zebu cattle, the Tukolor (8 percent) along the Senegal River in the north; the fiercely Islamic and warlike Mandingo (8 percent), who migrated centuries ago from the Niger River valley; and the Diola (8 percent) in the extreme southern part of the country, who are excellent rice growers and cultivators of palm wine.

Unifying these ethnic groups is the 600-year-old Muslim religious tradition, which claims 88 percent of the country's population. Islam was introduced into what is now Senegal in the twelfth century by North African traders crossing the Sahara looking for gold, ivory, slaves, and—with equal fervor—souls to convert for the glory of Allah.

Today, Islam is the most powerful influence in the country, affecting everything from politics to polygyny to peanuts. In every region of the country except the lower Casamance, Islam either controls or influences almost all aspects of life. The daily routine for almost all Senegalese begins with the morning prayer to Allah, the first of five prayer sessions every day. The Muslim practice of polygyny allows Senegalese men to have up to four wives, with important implications for the role of women in society. Even agriculture is affected. As Islam has spread in the southern areas of Senegal, many Diola and Mandingo have abandoned their traditional occupations as rice growers and herders for the uncertainties of peanut agriculture, a cash crop that yields a profitable share for the local religious leaders, the marabouts.

In political and economic matters, the marabout is as powerful as the parish priest was in Europe at the height of the Middle Ages. No matter how poor, the Senegalese peasant pledges a portion of his crop to the

At the bus depot in Dakar, travelers climb into open buses. (Photo: United Nations/ A. Rozberg.)

marabout who, in turn, supports his religious superiors. At the highest levels of the Islamic hierarchy in Senegal, the grand marabout of Touba controls enormous wealth and exerts considerable influence, even telling the faithful how to vote.

More important than any other influence, however, is the fatalistic view of life succinctly summed up in the phrase *in ch'Allah* (meaning "if Allah wills it"). Such an outlook controls and strengthens poor peasants, but it is a formidable psychological denial of the basic premise of development, i.e., that organized human effort can make the future better.

While Islam is the dominant religious influence in the country, the legacy of 145 years of French colonial rule pervades Senegal's culture and political economy. From Dakar's broad boulevards and excellent restaurants to the educational system in the most remote village schools, French influence is everywhere. The Senegalese are more comfortable with their French heritage than most Africans once under French colonial rule. When the French maintained Dakar as the capital of all their West African colonies, the Senegalese profited from the good schools and the economic opportunities that went hand in hand with a large expatriate population; the French came to look upon the Senegalese as the elite of their colonial subjects because they were the best educated and made the best soldiers and administrators.

Today, the results of that special relationship are clear. French and Wolof coexist as national languages, and a group of internationally known and respected artists, writers, poets, and even filmmakers flourish. The Senegalese have molded their own concept of African selfhood, negritude (in the famous phrase of the country's poet-President, Leopold Sedar Senghor), to the richness of French cultural and intellectual tradition.

President Senghor himself is a symbol of the Franco-African relationship. One of the best-known poets writing in the French language, in earlier years he was often criticized for being under the domination of the French. He has since emerged, however, as one of the most respected spokesmen for the problems of emerging Africa and the third world, pioneering his policies of African socialism, a blend of national control of the economy and cooperation with external—especially French—interests.

Even more impressive is the progress the country has made politically. A one-party democracy from independence through 1978, President Senghor and the ruling Senegalese Progressive Union (UPS)—now called the Socialist Party—have since opened up the nation's political system. By mid-1979, four political parties were officially recognized, including a Communist party.

At the village level, Senegalese life revolves around three major elements: the family, the seasons, and Islamic observance. The family is the most basic and most important social unit. The Senegalese define the family in its extended form to include three and sometimes four generations. Since a Senegalese man is allowed up to four wives, this means that a single

Senegalese women, dressed in handsome prints, harvest rice. (Photo: United Nations/ Ray Witlin.)

extended family may number 200 or more by the time all the siblings and in-laws are counted. Many smaller villages, in fact, may be composed of little more than a single family.

The physical appearance of the villages and huts varies. In the Wolof and Serer villages, compounds are grouped around a central clear area. The compounds are individually fenced and may include several square huts with rattanlike walls chinked and reinforced with dried mud, as well as a few smaller outbuildings for livestock or grain. The huts, covered with four-sided, thatched roofs, are basically sleeping quarters for the subfamily units. Cooking, eating, and socializing normally take place outdoors. In a typical village, there are no sanitary facilities, and the water is hand-drawn from an open well.

Farther to the south in the Casamance, the huts are strikingly different. In the eastern part of the region, the Peul huts are round, solidly built of distinctive red laterite mud, and have conical, thatched roofs. But by far the most dramatic constructions are those of the Diola in the lower Casamance. There one finds large, rambling, mud structures. Some have two stories, and most contain seven or eight rooms, including a granary that typically holds 8 to 10 tons of rice.

Throughout the country, women cook over small charcoal braziers. The staple is grain (millet or rice) mixed with fresh or (in the interior) dried fish, a few vegetables, and a sharp, piquant sauce. Most rural Senegalese do not eat well in terms of quality or nutritional balance.

Poor peasants not far from the brink of starvation, however, wear elegant clothing and even expensive jewelry. On festive occasions they wear versions of the *boubou*, which for men is an elaborately brocaded caftan and for women consists of a colorful sheath with an overgown. Dressed in their finest, even the poorest villagers underline the reputation of the Senegalese for grace and elegance.

Such nonproductive use of scarce income is common in Senegal, as it is in many poor countries. The pattern extends to the practice of polygyny and the "acquisition" of wives, the relatively large sums of money spent on rites like marriages and funerals, and the money spent on Islamic pilgrimages to Mecca in Saudi Arabia (the holiest of Muslim shrines) or Fez in Morocco. Clearly, fulfilling religious obligations and conforming to cultural patterns fill critically important needs for the Senegalese.

The agricultural cycle begins in April with the preparation of the fields for the year's planting. The techniques differ, depending on whether the land is being prepared for peanuts, millet, or rice, but hard work with primitive tools like the ancient *dabah* (short-handled hoe) or the formidable *katyandoh* (long-handled shovel) is the common factor. Recently, some of the more advanced farmers have started to use implements like seeders and animal-powered plows, but for the most part, tending and harvesting the crop follows centuries-old patterns.

The growing season extends through October/November for peanuts and into December for rice. The school year begins in November so that students can help with the harvest. Once the harvest is in, the Senegalese turn to other aspects of their lives—rebuilding their huts, attending school, or looking for work in the cities.

Since independence and the rise of Dakar and a half-dozen other cities, there has been considerable migration to the urban centers; villagers find the lure of steady employment in the cities difficult to resist. Some migrants find good jobs in urban factories or business establishments, but most find only marginal, part-time employment or no work at all. All Senegalese cities contain *medinas*, or poorer sections, where migrants live in cramped, difficult conditions, supported by their extended families.

While Senegal's industrial base is small, it has been growing at about 5 percent annually since independence and is located almost entirely in the Dakar area. The largest component is the processing of peanuts, primarily into peanut oil for export. In addition, a host of basic industries serve the local market—textiles, shoes, food processing, and breweries. Finally, the commerce and services sector, especially tourism and the civil service, are important sources of employment.

Employed or not, rich or poor, the Senegalese maintain strong links with their villages, even when they have been urbanized over several generations. Births, circumcisions, marriages, and deaths—the rites of passage—and the major holidays of the Islamic calendar bring important reunions of the extended family, and members come from all over the country. Those who have found work in the cities send money back to the village to support family members struggling to make ends meet.

The early influence of what is now Senegal rested on the sophistication of its political administration. As early as the fourteenth century, the Jolof Empire boasted an elaborate provincial organization complete with an army, local police, and a judicial system—all supported by taxation.

The first Europeans, the Portuguese, arrived in the fifteenth century, and for the next 200 years, several maritime powers fought to establish and maintain trading outposts along the Senegalese coast. The British held the Gambia River, and the Portuguese held the area south of the Casamance River. But the nineteenth century saw the French take control of most of the coast—especially Saint-Louis at the mouth of the Senegal River and the Cape Vert peninsula that would later become Dakar. From this powerful base, the French pushed north and east and, by the end of the nineteenth century, France controlled most of West and Central Africa.

Looking to the future, there are grounds for optimism over the short term. Barring unexpected oil or mineral discoveries, the economy will probably continue to make the same slow, steady progress that it has been making for the past 2 decades. The one major breakthrough is the prospect of the successful completion of the Senegal River project, breaking the country's centuries-old dependence on unreliable rainy seasons.

Politically, the big question is who will succeed Senghor. He was 74 years old in 1980 and has been Senegal's President since 1960. In very few countries is the personality of a single figure so intertwined with the character and development of the nation. Nonetheless, because of the country's long history of political stability and the recent liberalizing of its political system to include opposition groups, most observers believe that the transition, when it comes, will be orderly and positive.

Finally, Senegal's key strength—the ability of its people—will not be affected by rainfall or oil. It is the factor that has permitted the country to make impressive progress with very few resources. More than any other factor, it is the constancy of the people that will continue to fuel Senegal's development.

Geoffrey S. Howard

Sierra Leone
(Republic of Sierra Leone)

Area: 27,925 sq mi (72,325 sq km)
Population: 3.3 million
  Density: 118 per sq mi (46 per sq km)
  Growth rate: 2.5% (1970–1977)
Percent of population under 14 years of age: 40% (1975)
Infant deaths per 1,000 live births: 183 (1970)
Life expectancy at birth: 43.5 years (1975)
Leading causes of death: malaria and related diseases
Ethnic composition: Mende 33%; Temne 33%; 16 other ethnic groups (including Europeans, Lebanese, Creoles)
Languages: English (official), Krio, others
Literacy: 10% (1978)
Religions: animist 70%; Muslim 25%; Christian 5% (1978)
Percent population urban: 15% (1976)
Percent population rural: 85% (1976)
Gross national product: $690 million
  Per capita GNP: $210
  Per capita GNP growth rate: −1.3% (1970–1977)
Inflation rate: 15% (1972–1977)

Sierra Leone, a circular West African country about the size of South Carolina, is famous for the warm hospitality of its people and the fascinating story of the achievements of its Creoles in the nineteenth century. Its natural assets include its capital, Freetown, the third largest natural harbor in the world, and its famous gem diamonds. Sierra Leoneans are relying on these assets as they confront the more challenging aspects of their natural environment: fragile tropical soils, natural barriers to communication and endemic tropical diseases.

Most of Sierra Leone's rust-colored lateritic soils lack humus and certain minerals necessary for highly productive agriculture. Several centuries ago, nearly all of the country was covered by dense tropical forests. But the growing population gradually cleared much of the original forests to make farms, and vegetation today consists primarily of savanna in the north and low, secondary forests and thickets in the south. This man-made change in vegetative cover, the absence of a winter that would allow humus to be restored, and the country's ample rainfall that leaches minerals from the soil are the underlying causes of the generally weak soils. Rainfall exceeds 150 inches (391 cm) annually along the coasts and more than 100 inches (254 cm) in most of the rest of the country.

Sierra Leoneans are taking steps to reverse the gradual degradation of their land. Forest preserves have been set aside, and a reforestation program has begun. A major soil survey is in progress (only around 10 percent of the soil has been studied in detail), and a wide range of research is currently being carried out by the agricultural college at Njala. But concerted action must be taken quickly because the rapid growth in Sierra Leone's population means that less and less land is being left fallow. On the positive side, the leaching that removes some minerals serves to concentrate others, such as iron, bauxite, and rutile (the ore of titanium). Sierra Leone is thought to have the world's second largest reserves of rutile, but access to them is difficult.

Topographically, Sierra Leone resembles a giant green wedge. The elevation declines from the rolling plateaus 1,000 to 2,000 feet (305 m to 610 m) above sea level over the eastern half of the country to a narrow, low-lying coastal plain that slips gently into the Atlantic Ocean. The beaches along the coastal plain are extraordinarily beautiful and provide Sierra Leoneans with an important tourist attraction. Exceptions to this general picture include the mountainous mass nearly 3,000 feet (900 m) high forming the Sierra Leone Peninsula along the coast and the mountainous protrusions in the east, which include Mount Bintamani at 6,390 feet (1,950 m), the highest point in West Africa east of Cameroon.

Coursing down the wedge are nine roughly parallel rivers, but stretches of rapids just behind the coastal plain greatly reduce their usefulness for transportation. The rivers flow from the northeast to the southwest, while most of the country's commerce moves from the southeast to the northwest. As a result, the cost of building a national road network (which absorbed more than half of all development expenditure between 1964 and 1973) is high because so many bridges must be built.

Because nearly all of Sierra Leone's rain falls between May and November, there is a marked seasonal fluctuation in the levels of its rivers. Navigability is much improved at the end of the rainy season, when some rivers reach levels 50 feet (15 m) above their dry-season levels. The eventual construction of dams and locks will result in enormous benefits to Sierra Leone, including increased navigability through control of water levels, greater agricultural production from irrigation, increased supplies of fish, and abundant hydroelectric power. Sierra Leone is estimated to have a potential of more than 1 million kilowatts of hydroelectric power, a total 25 times greater than its present production of electricity, nearly all of which is based on the use of expensive imported oil. Finally, the coastal waters teem with fish, most of which are currently being caught by trawlers from various industrialized nations.

The well-watered and continually warm natural environment of the country is conducive to many tropical diseases and pests. The most serious is malaria, which, in association with malnutrition and other factors, causes a high rate of infant mortality and chronic ill health among the 80 percent of the adult population estimated to be afflicted by it. Schistosomiasis is also widespread, and, like malaria, it causes a general loss of energy among most adults. A third significant tropical disease is trypanosomiasis (sleeping sickness), which affects primarily cattle and horses. This disease is of major economic and historical importance because it deprives Sierra Leoneans (particularly in the south) of sufficient supplies of protein, milk and animal power for farm work and transportation. Pests like rodents and weaverbirds, which eat great quantities of rice, also flourish.

Sierra Leone's population, which passed 3 million recently, is growing rapidly, and the country is already among the most densely populated in Africa. More than 40 percent of the increasingly younger population is under 14 years of age and dependent on the relatively decreasing proportion of the population in the active labor force.

Sierra Leoneans include eighteen different ethnic groups. The Mende in the south and the Temne in the north each account for a third of the total population. Each group has its own language, but Krio, a language derived from English, Portuguese, Yoruba, and other African languages, serves as a lingua franca for the entire country. English, the official language, is the major medium of administrative, technical, and business communication and the language of instruction in the schools. In terms of economic development, English is useful, but some Sierra Leoneans find it politically and psychologically unsatisfactory as a national language. Like so many other African states, Sierra Leone wants an African national language but lacks a choice acceptable to all its people.

Sierra Leone's religious patterns are similarly diverse. Most Sierra Leoneans retain traditional beliefs, which include the idea of a supreme being but emphasize the importance of the life-force believed to be in everything and everyone living, dead, or yet unborn. There are also perhaps 1 million Muslims, living mostly in the north, and Islam is believed to be the fastest-growing religion. The approximately 200,000 Christians have an influence far beyond their numbers because of their longer association with modern education and technology. Many adherents of Islam and Christianity openly or privately retain various religious beliefs and practices from their traditional African cultures.

Throughout the country, Sierra Leoneans are experiencing pressures toward change in their ways of living. These pressures are most intense in the cities, towns, and mining areas, but even remote villagers no longer live as their ancestors did. Analysis of the 1963 census revealed that one in four Sierra Leoneans was living outside the chiefdom (there are 150 chiefdoms) in which he or she was born. Young males leave their homes first, usually in search of greater economic opportunities in the cities and mining areas, and other family members often join them later. The Freetown area, for example, has doubled in population since 1963 and now contains about 300,000 people. Some of the migration is seasonal, and in nearly all cases the migrants return to their original homes to visit relatives and participate in traditional ceremonies. When they do, they bring back new products and attitudes, thus accelerating the process of social change.

The role of the secret, or closed, societies in traditional Sierra Leone is clearly changing. The primary purpose of these social institutions (like the Poro for men and the Sande for women) is to ensure the health and prosperity of the community by dealing with the supernatural in special ceremonies and rituals, much

Women hold their infants while they wait at a government health center; tropical diseases and malnutrition cause a high rate of infant mortality. (Photo: United Nations/ B. Wolff.)

as a church functions. These societies also function as the traditional educational system, teaching young people to farm, dance, build houses, be proper husbands or wives, and, in general, to become productive and socially acceptable adults. While these traditional institutions retain considerable influence, their power, and prestige are waning under the impact of new religions and occupations, and modern schools. Enrollment in primary schools almost doubled in the 1960s, and the number of students in secondary schools grew even faster, from 7,800 to 35,500. At the same time, the period of traditional Poro instruction, the initiation process, declined from what was once several years to only a few weeks.

Similarly, the basis for social status is gradually but perceptibly changing. In Sierra Leone's traditional communities, age and important ancestors remain very significant if not exclusive requirements for high status. Increasingly, however, power and prestige may be achieved by nontraditional means, like obtaining a modern education or entering a modern occupation. In the cities, doctors, lawyers, and senior civil servants, whatever their age or ancestral line, generally occupy the top level of the social system. At the middle level are schoolteachers, middle-level government employees, nurses, and other salaried persons with high school educations. Below them are the semi-skilled, the unskilled and the unemployed, who usually have little formal training. While the new criteria for social status are most relevant in urban areas, their influence is increasingly a force for change in the countryside. Those seeking election to traditional political offices, like paramount chief, emphasize their level of modern education or modern skills as well as their age and genealogy.

In rural regions, the importance of the group exceeds that of the individual, and the focus of primary loyalty is the immediate kinship group. The crucial kinship group in Sierra Leone is the lineage, people of three or four generations related to each other via a common ancestor. Membership in this group determines much of one's life, such as where one lives, what traditional occupation one pursues (farmer, leather worker, blacksmith, "praise singer," and so on), what land one uses, whom one marries, and to whom one gives assistance. However, the new possibilities for personal gain on an individual basis by raising cash crops or working for wages in the cities and mining areas have undermined many of these traditional rights and obligations. Land-tenure practices are also increasingly being challenged by younger, more ambitious Sierra Leoneans, who want to move toward more permanent, individual ownership of land and away from the tradition that vests ultimate control in the elders of the major lineage groups in each chiefdom.

Marriage in rural Sierra Leone remains a social contract between two lineages, sealed by a transfer of resources (the so-called bride price) from the groom's lineage to the bride's lineage to compensate them for her departure. Polygyny is common in rural areas, because lineage bonds and wives are significant economic assets; in the cities, the impact of Christianity, the financial burden of maintaining multiple wives, and the weakening of lineage bonds have combined to increase the frequency of monogamous marriages.

There is no sharp division between rural and urban Sierra Leone, and traditional beliefs and practices still play a major role in the cities. What is remarkable is the continuing influence of kinship ties even among well-educated, highly urbanized Sierra Leoneans, who often retain close ties with their original villages. Moreover, some traditional patterns, such as the independent and powerful role played by women in many of the country's ethnic groups, are still functional in the modern world. In the southern half of Sierra Leone, particularly among the Mende, women have traditionally exercised greater independence and have performed political and economic functions often reserved for males elsewhere. They frequently control considerable economic resources, and they are also eligible for political office; in the early 1970s ten of the eighty-one paramount chiefs in southern Sierra Leone were women. This feature has been maintained in less traditional spheres, and Sierra Leonean women have served as Cabinet ministers and delegates to the United Nations and on numerous national boards and commissions.

There are fewer economic than social links between rural and urban areas. Most Sierra Leoneans are farmers who produce rice, palm oil, and cassava for local use and limited amounts of coffee, palm ker-

In a land where running piped water is scarce, a woman washes her vegetables at a community water pipe. (Photo: United Nations/B. Wolff.)

nels, and cocoa for export. Agricultural methods remain relatively unchanged and are not very productive. There are many small farms of about 4 acres, relying on rotational bush fallow (or shifting) cultivation. There are no chemical fertilizers or hybrid seeds; and farmers use simple tools and rely almost exclusively on human beings for energy inputs. The agricultural sector contributes less than one-third of the gross national product (GNP), even though three-fourths of the labor force consists of farmers.

The low productivity is, in part, a result of government policies. Government agencies, which control the purchase of rice and various cash crops, set the prices for the farmer below world market prices in order to earn profits and to keep the price of rice low for urban consumers. The result has been the smuggling of produce into Liberia, lower production than expected, and increased migration into the cities. An exporter of rice between the mid-1930s and mid-1950s, Sierra Leone imported 10 percent of its rice for consumption in the 1960s; and in most years since independence in 1961 the cost of agricultural imports has exceeded the value of agricultural exports.

The modern sector of the economy is dominated by mining, particularly diamond production, which accounts for more than half the value of the country's exports. Manufacturing remains insignificant, and foreign trade continues to be exceptionally important; thus the national economy is very vulnerable to fluctuations in the world prices of its primary products. This vulnerability, combined with the government's overspending, resulted in a major financial crisis in the mid-1960s and a minor one in the mid-1970s.

Much of the modern sector is owned by foreigners, and the outflow of repatriated profits exceeded new foreign investment by an average of $3.6 million (3 million leones) between 1963 and 1972. Europeans, mainly the British, play a major role in mineral production, banking, and specialized commerce; some 7,000 Lebanese dominate rural marketing and credit, motor transport, tourism and hotels, and the diamond trade.

A fundamental challenge is the wide and apparently growing gap between rich and poor. Per capita income in rural Sierra Leone is believed to be less than half that in urban areas. This is a major cause of the migration to the cities, and yet many illiterate and unskilled migrants fail to find productive work, and official unemployment ranges from 9 to 15 percent in the cities compared to only 1 percent in the countryside. This phenomenon continues despite the rapid growth of the civil service, which employs more than half of all salaried persons. One study estimates that 5 percent of the population receives more than 45 percent of the national income, a disparity which, if true, is extreme in comparison to other developing countries.

Despite Sierra Leone's difficult development problems, grounds for optimism may be found in the country's historical record. The ancestors of Sierra Leone's 50,000 Creoles (a racial mixture) were brought to the region around Freetown as liberated slaves by the British during the nineteenth century. By the end of the century, this talented and energetic group had earned for Freetown the title of the Athens of West Africa, recording a number of African "firsts" (first college, first doctor, first Christian bishop, first newspaper, and so on). By 1885, no fewer than thirteen Creole doctors were serving in the British Colonial Service in West Africa, and Freetown itself featured a flourishing press, a large measure of self-government, and a modernized, sophisticated society. Unfortunately, the remarkable progress of the Creoles collided with changing British interests and perceptions, as European racism reached its peak during the scramble for African colonies. Creoles were gradually but systematically excluded from positions of power and influence on the basis of their color, causing a decline in their self-confidence and dynamism, a decline from which they are only now recovering.

As part of the scramble for Africa, Sierra Leone was proclaimed a British protectorate in 1896. Two years later, most of the peoples of the interior rose in violent resistance to British rule. Throughout the first half of the twentieth century, Sierra Leoneans from all ethnic groups demonstrated initiative and adaptability, responding positively to pressures for modernization. After World War II, their continuing resistance to alien rule coincided with other pressures on the British for decolonization. After thousands of ordinary farmers poured illegally into the diamond areas in the mid-1950s, sparking a fivefold increase in diamond production, Sierra Leone's poverty could no longer be used as an argument against independence. Two other obstacles, the division between Creoles and non-Creoles and the division along north-south lines in the interior, were reduced, thanks primarily to the political skills of the country's first Prime Minister, Milton Margai, who led Sierra Leone to independence on April 27, 1961.

The first 15 years of political independence were not easy, and the country had its share of attempted and actual coups d'etat and sporadic violence. There was even a short period of military rule. But real progress has been achieved in training labor, building the physical infrastructure, and increasing administrative skills. Despite political instability, the depletion of iron-ore reserves, unfavorable world markets for several exports, a dramatic rise in the price of oil, and misguided policies, real growth in output has stayed a point or two ahead of the population growth of about 2.5 percent. Sierra Leoneans have learned from the mistakes of the 1960s. The country's first comprehensive development plan, 1974–1979, put a major emphasis on agriculture, and in 1975 the country became self-sufficient in rice production for the first time in 20 years, thanks to genuine price incentives for the ordinary farmer.

Long-term development in Sierra Leone will require much greater knowledge and better control of the natural environment, a continuing transformation of traditional values with a minimum of social repercussions, and increased regional cooperation to enlarge the market for Sierra Leone's products. The country's leadership has encouraged regional cooperation, and its large natural harbor should enhance its share of the benefits when and if better internal transportation and economic integration develop in West Africa.

The basic approach of the elite and the ruling political party, the All People's Congress (APC), might be termed regulated or reformist capitalism in an open society. While officially nonaligned and willing to accept aid from any source, Sierra Leone remains generally pro Western in its international outlook and essentially moderate in African circles.

So far, its commitment to the country's most pressing need—a more equitable distribution of goods and services—has been far more rhetorical than real. But social change, intensified by an apparently accelerating rate of internal migration, is gradually altering traditional ways of life, and the history of these friendly and easygoing people indicates that they can cooperate to act effectively when either danger or opportunity arises.   *John Collier*

Somalia
(Somali Democratic Republic)

Area: 246,199 sq mi (637,657 sq km)
Population: 3.7 million
   Density: 15 per sq mi (6 per sq km)
   Growth rate: 2.3% (1970–1977)
Percent of population under 14 years of age: 45% (1977)
Infant deaths per 1,000 live births: not available
Life expectancy at birth: 41 years (1977)
Leading causes of death: communicable diseases
Ethnic composition: Somali, over 90%
Languages: Somali, Swahili, Arabic, Italian, English
Literacy: 20%; 50% adult
Religions: Muslim, almost 99%
Percent population urban: 28.3%
Percent population rural: 71.7%
Gross national product: $470 million
   Per capita GNP: $130
   Per capita GNP growth rate: −1.1% (1970–1977)
Inflation rate: not available

The Somali Democratic Republic, commonly called Somalia, holds the strategic key to the Indian Ocean in the eastern Horn of Africa. Somalia is one of the world's poorest countries. Measures to promote economic self-sufficiency along socialist lines have the highest priority in the nation, whose natural environment provides meager resources for human life.

Somalia comprises the former British Somaliland Protectorate and the Italian-administered UN trust territory of Somalia. The British sector attained independence on June 25, 1960, and 5 days later merged with the Italian territory to form the Somali Democratic Republic.

Somalia covers an area of approximately 246,199 square miles (637,657 sq km) on the eastern Horn of Africa. Roughly the size of Texas, it is occupied by almost 3.7 million people, about 28.3 percent of whom live in urban areas. The country stretches along the southern shore of the Gulf of Aden to the easternmost corner of Africa, Cape Guardafui, and then for 1,180 miles (1,898 km) southwestward along the Indian Ocean to Ras Chiamboni. Somalia's neighbors are Djibouti to the northwest, Ethiopia to the west, and Kenya to the southwest. In the hot, sandy plains along the northern coast the limestone plateaus of the Mijertins rise to 7,500 feet (3,286 m) with an average annual rainfall ranging from 4 to 20 inches (10 to 50 cm). These lofty mountains together with sand dunes, valleys, regions of thorn growth, tsetse-infested swamps, and lifeless wastes (inhabited in a few places by nomads) make much of the terrain unsuitable for permanent settlement.

In the low-lying, humid and fertile southern extremity, there is enough rain [14 to 25 inches (36 to 64 m) a year] to permit grazing and sedentary cultivation. The country's two main rivers, the Juba and Webi Shebelle, originate in Ethiopian Ogaden. The 1,250-mile (2,011-km) -long Webi Shebelle vanishes in the marshy malarial swamps of the coastal areas, before reaching a submerged coral reef along the sea. The Juba River, which is 750 miles (206 km) long, wanders through the southern areas and ultimately disappears in the sea.

Semitic in origin, the Somali people penetrated the Horn of Africa centuries ago, possibly from southern Arabia. They replaced earlier pre-Hamitic Negroids and intermarried with the Hamite people to form their own homogeneous groups. The Somali resemble the pagan Galla, with whom they share many cultural and linguistic bonds. The Somali now compose more than 90 percent of the eastern Horn's population. They trace their ancestry to the families of Saab and Samaal, believed to have been members of the Prophet Muhammad's Qurayish tribe.

The pastoralist Samaal, an egalitarian and homogeneous group, occupy most of Somalia. Proud and warlike, they are ambivalent about the agriculturalist Saab, who are heterogeneous and less conflict-oriented and inhabit the regions between the Juba and Webi Shebelle rivers. The nomadic Samaal outrank the Saab who settled in Somalia some eight centuries ago and based their lineage structure on two classes—high and low—with a patrilineal kinship system.

Samaal clans constitute the most important political substructure. Their chiefs hold the title of sultan and perform primarily symbolic functions. Ethnic politics exhibit neither permanence nor stability. Land and access to water are considered essential for the survival of the clan. Since land is thought to be a gift from God, its use is restricted to those individuals who labor for its development. Social relationships, including interethnic loyalties and the settlement of conflicts, are based on material wealth. Conflicts that result in personal injury or death must be settled in writing by all parties.

Between 1973 and 1977, Somalia's GNP per capita income was estimated at $110. Somalia's economy is essentially rural; more than 80 percent of the population live on a subsistence level, based on income from animal husbandry. In 1977, the estimated relative poverty-level income per capita in urban and rural areas was $73 and $35, respectively. During the same period, 25 percent of the urban population were living below the poverty level; in rural areas, 30 percent were living in poverty.

The conditions of life for the cattle-raising nomads are precarious because of shortages of water and limited pasturage. Sources of water are varied. In northern and central Somalia, deep and shallow wells and artificial ponds are used seasonally or on a permanent basis. Home wells are owned through lineage. For rural Somalis, camels and sheep are the mainstay of the economy. If cattle are kept for reasons of prestige and power they become economic liabilities rather than assets. Intertribal conflicts over the ownership of herds and flocks are not infrequent. Claims and counterclaims result in disputes and inflict added burdens on the nomads' strained existence. The number of animals owned by nomads vary. Women own their own flocks, usually sheep and goats. At birth, a male member of the family is given a gift of a camel or other cattle with which to build a modest fortune in the future.

Until January 1973, the absence of a written language remained Somalia's greatest impediment to progress. In 1972, 95 percent of the population were illiterate. In 1977, however, adult literacy rose to an estimated 50 percent, according to Somali government figures. That year, 45 percent of the population were less than 14 years old. The Latinized Somali language is Hamitic, akin to Shoa Galla, with a considerable Arabic influence. Most Somali, including the ethnic Somali in Djibouti, Ethiopia, and Kenya, speak Somali dialects. Swahili is spoken in the south and along the coast; Italian and Arabic are trade languages.

Precolonial Somali education was Koranic, emphasizing Islam. Under British and Italian rule, separate, unequal, and inadequate school systems supervised by French and Italian Catholic missions were established. Today, education is considered the most im-

portant agent of social change. Under the 5-year development program (1974–1978), Somalia appropriated over $31 million for seventeen different educational projects, hoping to accelerate enrollment at all levels of education.

The Somali have adhered faithfully to the orthodox Sunni order of Islam for over 7 centuries. The impact of Islam, however, has not weakened pre-Islamic traditional values. Today, Muslim organizations are found throughout the country.

Since 1971, the government has given priority to primary sectors of the national economy: agriculture, livestock, fisheries and forestry. These sectors have not been developed enough to offset the country's adverse balance of trade. In recent years, the nation has received increasing foreign aid under bilateral and multilateral agreements. In 1977, Somalia's exports amounted to $71.3 million, while its imports totaled $175.1 million.

Somalia's main cash crops are bananas and sugarcane. Maize, sorghum, oilseeds, rice, wheat, cotton, tobacco, and grapefruit are also grown. With the exception of bananas, the products are grown for local consumption. In 1976, the government spend $16.5 million to diversify and reorganize the outmoded agricultural sector. Salination, the aging of the land, and a drought that lasted from 1972 to 1975 resulted in declining production. The adverse impact of the drought was felt also in the livestock sector, which includes cattle, sheep, goats, camels, various skins and hides, and meats. Under a short-term 5-year development program (1974–1978), the government intensified its efforts to improve the possibilities for livestock marketing.

With the second longest coastline in Africa, Somalia has an enormous commercial potential in sea resources. In 1973, the Ministry of Fisheries and Marines was established to expand the fishing industry, which had remained undeveloped since independence. Today, inadequate fishing equipment, limited

In a land of uncertain rainfall where water is invaluable, women and children wash at a water hole on the arid plain. (Photo: United Nations/Rice.)

local seafood consumption, the absence of modern fishing ports, and the shortage of trained fishermen impede the expansion of fisheries. In recent years, the United Nations, the World Bank, the Soviet Union, and Sweden have helped Somalia to develop its marine resources. In 1976. Somalia's fish production exceeded 76,000 tons (68,400 t).

Economic prospects for Somalia's mineral resources remain bleak because none of the known resources can be developed profitably. The Ministry of Mining recently studied the commercial potential of existing resources, including gypsum in Berbera and iron ore in Bur Galan and Daimir. The iron-ore deposits are estimated to have a potential reserve of 170 million tons (154 million t), most of which are considered unmarketable.

In view of the general water shortage, a survey of groundwater resources is continuing, and the government is funding projects for deep and shallow wells and basins. In 1977, probably only 38 percent of the population had access to safe drinking water.

Somalia depends on external sources of energy to satisfy its development requirements. In 1977, its oil imports amounted to $38.7 million. Recent energy development programs include the completion of oil depots at Berbera, Kismayu, and Mogadishu. Geological surveys for land and offshore exploration of oil, natural gas, and other energy resources have had little success. Hydroelectric projects on the Juba River, producing 5 million watts of energy potential, together with the Fanole hydroelectric project, have minimized dependence on external energy sources.

The Somali labor force is estimated at 1.25 million, 29.4 percent of whom are women. Of the labor force 77 percent are employed in agriculture and 7 percent in industry. It is estimated that by 1980 public as well as private sectors will absorb about 1.4 million workers.

Data on Somali health conditions are minimal. Available information indicates that the nation faces major health problems. Pulmonary tuberculosis, particularly in rural areas, malaria, and various contagious and communicable diseases have had disabling effects on national development. Lately, the incidence of mental illness has exceeded the nation's available treatment facilities. Malnutrition, parasitic diseases, leprosy, tetanus, venereal disease, and trachoma have impaired the nation's health. In 1974, it was estimated that 60 percent of the mortality rate was due to communicable diseases. In 1977, life expectancy was 41 years.

The initial European contact with Somalia took place during the sixteenth century when the adventurous Portuguese reached Berbera. During the seventeenth century, the Portuguese were replaced by Arab traders. In the arbitrary partition of the African Horn at the end of the nineteenth century, Somalia became the object of intense rivalry among the leading European powers: Britain, France, and Italy. British rule in Somalia began in 1884 when Anglo-Somali commercial treaties were signed. A year later, France concluded a treaty of friendship with the Somali clans of Dir and Issa, reinforcing earlier treaties that included the cession of their lands to France. By 1888, the Anglo-French agreements had defined their respective spheres of influence.

Italian expansion into Somalia began when Italy established a protectorate in 1889. In 1891 and 1894,

A woman takes care of her goats; in Somalia, women own their own flocks of sheep or goats, an asset in a land where animal husbandry supports more than 80 percent of the people. (Photo: United Nations/ Rice.)

the governments of Britain and Italy delimited common boundaries for their respective Somali protectorates, which made Ogaden dependent on Italy and Haud subject to British domination. Ogaden, occupied by the pastoralist Somali for centuries, became an object of dispute between Italy and Ethiopia.

In 1941, the British defeated the Italian forces invading Somaliland and established a British military and, later, civilian administration. During the British occupation of the Italian East African Empire, from 1942 to 1948, Ogaden was united with Somalia. The Anglo-Ethiopian treaty of 1948 set a provisional administrative line as the boundary between Somalia and the former Italian Somaliland. Somalia became independent in 1960, merging with Italian Somaliland to form the Somali Republic.

On October 21, 1969, a military coup ousted the last of three multiparty civilian regimes that had governed Somalia since independence. Once in power, the government of Muhammad Siad Barre suspended the constitution and issued a declaration known as the first charter, which outlined plans for economic and cultural development based on social justice and the elimination of illiteracy, poverty, and corruption. The second charter advocated scientific socialism and self-reliance. On July 1, 1976, the Somali Socialist Revolutionary Party, a Soviet-style party, assumed the government functions that had been assigned to the Supreme Revolutionary Council.

Somalia is a member of the United Nations and the Organization of African Unity. Its foreign policy advocates nonalignment, positive neutrality, support for international solidarity, and national liberation movements. It opposes colonialism and neocolonialism and maintains diplomatic relations with both Western and Communist states. The nation also has close ties with the Arab world.

The Somali are extremely nationalistic. In recent years, their efforts to unite Somali-populated regions in portions of Ethiopia, Kenya, and Djibouti have intensified. Territorial claims to the Ogaden sector of southeastern Ethiopia, about 80,000 square miles (207,200 sq km) and allegedly inhabited by some 500,000 Somali, and disputes over northeastern Kenya, nearly 94,000 square miles (243,460 sq km) and allegedly populated by about 100,000 ethnic Somali, led to bloody armed conflicts. Somalia's 8-month armed clash with Ethiopia and Ogaden, supported by external sources, ended on March 9, 1978.

After more than 70 years of European colonial rule and almost 2 decades of postindependence economic hardship and political instability, the Somali are feeling the pressure of development. Massive efforts to expand various undeveloped sectors of the nation's economy will continue if internal, regional, and international political factors permit. Somalia faces the arduous task of economic reconstruction with limited capital and meager inland mineral resources. It requires continuing and substantial foreign aid.

The future infusion of foreign aid will depend in large part on Somalia's internal political balance and on its ability to cooperate with its neighbors. Massive Soviet military aid to Ethiopia has undermined the balance of power in the area.

During the next decades, the nation may develop projects in agriculture, livestock, and fisheries, but the society will remain essentially pastoral, poor, and dependent on foreign aid. Lack of capital and acute shortages of trained workers and of technical facilities impede national progress. Livestock, marine resources, and hydroelectric projects remain the country's best prospects for long-range development programs.

Feraidoon Shams B.

Sudan

(Democratic Republic of the Sudan)

Area: 967,000 sq mi (2,505,813 sq km)
Population: 17.3 million
   Density: 18 per sq mi (7 per sq km)
   Growth rate: 2.6% (1970–1977)
Percent of population under 14 years of age: 43%
Infant deaths per 1,000 live births: 132
Life expectancy at birth: 42 years
Leading causes of death: tropical diseases, bilharziasis, some ethnic violence.
Ethnic composition: Afro-Arab, Negroid African
Languages: Arabic, English, African dialects
Literacy: 15–20%
Religions: Muslim 70%, animist 20%, Christian 10%
Percent population urban: 10% (est)
Percent population rural: 90% (est)
Gross national product: $5.54 billion
   Per capita GNP: $320
   Per capita GNP growth rate: 2.5% (1970–1977)
Inflation rate: in urban areas 20%; in rural areas 1%

The Democratic Republic of the Sudan is a microcosm of Africa. It occupies the largest territory of any state on the continent, and within its borders it harbors a variety of peoples who represent—in pure form and in mixtures—almost every racial community in Africa. In ethnic, geographic, and political terms, the Sudan is a crossroad of Africa.

Compared to its potential, however, the Sudan is still underdeveloped. Its major assets are the huge areas of relatively fertile ground and a considerable potential income from animal husbandry and marine resources. But it must obtain large-scale foreign capital investment to create the necessary infrastructure. This will be difficult because of the widespread skepticism of individual nations and multilateral donors, who worry about the stagnation of the Sudan's economy and the specter of political instability.

The Sudan covers almost 967,000 square miles (2.5 million sq km); it borders two Arab and six black African states and faces Saudi Arabia across the Red Sea. Because of its position, the Sudan's political elites act as a sort of bridge between the larger Arab states and the African states; at the same time, its government is involved in a myriad of cross-border tribal conflicts and problems of regional dissidents and secessionist movements in almost every neighboring state.

The country exhibits geographical variety, from the desert expanses in the north to the flat plains of the heartland and the rolling hills and mountain ranges along the western, southern, and eastern borders. Soils also vary, from sandy to tropical, with a wide range of vegetation in direct proportion to the annual rainfall, from desert scrubs in the northern region to lusher and thicker vegetation in the south, featuring steppe, savanna, bush, and thick jungle.

Yet two geographical factors predominate: the vast size—vast cotton fields, vast deserts, and vast swamps, making communications an overwhelming problem—and the Nile River. It is hard to overestimate the importance of the Nile (and its tributaries) to inhabitants of the countries through which it flows; it is a giver and taker of life, a natural barrier to expanding armies and raiding tribes, and the subject of international conferences and treaties. The Nile exudes an undefinable magic; it attracts both nomads and pilgrims from West Africa—the so-called

Using modern tractors, men cut sisal that will be processed into rope at a nearby factory. (Photo: United Nations/AM.)

Fellata—to settle along its banks, and it presumably casts a spell over those who have lived there for any length of time, in accordance with the ancient proverb that says, "He who has drunk from the River, shall return."

In the Sudan, climate regulates daily life. The Sudanese rise with the sun and normally begin work at 6 a.m. They retire around 2 p.m., when the heat has reached its maximum, almost never under 100°F (38°C) in the shade, in a country where shade is rare except inside buildings. (The only exceptions are office workers; civil servants arrive later at their desks and leave earlier, while business employees usually work a few extra hours in the evening.) Shortly before sunset, social activities (including politicking) begin. For various reasons, the Sudanese approach after-five activities with far greater vigor, enthusiasm, charm, and skill than they exhibit during working hours.

The annual rainy season also affects everyone who lives in the rain belt (from roughly 16° north latitude southward) except those living in the capital. Because there are virtually no all-weather roads, towns and smaller settlements are cut off from one another because no vehicles can move through the mud. Even rail service is heavily curtailed because of frequent washouts along the old-fashioned, narrow-gauge tracks. Farther south, the rainy season lasts longer, and all communications come to an absolute standstill. Plains turn into swamps, and swamps and rivers become immense lakes.

In contrast, the nonsedentary population—about 15 percent—welcomes the humidity-bearing southern trade winds. During the rainy season, the low reserves in the water holes and baobab trees are replenished, the scorched central plains sprout tall elephant grass at incredible speed, and the nomads once again change direction in their wandering in pursuit of pasture.

The country derives its name from the Arabic *bilad al-sudan*, i.e., "land of the blacks." Indeed, from an Arab perspective the Sudanese population appears black. The Sudanese, however, are acutely aware of nuances in the pigmentation of various ethnic groups. These nuances, plus other physical features and some tribal markings, distinguish the Sudanese in terms of ethnic origin. In fact, ethnic affiliation is one of the most important social identities, only less important than geographic location (village, hamlet, small town) and membership in the extended family. Ethnic affiliation is understandably of prime importance in this enormous country, where the nature of the terrain severely limits communication.

From a demographic point of view, the Sudan contains the most heterogeneous society in Africa and the Middle East, with divisions along ethnic, tribal, geographic, linguistic, and sectarian lines. There are more than 140 different spoken languages in the Sudan. Although some Sudanese are Arabs, some Hamites, and some Negroid Africans, most Sudanese are a mixture of two or all three groups. One authoritative source claims that there are 56 different groups in the Sudan, comprising 597 ethnic subgroups.

Sudanese are usually described as northerners or southerners. Northerners are almost all inhabitants of the 12 northern provinces. Racially Afro-Arab, they are overwhelmingly Muslim (Sunni) in religion and can speak Arabic. These factors have shaped a degree of identity among northerners and have created a common cultural heritage resembling that of other Arabs. Thus the Sudan has been an active member of the Arab League since its independence in 1956, yet remains distinctly Sudanese.

The southerners—living roughly south of 10° north latitude—have been protected from invasion by geographic and climatic barriers. Because of the difficult terrain, larger groups have scattered into smaller units with localized identities. All except for a very few educated southerners regard anyone outside their own clan as a potential rival or enemy. Clashes between southern groups have been fairly common until recently. Only in the last two decades have southerners developed a common animosity toward the new imperialists—the Arabs from the north who have supplanted the British as colonizers in the south. Animosity between northerners and southerners erupted in 17 years of civil war, from August 1955 to March 1972; an agreement accepted by both parties resulted in regional autonomy for the south.

Religious cleavages in the Sudan are almost as pronounced as ethnic conflicts, and, in terms of political impact, they are probably more damaging. In the northern Sudan, Islam is based on Tariqah, a type of sectarian organization. The most important Tariqahs are the Mahdiyyah (followers of the house of the Mahdi, also known as Ansar), from the central and western Sudan, and the Khatmiyyah, from the north and east. The suspicion and distrust between members of these two sects can hardly be overstated; each produced a major political party in the pre- and immediate postindependence era, drawing its support almost entirely from the Tariqah membership.

Between 10 and 20 percent of the southern population are Christian (roughly four-fifths Roman Catholic and the remainder Protestant). Most southerners are animists who worship a variety of deities, especially their ancestral spirits. Partly because these religions tend to be localized, political parties and movements in the south are based more on geographic and ethnic than on religious loyalties.

Compared with most other third world nations, the rural-urban distinction is not so important in the Sudan. At most, 10 percent of the overall population live in the six localities that might be characterized as normal cities: the capital area (Greater Khartoum), the lone port (Port Sudan), the railroad hub (Atbara), and three of the significant regional capitals (Wad Medani, El Obeid, and Juba). In these towns and even in metropolitan Khartoum, rural types of housing and lifestyle coexist with (and frequently overshadow) the urban indicators—modern transportation and govern-

ment offices. In fact, only a relatively small part of Khartoum Town and a similarly small portion of Khartoum North (in the industrial area) are reminiscent of urban life. Most urban dwellers even in the capital live in housing similar to housing in rural parts of the north and shop at markets that are distinguished from their rural counterparts more by size than by the quality of their wares. Thus, statistically, urban Sudan retains many rural features, and there has been only a relatively moderate population increase in the capital in the two decades since independence.

To be sure, the capital area, comprising three towns (Khartoum, Khartoum North, and Omdurman), has well over 1 million inhabitants, but its growth pales in comparison with other North African capitals. There is relatively less pressure from the countryside, because of the abundance of fertile land in proportion to the overall population, and less pull from the capital, because urban centers offer little more than cinemas, football clubs, and a few educational and health facilities.

Rural and private education in the Sudan depend on local enterprise; despite the tremendous efforts of the Ministry of Education and the soaring number of students of both sexes enrolled in public schools, overall literacy remains under 30 percent. Modern health care is virtually unavailable outside the principal towns, and there are abysmally few hospital beds. In the cities, medical treatment is dispensed at small clinics run by one doctor and an assistant; in rural areas, midwives and medicine men provide per-

Migrant subsistence farmers pound grain in front of their hut; nomadic and seminomadic people have little incentive to move into a more modern economy. (Photo: ILO/United Nations/ J. Mohr.)

haps 90 percent of the medical services. Not surprisingly, life expectancy is low, increasing from 30 years in 1960 to 42 years in 1975.

Despite the hardships faced by the average Sudanese, the country has been producing an admittedly small but qualitatively impressive elite. The top civil service posts are filled by well-educated graduates of the reputable University of Khartoum, many of whom receive attractive offers to work in senior positions for the governments of the oil-rich states on the Arabian Peninsula. Sudanese professors and college deans are working in many universities in West Africa and the Persian Gulf states. In contrast, the merchant class is undistinguished; except for a few large family-run enterprises, most businesses are small, and their proprietors are distinctly middle class. There is little, if any, conspicuous consumption.

The agricultural sector plays an overwhelming role in the Sudanese economy, and cotton is the outstanding cash crop. Approximately 85 percent of the labor force are engaged in agriculture, livestock production, forestry, and fishing, 6 percent in manufacturing, and 5 percent in services.

Sudanese cultivators—somehow the terms "farmers" and "peasants" seem equally inappropriate—can be divided into two groups: the large masses who are engaged in subsistence farming, and those affiliated with government-sponsored agricultural schemes, of which the Gezira (between the Blue and White Niles) is the largest and the most famous. Nomadic and seminomadic people can easily engage in subsistence peasant farming and animal breeding; this limits their incentive to shift to the modern economy. The cultivators affiliated with government schemes are far better organized. In Gezira, Rahad, and Khashm el-Girba, they are directly supervised by government inspectors, and their incentive for maximum output is substantial. For example, the Gezira tenants have an impressive history of economic productivity and political impact. Over the years, the Sudan has derived roughly 75 percent of its foreign exchange from its sales of cotton and cotton by-products. In addition, about 40 percent of all government revenue is based on cotton sales, virtually all from the Gezira. Other foreign exchange earners are sesame seeds, groundnuts, camels and cattle, oil cake, hides and leather goods, and gum arabic.

In the 1970s, the government recognized the need to diversify the economy, and development plans were drawn up to try to increase the production of cereals, sugar, tea, tobacco, and canned fruits. Toward that end, massive schemes involving mechanized farming, large-scale cattle ranches, and the resettlement of some rural groups have been started or are near completion. The World Bank, the Kuwait Fund for Arab Economic Development, and the Arab Fund for Economic and Social Development have poured over $10 billion into the necessary infrastructure, hoping that after the mid-1980s the Sudan may become a regional "food-basket," especially for the arid but oil-rich neighboring Arab states.

The greatest obstacle to this long-term goal has been the sluggish economy, which has been unable to generate the foreign exchange funds needed to finance imports and to pay off short-term debts on loans. In fact, the Sudan's inability to meet these short-term obligations led to the devaluation of the currency in mid-1978 and to an alarming drop in the country's creditworthiness. Even worse, the all-out rush into private and public development schemes produced both unbalanced growth and a shortage of supplies, leading to a shortage of basic food commodities in major areas for the first time in the country's modern history.

The loss of international confidence has been compounded by serious questions about political stability, a perennial worry since independence, equally applicable to the central government's ability to survive and to the simmering conflict between the northern and southern regions. Originally a collection of small states, the Sudan had been conquered and unified by the Egyptian Khedive on behalf of the Ottoman Sultan in 1820–1821 and remained under Turkish Egyptian control until 1885, when Khartoum fell to the forces of the Sudanese Mahdi. From 1885 to 1898, the Sudanese experienced self-rule under the Mahdi and his successor. In 1898, a joint Egyptian-British army reconquered the Sudan. In 1956, it became independent of Great Britain and Egypt.

Although the current regime under Ja'far Numeiri has been in power for more than 10 years—since the revolution of May 1969—it has been challenged by more than a half-dozen coup attempts and almost constant plotting, which has led to the purge of countless civil servants and military officers.

One of the Sudan's major dilemmas is the difficulty of accommodating the idiosyncratic demands and expectations of the various groupings in this highly pluralistic society. Sustained progress in economic and social development and national reconciliation and unification depend on strong centralized leadership. Given the Sudanese penchant for independence and rather well-developed democratic practices on the local level, military rule does not sit well with most citizens, especially educated groups in the larger towns. The Sudanese government, therefore, must try to create a political system that is at least reasonably open and can accommodate local interests without dissipating the momentum needed for economic development, especially in the poorer regions of the south, east, and west. The balancing act is challenging, and it is being carefully watched by observers in the Sudan and abroad.

Peter Bechtold

Tanzania
(United Republic of Tanzania)

Area: mainland: 362,688 sq mi (939,362 sq km); Zanzibar
  and Pemba: 1,020 sq mi (2,641 sq km)
Population: mainland: 16.9 million; Zanzibar and Pemba:
  400,000
  Density: 47 per sq mi (18 per sq km)*
  Growth rate: 3% (1970–1977)*
Percent of population under 14 years of age: 46%
Infant deaths per 1,000 live births: 160 (1970)
Life expectancy at birth: 44.5 years
Leading causes of death: contagious diseases,
  malnutrition
Ethnic composition: 120 different groups
Languages: Swahili (official), English
Literacy: 40–50% (1976)
Religions: Christian 35%; Muslim 35%; animist 30%
Percent population urban: less than 10%
Percent population rural: over 90%
Gross national product: $3.9 billion*
  Per capita GNP: $230*
  Per capita GNP growth rate: 2.1% (1970–1977)*
Inflation rate: not available

Tanzania is struggling to reconcile its stalwart egalitarian commitment with its meager natural resources and its absolutely low standard of living. Enjoying a real and strong sense of national unity, mainland Tanzania (once known as Tanganyika) has opted for an austere, socialist strategy. Since independence in 1962, its economy has moved in fits and starts, but there has been a widespread increase in the availability of social services. It has not yet proved possible to stimulate the economy without again stirring the class and social disparities that President Julius Nyerere is so anxious to downplay.

Mainland Tanzania is almost the size of Texas and New Mexico combined, with an area of 362,688 square miles (939,362 sq km) and a population of 16.9 million and increasing by nearly 3 percent a year. The islands of Zanzibar and Pemba, which formally united with the mainland in 1964, have a combined area of 1,020 square miles (2,641 sq km) and a total population of 400,000. The islands are 20 miles (32 km) off the Tanzanian coast, but in many respects they are worlds apart. For all practical purposes, Zanzibar is actually a separate state.

Tanzania's geography matches its demography. Nearly two-thirds of this huge, empty country is a dry, semiarid plateau, infested with animal and human trypanosomiasis for which there is yet neither an effective prophylactic nor a cure. The clusters of population are found along the long Indian Ocean coast and in the temperate southern and Mount Kilimanjaro highlands and the swampy plains that border Lakes Victoria and Tanganyika. These clusters of population are separated by vast tracts of wasteland,

*Figures refer to mainland only.

mangrove swamps fringing the coastal belt, and land plagued by the tsetse fly, the vector for trypanosomiasis. Geographically, Tanzania is an unattractive piece of real estate.

The coast is hot and humid with temperatures ranging from 80 to 95°F (27 to 35°C), cooled by Indian Ocean breezes. There is ample rain from March through May and in November and December, but the region suffers from poor, sandy soils. The central plateau is hot and dry, subject to periodic droughts and inadequate underground water supplies. Along the northern, southern, and western edges of the country highland area, climates are temperate or subtropical, and rainfall is ample.

Ethnically, Tanzania consists of 120 different groups of which the largest, the Sukuma who live near Lake Victoria, number only 1.2 million. No one ethnic group dominates the country, nor does any combination of several groups. Swahili language and culture, initially found on the coast, have spread nationally, facilitating ethnic intermarriage and a genuine sharing of customs. The achievement of substantial national cultural unity is perhaps Tanzania's most important postindependence accomplishment.

Population growth is a problem, but as yet there is no national effort to reduce fertility. Family planning services are available through government and private health programs, but they win slow acceptance in a society where life expectancy is only 42, infant mortality is very high, and extra hands can still be used to till the soil.

Tanzania still has an economy which is highly dependent on the export of agricultural products such as sisal, cotton, coffee, tea, and cashew nuts. Tourism, about which the government is ambivalent, brings in some revenue, although much less than in Kenya, in spite of Tanzania's beautiful parks and other attractions. Tanzanite and other precious gemstones are minor resources, and large deposits of noncoking coal in the south have not proved economical. All fossil fuels are imported at high cost and the cutting of firewood has caused a deforestation problem in several areas.

Industry is confined to the coast and produces consumer goods, such as textiles, mostly for the national market. Tanzania experienced a large and growing trade deficit with Kenya during the years of the East African Common Market and has practically closed the border to protect its home industries. Limited efforts have been made to develop small-scale rural industries and technologies, but these are still at an experimental stage. Per capita income was estimated at $166 in 1975, making Tanzania one of the poorest countries in Africa and the world.

In spite of its low level of economic development, Tanzania has a serious problem of urbanization. The capital, Dar es Salaam, has been growing at more than 6 percent annually, twice that of any other city in Tanzania, and has 5 times the population of Tanga, its sister port. A colorful and attractive port city, Dar is a beacon attracting the young from all over the country. The government has tried a variety of measures to curb the growth of Dar, even forcing the unemployed to return to their home areas. In recent years, it has selected the central plateau town of Dodoma, 700 miles (1,126 km) up-country from Dar, as a second capital. However, most government and commercial services remain on the coast; and Dodoma still lacks the infrastructure to attract the young.

Domestic transport is a major problem in Tanzania. The central railway line linking Dar to Lake Victoria was built by the Germans before World War I, and its equipment is obsolete. In this vast country, building all-weather roads is an enormous expense, and maintaining them is even more costly. The road south to the Zambian border from Dar was built with U.S. aid and carries a murderous load of heavy truck traffic. The famous TanZam Railway (TAZARA) built by the Chinese at a cost of $400 million to link the port of Dar to the Zambian copper mines has not been practical. Zambia prefers to export copper south through South Africa; the rail line has not generated much

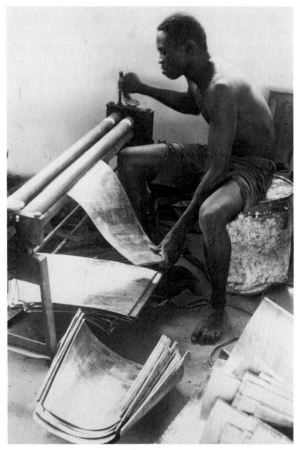

Small-scale local industry is being encouraged; a worker rolls out metal in a sheet metal factory. (Photo: United Nations/ Y. Lehmann.)

new commerce along its tracks, and its operating costs are high.

An even more important transport barrier is the lack of secondary and tertiary roads that would enable farmers to market their produce. In recent years, Tanzania has been a major net importer of grains, while transport bottlenecks keep local products from reaching their markets. Because imports of new passenger cars are prohibited and foreign exchange for buses and trucks is scarce, the deterioration of the vehicle stock is also a major problem.

Tanzania shares borders with Mozambique, Malawi, Burundi, Rwanda, Uganda, and Kenya. Although peaceful itself, Tanzania has had troubles at one time or another with all its neighbors. Hence national security is a concern, enhanced by Tanzania's commitment to the liberation of southern Africa from white minority rule and its position as one of the frontline states (states in direct conflict with apartheid South Africa).

At various times, conflicts between the Hutu and the Tutsi for power in Burundi and Rwanda have brought thousands of refugees into Tanzania. On a lesser scale, political violence in Malawi has brought a small Malawian refugee community into Tanzania, with some Tanzanian government support.

Relations with Kenya have been difficult because of the economic disparities between the two countries and the Tanzanian conviction that Kenya benefited at Tanzania's expense from the East African Community. President Nyerere's failure to bring about an East African Federation in 1963 led to a series of changes in the East African Common Market and changes in common air, railway, port, postal, and other services. By 1975, the common market and services had been abandoned, and Tanzania was operating at considerable cost its own railway, ports, and postal service. It remains to be seen whether the political changes in Kenya and Uganda in 1978 and 1979 will lead to a renewal of East African cooperation, an important but not essential Tanzanian goal.

During the 1962 through 1974 liberation struggle in Mozambique, Tanzania provided sanctuary and support for the Mozambique Liberation Front (FRELIMO). Since independence, Tanzania and Mozambique have continued to enjoy close, friendly relations based on the shared values and world views of their leaders. Air and sea links between the two countries have been initiated, but road travel is still difficult because of the remote borders.

Although Tanzania's land border with Uganda is less than 100 miles (160 km), it is this border that has been the most troubled. The coup that ousted Ugandan President Milton Obote in 1971 sent him into active exile in Dar. Nyerere soon clashed with Ugandan President Idi Amin, and their disputes precipitated the breakup of the East African Community. When Nyerere denounced the horrors of the Amin regime, Amin retaliated with threats, raids, and mock raids; finally, in 1977–1978, he launched a full-scale invasion of Bukoba in northwest Tanzania, 2,000 miles (3,218 km) from Dar. With a group of Ugandan exiles, the Tanzanian army finally invaded Uganda in March 1979, and 2 months later it swept Amin and his Libyan mercenaries from power. The rehabilitation effort in the war-torn Bukoba area will be long and expensive, but in 1979, for the first time in years, Tanzania enjoyed cordial relations with its two principal East African neighbors.

In spite of war and economic austerity, Tanzania's social and cultural life has made impressive strides since independence. Swahili and English are both official languages, but Swahili has become a national lingua franca. Government encouragement has promoted a Swahili press, a Swahili radio (Tanzania has no television), and an exciting spurt of Swahili poetry, drama, prose, and history. President Nyerere, known as *Mwalimu*, meaning "teacher" in Swahili, has translated Shakespeare into the national language. All primary school instruction is in Swahili, and primary enrollment as a percentage of the age-group rose from 24 percent in 1960 to 57 percent in 1975.

The emergence of a national language and culture has been promoted through the army, a national youth service for both sexes, and the media. Although ethnic identities remain important, Tanzanians from all parts of the country are acquiring national identities reflected in dress styles, in the use of Swahili, in the easy movement of government employees to new posts, and in other ways.

Some 90 percent of Tanzanians are rural, raising livestock and cultivating maize, cassava, bananas and other food crops. Protein deficiency is widespread, and malnutrition, especially after weaning, is common. The government and international organizations are experimenting with primary health care centers and preventive medicine to bring low-cost medical services to the rural population. Similarly, boreholes are being drilled to provide rural people with a safe and reliable water supply.

Except for the coffee-growing Chagga, who live on the slopes of 19,340-foot (5,879-m) Mount Kilimanjaro and 15,000-foot (4,572-m) Mount Meru, most Tanzanians traditionally have not lived in villages. Instead, pastoralists like the Sukuma and Gogo have followed their animals on regular migratory paths. Cultivators like the Nyakusa of the Southern Highlands or the coastal Zaramo built their homes next to their fields. A widely scattered rural population living in homesteads rather than villages has offered major obstacles to the delivery of economic services and the mobilization of human resources.

Since 1962, government measures have encouraged Tanzanians to form new communal villages. In a series of eloquent books and speeches, President Nyerere has made the case for *ujamaa*, "African village familyhood," or "socialism" in terms of traditional practices and modern needs. First relying on expensive new settlement villages, then turning to voluntary and at times coerced "villagization," the govern-

ment has tried to change the physiogonomy of the countryside. It is still early to judge the results, although most Tanzanians have moved closer together. Some villages are operated along communal or cooperative lines or both; others are simply regroupings of people closer to centers, clinics, and water holes. It is not clear whether agricultural productivity has been encouraged; lack of transport and roads remains a serious problem.

The Tanzanian approach to land and villages is the antithesis of that of Kenya, with its individual freehold capitalist system. Tanzania has abolished freehold land tenure and has nationalized most retail and wholesale trade. The Asian merchant population, which once numbered 120,000, has dwindled to a few thousand.

Are Tanzanians happier in their ujamaa villages? It is hard to say, because conditions vary so sharply from village to village and from region to region. The Tanganyika African National Union (TANU), the single party that mobilized the preindependence nationalist movement, is stagnant in some villages and active in others. Distinctions of wealth and possession of property have been replaced in some villages by new distinctions based on party or government bureaucracies. Some argue that the lack of material incentive is a major factor retarding rural output; others contend that cooperative and communal efforts are more efficient than individual capitalism. Concerned to limit the growth of privileged groups and classes, the government has alternately removed and restored rural incentives, such as fixed versus free prices for maize and other crops.

Nyerere's evocation of an idyllic African past has its echoes in Tanzania's (then Tanganyika's) own past. Louis Leakey's excavations at Olduvai Gorge on the Serengeti Plains date the human race back at least 2 million years. There is evidence that for many centuries Tanzania's plains were crisscrossed by semi-

Workers pack fish on a boat on Lake Tanganyika. Fishing is a major industry and fish are an important source of protein. (Photo: United Nations/ Y. Lehmann.)

pastoral Bantu groups. Because of problems of transport and communication, isolated settlements that practiced a particular lifestyle were able to persist, even to our times.

Along the coast, the urban Swahili culture emerged nearly 2,000 years ago, a product of Bantu, Arab, and Asian intermingling. The city-states of Kilwa Kivinje, Bagamoyo, and Lindi were trading with the Arabian Peninsula, Persia (now Iran), India, and even China, as well as other states along the Indian Ocean coast. The fifteenth-century Portuguese entry into the Indian Ocean trade and conquest altered but did not upset the balance of power. Eventually, in the mid-nineteenth century, Zanzibar Island under the rule of the sultan of Oman and Zanzibar, emerged dominant over much of the coast. Zanzibar served as the entrepôt center for a flourishing slave trade that devastated the interior and weakened several key ethnic groups.

While Britain took Kenya, Germany settled for Tanganyika in the 1890s colonial division of power. Harsh but efficient German rule lasted until 1918, providing a transport infrastructure, plantation agriculture, and the new capital at the once humble port of Dar es Salaam.

After World War I, the British governed Tanganyika, first as a League of Nations mandate and then (after World War II) as a UN mandate. But Britain was reluctant to invest in a colony that might be taken away, and prospective white settlers were kept at bay while the economy stagnated.

In 1954, TANU launched its nationalist drive under the leadership of schoolteacher Julius Nyerere, one of the first Tanganyikans to study abroad and a practicing Catholic. Taking advantage of the widespread resentment of compulsory colonial rules concerning cultivation, TANU quickly amassed 1 million members and swept a series of preindependence elections. Significantly poorer but more unified than either Kenya or Uganda, Tanganyika achieved independence peacefully on December 9, 1961, with Nyerere as its first and still its only President.

The first years of independence were marked by Tanganyika's failure to achieve an East African Federation and its subsequent desire to make separate trade and services arrangements. An abortive army mutiny in 1964 required British and then Nigerian intervention and revealed the fragility of the new political order. Meanwhile, the island of Zanzibar gained independence in December 1963. Zanzibar's Arab minority government, which was hostile to Nyerere, was overthrown in a lightning coup in January 1964. Seeking to control spreading disorder, Tanganyika and Zanzibar agreed to a loose political union under

the name of Tanzania. Although Zanzibar has a voice in the National Assembly and the Cabinet, Tanzania has little influence on the island, which has moved from a fanatically anti-Arab leadership to a more moderate regime. Exotic Zanzibar still lives on the proceeds of its clove exports, but since 1964 its Arab and Asian elites have been supplanted by Afro-Zanzibaris.

In 1967, Nyerere launched the Arusha Declaration to outline the new policies of self-reliance, ujamaa (communal) villages, and agricultural development. TANU was restructured as a single party that encouraged multiple candidates and open discussion. Limits on wealth, salaries, and inheritance curbed the appetites of the growing government elites. Tanzania became the favorite country of many Western radicals, especially because of its militant support for the liberation of southern Africa. Nyerere earned a deserved reputation as one of Africa's outstanding political leaders.

Yet economic performance has been disappointing, partly because of poor weather and other climatic variables. The civil service and party elites often confuse ideology with gain, and the swollen public sector has been ineffective in delivering goods and services to rural areas. Egalitarianism based on shared poverty does not attract all Tanzanians equally, and there is little room for any political dissent that questions the fundamental tenets of the regime. When resources were diverted for a military buildup against Amin's Uganda, the austerity deepened but was compensated for by Tanzania's decisive military victory.

Tanzania's future is not clear. Given its limited natural resources and manpower restraints, it is difficult to see how Tanzania can achieve rapid, sustainable economic growth. However, some sections of the country, especially the highlands and Dar, and specific sectors of the economy could maintain far higher growth if current controls were relinquished. The price might very well be the precious national unity that has been achieved partly through a shared austerity and poverty.

Nyerere's commitment to egalitarianism is unquestioned, but he has been in power since 1961 and turned 55 in 1980. Whether younger generations share his goals remains to be seen, especially because a stagnant economy maximizes the gains of opportunist behavior. Whether Tanzania's government and party elites if unrestrained would be less avaricious than their Kenyan capitalist counterparts is also an open question. Tanzania may well evolve more pragmatic and less ideological policies on tourism, light industry, and large-scale commerce.

Aaron Segal

Togo
(Republic of Togo)

Area: 21,853 sq mi (56,600 sq km)
Population: 2.4 million
  Density: 110 per sq mi (42 per sq km)
  Growth rate: 2.6% (1970–1977)
Percent of population under 14 years of age: 43%
Infant deaths per 1,000 live births: 121 (1975)
Life expectancy at birth: 40 years (41)
Leading causes of death: malaria
Ethnic composition: Ewe, Mina, Kabre
Languages: French (official), tribal
Literacy: 10%
Religions: traditional 60%; Christian 20%; Muslim 20%
Percent population urban: 10% (est.)
Percent population rural: 90% (est.)
Gross national product: $770 million
  Per capita GNP: $320
  Per capita GNP growth rate: 5.3% (1970–1977)
Inflation rate: not available

Togo, a former German and French colony in West Africa, has followed a stormy political path and remains a politically divided nation. Togo's politics stem from the enforced merger, in one nation, of two radically different ethnic groupings, long at odds with one another, and from the country's tortured history under German, then British, then French rule.

Togo (and Benin) are sandwiched between two far better-known countries—Ghana and Nigeria—both of which have been more successful in attracting foreign investment, and the Togolese as a people have a sense of national insecurity that is often manifested in demonstrations of indifference or feigned superiority toward their neighbors. Most Togolese regret that Togo did not remain the *Meisterkolonie* ("master colony") of Germany, Europe's most successful contemporary nation. But although politicians regularly refer to the nation as a future "West African Switzerland," Togo's resources are limited, and most of its soil is so poor that it is hard for the Togolese even to feed themselves adequately.

Over 360 miles (579 km) long from north to south and only 31 miles (48 km) wide at the coast, about the size of West Virginia, Togo consists of approximately three-fourths of the former *Schutzgebiet* (protectorate) Togo, which was seized by Berlin shortly before the Berlin Conference of 1884–1885.

Occupied in 1914 by French colonial forces coming from neighboring Dahomey (now Benin) and by British colonial forces coming from the neighboring Gold Coast (now Ghana), Togo was divided after World War I into a French-mandate and a British-mandate territory under the League of Nations. The smaller British territory, which was to all intents and purposes administered as a region of the Gold Coast, voted in 1956 to join the Gold Coast, then soon to become independent Ghana. The French-mandate territory,

which had been administered as a separate unit, is now the modern Republic of Togo. Reunificationist irredentism by the Ewe of former British Togo and the southern third of the Republic has created friction with Ghana in the past and may do so again.

Togo is bordered by Ghana, Benin, Upper Volta, and the Atlantic Ocean. The country consists of two savanna plains divided by a modest range of hills. The southern half of the country is adequately watered, but agricultural production is poor, and the principal natural resource is phosphates.

Togo was conceived by the German administration as its Meisterkolonie, and at the time of Germany's eviction in 1914, the Ewe tribe was being trained to staff the administration of South-West Africa (now Namibia), Tanganyika (now the mainland portion of Tanzania), and Cameroon. After the departure of the Germans, Togo's limited economic potential and its status as a League of Nations and UN territory limited its achievements to the export of teachers, administrators, and other white-collar professionals to other parts of French-speaking Africa or to Ghana.

A population of approximately 2.4 million, growing

Workers take a break at a phosphate plant. Phosphate ore is the country's principal export and is mined by a German-led consortium. (Photo: United Nations/BZ/BME.)

at a rate of 2.6 percent annually, includes three main ethnic groups: the Ewe (who are divided by dialect into four groups), the related Mina, and the dominant Kabre of the north. About 10 percent of the population is functionally literate in French, the official language.

Life expectancy is 40 years, largely because more than 35 percent of the children die before the age of 5, directly or indirectly from malaria. Roughly half the population is less than 17 years old. The only towns of significance are Lomé, the capital (with a population of 150,000), Anécho, Atakpamé, Sokodé, Lama-Kara, and Sansanné-Mango.

Islam claims about 20 percent of the population, mostly among the Kabre and other northern tribes. Christianity, especially Roman Catholicism, claims an equal number, almost entirely among the southern Ewe and Mina. About 60 percent of the population follow traditional African religions. Traditional black African family patterns prevail, although the power of paramount and village chiefs has gradually eroded since independence, particularly in the south.

Since 1967, President Etienne Eyadema, an army general, has ruled by decree, on the advice of ministers whom he selects, and without a legislature. The internal administration and the judicial system are patterned on structures introduced by France. Political parties were banned between 1967 and 1969, when a single party was formed, the Togolese People's Rally. Government remains tightly centralized; but, since 1976, all members of Eyadema's Cabinet except himself have been civilians.

Most Togolese are subsistence farmers, although there is a small but rich cocoa-growing area in the southwest. Coconut oil and copra exports have declined because of yellow leaf disease, but some low-grade robusta coffee (for instant coffee) is now exported. A few light industries cater to local consumption.

Most Ewe-Mina folklore of the coast relates to the sea and the salt lagoons, and fishing is a traditional skill. But the lagoons are drying up and are mostly fished out; inshore fishing, by hand trawl, yields only enough for local consumption, and deep-sea fishing has been better capitalized in Ghana and Nigeria. The new 200-mile (322-km) offshore limit will preserve extensive new waters for Togolese fisherman only, but with a 31-mile (48-km) coast, even this blessing is limited.

The country's principal export is phosphate ore, originally mined by a German-led international consortium that was nationalized in 1974. Over 2 million tons (1.8 million t) of the ore are shipped each year. Limestone quarrying is being developed with a view to exporting clinker, starting in 1980. An oil refinery was completed in 1978, and a steel mill in 1979. A sugar mill is planned for 1982. Offshore oil exploration is in progress, and there is prospecting for ura-

At an open market, boys rest among the pigs being offered for sale. (Photo: United Nations/ B. Wolff.)

nium. Foreign firms continue to operate in the distributive and retail sectors, and the country has tourist potential. There are French restaurants and French-managed hotels in Lomé and in a few other cities. In all, there are four international-class hotels. Two more are planned for Lomé, one for Anécho, and another for Lake Togo. Lomé and the nearby coast are favorite resorts for visitors from Ghana and Nigeria. Togo is actively seeking foreign investment in mining, manufacturing, and tourism. The capitalist system has been largely preserved.

Togo's relations with France and Germany stem from historical ties. German rule, although it was efficient by colonial standards, was harsh, and after World War I, French administration was initially welcome. After World War II, however, as the English-speaking West African colonies, including former western Togo, moved toward nationhood, the Togolese southern elites became dissatisfied with France's oft-repeated determination to resist independence. Togo's maverick situation, first as a ward of the League of Nations, then of the United Nations, divided it from the rest of French-speaking Africa. Most Togolese refused to join French African confederal political parties. France was reluctant to invest in the territory on the same scale of investment as in its other colonies, which until 1960 it expected to retain forever.

In the 1950s, Togo's political leadership crystallized in an unusual figure, more at home in a company boardroom than in a party caucus. This was Sylvanus Epiphanio Olympio, the only African to become the general manager of a large foreign enterprise in West Africa. Olympio, who had learned German and Portuguese as well as Ewe in childhood, was the descendant of a Brazilian mulatto slave trader, raised to respect both his African and Portuguese heritages. Having spent 4 years in high school under the British during the 1914 through 1918 occupation of Lomé, Olympio learned English and went on to study at, and graduate from, the London School of Economics. He learned French on his return home and subsequently headed the United Africa Company of Togo, a subsidiary of the global British conglomerate Unilever, for whom he had also worked in the Gold Coast and Nigeria.

His principal political opponent was his brother-in-law, Nicolas Grunitzky, the half-German, half-Kabre brother of Olympio's wife. Grunitzky, a pro-French moderate, became Prime Minister of the territory in 1956. Olympio, as leader of the opposition Togolese Unity Party (favoring reunification of the two Togos), appealed regularly to the United Nations to force France to give Togo independence. Despite heavy French-organized electoral fraud in 1958 in favor of Grunitzky, Olympio, campaigning under the slogan *ablode* (Ewe for "emancipation"), won in a 2 to 1 landslide. French President Charles de Gaulle announced Togo's immediate independence; but Olympio, through the United Nations, forced France to

continue to govern the country for another 2 years and prepare it for independence. This was achieved on April 27, 1960.

Olympio at once began an active courtship of West Germany, appealing to old sentiments about the *Schutzgebiet*, and Bonn agreed to build the country's first deep-water port near Lomé. This German aid and many other factors soured Olympio's relations with France.

In 1962, when France was driven out of Algeria, about 600 Togolese veterans of the French army in Algeria returned to Togo and, with French military encouragement, urged Olympio to expand his 250-man force to absorb them and give them employment. When Olympio refused, they overthrew him in a swift, sharp coup d'état early on Sunday morning, January 13, 1963. Olympio was slain on the grounds of the U.S. embassy, next door to his residence.

The coup leaders invited Grunitzky, then a businessman in the Ivory Coast, to return as figurehead President. However, Grunitzky's post was abolished 4 years later in a bloodless coup led by Lieutenant Colonel Etienne Eyadema, who as an ex-corporal had fired the shot that killed Olympio. Eyadema, relying on military support from the Kabre tribe, seized all the reins of power, later declaring himself President and promoting himself to General. Since then, Eyadema has sought to dampen Ewe passions against his leadership; but irredentism remains a force, and political discontent is fanned by the country's economic difficulties.

Togo's chief trading partner is still France, and the country has an annual trade deficit of about 20 percent. It enthusiastically supports the creation of a regional common market, and Lomé is the headquarters of the Development Fund of the Economic Community of West African States (ECOWAS). A small university has been established.

Greater agricultural self-sufficiency is also sought, and land-tenure reform has begun, but most of the country's land is not particularly fertile. The substantial increase in phosphate prices in the 1970s compensated Togo for increases in oil prices and in finished goods imported from industrialized countries. Phosphate prices have also permitted an annual economic growth rate in recent years of nearly 6 percent, and per capita gross domestic product was estimated in 1978 at $260. But Togo has overextended itself in capital investment and currently has a foreign debt of over $570 million—up about 33 percent in 12 months. The principal expenditures have been on infrastructure, a cement plant, and a higher level of imported consumer goods than most similar African countries.

Togo's principal sources of aid have been France, West Germany, the European Development Fund (EDF), the World Bank, and the United States. United States aid for 1979 is $1.3 billion, together with $2.3 billion worth of food supplied under PL 480, the U.S. food-aid program. China is helping with irrigation, rice-growing and sugar-production projects, and medical facilities. Togo's relations with Bonn are good, despite Togo's recognition of East Germany.

Togo's future is uncertain. Relations with Benin next door are poor, and there is a continual border problem with Ghana. Many of the self-confident, politically fractious Ewe elite have left the country; but sharp divisions between the Ewe-Mina, on the one hand, and the Kabre and other northern ethnic groups, on the other, remain. Eyadema has successfully developed youth, female, farmer, and shopkeeper organizations within his single party, but he continues to depend heavily on the loyalty of his expanded, northern-dominated army to remain in power.

Russell Warren Howe

Uganda
(Republic of Uganda)

Area: 91,076 sq mi (235,889 sq km)
Population: 12.4 million
   Density 136 per sq mi (53 per sq km)
   Growth rate: 3.0% (1970–1977)
Percent of population under 14 years of age: 41%
Infant deaths per 1,000 live births: 110 (1974)
Life expectancy at birth: 50 years
Leading causes of death: infants: protein malnutrition, enteritis, measles, pneumonia; adults: parasitic diseases, e.g., malaria
Ethnic composition: Baganda, Iteso, Basoga, Banyankole, Bakiga, Bagisu, Acholi, Lugbara, Banyoro, Batoro, Karamojong, Alur
Languages: English (official), Swahili, diverse tribal languages
Literacy: 30%
Religions: Christian 50%; Muslim 10%; traditional 40%
Percent population urban: 7%
Percent population rural: 93%
Gross national product: $3.2 billion (1977 est.)
   Per capita GNP: $260 (1977 est.)
   Per capita GNP growth rate: −3.1% (1970–1976)
Inflation rate: 50%

A landlocked country, Uganda shares many of the characteristics of developing African economies. It is heavily dependent on agriculture, and the agricultural export sector has received most attention. Development is grossly uneven and often leads to political decisions that misallocate scarce resources, and the need to redirect the economy has meant a heavy government presence.

Uganda is a country of great natural beauty and ecological diversity and certainly deserves its tourist name, "the pearl of Africa." The beauty of Uganda lies in its well-drained, rolling hills; its majestic mountains of which the Ruwenzori (the snow-capped "mountain of the moon") and Mount Elgon are the most important; its many lakes; and its breathtaking Rift Valley scenery, especially the waterfalls. The Murchison (Kabalega), the Ripon, and the Owen are the important waterfalls, the Owen providing about 90 percent of the hydroelectricity currently generated in the country.

Lake Victoria, 3,938 square miles (10,200 sq km) in area, the world's second largest inland freshwater lake (ranking after Lake Superior), provides the upper waters of the Nile—Victoria Nile, Lake Kyoga, and Lake Kwania. The Rift Valley contains Uganda's elongated lakes—Albert, Edward, and George (the first two renamed Lake Mobutu Sese Seko and Lake Idi Amin Dada, respectively, by President Amin before he was deposed). The equator crosses Uganda at Lake George, a few kilometers south of Entebbe, leaving a disproportionate area of this plateau country in the northern hemisphere. Uganda has an area of 91,076 square miles (235,889 sq km) of which 16,364 square miles (42,383 sq km) is open water and swamps; in size it is comparable to Ghana, the United Kingdom, or West Germany.

Uganda is a part of the heart of Africa—the equatorial zone of permanent low pressure and convectional storms—fringed by mountainous country and separated from the Indian Ocean by 700 miles (1,129 km) of mostly arid land. But Uganda's high altitude, ranging from about 3,000 to 5,000 feet (914 to 1,526 m), combines with the presence of large bodies of water to produce a warm, equable climate. Uganda is well watered. Mean annual rainfall varies from 20 inches (51 cm) to 85 inches (216 cm), and most rains occur around Lake Victoria, near the slopes of Mount Elgon, and in a broad belt of country lying along the northeast to southwest axis. Rainfall varies in amount, duration, and locality, decreasing from the south to the north. The south and the east experience two peaks of rainy season, in April and May and in October and November, allowing two crops a year. The single rainy period occurs from April to October, mostly in the north.

The climate produces a diversified vegetation. There is a small band of equatorial rain forest on the Uganda-Zaire frontier. Most of the southern country is tropical forest, modified by human activities—settlement, agriculture, and bush-burning. Uganda's 5,598 square miles (14,504 sq km) of swampland is full of papyrus. The wooded savanna and parklands of mid-Uganda give way to acacia and cacti woodland in the north. Uganda is a great cattle country and a good farming area.

Uganda is a meeting place of three major African linguistic groups; its human populations and their cultural traditions and orientations are diverse. The indigenous populations of Uganda are often discussed in terms of linguistic categories: the Bantu, the Nilotic, and the Nilo-Hamitic. However, modern Uganda also includes Indians and Pakistanis, who are called "Asians"; there are also Europeans and Arabs.

The ethnically diverse Bantu-speaking peoples account for about 70 percent of the total population. They occupy the whole southwestern half of the country and extend into the southeast, which they share with the speakers of Nilotic and Nilo-Hamitic languages.

Current estimates put the population of Uganda at 12.4 million. Estimates based on a rate of population growth of 2.5 to 3 percent per annum would lead to a doubling of Uganda's population within 20 to 25 years. None of Uganda's major ethnic groups dominates the country demographically. The Buganda, the largest ethnic group, contributes no more than about 18 percent of the population; the Iteso, the second largest, makes up about 9 percent. About 7 percent of the population lives in urban and peri-urban areas. The major population centers are in the south, in Kampala, Jinja, Mbale, and Entebbe. Kampala, the capital of Uganda, is the major urban center and accounts for over one-third of the total urban population. Kampala provides an exciting nightlife and remains the cultural and intellectual capital of the country. Churches, mosques, schools, theaters, and museums are the principal institutions for cultural expression. According to the 1969 census, Kampala had a population of 330,700; Jinja 52,509; Mbale 23,544; and Entebee 21,096. Each of the eighteen district capitals is developing its own urban character, but the urban population remains relatively small because Ugandans in the peri-urban areas tend to live on their farms and commute to the city for work and pleasure.

Makerere University and its distinguished medical college and the Institute of Social Research provide opportunities for higher education and research for over 5,000 students. Primary and secondary education is being extended as fast as limited resources of funds, space, and teachers allow. The political goal is free education for all, a goal that is paradoxically being realized at the university level rather than at the secondary level because of the urgent need to produce the skilled manpower needed for economic and social development.

Because of the enormous opportunities of Uganda's agriculture, the people of Uganda are not interterritorial migrants. Rather, their expanding economy attracts and retains migrants, largely from Rwanda and Burundi. Internal migration is southward to the banana-coffee agricultural zone, and to the big cities. Before the emergence of the modern state, religious wars and political strife led to a redistribution of population, particularly in the south. In the nineteenth century three world religions—Islam, Catholicism, and Protestantism—met and clashed among themselves and with traditional kingdoms.

The human populations and traditional institutions that built Uganda are varied and ancient indeed. Colonial rule added new complexities to the social system. It brought purveyors of new religions, administrators, traders, and seekers of fortune. The goods it brought created new value systems that are challenging and sometimes replacing the traditional symbols of prestige and power. By creating wage labor and the opportunity to earn an independent income, it correspondingly reduced the traditional dependence on the polity for upward mobility. It has also created new roles of competition in society, and some of them are radical enough to undermine traditional authority. The educational system has produced a new class, men and women who derive their status from their "new knowledge" and whose claims on the resources of society more often reflect the scarcity value of this knowledge rather than its utility.

Uganda's inherited social structure is complex and unstable, but its economy has a more solid foundation. Uganda has important natural and human assets. The soils are generally productive; rainfall is adequate in most places. A long period of interaction with Arabs and British traders stimulated interest in foreign goods, and many Ugandans went to work for them.

Since Ugandans were self-sufficient in foods, the immediate challenge was the development of an export capacity. The British policy of leaving Uganda's lands in the care of its indigenous population paid off, and the 1900 Settlement Agreement with Buganda, which was extended with modifications to other

In a village in rural Uganda, government health workers teach the villagers about nutrition and sanitation. The government is working to improve health and education, particularly in rural areas. (Photo: United Nations/ WHO/J. Rohr.)

kingdoms and polities, made clear that Uganda was not another Kenya—a country for white settlement. The history of Uganda's export economy since 1900 is the story of the development and expansion of cotton and coffee, the two most important export crops of the country. The commercial development of tea, tobacco, and sugar came much later.

Uganda's agricultural production is dominated by Africans who work on small farms averaging 5 to 10 acres (2 to 4 hectares); but marketing and processing have passed from the hands of Indian traders to cooperatives and government boards. About 90 percent of the people are employed in agriculture, and about 85 percent cultivate less than 5 acres (2 hectares per family) in Uganda's five agricultural systems. The banana-coffee system, located in the south, primarily in Buganda, produces most of Uganda's robusta coffee and depends heavily on migrant labor. On its northern frontier, production becomes a combination of bananas, millet, and cotton. The Teso system, based on ox breeding, produces finger millet and cotton and involves large numbers of cattle. The northern system, a household economy practiced in the short-grass region, depends on family labor for the production of finger millet, manioc, and cotton. The Montane system, practiced in the foothills and on the brows of Ruwenzori and Elgon and in the Kigezi highlands, is noted for its terrace agriculture and produces Arabica coffee, bananas, and sorghum. The pastoral system is practiced by the pastoral populations of Ankole and Karamoja.

Uganda's domestic economy is diversified. Food crops are linked to ecology and cultural preferences.

Bananas are produced and eaten in the south and west, sesame in the north, sorghum in the northeast and southwest, and finger millet in the southeast and northwest. Manioc and peanuts are grown and eaten practically everywhere. The lakes and streams teem with fish, and the export of smoked and dry fish to Zaire is a thriving business. Uganda is also a rich cattle country, and the production and sale of livestock make an important contribution to its economy. The agricultural economy contributes an estimated 42 percent to Uganda's monetary gross domestic product (GDP) and nearly 90 percent of the nonmonetary GDP. Thus agriculture, as the major source of foreign exchange and development capital, is an important engine of growth.

Uganda's agricultural wealth is not matched by its mineral resources. Its two most important minerals are copper and tin ores, the former accounting for over 65 percent of all mining. Sand, stone, limestone, and clay are exploited for the building industry, and phosphates are used for the manufacture of fertilizers. With practically no workable coal deposits, Uganda depends on its waterfalls for the generation of hydroelectricity. About 90 percent of the hydropower is produced by Owen Falls at Jinja, from which power is exported to Kenya. There are small power plants in Kabale and Kikagati in the southwest.

The expanding trade networks that Uganda maintains with the outside world illustrates its policy of economic redirection. Before independence in 1962, Britain was Uganda's chief market; since independence, the United States, West Germany, Japan, and India have become increasingly important. The eco-

Workers pick tea on a large plantation in Uganda. (Photo: United Nations/ Nagata.)

nomic hardships of a landlocked state were mitigated by Uganda's membership in the East African Community, a regional grouping that was dissolved in 1977. Uganda is a member of the Commonwealth and of the African-Caribbean-Pacific states that have a special trade relationship with the European Community, and it is entitled to the economic benefits of these associations. Ugandan trade follows multiple channels: the principal commodities (coffee, cotton, copper, tea, hides, and skins) are exported to the Common Market, the European Community, and other foreign markets. Imports from these markets are machinery, vehicles, and fabrics. The East African Community supplied petroleum products, unmilled wheat, processed foods, paper, and sacks, while Uganda sold to it cotton fabrics and iron and steel bars, which are economically made from scrap metal using Uganda's reserves of hydroelectric power.

The political direction of Uganda's economy includes a series of 5-year development plans which were initiated in 1961–1962. The Common Man's Charter, which was not implemented because President A. Milton Obote was deposed by General Idi Amin, indicated the intention of the ruling Uganda People's Congress (UPC) to seek socialist economic solutions. The first 5-year development plan (1961 to 1966) intended to raise the national product per capita by concentrating on the agricultural export sector, improving the basic infrastructure that supports this sector as well as improving health and education. As an investment proposition, this first plan was an outstanding success. The second 5-year development plan (1966 to 1971) called for a change in the structure of the economy through a strategy of crop diversification and import substitution industrialization.

In 1970, the fourth year of the second development plan, the ruling Uganda People's Congress declared that the state had to take over all the means of production, including land, and that it would use parastatals (government-owned corporations) and cooperatives to build a socialist society for Uganda.

The intervention by Uganda's military forces in the political process and the subsequent dictatorship of President Idi Amin put a temporary end to the move to the left in Uganda. But it also created a regime of terror that for 7 years (1972 to 1979) practically eliminated Uganda's export economy and reduced the population to a near-subsistence existence. The third 5-year development plan (1971 to 1976) extended the goals of the second plan and aimed at achieving some of its unrealized promises. Improvement in the quality of agricultural export was emphasized, and the growth rate for this sector was targeted at 4.9 percent per annum. But political problems during the years of the third plan put the economy in a state of seige, and many observers described the economy as "a total disaster."

The government of Uganda plays an active role in economic management, and this role is expected to increase. Government dominates the public sector of the economy. Through its parastatals—the Uganda Development Corporation, the Uganda Electricity Board, the Coffee Marketing Board, the Lint Marketing Board, the State Trading Corporation, and the Export and Import Corporation—the government participates directly in industrial, commercial, and manufacturing activities. Government financial and political support for the cooperatives has extended its power to police and to local economic activities.

Uganda Tourist Development Corporation (UTDC), another parastatal, runs the country's tourist industry. Exploiting the natural beauty of the country and its rich game resources, UTDC currently operates three national parks, at Murchison Falls (Kabalega), Queen Elizabeth, and Kidepo, each equipped with first-class lodges. Expansion of the national parks was halted because worldwide revulsion against the actions of the government of Idi Amin meant that few tourists visited Uganda.

The roots of Ugandan social dynamics lie in the nineteenth century. It was the search for the source of the Nile—a European mystery solved by John Speke in 1882—that opened Uganda to European explorers. The acquisition of Uganda for Britain followed the familiar pattern of colonization. Explorers, missionaries, and traders were followed by traders backed by political officers who negotiated treaties of commerce and friendship with African kings and princes, a role which Captain F. D. Lugard played successfully for the Imperial British East Africa Company. The trading treaties led to political alliances between African rulers and the European trading companies and later justified claims to spheres of influence that eventually ended in protectorate rule.

Britain established modern Uganda through a combination of treaties or agreements with traditional rulers and by military conquest, often mistermed "pacification" action. Buganda, Ankole, Toro, and Bunyoro were the treaty or agreement kingdoms. Because of its precolonial power, Buganda was accorded special political privileges that later became an obstacle to the political integration of modern Uganda.

The British protectorate over Buganda was announced in 1894, and by 1914 the outline of modern Uganda was unmistakable. After over 60 years of colonial rule, Uganda became independent on October 9, 1962. The colonial structure that Uganda inherited at independence was a stratified racial system in which the British colonial elite, with a monopoly of political power, was on top; the Asian immigrants, who dominated the retail trade, were in the middle; and the majority of the Africans, mainly cultivators, were on the bottom stratum.

Under the independence constitution of 1962, each kingdom was ruled by its traditional ruler, called *kabaka* in Buganda, *omukama* in Bunyoro, *omugabe* in Ankole, and *mukama* in Toro. The two power centers did not coexist for long. In 1976, A. Milton Obote, the Prime Minister of the central government, suspended the 1962 independence constitution and persuaded

Parliament to make him an executive President after adopting a new constitution. The kingdoms were abolished in 1967, and in 1971 Milton Obote was deposed by General Idi Amin. The following year, Amin expelled the Asian population, the nation's traders, and Uganda's social system broke down. President Amin was removed from power by the combined military operations of the Tanzanian army and the Uganda National Liberation Front in April 1979. His successor, President Yusufu Lule, resigned from office after 2 months; Lule's successor is Godfrey L. Binaisa.

A post-Amin government must reassert the rule of law, rebuild the nation and its economy, and restore regional and external confidence in its ability to govern fairly. From an economic perspective Uganda suffers more than Tanzania or Kenya from the political death of the East African Comunity. Economic realities inspired the evolution of this community, and it is likely that something resembling it will be reconstituted in the near future.

Victor C. Uchendu

Upper Volta
(Republic of Upper Volta)

Area: 106,000 sq mi (274,500 sq km)
Population: 5.5 million
  Density: 52 per sq mi (20 per sq km)
  Growth rate: 1.6% (1970–1977)
Percent of population under 14 years of age: 35%
Infant deaths per 1,000 live births: 260
Life expectancy at birth: 38 years (1978)
Leading causes of death: malaria, measles, meningitis
Ethnic composition: Voltaic-speaking tribes, Mande-speaking tribes, others
Languages: French (official), Voltaic, Mande, Hausa, Bambara
Literacy: 5–10% (1978)
Religions: traditional (majority); Muslim 20%; Christian
Percent population urban: 5–10%
Percent population rural: 90–95%
Gross national product: $760 million
  Per capita GNP: $160
  Per capita GNP growth rate: 1.6% (1970–1977)
Inflation rate: 12% (1972–1977)

On August 5, 1960, the geographical region in the bend of the Niger River became the independent Republic of Upper Volta. Significant factors that influenced this political entity include the region's relatively poor and semiarid soils; the experience of a landlocked nation with few resources; the precolonial resistance to Islam of the majority of the region's inhabitants; and French colonial rule (1896 to 1960). These four factors, among others, contributed to the process that transformed a geographical region with distinguishing cultural and ethnic characteristics into the postcolonial state of Upper Volta.

Bordered on the west by Mali, on the east by Niger, and by the Ivory Coast, Ghana, Togo, and Benin to the south, Upper Volta covers approximately 106,000 square miles (274,500 sq km) and compares in size with Colorado. Most of the country is a granite and gneiss plateau—650 to 1,000 feet (198 to 305 m) above sea level—covered by primary and anteprimary sedimentary layers. It is drained by three rivers: the Black Volta, the Red Volta, and the White Volta, none of which is navigable. Situated between 10 and 15° north

latitude, southern Upper Volta has a tropical climate, with alternating rainy (June to October) and dry (November to May) seasons. In the south and southwest, where rainfall is heaviest, annual averages are approximately 40 inches (102 cm); in the extreme north and northeast, a near-desert semiarid (Sahelian) climate prevails. Corresponding temperatures average 75 to 80°F (24 to 27°C) in December and January, and 80 to 85°F (27 to 30°C) in April toward the end of the dry season. In the semiarid and arid north and northeast, temperatures may rise higher. Voltan vegetation corresponds to the ecological zones: forest and fruit trees in the south; spiny and mimosa-type vegetation in the plateau area; desert scrub and bush in the north and east.

A per capita income of approximately $160 (World Bank estimate) means that the country is numbered among the world's poorest. With mainly lateritic soils lacking essential nutrients and with few mineral, energy, forest, or water resources, Upper Volta's gross national product is a mere $760 million. The people of the central plateau—where agricultural yields are low—tend to grow drought-resistant cereals, such as sorghum and millet, and peanuts. During the last decade, cereal production was adversely affected by the droughts, and food imports were necessary. In the arid and semiarid north and northeast, about 80,000 seminomads raise livestock. In the west and southwest, where rainfall is heavier, beans, sweet potatoes, yams, maize, and rice are grown, together with cash crops such as cotton, sugar cane, and sesame seeds. Livestock breeding is also practiced in the south by approximately 70,000 sedentary herdsmen, who raise cattle, sheep, goats, and donkeys. Because many segments of the population are non-Islamic, pigs are also bred. In the wake of recent droughts, herders are rebuilding their stock. Fish are not a significant dietary item, and there is a severe shortage of clean drinking water.

Like most African countries, Upper Volta has considerable ethnic, cultural, and linguistic diversity. Of a total population of 5.5 million, the majority are Voltaic-speaking people, such as the Mossi—about 67 percent of the total population—who live on the central plateau between the Black Volta and the White Volta Rivers.

The Mande, who represent a separate linguistic and cultural identity, include the Boussane (or Bisa) near the Ghana frontier, the Senoufu near the Ivory Coast, and the Samo and the Marka. Hausa and Bambara are lingua francas spoken mainly by trading communities, but French is the official language.

Population densities are highest in the south and on the plateau in areas where soils are poor. Here a density of 104 people per square mile (48 per sq km) overtaxes the land. In the north, mainly occupied by the Tuareg, the Peul, and the Bella, population density is low.

Although Islam penetrated the West African Sudan after the eighth century, Voltans have tended to resist conversion. Only one-fifth of the population is Muslim; and aside from the 250,000 Roman Catholics and Protestants, the majority of the population adheres to African traditional religions. The population is young, with a life expectancy of 38 years and an annual growth rate of 2.2 percent. Despite growing modernization, characteristic urban and rural social structures focus on the extended family; in the north, the clan is still the principal social institution. Traditional elites, chiefs, and elders dominate rural areas, while traditional religions and Islam reinforce social relationships.

Between 90 and 95 percent of the people live in rural areas, and approximately 95 percent of the overall population is engaged, at one time or another each year, in agriculture and herding. Rural poverty is pervasive, and the average rural per capita income may not exceed $60 a year. Smaller segments of the rural population also engage in trade and fishing.

Women play a prime role in the labor unit, and most agricultural maintenance is done by women. Additionally, women frequently work their own fields. They may also engage in petty trade and raise small animals. Where conditions permit, they keep the earnings from their personal labor. But modernizing trends in the agricultural sector may adversely affect women's economic status. For example, since new techniques for weeding and spreading fertilizer on family fields are more time-consuming than traditional methods, women are putting less labor into their own market gardens than previously, which may ultimately affect their earning power. Moreover, agricultural instructors—mainly male—work only with men, and with the present rate of deforestation for wood fuel, women's age-old economic role as gatherers of fruits, roots, and berries is likely to suffer.

But it is not only women's role in the labor unit that is being affected by modernization. Poverty, unemployment, and underemployment are linked to large-scale migratory labor, mainly of males between the ages of 20 and 40. It is estimated that more than 460,000 Voltans migrate to another country each year for employment. Of these, approximately 100,000 never return, and there are about 1 million Voltans in the Ivory Coast and in Ghana. Migrants frequently gain their livelihood as skilled or unskilled workers in the towns or in agricultural sectors. Remittances from migrant laborers amount to about 6 percent of the gross national product.

Moreover, in recent years, land-tenure systems have conflicted with social realities. According to the traditional laws recognized under national law, usufruct rights to land held by the lineage (people of three or four generations related via a common ancestor) are allocated according to need and demonstrated use. In some areas, however, traditional land law is now in conflict with the Western practice of individual ownership and land transfers, a practice that reflects the changing needs of the young. On the cutting edge of change, some youth resolve the conflict by migrating to towns, or they are absorbed into the neighboring work force in the Ivory Coast and Ghana.

Of the school-age population, rural as well as urban, only 13.3 percent (1977) attend primary schools, where boys outnumber girls by more than 2 to 1. Only about 5 to 10 percent of the entire population is literate. In the absence of data, it is safe to assume that the majority of the functionally literate migrate to urban areas. There are some secondary schools, and in 1974, the University of Ouagadougou was established. As is true of education, rural health facilities are poor, and the health of the rural population is a cause for concern. Endemic diseases such as malaria, measles, meningitis, and, to a lesser extent, leprosy,

Women wait their turn with their bowls of millet at a portable huller; millet and sorghum, both drought-resistant cereals, are grown on the central plateau. (Photo: United Nations/Ray Witlin.)

trypanosomiasis, and tuberculosis take their toll on a population where the infant mortality is 260 per 1,000 (compared to 17 per 1,000 in the United States). Moreover, in a country where the daily per capita intake is an estimated 2,200 calories, including 45 grams of nonanimal protein, severe malnutrition continues. Health prospects for the immediate future are not promising; there is only 1 doctor—including foreign doctors and those principally engaged in administration—for every 52,000 people, and 1 Voltan physician for every 142,000 inhabitants. In some areas, e.g., the Sahel (a semiarid zone that rings the southern edge of the Sahara), the estimated 186,000 inhabitants have no doctors. In many rural areas, women walk miles each day for impure drinking water that continues to spread waterborne diseases.

In urban areas, Voltan populations are small—less than 10 percent of the overall population—and they are mainly concentrated in Ouagadougou, the capital (population 200,000), Bobo-Dioulasso (150,000), and Koudougou (60,000), which were either precolonial capitals or trade centers. Urban poverty is also widespread. It is estimated that with the exception of the 23,000 public employees, whose yearly income averages $1,800, and the 200,000 registered employees of the nonfarming sector, the incomes of most urban Voltans barely exceed the International Labor Organization's poverty line for Africans of $205 (1972) per annum.

Migrating workers frequently form linkages between urban and rural populations, and there is an urban-rural continuum. Accordingly, the lives of most urban people are still subject to rural social institutions, especially polygamy (in the case of non-Christian households) and the extended family. Modifications of urban-rural social institutions are more likely to be found among elite families, which are distinguished by their functions and by their relative wealth.

Workers harvest peanuts, one of the principal market crops in Upper Volta. The people of Upper Volta also grow cotton, rice, and karite to sell in the markets. (Photo: United Nations/Ray Witlin.)

Industries are small; they contribute no more than 36 percent of the gross national product and 19 percent of the gross domestic product. They are limited to Ouagadougou and Bobo-Dioulasso, where small private enterprises also exist. Raw materials such as peanuts, peanut oil, and shea butter are processed for the domestic and export markets. Other industries include a soap factory, breweries, carbonated-beverage plants, a rice factory, a commercial dairy, and two refrigerated slaughterhouses that also manufacture animal food.

Commerce and services account for 21 percent and 16 percent of the gross domestic product, respectively. Exports are small, and in 1977, when sales totaled $89 million, livestock still accounted for most exports. There are no natural sources of energy in Upper Volta, with the possible exception of the potential hydraulic energy of the Kemoe River near Banfora and the Black Volta River near Dedougou. Electricity is produced by thermal power stations in Ouagadougou (9,620 kilowatts in 1973), Bobo-Dioulasso (5,094 kilowatts in 1973), and Ouahigouya.

Despite recent expansion, the lack of internal and external communications in this landlocked country continues to impede economic growth. In the absence of a good road system, railways provide the principal means of external transport. The Abidjan (Ivory Coast) to Ouagodougou line (712 miles [1,150 km]) begun in 1904, was not completed until 1954, when Voltans were provided with their first railway to the sea. Airports at Ouagadougou and Bobo-Dioulasso have since linked them to international airways. Upper Volta has about 10,000 miles (16,090 km) of internal road communications, about 2,500 miles (4,022 km) of which are all-weather roads. Nonetheless, large sections of the rural population are cut off from health facilities, consumer goods, markets, and, in the case of school-age children, from school. This is especially true during the rainy seasons.

With these communication and energy contraints—not to mention inadequate capital accumulation—it is hardly surprising that Voltans today are in no position to develop extractive industries. Exploitation of the 450,000 tons (415,315 t) of high-grade manganese deposits with a deposit life of 20 years awaits the northern expansion of the railway line to Tambao. Limestone deposits in the neighboring region which, when combined with manganese, could expand the Voltan industrial base to include a cement plant with a capacity of 130,000 tons (117,910 t) per annum, are unexploited. Other scattered ore deposits include uranium, bauxite, copper, marble, and gold, none of which has been mined for industrial purposes.

Historical as well as geographical factors contributed to Upper Volta's current situation. Relatively isolated in the Niger bend, the empire-building Mossi, who reached the area in or after the eleventh century from a northeasterly direction, dominated the area. Although they participated in the politics of the Islamized belt of the West African savanna and in the age-old trans-Sahara trade, the Mossi invested more of their creative energies in developing political and warrior institutions in the precolonial kingdoms of Fada-Ngourma, Ouagadougou, Tenkodogo, and Yatenga. As part of this process, they resisted the expansion of the neighboring states of Mali (twelfth to fifteenth centuries) and Songhai (fourteenth to sixteenth centuries), holding at bay the Islamic influences that came to dominate neighboring regions. Consequently, non-Islamic politico-religious institutions, of which the *moro naba*, or "sovereign," was the chief executive, became the focus.

With the capture of Ouagadougou by the French in 1896, Upper Volta became part of the French Sudan. By 1904, it was incorporated into the newly created French West African Federation (1895) and became part of the Upper Senegal and Niger Administration, along with Niger, Mauritania, and Mali. In 1919, the colony of Upper Volta was created from territory separated from the Ivory Coast and Niger. Its administrative life was short-lived, however; by 1932, it was dismembered and reabsorbed into the colonies of Niger, the Sudan (modern Mali), and the Ivory Coast. Between 1937 and 1947, the colony, called the "Upper Coast," reemerged as part of a new administrative division.

After additional reorganizations, the Overseas Reform Act of July 23, 1956, established a Government Council and a large degree of self-government in Upper Volta. On December 11, 1958, Upper Volta became an autonomous republic in the French Community, and in August 1960 the Republic of Upper Volta was proclaimed.

Subject to military-civilian rule from 1966 to 1970 and from 1974 to 1978, Upper Volta's 1960 constitution nonetheless provided for an Executive and National Assembly elected by universal suffrage. Accordingly, after the military coup d'état of January 3, 1966, which removed President Maurice Yameogo from office, abortive attempts were made to restore the electoral provisions of the constitution. However, since May 28, 1978, the date of the openly contested elections, Upper Volta has been governed by President Major General Aboubakar Sangoul-Lamizana, now elected to the office that he held after the coup of 1966, and by an elected unicameral National Assembly.

The present constitution (1977) is one of the few in Africa that provides for a division of power among the executive, the legislature, and an independent judiciary. Structurally, it owes little to the unicameral rule of Islam or to the authoritarian Mossi political traditions. The President is elected by universal suffrage for no more than two 5-year terms. His nomi-

nations to the posts of Prime Minister and to the Cabinet are subject to the absolute majority approval of the 57 National Assembly deputies, who also are elected by universal suffrage. While the President has powers to dismiss members of the executive and the National Assembly, a two-thirds vote of censure or an absolute majority vote of no confidence in the Assembly can remove the Prime Minister and Cabinet members from office.

The 1977 constitution also provides for a limited multiparty system and recognizes the three political parties that receive the most votes. Since 1978, the parties gaining recognition, which control nearly 50 percent of the Assembly seats, are the revived Voltan Democratic Union (RDA/UDV), the National Union for the Defense of Democracy (UNDD), and the Voltan Progressive Union (UPV). It remains to be seen whether elected public officials will govern effectively in the intended spirit of the constitution.

Upper Volta's national aspirations include the economic development and improvement of the quality of life for the masses, although immediate prospects are not encouraging. Not known for ideological stridency, pragmatic Voltan officials agree on the need for controlling state influence over the allocation of scarce resources. Recovering from the aftereffects of the Sahelian droughts (1969 to 1974)—which were less devastating in Upper Volta than in the central and northern savanna—decision makers want to develop the country's mineral resources and the agricultural potential of the underpopulated Volta River valleys. For the time being, however, the government is heavily dependent on profits from the $89 million (1977) export trade, primarily to the Ivory Coast, the European Economic Community, France, and Ghana. It also depends on aid, loans, grants, and gifts, principally from France, the United States, and other industrial countries, to fuel its annual actual economic growth rate of 5.8 percent (1979).

But the greatest obstacles to development remain pervasive hunger, poverty, disease, widespread illiteracy and inadequate educational facilities. The adverse effects of weather have only exacerbated these long-standing problems. And although the populations in the west and southwest—where soils are richer—have slightly higher living standards, an inflation rate of 12 percent in the last 5 years has reduced the real effects of economic gains. In the country as a whole, major infrastructure projects, such as the railway line to the ore deposits at Tambao, have been delayed by recurring rising costs and unfavorable manganese prices that continue to reduce the potential of the yet unexploited deposits.

B. Marie Perinbam

Zaire
(Republic of Zaire)

Area: 905,063 sq mi (2,344,102 sq km)
Population: 26 million
  Density: 29 per sq mi (11 per sq km)
  Growth rate: 2.7% (1970–1977)
Percent of population under 14 years of age: 44%
Infant deaths per 1,000 live births: 104 (1960)
Life expectancy at birth: 44 years (1978)
Leading causes of death: not available
Ethnic composition: Bantu tribes 80%; over 200 tribal
  groups
Languages: French (official), Lingala, Kikongo, Tshiluba,
  Swahili
Literacy: 20%
Religions: Christian (majority); traditional
Percent population urban: 25%
Percent population rural: 75%
Gross national product: $5.5 billion
  Per capita GNP: $210
  Per capita GNP growth rate: −1.4% (1970–1977)
Inflation rate: 75%

Zaire, once the Belgian Congo, is a huge country, the second largest in Africa (after the Sudan), occupying the very heart of the continent. At the time of independence, Zaire had one of the most highly developed and diversified economies in sub-Saharan Africa. Its literacy rate was high, upwards of 80 percent, but its stock of skilled and professional workers was desperately low. The new nation of some 15 million people had only a dozen college graduates and virtually no indigenous doctors, lawyers, or engineers.

At present, despite its potential, Zaire's economic problems are pushing the state to the brink of bankruptcy. Zaire confronts security problems in the wake of two invasions from neighboring Angola and political difficulties stemming from dictatorial rule.

Zaire's 905,063 square miles (2,344,102 sq km) make it approximately the size of the United States east of the Mississippi River. While bordering nine different states, Zaire has only one outlet to the Atlantic Ocean: a short, 23-mile (37-km) strip of land on the north bank of the Zaire (Congo) River estuary.

Zaire's large central area is covered by a tropical rain forest and is surrounded by mountainous terraces in the west, plateaus merging in the savannas in the south and southeast, and dense grasslands in the northwest. Nearly half the total land is considered suitable for farming but only 1 percent is under cultivation. Because Zaire lies on the equator, with one-third of the land to the north and two-thirds to the south of it, the country is hot and humid.

The Zairian government estimates the total population at 26 million (which may be exaggerated) and the average annual population growth rate at around 2.7 percent (which may be more accurate). The nation's indigenous population includes some 200 tribal

groups, four-fifths of whom are Bantu and the remainder, Pygmies and Hamites.

Those with some education, which is still largely conducted by the Christian (and predominantly Catholic) churches, speak French. Some 5 percent of the population speak French fluently, and one-third understand French. Most individuals speak one of the four tribal languages: Lingala, the commercial language spoken along the Zaire River including the capital city (Kinshasa), and officially used by Zaire's police and army; Kikongo, the language of the tribe found in Bas-Zaire, south of Kinshasa; Tshiluba, the tongue of the tribes in south central regions; and Swahili, spoken in eastern Zaire and all across East Africa. Some 80 percent of the population also speak 1 of 200 different languages and live in the rural areas in a traditional lifestyle.

Those Zairians who live in rural areas generally work subsistence farms. Using traditional methods of cultivation, they produce staples for their families, including manioc, the starchy food that is the main diet of most Zairians, rice, and maize.

The beliefs, practices, and ethnic cohesion brought about by traditional religions influence the life and thought pattern of almost all Zairians and are perhaps the most important factors in their lives. Even though most Zairians consider themselves Christians, they retain the basic beliefs of African traditional religions, follow the traditional ethical commandments, use the fetishes, and consult the *ngangfa*, or "fetisher."

The traditional religions have a tremendous influence even in the urban areas, where the lifestyle is quite different. While the multitude of peoples in the city breaks the exclusiveness of traditional society, the urban dweller still retains strong ties with traditional religion and the family group. Members of a family group often live together in the city. Villagers coming to the city seek out those they know and live with them. This creates a small-village environment in the city. The vast majority of marriages in Kinshasa, the largest and most modern Zairian city, still link members of the same ethnic group.

The tremendous economic, social, and cultural pressures of city life often encourage a Zairian to find comfort and stability through traditional ways and ceremonies. These same pressures also increase the practice of *kindoki*, or "witchcraft." Many city dwellers, earning the equivalent of $1 a day, support large families in both the city and the village. This places impossible burdens on them, makes it inevitable that they cannot meet all their responsibilities, and opens them to charges of invoking harm through witchcraft. Because there is no subsistence farming in a city, the city dwellers often believe they need help from their ancestors to make a living and will thus petition the divinities continually for material assistance.

Mining is the heart and soul of Zaire's economy. Copper production is in the hands of two state-owned companies: the Congolese General Mining Society (GECOMINES), formed in 1967 after the nationalization of the Belgian-owned Mining Company of Upper Katanga (UMHK), and the Society for Industrial Development and Mining in Zaire (SODIMIZA). These companies are responsible for Zaire's copper exports, which in 1976 accounted for some $250 million of the country's $600 million in total exports.

Kolwezi, the scene of the second invasion (June 1978) of Katangans based in Angola, is the home of five of the six open-pit copper mines in Zaire and of the largest underground copper mine. More than 75 percent of the approximately 425,000 short tons (385,475 t) of Zairian copper produced annually originates in the Kolwezi district, or is refined there.

Zaire provides two-thirds of the non-Communist world's supply of cobalt, a vital mineral in steel production. As is the case with copper, over 90 percent of Zaire's cobalt is found in the Kolwezi district, although deposits also exist throughout the Shaba. The Shaba also contains sizable quantities of tin, columbium, manganese, and several other rare minerals. In addition, Zaire's mineral riches provide the West with half its industrial diamonds, and approximately one-third of its tantalum and germanium.

Zaire's uranium provided the radioactive material used in U.S. atomic bombs in World War II. Both Zaire's uranium and its vast and as yet unexploited deposits of iron interest Western powers. Finally, offshore oil has been discovered in Zaire, but oil production to date is sufficient only for domestic use.

Other Zairians in the money economy are involved in large-scale agriculture. Recently, the government has encouraged plantation owners who left in 1973 to return, offering inducements like ownership rights and repatriation of profits. The main cash crops produced by the large plantations are coffee, manioc, bananas, and corn. Coffee leads the exports of agricultural products.

Compared to many other black African nations, Zaire has a well-developed and diversified manufacturing sector. Its industries are concentrated in the big cities—primarily Kinshasa and Lubumbashi (in the Shaba)—where labor supplies are plentiful, electrical power is inexpensive, and transportation outlets are readily available. The largest manufacturing production increases have occurred in consumer goods, particularly processed food, beverages, and clothing. A cement factory and a steel mill are in operation, as are truck and automobile assembly plants, a tire factory, and a host of medium-sized concerns.

Zaire has great economic potential; it was this potential, in fact, that prompted King Leopold II of Belgium to appropriate the territory, then called the Congo Free State, as his private domain in 1878. The Belgian government took legal possession of the area in 1908, renaming it the Belgian Congo. Belgium retained the most squalid practices to exploit the ivory, minerals, and agricultural wealth, while offering a bare minimum of training and improvement in the living conditions of the local inhabitants.

The country's independence from Belgium in June 1960, was accompanied by army mutinies, riots, successions, revolutions, and the intervention of UN peacekeeping forces. The chaos continued after General Mobutu Sese Seko assumed power in November 1965, even though over time his political acumen added a measure of stability. The state's 1967 constitution proclaimed the Popular Movement of the Revolution (MPR) as the sole political party and the country's primary institution, under the firm control of its founder, President Mobutu. In 1971, the country was renamed Zaire.

In late 1974, Mobutu radicalized the economy, that is, nationalized all enterprises exceeding $2 million in turnover. Most plantations and businesses were subsequently handed over to party loyalists of the Zairian elite, who often managed them poorly and sold existing stock without reordering. The government handled its own treasury in much the same manner, using scarce foreign exchange for large prestigious purchases or ostentatious luxury items. Corruption has also long been rampant in Zaire's government, flourishing from the very highest to the lowest levels.

Such a precarious situation could not long endure. Zaire's economic house of cards began to crumble in the 1970s. In the spring of 1976, after Zaire had defaulted on loan principal and interest payments for more than a year, the Zairian government altered its direction by returning nationalized enterprises to their former owners, who are now authorized to maintain 60 percent ownership.

In March 1976, the President accepted a stabiliza-

Wagenia fishermen haul in their net on the Zaire River. Fish catches enable poor Zairians to eke out a meager living and to add protein to their very limited diet. (Photo: United Nations/ Y. Lehmann.)

tion package from the International Monetary Fund (IMF), which provided some relief. Soon after adopting its provisions, Zaire cleared all arrears, made payments on time, and established a National Debt Management Office to ensure a coherent policy in the future. In return, the international banking community agreed to extend the period of Zaire's debt payments and to lend the Bank of Zaire an additional $250 million (contingent on good performance).

In November 1977, the President unveiled his Plan Mobutu, a 3-year emergency program. The plan's objectives were to improve the management of the economy; to reduce food deficits and make the country self-sufficient in basic staples; and to raise the average Zairian's standard of living, particularly in the rural regions. The government aimed at decentralizing economic decision making, reorganizing state agencies involved with import controls and payments, and establishing an audit office to authorize and verify all expenses in the public sector. Particular attention was given to transportation and agriculture.

However, despite the new plans, Zaire's economy remained extremely weak. Inflation was severe—75 percent annually—and the currency (called the zaire) was overvalued, creating an active black market. Shortages of essential commodities were aggravated by a lack of foreign exchange and the deterioration of transportation networks. Factories were said to be operating at less than half capacity because of a lack of spare parts and adequate transportation.

Yet another international program by the IMF is under way to prevent bankruptcy in Zaire. IMF officials have been installed in the top levels of Zaire's government, and all Zairians must receive their permission before spending scarce foreign exchange. Whether this newest and most stringent of contingency plans will prove successful remains in doubt, though its chances are far brighter than those of previous plans. Still, Zaire's economic picture remains quite dismal.

Such economic crises and the recurrent military crises—including two invasions by Angola-based Katangans (in May 1977, dubbed Shaba I, and in June 1978, Shaba II)—have shown Zaire's excessive political centralization and military weakness, while highlighting the President's political skills.

Over the years, Mobutu has maintained good relations with his top government and military officials. He generously shares the copper revenues with his elite corps. While inducing loyalty with such incentives, Mobutu employs harsh measures when obedience is not forthcoming. The country's secret police is considered one of its best-run agencies, and it maintains a thorough dossier on all top officials.

The President is a master politician, juggling government and military leaders to prevent any threatening local or command base of support. His regional commissioners (equivalent to U.S. state governors), who are all assigned to locales outside their tribal areas, usually cannot speak the local dialects and are thus unable to build up any personal base of support. The same is true of their subordinates right down to minor functionary levels. One military officer is frequently played off against another, and the normally rigid command lines of authority and areas of functional responsibility are often blurred. This, too, prevents any concentration of power in hands other than Mobutu's.

Such maneuvering has aided Mobutu's retention of unrivaled power. Nonetheless, it has tended to weaken both Zaire's political system and its armed forces. Top political leaders are so busy scheming, so distrustful of one another, and so fearful of making a decision offensive to the President that little time or energy is left for effective implementation of government programs. As a result, there is all too little evidence of development projects or even governmental presence outside the large cities. Popular discontent is very widespread.

In large part because of President Mobutu's colossal mismanagement and the corruption within his regime, Zaire remains a poor nation despite enormous mineral wealth. Its per capita income of some $200 a year qualifies it as one of the United Nations' least-developed states. Zairians in both urban and rural areas face greater hardships today in eking out a living than they did during either the colonial or immediate postcolonial periods. Some estimates place today's standard of living for the average Zairian at a level comparable to that of 1910–1915.

Prospects for the future are not bright either. Even if the world price of copper remains high, Zaire may not be able to benefit sufficiently to escape economic disaster. The Benguela railroad, Zaire's main means of transporting copper for export before the 1976 civil war in Angola, is closed for the foreseeable future. Angola announced that the railroad would open in 1978, but continued disruptions by the resistance group UNITA (National Union for Total Angolan Independence) have made that impossible. Should wide-scale civil disturbances erupt in Zimbabwe, as many observers predict, Zaire will suffer still more. Over one-third of its copper is transported through Zimbabwe, and nearly all of its imports to the Shaba—maize, coke, coal, and sulfur products—come directly from Zimbabwe or through Zimbabwe from South Africa.

So Zaire teeters on the brink of bankruptcy and internal upheaval as it attempts to recover from the government's egregious decisions and the Shaba invasions. In this huge central African state, the continuing crisis overshadows the country's staggering potential.

Kenneth L. Adelman

Zambia

Area: 290,724 sq mi (752,975 sq km)
Population: 5.3 million
   Density: 18 per sq mi (7 per sq km)
   Growth rate: 3% (1970–1977)
Percent of population under 14 years of age: 47.6%
Infant deaths per 1,000 live births: not available
Life expectancy at birth: 44.5 years
Leading causes of death: malnutrition, bilharzia, malarial
   parasites, alcoholism
Ethnic composition: African 98%; over 70 Bantu-speaking
   tribes
Languages: Bemba, Tonga, Nyanja, northwestern lan-
   guages, Barotse, English
Literacy: 20% (1975)
Religions: Christian 25–33%, traditional
Percent population urban: 40%
Percent population rural: 60%
Gross national product: $2.5 billion
   Per capita GNP: $480
   Per capita GNP growth rate: −0.2% (1970–1977)
Inflation rate: 17%

Geographical features shape life in Zambia. First, Zambia is a vast, relatively sparsely populated territory. Although it is about the size of Texas, its total population is around 6 million. Since about 40 percent of the population is urban, concentrated in the Central and Copperbelt provinces, there is relatively low rural population density and little pressure on agricultural land.

Second, Zambia has significant mineral resources, particularly copper. It has more than 20 percent of the known world reserves of copper, and as much as 25 percent of the proven reserves outside the Soviet Union, much of it extremely high-grade. Zambia holds first place among the net exporters of refined copper and is the world's largest producer of smelted and refined copper. It ranks third in copper mining. Thus copper plays a commanding role in the economy, in normal times contributing over 90 percent of merchandise exports, 30 percent of government tax receipts, and 25 percent of real gross domestic product. The continuing importance of copper and the chronic volatility of copper prices have led to the instability of foreign exchange earnings and government revenues and have made long-term development planning difficult. The country also mines lead, zinc, cobalt, limestone, coal, manganese, and smaller concentrations of minerals.

Zambia's third major geographic feature is its location as a landlocked territory, surrounded by relatively unstable governments. This has meant that Zambia's transport routes have long been insecure and unreliable, that its territory has been violated regularly by hostile neighbors (Zimbabwe-Rhodesia, South Africa, Zaire, and Portugal before the independence of Angola and Mozambique), and that it has become a haven for refugees fleeing political unrest

in nearby states and a sanctuary for guerrilla movements aimed at minority regimes to the south.

Zambia is a high-plateau country, with an elevation of 3,000 to 4,000 feet (914 to 1,219 km) above sea level. The climate, although modified by altitude, is subtropical. Two-thirds of Zambia is savanna woodland suitable for grazing, *citemene* ("slash-and-burn" methods), and modern agriculture, although soils and climate limit all types of land use. The other third consists of swamps, specialized forests, and the Luangwa and Zambezi valleys, part of a major geological rift complex. Most of the rivers and streams flow into the Zambezi River (along the southern border), and there is no significant shortage of water for electrical power and for irrigation, although uneven seasonal rainfall makes traditional agriculture difficult. Average rainfall ranges from 25 inches (63.5 cm) in the south and southwest to 50 inches (127 cm) in the north. Rain is almost unknown from May to October.

About 99 percent of the total population is black, belonging to over seventy Bantu-speaking ethnic groups. The five major languages spoken by Zambians are Bemba (35 percent); Tonga (17.5 percent); Nyanja (16 percent); northwestern languages (12 percent); and Barotse languages (9.7 percent). For the most part, the languages are not mutually intelligible, so Bemba is spoken in the Copperbelt cities, Nyanja in the Lusaka region, and English is the national lingua franca.

Ethnic identity is not absolute because of migration, association in new locales, and circumstances of conquest. It has been partly simplified by the fact that a few powerful ethnic groups conquered smaller ones, dominated them politically, and transmitted to them their language and parts of their culture. Each group has usually concentrated in a specific area, but there was considerable turbulence in the eighteenth and nineteenth centuries, and today villages of one group may be found in the territory of another. There is also considerable mixing in the transitional areas between groups and, since the 1920s, in the towns and cities. In addition, there are some 44,000 Europeans, many of South African, Rhodesian, and British origin, working with the copper firms and in government positions, and some 17,000 Asians, mostly from India, chiefly engaged in commerce.

Between one-fourth and one-third of the population are either Christian or members of a Christian community. Most others are followers of traditional religions, but in only a few cases have traditional belief systems remained untouched by Christian practices and vice versa. The belief in witchcraft and sorcery is common and persists among many Christians as well as non-Christians. Most churches participate comfortably in Zambian life, although two groups have resisted fealty to colonial or independent Zambian authority. The Lumpa, formerly led by Alice Lenshina, have rejected state authority, and this has led to their imprisonment, violent conflicts, and exile. The Watch Tower Bible and Tract Society (Jehovah's Witnesses) refuses to cooperate with the state and its agencies and for this reason is resented by some Zambians and is occasionally repressed by the authorities (especially at the local level).

Before independence Zambia, then known as Northern Rhodesia, was a radically stratified colonial society. Europeans were politically, economically, and socially dominant. Africans were mostly confined to subsistence farming and low-wage urban and mine employment. In contrast to people of other British colonies, Zambians had practically no opportunities for higher or even secondary education. Virtually no preindependence African elite existed. Asians (Hindus and Muslims) were usually small-scale merchants, who participated little in political life.

Despite significant alterations in Zambian life since independence, many features of the colonial period still prevail. Africans may dominate internal political life (although their political alternatives are deeply constrained by international economic realities), but Europeans are still active in skilled, managerial, and professional posts, especially in the copper industry.

Developments since colonial contact have eroded local structures. The authority of chiefs has diminished, unilineal kinship principles are less important, and polygynous marriages are fewer. Because of the changing characteristics of commerce and industry, village life is also different. But modern institutions may make deep inroads into village life without greatly affecting ordinary lives.

Zambia has not yet fashioned a real national society despite the official motto, "one Zambia, one nation." Zambia lacks integrated social institutions, common cultural practices, and a feeling of national identity.

The major cultural institution in terms of residence, language, and individual self-identification remains the ethnic group. National society centers on politics, higher education, and the economy.

Each of Zambia's ethnic groups has its own traditional practices and attitudes regarding marriage, the status of women, family composition, and other aspects of social interaction. These are being affected by economic change, education, and urbanization, and common patterns are beginning to emerge in zones of intense ethnic interaction.

In many groups, the nuclear family (husband, wife, and unmarried children) is embedded in a larger, or extended, family. This occurs less frequently today as younger people assert their independence of parental authority. Likewise, the polygynous family, consisting of a man and two or more wives and their children, is now rare because of changing attitudes, the impact of Christianity, and the economic burdens of maintaining more than one wife. Today, five forms of marriage are recognized as legal—tribal (customary), civil, and, although the law makes no specific mention of religious denominations, Christian, Muslim, and Hindu.

Most Zambian tribes are matrilineal. Succession to traditional offices and the inheritance of property generally go from a man to his sister's son or sons. Lineages and clans are based on matrilineal descent, although some clans in the east are organized in a patrilineal system. A rare exception to Zambian patterns are the Lozi of Barotseland, who trace their descent through both men and women. In unilineal systems, traditional African marriage is viewed as an alliance of two kin groups or lineages, often a product of negotiations between the two groups and the payment of an agreed upon *impango*, or bridewealth.

In an increasingly urbanized and materialistic cash-oriented society, matrilineal descent patterns are under fire. A man who acquires money and property usually wants his own sons, not his sisters' sons, to inherit his earthly savings. A transitional system is evolving.

In most Zambian tribes, the status of women is higher than it is in many other parts of Africa. Still, women are expected to defer to their husbands, and they are not considered the social equals of men. As a result, they are less likely to be educated or involved in community affairs at higher levels. Most women are engaged in the subsistence or cash-crop economy. In some areas, one-fourth or more of the men are away from home working for wages. Much of the subsistence work is left to women, boys, and old men.

Despite rapid urbanization since independence (20 percent urban in 1963, 35 percent in 1974, and 40 percent in 1979), most Zambians earn their living by farming, cattle raising, and fishing. There are some 600,000 smallholder subsistence farmers. Yet over 55 percent of Zambia's marketed food is produced on large state farms and on some 800 commercial farms (65 percent of which are owned by expatriates). With

Workers are busy in a copper refinery in Ndola. Copper is Zambia's chief export and Zambia is one of the world's leading copper exporters. (Photo: United Nations/ Y. Lehmann.)

an average of 4 acres (1.62 hectares) to cultivate, the villager normally produces enough food for the family. Seasonal surpluses provide modest funds for children's school fees, clothing, and utensils. Sometimes there is enough for some furniture, transportation, and maybe a radio or a bicycle.

When increasing copper prices in the 1960s contributed to urbanization, and when many European farmers left because of food price controls, Zambia found itself increasingly dependent on imported foodstuffs, including corn, wheat, rice, potatoes, meat, cooking oils, and dairy products (most of which could have been produced locally). Imports average about 25 percent of the marketed food. With the fall in copper prices from 93 cents per pound to 56 cents in 1975, and the consequent decline in foreign exchange earnings, the importation of foodstuffs was difficult, and periodic shortages of key commodities became a regular occurrence.

In rural areas, the diet consists largely of carbohydrates, mostly corn, millet, and cassava, with some yams, peanuts, beans, and seasonal fruits. The standard diet includes little protein and still less meat, even in cattle-raising regions. As a result, the major threat to Zambia's health is malnutrition, which is said to cause the deaths of four out of ten children before the age of five and to affect seriously two of the remaining six. In addition, it is estimated that half a million Zambians suffer from bilharzia and about 50 percent of the schoolchildren have malarial parasites in their blood. Alcoholism and excessive drinking are also serious and long-standing problems, and, especially in urban areas, drinking contributes to absenteeism, violence, and high accident rates.

To many Zambians, the city represents a beacon of affluence and improved living standards. About half a million Zambians live in Lusaka, the capital city, about a quarter of a million live in Kitwe, and another quarter of a million in Ndola. With half a dozen or more cities, Zambia is more urban than most African states. Income disparities between urban and rural sectors are great. According to a 1972–1973 survey, average annual household income in urban areas was more than 4 times that in rural areas, although in urban areas income distribution was more skewed. Towns and cities have had a powerful attraction for migrants since before independence. Migrants have drifted to the line-of-rail areas, particularly to the Copperbelt and to Lusaka. Shantytowns and squatter settlements have mushroomed.

Insufficient housing is the major urban problem, followed by unemployment and underemployment and unequal distribution of the nation's wealth. There is little housing available for job seekers, who must crowd into the shantytowns. The government (at various levels) has developed programs for upgrading squatter settlements in cooperation with the occupants themselves, and these programs are successful in some areas. Because of growing unemployment, especially in view of depressed copper prices, more

Zambians have sought work in the informal sector of the economy.

The modern sector of the economy (manufacturing, transportation and communication, and services), concentrated in towns and cities, at first grew rapidly but since 1970 has grown at a slower rate. With the introduction of increasingly capital-intensive industries, capital-labor ratios have risen in all subsectors at the cost of many potential jobs. Parastatals (government-owned corporations) including INDECO, the Industrial Development Corporation created in 1966, and MINDECO, the Mining Development Corporation, play an increasing role in manufacturing and mining.

The private sectors, still important, tend toward a smaller-scale, more labor-intensive sector of production. Not many parastatals, however, have shown profits. A more diversified economy is needed. As long as the economy remains dependent on copper, the likelihood of periodic foreign exchange and budgetary crises is great.

Unfortunately, there has been an urban bias in the government's development and welfare programs and plans. Despite all the talk about using copper revenues to diversify the economy and to fuel agricultural self-sufficiency, little has been accomplished in rural areas. By and large, despite the government's conscious decision to disperse health expenditures to the rural areas, and despite more than 500 rural health centers and clinics, the best health care is available in larger towns and cities where hospitals and medical doctors are concentrated. Traditional and Western medicine coexist in urban and rural areas, complementing and competing with one another. Other social services, such as day-care nurseries, recreational

Farmers use modern machinery for harvesting on a large state farm; some 600,000 subsistence farmers with small holdings produce only enough food for their families. (Photo: United Nations/ Y. Lehmann.)

facilities, communications, and adult specialized and secondary education, are more available in the urban areas. This contributes to the pace of urbanization.

Education in Zambia was neglected by the colonial authorities. Mission societies that were generally short of funds and trained personnel sought to fill the gaps, but deficiencies were acute. Racially segregated schools lasted until independence and seriously retarded the development of African education. Since 1964, however, significant progress has been made at all levels. With the assistance of the World Bank and other foreign sources of funds, educational facilities have been expanded (today around 75 percent of primary-age children complete 7 years of schooling), teacher training has increased, and the curriculum has been revised to emphasize Zambia. Vocational education and agricultural training have also grown. In 1966, the University of Zambia (at Lusaka) was completed.

Zambia was organized as a clearly defined territory and its present boundaries were set in 1905. Early missionary interest in the area, largely stimulated by David Livingstone, was followed in the 1880s and 1890s by a drive for European settlement and the exploitation of agricultural and mineral resources. Cecil Rhodes and his British South Africa Company (BSAC) was given a royal charter to explore, administer, and develop the territory, which eventually became Northern and Southern Rhodesia. By the mid-1920s, BSAC was replaced by the British Colonial Office.

By the 1950s, a small but articulate group of Africans began to resist the white domination of their affairs, and a coalition of educated Africans and mine workers became increasingly militant. Meanwhile, the white settlers pressed for a union between Northern and Southern Rhodesia, achieving this aim in 1953 over black protest in all three territories. Thus the Federation of the Rhodesias and Nyasaland was established.

During the 10 years of the federation, Southern Rhodesia clearly benefited at the expense of its northern partners. Although the economy boomed after World War II, Africans were not sharing equitably in its fruits. In the Copperbelt, for example, wages earned by black miners were about one-tenth of those earned by white miners. Trade union politics propelled much of the subsequent conflict. Wage discrimination, job insecurity, economic depression, segregation, and political dictation contributed to a growing atmosphere of tension, strike, and unrest, which coalesced in an independence movement led by Kenneth Kaunda and, at first, Harry Nkumbala and later, Simon Kapwepwe.

Nationalist activities led to the March 1959 banning of the Zambian African National Congress and the imprisonment of some of its leaders. Out of this emerged the United National Independence Party (UNIP) that was dominated by the followers of Kaunda and campaigned against the Federation. Kaunda was released from prison in January 1960.

Disturbances continued until the federation was dissolved by the British government on December 31, 1963. A January 1964 parliamentary election brought UNIP 55 of the 75 seats. Kaunda was made Prime Minister of the first African-dominated Cabinet, and on October 24, 1964, Zambia gained its independence.

In the years since independence, UNIP and President Kaunda have consolidated their tenuous positions at the center of the Zambian political system, although political violence has been frequent and sometimes severe. In December 1972, a constitutional amendment bill designated Zambia a one-party participatory democracy. A new constitution for the republic and for UNIP came into force in May 1973, linking those two institutions in the person of the party's president who became, ipso facto, the sole candidate for election to the presidency of the republic.

Ethnic competition within UNIP is acute, along a Bemba/anti-Bemba fault line. Party congresses occasionally become open struggles for control, with Kaunda serving as referee, peacemaker, and stern parent. Despite provisions of preventive detention, dissent and dissatisfaction may be expressed and, within limits, freedom of press and speech prevail. To be sure, the media are largely owned and controlled by the party and the government (radio, television, and the two daily newspapers), but editorials sometimes express views critical of top officials and government policies.

Perhaps the most significant development policy shift began with Kaunda's April 1968 Mulungushi Declaration, announcing government acquisition of a 51 percent interest in some 26 commercial firms and pressing Zambianization, especially in the private sector. This was followed in August 1969 by the government's demand for a 51 percent share in the copper mines. These and other takeovers went smoothly. By the time the government launched its second national development plan in 1972, the state was ostensibly in control of the commanding heights of the economy.

The tasks of development, however, proved difficult. After an all-time high in April 1974, copper prices fell 60 percent by December. In January 1973 the principal railway route through Zimbabwe-Rhodesia and Mozambique was closed. In August 1975 the Benguela railway through Zaire and Angola was damaged in the civil war and has not yet been reopened. Despite the 1976 opening of the TanZam Railway (TAZARA), built by and with aid from the People's Republic of China, to Dar es Salaam, shipping problems continued. The reopening of the route through Zimbabwe-Rhodesia in October 1978 relieved a terribly congested TAZARA and the port of Dar es Salaam, and enabled the Zambian government to survive increasing domestic pressures for economic relief.

Zambians have suffered through lean years. Shortages of a variety of important products and goods make life difficult, and they prompt second thoughts about the government's commitment to the liberation of settler white Africa. Are Zambians willing to sacrifice to assist their neighbors to the south? So far the answer has been "yes," although not without a great deal of grumbling. President Kaunda's philosophy of humanism stresses egalitarianism and the dignity of the individual, and discourages class differences. In reality, humanism has proved to be an umbrella covering a variety of programs, some apparently paradoxical and few well organized or well managed.

By 1977 and 1978, the economic crisis in Zambia had reached an alarming proportion. In desperation, the government turned to the International Monetary Fund, which agreed to reschedule previous loans. In return, Zambia pledged to reduce its budget deficits; thus government spending and borrowing were cut, social services were trimmed, government employees (including miners) were laid off, and the government tried to strengthen its grip on the economy. Western governments also pledged assistance to help Zambia.

Zambia has considerable promise for long-range economic growth and development, despite its landlocked vulnerability. Its mineral resources are substantial, and its climate and soil could enable it to be self-sufficient in food and to export agricultural and manufactured products. A great deal depends on two factors: the ability of the government to keep the fragile social fabric intact and to provide sound and creative leadership and economic management; and the extent to which Zambia can be insulated from the unrest in neighboring states (especially in Zimbabwe and Zaire).

So far Zambia borders have been penetrable, allowing refugees, guerrilla fighters, hostile neighboring armies, and aircraft to enter and leave virtually without resistance. But Zambia's commitment to majority rule throughout southern Africa is not likely to be abandoned because of such provocations.

Kaunda's singleness of purpose has given him a continental, indeed, a worldwide forum as the leader of the front-line states, states in direct conflict with apartheid South Africa. His continuing leadership and the development prospects for Zambia depend on the character of any new Zimbabwe government. A rise in world copper prices will help. So Zambia's future is once again locked into decisions made and events occurring beyond its boundaries.

Kenneth W. Grundy

Zimbabwe

Area: 150,886 sq mi (390,759 sq km)
Population: 6.9 million
  Density: 46 per sq mi (18 per sq km)
  Growth rate: 3.3% (1970–1977)
Percent of population under 14 years of age: 48%
Infant deaths per 1,000 live births: not available
Life expectancy at birth: 51.5 years
Leading causes of death: not available
Ethnic composition: Shona 71%; Ndebele 16%; white 3.0%
Languages: Shona, Ndebele, English (official)
Literacy: not available
Religion: Christian
Percent population urban: 20%
Percent population rural: 80%
Gross national product: 3.3 billion
  Per capita GNP: $480 (est.)
  Per capita GNP growth rate: −0.1% (est., 1970–1977)
Inflation rate: 16%

The landlocked country of Zimbabwe in southern Africa, once known as Rhodesia, continues to be torn by racial and ethnic strife. From December 1972, to independence under African majority rule in April 1980, Zimbabwe labored under a debilitating guerrilla war. Since then, the country has struggled to mend its wounds, under Prime Minister Robert Mugabe. This former guerrilla and Marxist ideologue has pragmatically sought reconciliation with whites by allowing them to retain their land, businesses, and even a share of governance. He has also tried, with only limited success, to integrate the former guerrilla factions and the old Rhodesian army into a national defense force.

The nation's assets are rich mineral resources; a fine climate; productive arable land; a well-developed transportation and communications infrastructure; skilled workers; and a modern, sophisticated manufacturing sector. Its liabilities include a high level of black unemployment; urban overcrowding; an unequal distribution of wealth, especially in land; and diplomatic and geographical isolation, expressed in Zimbabwe's heavy dependence on South Africa's distant ports for its trade.

Despite independence, about 80 percent of the economy remains dependent on white-controlled and -managed businesses, and whites contribute more than 90 percent of all personal income tax. The nation is faced with one of the highest population growth rates in the world, an astounding 3.6 percent per annum among the Africans. In no way can the economy expand rapidly enough to absorb the flood of school leavers coming onto the labor market each year.

Physically, Zimbabwe is a compact, mainly plateau country of 150,886 square miles (390,759 sq km), about the size of California. It is bordered on the north by the mighty Zambezi River and its Lake Kariba and on the south by the Limpopo River. Man-made Lake

Kariba is formed by a vast dam that generates hydroelectricity for both Zimbabwe and Zambia. The country's climate varies with altitude. The gently rolling highveld, which extends diagonally across the country in a west to a northeast direction, is generally more than 400 feet (1,219 km) above sea level, with an invigorating, malaria-free, cool climate where mean annual temperatures seldom exceed 68°F (20°C). Much of the nation's most fertile land is located on the veld and is under white ownership. The lowlands, in the north near the Zambezi and in the south toward the Limpopo, are hotter and drier, and in many places require costly irrigation. Rains usually fall between November and March.

Zimbabwe is the ancient Shona word for the many stone-built towns in the fifteenth-century Rozwi Empire of Mwenemutapa. Since the onset of the guerrilla bush war in December 1972, Zimbabwe has been weakened by racial and ethnic strife. The whites, who number only 210,000 out of a population of 7 million, have failed to produce an integrated society based on human, economic, and political equality. The two largest components of the black African population are the Shona-speakers and the Ndebele-speakers who make up approximately 71 percent and 16 percent of the total population, respectively. The Shona, who were the earliest inhabitants, comprise several powerful clans, each speaking a distinct dialect; most important are the Karanga, Manyika, and Zezuru. The whites, primarily of British descent, are outnumbered by the Africans by a 30 to 1 ratio. Less than one-fourth of the whites were born in the country; a majority hold foreign passports, and most of them arrived after 1953. There is no clear sense of national or cultural unity.

Young Africans wait outside a factory gate in Salisbury, hoping for work despite the "no work" sign; unemployment is a major problem for Zimbabwe's urban youth. (Photo: United Nations/ CIRIC-Geneva.)

Zimbabwe's economy, though mainly rural and agricultural, is the most modern, dynamic, and industrialized on the continent, except for South Africa's. It enjoyed a high growth rate until 1974. Since then, there has been a negative growth rate in real terms. In 1978, there was a fall in real GNP of 3.6 percent. Living standards in terms of per capita income dropped 25 percent over 4 years (1974–1978), reflecting falling output, a fast-rising population, and the escalating war. The budget deficit for 1980–1981 is estimated at $US 699 million, and the country will need at least $1 billion over the next five years for postwar reconstruction. The nation's extractive industries, mainly American- and British-owned, are highly technological and require considerable expertise. Major mineral exports are asbestos, iron ore, gold, copper, chromium, nickel, and tin. Historically, most minerals were exported to Great Britain or the United States. Zimbabwe holds 86 percent of the non-Communist world's known reserves of high-quality chromium and is one of the world's main producers of asbestos.

After the nation's Unilateral Declaration of Independence (UDI) from Great Britain in November 1965 and the imposition of international sanctions, the nation undertook an ambitious and extraordinarily successful program of import substitution. Consequently, the manufacturing sector boomed; by 1978, manufacturing, which is mainly under local white ownership and management, had become the biggest contributor to the GNP. The nation became remarkably self-sufficient in basic food staples and consumer goods.

Oil is the nation's Achilles heel. Zimbabwe has no petroleum resources and is totally dependent on imports via South Africa, which has no petroleum deposits either. The closure of Iranian oil fields to South Africa in late 1978 and the ensuing guerrilla attacks on Zimbabwe's fuel depots resulted in severe shortages and exorbitant prices for both countries. These placed crippling restraints on the economy and caused a further deterioration in the already precarious balance of payments situation. Moreover, the closure of the Zambian and Mozambique borders in 1973 and 1976, respectively, forced Zimbabwe-Rhodesia to rely almost entirely on South African ports for its foreign trade. With peace restored and the border with Mozambique reopened, the economy is expected to improve rapidly.

Zimbabwe has been self-sufficient in food production since the 1930s and has been able to export large quantities of agricultural produce to other African nations and overseas. The white agricultural sector is highly developed and regionally specialized. Most commercial agriculture, like politics, is controlled by white farmers. Their farms, plantations, and ranches embrace the most fertile lands, are highly capitalized, efficiently managed, and profit from cheap, non-skilled African labor, much of which is of an oscillating migratory nature. In the early 1970s, white farms employed 1.4 million blacks, 38 percent of all African wage earners.

The principal commercial crops are tobacco (a major source of foreign revenue), maize, cotton, wheat, tea, coffee, meat, sugar, and citrus fruits. The latter two crops are grown on irrigated farms in the southeastern lowlands. Tea and coffee are cultivated on large plantations in the eastern highlands. As recently as mid-1980, 4,500 white farmers and estate-owning multinational corporations accounted for more than 80 percent of the country's agricultural output and 50 percent of its export earnings.

For half a century, after the Land Apportionment Act of 1930, Africans were discouraged from growing export-oriented cash crops that might compete with those grown by the whites. Consequently, African peasants confined themselves to the cultivation, on communally owned lands, of maize (their major crop), millet, sorghum, beans, and peanuts.

The Africans' agricultural productivity is extremely low; their land is poorly suited for crops and under cultivation tends to be overworked and overgrazed; combined with overpopulation, poor farming practices have led to soil erosion. Only a handful of Africans have sufficient capital to buy large commercial farms. Moreover, white lands are mostly contiguous and near transportation centers, while African lands are scattered into over 100 tribal trust lands, or native reserves, and 71 purchase areas. Much African agriculture is still subsistence and communal.

In 1969, the Land Apportionment Act was abolished, and Africans were given about 60 percent of all land in the country. But the best properties remained in white hands, and whites held 40 percent of all land, although they comprised less than 3.8 percent of the nation's population. Rural classification of land was abolished in 1977, and a year later land was open to all races, although it was priced far beyond the reach of most Africans.

Not surprisingly, a growing number of Africans are leaving the crowded and poverty-stricken rural ghettos and drifting to the urban areas to seek employment in mines, factories, and in the service occupations. Consequently, many of the African farms are cared for by women and children.

For decades agriculture has been vital to the country's economy. In 1974, it accounted for 18 percent of GNP, second only to manufacturing's 23 percent share. But the war took a terrible toll. Many tea and coffee estates in the east were destroyed or abandoned in the wake of escalating guerrilla attacks. Everywhere, Africans were reluctant to work for whites for fear of guerrilla reprisals.

The government has failed to stem the continuing drift of African peasants to the cities. The process of urbanization is well under way and has developed further than it has in most African nations save Nigeria. Salisbury, with a population of approximately 500,000, is the capital. The second largest city is Bulawayo, with some 290,000. Mining and manufacturing centers are densely concentrated on a geographical basis. Gatooma and Umtali are centers of textiles and clothing manufacturing; Que Que and Redcliff have an iron and steel complex; Gwelo and Selikwe boast mining and heavy industry. Manufacturing, like farming, has been greatly diversified since the 1965 UDI and is concentrated along the rail line between Salisbury and Bulawayo.

The central portions of Zimbabwe's cities, where most whites live, are well planned and spacious, with wide tree-lined boulevards, sidewalks, and immaculately maintained public gardens. In contrast, the African suburbs resemble overcrowded shantytowns, and have inferior public amenities. The war, fought mainly in the black rural areas, created an enormous and explosive refugee problem. By late 1978, more than one-fifth of the African population had been uprooted and many had fled to the safety of the cities. The government's protected-village program, similar to the unsuccessful American program in Vietnam, failed to restore a sense of security among the peasants. In 1979, three refugee camps mushroomed outside Salisbury alone. Some camps held populations exceeding 40,000.

Whites have also been gravitating toward the cities. Salisbury and Bulawayo hold more than two-thirds of

On a tea estate in the Honde Valley, women wash dishes at a communal spigot. Tea is a major commercial crop in Zimbabwe. (Photo: United Nations/Contact.)

the total white population, and more than 80 percent of all whites now reside in urban areas. But while the African urban population grows at an alarming rate, an increasing number of whites are leaving the country. By March 1979 whites were leaving at the rate of 2,000 a month. This accelerating rate of emigration, especially among the economically active white young, caused a fall in industrial production, a critical work force shortage, and the near abandonment of certain enterprises.

Zimbabwe is a spectacularly beautiful land. Tourism was once a major source of black employment and government revenue. But the escalating violence of the war and shortages in fuel brought that industry to an end. However, by late 1980 with the restoration of peace, tourism began to increase again.

Education has always been a burning issue. Educational facilities for whites have always been vastly superior. Until recently, government expenditure on African education has nowhere nearly matched that spent on whites. It was assumed that missionaries would bear the responsibility for educating the Africans. Nevertheless, Zimbabwe has a good record of providing primary education. The literacy rate is higher than in nearly all African nations. But the government has been neglectful of secondary and university education. In spite of this, since its founding in 1953, the University of Rhodesia has graduated more than 1,000 Africans; others have been sent to overseas institutions for training.

Culturally, there is a great dichotomy. The whites live in an almost Victorian setting and are formal in their lifestyle. Their many theaters, art galleries, and recreational centers traditionally excluded even educated Africans. Urbanized Africans have become Westernized in their lifestyle and disdain traditional music, art, and dancing. Rural Africans, particularly men, also wear Western-styled clothing, but cultural traditions persist.

The concept of the extended family weakened with the penetration of a cash economy. Nuclear family life is becoming more common, and in the mining areas family life in general is breaking down. The war also weakened the family.

Zimbabwe is predominantly a Christian country. Christianity was first introduced to the people in 1859 when the Ndebele allowed the London Missionary Society to open a mission station at Inyati. It did not spread rapidly until after the Matabele Wars of the 1890s when the traditional religious authorities, who had led the rebellions, were defeated and the people lost faith in them. Africans were excluded from the white settlers' churches and many broke away from the paternalistic missionary orders to establish their own African Christian church organizations. The Watch Tower Bible and Tract Society was introduced into Shona areas in the 1940s and 1950s by domestic servants from Nyasaland, and today is a powerful religious force in the country. During the war, many churches, especially the Roman Catholic Church, attacked the white government and gave financial and moral support to the African nationalists.

Health care, almost the best in tropical Africa before the war, has deteriorated alarmingly. The disruption of rural life created by the war and the massive relocations of the populations led to an almost complete breakdown of rudimentary social and health services. In early 1979, the Rhodesian Medical Association reported that the government had closed down clinics in many areas to prevent medical supplies from falling into the hands of the Patriotic Front guerrillas. Raids on farms by both guerilla and government forces reduced food supplies and contributed to spreading malnutrition. Malaria eradication programs ceased in most rural areas, and malaria increased dramatically. The war also led to the closure of Rhodesia's excellent veterinary programs. In the first 4 months of 1979, nearly 500,000 African-owned cattle died either from tick-borne diseases or because of the destruction by guerrillas of cattle-dipping tanks. Foot and mouth disease is rife, and diseases unknown for half a century have reappeared.

The nation's long history has been punctuated tragically by strife. The Shona's Mwenemutapa Empire successfully fought against Portuguese intrusions in the late sixteenth and early seventeenth centuries, but at the cost of disunity and the disintegration of the empire. In the 1830s and 1840s the Shona people were defeated by Ndebele warriors, who established a conquest state, called Matabeleland, and forced the Shona into a tributary position. Later, the South African imperialist Cecil Rhodes sought control of Matabeleland, and in 1888, King Lobengula signed a treaty with Rhodes's agents giving them a monopoly over Matabeleland's subsurface minerals. Inevitably, white settlers and Africans competed for land and raided each other's cattle. In two subsequent Matabele Wars (1893–1894, 1896–1897), the Matabele Empire was destroyed, much African land was confiscated, and the area, soon to be called Southern Rhodesia, was taken over by the British South Africa Company. A hut tax, imposed on the Africans, forced many of them to work on the white settlers' farms in order to meet their tax obligations. Thus the Africans became a landless proletariat on the lands of their ancestors.

In 1923, whites voted to transform Southern Rhodesia into a self-governing Crown Colony with a constitution giving the British Crown a veto over constitutional matters and racial policy, thus enhancing the white settlers' power. Africans continued to lose land in the face of rising white immigration and an accelerating black population increase.

In 1953, Southern Rhodesia and the British Protectorates of Northern Rhodesia and Nyasaland were joined in the white-dominated Federation of the Rhodesias and Nyasaland. African nationalism grew in all the territories and led to the breakup of the federation in 1963, and to a tragic split in the nationalist movement.

Northern Rhodesia and Nyasaland became, respectively, the independent African nations of Zambia and Malawi. Southern Rhodesian whites unilaterally declared their independence (UDI) in November 1965, and established the white-dominated Republic of Rhodesia under Prime Minister Ian Smith. African nationalist parties were banned and driven into exile. Not a single nation in the world extended diplomatic recognition, but many nations did not join the boycotts of Rhodesia, and the country's economy boomed.

All went well for Rhodesia until 1974, when five centuries of Portuguese colonial rule in Africa ended, and neighboring Mozambique, crucial to Rhodesian access to the sea, became a hostile African-ruled nation. Recognizing the changing political situation, South Africa's Prime Minister, John Vorster, forced the hitherto intransigent Ian Smith to negotiate with the African nationalists and move toward African majority rule.

After June 1979, the country was ruled by an American-educated Methodist Bishop, Abel Muzorewa, who served as Prime Minister in a multiracial government. The 1979 constitution provided for African majority rule, based on universal adult suffrage, and reserved for whites one-fourth of the Prime Minister's Cabinet and 28 of the 100 parliamentary seats, even though whites represented less than 4 percent of the total population.

This document grew out of the March 1978 Internal Agreement between the white government of Prime Minister Ian Smith and three moderate African nationalists: Chief Jeremiah Chirau of the Zimbabwe United People's Organization, Reverend Ndabaningi Sithole of the African National Council, and Bishop Abel Muzorewa of the United African National Council (UANC). It was ratified by a referendum in which only the 90,000 white voters were allowed to participate. However, in national multiracial elections in April 1979, when nearly 70 percent of the country's eligible voters cast their ballots, Muzorewa's UANC won 67 percent of the votes and thus secured 51 of the 100 parliamentary seats. Smith's Rhodesian Front party won all 28 seats reserved for whites. Despite the impressive turnout, many Zimbabweans, including Reverend Sithole, labeled the election a sham.

Strongest opposition to the Muzorewa regime came from the Patriotic Front, an uneasy alliance formed in 1976 between Joshua Nkomo of the Zimbabwe African People's Union and Robert Mugabe of the Zimbabwe African National Union. Together, they constituted the guerrilla movement. They were supported by the Organization of African Unity (which had repudiated the Zimbabwe-Rhodesia regime), the Soviet Union, China, and the Front Line States of Zambia, Tanzania, Mozambique, Angola, and Botswana.

The guerrilla struggle, which began in 1966, escalated dramatically in 1979, and by mid-1979, nearly 16.5 percent of the country had been liberated and 80 percent was under government-imposed martial law. But all groups were suffering from war weariness and internal strife, and outside powers were increasingly impatient. Zambia, unable to receive supplies from the south, was on the verge of starvation and bankruptcy.

The stalemate broke in October 1979 when the British government, supported by most members of the British Commonwealth, persuaded the contending factions (including the Patriotic Front) to accept a cease-fire, a new constitution, and a new election supervised by the British government and a Commonwealth peacekeeping force. Britain and the United States then quickly lifted economic sanctions, and in December 1979, the country was restored temporarily to the status of a British colony, again called Rhodesia, under the British governor Lord Christopher Soames. In January 1980, leaders of the Patriotic Front returned to Salisbury and the tense and frustrating process of campaigning for new elections began.

The elections in March resulted in a stunning and unprecedented victory for Marxist leader Robert Mugabe and his Zanu party. His candidates won 57 of the 80 African seats in the 100-member legislature to Nkomo's 20 seats and Muzorewa's 3. Twenty legislative seats were reserved for whites, almost all of which were won by Ian Smith's Rhodesian Front. But real power had passed at last to the African majority, and Great Britain formally gave Zimbabwe its independence on April 18, 1980, with Robert Mugabe as Prime Minister.

For the next six months Mugabe steered a pragmatic middle course, balancing white interests against black and Nkomo's faction against his own, while contending with more radical Marxist elements in his own party. Mugabe masterfully defused the widespread African labor strikes in May 1980, and actively sought Western aid while rebuffing the Soviets. He broke diplomatic relations with South Africa, yet allowed South African trade to increase. By late 1980, the Prime Minister had only begun to turn attention to the thornier and more delicate problems of land reform, health, education, and the integration of the tens of thousands of frustrated and impatient former guerrillas into civilian society.

Richard W. Hull

North Africa
and
the
Middle East

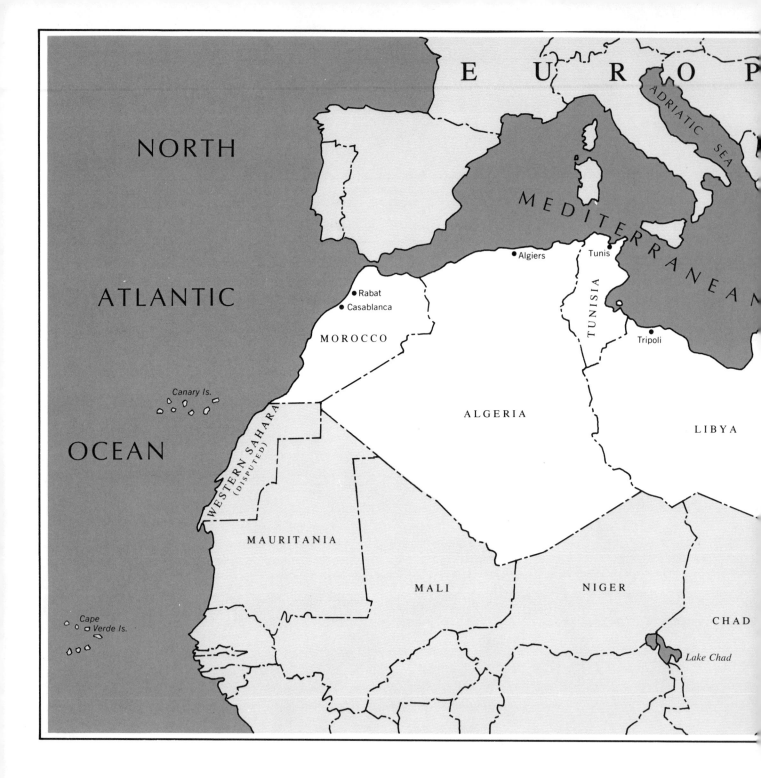

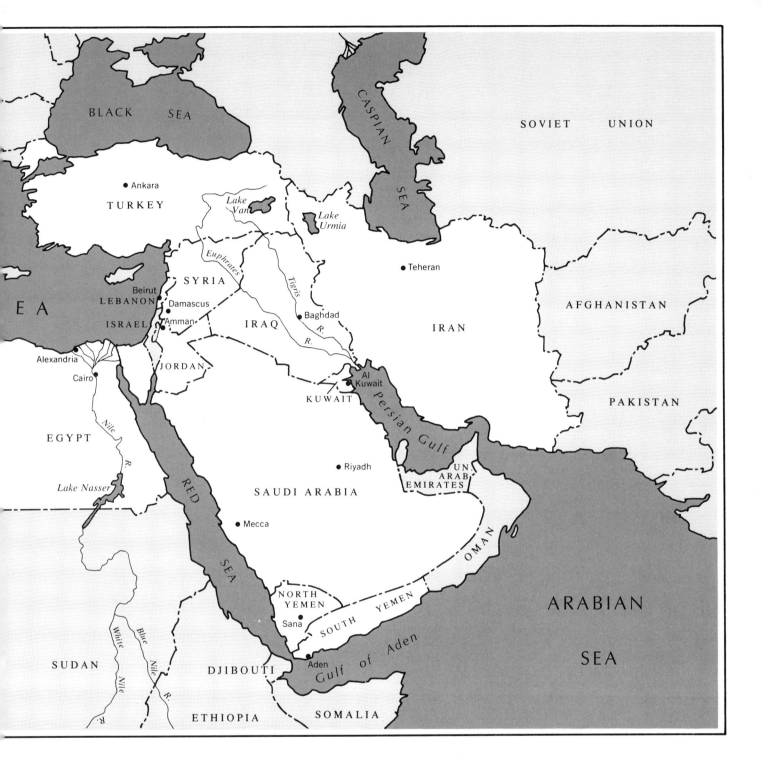

Algeria
(Democratic and Popular Republic of Algeria)

Area: 919,590 sq mi (2,381,738 sq km)
Population: 17.7 million
 Density: 19.2 per sq mi (7.4 per sq km)
 Growth rate: 3.2%
Percent of population under 21 years of age: more than 33%
Infant deaths per 1,000 live births: not available
Life expectancy at birth: 53.6 years (1976)
Leading causes of death: not available
Ethnic composition: Arab; Berber
Languages: Arabic; Berber; French
Literacy: 25%
Religions: Muslim
Percent population urban: not available
Percent population rural: not available
Gross national product: $22.3 billion
 Per capita GNP: $1,260
 Per capita GNP growth rate: 2.1% (1970–1976)
Inflation rate: not available

The North African state of Algeria has a powerful voice in third world councils and in the Arab League. Linked by its geographic location, economic resources, and foreign policy orientation to Europe, the Near East, and sub-Saharan Africa, Algeria speaks for the redress of grievances against vis-à-vis the industrialized nations, for the rights of the Palestinian people, and for the liberation of black people in southern Africa.

The current prestige of the Algerian leadership in the third world derives from its lengthy struggle against French colonialism. Out of the throes of more than 7 years of conflict (1954–1962), a war-ravaged Algeria emerged to build a new life and a new political system. In the nearly 2 decades since, this dynamic country on the southern shores of the Mediterranean has met both challenges successfully. In the process, Algeria has established a measure of economic growth and political stability that makes it the envy of many other states in the Mediterranean basin.

Physically, Algeria is a land of great beauty and startling contrasts. Within its confines are verdant coastal zones with magnificent agricultural enclaves reminiscent of southern California. Not far from its coastline, the traveler encounters gentle upland slopes, craggy mountains, and deep, crosscutting ravines—the refuge of the Berbers, Algeria's original, non-Arab population.

With a land area of 919,590 square miles (2,381,738 sq km), which is about one-third the size of the United States, Algeria is among the largest nations in the Middle East and Africa. Geographically, it is divided into four zones: (1) a narrow coastal region of some 600 miles (966 km), called the Tell, where most of Algeria's major cities are located and where most

of the modern agricultural activities are clustered; (2) the adjoining high plateau region—averaging 3,000 feet (914 m) above sea level—a rocky, barren area; (3) the intersecting Atlas Mountains; and (4) the interior Saharan desert region. Approximately 80 percent of Algeria's total land area consists of steppes, desert, and mountainous terrain. Rainfall, except along the coastal belt, is irregular, leading the interior population to follow pastoral pursuits and oasis farming.

Because of the country's geography, the bulk of Algeria's population is concentrated in the coastal zone and in mountain regions such as the Kabylia and Aurès. In 1976, the government estimated that Algeria had a total population of 16.2 million and that the annual growth rate was 3.2 percent. The principal urban agglomerations were Algiers, 2 million; Oran, 600,000; Constantine, 500,000; and Annaba, 250,000. In addition, the government estimated that almost 500,000 Algerians lived in France, working in factories, mines, and other sectors requiring unskilled laborers. Like other third world nations with a substantial growth rate, more than one-third of Algeria's population is less than 21 years old. With its high population growth rate, much of Algeria's excess population has been forced to move to the cities and towns or emigrate to France.

The government is trying to cope with this problem by establishing a modern industrial sector in petrochemicals, electronics, and related fields. Because of the shortage of skilled managers, technicians, and planners, some projects have been ill-conceived; nevertheless, the government intends to press on with its program. Currently, efforts to transform Algeria into a modern industrial nation have left the country with a foreign debt of $13 billion.

The management and direction of the Algerian economy are almost entirely in the hands of the government. In the period 1962–1972, the government nationalized all major foreign business interests and many private Algerian firms. State enterprises (over 75 of them) and government agencies oversee all the nation's industries, much of its foreign trade, and a substantial portion of its retail, banking, and credit systems.

The government's development strategy includes attempts to improve the quantity and quality of its agricultural output. Wine remains the principal agricultural export—a reflection of Algeria's colonial past—but the country is expanding its production of wheat, barley, olive oil, and citrus fruits. While more than half the population relies on agriculture for a livelihood, less than one-tenth of Algeria's gross domestic product (GDP) derives from this sector.

Algeria's gross national product (GNP) rose to $17.4

billion in 1978; its per capita distribution exceeded $850. Much of the country's impressive growth is directly attributable to its oil and natural-gas sectors, where Algeria ranks tenth and fourth, respectively, as a world producer and in terms of proved reserves. A member of the OPEC oil cartel, Algeria has steadily increased its prices, thereby strengthening its balance of trade position and foreign exchange holdings.

Since the death of President Houari Boumediene in December 1978 and the selection of Colonel Chedli Benjedid to succeed him, the governing team has followed past policies on energy. This involves heavy reliance on the country's hydrocarbon reserves—7.5 billion barrels of oil, 3.4 billion barrels of condensate, 1.8 barrels of liquefied petroleum gas, and 100 trillion cubic feet (2.83 trillion cu m) of natural gas—to sustain its economic growth. (The GDP reached $21.8 billion in 1978, an impressive 8 percent growth rate.) The United States has a particular interest in Algeria's development prospects because it is an important trading partner, absorbing one-fourth of Algeria's productive capacity in liquefied natural gas, with contracts already signed for 1.8 billion cubic feet (50.9 million cu m) a day.

Algeria is a Muslim country. There are mosques in every town and village. Algiers has a center of higher Islamic religious instruction, and there are many holy leaders and religious savants.

However, the country also mirrors two other cultures—traditional Berber and tribal society on the one hand and modern French and Mediterranean civilization on the other. The traditional underpinning is reflected in the preservation of Berber customs and language in the Kabylia and Aurès mountain regions, the preservation of the *djemaa* (council) as a viable and venerable tribal institution, and the maintenance of the Berber's close familial ties when abroad or working in Algeria's major urban centers. The modern overlay is reflected in the use of the French language, the matriculation of Algerian students in European universities, and the constant search for ways to adapt advanced technologies to Algerian needs.

Thus far, there has been a relatively harmonious

blending of all these cultural influences, but Muslim fundamentalists occasionally object publicly to the growing secularization of life and what they regard as the corruption of basic Islamic values and precepts.

In rural areas, the souk, or "market," is the focal point of communal social and commercial relations. Each town has its weekly souk day, when gossip is exchanged, local political news is transmitted, and products are bartered or sold. In urban centers, in contrast, social life centers around the cinema, sports contests, and family affairs involving marriage, birth, and death.

Algerian women are becoming increasingly emancipated. While the veil is still used in rural areas, Western education and modes of dress are available. Women participate in local elections and compete with men for positions where advanced training and expertise are required. However, as is true in most Mediterranean countries, women do not possess full freedom and cannot enter into informal relationships with males without observing local conservative conventions and restraints. In short, although the position of women remains inferior, significant improvement has occurred.

Since independence, Algeria has developed an increasingly sophisticated educational infrastructure. About 25 percent of the population are literate. Almost 15 percent of government expenditures are allocated to education, with special emphasis on technical instruction. Primary schooling includes courses for children 6 to 11 years old. High school (secondary school) extends through a 7-year period. In addition, university training is available in Algiers and Oran, as well as abroad. The government has not yet overcome a severe shortage of teachers.

In rural communities, the dominant social and class distinctions tend to follow traditional lines. Status is ascriptive, based on religious title, landholding, size of herd, occupation, and reputation of family in terms of the local history. In urban communities, status is achieved, with high ranking given to military professionals, government officials, educated technicians, and middle-class merchants. Throughout Al-

Bedouin camels and sheep graze on the road between Sètif and Constantine. Traditional agricultural practices contrast with modern worker-managed state farms in Algeria. (Photo: United Nations.)

geria, the highest status is accorded to the *mujahadeen,* the guerrilla warriors who fought to liberate Algeria from French rule.

Old class distinctions are essentially the product of Algerian history. Like most North African countries, Algeria has served historically as a gigantic funnel through which conquering armies and civilizations have passed. The country experienced, in turn, the rule of Phoenicians, Romans, Vandals, Arabs, and Turks. Each left a patina of cultural influence, but the tribes and people of the interior regions, the Atlas Mountains and the Saharan steppes, resisted the conquering armies and maintained a measure of independence. The Arab conquests in the seventh and eleventh centuries, however, resulted in a general conversion to Islam (the religion espoused by the Prophet Muhammad) and the adoption of Arabic as the language of religion, commerce, politics, and learning.

It remained for France, which launched its colonial conquests in the fourth decade of the nineteenth century, to draw the diverse peoples and territories together and to begin to implant a sense of national consciousness. Previously, personal loyalties and political identities were aligned with tribal groups, clan factions, or the extended family. No national identity in the modern sense existed in Algeria. However, the arrival of almost a million European settlers, the creation of a modern economic system (albeit under French domination), the settlers' seizure of the best agricultural lands, and the establishment of a political and social system that blatantly discriminated against the Muslim population led to rising protest. Northern Algeria was ultimately organized as an Overseas Department of France with representatives in the French National Assembly, and control of Algeria passed almost entirely into French hands.

Following World War II, Algeria's failure to secure equal political and social status led to the growth of nationalist agitation in the Muslim population—a development that was greeted with increased repression. On November 1, 1954, Algerian nationalists launched their military campaign against French police posts and military caserns.

Over the next 7 years, the Algerians organized a liberation force, the National Popular Army (ANP), and a political party, the National Liberation Front (FLN), to sustain the conflict. France responded by rushing 500,000 troops to Algeria. During the war, almost 250,000 Muslims were killed; 2 million were resettled in relocation centers; and 300,000 fled to neighboring Morocco and Tunisia to await the outcome of the war. The strains of the conflict led to the collapse of France's Fourth Republic in 1958 and the return to power of President Charles de Gaulle, who subsequently offered the "peace of the brave" to the FLN. On March 12, 1962, peace accords were signed at Evian, France; and, after a referendum was conducted, independence was announced July 3.

Tragically, in an expression of opposition, the European settler population engaged in a round of violent attacks against the Muslims; subsequently, during the summer of 1962 virtually all Europeans fled to France. Thus, at independence, war-ravaged Algeria lacked the technical and specialized expertise needed to maintain effective government and manage the country's modern economic sector.

Algeria had few conventions or institutions to guide it through its difficult postwar period of institution building and economic rehabilitation. A sturdy democratic tradition had not been implanted; politics had largely been the preserve of the Europeans. Algerian experience in the art of governing was limited, and no meaningful effort had been made during the 7-year period of the liberation struggle to organize cadres of administrators, technicians, and bureaucrats.

No politically integrative mechanism emerged from the early nationalist experience; the FLN was a loose amalgam of diverse and quarreling interest groups. The country was subsequently brought to the brink of civil war as rival leaders competed for political power. Ultimately, Ahmed Ben Bella (one of the founders of the liberation movement), supported by Boumediene, leader of the so-called external army, assumed full power.

The political relationship between Ben Bella, who assumed the post of President, and Boumediene, who was appointed Minister of Defense, was an uneasy one. On June 19, 1965, Boumediene deposed his superior after securing the support of the Army. He directed the government until his death in December 1978. As a result of a special Congress convened by the FLN in January 1979 and national elections held

Trainees are instructed in the telegraphy workshop of the Algiers Telecommunications Training Center. (Photo: United Nations.)

the following month, he was replaced by Colonel Chedli Benjedid, another military man.

Today, Algeria has a well-structured government. A constitution, drawn up in 1976, provides for a President, a Ministerial Council, and a National Revolutionary Council. At the local level, communal assemblies and *wilaya* (provincial assemblies) provide the underpinnings of popular participation in the decision-making process. At the same time, efforts have been launched to revive the FLN as a vanguard party to provide guidance and advice to government ministers. However, at present, the military serves as the most influential institution, providing officers for service as provincial governors and in various ministerial posts. Working with Western-trained technicians and bureaucrats, the military has fashioned a relatively cohesive government, one which provides stability and coherence in the planning and management of most agencies.

The future of Algeria depends on a host of factors, only a handful of which can be controlled by its existing leadership. The regime must decide whether it wishes to continue its support of the Polisario liberation movement and its military campaign against Morocco and Mauritania, which partitioned and annexed the Spanish Sahara in 1975–1976. Continued support means the risk of a confrontation with Morocco and possible hostilities. A second potential problem area involves the establishment of a viable system permitting Algerians to participate effectively in the processes of government. Critics of the existing leadership are convinced that there is not sufficient opportunity to express dissent over government policies and performance. A third area of concern—one which the leadership has little control over—relates to the world economic outlook. A major recession in the international community would diminish the current demand for Algeria's energy exports and would undermine its balance of payments position. A slackening of Algeria's hitherto impressive growth rate could weaken public support for the existing leadership and, conceivably, create a political situation which would bring about major changes in the power structure. *William H. Lewis*

Egypt
Arab Republic of Egypt

Area: 386,000 sq mi (999,730 sq km)
Population: 38.7 million (1978)
  Density: 100.2 per sq mi (38.9 per sq km)
  Growth rate: 2.1% (avg. 1970–1976)
Percent of population under 14 years of age: 41 (1975)
Infant deaths per 1,000 live births: 101 (1974)
Life expectancy at birth: 52.4 years (1975)
Leading causes of death: not available
Ethnic composition: Egyptians; Copts (Egyptians); Bedouin (Arabs) (1%)
Language: Arabic
Literacy: 40% (1970)
Religions: Muslim (93%); Christian
Percent population urban: not available
Percent population rural: not available
Gross national product: $15.5 billion
  Per capita GNP: $1400
  Per capita GNP growth rate: 5.2% (1977)
Inflation rate: not available

"Egypt is the Nile and the Nile is Egypt." This often-quoted remark says a great deal about the country in developmental terms. The Nile has had a major impact on the land and the people; Egyptians can live only along its banks, although its waterborne parasites endanger their health. Although the continued scientific management of its water holds promise for further agricultural development, its potential is limited.

If the Nile is Egypt's womb, then the key to full development of the country lies in severing the agricultural umbilical cord and seeking sustenance from other sources, including oil and other natural resources, services like passage through the Suez Canal, and steel and manufacturing industries.

The Nile creates a green sliver below Cairo called Upper Egypt and a green fan above Cairo called the Delta (or Lower Egypt). Together, these two areas constitute the 3.5 percent of Egypt's land that is habitable and contain 99 percent of Egypt's roughly 40 million people. Over 50 percent of the population are engaged in agricultural pursuits, raising cotton, onions, and rice, the country's main crops. Egyptian farmers are among the most accomplished in the world, and the combination of their skill and the richness of the soil gives Egypt some of the highest per acre crop yields in the world. Egypt long ago shifted from subsistence agriculture to commercial agriculture by growing cotton for export—a move that many third world countries have yet to make.

While the ready availability of Nile water has been an advantage to Egypt, until recently Egypt had little else in the way of natural resources. With Israel's release of the Sinai oil fields captured in the 1967 war, Egypt became self-sufficient in oil production in the 1970s. In the 1980s, Egypt may even become a small exporter of oil. Aside from oil, the major source of energy is the hydroelectric power generated by the Aswan High Dam. Phosphates are another significant natural resource; they are used as fertilizer to replace the natural nutrients that the annual flooding of the Nile provided until the Aswan High Dam began partial operation in 1965.

Egypt is remarkably free of ethnic and religious divisions. The Egyptians are distinct among Arabs; their darker skins undoubtedly reflect the historic communications link between the Nile valley and black Africa. The 93 percent of the population which are Sunni (orthodox) Muslim identify culturally with the Arab Middle East and the Monophysite Coptic (Eastern) Christians accept the Arab identification because of a common sense of Egyptian cultural and nationalistic identity. The word Egypt itself is the ancient Greek word for "Copt."

Reinforcing this remarkable social homogeneity is Arabic, the universal language of the country. The nomadic Bedouin, a source of social division elsewhere in the Middle East, comprise less than 1 percent of Egypt's population. Social stratification in Egypt has changed fundamentally since 1805, but a distinction between the elite and the masses remains.

The classical Arabic word *ayan* ("notables") and the colloquial Arabic expression *kubbar* ("big shots") are used to describe the elite, which includes the ruling class, supporting or ancillary elements like the middle class (technobureaucrats, military and professional people, and students and entrepreneurs), the resident landowning class, and the religious class. As a component of this middle class, the military remains most important in political terms. Since 1970, however, the army has been an arbiter of Egyptian

politics rather than an active participant, and professionals (especially lawyers), students, and entrepreneurial elements have achieved increased prominence.

The resident landowning class is perhaps the most enduring element of the elite. Politically prominent before 1952, the landowners survived the successive land-reform programs of 1952, limiting ownership to 300 acres (121 ha); 1961, limiting ownership to 100 acres (40 ha); and 1969, limiting ownership to 50 acres (20 ha). The land-reform programs eliminated absentee landowners, who represented less than 1 percent of the population and owned 19.7 percent of the land in 1952. But resident landowners, possessing between 5 and 50 acres (2 to 20 ha) and comprising 5.5 percent of all landowners, still hold 43 percent of the land. Ownership of 3 acres (1.2 ha) is considered necessary for subsistence; thus this politically important resident landowning element also produces the country's agricultural surpluses.

The religious class *ulama* (meaning "learned men of Islam") is important because of the religious character of Egyptian society. Any regime or political leadership in Egypt needs a religious legitimacy, meaning that the ulama must at least not oppose the regime. Egyptian regimes are therefore careful not to invite the antagonism of the ulama. The resurgence of religious feeling throughout the Islamic world is reflected in Egypt. The religious class centered at Cairo's Muslim University of El-Azhar (founded A.D. 196) has assumed greater political importance. How-

A woman washes clothes in front of shanty housing built on a garbage dump in Izbit el Nakhl. Rapid urbanization and population growth have led to inadequate housing. (Photo: United Nations/B. P. Wolff.)

Using a bullock-drawn plow, an Egyptian farmer tills the soil at the oasis of Al-Faiyūm. Egyptian farmers produce some of the highest agricultural yields per acre in the world. (Photo: United Nations/ B. P. Wolff.)

An irrigation canal in Tanta, part of a tile drainage project covering 1 million acres (400,000 hectares) of land in the Nile Delta, makes possible a 20 percent increase in crop production for farmers in the area. (Photo: World Bank/ Ray Witlin.)

ever, there is a wide spectrum of religious views in the country, ranging from the modernist and, to some extent, mystical views of the Sufi Muslims of El-Azhar to the fundamentalist but progressive views of the outlawed but condoned Muslim Brethren and members of other extreme fundamentalist groups. The overall political result is lack of effective unity.

The masses include the urban proletariat, peasants and nomads. Since the 1920s, urban workers have been an important feature of national and urban politics. In January 1975 and January 1977, economic grievances resulting from the high cost of living and the decision (quickly rescinded) to reduce food subsidies led to violence in urban centers from one end of Egypt to the other. The unemployed urban masses, like the masses in many other third world countries, tend to retain their rural values and social organization. As a result, in spite of poor housing, disease, and

poverty, this group remains politically stable and perhaps even politically conservative.

Peasants benefited significantly from the 1952 coup. Before 1952, peasants received little in the way of government services and hardly participated in politics. Since 1952, village electrification, potable drinking water, agricultural technical services, and health services have helped alleviate the poverty, disease, and animal-like existence of the peasant. In spite of this, a visitor to an Egyptian village would still note the dust and dirt, the prevalence of straw, mud, and brick houses, and the absence of toilet facilities, internal water outlets, and electrification. In short, although improvements have been revolutionary, they are still marginal.

Informal and formal group identification radiates outward from family to peer group and cohorts, neighborhood, religious organization, trade union, political party, and then nation. The family is important in establishing solidarity and as an agent of socialization in the political culture of the society. The Egyptian family is an extended family. It includes grandparents, aunts, uncles, and cousins, all living within a single dwelling or on the same street or alley. (In one quarter of Cairo, an entire modern apartment building is occupied by members of the same family.) The solidarity of the family is reinforced by the common Middle Eastern custom of arranged first-cousin marriages. These marriages cement family relationships; keep the economics of dowries, bride prices, and inheritance under family control; and maintain informal social controls in case of marital difficulties. Families are also influence networks. Thus, if a service is needed, the first question asked is whether a relative can provide the service or whether a relative knows someone who can.

The father dominates the family, especially his sons. The result is a receptive attitude toward authoritarian and paternalistic leadership. Thus, Sadat's speeches frequently refer to the Egyptian nation as a family, with the obvious implication that he is its head.

When a male reaches puberty, he abandons his close relationship with his mother and moves into relationships with boys of his own age on his own street. When he enters high school or a university, he becomes part of a solidarity group or "old boy network." Thus Nasser, Sadat, and virtually all the officers leading the July 1952 coup were members of the Royal Military Academy class of 1938.

Egypt's developmental problems are staggering. With per capita income of $236 a year, a literacy figure of only 40 percent (1970) and a 1974 infant mortality rate of 101 per 1,000 (the highest in the Middle East), Egypt faces formidable problems. The root of these problems is the population growth rate. With a 2.2 percent annual growth (average 1970–1976), Egypt's rate is not so high as some nations' (Algeria's population is growing 3.2 percent a year); but with a habitable area of only 3.5 percent, Egypt has some of

Egyptian peasants walk in front of the main pumping station at Tanta in the Nile Delta, where a land drainage program helps some 3 million farmers. (Photo: World Bank/ Ray Witlin.)

the highest population densities in the world, for example, 3,035 per square mile (1,172 per sq km) in the agricultural area of the country. Social resistance to family planning is so strong that in spite of repeated government statements of support for birth control there has been little follow-through.

Against a background of a declining gross national product (GNP) growth rate before 1974 (4 percent in the period 1960–1973 and 3.3 percent in the period 1965–1973), a reported GNP growth rate of 8 percent for 1978 was spectacular. Nonetheless, the figures for infant mortality, literacy, and birthrate, combined with other indices of development, caution against premature expectations for rapid development.

The size of Egypt's foreign debt is another basic structural economic weakness. Total hard currency receipts in 1977 from oil, the Suez Canal, tourism, and, most important, remittances of Egyptians working abroad ($1.56 billion) amounted to about $3 billion, only a little more than the $2.8 billion needed for debt servicing. The International Monetary Fund (IMF) and the Gulf Organization for the Development of Egypt, however, agreed that their funds could be used for debt servicing until 1981. Thus the Egyptians had a brief respite in which they could direct attention to obtaining the funding needed for economic assistance and development.

The extraordinary feature of Egypt's historical development is its length and continuity. It began with the coming to power, in 1805, of a remarkable Albanian officer in the Ottoman Turkish army, Muhammad Ali. With intelligence and vision, he created a modern army to prevent the return of the French (Napoleon) and the British. This essentially political decision led to the creation of a modern economic system, a transformed social structure, and increased opportunities for social mobility. A modern army meant training officers in Rome or Paris and procuring war matériel. The need for hard cash, in turn, led to the shift from traditional subsistence agriculture to modern com-

mercial agriculture—growing cotton as a cash crop. Even this did not satisfy Egypt's urgent need for cash.

During the 1830s, the land-tenure system gradually shifted from state or collective ownership to individual Egyptian (as opposed to Turkish) ownership. This system of land tenure represents a stage of development yet to be achieved in many areas of the third world, especially in Africa. Behind the creation of a modern economic system and the modernization of the system of land tenure was the impulse to expand the authority and function of the state. To this end, Muhammad Ali deprived the ulama of many of their

Rush hour traffic jams the streets in a business section in Cairo. (Photo: United Nations/ B. P. Wolff.)

traditional functions (social welfare, education, and even public health). The resulting secularization further modernized Egyptian society, but religious sentiment remains strong and politically relevant.

Egypt resisted British occupation of the country from 1882 to its nominal independence in 1922, which followed widespread uprisings in 1919. In fact, continued British interference in Egypt's internal affairs was a contributing factor in the 1952 coup, led by the Society of Free Officers, which toppled King Farouk. In 1953 Egypt became a republic under President Muhammad Naguib; in 1954 Gamal Abdel Nasser replaced him.

Clearly, even before 1952 Egypt had embarked on a course of economic modernization, however beset by stresses and inequalities, but so long as there was foreign interference there was no opportunity for the creation of a national sense of development. Political turmoil, however, did not prevent the emergence of a nascent modern entrepreneurial class. In addition, political manipulation and the fragmenting effects of Islamic inheritance law (land must be equally divided among the heirs) had led to inequalities in the size of landholdings.

The 1954 Anglo-Egyptian Treaty ended British interference (the final spasm was the British and French attack upon Egypt in 1956), while land reforms eliminated the worst abuses of land-tenure inequalities. Meanwhile, in the 1950s, the essentially middle-class military leadership tried to perpetuate the modern free-enterprise system and to foster a greater role for the native Egyptian entrepreneurial class. But perhaps because of their own inabilities and distrust of the young upstart revolutionaries, the entrepreneurs failed to respond. Instead, in the period of union be-

The Aswan High Dam, completed in 1970, is Egypt's major source of hydroelectric power. (Photo: United Nations/P. Pittet.)

tween Egypt and Syria (1958–1961), Egypt came in contact with more radical socialist ideas.

In July 1961, socialist decrees nationalized most industry, large-scale urban real estate holdings, banks, and insurance companies. While these decrees were carried out in the name of socialism, the result was more reminiscent of state capitalism, for the most part benefiting the military and technobureaucratic middle class.

Egypt's devastating military defeat in 1967 at the hands of the Israelis set in motion developments that took new direction after the death (by natural causes) of Nasser in September 1970. The last survivor of the Free Officers of 1952, Anwar Sadat, who succeeded to the presidency, professionalized the military and led it to withdraw from active politics. In 1974 Sadat announced a policy of economic liberalization that called for foreign private investment and for native Egyptian investment as well.

This economic shift in direction was accompanied by a political shift. After an abortive coup attempt against him by Nasserite elements in May 1971, Sadat declared that his regime was one of law and freedom. The rule of law meant restoring the prerevolutionary integrity and independence of the Egyptian legal system. Freedom meant the closing of political detention camps and the movement toward a multiparty system. In 1975, forums of the political left, right, and center were permitted within the Arab Socialist Union's single-party structure. By the following year, these forums were permitted to organize as political parties; and parliamentary elections were held in 1976 and in 1979. Freedom, however, did not preclude harassment, especially of the left wing.

In the June 1979 parliamentary elections, Sadat's own National Democratic Party gained 330 seats; the right-of-center opposition Socialist Labor Party, 29 seats; and the right-wing Liberal Socialist Party, 3 seats. The left-of-center Progressive Union Party was left without the few seats it previously held. After a referendum in May 1980, Sadat became President for life.

With the abrogation of the Soviet-Egyptian Friendship Treaty in 1976 and the decision to suspend payments on the debt to the Soviet Union, Egypt shifted from a reliance upon the East to a reliance upon the West. In economic terms, this meant submitting the Egyptian economy to Western demands for efficiency, discipline, and greater freedom from government regulation. In exchange, the IMF and the Gulf Organization for the Development of Egypt have provided major financial assistance.

As part of the Sinai I (1974) and Sinai II (1975) disengagement accords and the Egyptian-Israeli peace treaty (March 1979), the United States gave Egypt more than $1 billion a year in assistance. Saudi Arabia and Kuwait also provided Egypt with $2 billion annually before 1979, when they suspended their support in protest against the Egyptian-Israeli peace treaty. Currently committed Saudi and Kuwaiti

funds, however, can continue to be used, and private Saudi and Kuwaiti capital can and has continued to flow into the country.

Foreign aid has been used for infrastructural projects like the construction of sewer, telephone, and road systems, but it was hoped that private foreign investment would also stimulate industrial development. The result so far has been disappointing, with the exception of the establishment of tax-free zones where foreign goods bound for other nations in the Middle East are warehoused and factories for the assembly of such goods are operated.

Progress in rural areas has been more spectacular in design and possibly in accomplishment. Under a law passed in 1972 (Law 52), Egypt committed itself to the decentralization of its cumbersome, highly centralized and inefficient administrative structure. The governors of Egypt's 25 provinces were given more executive authority; more important, direct responsibility for village-level development was given to popularly elected village councils. Furthermore, in an Egyptian form of revenue sharing, 75 percent of central government taxes collected locally can now be retained for purposes of local investment. The result of Law 52 has been to increase economic activity at the local level. Whether it will serve to alleviate the grinding poverty of the Egyptian peasant, however, is a question still to be answered. If development in the rural areas simply reflects middle-class dominance, it may lead to social unrest.

The potential for social unrest remains real and must be considered against the background of Egypt's efforts to seek a peaceful resolution of its conflict with Israel. These efforts, although criticized bitterly by other Arab states, have had widespread support in Egypt. A major expectation of an Egyptian-Israeli peace, however, is the prospect of greater domestic prosperity. Should this expectation not be realized, the political right and the religious right may merge their forces, creating an explosive political situation.

In the 1980s, Egypt must meet economic expectations; reconcile political liberalization with political stability; and liberalize the economy, giving a greater role to the private sector while providing for equitable economic distribution.

Louis J. Cantori

Iran

(Islamic Republic of Iran)

Area: 620,000 sq mi (1.6 million sq km)
Population: 35.8 million
   Density: 58 per sq mi (22 per sq km)
   Growth rate: 3% (1970–1977)
Percent of population under 15 years of age: nearly 50%
Infant deaths per 1,000 live births: 120 (1975)
Life expectancy at birth: 51 years (1975)
Leading causes of death: not available
Ethnic composition: Persian, majority Turkish; Kurdish; Arab; Qashqai; Bakhtiari; Baluchi; Turkoman
Languages: Persian, about 50%; Azerbaijani; Gilani; Luri-Bakhtiari; Kurdish; Mazanderani; Baluchi; Arabic; Turkomeni; Armenian; Assyrian
Literacy: 36.9% (1971)
Religions: Shiite Muslim 97%; Sunni Muslim; Bahai; Christian; Jewish
Percent population urban: 48% (1978)
Percent population rural: 52% (1978)
Gross national product: not available
   Per capita GNP: over $2,000 (mid-1970s)
   Per capita GNP growth rate: not available
Inflation rate: not available

The desert lands of Iran are among the most desolate in the world, shaping its economy and its history. Only 10 percent of Iran's land is arable, and only one-half of that is cultivated. Even that soil is poor, highly saline, and subject to waterlogging, which keeps agricultural productivity low. Scarcity is ever present, and security is elusive. Today, Iran's leaders argue about the path to economic and social development, given the fact that the country has few natural resources except for its nonrenewable oil.

Iran is a large country, almost equal in size to West Europe. Its territory, 620,000 square miles (1.6 million sq km), lies south of the Soviet Union. Its southern coastline follows the Persian Gulf and the Arabian Sea for 2,000 miles (3,219 km) linking the Indian subcontinent and the Middle East. The interior of the country is divided by mountains that influence its climate and provide summer grazing grounds for a dwindling nomadic population. The Elburz Mountains face the landlocked Caspian Sea. Their northern slopes define Iran's richest agricultural region, the provinces of Gilan, Mazandaran, Gorgan, and Khorasan. On the Caspian coastline, the annual rainfall may exceed 80 inches (200 cm); in the southern part of the country precipitation seldom exceeds 8 inches (20 cm).

The Zagros Mountains divide Iran's central plateau, geographically dominated by the Dasht-e-Kavir (Great Salt Desert) from Khuzistan, Iran's oil producing province. The Zagros Mountains also form a rough boundary between several distinct ethnic groups—the Persian majority in the plateau area and the peoples in the western provinces, who are predominantly Turkish (Azerbaijan), Kurdish, and Arab (Khuzistan). The Persian center is also surrounded by the Qashqai in the southwest, the Bakhtiari in the south-central, the Baluchi in the southeast, and the Turkomans in the northeast.

Language is the major factor that distinguishes one ethnic group from another, although ethnic identity is also reinforced by social custom and marriage within extended families. Within the Persian population, too, regional differences exist that affect social relationships.

The Persian cultural heritage and Shia Islam are the two sources of community. Nearly half Iran's population of 35 million speak Persian (Farsi). In a country where television is still uncommon, story telling thrives. The favorite stories have been passed down from the Middle Ages, stories like Omar Khayyam's *Rubaiyat* and Ferdowsi's epic *Shah-nama* (*The Epic of the Kings*), recounting the bravery of Iranian heroes. Proposals to change written Persian from Arabic to Roman script have been consistently defeated in deference to the authority of Persian literature.

Some 97 percent of all Iranians follow Shia Islam. Most apparent in the Islamic Republic established in 1979, Shiite doctrine emphasizes community and the inseparability of government and society. Religion also dictates social behavior through the *hadith* (the words and customs of Muhammad as recorded by his followers). These religious norms help to contain social conflict and strengthen the family.

Relations between the Shiite Muslims and minority religious groups in Iran have usually been peaceful. One historical tradition venerates Iran as a haven for persecuted groups from neighboring countries: Jews, Armenians, and Assyrian Christians. Yet virtually no intermarriage takes place between Muslims and these minorities; and sporadic incidents of violence have resulted in the destruction of property. The most intense discrimination, however, is re-

Waste gases are burned off at oil fields in Iran. (Photo: United Nations/E. Adams/ Contract.)

served for the Bahais, who adhere to a universalist religious doctrine indigenous to Iran. Shiite Muslims regard Bahaism as an illegitimate Islamic sect and a vehicle for foreign influence in Iranian politics.

Religion and the family are integral parts of the everyday lives of most Iranians. Several generations of a family often live under the same roof. First-cousin marriages are still common, and one's mother-in-law is likely to be one's aunt as well. This custom helps to ensure that wealth is preserved within the family and that all parties to a prospective alliance have an equal investment in keeping the family honor intact. The family is particularly important in rural Iran, but even in the cities families try to live together, often on separate floors in one apartment building.

Despite limited farmland, agriculture plays an important role in Iran's economy. Of Iran's labor force 47 percent are employed in the agricultural sector. The gap between the profitability of the agricultural sector on the one hand, and oil and industrial wealth on the other is evidenced by the vast differences between rural and urban incomes. Government statistics for the period 1970–1971 show the ratio between rural and urban household expenditures to be 1 to 2.3; unofficial statistics place the ratio at 1 to 5. The inequality between Teheran and the poorest provinces is far greater. While per capita annual income for the country as a whole passed the $2,000 mark in the mid-1970s, per capita income in rural Baluchistan hovered around $100 per year.

Food crops constitute the largest part of Iran's agricultural production. Of these, wheat, barley, and rice are the most important. Production of all three grains increased in the twentieth century, and famines became rarer. The last widespread famine was a result of the Allied occupation during World War II, when food production fell and demand for food for the occupying troops rose. Low levels of agricultural productivity make nonfarm income important for the 19 million Iranians who live in rural areas.

More than 3 million Iranians received land under a redistribution program that began in 1962. But peasant farms are still small; 67 percent of Iran's farms contain fewer than 12 acres (4.9 ha) each and occupy only 16 percent of the total cultivated land. The land-reform program confronted neither the problem of landless rural laborers (perhaps one-half the rural labor force) nor the issue of food prices (the rural-urban terms of trade). Good farmland is scarce in Iran, and what land was available went to sharecroppers who had established their right to farm their landlords' plots, not to day laborers. The landless migrated to the cities, placing the government under pressure to keep urban food prices down, a policy that was especially hard on small farmers.

After 1960, nonagricultural production grew more rapidly than agriculture, oil exports became more profitable, and industrial investments began to take hold. Agriculture represented 24.5 percent of the gross domestic product (GDP) in 1967; it had fallen to 18.1 percent in 1972. Actual food production rose; but food imports also rose, reaching $2 billion worth in 1978.

Agriculture is a persistent concern of Iranian planners because it is culturally important in Iranian life. Even though it may not be economically productive, agriculture is also regarded as a stabilizing force because urban migration, which swells the ranks of unskilled labor in the cities, has raised fears of increased social conflict and political instability. Despite agreement on the need to improve rural conditions, however, there is little agreement about how to proceed.

At least two distinct agricultural sectors compete for limited investment resources. The peasant sector consists of small farms that typically are fragmented into nonadjacent plots (an inheritance from the traditional practice of dividing the most fertile lands of a village equitably among the several village households). The highly capital-intensive agribusiness sector specializes in sugar beet and, to a lesser extent, wheat production; its growing animal-husbandry and dairy farms compete with peasant production.

The new Islamic government finds it just as difficult to establish agricultural priorities as did Muhammad Riza Shah Pahlavi's regime. Abolhassan Bani-Sadr, President of the Republic, has given verbal support to both peasant agriculture and mechanized farming. But like its predecessor, the regime of Ayatollah Ruhollah Khomeini has been forced to import food despite its nationalistic doctrine.

Resentment of the foreign investments made in Iranian agribusiness under the Shah runs high, but the alternative is massive government investment in impoverished peasant agriculture. Illiteracy, a high birthrate (about 3 percent), and poor educational and health facilities are features of rural poverty. Rural schools are badly understaffed; the buildings are in poor condition (some have broken windows, few seats, and no heat or electricity); and materials for agricultural education are scarce. Peasant farmers know how far behind they are in terms of agricultural technology and capital, but they have virtually no political influence over development planning.

The Iranian government must combat illiteracy before it can address the problem of the shortage of technical skills. Three-fourths of Iran's women and more than half of its men are illiterate. In 1971, illiteracy in rural Iran was as high as 79.6 percent, while in the cities only 41.4 percent of the population over 6 years old could read and write. Some progress has been made in this area in recent years, but it has not been dramatic. The proportion of the total population that was literate rose from 29.4 percent in 1966 to 36.9 percent in 1971. The number of school-age Iranians attending classes at all levels rose by 66 percent during the same period.

Progress in technical education is hindered by a preference for the traditional academic fields. Competition is keen for places in universities in established fields—medicine, law, literature, and (recently)

management. Students from rural areas find it difficult to compete because most of them do not have access to high schools and must live with relatives in the cities if they wish to complete their high school educations. In 1978, 290,000 students took the *Konkur,* a nationwide college entrance examination, vying for 60,000 places at universities in Iran. Those who are unsuccessful study abroad or wait until the following year to try again.

Land redistribution, which began in 1962, was one step toward agricultural reform and rural development. Redistribution undermined the power of the traditional landowning class over the peasantry, but it did not actually increase agricultural productivity and income. Many of the former landowning families transferred their wealth into construction and industry in the cities, while in rural areas, the gap between the new peasant-landowners and agricultural day laborers widened.

Over the period of redistribution, agricultural mechanization increased. The number of two-wheel tractors imported into Iran jumped from 400 in 1962 to 4,000 in 1972. Most mechanization is in the agribusiness sector. Cooperatives, very weak in Iran, and independent owner-cultivators use less machinery.

On the smaller farms, most of the work, including the planting, fertilizing, and harvesting, is done by hand. Basin irrigation is used. Open ditches carry water to the crops, and much water is lost through evaporation and seepage. In many regions, the primary source of water for the ditches is the underground *qanat,* a water tunnel that is graded to permit water to flow to the village farmlands from a spring

On Taibad, a tiny village at the Afghanistan border, children tend the flocks instead of attending school. (Photo: United Nations/A. Jongen.)

some distance away. The qanats require frequent repair and, more serious, much of the water is lost through seepage before it reaches the fields.

In an attempt to rationalize the use of water for agriculture, an agricultural development policy was initiated in 1975, under Mansur Rouhani, who became Minister of Agriculture. Legislation was enacted to encourage farmers to move to land with sufficient water and fertile soil if their own lands were not productive. Rural-development funds were distributed to the villages that were in line for development under the new policy. It was hoped that the villages receiving more social and public services would attract farmers from less productive areas. Rouhani's policy generated an enormous amount of controversy because it threatened to disrupt peasant work groups and informal community planning.

Many Iranians responded to rural poverty by migrating to the cities. Between 1963 and 1978, Iran's urban population increased from 25 to 48 percent of the total population. Teheran, the capital, doubled in size between 1968 and 1978. Urban migrants were exposed to very different lifestyles in the cities. In the villages in Iran, villagers share their public bath, mortuary, teahouse, and mosque (in the larger villages). By contrast, few urban dwellers have any such community life. Urban unemployment also has more severe repercussions because the cost of living is higher in the cities.

The industrial growth favored by the Shah's regime contributed to the disparity between urban and rural Iran. Foreign capital was encouraged to promote industrialization, but the impact of Western culture that accompanied foreign investment made a mockery of modernization. Western-style dress was exaggerated in Teheran: miniskirts were shorter, women's

heels were higher, and jeans were tighter. In a country where dating is not generally accepted, modern couples shared vodka limes during long afternoons at ice cream/alcohol bars along Pahlavi Avenue.

Before the oil boom, Iran's chief industrial products were clothing, textiles, and food. During the early 1970s, industrial production also included chemical and mineral products, electrical machinery, and motor vehicles. Consequently, rural industry began to play a lesser role in production. The new industries are capital-intensive, and rural workers are unskilled. In 1972, rural industries employed roughly one-half the industrial workers in Iran, but they produced only 20 percent of the country's total industrial product.

During the period of the fifth development plan (1968–1972) the government offered tax incentives to firms that moved away from Teheran, hoping to spread industrial development more evenly throughout the country. Most managers were unwilling to leave the Teheran environs, however, and a ring of industrial plants grew up just beyond a 75-mile (120-km) radius of the capital. The manufacturing plants that did locate in rural areas did so in order to take advantage of the lower wage rates there and to escape government regulations regarding working conditions.

Manual labor, even skilled labor, has a very low status in Iran. The absence of a strong labor movement perpetuates the value placed upon white-collar desk jobs. Labor union organizations were tightly controlled by the government under the Shah and are still restricted by the Islamic Republic. Union members do not have the right to strike, and under the monarchy the Iranian Security and Intelligence Organization (SAVAK) was actively involved in the selection of union leaders. In 1975, the government pro-

In the old city of Ray, a worker lays out carpets to dry in the sun. Handmade carpets are a traditional industry. (Photo: United Nations/Witlin/PAS.)

mulgated a profit sharing plan that applied to all industrial establishments employing more than 100 workers. According to the plan, workers were to receive shares in the corporation they worked for and enjoy the profits from their labor. Managers in many companies were able to get around the law by reorganizing, establishing a "selling" firm that received profits but employed few workers and a "producing" firm that distributed shares to workers but received no profits. The weakness of the industrial labor force in Iran is a result of a very close alliance between private enterprise and the state over several centuries.

In Iran, economic planning in the 1970s was a result of the oil-based economy. In 1977, oil revenues accounted for 97.3 percent of Iran's exports and over 50 percent of its gross national product. By the fall of 1980, Iran's oil production had dwindled from 5.5 million barrels a day to 1.2 million barrels a day. And in late 1980, because of the widespread damage caused by the war between Iraq and Iran, Iran stopped exporting oil.

After the 1978 revolution, banks, large industrial establishments, and insurance companies were nationalized. Even before the revolution, many of these enterprises had been under joint public-private ownership.

The government dominates the capital market in contemporary Iran. Under the fifth development plan, the programs were divided into national, regional, and special regional projects. The lion's share—99 percent—of the development budget went to national projects such as a steel mill, atomic energy programs, and the aircraft industry—projects that contributed to national industrial growth. Special regional projects on the other hand were designed to lessen the impact of urban industrial growth on backward rural regions. Through these special regional projects, schools and roads were built, rural medical centers were established, and a minimal planning-administrative apparatus was set up at the grass-roots level.

Opportunities outside the modern sector dwindled as the vitality of the traditional economy deteriorated. Traditional Iranian bazaars had always been constructed in concentric circles around the local mosque (which once also functioned as the local school). In these bazaars, there were cottage industries, shops, credit institutions, and even apprentice training. The Shah's decision to revamp Iran's commercial and financial institutions along Western lines undermined the economic power of the bazaars. The Shah assumed that the bazaar economy was inefficient and incompatible with a modern, industrial Iran. Provincial officials in the Ministry of Commerce, therefore, were directed to give business licenses only to stores outside the bazaars; government bank loans were also directed toward modern enterprises. As the bazaar declined, so did the interests of a significant commercial sector.

Before the revolution, Iran was a striking example of the deliberate creation of a military-industrial complex to foster economic growth. The central vehicle of the industrialization program in the mid-1970s was the military sector. Military imports have consumed over $20 billion since 1970. Aircraft assembly and repair plants were being built in Iran by three American manufacturers (Bell, Grumman, and Northrup) when the revolution occurred. The plants were located in Isfahan, a city of historical and architectural importance that was being transformed into a military-industrial center. Defense contractors were undertaking the technical education of army recruits, who would later be available for civilian jobs. A missile plant (Raytheon) in Shiraz was to serve as a model for a growing Iranian electronics industry.

Many Iranian planners dissented from the military-industrial strategy, partly because the initial import costs for military equipment, technical assistance, and training were so high. Officials in the central Plan and Budget Organization were concerned with increasing Iran's non-oil exports in order to sustain the import requirements of rapid industrialization. By 1977, Iran had begun to increase its exports of buses, detergents, iron and steel structures, and prepared foods. It had also begun to develop markets in non-industrialized countries in the Middle East and Africa, becoming less dependent on the Soviet Union and Japan for non-oil trade. Iran also played an increasingly important role in profitable Asian capital markets through the Asian Development Bank and the Association of Southeast Asian Nations (ASEAN).

The impetus for industrialization and international influence has strong historical roots in Iran. The Shah linked the country's future prospects to the Persian Empire of Darius and Cyrus, Xerxes and Artaxerxes, 2,500 years earlier. More vivid was the memory of the foreign occupations of Iranian soil during the two world wars. The Shah's father, Riza Shah Pahlavi, took power in a military coup d'état following World War I, bringing to an end the weakened Kajar dynasty. He was forced to abdicate in 1941 when he refused to accept Allied intervention during World War II. The throne that his son inherited was not secure, nor was his country intact. Russian troops controlled the north, and British troops controlled the south.

Corruption plagued the bureaucracy under the Shah; it mushroomed along with the oil boom. The negative impact of corruption on Iran's economic growth was one factor leading to the overthrow of the monarchy. More important, however, was United States military and economic involvement in Iran. This became the central issue for the next generation of Iranians because of the way it permeated economic planning decisions and social life. Hence, the Khomeini revolution led to the termination of United States–Iranian relations, especially after the November 1979 capture of the American embassy in Teheran by Muslim militants, who held some 52 Americans hostage before releasing them on January 20, 1981.

The political instability plaguing Iran was exacerbated by its 1980 war with Iraq, which led to the Iraqi seizure of Khurramshahr, the Iranian oil port, and Abadan, site of Iran's major oil refinery.

Political stability is one prerequisite for planning and growth, but it is not enough. Establishing planning priorities will always be difficult in Iran because of its scarcity of land and water and because of the continuation of foreign interference in its political life. Despite Iran's continuing social conflict, however, its cultural integrity is strong. The prospects for future economic development depend in large measure on whether government leaders can build an economy that has the same integrity.

Ann T. Schulz

Iraq
(Republic of Iraq)

Area: 172,000 sq mi (445,500 sq km)
Population: 12.2 million (1977)
 Density: 71 per sq mi (27 per sq km)
 Growth rate: 3.4% (1970–1977)
Percent of population under 14 years of age: 47% (1975)
Infant deaths per 1,000 live births: 28 (1975)
Life expectancy at birth: 53 years (1975)
Leading causes of death: not available
Ethnic composition: Arab, Kurdish, Turkish, Turkoman
Languages: Arabic, Kurdish
Literacy: 51% (1978)
Religions: Shiite Muslim 50%; Sunni Muslim 50%
Percent population urban: 60%
Percent population rural: 40%
Gross national product: $22.7 billion
 Per capita GNP: $1,860
 Per capita GNP growth rate: 7.1% (1970–1977)
Inflation rate: 10% average last 3 years

Iraq, regarded as the site of the Garden of Eden and the scene of much of the history recounted in the Bible, is today one of the most important countries in the Middle East. Its more ancient name, Mesopotamia (meaning land between the rivers) is a reminder that until very recently its economic life revolved almost entirely around two great rivers, the Tigris and the Euphrates. Their abundant water, running through a torrid desert, created a fertile plain and made irrigation possible; the country became a granary for many empires. Agriculture is still important in Iraq, but in the twentieth century it has been the development of oil fields that has boosted the country's importance and vastly enhanced its economic possibilities.

Oil is nature's one great gift to Iraq; it has no other economically significant minerals. The diversity and rapid pace of its recent economic development stem from its oil revenues. Petroleum resources have generated such enormous export revenues in recent years that glass-fronted skyscrapers now look down on mud huts, and the traditional, almost feudal social order has crumbled.

The western and southwestern parts of the country are desert. This inhospitable area, about half the surface of the country, is largely uninhabited save by wandering nomads. In the desert regions, Iraq borders on Syria, Jordan, Saudi Arabia, and Kuwait, with no significant geographical features to mark the end of one country and the beginning of the next. The soil in the desert, composed of ancient rock that has been much eroded, is unsuitable for cultivation or even grazing. The other three geographical regions are lower Iraq, upper Iraq, and the northeastern mountain region. In general, the country slopes upward from south to north, from the reed-matted marshes on the Persian Gulf to the 10,000-foot (3,050-m) mountains on the borders of Iran and Turkey.

The economic heart of Iraq, as far as agriculture and oil are concerned, lies in the regions known as lower and upper Iraq, where the Tigris and Euphrates made agriculture and civilization possible. Lower Iraq extends for about 350 miles (563 km) from Baghdad, the capital, southeastward toward the Persian Gulf; upper Iraq stretches northwest from Baghdad for about the same distance and is bounded on the north and east by the mountainous region.

It is impossible to exaggerate the importance of the Tigris and Euphrates Rivers; Iraq depends on them as absolutely as Egypt depends on the Nile. They rise in the highlands of eastern Turkey, and their upper courses are widely separated, the Euphrates running for several hundred miles through Syria. In lower Iraq, until they join to form the short Shatt-al-Arab near the Gulf, they follow roughly parallel courses, separated by a broad strip of land that at some points is more than 100 miles (161 km) wide. This is a region of intensive agriculture based on irrigation. Most of Iraq's 12 million people live here and in upper Iraq, toiling in the heat in the low-lying fields just as their ancestors toiled for countless generations.

The waters of the Tigris and Euphrates Rivers are made available in lower Iraq through a complicated maze of canals and distribution channels, the water being retained in the channels by levees raised above the plain. These irrigation channels have been enlarged and altered innumerable times through the ages. They have also been destroyed many times as a result of war. Damage to these channels created the many lakes and marshes that dot the area.

The Tigris and Euphrates Rivers follow twisting courses because there is little natural drainage in lower Iraq: Baghdad, 350 miles (563 km) inland from the Gulf, is only 112 feet (34 m) above sea level. Recent decades have seen the completion of the Wadi ath-Tharthar river-control project (1956), involving the building of a canal 40 miles (64 km) long; and more ambitious projects financed by oil revenues are now underway, including a large barrage at Kut.

Irrigation in lower Iraq is difficult. The seasonal rise of the Tigris River at Baghdad is about 23 feet (7 m), and the maximum river flow occurs when the crops are already partially grown; thus surplus water must be stored for the next season. As in all areas of intensive irrigation, excessive salinity is also a problem that has never been (and perhaps may never be) completely solved. In the case of Iraq, salinity has been exacerbated by the breakdown of the irrigation works.

In upper Iraq, agriculture is dependent on rainfall. This part of the country consists of undulating plains, with heights varying from 700 to 1200 feet (215 to 365 m). Upper Iraq has good soil, and lower Iraq possesses heavy alluvial deposits. Elsewhere, the soil of Iraq is light and poor.

The most valuable product of Iraqi agriculture is the date, second only to oil in the amount of export revenue it generates. Iraq produces about 500,000 tons (455,000 t) of dates per year; the extreme south is the greatest center of date production. Barley, wheat, linseed, lentils, beans, and many other crops are grown; and cattle and other livestock are also raised. The government recently made an effort to emulate Egypt by embarking on large-scale cotton production; its success cannot yet be evaluated. Iraq's natural vegetation is restricted in range, a consequence both of aridity and of the shortsighted treatment of natural flora in the past; timber for building purposes must be imported.

Iraq's extreme summer heat and scant rainfall demand great endurance from its people. Rain falls only between November and April and averages only about 6 inches (15 cm) in lower Iraq and 20 inches (51 cm) in upper Iraq. In Baghdad, summer temperatures of 110 to 120°F (43 to 49°C) are normal. Throughout the summer, there is a disagreeable and persistent northwest wind called the *shamal*. In the northern areas, at higher altitudes, the climate is less demanding.

Iraq is an Arabic country. Almost three-fourths of its population consists of Arabs, and Arabic is the language of a far greater percentage of its people. The country is overwhelmingly Muslim, divided evenly between Shia Muslims (who are dominant in Iran) and the Sunni Muslims (who are dominant elsewhere). No other Arabic country has so many Shiite Muslims.

Tides of migration and conquest have resulted in a considerable admixture of peoples in Iraq, but the recent tendency has been to emphasize national unity (even uniformity) on a socialist basis and to discourage diversity (sometimes by force). Large numbers of Persians settled along the eastern edge of Iraq, but perhaps 100,000 of them were deported to Iran in the early 1970s. Most of the once considerable Jewish population moved to Israel after its establishment in 1948. The largest and least assimilable minority today (and also the hardest to coerce) consists of 2 million or more Kurds, who live in the northwest, have their own language and culture, and are engaged in a struggle for independence. There are also Turks and Turkomans living in areas adjacent to Turkey.

A population of about 12 million with an annual growth rate of about 3.1 percent make Iraq one of the more populous Middle Eastern states, though it is far behind Egypt, Turkey, and Iran. It is also among the most ancient centers of urban culture. About three-fifths of all Iraqis live in towns, and there has been a marked drift to the towns in recent decades. Baghdad is by far the largest city, but five other cities have populations of more than 500,000. Yet there is a curious lack of a sharp distinction between town and country. Many townspeople, in fact, follow agricultural callings, and nomads and religious pilgrims swell the urban population at some seasons.

The patterns of landholding and associated social relationships have changed markedly since the revolution of 1958. Large estates have been broken up, and a new class of small to medium-sized landowners has been created. Wealth has been more evenly distributed, and traditional social stratification is less marked.

The development of Iraqi oil has transformed the face of the country in the last few decades. In 1927, when Britain administered Iraq as a mandate under the League of Nations, the Kirkuk oil field was opened up in the north by the British-owned Iraq Petroleum Company. The Kirkuk oil field was Iraq's

Workers set bricks out to dry in the sun; bricks were invented in Iraq. (Photo: United Nations.)

most productive field, but there was also oil in the northwest (the Mosul field) and in the south (the Rumailah oil field). The Iraq Petroleum Company was nationalized in 1972, and all development of the country's oil resources is now in the hands of the National Petroleum Authority.

Until the 1980 war between Iraq and Iran, Iraq was the fifth largest petroleum producing country in the world, with an annual output of some 840 million barrels. Oil accounted for some 94 percent of total exports by value and for about half of all government revenues. The proven oil reserves of Iraq, estimated at 4.5 billion tons (4.08 billion t) constitute about 6 percent of the total known world reserves. The war severely damaged Iraq's oil facilities.

Since World War II, oil revenues have financed ambitious plans for industrial expansion and economic diversification. Iraq's recent economic history was thus strikingly similar to the history of Iran, its larger neighbor. Its economy once depended almost entirely on agriculture, but later manufacturing and service industries began to flourish. At the same time, Iraq probably more successfully than Iran devoted some of its rapidly increasing wealth to the modernization of agricultural methods.

In the mid-1960s, a series of 5-year plans for economic development were launched. Baghdad acquired a steel mill in the 1970s. Textile factories, breweries, asphalt and cement plants, and sugar, fertilizer, and paperboard mills have sprung up in the last decade or two. The government plays the major role in all large-scale economic enterprises, and nearly half the new industries are located in the Baghdad area.

Iraq has moderately good transportation and communications systems. There are some 30,000 miles (48,300 km) of roads, about one-third paved. On many routes, it is possible to drive across the hard surface of the desert. All major routes, both road and rail, center on Baghdad, as did the great historic caravan routes of earlier ages. Oceangoing ships can reach Basra, 85 miles (137 km) upstream on the Shatt-al-Arab at the confluence of the Tigris and Euphrates. River steamers ply upstream to Baghdad.

The culture of Iraq is Arabic, but with unique features that are cultivated and encouraged by the government through the government-owned mass media. This culture is expressed in Iraqi literature, rug design, folk art, and dance.

Fought over through the centuries, the great river valley of Mesopotamia formed part of several ancient empires before it fell to the Ottoman Turks in the seventeenth century. With the breakup of the Ottoman Empire, Iraq became a British mandate ruled by Faisal I, a member of the Hashemite royal family. Iraq became independent in 1932, but British and Western influence remained strong until 1958. The revolution of that year, when General Abdul Karim Kassem came to power, is the great watershed in recent Iraqi history, an event comparable to the revolution 20 years later in Iran. Since the overthrow of the monarchy (and King Faisal II) and the pro-Western government led by Premier Nuri Said, a succession of revolutionary regimes fanatically devoted to socialist principles has ruled in Baghdad. The Baath (Arab Socialist) Party has been in power since the 1960s. Despite its radical nature, the government in Baghdad displays a strong admixture of pragmatism. In 1975, for example, it brought to an end a long period of unfriendly relations with Iran. But this respite was shortlived. In September 1980, Iraq attacked Iran and claimed sovereignty over the Shatt-al-Arab, the waterway that divides the two countries. Iraq subsequently seized the Iranian oil port of Khurramshahr and the major oil refinery center at Abadan.

Both before and after 1958, the main emphasis in Iraqi internal policies has been on economic development, and very substantial and continuing progress has, in fact, been made. Iraq is not overpopulated (the people-land ratio is relatively low); it has a substantial agricultural base and a vast oil-derived wealth to draw upon. Thus, the prospects for its people justify a cautious optimism. This impression was reinforced by a change in political leadership in the fall of 1979, when President Ahmad Hasan Bakr's place was taken by former Vice President Saddam Hussein. Under Hussein, the first parliamentary elections since the fall of the monarchy in 1958 were held in June 1980, to fill the 250-member National Assembly. The new President's policies apparently indicate his determination to improve relations with the industrial powers of the West and to keep the Communist Party in Iraq under even stricter control. In all probability, Iraq will continue its present trend toward secular government and economic development.

Arthur Campbell Turner

Jordan

(Hashemite Kingdom of Jordan)

Area: 37,737 sq mi (97,740 sq km)
Population: 2.98 million
  Density: 79 per sq mi (30 per sq km)
  Growth rate: 3.3% (1970–1977)
Percent of population under 14 years of age: 46% (1975)
Infant deaths per 1,000 live births: 23 (1975)
Life expectancy at birth: 53.2 years (1975)
Leading causes of death: not available
Ethnic composition: Arab
Languages: Arabic
Literacy: 65%
Religions: Sunni Muslim 94%; Christian 6%
Percent population urban: less than 20%
Percent population rural: more than 80%
Gross national product: $2.27 billion
  Per capita GNP: $1,050 (East Bank only)
  Per capita GNP growth rate: 6.5% (1970–1977)
Inflation rate: 13% (1973–1976)

Jordan is a small, pro-Western Middle Eastern monarchy with a resolute ruler who has survived half a dozen assassination attempts. Jordan—officially called the Hashemite Kingdom of Jordan—stands in terms of size somewhere between the large states of the region, such as Egypt, Saudi Arabia, and Iran, and the several very small states. Jordan has no oil, and much of its area is unproductive desert. Its access to the sea is limited to one port in the extreme south. Given its lack of natural advantages, Jordan has performed remarkably well in the area of economic development in recent decades. With external aid and an alert and enterprising government, Jordan has rapidly raised its standard of living, and there is reason to believe that its progress will continue.

Jordan's neighbors are Syria to the north, Iraq to the east, Saudi Arabia to the east and southeast, and Israel to the west. Jordan's borders are not defined by any obvious natural features and are, to a large extent, arbitrary—that is, they rest on international agreements.

Jordan is divided into two main geographical regions, which differ in their topography, their inhabitants, and their present status. The dividing line is the Jordan River. Before 1948, the territory to the west of the Jordan, known as the West Bank and including the old City of Jerusalem, formed part of the Palestine mandate. In that year, during a war with the nascent state of Israel, it was conquered by what was then called Transjordan and incorporated into the Kingdom. But in the Arab-Israeli War of 1967, the West Bank and the Jordanian sector of Jerusalem were conquered by Israel and have been under Israeli occupation and administration ever since.

The official Jordanian view, which is also the U.N. official view, is that the West Bank territories are de jure part of Jordan. Actually, however, the West Bank

was under Jordanian rule for only 19 years, and has been out of Jordanian hands since 1967. Even in the event of the desired reunion (an objective of no particular urgency in Jordan), the differences between the two areas might make it difficult for them to function smoothly as parts of the same monarchy. Such stresses were obvious when they were united, between 1948 and 1967. However, during most of the Israeli occupation, the West Bank has not been totally cut off from east Jordan. Since the early 1970s there has been an "undeclared peace" between Jordan and Israel, and economic links and the movement of people back and forth have usually been permitted.

In area, the Israeli-occupied West Bank is a very small part of the Kingdom. The total area of Jordan is 37,737 square miles (97,740 sq km), of which 2,270 square miles (5,879 sq km), or about 6 percent, is occupied by Israel. This gives little idea of the West Bank's significance, however, because the 6 percent includes about half of Jordan's agriculturally useful land. About 750,000 people live on the West Bank and in the part of Jerusalem that was formerly Jordanian.

Jordan's central topographical feature is the Jordan Valley, a relatively narrow and well-marked valley that is part of the Great Rift Valley system that extends south through much of East Africa. The Jordan River originates in the north in the Sea of Galilee and meanders south on a tortuous course. In the rainy season it is deep and turbulent, but during the dry season it is not much more than a muddy stream. The salinity of the Jordan increases as it flows south, and it ends its course in the Dead Sea, nearly 1,300 feet (396 m) below sea level, the lowest point on the earth's surface. The shores of the Dead Sea consist of salt marshes that are hostile to vegetation. South of the Dead Sea, the Great Rift Valley continues toward the Gulf of Aqaba in the form of the Wadi el-Araba, a totally dry and inhospitable valley with potential mineral wealth.

On both sides of the Jordan are uplands; their soil is not particularly good, but alluvial deposits in the hills and in some basins make agriculture possible. In the West Bank uplands, the major valleys drain toward the Mediterranean.

The Jordan River Valley is the country's most important agricultural area, with great potential wealth. The Jordan Valley, which is 75 miles (120 km) long and from 3 to 10 miles (5 to 16 km) wide, has been described as a huge natural farm. The alluvial soil is rich, and the climate is conducive to year-round agricultural operations. Given adequate irrigation and technology, this valley could rival the productivity of the Imperial Valley in California, which it resembles.

The remaining areas of Jordan are the eastern grassland slopes and the desert. The grassland is the eastern slope of the East Bank uplands, which merges slowly into desert. The effective boundary between the two areas, grassland and desert, is the Hejaz railway (famous as the perennial target of T. E. Lawrence in World War I), which follows a course roughly parallel to the Jordan about 40 miles (64 km) to the east. The high grassland forms summer pasturage for the Bedouin, who move east in winter. The desert territory of Jordan, which occupies about four-fifths of the country's East Bank territory, extends eastward in two great butterfly wings, with a large salient of Saudi Arabian territory between them.

There is considerable variety in the Jordanian climate. In the uplands on either side of the river, the climate is Mediterranean, with hot summers and cold winters with occasional snow. Snow seldom falls in the Great Rift Valley. In the hilly areas, rainfall ranges from 15 to 35 inches (38 to 89 cm); but as one moves east and south, there is less and less rain, averaging only 2 to 4 inches (5 to 10 cm) in the extensive desert areas.

Thus, Jordan has little in the way of water resources. Miracles of agricultural development could nonetheless be accomplished if there were an integrated regional plan for the water resources of the Jordan Valley. Political conditions have so far made such a sensible solution impossible. Syria and Lebanon divert water from the headwaters of the Jordan; Israel and Jordan each have their own schemes, which are, to some extent, mutually harmful. In Jordan, three reservoirs have been built by the government on the smaller west-flowing tributaries of the Jordan, but the centerpiece of the irrigation system is the East Ghor Canal, which draws most of its water from the Yarmuk River and some water from the recently completed King Talal Dam on the Zarqa River. A project at present under way will extend the East Ghor Canal south to the Dead Sea and will make possible the irrigation by sprinkler systems of about another 50 square miles (130 sq km).

The varieties of vegetation in Jordan correspond to the climatic regions: Mediterranean-type vegetation, including olive and fruit trees, in the uplands; grass and sagebrush on the high slopes; scanty desert vegetation as one travels farther east or south. In earlier times, there were many forested areas, which are now exhausted. The Jordanian government began a reforestation program in 1948. In addition to a great variety of wild animal life, the country has several hundred thousand sheep and goats, about 30,000 head of cattle, and some horses, camels, and other draft animals. The livestock population is subject to great fluctuation because herds cannot be maintained in arid years.

Jordan has, as yet, discovered no oil resources. Its richest mineral resources are its phosphate deposits. There is also considerable cement available, as well as iron, phosphorus, and some more or less exotic metals. Exploitation of these resources is being pushed forward rapidly. The mining industry is small but growing.

Most Jordanians on both sides of the Jordan are Arabic-speaking Arabs. There are, of course, different dialects, but these differences are less important than they used to be. About 94 percent of all Jordanians are Sunni Muslims; the other 6 percent are Christians, most of them members of the Greek Orthodox Church. The Jordanian constitution makes no distinction on religious grounds, and there is little sectarian friction.

There is a more serious cultural and political division between the residents of East Bank and West Bank Jordan. East Jordan is the historic nucleus of the Hashemite Kingdom and the real base of the Hashemite monarchy's support. The people on the West Bank, in many (perhaps most) cases, prefer to think of themselves as Palestinian rather than Jordanian; but the term Palestinian also applies to inhabitants of the Gaza Strip, who have been under Egyptian (but never Jordanian) rule and to many inhabitants of Israel. Jordanians living on the West Bank tend to be more politically sophisticated and active, more vocal, and more Mediterranean, while East Jordanians tend to be conservative and more respectful of traditional values and authority.

The Palestinian problem is physically present in East Jordan in the form of the Palestinian refugees. In 1976, the UN Relief and Works Agency for Palestinian Refugees in the Near East (UNRWA) estimated that there were 644,669 Palestinian refugees in East Jordan, about one-third of them living in camps.

Near Amman, Jordanians labor in the heat to bale hay at harvest time. Most of the land is desert, and irrigation is necessary. (Photo: United Nations/ B. Cirrone.)

These refugees are supported on a minimal basis by funds channeled through UNRWA. Although all the refugees have been granted full Jordanian citizenship, they are an alien and unassimilable element.

The future of the West Bank is a formidable political problem for Jordan's King Hussein. He has advanced compromise proposals for a semi-independent Palestinian state linked to the Jordanian monarchy, but at a 1974 Arab summit meeting he agreed to relinquish all authority to negotiate for the future of the Israeli-held West Bank to the Palestine Liberation Organization (PLO). Subsequently, there was a partial reconciliation among Jordan, the PLO, and Syria. Hussein cannot afford to accept the PLO unconditionally because a radical Palestinian state would make a worse neighbor than Israel; nor can he flout the PLO completely because that would mean alienating other Arab nations and forfeiting much needed subsidies from oil-rich Arab states.

The natural rate of increase of the population of Jordan is about 3.3 percent a year. The population has approximately doubled since 1952, from 1.4 million to the present 2.9 million. More than 80 percent of the people depend for a living on herding or agriculture.

In the desert and semidesert areas of East Jordan, there are many nomadic and seminomadic people. More than any other group in the Middle East, these nomads are true Bedouin. They now number less than 100,000, and their numbers are diminishing. The western Bedouin herd sheep and goats, the eastern Bedouin breed and herd camels. Some are seminomadic, living in houses during the planting and harvest seasons and moving into tents in the winter. Some confine their peregrinations to Jordan, but the Rwala tribe passes through the country yearly on its way from Syria south to Saudi Arabia. International agreements concluded at the end of World War I provide for free grazing and the free movement of nomadic tribes across the Syrian Desert.

Not quite half the population of Jordan live in the dozen or so major towns and cities. There has been considerable movement from rural to urban centers. The chief city and capital of Jordan is Amman, which has grown rapidly and is now a bustling, largely modern city of 750,000. Though modern in appearance, it is believed to be one of the oldest continuously inhabited cities in the world. It was called Philadelphia in Greco-Roman times, but Amman is a still older name—it is the Rabbah Ammon of the Old Testament. Periods of civilization are embalmed layer upon layer in Jordan. Besides Amman, the chief cities are Zarqa (300,000), a fast-growing city with new industries, and Irbid (116,000).

More than half the population of Jordan live in often primitive villages. There are about 400 villages in East Jordan and 800 on the West Bank. Jordanian society is patriarchal, and family ties are supremely important.

A network of hard-surfaced roads links Jordan's major cities and towns. The main north-south road links Amman with Syria to the north; south, it is a five-hour drive to Aqaba, Jordan's one port. The main east-west road links Amman with Jerusalem by way of the King Hussein Bridge across the Jordan. The single-track, narrow-gauge Hejaz railway is Jordan's only rail line. The international airport is near Amman.

The land of Jordan is one of the most ancient homes of man, but the state is new. A part of the Ottoman Empire since the 1500s, Jordan was one of several states that came into existence when that empire disintegrated in defeat at the end of World War I. The League of Nations awarded Britain the mandate for Palestine and Transjordan, but Transjordan was administered separately. In May 1923, Britain recognized Abdullah ibn-Hussein, a member of the noble Hashemite family descended from Muhammad, as Emir of Transjordan, an independent ruler under British tutelage. His brother became king of Iraq. British financial aid set the Emirate on the path of economic progress, and a small but efficient Jordanian army called the Arab Legion was trained by Sir John Bagot Glubb ("Glubb Pasha").

The mandate ended in 1946, and the Emirate became the Hashemite Kingdom of Transjordan. In the war of 1948, Abdullah's forces won over 2,000 square miles (5,180 sq km) of Palestine, including the Old City of Jerusalem. This area and its nearly 1 million inhabitants were annexed to the Kingdom, which was renamed Jordan. Since then, Jordan has been ruled by Talal's eldest son, King Hussein ibn Talal, born in 1935, thirty-ninth in line of descent from the Prophet. According to the constitution of 1952, Jordan is a constitutional monarchy; but major decisions are made by the King, and he has proved himself an able and effective ruler.

Jordan's rapid economic expansion in the 1950s and

In this landlocked Hashemite Kingdom, with its arid and infertile soil, a Bedouin woman and her donkey rest at a water hole near the Q'a Disi pilot farm. (Photo: United Nations/Rice.)

1960s attests to the effectiveness of the wise use of foreign aid. Between 1954 and 1967, Jordan's gross national product (GNP) nearly quadrupled, but defeat in the war of 1967, the consequent loss of territory and its agricultural income, the sporadic fighting that took place in the Jordan Valley for three years after the war, and a new refugee influx proved to be severe setbacks. In 1970 and 1971 there was internal warfare as Hussein restored his authority by smashing PLO guerrilla bands in Jordan. However, surprisingly, economic recovery in the 1970s has been steady. Jordan still operates with a budget deficit ($415 million in 1977) and has a heavy deficit ($186 million in 1977) on external account—visible exports are about one-sixth of visible imports. The difference is made up from various sources: external subsidies, originally (before 1956) from Britain, later from other Arab states, and from the United States; profits from tourism, which is rising rapidly; and substantial amounts in remittances from Jordanians abroad. Tens of thousands of Jordanians work in other Arab states, principally on the Gulf. Jordan has a high educational level and is an exporter of talent.

A modern emphasis on education and health care is evident. Education for the first nine grades is free and compulsory; and, in response to an energetic government campaign, literacy increased from 32.5 percent in 1961 to 65 percent in 1977. The Ministry of Health expanded medical clinics from 46 in 1951 to 332 in 1976.

The primary support of the Jordanian economy is agriculture, which is being developed by the extension of irrigation. The second major support is the mining of phosphates and the third is tourism. Jordan produces large amounts of cereals, fresh vegetables, fruits, and olive oil (though it must still import some foodstuffs). Its principal exports are fruits, vegetables,

and phosphates, the last shipped through new facilities built at the port of Aqaba.

The diversification and development of the Jordanian economy are, on the whole, progressing well. The evidence can be seen in new schools and hospitals; in new developments in business, industry, and agriculture; and in the growing self-confidence of the people. The government values the principle of free enterprise and holds itself responsible for maintaining favorable conditions, internal security, and a stable currency.

During the last 25 years new business and industry have expanded, and the economy is improving. New industries include a large cement factory, a petroleum refinery, several foundries and marble factories, a tannery, and more phosphate-mining plants. Other industrial activities include milling, oil pressing, brewing, printing, and publishing. Manufactures include footware, metal products, furniture, processed food, and glass. Although two-thirds of Jordan's factories produce clothing and comestibles, the bulk of industrial income is derived from three sources: phosphate extraction, cement manufacturing, and petroleum refining.

Political problems remain intractable. Relations with the Palestinians have deteriorated since Hussein destroyed the Palestinian movement inside Jordan (a militant threat to his throne) in 1970–1971. Consequently, Hussein may be the target of an assassination attempt. Jordan is a monarchy (as once were Egypt, Iran, and Iraq), and monarchies are becoming increasingly scarce in the Middle East. Jordan's conservative, pro-Western government is trying to maintain its equilibrium in a time of political turbulence, and this will require all the considerable political skill of the Hashemites.

Arthur Campbell Turner

Kuwait

(State of Kuwait)

Area: 6,886 sq mi (17,835 sq km)
Population: 1.2 million (1980)
   Density: 174 per sq mi (67 per sq km)
   Growth rate: 6.2% (1970–1977)
Percent of population under 14 years of age: 47% (1975)
Infant deaths per 1,000 live births: 44 (1975)
Life expectancy at birth: 67.2 years (1975)
Leading causes of death: not available
Ethnic composition: Arabs, Palestinians, Pakistanis, Indians
Languages: Arabic (official), English
Literacy: 80%
Religions: Sunni Muslim
Percent population urban: 95%
Percent population rural: 5%
Gross national product: $18.04 billion
   Per capita GNP: $14,890
   Per capita GNP growth rate: −0.9% (1970–1977)
Inflation rate: not available

Enormous oil resources have endowed Kuwait—a diminutive country with a small population—with a level of national wealth unparalleled elsewhere and difficult to imagine. There are now no capital restraints at all; the average per capita income of Kuwaiti citizens is probably the highest in the world, being rivaled only by the per capita income in Abu Dhabi (whose situation is similar) and Switzerland. For Kuwait, the problem is not the normal one of scarcity but the rarer and headier problem of absorptive capacity. The only constraints on Kuwait are those of time, available labor, and the capacity to organize the handling of such wealth.

Kuwait, an independent Arab monarchy since 1961, is situated in the northeast corner of the Arabian Peninsula and faces the northwest corner of the Persian Gulf. Even before the advent of oil, it had strategic significance as a gateway from the south to the Middle East, being near the mouth of the Shatt-al-Arab, the common channel through which the waters of the Tigris and Euphrates Rivers reach the Persian Gulf. Kuwait has the only really good harbor on the entire Gulf coast.

A peculiar feature of Kuwait's international borders is the area in the south called the Partitioned Zone (formerly known as the Neutral Zone). This area, about 37 square miles (95 sq km), was in dispute between Kuwait and Saudi Arabia following World War I. After 1922, it was jointly owned and administered by the two countries. In the early 1960s, the zone was formally partitioned between Saudi Arabia and Kuwait, but there was an agreement for continuing joint exploitation of the oil resources on a 50-50 basis.

There is little variety in Kuwait's limited and harsh terrain. The whole area is desert, and the land is flat or slightly undulating, rising from sea level at the coast to about 1,000 feet (305 m) in the south. There are salty marshes near the coast and inland shallow depressions that fill with water in the rainy season and serve the camels of the Bedouin. The rainfall everywhere is trivial and variable, ranging from 1 to 7 inches (2.5 to 18 cm), and falling in the period from October to April. In summer the climate is extremely hot, commonly reaching 125°F (52°C) in the daytime. The temperature has been known to go as high as 150°F (66°C) or higher. Winter is fairly pleasant, but it is often accompanied by dust storms brought by the prevailing northwest wind. Vegetation is minimal, natural vegetation consisting only of scrub, bushes, and some grass.

Since the local water supply is totally inadequate, water was one of the first problems faced in the recent decades of modernization. Before the 1950s, the people of Kuwait depended (as they had for centuries) on the brackish water of desert wells, on rainwater, or on the expensive (and often unhygienic) supplies brought occasionally from the Shatt-al-Arab by boat. In 1953, the Kuwaiti government commissioned the first desalination plant to transform seawater into drinkable water by distillation. The first plant could produce 1 million gallons (3.8 million l) of potable water a day; by 1978, Kuwait's daily production of desalinated water had reached 102 million gallons (385 million l), which is over 90 percent of the water used in Kuwait. The desalination plants are linked to turbo-generators, so the expansion of power-generating capacity has also been phenomenal. From levels of 2.5 million watts in the early 1950s and 500 million in 1967, power generation has reached the amazing level of 2.6 billion watts. The demand for electric power has, of course, risen step by step with the growing affluence of the Kuwaitis, and a very high proportion of this electric energy is expended on air conditioning.

The population of Kuwait, estimated to be 90,000 in 1946 and 740,000 in 1971, is estimated to be slightly over 1 million today. Kuwait's population has, on the average, been increasing at a compounded annual rate of more than 8 percent for the past 30 years because of three main factors: a high rate of natural increase, an increase in the number of Kuwaitis through a concerted effort to bring in and naturalize tribesmen scattered on the fringes of the country, and a massive influx of workers from other countries in the region. These workers help with the construction of new projects and fill administrative and supervisory posts.

The proportion of non-Kuwaitis in the total population rose to 45 percent in 1957, 50 percent in 1960, and 53 percent in 1965, and remained steady thereafter. The oil industry required an increase in the labor force in the early years of this period; later, workers were needed for construction and infrastructure development. In its productive phase, the oil industry is capital-intensive, not labor-intensive, and only about 5,000 persons were employed directly in the oil sector in 1975.

Government policy makes it very difficult for a non-Kuwaiti to acquire Kuwaiti citizenship, but it is easier if the non-Kuwaiti is an Arab. Because of the enormous influx of foreign workers, the Kuwaitis are anxious to protect their national identity. While some foreign workers are in Kuwait only for a short time, most of them are there on a long-term basis or intend to remain there for life. Women represent about 45 percent of the noncitizen resident population, an indication that the foreign population has become less transitory. The noncitizen population have varied national origins. Palestinians represent about 40 percent of the non-Kuwaiti population and almost 20 percent of the total population. There are also many Pakistanis and Indians (who are Hindu in religion), some Egyptians and other Arabs, and a few Britons and Americans.

The labor force—that part of the population that

In this flat desert country, a Bedouin nomad tends his sheep and maintains an age-old way of life. (Photo: United Nations/Rice.)

actually holds jobs—numbered 304,582 in 1975. Of this number, Kuwaitis represented 30 percent and non-Kuwaitis 70 percent. Of the Kuwaiti citizens who held jobs, 52 percent worked for the government. Hardly any Kuwaiti citizens work as laborers or in less desirable jobs. Non-Kuwaitis are more evenly distributed among the major activities: government service, trade, manufacturing, service industries (a rapidly increasing sector of the Kuwaiti economy), and construction. There are no strong ties among the different elements in the non-Kuwaiti population; non-Kuwaitis, as a whole, do not mix with the indigenous population. They are not allowed to own real estate or shares in Kuwaiti enterprises. Their incomes are lower, on the average, than the incomes of Kuwaiti citizens. The median income for a Kuwaiti family is estimated to be 50 percent higher than the median income for a non-Kuwaiti family.

In the last few years, as the government has become aware of the dangers of an entirely negative policy toward the enormous alien element in its midst, it has made it easier for aliens to acquire the security of permanent resident status and to become citizens.

Women have played a larger role in the economy in recent years. In 1975, 11 percent of all women in Kuwait were employed. This included 25 percent of non-Kuwaiti women, but only 6.7 percent of women who were Kuwaiti citizens. Twenty years earlier, however, only 1.4 percent of Kuwaiti women were employed.

Kuwait was not the arbitrary creation of a colonial administration. Because it had exercised substantial autonomy for two centuries before independence in 1961, its society possessed the elements of social

cohesion essential for political stability. The native Kuwaitis are Arabs; nearly all are Sunni Muslims and think of themselves as Kuwaitis. The sheikhdom has been held by the same family (the Sabahs) since the middle of the eighteenth century.

Before the production of oil, Kuwaiti lives centered not on the desert but on the port of Kuwait and its activities—fishing, trading, and smuggling. The people of Kuwait therefore developed skills as sailors, traders, and fishermen. With little agriculture, the customary Middle Eastern pattern of a large peasant class and a small landowning class never developed; and there is still little class stratification in Kuwait. The family is important, and the population is so small that a strong family feeling unites all the people, linking the ruler to those he rules.

The first oil well was drilled in 1936, and oil was first struck in 1938 in the Burgan oil field, later to be recognized as the world's largest single oil field. After 1945, development of the oil fields began. The main development was in the hands of the Kuwait Oil Company (KOC), granted a 65-year concession in 1934. The KOC was owned equally by the British Petroleum Company and the American Gulf Oil Corporation. In the Neutral Zone, concessions were held by Getty interests and other independents, and oil was struck there in 1953. Later, offshore drilling concessions were granted to other interests. Like other oil producing states, Kuwait nationalized its oil industry in the 1970s, purchasing 60 percent of the KOC in 1974 and the remaining 40 percent in 1975.

Kuwait ranks sixth in the world in terms of crude oil production. Production rose from a modest 6 million barrels in 1946 to over 600 million barrels in 1960. It reached its highest level—1.2 billion barrels—in 1972. Since the early 1970s, oil production has been deliberately kept at a lower level. Through the late 1970s, it totaled 700 million to 800 million barrels per year; in January 1979, the Oil Minister announced a production level of about 2 million barrels per day. What distinguishes Kuwait from other oil producing countries is the fact that it possesses one-fifth of the world's known oil reserves. No other oil producing country has so high a ratio of reserves to current production. At current levels of production, the known reserves have an estimated life of well over 80 years.

The enormous rise in the selling price of oil has produced an astounding bonanza for Kuwait and has stimulated every part of its economy. Measures have been adopted to distribute the wealth among the people and to create a state welfare system. Originally established in 1956, the welfare system has been expanded. Broadly speaking, the Kuwaiti citizen is protected against all major ills and enjoys an amazing range of free or subsidized services. Citizens pay no personal taxes and are provided with free education, almost free housing, and free telephones. The Kuwaiti social and economic system combines a highly successful capitalism with welfare-state provisions of unparalleled generosity. In Kuwait, the welfare state does not connote a socialist ideology. It reflects,

The ultramodern capital city of Kuwait is growing rapidly because of the great wealth created by oil exports. (Photo: United Nations/ Rice.)

rather, the ancient Kuwaiti tradition of close community relations and interrelated mutual responsibilities.

The government provides free education at all levels. A massive school construction program began early. Forty-one schools had been completed by 1954, and the student population increased from 3,600 in 1945 to 45,000 in 1960 and to about 250,000 in 1975. In 1945, females made up only 5 percent of the school population; today, they represent more than 45 percent. In the 1960s, an ambitious adult education program was initiated to eradicate illiteracy. The University of Kuwait was established in 1966 and now has over 6,000 students. All young men are under obligation to perform military service, but the government does not seem to be entirely successful in enforcing this obligation.

The government has been active since 1953 in carrying out programs for low-income housing. By 1975, about 15 percent of the Kuwaiti people had benefited from these programs. In addition, low-interest loans are extended by government agencies to enable Kuwaitis to buy land at low prices and to construct homes.

Government financial assistance to needy families started in the 1950s. About 9,600 families currently benefit from this program. Basic commodities like water, electricity, and gasoline are heavily subsidized; in recent years, the system has been extended to cover many essential food products. A social security program provides for generous retirement pensions and other benefits. In the field of health, a campaign has been mounted to eradicate the two endemic diseases of the desert, smallpox and tuberculosis.

Kuwait's wealth has increased so dramatically in the recent past that it would hardly be possible, even were it desirable, to spend it all on domestic programs. Kuwait has therefore created a broad program of overseas investments and makes loans or grants to its less-fortunate Arab neighbors through the Kuwait Fund for Arab Economic Development. Created as a public corporation in 1961, this fund now has at its disposal a capital sum approximately equal to $3.7 billion.

The Sabah family, members of which have ruled Kuwait as semi-independent lords of the port and its hinterland under the Ottoman Empire since the 1750s, has produced in the recent past four successive sheikhs whose policies have been essentially consistent. The oil industry began under Sheikh Ahmad Jabir, who was succeeded in 1950 by Sheikh Abdullah al-Salim. In 1965, the throne passed to Sheikh Sabah al-Salim, who ruled for a crucial 12-year period (1965–1977). The present ruler, Sheikh Jabir Ahmad, succeeded on December 31, 1977.

It is only since 1961 that Kuwait has been an independent state. In 1899, the ruler of Kuwait signed an agreement with the British, chiefly in order to ward off any serious assertion of Turkish control. Kuwait was a British protectorate from 1899 to 1961, but it was never a British colony, and British troops were never stationed there. In a curious incident immediately after independence in 1961, British troops were sent for a short time to Kuwait at the invitation of the ruler to discourage a threatened Iraqi takeover. (Iraq has traditionally regarded Kuwait as ripe for annexation).

Kuwait is small, vulnerable, and almost incredibly rich. It is possible that it may succumb to an Iraqi or other takeover. Britain withdrew in 1971, and Kuwait lost another protector when the Shah of Iran was ousted. But barring a takeover, the future seems to hold only the promise of continued progress in the Kuwaiti paradise. Few countries, perhaps none, have ever been so blessed.

Arthur Campbell Turner

Lebanon
(Republic of Lebanon)

Area: 4,000 sq mi (10,350 sq km)
Population: 3 million
  Density: 750 per sq mi (290 per sq km)
  Growth rate: 2.5% (1970–1977)
Percent of population under 15 years of age: 43% (1975)
Infant deaths per 1,000 live births: not available
Life expectancy at birth: 63.3 years (1975)
Leading causes of death: not available
Ethnic composition: Arab 93%; Armenian 6%
Languages: Arabic (official), French
Literacy: 68% (1974)
Religions: Muslim, Christian
Percent population urban: 60% (1975)
Percent population rural: 40% (1975)
Gross national product: not available
  Per capita GNP: not available
  Per capita growth rate: not available
Inflation rate: 4.4% average (1970–1976)

Lebanon is the smallest of the Arab states. From the beginning of recorded history, Mount Lebanon has been the "crossroads of the Middle East"; location and geography have been the primary factors in Lebanon's national development. Sidon and Tyre have been important commercial centers for over 3,000 years, and today Tripoli, Beirut, Sidon, and Tyre are important ports of entry to Syria, Iraq, Jordan, and the Arabian Peninsula.

Lebanon occupies a strip of land about 124 miles (200 km) long and 25 to 50 miles (40 to 80 km) wide along the eastern end of the Mediterranean Sea, an area about the size of Yellowstone National Park. Bordered by Syria and Israel, Lebanon is divided into four zones. A thin coastal strip varies from 1,100 yards (1,000 m) to 6 miles (10 km) in width and is traversed by 10 small rivers. The second zone is formed by the Lebanon Mountains, a rugged range with steep slopes and peaks rising to about 9,840 feet (3,000 m). These mountains run parallel to the coast from south of Sidon to the Syrian border east of Tripoli. East of the Lebanon Mountains, at an average elevation of 3,280 feet (1,000 m), lies the Bika plateau (Bika Valley). This fertile plain, about 75 miles (120 km) long and 6 to 9 miles (10 to 15 km) wide, forms the third zone. Another, slightly lower range, called the Anti-Lebanon Mountains, constitutes the fourth zone. Because of the mountainous terrain of their country, the Lebanese call themselves "people of the mountain."

Lebanon's climate is subtropical Mediterranean with rainy, cool winters and dry, hot summers. The mountains cause significant climatic differences. In the early spring and late fall, it is possible to swim in the sea and ski in the Lebanon Mountains on the same day. Vegetation is plentiful. About 9 percent of the nation is covered with forests. Flowering trees, oak, poplar, and other trees grow in the mountains. Despite adequate rainfall, only 27 percent of the land is arable, the rest (64 percent) is uncultivable mountain terrain and waste.

The country has no significant natural resources. Some iron-ore deposits have been found, but they are hard to work and of only marginal importance. Little is known about other minerals, and there are probably no commercially important mineral deposits.

The terrain has been an important factor in the development of the people. Many religious and ethnic groups fled from their original homes and sought refuge in Lebanon's rugged mountains. Fiercely independent, these groups established individual zones of influence and learned to tolerate, if not to trust, their neighbors. Occasionally they banded together to meet

a common threat, and as long as they paid tribute to the ruling power, they remained free.

Yet despite their religious divisions, the Lebanese share a common culture. Lebanese Christians may stress their relationship with Europe or their Greco-Roman heritage, but they speak Arabic and share many of the cultural traits of the Muslims. Ethnic divisions are unimportant among the Christians, but in the south and in the east, Muslim feudal families draw their national power from their ethnic groups. Some of the ruling families among the Druze, like the Jumblat, trace their roots to tribes that inhabited the Mount Lebanon area before the arrival of Islam. Arabic is the national language, but many Lebanese, especially in the Beirut area, speak French fluently.

Religious differences are the basis of Lebanon's political structure. Seventeen religious sects are officially recognized. Three Muslim sects—Sunni, Shiite, and Druze—and three Christian sects—Maronite, Greek Orthodox, and Greek Catholic—constitute over 90 percent of the population. Religious affiliation determines social and political relations; religion is the focus of loyalty, self-definition, and social identity, although most Lebanese would find it difficult to explain sectarian differences. Each sect is generally concentrated in a geographic area. When the various sects are gathered in the same city, as in Beirut, each community confines itself to a particular locality.

The legal system protects and supports representative government based on religion (confessionalism). All religious sects are legally recognized, and any person or organization engaging in any activity deemed to cause religious conflict is subject to fine, imprisonment, or the loss of civil rights. An individual registers as a member of a certain sect; and marriage, divorce, separation, child custody, or inheritance are subject to the law of that sect.

The only official population census, taken in 1932, is still the basis for apportioning political power. It showed the distribution of the major confessions as follows: Maronite Christian, 28.5 percent; Sunni Muslim, 22.3 percent; Shiite Muslim, 19.4 percent; Greek Orthodox, 9.7 percent; and Druze and Greek Catholic, 5.9 percent each. Overall, including splinter groups, the census showed slightly more Christians than Muslims, and political power was apportioned accordingly. Since 1932, however, Islam has become the religion of the majority: it has been estimated that the number of Shiite Muslims has increased fourfold since 1932, and evidence indicates a considerable increase in the number of Sunni Muslims as well. The failure to redistribute political power in accordance with current demographic reality is one cause of today's civil strife in Lebanon. Family and religion are the basis of the nation's social structure. In recent years, migration to the cities and emigration abroad have loosened family ties. However, most emigrants maintain close connections with their hometowns or villages, and many emigrants return periodically or permanently to their homeland. Family ties are

In Basharri, women spread grain to dry in the sun on the building's rooftop; age-old agricultural methods are still common. (Photo: United Nations/ B. Cirone.)

strengthened by family associations, some of which number as many as 15,000 members (the Atallah Association). In 1968, over 450 associations were registered with the government.

In rural areas, the extended family is the primary production unit, and even in urban areas single-owner family enterprises predominate. Partnerships and corporations are often based on kinship ties. Anyone not connected with a family is an outsider in Lebanese society.

Lebanon's economic structure is unlike any other in the Arab world. It does not export crude oil, nor does it have a large agricultural sector. In 1972, agriculture and industry accounted for only 9.9 and 15.9 percent, respectively, of gross domestic product (GDP), while services accounted for an amazing 69.6 percent. Because of external forces such as political instability in neighboring countries, the imposition of socialism in Egypt, Iraq, Libya, and Syria, the creation of Israel, and the acceleration of development in the Arabian Peninsula, relatively stable Lebanon became a haven for capital investors and for many well-educated technicians. (However, the influx of Palestinian refugees, most of whom are poorly educated, has been a burden to Lebanon.)

Between 1970 and 1976, real GDP (constant prices) grew at an annual rate of 8.6 percent, up from 4.9 percent during the previous decade. This was the third highest growth rate of any Middle Eastern country, including Israel. Only two oil producing states, Iraq (9.5 percent) and Saudi Arabia (14.4 percent), achieved a higher growth rate.

Agricultural productivity is low: 20 percent of the labor force produces one-tenth of the GDP, while 56 percent of the labor force produce over two-thirds of the GDP in the service sector. Because of its location and the absence of controls over business and industry, Lebanon became the banking and service center of the Middle East. Since 1975, however, the continuing civil war has destroyed much of the Lebanese economy.

Given the strength of private business enterprise, the distribution of political power, and the competing ethnic interests, it is unlikely that formal economic development planning will be adopted in Lebanon. This lack of government planning has retarded economic development, distorted income distribution, and thrown doubt on the future of the economy. In 1960, private consumption accounted for 85 percent of GDP, public consumption for 10 percent, and gross domestic saving (an important factor in economic development) for only 5 percent. Income is unevenly distributed in favor of the Christian minority, partly because of the higher level of education among Christians. Free public education is available, but because of its poor quality most parents send their children to private, sectarian schools.

Many villages still lack modern amenities, but some contain telephones, electricity, piped water, radios, and refrigerators. Nearly all Lebanese villages have some contact with the towns and cities, primarily through the migrants who left their villages for the towns but retained firm ties. Villagers are concerned about family prestige, loyalty to their communities, landownership as a status symbol, and educational and employment opportunities. Most villages are inhabited by a single religious sect, and several villages of coreligionists may be clustered together. Class distinctions are not drawn according to residence but according to family prestige, religious sect, and position of power.

Despite its social significance, the extended family is losing importance. In many parts of the country, there has been a shift away from the traditional patrilineal male-dominated family to a contemporary patrilineal male-dominated nuclear family, a change linked to the modernization of the Lebanese economy. As lucrative professional employment becomes available outside the village, the land fixation of the family head weakens and he becomes less concerned with preserving the family patrimony in land. Instead, today his bequest to his children is often a professional education. Once the tie to the land was broken, the extended family became less important and the accumulation of assets became a function of individual effort. In some villages, this has already led to the sale of land outside the family.

In the village, the head of the family still earns most of the cash income and makes all decisions regarding its disbursement. Women occupy an inferior position, but they are beginning to participate in the decision-making process. Furthermore, women's rising educational level is advancing their emancipation. Rela-

On the banks of the Karaoun Reservoir, formed by the construction of the Litani Dam, a farmer threshes a field of grain. (Photo: United Nations.)

tionships among family members are close, and there is a commitment to family welfare. Religion and tradition control rural culture; however, it is difficult to generalize because their influence depends on the religious sect or ethnic group in a given village.

Agricultural pursuits predominate; but there is a small but growing industrial sector in some villages. Multiple employment is common. In 1961, more than half the landowners held nonagricultural jobs as a main occupation. Unpaid family help makes up a considerable part of farm labor.

Land is privately owned, and owner-operated farms predominate. Farm sizes vary from an average of less than 2.5 acres (1 ha) in the Mount Lebanon region to about 12 acres (5 ha) in the Bika Valley. Regional differences in ownership patterns are due to a variety of factors: topography, history, inheritance practices and laws, politics, and population density. Inheritance laws vary according to religion, and Muslim-owned farms tend to be smaller because Islamic inheritance law requires an even distribution among one's heirs.

The adoption of modern cultivation methods varies by region. In southern Lebanon mechanization has proceeded slowly, while in the Bika Valley it has been more rapid. Especially in the south, topography, tradition, and the lack of investment capital have led to a general disinterest in technological change and a preference for the status quo.

The rate of urbanization in Lebanon is one of the highest in the Arab world. Between 1960 and 1975, the urban population rose from 35 to 60 percent. In 1975, 43 percent of the population were under 15 years of age, placing Lebanon third lowest among Arab states in the proportion of individuals in that category.

Until 1975, Lebanon's cities were among the best developed in the Arab Middle East. Beirut, the capital, was a vibrant, attractive city with many job opportunities and cultural and intellectual attractions. Tripoli, Sidon, Tyre, and Baalbek did not rank with Beirut, but they also offered an interesting environment for urban living. Unfortunately, the civil war of 1975–1976 and the continued fighting in southern Lebanon have destroyed large sections of Beirut, and commerce and industry have slowed down or stopped completely. The city is divided into hostile enclaves, across whose boundaries the militias of various factions eye each other suspiciously and fight occasional pitched battles despite the presence of the largely Syrian Arab peacekeeping force. There was less damage in the other major cities, but Tyre, the largest city near the Israeli border, is slowly being destroyed in the battles between Israel and the Palestinians.

Since the time of the Prophet Muhammad, the Middle East's social structure has been divided along religious and ethnic lines. Because Islam tolerates the "people of the book," Christians and Jews were able to maintain their religion and their communal autonomy under Islamic rule, but they survived only at the fringes of society as second-class citizens. In the period of the Ottoman Empire, non-Muslims were recognized as separate *millets* (communities). In Lebanon, each community developed under the leadership of a ruling family.

The history of modern Lebanon begins in the early sixteenth century with the establishment of the *imarah* (princedom) under the leadership of the Ma'n family. For the first time, a number of feudal families united under the rule of a local prince who stood above his own community and offered protection to religious men and laity of all faiths. The *imarah* united Maronite Christians and Druze politically while leaving each sect free to govern its own social, religious, and cultural affairs. By 1830, external and internal events threatened to destroy the *imarah*. The ruling emir (Bechir II, 1788–1840) allied himself with the Egyptians, who had expanded their influence into Syria. The British supported Ottoman attempts to regain Syria and encouraged local discontent, which culminated in the revolt of 1840 and the end of the *imarah* in 1842.

At about the same time, the spirit of cooperation between the Druze and Christians faded. The southward expansion of Maronite peasants into Druze districts created friction between the two sects, forcing the Ottoman rulers to change the region's administrative structure. The country was divided into two districts, Druze and Maronite, each governed by a member of the majority sect. But the solution did not bring peace to the area, and sectarian strife continued.

Following World War I, Lebanon came under French control, and in 1922 the League of Nations created Greater Lebanon under French mandate. The mandate expanded the former Ottoman administrative district by adding the coastal regions, including Beirut and Sidon, the Bika Valley, certain areas south of Sidon, and Tripoli plus its environs. These additions strengthened the country economically but weakened its fragile political structure. Mount Lebanon had been predominantly Christian and overwhelmingly Maronite. The mandate added many Muslims, reducing Christians to a bare majority; Shiite and Sunni Muslims outnumbered the Druze, and the Maronites were reduced to 30 percent of the population.

Between 1922 and 1943, the distribution of political power according to confession was formalized. Under the often amended 1926 constitution, the President is a Maronite Christian, the Prime Minister is a Sunni Muslim, and the speaker of the Chamber of Deputies is a Shiite Muslim. Parliamentary seats are distributed in proportion to the numerical strength of each sect, but 6 to 5 in favor of Christians. Independence, proclaimed in 1941, was confirmed by agreement with the Free French in 1943, and became an actuality in 1946 when French troops withdrew.

Despite its precarious nature, the Lebanese political system survived until May 1958, when civil war erupted between Christians and Muslims. The revolt lasted from May to October. In July, U.S. Marines landed on the beaches near Beirut in response to a government request. The situation remained tense, but a compromise was worked out preserving the status quo among the confessions and reaffirming Lebanon's position as an unaligned independent Arab nation. The compromise thus ended the revolt without solving the basic problems. The Christians retained too much power and the Muslims were dissatisfied because Lebanon remained uncommitted to the Arab nationalist movement. In May 1975, civil war erupted again.

Following almost a year of fierce fighting between Muslims (supported by Palestinians) and Christians, an uneasy truce was established by the Syrian army and forces of the Palestine Liberation Organization (PLO). To prevent further fighting and reduce Syrian involvement, the Arab states interposed an Arab peacekeeping force between the warring factions.

In 1976, a new National Covenant was adopted.

The three highest national offices were retained by representatives of the three most important sects. To rebalance relations between Christians and Muslims, the seats in the Chamber of Deputies were divided equally among Christians and Muslims and proportional representation of the sects was provided. Fiscal, economic, and social reforms were also promised.

But the conflict and bitter fighting between Christians and Muslims continue. If the Arab-Israeli question could be settled and if the Arab nations were to return to the principles of the Arab League Pact of 1945 (which pledges noninterference in each member's internal affairs), Lebanon might have a chance to reestablish domestic tranquility. Unfortunately, the longer the turmoil continues the greater the possibility that a viable confessionalism cannot be resurrected, and Lebanon may cease to exist as an independent state.

Ramon Knauerhase

Libya

(Popular Socialist Libyan Arab State of the Masses)

Area: 679,217 sq mi (1,759,164 sq km)
Population: 2.8 million (1978)
  Density: 4 per sq mi (1.5 per sq km)
  Growth rate: 4.1% (1970–1977)
Percent of population under 15 years of age: 44%
Infant deaths per 1,000 live births: 80 (1975)
Life expectancy at birth: 37 years
Leading causes of death: not available
Ethnic composition: Arab and Arab-Berber 97%
Languages: Arabic
Literacy: 35%
Religions: Muslim 97%
Percent population urban: 25%
Percent population rural: 75%
Gross national product: $18.96 billion
  Per capita GNP: $7,000
  Per capita GNP growth rate: 4.5% (1970–1977)
Inflation rate: not available

Libya is a land of vast deserts, sparse population, and immense wealth generated by native petroleum resources. Its leader, Colonel Muammar Qaddafi, believes himself to be a prophetic figure in Arab circles, a benefactor to the world's liberation movements, and the architect of third world defenses against the depredations of American and Western imperialism. When weighing Libya's assets against its liabilities, petroleum must be placed on the plus side of the ledger; Colonel Qaddafi may well be a national liability.

A creation of the United Nations, Libya has struggled for political and economic viability ever since it acquired independence in December 1951. The discovery of commercially exploitable quantities of oil in the late 1950s helped to lighten Libya's economic burdens, although the country has not yet established an integrated national infrastructure. The struggle to establish a stable political system continues almost three decades after independence. Unless stability is established in the next few years, the country may face serious political disorientation and disorder.

Libya is bound by the Mediterranean Sea to the north and the Sahara Desert to the south. More than 90 percent of the country's 679,217-square-mile (1,759,000-sq-km) territory is rock-strewn desert or barren semidesert. The principal agricultural belt lies along the coastline of Tripolitania; the highlands of Cyrenaica are useful for pasture. The desert reaches to the sea in the Gulf of Sidra region, bifurcating the 1,097-mile (1,770-km) coastline.

Libya has no permanent rivers because of its flat terrain and inadequate rainfall. Rainfall is irregular and operates on a three-year cycle. The *ghibli*—a hot, dusty southern wind lasting up to five days at a stretch—has a desiccating influence. There are only two significant elevations in the country. The Jebel Nafusa, located east of the main Cyrenaican city of Benghazi, have a maximum height of approximately 3,000 feet (915 m). To the extreme south, a generally inaccessible string of Saharan zone mountains rises to a height of some 10,000 feet (3,050 m).

The climate in the coastal belts of Tripolitania and Cyrenaica is mild and Mediterranean—somewhat like that of southern California. Except for periods in the spring and fall when the ghibli appears, temperatures are moderate. The desert zones, by comparison, are comparable to California's Death Valley. Temperatures will sometimes climb to more than 110°F

(43°C). In the Cyrenaican Jebel, the climate is somewhat more moderate because of the elevation of the area and the availability of shade trees. In the south, oasis culture and climate prevail.

Libya's population, which numbered 2,758,000 in mid-1978, is predominantly Arab-Berber. Its growth rate—reportedly 4.1 percent—is one of the highest in the world. Population density is 4 persons per square mile (2 per sq km). Because the country is mostly desert and semidesert, 90 percent of the population occupy the 10 percent of the land area on the coastal belt. Approximately 25 percent of the population is urban, and 44 percent is less than 15 years old.

The population reflects a heavy overlay of Arab and Islamic influences. Conquered in the seventh century, the indigenous Berbers were quickly converted to Islam, a monotheistic religion that follows the teachings of Muhammad and submission to the will of Allah, the need to avoid secularism, and the desirability of abstaining from alcohol and other indulgences that corrupt spiritual values. Colonel Qaddafi's military regime has stressed the need to return to these hallowed precepts and, since coming to power, Qaddafi has embarked on a campaign of religious and secular purification. Arabic has been restored as the primary language of learning, government, and commerce; Western-style bars have been closed; and all manifestations of Western, secular influence seen as potentially corrupting have been eliminated.

The extended family, the clan, and the tribe retain their central place in the lives of most Libyans despite the social transformations of the past two decades. These traditional social units, which provide a sense of identification, pride, and status, still enjoy the basic loyalties of most Libyans. Continuing local rivalries among tribes, clans, and families reinforce these loyalties.

There are three forms of education in contemporary Libya. Traditional Islamic or *Sharia* schools continue to provide a fundamental grounding in religious precepts. In the interior, tribal schools indoctrinate youths with local customs and behavior. Finally, the government has developed a more modern school system, which has raised the literacy level from 5 percent at independence to 35 percent today. The modern schools have produced high school and college graduates with excellent grounding in the social sciences. Students wishing to pursue more technical studies matriculate in foreign universities, most often in Europe and the Arab world.

Because of the persistence of traditional tribal and religious proscription, most rural women do not enjoy emancipated status. Their life is harsh and difficult. They till the soil, tend local animals, produce offspring, and have few privileges. Because of the difficult natural environment, the lot of the men is not appreciably better. The average life expectancy in rural areas is less than 35 years.

In urban Libya, principally in the cities of Tripoli and Benghazi, social relationships are more relaxed and the status of women is substantially less menial. Nevertheless, the tradition of plural marriage persists, and women are still restricted in public and subordinated to male direction on social and political issues.

Today, Libyans are waiting for the "good life"—social and educational betterment, an opportunity to acquire new material possessions, and the prospect of occupational mobility—that the extraction of oil promises. As a result, over the past two decades, an increasing number of young Libyans have left rural areas in search of education and jobs in Libya's few cities. This migration has reduced agricultural productivity and added to the problems of housing, training, and social integration in the urban centers of Tripoli and Benghazi.

To cope with the problems attending social and economic change, the government is spending large sums to improve agriculture, industry, and social conditions. Consonant with its dedication to a better distribution of wealth and amenities, the government has embarked on a program to build health facilities, schools, community centers, and low-cost housing (for which generous loans are provided).

The key to all these efforts is Libya's oil. Beginning with limited production in 1959, crude oil production has risen to more than 3 million barrels a day (a level that has recently declined because of government conservation measures). As a result, the country's economic growth rate and the income of the average Libyan have risen markedly. The gross domestic product of Libya rose to $5,000 per capita in 1975. Today, total GDP exceeds $15 billion, a significant reversal of the situation at independence in 1951, when Libya's deficit compelled it to look abroad for loans

In this family-oriented society, all members assist in cleaning and packing onions. Other crops grown on the farms include wheat, barley, and oats in winter, and vegetables and fruit in summer. (Photo: United Nations/ Rice.)

and economic assistance to sustain an impoverished economy.

Indeed, at independence, there were few indications that Libya would become relatively self-sufficient. And there was little in Libya's background to suggest that the country would ever play an influential role on the world stage. For much of its history, Libya served as an avenue through which foreign invading armies marched. In antiquity, it knew Phoenician, Carthaginian, Roman, and Vandal rule. More recently, Libya experienced conquest by Arab, Ottoman, Turkish, and Italian forces. Freed from Italian rule during World War II, the area fell under British and French military administration while the United States, Britain, France, and the Soviet Union negotiated the fate of Italy's former colonies in Africa. When they failed to agree, the UN General Assembly passed a resolution, on November 21, 1949, proposing to make Libya an independent nation. Libya achieved independence on December 24, 1951.

Under the auspices of the United Nations, a federation unified the three provinces of Tripolitania, Cyrenaica, and Fezzan. King Idris—previously the leader of the Sanusi religious brotherhood and emir of Cyrenaica—was made ruler, with wide-ranging political powers. A frail and modest monarch, Idris delegated some of his powers to ministers who served at his personal behest and he remained secluded in his native province of Cyrenaica. He ruled an impoverished land that numbered slightly more than 1 million people at independence; the per capita income was $35, and the country could boast but a single Libyan college graduate (excluding the Italian community of 30,000, which has since left the country).

The discovery of commercially exploitable quantities of oil in the late 1950s and the consequent growing wealth drastically transformed Libyan society. A process of social change led to rapid urbanization, the emergence of new social classes, the appearance of an educated elite, and the growth of a national consciousness and national pride not evident at independence.

Because Idris was increasingly unable to cope with the transformation of Libyan society, these changes ultimately led to the downfall of the Idris government. In 1969, the intervention of the army, led by Muammar Qaddafi, overthrew the King and produced other unforeseen changes. Colonel Qaddafi and the Revolutionary Command Council drew their initial inspiration from the political philosophy of Gamal Abdel Nasser, President of the United Arab Republic from 1958 to 1970. Like Nasser, they endorsed Arab unity, the forces of revolutionary change, and a doctrinaire anti-Zionism. Qaddafi believes that peace will not be realized until the Palestinian people return to Palestine and Arab unity is reestablished. In September 1980, Qaddafi and Syrian President Hafez Assad agreed to unify their two countries.

On March 3, 1977, Libya was proclaimed a people's republic and all powers were vested in the General People's Congress—a shadowy body that is apparently intended to operate on a town meeting discussion basis. Qaddafi was appointed secretary-general of the secretariat of the Congress; he remains chief of state. The Revolutionary Command Council was abolished, but its members were named appointees of the Secretariat and serve in an advisory capacity. Each community has a local council in which labor organizations and professional associations as well as groups such as students and farmers are represented. This democratic pluralism has yet to be proved a viable or effective system. Nor has the formal adoption of the Koran (the holy book of Islam) proved a coherent guide in shaping the country's political and legal systems.

The philosophy of the Libyan revolution is based on a form of "people's power." The term *jamahiriya*, part of the title of the country, is defined by Qaddafi as a "state run by the people without a government." In the colonel's terms, peace depends on the disappearance of government.

Qaddafi believes that Libya must use its oil wealth freely to influence other nations. Nothing more clearly exemplifies the Libyan sense of mission than

Using a large tractor-drawn plow, farm workers seed a wheat field in Libya, which is primarily an agricultural country. (Photo: United Nations/ Kay Muldoon.)

the role that Qaddafi has played in Chad. Taking advantage of the traditional animosities that until recently characterized relations between the Arabized Saharan tribes of northern Chad and the black-dominated government at N'Djamena, Qaddafi has used military force to seize border territory long claimed by Libya, while providing arms, financial support, and sanctuary to Saharan insurgent groups. Because of Libya's largesse and Soviet arms, the principal insurgent force, Frolinat, has been able to seize control of two-thirds of Chadian territory. While French troops tried to stem the tide, the rebels prevailed and toppled the regime of Chad President F. Malloum Ngakoutou Bey-Ndi. Currently, under the auspices of Nigeria, efforts are being made to fashion a government of national reconciliation. Recently, the Libyan government has announced plans to merge with Chad.

Qaddafi also tried to prevent the overthrow of Uganda's Field Marshal Idi Amin by Tanzanian forces in April 1979. Responding to urgent appeals from Amin, a professed Muslim, Qaddafi dispatched 3,000 Libyan troops to help him. In the ensuing struggle, more than 1,000 Libyan troops were killed or wounded, and the remainder were captured. This incident confirmed the general impression that Qaddafi is an unstable leader, without the knowledge, experience, or temperament needed to create a viable political system in Libya or to establish a constructive foreign policy.

Libya's fate will be determined by Qaddafi's tenure. His protracted rule would ensure that despite its oil wealth Libya would remain a pariah in international society; the end of his regime could lead to the formation of a more open, dynamic political system.

William H. Lewis

Morocco
(Kingdom of Morocco)

Area: 171,953 sq mi (445,356 sq mi)
Population: 19 million
  Density: 110 per sq mi (43 per sq km)
  Growth rate: 2.7% (1970–1977)
Percent of population under 14 years of age: 47% (1975)
Infant deaths per 1,000 live births: 130 (1975)
Life expectancy at birth: 53 years (1975)
Leading causes of death: not available
Ethnic composition: Arab-Berber 99%
Languages: Arabic (official), French, Berber dialects
Literacy: 25% (1978)
Religions: Sunni Muslim 99%
Percent population urban: 38%
Percent population rural: 62%
Gross national product: $12.6 billion
  Per capita GNP: $670
  Per capita GNP growth rate: 4.2% (1970–1977)
Inflation rate: 13% (1977 est.)

Morocco's more than 19 million people blend Mediterranean, Arab, European, and pre-Saharan cultures and reflect the influences of Andalusia, of Cairo and Damascus, and of the Berbers, Morocco's original inhabitants. Morocco is a nation in the process of establishing its geographic boundaries in the Sahara, its government's parameters, and the extent of its role in Africa. The continuing drain caused by its war in the Western Sahara, the constraints of an Islamic tradition, and the stagnating economy all hinder Morocco's development.

A fabled land in the northwest quadrant of Africa, Morocco once served as the land bridge for the Arab invasions of West Europe; in more recent times Morocco has suffered the depredations of the notorious Barbary pirates, the raids of the freebooter Raisuli, and the "romantic" activities of the French Foreign Legion. During World War II, Morocco was the landing point for American troops initiating the first major Allied military offensive against the Axis armies of Germany and Italy. Because of its geographic location, Morocco has provided the stage on which African, Arab, and European forces have acted out their ambitions.

Morocco has four basic geographic zones. The Mediterranean zone embraces one-fifth of the nation and enjoys balanced rainfall, ample vegetation, and fairly productive agricultural soil; the Rif mountain region of northern Morocco forms the heartland of this zone. Adjacent to the Mediterranean zone is an intermediate area of steppes, where rainfall is somewhat more irregular, occurring mostly in spring and fall, and where cultivation is less certain. The Atlas Mountains, which traverse Morocco on an east-west axis, are the geographic heartland of the country. Extending over a distance of 465 miles (750 km) the Atlas Mountains have an average elevation of more than 6,560 feet (2,000 m), and the highest peak, the Toubkal, rises to more than 13,600 feet (4,150 m). The fourth zone is the region of the Sahara Desert to the extreme south, which includes a substantial portion of the former Spanish Sahara, incorporated into the Kingdom of Morocco in 1975. This is a rocky, sandy area; in its interior, the daily temperature ranges from 52 to 112°F (11 to 44°C).

Morocco has a population approaching 20 million, of which 99 percent are Arab-Berber and Muslim; 0.2 percent is Jewish; the remainder, 0.7 percent, is non-Moroccan. The population grows at an average annual rate of almost 3 percent; approximately 60 percent of the people are less than 21 years old. About 38 percent of the population live in urban centers—the largest of which are Casablanca (population, 1.4 million), Rabat (population, 370,000), Marrakesh (population 300,000), and Fès (population 250,000). About one-third of the population are in the active labor force: 70 percent in agriculture; 12 percent in industry; and 18 percent in the service sector.

Morocco offers startling contrasts in living standards and lifestyles. The Western-educated elite and the older merchant families have a high standard of living, reflected in their modern villas and modern appliances and conveniences. There is a substantial Moroccan middle class, which holds positions in the middle reaches of government, in the management ranks of private enterprise, and in the academic community. The main symbol of middle-class status is the possession of a small home or apartment in one of the principal cities or fashionable suburbs. In rural areas, a modest landholding class follows modern agricultural practices and commands a secure income.

However, rising living costs, inflation, uncertain employment, and limited prospects for self-improvement condemn the overwhelming majority of Moroccans to a marginal existence. A relatively stagnant economy has produced a large underemployed urban working class—a Lumpenproletariat barely able to sustain family life. In rural areas, casual day laborers abound. And there is a sharecropping class, the *khammes* workers, who receive one-fifth of an agricultural crop for their services. When crop yields diminish, the sharecropper falls into serious debt and often cannot escape the poverty that robs farm families of their vitality and hopes for self-improvement.

Since independence, the Moroccan government has embarked on an ambitious program to unify, modernize, and expand the nation's educational system. Virtually all hamlets and towns have grade schools where a rudimentary education is offered; larger centers contain secondary schools; the main cities have university or technical-training facilities. Approximately 45 percent of Moroccans of primary school age are enrolled in classes, but the percentage enrolled at secondary and college levels is far lower. Only 25 percent of Morocco's overall population were classified as functionally literate at the end of 1978. This is in part due to the fact that because of traditional constraints in rural areas, young women do not usually enjoy the same educational advantages as young men.

Indeed, as in most Muslim countries, a wide gulf exists between males and females, in terms of freedoms accorded and standards imposed. In rural areas, particularly, ethnic and family custom weigh heavily on women; the veil is commonplace as are social and sexual taboos. The average Moroccan woman is responsible for child rearing and for preserving and transmitting social customs. Women labor at menial tasks in the household and in the fields and are subservient to male authority.

Lifestyles are changing, however, particularly in Morocco's urban centers. Radio and television, motion pictures, and the foreign press offer attractive models for many young Moroccans. The disco phenomenon, for example, has an increasing appeal. The automobile has also become a symbol of liberated status for young Moroccans—as has a summer vacation in Europe, where many trek to youth hostels to enjoy freedom from family restraints and customary taboos. French authors, lifestyles, and values are particularly admired and have a strong attraction.

Despite these changes in outlook, Islam and local custom exercise a restraining influence on the course and speed of change. *Islam*, which means "submission," emphasizes the avoidance of corrupting secular values and actions that might bring shame to the individual and his family. Local customs also reinforce tradition, restraint in public behavior, and respect for the authority of older members of the family. These constraints naturally produce occasional tensions between younger Moroccans and their elders.

In this context, the government acts as an important bridge. King Hassan II serves as a link between Arabs and Berbers, the modern sector and the traditional, the secular and the nonsecular. The latest in the line of Alawite rulers who established their dynasty in the seventeenth century, Hassan is expected to serve as the defender of the Islamic religion, the mediator of disputes between major tribal factions, the interpreter of the modernizing impulses of the youthful, and the general architect of government planning and policy. His father, Muhammad V, was

Despite the stagnating economy, the Atlantic port of Casablanca, Morocco's largest city, bustles with activity. (Photo: United Nations/ J. Slaughter.)

instrumental in rallying Morocco's nationalist organizations and diverse tribal factions against French rule, an action that enhanced immeasurably the popularity of the royal family.

The monarchy remains the central institution in Moroccan public life and the pivot for decision making in government. Under the existing constitution, King Hassan appoints the Cabinet, approves legislation, and personally directs Morocco's armed forces. There are few institutional restraints on the King's authority. A National Assembly includes representatives from Morocco's many political parties, but its capacity to function independently of the King is limited by factionalism, personal rivalries, and a lack of consensus on national goals.

The King faces two major problems: the first concerns Moroccan control over the Western Sahara, the second economic stagnation. In the Western Sahara, Morocco is hard-pressed by a guerrilla movement— the Polisario—that wants to end Moroccan control over the northern reaches of the former Spanish Sahara on the Atlantic coast of northwest Africa. An area of 102,703 square miles (266,000 sq km, slightly smaller than Colorado) with an essentially nomadic population of some 70,000 people, the Spanish Sahara became a source of contention when Spain decided to relinquish its control in the early 1970s.

Ultimately, Morocco and Mauritania occupied the former Spanish Sahara and annexed it (with two-thirds of the territory taken by Morocco). The local population were not afforded a full opportunity to express their preferences, and many of them fled to neighboring Algeria, where they formed the Polisario resistance movement. This "liberation" force has been waging intermittent but increasingly effective warfare against Morocco (which has more than 20,000 troops in the region). As the war has dragged on, Moroccan resentment against Algeria's support of the Polisario has mounted. Thus far, King Hassan has sought to establish a basis for a negotiated settlement to the dispute.

Morocco's economic woes are legion. Despite substantial recent growth in the industrial and service sectors, the country is basically agricultural. Its principal crops are cereals (wheat and barley), citrus fruits, and wine grapes. Wines and minerals, primarily phosphates, also contribute to the country's exports. France, West Germany, and Italy have been Morocco's major trading partners. As of 1978, the gross national product was $12.6 billion, or about $670 per capita. The average annual rate of the nation's real growth was 4 percent during the period from 1970 to 1973; 9 percent in 1974; and less than 3 percent during the period from 1975 to 1977.

Particularly disturbing to its modern economic sector has been Morocco's limited ability to provide goods and services and to control the rising rate of inflation and the spreading unemployment in urban centers. Frustration and resentment are directed toward the government ministries. But, as the war in the Sahara continues and the armed forces command increasing shares of government resources, resentment may shift to the King. The historic unity of Morocco may be threatened.

In antiquity, Morocco was an outpost of Phoenician and Roman conquests. But because of its distance from the central Mediterranean basin, the imprint left by Phoenician and Roman civilization on Morocco was slight. The original inhabitants of the region, the Berbers, maintained their institutions by retreating into the interior, particularly into the ancient refuge, the Atlas Mountains and the pre-Saharan steppes. The surge of Arab armies out of the Arabian Peninsula in the seventh and in the eleventh centuries led to the conversion to Islam of the original Berber population and to their partial Arabization. Still, the Berbers retained their separate identity and distinctive institutions. Successive empires, including the Almoravids and the Almohades embraced much of North Africa, but their imprint was shallow and their contributions did not last. It was not until the establishment of the Alawite dynasty in the seventeenth century that a sense of historical continuity developed.

Despite the durability of the Alawites, who still rule Morocco, the country suffered frequent political upheavals and tribal unrest. Nevertheless, unlike other North African nations, Morocco retained its separate identity and was never conquered by Ottoman Turkey.

By the end of the nineteenth century, tribal dissi-

Moroccan farmers use modern machinery to harvest wheat, one of the principal crops in this primarily agricultural country. (Photo: United Nations/Bill Graham.)

dence, an impoverished government, and weak monarchical rule had led to growing European encroachments. Finally, in 1912, the sultan signed a treaty with France establishing protectorate zones in the north and in the south. An international consortium, including the United States, administered Tangiers.

The rise of nationalism movements after World War II led Morocco to an inevitable clash with France. The leaders of the principal nationalist party, the Istiqlal, were imprisoned. When King Muhammad V of Morocco, Sultan Sidi Muhammad ben Youssef, aligned himself with Istiqlal in 1953, he was deposed and exiled to Madagascar. This action rallied the Moroccan population; after 27 months of rising agitation, Muhammad V was restored to the throne. On March 2, 1956, Morocco was granted full independence. In the months that followed, Tangiers and the two Spanish zones were returned to Morocco. The United States, however, continues to maintain access to several small communications facilities outside the capital, Rabat.

Independence offered Muhammad V his second major challenge—making Morocco a viable political entity. In this he was successful. However, the conflict in the Western Sahara and the stagnating economy may undo his accomplishments. Hassan II, who succeeded to the throne in 1961, confronts complex and demanding problems. Unless he can end the Saharan conflict without relinquishing control of the disputed territory (relinquishment would be a personal defeat), he will not be able to plan Morocco's economic development effectively. And without progress in the economic area, Hassan may find it increasingly difficult to hold Morocco's delicate constellation of political forces together.

William H. Lewis

Saudi Arabia

(Kingdom of Saudi Arabia)

Area: **864,000–870,000 sq mi (2,237,750–2,253,290 sq km)**
Population: **7.9 million**
  Density: **9 per sq mi (3.5 per sq km) (1978)**
  Growth rate: **2.7% (1970–1977)**
Percent of population under 15 years of age: **45% (1975)**
Infant deaths per 1,000 live births: **not available**
Life expectancy at birth: **45 years**
Leading causes of death: **not available**
Ethnic composition: **Arab**
Languages: **Arabic**
Literacy: **15%**
Religions: **Sunni Muslim**
Percent population urban: **35%**
Percent population rural: **65%**
Gross national product: **$63.3 billion**
  Per capita GNP: **$8,040**
  Per capita GNP growth rate: **13% (1970–1977)**
Inflation rate: **33.3% (average 1970–1976); 4% (1977)**

Wahhabism and crude oil are the foundations of modern Saudi Arabia. Wahhabism, a puritanical, fundamentalist religious reform movement that began in central Arabia about 1750, was the bond uniting the warring tribes of the desert under the banner of the house of Saud; it led to the creation of the Kingdom of Saudi Arabia under the leadership of Abdul Aziz Saud (ibn Saud). Crude oil, discovered in commercial quantities in March 1938, is the means by which Saudi Arabia can develop the basis for a modern, industrial economy and become a major force in the economy and politics of the Middle East.

Saudi Arabia covers approximately 80 percent of the Arabian Peninsula. Because most of its borders are undefined, its exact size is unknown. Estimates vary from 864,000 to 870,000 square miles (2,237,750 to 2,253,290 sq km), an area about the size of the United States east of the Mississippi. The country is mostly desert, and water is by far its most precious resource. Less than 1 percent of the land area is suitable for settled agriculture. Along the west coast, a narrow, fertile plain extends from the border with Yemen north to the Gulf of Aqaba. East of this plain, running about 10 to 40 miles (16 to 64 km) from the coast, a mountain range rises almost vertically out of the coastal plain, varying in height between 9,000 feet (2,743 m) in the Asir and 3,000 feet (914 m) north of Medina. East of the Hejazi Mountains stretches the Nejd Plateau with an average elevation of 4,000 to 6,000 feet (1,220 to 1,830 m). The elevation decreases from west to east. Taif, the summer capital, located in the Hejazi Mountains, is 4,500 feet (1,370 m) above sea level; Riyadh, the permanent capital, 950 miles (1,530 km) east of Taif, is about 2,000 feet (610 m) above sea level; and Dhahran, the center of the oil fields, is 72 feet (22 m) above sea level.

Saudi Arabia's climate is controlled by the subtropical high pressure system. In the interior, the summer is hot and dry and the winter is relatively cool; temperatures often rise above 130°F (54°C) in July and August and rarely fall below 32°F (0°C) in winter. In the coastal regions, temperature differences are modified by the sea; humidity is high and temperatures seldom rise above 100°F (38°C). In the eastern sections, sandstorms occur frequently, reaching their peak each June.

Except for the southwestern region (Asir) rainfall is scarce, and for thousands of years the seasonal rainfall has determined the annual migration of the nomadic

Bedouin. While the average annual rainfall is 4 inches (10 cm), many areas often receive no rain for several years. Sometimes the rainfall results from one or two violent storms, causing severe flooding and damage. The rainfall is sufficient, however, to sustain forage vegetation for goats, sheep, and camels. Regional water resources depend on geology. Most usable sources are confined to aquifers and springs.

Saudi Arabia possesses the world's largest oil reserves. Its 150 billion barrels of proved reserves (well over five times United States oil reserves) amount to 22.8 percent of world oil reserves and 39.1 percent of Middle East reserves; they constitute 32.3 percent of the reserves controlled by the Organization of Petroleum Exporting Countries (OPEC). Copper, gold, silver, iron, sulfur, phosphates, and rare earths also exist in commercial quantities. A major deposit—estimated at 1.5 billion tons (1.36 billion mt)—of low-grade iron ore has been discovered west of Jidda.

In contrast to most developing countries, the kingdom is sparsely populated. Sixty-five percent of the population live in rural areas, three-fourths in agricultural villages; the rest are nomadic. The nomads have turned to farming most rapidly in the eastern and western provinces. Approximately 35 percent of the population live in seven large and nine smaller urban concentrations. Geographic population patterns are determined entirely by the availability of water, and because the number of oases is small, permanently habitable regions are densely populated. In 1970, the population growth rate was estimated at 2.75 percent; it is probably around 3 percent today.

The population is young. In 1975, 45 percent of the population were less than 15 years old and 53 percent were of working age (15 to 64 years).

The extended family is the basic unit of social organization, and kinship ties are of primary importance. Marriages are arranged, and often bride and groom meet for the first time on their wedding day. Polygamy is declining because Islamic law asserts that a man must maintain his wives equally. With rising demands for consumer goods, it has become increasingly expensive to provide equally for several wives. Thus the number of plural marriages has fallen, especially among the younger, better-educated members of the middle class.

Because the society is male-oriented, the status of women is low. Isolated from nearly all outside influence, a conservative, dutiful Saudi woman confines herself to the traditional role of mother and housewife and plays virtually no public role. Because Saudi women are usually illiterate, they have little influence on the education of boys. At age eight or nine, a boy passes from his mother's care and his education becomes his father's responsibility. Girls remain under a mother's tutelage in order to learn women's duties in the household.

This pattern is beginning to change. In 1960, slightly over 5,000 girls attended school. By 1975, the number had risen to over 241,000. Most women complete only the first few years of primary grades; but about 9 percent of women enrolled on all levels of education in 1974 were granted certificates. The most significant aspect of the rising educational level of women is that the number of women graduating above primary school level in many technical fields has risen substantially since the mid-1960s.

Racially, religiously, and linguistically the population is homogeneous; the most important difference is the spoken dialect that easily identifies a person's regional origin.

Islam is the state religion. In theory the Koran and the Sharia (Islamic law) cover all aspects of religious, political, and civil life; therefore, the Koran is the constitution, and the judicial system is based on the rules of the Sharia as codified by ibn Hanbal. Criminals are punished according to the rules laid down in the Koran. The religious authorities (*ulama*) have considerable influence in educational and cultural matters.

Most Saudis still adhere firmly to prescribed ritual obligations. But change is coming. With the shift from rural to urban lifestyles, the power of the religious authorities to enforce the observation of prayer and other rituals has declined in the cities. Interest on loans is prohibited by the Koran, but private banks charge and pay interest on deposits. Religious conservatism is stronger in the rural areas, especially in the Nejd, than in the cities. And it is weaker in the western cities of Jidda, Taif, and even in the holy cities Mecca and Medina than in the centrally located cities of Buraidah, Hayil, and Riyadh.

At a desert oasis, people wash and bathe. Oases create year-round habitable areas in a land where water is scarce. (Photo: United Nations/WHO/Scheidegger.)

The social structure is divided into a primary nomadic group and a secondary group of peasants and city dwellers. First and foremost in the determination of social position is descent on the father's side from an independent, camel-breeding Bedouin tribe. This is the only legitimate ground on which a person can claim to be an Arab. The relationship among ethnic groups is determined by pride, wealth, ability, and lineage.

Although the city dwellers value their descent from the Bedouin, the usual social division between city and country exists. Apart from such exceptions as tribal chiefs, the Bedouin and the settled rural population are considered inferior by the urban population.

Next in the determination of class position is membership in a religious sect: Sunnis rank above Shiites, Wahhabis above Shafiites. Third is land ownership. Ownership of animals and town houses yields less prestige. Finally, there is a person's occupation. Trade, service, intellectual occupations, and animal husbandry are held in high esteem. Manual occupations, with the exception of mechanics, are held in relatively low esteem.

Since the turn of the century, the royal family of the house of Saud and its branches have formed the upper class, which includes top members of the Al-Shaykh family (descended from Muhammad ibn Abdul Wahhab, the eighteenth century religious reformer), and a few important tribal sheikhs.

A modern education has become an additional factor in the determination of class position. Until the 1950s, the country's small middle class consisted of those with a traditional education: judges, lawyers, and teachers of Arabic and religion. The middle class has been augmented in recent years by other professionals, such as physicians, economists, managers, skilled technicians, and higher government officials. In 1975, about 90,000 persons (6 percent of the labor force) were employed in professional, technical, administrative, and managerial positions.

Oil is the foundation of the economy. In 1977, total crude oil and refined-product exports amounted to 3.3 billion barrels, which generated $36.5 billion in revenue. Measured in terms of growth of the economic aggregates, economic development has been successful. The gross domestic product grew 9.9 percent during the 1960s; stimulated by growth in the construction, transportation, communication, and oil-producing industries, the annual growth rate has averaged 14.4 percent since 1970. In fiscal year 1975–1976, the GDP amounted to $44.6 billion, of which about 74.5 percent originated in the oil sector, 8.8 percent in the industrial, and 10.1, 5.6, and 1.0 percent in the service, government, and agricultural sectors, respectively.

The economy is based on a free market, private enterprise system. To coordinate the development effort and to achieve economic self-sufficiency before oil reserves are exhausted, formal planning for development was introduced in 1970. The first 5-year plan (for the period from 1970 to 1975) called for expenditures of $9.2 billion, and the second plan (for the period from 1975 to 1980), formulated after the first oil price declaration of the Persian Gulf states on January 1, 1974, budgeted expenditures of $140 billion. The major goal of both plans was the diversification of the economy to be accomplished by improving agricultural and industrial output. To match the specific needs of the various regions and to maximize the benefits of the planning effort, the country was divided into five socioeconomic regions according to resources. The third 5-year plan calls for an expenditure of $240 billion to bolster the economy.

A keystone of the regional development concept is the creation of growth poles in the eastern and western regions. In addition to the existing facilities at Ras-Tanura and Dammam, a major hydrocarbon complex is now under construction at Jubail near the east coast oil fields. Negotiations are underway for another hydrocarbon complex at Yanbu, in the eastern region, with the required raw material to be supplied from the east coast via pipeline.

The most serious constraint on development is the lack of a trained labor force. Thus, the first 5-year plan placed great emphasis on education at all levels and in all categories, and the second plan called for the employment of 812,600 expatriate workers by 1980. This means that about one out of every two workers and one out of every five or six persons in Saudia Arabia will be a foreigner.

The results of the 5-year plans have been uneven.

Construction workers build an oil tanker terminal. Saudi Arabia's oil reserves are the largest in the world. (Photo: United Nations/J. O'Brien.)

The oil sector continues to overshadow the rest of the economy, and industrial diversification has lagged behind plan goals. In fact, recent evidence indicates a departure from the timetable and goals of the second plan. The government has largely abandoned most major development projects except petrochemicals and metals for export. Several major projects have been canceled or scaled down. Production for the consumer goods market has been left to the private sector, and medium and light industry will be concentrated in five industrial parks located in the major population centers.

One consequence of rapid development has been inflation. Between 1970 and 1977, prices rose 200 percent. Capital formation has been rapid, and considerable progress has been made in social overhead capital formation. The trunk road system is nearly completed. Almost 4,340 miles (7,000 km) of paved primary roads connect the major population centers. These primary roads are supplemented by over 4,960 miles (8,000 km) of secondary roads.

At least three major university campuses are under construction, and the number of primary and intermediate (junior and senior) high schools has increased considerably, as is indicated by a nearly 80 percent rise in the number of classes from 1970 to 1975. During the same period, the number of teachers rose by 78.3 percent and the number of students by 52.2 percent, lowering the average student-teacher ratio from 23 to 1 to 20 to 1. Despite a significant increase in school enrollments since 1960, the adult literacy rate is only 15 percent.

Important advances have also been made in the agricultural infrastructure. Numerous deep wells have been drilled in the villages, and a number of dams have been constructed to catch and store the seasonal rainfall. In the Southern Province, irrigation systems have brought over 12,350 additional acres (5,000 ha) of land under cultivation, and in the Al-Hasa region of the Eastern Province, irrigation and drainage projects added 7,410 acres (3,000 ha) to the arable land by the end of 1975. These developments have been tempered by the continued inefficiency of the agricultural sector (illustrated by the small average annual growth rate of the agricultural sector as compared to the rest of the economy as well as by the relatively high percentage of the population still engaged in agriculture).

In the major cities, water-supply systems have been completed. Furthermore, several water-desalinization plants have become operational, and a number of others are under construction.

To make rudimentary medical services available to everyone, the number of health centers and dispensaries has been increased throughout the country. In the major cities, fully equipped hospitals provide free medical services to all. The buildings have been staffed and filled with trained technicians; the number of physicians and medical technicians more than doubled between 1970 and 1975, reducing the number of persons per physician from 13,000 in 1960 to about 6,000 in 1975.

Overall, the people have benefited from the sale of oil, and if the effects on real income of free medical care, social security, free education and generous support payments to students attending universities and other institutions of higher learning, and many other transfer payments are considered, there can be no doubt that the government has provided an adequate if minimum standard of living for all citizens. The gross national product grew at an annual rate of 7 percent between 1960 and 1976. Since 1960 life expectancy at birth has risen from 37 to 45 years. The government subsidizes the price of essential food items and makes interest-free home construction loans to low and middle income private individuals, to Saudi employers for company housing, and to city governments for urban renewal.

Saudi Arabia is the only Arab state never touched directly by Western imperialism. The Arabian Peninsula was a backwater of the Ottoman Empire, and even during the height of nineteenth century European imperialism, it was of little interest to the competing imperialist powers. Until the discovery of oil, Arabia Deserta—as the section of the peninsula now called Saudi Arabia was called—was unknown territory to Europeans.

At the turn of the century, Abdul Aziz ibn Saud regained the patrimony that his father had lost to the Rashidi family. In a series of fiercely fought campaigns, he extended his influence from Riyadh across the Arabian Peninsula. In 1921, he assumed the title "Sultan of Nejd and Its Dependencies"; in 1926, he was proclaimed King of the Hejaz and Nejd; in 1927, Great Britain recognized his kingdom as a sovereign state; and on September 22, 1932, the country was renamed the Kingdom of Saudi Arabia, the only country in the world named after its ruling family.

The puritanical influence of Wahhabism and the location of the holy cities Mecca and Medina within its boundaries have made Saudi Arabia one of the most conservative Arab states. Wahhabism has been a major factor in the development of Saudi Arabia. Today, Wahhabism is a conservative social force, but its influence is slowly declining because it has been unable to moderate the corrupting effect of the nation's oil wealth.

After Abdul Aziz died in 1953, the succession was passed among his sons according to age. His first successor, Saud ibn Abdul Aziz, who reigned from 1953 to 1964, was an incompetent, profligate ruler and was deposed in favor of Faisal ibn Abdul Aziz. Under Faisal's leadership the kingdom emerged from its backwardness and isolation. The current king, Khalid ibn Abdul Aziz, succeeded to the throne after Faisal's assassination in 1975. Attempts to modify the theocratic and feudalistic structure of the government failed during the 1950s. The oligarchy is based on a policy of marriage and the basis for succession rests on consensus in the 3,000-member family.

It is not known how policy is made, but basic policy decisions apparently result from an interchange of views among the family's many branches and factions and a balancing of their ideas. There is some evidence that outsiders are consulted, but how much influence they exert is unknown.

The government consists of three elements: the royal family, the ulama (religious leaders), and the armed forces. The royal family in fact controls the other elements. The crown prince is the Prime Minister, and the army, the national guard, and the foreign ministry are headed by senior family members. Family members occupy other important positions.

There has been some domestic opposition, but on the whole the people support the monarchy. Radio, television, and the press are controlled, and it is unlikely that there will be any major social upheavals in the near future. Nevertheless, it is by no means certain that the royal family will retain its hold. Two factors related to rapid economic development threaten the nation's tranquility: the large number of expatriate workers and the failure of native labor to fill many skilled and unskilled blue-collar positions because of a preference for trade and white-collar jobs.

Foreigners threaten to dissolve the social relationships upon which the current power structure is based; thus, the faster native labor takes over many of the jobs currently held by Palestinians, Pakistanis, Indians, Egyptians, and other nationals the sooner the pressure will be relieved. Unfortunately, the decision to industrialize the country by the year 2000 requires many foreign workers, given Saudi unwillingness to take blue-collar jobs.

Saudi Arabia is in a difficult international position. It is a first-rank economic power, but it is militarily weak. The leader of the conservative Arab states, it is engaged in a delicate balancing act among its neighbors to fend off the radicals and to keep the Middle East out of the Soviet orbit. Until recently, the central themes of its policy were maintaining close relations with the United States and offering financial support to all moderate Arab regimes. To this end, the government supplied billions of dollars of aid to Egypt, Jordan, and the Yemen Arab Republic (Sana).

Saudi Arabia has also been a moderating force in OPEC. However, the downfall of the Shah of Iran in 1979 weakened Saudi Arabia's position. Saudi closeness to the United States has recently been deemphasized, and a limited rapprochement with the radical Arab states has been attempted.

With respect to Israel and the West Bank, Saudi Arabia faces a dilemma. It is committed to the return of East Jerusalem and the West Bank to Arab control. But this could result in a radical Palestinian state governed by the Palestine Liberation Organization (PLO) and supported by Libya and Iraq. The establishment of such a state would surely threaten the continued existence of a conservative Saudi Arabia. At the moment, the Saudis have joined the militant opposition against the Egyptian-Israeli peace treaty. They are using their economic and financial power against Egypt in support of the radical Arab states which reject the treaty. (In Lebanon, Saudi mediation efforts between Muslims and Maronite Christians continue in an attempt to bring peace to that troubled nation.)

Saudi economic aid extends beyond the Arab Middle East. Islamic countries such as Pakistan, Bangladesh, and certain African nations have been recipients of aid. Saudi Arabia has also contributed generously to the Islamic Development Bank, the Saudi Arabian Fund for Development, and other institutions dispensing foreign aid. Estimates indicate that Saudi Arabia has disbursed $5.2 billion in aid since 1974; of this amount, three-fourths took the form of outright grants. The Saudi government is also spending hundreds of millions of dollars on Islamic education. In Mecca, a university is being established that will be dedicated to Islamic scholarship and is intended to eclipse El-Azhar University in Cairo, the oldest and most distinguished institution of higher Islamic learning.

Saudi Arabia's economic future is bright, but despite the closer relationship between the kingdom and the radical Arab states, its political future is insecure. Radical elements may attempt to subvert the royal family and to supplant it with an extremist regime totally committed to the Arab cause. Economic development and modernization are also antithetical to religiously based conservative rule.

The attempt to promote economic development by means of capital-intensive industries has not benefited the majority of people, although there has been improvement in the standard of living. The presence of foreigners and the modernization of the economy are slowly dissolving the relatively homogeneous social fabric. Unless the royal family shares power and distributes the gains from oil exports faster and more equitably, it will have to relinquish control. The new ruling class and its supporters, not the people, will probably be the beneficiaries.

Ramon Knauerhase

Syria
(Syrian Arab Republic)

Area: 71,500 sq mi (185,184 sq km)
Population: 8.1 million
   Density: 113 per sq mi (44 per sq km)
   Growth rate: 3.3% (1970–1977)
Percent of population under 15 years of age: 49%
Infant deaths per 1,000 live births: 114
Life expectancy at birth: 57 years
Leading causes of death: not available
Ethnic composition: Arab 90%; Kurd; Armenian; Circassian; Turk
Languages: Arabic, Kurdish, Armenian, Circassian, Turkish
Literacy: 41% (1977)
Religions: Sunni Muslim 70%; Shiite Muslim 15%; Christian; Jewish
Percent population urban: 48%
Percent population rural: 52%
Gross national product: $7.49 billion
   Per capita GNP: $930
   Per capita GNP growth rate: 6.1% (1970–1977)
Inflation rate: 10% (1978–1979)

Syria did not exist in its present form until 1920, when it was created by the Western powers. Carved out of the Ottoman Empire, Syria remained under French mandate from 1920 until independence in 1946. Earlier, however, the Greeks used the term "Syria" to refer to the region at the eastern end of the Mediterranean between Egypt and Anatolia, a region which has one of the world's richest and longest recorded histories. Damascus, the present capital of Syria, occupies a site that has been continuously settled for thousands of years. Population pressure, rapid urbanization, rural poverty, and continuing political strife challenge this small nation, which is enjoying a period of relative political stability and rapid economic growth.

Past and present are linked in the area's geography, the broad physical outlines of which have changed little through the centuries. Syria is a country of impressive environmental contrasts. Its westernmost portions are dominated by the mighty Jabal Alawi Mountains, which rise gradually to over 5,000 feet (1,525 m) from a thin Mediterranean coastal plain 110 miles (177 km) long. To their south and southeast are the even more imposing Anti-Lebanon Mountains, which straddle Syria's boundary with Lebanon and reach an elevation of over 9,000 feet (2,745 m) at Mount Hermon. Most of Syria is steppe and desert plateau, however, and lies to the east of these two mountain ranges. Here the landscape is less dramatic, even if its most desolate parts often have a stark beauty of their own. More important, most of Syria's people and their agriculture and industry are located in the interior, concentrated in a narrow belt that stretches from north to south through the cities of Aleppo, Homs, Hama, and Damascus at the edge of the desert.

Syria's location and surface configuration shape its climate. Lowland areas immediately adjacent to the Mediterranean remain mild and pleasant in winter but suffer oppressive humidity and temperatures in the high 80s°F (low 30s°C) in summer. The mountains offer relief from summer discomfort, but they also cut off the areas to their east from the ocean's moderating influence. Consequently, the interior is much colder in winter (occasionally below freezing) and notably hotter in summer (typically ranging from 90 to over 100°F (32 to 38°C).

A far more critical difference is varying precipitation, which has a profound effect on human settlement patterns and agricultural production. Virtually all the country's rain (or snow at higher elevations and sometimes even in inland cities) falls during the winter months. The amount of precipitation varies sharply, geographically and from year to year. Because the mountains that parallel the coast lie athwart the moisture-bearing winds from the west that bring Syria almost all its precipitation, the coastal provinces are consistently well-watered, receiving between 25 and 40 inches (63 and 102 cm) annually. Their adequate rainfall is reflected in their rich green vegetation and in their high population densities. The mountains, however, decrease the quantity and reliability of rainfall from west to east and from north to south in the interior. Partly because of their blocking effect, 30 percent of the country is semiarid steppe and another 60 percent is true desert, receiving considerably less than 10 inches (2 cm) of rain in most years. Population density accordingly declines abruptly in areas distant from the so-called fertile crescent that rims the western and northern parts of the country. Much of the interior is inhabited only by nomadic tribes.

The Levant, of which Syria is part, has historically been a strategic land bridge connecting Europe, Asia, and Africa, and a place of interchange and contact between the seas of sand and water. As a passageway for peoples, ideas, and conquering armies, it has been a zone of interaction. This is reflected to some degree in the cultural heterogeneity of the present population. Since the seventh century, when Syria was conquered by armies carrying the newly born Islamic religion from the Arabian Peninsula, a majority of Syrians have been Arabic-speaking Muslims. Nevertheless, over 15 percent of the population speak non-Arabic languages—Kurdish, Armenian, Circassian, and Turkish.

Religious divisions are even more numerous. Approximately 70 percent of the Syrians are orthodox Sunni Muslims. Although most are Arabic-speaking, some speak Kurdish, Circassian, or Turkish. Another 15 percent of the Syrians are heterodox Shiite Muslims, belonging to the Alawi, Druze, and Ismaili splinter sects, all of which speak Arabic. Many Sunni Muslims view these sects as heretic. With the exception of a tiny Jewish community in Damascus, the rest of the population belongs to one or another of the many Christian denominations in the region. Most Christians speak Arabic; they tend to be more prosperous and are well-represented in the professions. Although a much larger proportion of Christians than Muslims live in the cities, there are Christians in almost every part of the country.

Other minorities, by contrast, are often concentrated in particular regions. The Alawis, for instance, dominate the impoverished, mountainous, coastal provinces; and the Druze dominate an inaccessible, backward upland area southeast of Damascus. Historically, these geographically compact minorities have fiercely resisted the imposition of central government authority.

The religious sect has traditionally been a primary unit of social interaction. Marriage typically is restricted to members of the same sect, and often sects are associated with particular occupations. In the past, most sects operated their own schools and had their own courts, with laws governing marriage, divorce, and inheritance. Until the late 1940s, sects were proportionally represented in Parliament. While this compartmentalization has been greatly undermined in recent years, Syrian society remains a mosaic society. The persistence of strong sectarian, linguistic, and regional allegiances has often been a source of internal political friction and a cause of problems that have plagued Syria's attempts at social integration. (The intensity of these problems has diminished since independence.)

A majority of Syrians dwell in rural areas and live directly off the land. Agriculture accounts for about 20 percent of gross domestic product, but it employs over one-half the labor force. Because of environmental constraints, less than one-third of the country is cultivable, and even less is actually farmed. Far and away the most widely grown crops are wheat and barley, which cover about two-thirds of the cultivated area and are consumed locally. Cotton crops are cultivated over a far smaller area but are much more valuable, forming the basis of Syria's textile industry. Cotton crops accounted for the largest part of Syria's export earnings until the early 1970s.

Among other leading agricultural products are the fine, fragrant tobacco grown in the Jabal Alawi, olives, figs, various citrus fruits, grapes, lentils, tomatoes, onions, chick-peas, and a wide range of other vegetables. Animal husbandry is also important. Sheep are the principal source of meat, and goats provide Syrians with their much-loved cheese and yogurt-type products.

Compared to the cities, the countryside remains desperately poor and underdeveloped. Numerous hardships bedevil peasant existence. One of the most serious is the effect of climate on agriculture; since annual rainfall varies tremendously and drought is frequent, agricultural output fluctuates wildly. Only one-third as much wheat and one-seventh as much barley were produced in 1973 as in 1972. Such periodic, precipitous drops in output have prompted a massive government effort to develop and extend irrigation by tapping such rivers as the Euphrates, Orontes, Khabur, and Yarmuk, which rise in areas where rainfall is less capricious and more abundant.

As a result of government efforts, the total irrigated area has increased by over 494,000 acres (200,000 ha) since independence. Much of this increase has been in the Ghab area of the Orontes. Since the late 1960s, development plans have given pride of place to the recently completed Euphrates Dam. In coming years, this massive structure will increase the irrigated area by as much as 1,580,800 acres (640,000 ha) and will meet most of Syria's electricity needs. The Jazirah region of the northeast will be the principal beneficiary of this and related irrigation schemes. If projections are correct, Syria's irrigated area (less than 15 percent of the total cropped area) will more than double.

For most of this century, gross inequalities in land ownership have been another source of difficulty in the countryside. Traditionally, most peasants eked out a pitiful existence as debt-ridden, exploited sharecroppers on large estates owned by a few absentee urban landlords. By the late 1950s, less than 1 percent of the rural population owned 35 percent of all agricultural land; some 70 percent owned no land. In the Hama region, where conditions were particularly appalling, four families fully or partly owned 108 out of

A woman feeds cattle at a dairy farm; the government helps to develop dairy production. (Photo: United Nations.)

114 villages. Since the socialist Baath party came to power in 1963, however, the lot of the peasant has been improved. The Baath regime expropriated all holdings exceeding a certain size and eventually redistributed almost 500,000 acres (202,000 ha) to more than 100,000 families. At the same time, it greatly expanded and formalized the legal rights of landless peasants and channeled rural development through the more than 3,000 agricultural cooperatives it established. With over 250,000 members, these cooperatives have made it easier to market crops, to spread new techniques, seeds, and ideas, to pool labor and equipment, and to distribute low-interest loans.

Some aspects of rural existence are harder to ameliorate. The poorest peasant may shelter a family of six, as well as his animals and possessions in a single windowless mudbrick room. A more prosperous peasant may have two rooms and a courtyard for cooking, entertaining, and sleeping; he may own a couple of simple wooden chairs and a table, a few functional clothes, and if he is very fortunate, a radio or bicycle. But like most rural Syrians, he will probably not have easy access to electricity, potable water, or adequate sewage disposal. Not surprisingly, life expectancy in rural areas is often far less than the national average of 57 years, and infant mortality rates in these areas are usually significantly higher than the national average of 114 per 1,000.

Farm workers walk along an irrigation canal that supplies water to cultivated fields in the Euphrates Basin; most Syrians are farmers. (Photo: United Nations.)

The plight of women in Syria's fiercely male-dominated, tradition-bound society is unenviable. Marriage is invariably arranged and young people marry very early. In the absence of birth control, a peasant woman may have five or six children. Divorce remains a male prerogative. Although the Baathi government has made a serious effort to change attitudes, women do not have equal access to education. According to the 1970 census, 84 percent of all females in rural areas were illiterate; only 39 percent of all males were illiterate. In the country as a whole, 50 percent more boys than girls were enrolled in primary schools in 1977.

The proportional contribution of agriculture to the gross domestic product has declined in recent years, while the share of manufacturing and mining has, with active government encouragement, increased. Between 1970 and 1977, these two sectors grew by over 11 percent annually in real terms. Industry, which has been largely state-controlled since sweeping nationalization in the mid-1960s, is concentrated in the areas of food processing and the production of cement and textiles and, more recently, the production of petrochemicals and fertilizers and the assembly of tractors, refrigerators, and television sets. Virtually all industrial activity is concentrated in Damascus, Aleppo, Homs, and the booming port city of Latakia.

The mining sector has expanded particularly rapidly since the late 1960s because of increased production in the Palmyra region east of Homs and, more especially, because of increased production of oil in the Karachuk and Suwaidiyah fields in the northeast. With estimated reserves of approximately 2 billion barrels and a daily production of only 180,000 barrels, Syria is clearly not among the top-ranking oil producers. (Neighboring Iraq, for example, has reserves of 36 billion barrels and produces approximately 2.5 million barrels daily.) Nevertheless, crude oil accounts for almost two-thirds of the value of Syria's exports and is a major source of government revenue.

Rural poverty, industrial expansion, improved communications, and the many attractions and advantages of city living have fueled rapid urbanization. Between 1960 and 1977, the urban population increased from 37 to 48 percent and the number of urban dwellers rose by over 2 million. This has caused severe problems, especially in the largest cities like Damascus and Aleppo. There, huge, uncontrolled shanty settlements have sprouted, and pollution, congestion, and underemployment are chronic.

Rural to urban migration is not the only culprit, however. With a birth rate of 44 per 1,000 and a death rate of only 13 per 1,000, Syria's annual population growth (3.2 percent) is one of the world's highest. The population as a whole may double in only 22 years, climbing from 8.4 million in 1979 to a projected 16.3 million by the year 2000. An extraordinarily high proportion of the population, 49 percent, is less than 15 years old.

173

Syria

Since the economy has grown impressively, Syria might seem to be keeping ahead of its population pressures. By 1979, per capita gross national product was a respectable $930. However, prosperity is not enjoyed equally in all parts of the country, and industrialization and urbanization have widened regional inequalities. More than ever, cities are islands of growth and privilege in a sea of underdevelopment. This is illustrated by the distribution of health-care facilities. While access to modern medicine has greatly improved nationally, in 1977 Damascus and Aleppo provinces still had 72 percent of Syria's doctors and 64 percent of its hospital beds. There were 10 times more people for each doctor in Dara province than in nearby Damascus.

Syria's recent political history has been stormy. From the time of the country's birth after World War I, most Syrians refused to accept the legitimacy of the colonially drawn, arbitrary boundaries that separated them artificially from their fellow Arabs in Lebanon, Jordan, Iraq, and elsewhere. Many even denied Syria's right to exist and sought to join a larger entity that would give concrete political expression to their pan-Arab sentiments. Their underlying antipathy to the state bestowed on them by European imperialism was a fundamental cause of Syria's acute political instability and the many military coups d'état it experienced after independence.

Not until after 1961, when Syria's brief union with Egypt ended in bitter failure, did a sense of national identity emerge. But Syria has not forgotten that it was the birthplace of Arab nationalism. Even now it plays a major role in the Arab world and is the leader of those Arab countries seeking greater coordination of their foreign policies and closer economic integration.

No single issue has dominated political life so completely during the past 30 years as the Arab-Israeli conflict. Syria has been in a semipermanent state of war ever since Israel was carved out of portions of Arab Palestine in 1948 and the first 800,000 of what are now 4 million Palestinian refugees fled their homes. Each outbreak of fighting—in 1956, in 1967, and in 1973—has been more destructive than the last. The costs of keeping 227,500 soldiers equipped with the most modern, sophisticated weaponry that the Soviet Union is willing to provide have been enormous. Defense expenditures account for about one-fourth of Syria's entire budget and over 16 percent of its gross national product, one of the highest ratios in the world. The stationing of 30,000 peacekeeping troops in Lebanon is also a financial drain on Syria.

Aid from richer oil-producing Arab states—amounting to approximately $500 million annually in recent years—has helped to ease the burdens of being a front line confrontation state and policeman of the Palestinians. Nevertheless, Syria's development has been hindered by the massive diversion of resources to the war effort. Continued Israeli occupation of the Golan Heights after the extensive aerial bombardment of industrial and port facilities during the fighting in 1973 graphically illustrates the costs of modern warfare to still-underdeveloped Syria.

The first 17 years after independence witnessed a complex, bitter, and protracted struggle for power between a reactionary landowning elite that was indifferent to Syria's development problems and a rising middle class committed to reform and modernization. The most active proponent of change was the Baath party, whose blend of pan-Arabism, socialism, and secularism won increasing support during the 1950s, especially in the politically active, multifactioned armed forces, and among minorities, and rural Syrians. The Arab-Israeli conflict, great-power rivalry in the Middle East, and Syria's problematic identity as a nation all aggravated and complicated this contest, which was not settled decisively until a group of Baath officers seized power in 1963.

Since this Baath revolution, Syria has undergone a radical transformation. The traditional ruling class was quickly destroyed by comprehensive land reforms and by large-scale nationalization of industry, trade, and finance. The elite that replaced the traditional ruling class was made up of young officers and civilians from the lower middle class, a disproportionate number of whom came from underdeveloped peripheral provinces, from rural areas, and from the Alawi and other minority communities. Under the leadership of this new elite, Syria has become a relatively stable, authoritarian, one-party socialist state, within which the military is final arbiter.

Although Syria has lived under continuous Baath rule for over a decade and a half, the regime has itself changed as a result of intraparty power struggles, which culminated in "corrective" coups d'état in 1966 and in 1970. The most recent of these coups brought the pragmatic and popular Hafez Assad to power. He has pulled the regime sharply back to the center and broadened its base of support, relaxed rules governing private and foreign investment, and put Syria on good terms with even the most conservative Arab countries. Under his presidency, the country has enjoyed relative stability, which in turn allowed it to tackle some of its intractable development problems more vigorously.

Despite its many accomplishments, the Baath regime is vulnerable. Most important, the Baathi are unpopular with the Sunni majority; since 1963, the regime has tended to rely heavily on the appointment of Alawis to key positions, especially in the armed forces. Assad and many of his closest supporters come from this underprivileged minority. Second, the Assad regime has shown signs of decay since the peak of its popularity after the 1973 Arab-Israeli war. Party organization and discipline have weakened, a fact reflected in the abysmally poor voter turnout in recent parliamentary elections and widespread high-level corruption.

Finally, bitter opposition to Syria's continued deep involvement since 1976 in the Lebanese civil war, which some have called "Assad's Vietnam," may bring other grievances to the surface. In this light, the assassination of several leading Alawis since Syria intervened in Lebanon has deeply worried the regime.

Nevertheless, Syria has made progress in solving some of its problems, especially since the 1963 Baath revolution. Politically, the chronic instability of the first two decades after independence has given way to the stability of an authoritarian military regime that has successfully and often ruthlessly fought off all challengers and used its considerable power to initiate structural economic reforms and to define specific goals for the development of the nation. Rural areas have unquestionably benefited from land reform and from the establishment of cooperatives; from state financial, technical, and marketing assistance; and from large-scale investment in public works, irrigation, and social welfare projects.

Simultaneously, exploitation of oil and phosphate

resources, the construction of the Euphrates Dam, port expansion, and substantial improvements in the communications infrastructure have laid solid foundations for Syria's future industrialization and balanced economic growth. In September 1980, Assad and Libyan President Muammar Qaddafi agreed to unify their countries.

On the other hand, many of the problems that have afflicted Syria in the past seem destined to constrain its development in the future. Fluctuations in agricultural production because of the unreliability of rainfall, rapid population growth, rural poverty, uncontrolled urban growth, and regional inequalities will persist for many years to come. Similarly, stubborn political problems, particularly Syria's poorly developed sense of national identity, ethnic and regional rivalries, and the enormously expensive Arab-Israeli conflict, will continue to plague Syria's leaders.   *Alasdair Drysdale*

Tunisia
(Republic of Tunisia)

Area: 63,378 sq mi (164,148 sq km)
Population: 6.1 million
  Density: 96 per sq mi (37 per sq km)
  Growth rate: 2% (1970–1977)
Percent of population under 21 years of age: more than 50%
Infant deaths per 1,000 live births: 63 (1975)
Life expectancy at birth: 57 years (1977)
Leading causes of death: not available
Ethnic composition: Arab 98%; French 1%; Jewish 1%
Languages: Arabic, French
Literacy: 60% functionally literate
Religions: Muslim 98%
Percent population urban: 48% (1975)
Percent population rural: 52% (1975)
Gross national product: $4.58 billion (1975)
  Per capita GNP: $950
  Per capita GNP growth rate: 6.5% (1970–1977)
Inflation rate: 7.2% average (1960–1977)

Tunisia is a country of contrast. Nestled in the middle reaches of North Africa and adjoining the Mediterranean, it has experienced the trauma accompanying the dynastic and imperial struggles associated with that turbulent region. Not surprisingly, Tunisia has known many cultures and civilizations. Its northern ports face toward Europe; its many towns are on the highway between West Europe and Cairo; and its interior oases abut the Sahara and face sub-Saharan Africa. However, Tunisia has its own distinctive charm, which reflects a blending of other cultures with a strong sense of its own élan and purpose.

Among contemporary Tunisia's many assets are its geography, its strategic location, its people, and its capacity to adapt to changed circumstances. Unfortunately, its natural resources are limited. Not a large

country, it covers only 63,378 square miles (164,149 sq km) and is about the size of New York State. Tunisia is only 90 miles (145 km) across the Strait of Sicily from Italy; its long 1,000-mile (1,610 km) coastline on the Mediterranean and Gulf of Gabes is adjacent to excellent fishing grounds and potential offshore petroleum resources; its position between Libya and Algeria allows it potential and actual influence in the affairs of these neighbors.

Tunisia is subdivided into a well-watered and fertile northern area, in which most of the country's agricultural production is concentrated; a central coastal plain, which is noted for livestock and olive groves; and a semiarid central steppe that gradually blends into the Sahara. The semiarid region, more than one-third of Tunisia's land surface, lacks sufficient rainfall to support more than sparse grazing and seminomadic peoples. South from the town of Monastir, the birthplace of Tunisia's President, Habib Bourguiba, the coastal area curves in a lazy S—this is the 12-mile (19-km) deep coastal strip known as the Sahel (or shore), dotted with olive orchards, small mixed farms, towns, and harbors. Here is the center of Tunisia's culture, where population density is greatest. Sousse, the capital of the region, is nicknamed "the smiling city." Tunisia derives much of its economic resources and many political leaders from this region.

The Tunisian people themselves reflect the vast tapestry of their history. They are descended primarily from indigenous Berber tribes and from the Arab tribal groups that migrated into North Africa during the seventh century. Today there are more than 6 million Tunisians, of whom 98 percent are Muslim, a reflection of these migrations and subsequent conversion; 1 percent, or 60,000, of the Tunisians is principally French in origin, a reflection of the more than 70 years of France's protectorate rule (from 1881 to 1956); and less than 1 percent of the population is Jewish. Most of the population live in Tunisia's coastal region, where the major urban centers are located: in Tunis (population 1 million) and in Sfax and Bizerte (each having a population of 250,000). The country's population is growing at a yearly rate of 2 percent; more than one-half of the people are less than 21 years old. Improved health facilities have raised life expectancy to 57 years.

Because Tunisia has been conquered by Phoenicians, Romans, Vandals, Byzantine Christians, Arabs, and Turks, its people have developed a tolerance for other cultures. While Islam and Arabism are the bedrock of their culture, Tunisians evince a more Western outlook and a stronger desire for material improvement than any other Arab nation. This is reflected in Tunisian education, which is compulsory; 85 percent of the school-age population is enrolled in classes and 33 percent of the national budget is allocated to the schools. At present more than 60 percent of Tunisia's people are functionally literate.

Islam is a pervasive influence; its strength is reflected in the inland city of Kairouan, located midway between north-central Tunisia and the sea, on a featureless plain called the Bled (countryside). Founded 40 years after the death of the Prophet Muhammad, Kairouan has become a center of religious instruction and a holy city for North African Muslims. Many believe that four or more visits to Kairouan equal the required pilgrimage (or hajj) to Mecca. Within Kairouan's ocher walls are innumerable mosques, a thriving rug industry, and a university renowned throughout the Muslim world.

The ninth century was the golden age of Kairouan: in 800 A.D., it became the capital for the Aghlabite dynasty, which subsequently extended its rule over one-half of North Africa; the Great Mosque was constructed; and Arab jurisprudence in the form of Sharia law achieved distinctive form. Kairouan's only rival in the intellectual power and brilliance of its court was Córdova in Muslim Spain.

The distinctive period of Kairouan has passed, and Tunis, the nation's capital, is the center for government affairs, the arts, education, and modern commerce and trade. Within its traditional quarter, the *medina*, is the well-known Rashidiya, a conservatory of Arab music. In the confines of the city is the University of Zitouna, which is also a mosque, where the famed fourteenth-century Arab historian and scholar ibn Khaldun studied. (Zitouna means "olive tree.") Schools in modern Tunis now rival the University of Zitouna, but the luster of history remains.

Many of the external precepts and forms of Islam have been discarded under the tutelage of President Habib Bourguiba, Tunisia's first and only President since it became independent on March 20, 1956. The President has worked prodigiously to remove the constraints that he believes reduce the productivity and openness of modern Tunisian society. Thus, the traditional system of plural marriage has been banned; women no longer wear the veil (at least in Tunisia's cities and towns); modern education is stressed and the power of traditional religious leaders has diminished; and the ancient practices associated with the holy month of Ramadan have been played down. No longer, for example, does social convention applaud total abstention from food and drink in the daylight hours during Ramadan; nor is evening-long carousing condoned. Rather, in the interest of national productivity, men and women are enjoined to shun these practices and to make more modest accommodations to Islamic precepts.

Despite these efforts at modernization and rapid economic growth, Tunisia's progress in the economic field has been slow. During the first years following independence, Tunsia's economic policies had only limited success. A drive in the 1960s to collectivize agriculture, directed by Tunisian economic czar Ahmed Ben Salah, was badly conceived and hastily implemented, and it stimulated wide criticism and unrest. Ben Salah was removed in 1969, and Bourguiba adopted a more relaxed approach, involving a mixed economy. The result was more favorable economic growth. But Tunisia's limited natural resources—consisting of low-grade phosphates, iron ore, zinc, wheat, olives, and citrus fruits—inhibit prospects for overall development. Oil, which was

Construction workers build a house and dig a foundation. (Photo: United Nations/ Bill Graham.)

discovered in modest quantities in 1964, is sufficient for the requirements of domestic consumption and accounts for one-third of Tunisia's export revenues. Tourism is an additional money earner; in 1977, approximately 1 million people visited Tunisia.

In 1977 the Bourguiba government embarked on an ambitious fifth development plan. However, during its initial year, real growth was only 4.1 percent, in part because of a severe drought that caused the loss of 40 percent of the country's cereal crop. While 1978 saw some improvement, especially in the production of construction materials, agricultural crops, and phosphates, the inflation rate remained high (10 percent) and the ranks of the unemployed continued to swell. An estimated 25 percent of the national work force was unemployed or underemployed in 1978.

In January 1978, a group of trade union leaders, dissatisfied with conditions in Tunisia, sparked wide-ranging riots that directly challenged the authority of the Bourguiba regime and led to hundreds of arrests. In due course, more than 100 trade unionists, members of the General Union of Tunisian Workers (UGTT), were placed on trial and many, including their former chieftain, Secretary General Habib Achour, were convicted and sentenced. While the storm has been contained for the present, pressures for economic improvement and political change are building.

To cope with these looming difficulties, Tunisia relies on its Supreme Combatant, President Habib

Workers attend an open-air class in animal husbandry near an earthen dam. (Photo: United Nations/ W. Graham.)

Bourguiba, founder of the national party, the Destourian Socialist Party (PSD), leader of the country's independence struggle and a father figure for many Tunisians. Bourguiba has ruled since July 25, 1957, when the constituent assembly voted to abolish the monarchy and to establish a republic. The assembly named Bourguiba President and, under his guidance, drafted a constitution creating a strong presidential system.

Bourguiba has since dominated the political scene. His overall dominance was reflected in Tunisia's national elections in 1974, when the PSD won all 101 seats unopposed. That same year, a constitutional amendment made Bourguiba President for life.

Unfortunately, Bourguiba is infirm, and his stewardship may be drawing to a close. Beset by uncertainty, anxious to avoid the anger of an ailing President, and unable to revive the PSD (which fell into disuse by presidential fiat), the Cabinet is not filling the void for fear of alienating the presidential family. Pending the inevitable postsuccession political confusion, the Cabinet is functioning on a caretaker basis.

The potential for turmoil is substantial, given the absence of a clearly designated successor, the malaise within the PSD, and the active interest of militant neighbors like Libya's Colonel Qaddafi. The real tragedy, should instability materialize, will be its threat to political moderation in North Africa. Symbolically, at least, the government of President Bourguiba has long been regarded in the United States as a model of moderation. The high level of United States economic assistance to Tunisia—more than $950 million since 1957 (American aid to Tunisia has been among the highest per capita offered to any foreign recipient during the past two decades)—has been material testimony to the U.S. government's endorsement of Bourguiba's policies. France, however, continues to be Tunisia's principal trading partner; it supplied 33 percent of Tunisia's total imports in 1978. The United States was fourth, behind West Germany and Italy, providing on an annual average somewhat less than 7 percent of Tunisian imports.

Tunisia has a lengthy history of overcoming adversity. In 1574, the Turks invaded Tunisia and incorporated it into the expanding Ottoman Empire. For three centuries thereafter, the Tunisians were compelled to pledge their fealty to the Ottoman ruler at Constantinople. Distance and other distractions ultimately permitted the local Ottoman representative, the bey, to establish his own dynastic order and to assert a measure of autonomy from the sultan.

In due course, Turkish domination was replaced by that of France which, having conquered Algeria, sought to exercise influence over the bey. In 1881, the Treaty of Bardo permitted France to establish protectorate rights in Tunisia. The growth of French hegemony was relatively smooth, but as young Tunisians acquired a French education and were attracted to French political values, they began to agitate for increased Tunisian autonomy. The French response was to imprison leading agitators, including Habib Bourguiba. The rivalry between the French governing authority and the young nationalists persisted through the 1930s. Subsequently, during World War II, Tunisia became a battleground.

After the war, although France's protectorate over Tunisia was reaffirmed, the nationalist movement in the form of Bourguiba's Neo-Destour Party gathered a popular following. The French imprisoned Bourguiba again, but popular demonstrations continued. In July 1954, the French government under Prime Minister Pierre Mendès-France promised Tunisia full autonomy and Bourguiba accepted. Bourguiba's gradualist approach was vindicated when Tunisia was granted full independence on March 20, 1956.

Bourguiba's tactics and gradualism made him the object of considerable controversy. He was one of the first Arab leaders to admit that Israel was a reality in the Middle East and to conclude that Arab governments should accommodate themselves to Israel's existence. This conclusion earned Bourguiba the op-

probrium of Egypt's President Gamal Abdel Nasser and Tunisia's partial suspension from membership in the Arab League. More recently, Bourguiba collided with Libya's Colonel Qaddafi over a wide range of issues, including Qaddafi's desire to form a political federation with Tunisia. Bourguiba's relations with Algeria are strained as a result of the radical socialist doctrine adopted by President Ahmed Ben Bella and his successor, the late President Houari Boumeddiene. Nevertheless, until recently, Bourguiba has maintained a substantial degree of political equilibrium in Tunisia.

Whether Tunisia, which has developed a sophisticated managerial and planning elite, will be able to find an able successor to Bourguiba is the critical question. The economic woes that confront the existing leadership are likely to persist. These difficulties would be immeasurably compounded if a struggle for power in the succession period attracted the intervention of Tunisia's more militant neighbors.

William H. Lewis

Turkey
(Republic of Turkey)

Area: 301,160 sq mi (780,000 sq km)
Population: 43 million
    Density: 143 per sq mi (55 per sq km)
    Growth rate: 2.5% (1970–1977)
Percent of population under 14 years of age: 42 (1975)
Infant deaths per 1,000 live births: not available
Life expectancy at birth: 56.9 years (1975)
Leading causes of death: not available
Ethnic composition: Turkish 87%; Kurdish; Arab; Armenian; Greek
Languages: Turkish 87%; Kurdish; Arabic; Armenian; Greek
Literacy: 65%
Religions: Sunni Muslim, Shiite Muslim, Christian, Jewish
Percent population urban: 33%
Percent population rural: 67%
Gross national product: $51.75 billion (1976)
    Per capita GNP: $1,210
    Per capita GNP growth rate: 4.5% (1970–1977)
Inflation rate: 40% (1978)

The future of Turkey is bright. An ancient empire transformed into a modern republic, Turkey will nonetheless continue to suffer the growing pains normally accompanying significant economic development, industrial and social modernization, and rapid urbanization. Fortunately, the economy is solidly based on plentiful natural resources, an adequate and expanding skilled labor pool, and highly competent entrepreneurial management. The political process is fundamentally democratic and resistant to extremism, although the military, with obvious reluc-

tance, staged a bloodless coup in 1980 to curb mounting extremist violence, for the third time in 20 years.

Turkey is a large country (about one-tenth the size of the continental United States) with a population of approximately 43 million. Part of its territory is in Europe, and part is in Asia. Ethnically distinct from Arabs and Persians, Turks are Muslims of the Sunni

Peasants gather around a spigot, the only water supply in this village, which is one of the thousands of primitive villages in Turkey. (Photo: United Nations.)

Workers move logs at a sawmill at Bolu. A government program helps develop forestry and forest industries. (Photo: United Nations/FAO/ H. Rabben.)

Sheep are bought and sold in the market at Adana on the Adana Plain. (Photo: World Bank/ Mary M. Hill.)

rite who adopted Islam more than 1,000 years ago. Originally, the Turks were settled in what is now the Xinjiang area of China. Starting in the eighth century, they migrated westward; and the Republic of Turkey is the high-water mark of their westward expansion.

Turkey covers 301,158 square miles (780,000 sq km), with many distinct regions and a considerable variation in climate. Western Turkey, a rectangle bounded by the cities of Ankara (the capital) and Antalya in the east and by Istanbul and Izmir in the west, is a well-watered, agriculturally productive land, with a mild climate. Half the population and three-fourths

of the country's industry are concentrated in this area, the most-developed sector of the country. The style of life here is uniformly Western in appearance and practice, and the standard of living is significantly higher than it is in eastern Turkey. Western Turkey's rainfall is sufficient to support extensive agriculture, including the cultivation of citrus fruits, olives, and other fruits and vegetables. Western Turkey also has significant coal and lignite deposits, iron ore, substantial chromium ore, copper, and other metals of industrial importance. Turkey's major steel-making plants are also in the west, and so are its best highways, rail lines, power generation and transmission facilities, and most of the rest of the infrastructure of a developing modern industrial state. Western Turkey's industrial output includes a wide variety of manufactures, textiles, electrical equipment, consumer goods of all kinds, and even locally assembled automobiles and trucks. Altogether, western Turkey presents a picture of rapid, if not wholly uniform, industrial and agricultural development.

Eastern Turkey is a different matter. The central Anatolian plain stretches eastward from the capital city of Ankara for a distance of 500 miles (805 km). It is a semiarid, barren steppe that provides the peasants who live in thousands of primitive, backward villages only a bleak existence. The climate of the Anatolian plain is extremely harsh—blazing hot in the summer and freezing cold in the long winters. As the plain rises to the Caucasus Mountains in the east, where Turkey shares a border with the Soviet Union, winter snowfall is so heavy that vast sections of the country are isolated for weeks on end.

Eastern Turkey's peasant population is almost wholly agricultural; the peasant is a subsistence farmer, producing little or no agricultural surplus. Many peasants are landless and are employed as agricultural laborers, usually at very low wages. Their employment is seasonal; after the planting and harvesting seasons, there is little work. Other eastern Turkish peasants are herdsmen, tending flocks of sheep, goats, or cattle.

The southern coast of Turkey, bordering the Mediterranean Sea, has a hot, humid climate and adequate rainfall, and is the center of the citrus- and banana-growing region of the country. The great Cukurova Plain, extending inward from the sea to the Taurus Mountains, in the vicinity of the city of Adana, is the site of large-scale cotton and rice production. Because of the high market value of these crops and the relatively more efficient agricultural methods employed, the southern coast is prosperous. Adana, the focal point of the productive agricultural region, is flourishing, unlike many other eastern Turkish cities.

The northern coast of Turkey, bordering the Black Sea, has a humid climate also, but temperatures are milder than in the region of the southern coast. Agriculture on the northern coast, the economic mainstay, is notable for the production of tea and tobacco. Much of the tobacco is exported, primarily to the

United States and to West Europe, whereas nearly all of the tea is consumed locally.

Ninety percent of Turkey's 43 million people are of Turkish ethnic stock, speak Turkish in a variety of dialects and accents, and are linked by their common cultural and Islamic heritage. The Kurds are the largest minority, numbering between 3 and 5 million. They live in the extreme eastern provinces of the country. Although the Kurds are Muslims, like the Turks mostly of the Sunni rite, they are ethnically, culturally, and linguistically set apart. Their ancient tribal system of organization continues to dominate their communities. Other minorities in Turkey include Muslim Arabs and Christian Armenians and Greeks. Each of these groups has, to an important extent, preserved its own culture, language, and traditions.

Among Turks and non-Turks, urban or rural, the extended family structure, patriarchal in nature, is of great importance. In the major cities where educational, employment, and cultural opportunities have had transforming effects, traditional family structure has changed, but among the two-thirds of Turkey's population that remain rural, traditional, male-dominated family life remains intact. Most women, especially peasant women, undertake traditional tasks: motherhood, child-rearing, household management, and selected farming. Among the peasants, marriages are most often arranged by the male elders of the family. Women defer to their fathers, husbands, and older brothers; as a general rule, peasant women receive little formal schooling.

Illiteracy is still a serious problem in Turkey. Perhaps 35 percent of the population is illiterate, and many of the literate majority have only rudimentary reading and writing skills. The literacy rate is far higher in the cities.

Although the Turkish constitution specifically provides that Turkey is a secular country and state-supported schools are rigidly and exclusively secular, Islam has a pervasive influence. In the past 10 years, there has been a significant resurgence of religious influence in private life and in public institutions. For instance, the recently formed National Salvation Party, led by Necmettin Erbakan, emphasizes an intensified religious commitment, although the constitution specifically forbids the exploitation of religion for political purposes. Erbakan's religiously oriented party received 9 percent of the votes in the 1977 election and controlled 24 seats (out of 455) in the Parliament. Erbakan was a member of the coalition government led by Prime Minister Bulent Ecevit. Ecevit was succeeded as Prime Minister by Suleyman Demirel in the 1979 election but, like Ecevit, Demirel was also forced to resort to a coalition government, which included Erbakan.

Turkey's population is growing rapidly, at approximately 2.7 percent annually. Unless this rate soon slows sharply, Turkey's 45 million people will be 80 million in 25 to 30 years. Improved health conditions and better child care mean that an increasingly high percentage of those born reach adulthood. Consequently the average age of the Turkish population is dropping and approximately one half of the population is less than 20 years old.

At least two-thirds of the population is working in agriculture or related fields. Most Turkish land is held by individual peasants in small parcels. In accordance with the Land Reform Act of June 11, 1945, inheritance is based on the principle of primogeniture; the land passes to the firstborn son. The state holds large tracts of land for experimental and demonstration purposes. Important agricultural research and development take place on state-operated farms. There are also large landholdings in private hands for the production of crops, like cotton, that require large-scale operations. In the past 20 years, mechanization, in the form of tractors, combines, and mechanical seeders and pickers, has increased total agricultural production significantly.

The living standards of the peasants are low in comparison to those of their urbanized fellow Turks. All the usual measurements—per capita income, material-consumption patterns, savings, and investments—indicate that life in Turkish cities is more comfortable than it is in the countryside. Hundreds of thousands of peasants are leaving their villages and flocking to the cities in search of a better life. In the major cities of Turkey—Istanbul, Ankara, Izmir, and

A woman aligns thread at the Bosser Textile Mill near Adana; the mill is one of the largest users of power from the Cukurova Electric Power Company. The textile industry is important to Turkey. (Photo: World Bank/ Mary M. Hill.)

After working in the fields all day, a Turkish woman wends her way home. The irrigated fields of the Adana Plain are one of Turkey's richest areas. (Photo: World Bank/Mary M. Hill.)

Adana—explosive population growth strains the social structure. Every major city in Turkey is ringed with shantytowns (*gecekondu*), the newly created "villages in the cities."

Turkey is a full member of the NATO alliance, and the southern headquarters of NATO is located in Izmir. Moreover the Turkish land army is, after the United States, the largest in the alliance. Turkey also has important bilateral treaties with the United States.

Turkey is an associate member of the European Economic Community (EEC) and is scheduled to gain full membership within 10 years. This timetable has imposed on Turkey an even broader and more rapidly paced program of modernizations in industry and agriculture. Thus far, annual goals have been met.

A unique aspect of Turkey's increasingly close relationship with the EEC is the annual export of significant numbers of its labor force to work under contract in the countries of northern Europe. In 1979, for instance, over 500,000 Turkish laborers were working in the factories and mines of Germany, France, Holland, and Belgium. Not only are these workers acquiring a very large range of industrial skills, but they are also earning large amounts of foreign currency, a phenomenon which has a favorable impact on Turkey's international balance of payments.

Kemal Ataturk, the republic's first President (from 1923 to 1938), was a brilliant soldier, the father of his country (his name literally means "Father of the Turks"), philosopher, scientist, modernizer, and nation builder. With the catastrophically defeated Turkish Ottoman Empire in ruins after World War I, Ataturk assumed the leadership, drove out Turkey's would-be foreign occupiers, and united the people. He then proceeded to revise the country's entire social, economic, political, and cultural structure. A new nation, the democratic, secular, and progressive Republic of Turkey, was born. Since Ataturk's death in 1938, Turkish history is the record of the Turkish people's attempts to fulfill and to consolidate his legacy.

In 1980, for the third time in 20 years, the Turkish military (this time led by pro-West General Kenan Evren) took over the government to curb the growing violence, after thousands of people had been killed in fighting between left-wing and right-wing extremists. In September, the entire country was placed under martial law and the constitution was suspended. About 250 senior politicians, including Prime Minister Demirel and opposition leader Bulent Ecevit were temporarily placed under house arrest.

The military intervention was prompted by the Army's fear that factional violence was endangering the safety of the modern republic. The Turkish army has no political aspirations of its own and is in fact an important bulwark of political democracy and the process of modernizing the economy.

Thanks to international financial aid and internal economic reforms, the Turkish economy may stabilize and expand in the 1980s. But tension continues between those who want to follow Western-oriented guidelines and those who want Turkey to develop as a semi-theocratic Islamic state.

Despite chronic and sporadic violence, the prognosis for Turkey at the beginning of the 1980s is optimistic. Barring a series of unforeseeable catastrophes, by the twenty-first century Turkey should be enjoying political stability, reasonable economic productivity and affluence, and full integration into the European community.

Dwight James Simpson

Yemen, North (Sana)
(Yemen Arab Republic)

Area: 72,000 sq mi (186,480 sq km)
Population: 5.1 million
  Density: 71 per sq mi (27 per sq km)
  Growth rate: 1.9% (1970–1977)
Percent of population under 14 years of age: 45% (1975)
Infant deaths per 1,000 live births: 159 (1975)
Life expectancy at birth: 37 years (1975)
Leading causes of death: not available
Ethnic composition: Arab
Languages: Arabic
Literacy: males 26%; females 3%
Religions: Shiite Muslim, Sunni Muslim, Jewish
Percent population urban: not available
Percent population rural: not available
Gross national product: $2.96 billion
  Per capita GNP: $580
  Per capita GNP growth rate: not available
Inflation rate: 40%

The Yemen Arab Republic, deliberately shut off from outside contact until 1962, is in some respects a land still living in the fifteenth century. Also called North Yemen or Yemen (Sana), it is one of the poorest and least-known countries in the world. Although Yemen is not entirely devoid of natural advantages of soil and climate, it makes very little use of them. A source of potential wealth, however, is its relatively large population: a surprising number of Yemenis work outside their homeland, and their remittances help to defray a deficit in its balance of payments.

Yemen, which is generally believed to have been the realm of the Queen of Sheba, is located at the southwestern corner of the Arabian Peninsula. It is one of two adjacent states both called Yemen; the other is the Marxist People's Democratic Republic of Yemen, also known as South Yemen or Yemen (Aden). (In the remote past, the Yemens were not divided, and today projects for unification are being discussed.) Yemen is bounded on the north and east by Saudi Arabia, on the east and south by Yemen (Aden), and on the west by some 300 miles (483 km) of the Red Sea coastline. Yemen is over 300 miles (483 km) from north to south and has an average east-west width of some 200 miles (322 km). Its area is roughly 72,000 square miles (186,480 sq km). The area can be stated only approximately because Yemen's northeastern frontier with Saudi Arabia along the Rub al Khali ("empty quarter") desert has never been accurately defined.

Known to the Romans as Arabia Felix ("fortunate Arabia"), Yemen differs sharply from the rest of the Arabian Peninsula. Most of the country has adequate rainfall. A considerable altitude provides a reasonable climate and makes various kinds of agriculture possible. As a consequence, the population is fairly large.

The topography of Yemen contains two main zones—the coastal strip and the highlands, the latter comprising most of the country. The coastal strip, known as the Tihama, runs along the edge of the Red Sea from north to south. Varying from 20 to 30 miles (32 to 48 km) in width, it is arid and unpleasantly hot and humid. There are a few oases and some agriculture, but much of the area consists of sand dunes and scrub. To the east, the Tihama rises through an intermediate region known as the Upper Tihama, where there are jagged, eroded valleys and low plateaus.

Eastward lie the highlands, the home of most of the population. High mountains rise to over 12,000 feet (3,660 m); the landforms are varied, rugged, and complicated; valleys alternate with plateaus. In the valleys and on terraced slopes, the people are farmers. Three-fourths of the country's population live in the western highlands, with a more intensive pattern of cultivation than in any other part of Arabia. To the east of the Yemeni Highlands, the land gradually slopes down, agriculture disappears, population density decreases sharply, and desert conditions increasingly prevail. This is the area where the Rub al Khali desert begins, and Yemen merges into Saudi Arabia along an undefined frontier.

Yemen is in a region affected by the southwest monsoon, which brings reliable rainfall in late summer. (A lesser rainy season occurs in March and April.) Only a negligible amount of rain falls in the Tihama, but in the highlands rainfall varies with altitude and other conditions and ranges from 15 to 30 inches (38 to 76 cm).

Workers tend a newly constructed irrigation system carrying water to a cotton and sorghum field. Cotton is Yemen's major cash crop. (Photo: United Nations/ Kay Muldoon.)

Agriculture and human settlement favor the southwestern slopes, where the rainfall is highest. There are seasonal rivers in the innumerable wadis, but evaporation is so rapid that Yemen has no real rivers. In ancient times, water was stored in dams. Near Marib in the eastern highlands, there are impressive remains of a great dam that stood for 1,000 years until it was destroyed in the sixth century. It stored floodwaters to irrigate thousands of acres of what is today dusty and unproductive desert.

To speak with precision about the number of Yemenis is impossible, because no census has ever been taken. Estimates of the population range all the way from 5 to 10 million; but a figure of about 6.5 million seems the most reasonable. In any event, rainfall and climate make Yemen the most heavily populated country of the Arabian Peninsula; Yemen contains about half the population of Arabia. The rate of natural population increase—3 percent—is fairly high, and emigration is a common pattern. Probably about one-third of the population of neighboring South Yemen originated in North Yemen. Some 1 million Yemenis have been working in recent years in Saudi Arabia, and many Yemenis live in other Arab countries and in eastern Africa.

The Yemenis are Arabs, speaking Arabic, and are fairly homogeneous (with a considerable Negroid strain among those living along the coast). Almost all are Muslims, though they are divided between Sunni and Shia branches of Islam. The majority are Shiites of the Zaidi sect, and the minority, who live mostly in the lowlands, are Sunnites of the Shafi sect. About 60,000 Jews had lived in Yemen since ancient times. But most Jews left for Israel in the 1950s, and now there are perhaps only 1,000 to 2,000 living in the upland districts. The Zaidi Muslims are tolerant toward Jews, and though the Shafi Muslims are not, there is no apparent persecution.

Yemen is an unusual Arab country because its population is settled and not nomadic. Although there is a small nomadic element, perhaps 5 percent or less, in the arid northeast, most Yemenis are settled farmers or townspeople of various occupations.

Yemen has several sizable cities, nearly all of great antiquity; they are not modern cities, but are traditional communities of traders, small-scale manufacturers, rulers, and servants. The capital city, Sana, is the largest and most important, with a population estimated at 150,000. Taiz, in the south, with about 60,000 people, is near the border with South Yemen, and most of the trade from Yemen to Aden passes through it. Hodeida, the chief port, has only come into its own with the decline of Aden, although the Turks developed it in the nineteenth century. North Yemen's vast import trade and modest export trade are funneled exclusively through Hodeida. Lesser towns are scattered over the western part of the central highlands; their sites were often chosen with an eye to defense, and they are often still fortified. With houses built of stone or brick, often three or four stories high and decorated with geometrical patterns, these lesser towns have a picturesque and archaic appearance. The country has many of these square castles on commanding heights.

Kinship is the cement of village and small-town social organization. There is a sharp division between the sayyids ("lords"), descended from the Prophet, who are the aristocratic leaders of the rural people, and the tribespeople who are their followers. The government's authority outside the cities is virtually nonexistent—everything depends on the local tribal leaders (sheikhs). Yemeni men customarily carry rifles. (At the start of commuter flights inside Yemen, arms are collected from the passengers and are handed back upon landing.)

Roads in Yemen are rudimentary, and travelers in

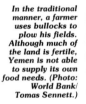

In the traditional manner, a farmer uses bullocks to plow his fields. Although much of the land is fertile, Yemen is not able to supply its own food needs. (Photo: World Bank/Tomas Sennett.)

the countryside may encounter casual and rather random brigandage. The only all-weather permanent roads link the triangle Sana-Taiz-Hodeida. Foreign aid from China, the Soviet Union, West Germany, and the United States financed these roads. Buses and overloaded trucks create a considerable volume of traffic.

Women in Yemen have the traditional and restricted role characteristic of Islamic society. Women do not appear without the veil before men who are not close relatives. The social lives of the sexes are separate: women are excluded from male social gatherings, and men are excluded with even greater rigidity from the female world. One recent woman observer reported that the behavior of Yemeni women is far from constrained, and noted that a striking feature of female society in Yemen was the relaxed atmosphere.

Change is occurring, but it occurs more slowly in Yemen than in any comparable developing society. In Sana and Taiz, women are working in offices and hospitals and studying at the university. The Sana textile factory, founded by the Chinese in 1967, employs about 400 women. When Sana University (funded by Kuwait) opened in 1970–1971, it had only 3 female students; in 1973, it had 125, and in 1976, 300. Working or studying, women wear the veil, but the veil can after all be manipulated.

Upper-class and middle-class women and girls have opportunities to go to the university, to work, and to travel abroad, but more than 97 percent of all Yemeni women are illiterate (74 percent of Yemeni men are illiterate). Even now, girls comprise only about 10 percent of the school population. Rural women play an active part in agricultural work. Girls are married very young, 5 percent of them between the ages of 10 and 14, and more than 50 percent by the age of 19. Their bridegrooms may be very young or considerably older.

Television was introduced in Yemen in 1975. It is enthusiastically watched and, inevitably, has had a destructive impact on traditional ways of thought and behavior. Another technical innovation that has become wildly popular is the cassette player, now the principal source of music on all social occasions.

In Yemeni society, particularly in the towns, afternoon visits are the main social activity, and on these occasions the drug kat (*Catha edulis*) is chewed. Addiction to kat is common, especially in the cities. An amphetamine, kat is a mild stimulant said by its champions to be no more potent than coffee, and described by its critics as noxious in its physical, moral, and social effects. It reduces the appetite, which helps account for the fact that no evening meal is normally taken in Yemen.

Economically, the culture of kat has had pernicious results. Kat grows fairly easily; the profit yield is high; and it has been replacing the culture of coffee, cotton, and food crops. Yemeni coffee is one of the most famous coffees in the world, as the name Mocha (a Ye-

meni port, now much decayed, on the Red Sea) testifies. In the 1950s and earlier, Yemen was self-sufficient in food, but it now imports large quantities of foodstuffs because of a slight rise in population, the increasing cultivation of kat and higher standards of living, which lead to a demand for better and more varied food supplies. The value of the imports of food and manufactured goods far exceeds the value of Yemen's exports.

The consequent deficit on external account is mostly made up by the remittances of the million or so Yemenis who work in Saudi Arabia and send home an estimated $1,500 million every year from that country. Yemen has no oil; and Yemen's growing prosperity in the past half-dozen years is largely a side effect of Saudi Arabia's oil-based prosperity. The government of Yemen has no regular source of revenue, since there is no general income tax and only a very sketchy administration. The government habitually operates in the red. It is subsidized to the extent of about $200 million a year by Saudi Arabia and receives some help from other countries, including the United States. There is a very high rate of inflation, roughly 40 percent.

Yemen has had a long, picturesque, complicated, and often violent history. It was famous in antiquity because it controlled the trade routes for frankin-

A turbaned vendor sells his goods at the main marketplace in Sana. (Photo: World Bank/ Tomas Sennett.)

cense, myrrh, gold, ivory, and spices. In the seventh century, Yemen was converted to Islam. In 1918, after a prolonged revolt against the Ottoman Empire, it became independent. From 1918 to September 1962, it was ruled ruthlessly by the Imam of Yemen as a theocratic monarchy, entirely closed to external influences. In 1962, a successful revolt drove the Imam from his capital, and a republic was proclaimed. This was the beginning of the present era; in Yemen, "the revolution" refers to the events of 1962. However, a civil war against royalist forces dragged on until the end of the 1960s. A constitution was promulgated in 1970, and although there have been several internal coups and Lieutenant Colonel Ibrahim Muhammad Hamadi, the President of Yemen, was assassinated in 1977, the republic seems reasonably stable.

Yemen, a member of the United Nations since 1947, has flirted with the Soviet Union and with the Marxist government of South Yemen. Plans for union with South Yemen—about which most observers are skeptical—were announced in 1972 and again in 1979. During a brief war in the spring of 1979, South Yemen successfully invaded Yemen but was later persuaded to withdraw by the united pressure of the Arab League. In 1979, the United States began to give military aid to the Sana government. Yemen occupies a strategic position; and because of Soviet influence in Afghanistan, South Yemen, and Ethiopia and the upheaval in Iran, the future of Yemen is a cause of concern for the West.

Yemen has been making some progress in ameliorating its appalling poverty, but with a per capita income estimated at $580 in 1978, Yemen remains a very poor country. The economy is dominated by agriculture, which produces about 50 percent of the GNP, employs 73 percent of the labor force, and produces over 80 percent of the visible exports.

The best-known crop is coffee, but the amount of land devoted to it has decreased in recent years, because kat is more profitable and easier to grow. In any case, cotton has replaced coffee as the major cash crop. In 1976, cotton exports totaled approximately $5 million, and coffee exports, approximately $1.5 million. Actually there is an enormous deficit on external account on visible items; in 1977, imports totaled $600 million and exports totaled $10 million. Remittances from expatriates and aid from other Arab states more than make up the deficit, and leave Yemen with a surplus on external account.

Yemen's 5-year development plan (1976–1977 to 1980–1981) concentrates not only on the improvement of agriculture but also on industrial projects, including an oil pipeline linking Sana, Hodeida, and Taiz; a Yemeni-Kuwaiti Bank; a cement plant with a capacity of 500,000 tons annually; a textile plant; and a number of hotels.

Yemen has no large-scale industry, but about 100 new small artisan industries were started each year during the 1970s, compared with the 10 or 20 started each year during the 1960s. There has been a massive building boom since 1973. The educational level is slowly rising and so is the level of health care. The people chew a great deal of kat (which makes them lethargic), they watch television, and they listen to music on their cassettes.

Yemen has no oil, and no other mineral resources have yet been developed. Although it has a great deal of fertile land, it is less able to meet its own food needs than it was a generation ago. However, largely because of the activities of its expatriated workers, Yemen claims that its GNP has doubled in real terms during the 1970s and the per capita income has substantially risen. The conditions of life in Yemen's hardy, traditional society are slowly improving.

Arthur Campell Turner

Yemen, South (Aden)
(People's Democratic Republic of Yemen)

Area: 111,000 sq mi (287,490 sq km)
Population: 1.7 million
  Density: 15 per sq mi (6 per sq km)
  Growth rate: 1.9% (1970–1977)
Percent of population under 14 years of age: 45% (1975)
Infant deaths per 1,000 live births: 40 (1975)
Life expectancy at birth: 44.8 years (1975)
Leading causes of death: not available
Ethnic composition: Arab, Veddoid
Languages: Arabic, other Semitic
Literacy: 10–20%
Religions: Sunni Muslim, Zaidi Muslim
Percent population urban: not available
Percent population rural: not available
Gross national product: $740 million
  Per capita GNP: $420
  Per capita GNP growth rate: 11.2% (1970–1977)
Inflation rate: not available

South Yemen, also called Yemen (Aden) and officially styled the People's Democratic Republic of Yemen, is a large and very sparsely inhabited country on the southern coast of the Arabian Peninsula. Independent only since 1967, South Yemen now has an economy which is probably in far worse shape economically than when South Yemen was a colony, and there is little prospect of substantial improvement. South Yemen has almost no natural advantages, and the pro-Soviet policies of its regime inhibit it from making the most of the opportunities it does have. As a state attempting to reconcile explicit Marxism and militant Arab nationalism based on Islam, it is unique in the Arab world.

Yemen (Aden) is bounded on the north and northwest by Yemen (Sana), and the boundary between the two states runs down to the sea at the Strait of Bab el Mandeb, the narrow entrance to the Red Sea. To the south, there is a coastline along the Gulf of Aden and the Arabian Sea more than 700 miles (1,127 km) long. Inland, to the north, South Yemen's neighbor is Saudi Arabia. The border, which has never been demarcated, lies along the southern edge of the Rub al-Khali, the vast desert in the south of the Arabian Peninsula, where the country is virtually uninhabited. To the northeast, also bordering the Arabian Sea, lies the monarchy of Oman. The western end of South Yemen is very much narrower than the rest of the country. In the eastern part of the nation, the north-south distance is very much greater, and is as long as 250 miles (402 km) in some sections. Since the coast slants northeast rather than east, the northernmost point in South Yemen is substantially north of the northernmost point in North Yemen. The names, however, make sense in terms of the western region of South Yemen (where Aden, the capital, is located), the part of the country which is its administrative and economic center as well as the region of greater population density.

South Yemen is, in general, an inhospitable country, with little rainfall, generally poor soil, and a harshly hot climate. Because of the undefined border with Saudi Arabia, estimates of the total area vary widely, but the approximation of 111,000 square miles (287,490 sq km) is generally accepted. In addition to its mainland area, South Yemen's territory includes the islands of Socotra, Perim, and Kamaran as well as several other smaller islands. Socotra, by far the largest of the islands under South Yemeni sovereignty, is some 75 miles (120 km) long from east to west and has an average breadth of 20 miles (132 km). Socotra is located over 250 miles (402 km) south of the nearest point on the mainland of South Yemen and about 150 miles (241 km) east of Ras Asir (formerly, Cape Guardafui). Perim is a small island that lies right in the throat of the Strait of Bab el Mandeb. Kamaran is about 200 miles (322 km) north of the Strait of Bab el Mandeb in the Red Sea, just off the coast of North Yemen. It has a sheltered harbor and was administered as part of the Aden Protectorate because the British used it as a staging point on their air routes.

The main topographical division is between the coastal belt and the inland highlands. The coastal belt runs for 740 miles (1,191 km) from the Strait of Bab el Mandeb to Ras Dhurbat Ali, at the frontier with Oman. The climate of the coastal belt is intensely hot and humid in summer, with temperatures normally reaching 100°F (38°C), humidity around 80 percent, and virtually no rainfall. However, considerable stores of underground water can be made available through modern wells. The width of the coastal belt varies from 4 to more than 40 miles (6 to more than 64 km). In its western end, the belt tends to be stony; toward the east, it is sandy.

Inland from the coastal belt rises a mountain range with peaks varying from 1,000 to 2,000 feet (305 to 610 m). Beyond this are high plains, rising to the main massif. This plateau averages around 6500 feet (1,980 m), and there are peaks rising to heights between 8,000 and 9,000 feet (2,440 and 2,754 m). To the northeast, the altitude diminishes gradually toward the Rub al Khali desert.

In the eastern two-thirds of South Yemen, four great dry watercourses—or wadis—run for hundreds of miles eastward and northeastward. Gouged out by large rivers, the wadis are probably relics of a period when the climate of Arabia was much moister. The most impressive wadi is the Hadhramaut, and Hadhramaut is the name often applied to the whole east-central part of the country. The outstanding scenic feature of South Arabia, the Wadi Hadhramaut is a remarkable system of deep canyons, with almost vertical cliffs rising from steep scree slopes. Over considerable stretches of its course, there is a perennially flowing river. In the interior highlands of South Yemen, the rainfall averages 12 inches (30 cm) a year, shading off to 8 inches (20 cm) in the east. Vegetation is watered by night dews and mists.

Estimates of the total population of South Yemen are as uncertain as estimates of its precise area. No census has ever been taken, but a figure of just under 2 million is thought to be probable. About 15 percent of the population live in greater Aden, and most of the rest live along the coast, although many people live in the Hadhramaut.

The people of South Yemen are almost uniformly Arab and speak Arabic, but in the eastern end of the country there is a strong Veddoid (Australoid) group, speaking a Semitic language older than Arabic. Nearly all native South Yemenis are Sunni Muslims of the Shafi sect; some Zaidi Muslims are to be found in the towns, especially Aden. In the great days of Aden's prosperity (before 1967), Hindus, North Yemenis, and Jews and other foreigners worked in the port area, but they have almost all left. (The many thousands of Russian, East German, Czech, Cuban, and other advisers and specialists from the Communist bloc in South Yemen should not be counted as permanent residents.)

Except in the only large urban area, Aden, the chief sources of national income are agriculture, animal husbandry, and fishing. The people farm where the wadis and their waters reach the coastal strip, at oases and on river banks in the upland areas, and on terraced land where water is collected. In the highest and most arid areas, where agriculture is not possible, there is a small nomadic population. Everywhere, farming depends on a highly developed system of water management. Agriculture (mostly subsistence farming) produces crops like sorghum, sesame, millet, wheat, barley, and dates. The chief cash crop is long-staple cotton.

Aden, which has an excellent harbor, is the historic capital of its region, although the actual seat of government is Madinat el-Shab, a few miles west of Aden. Aden is the center of a complex of satellite towns and is the chief urban area, with a population of about 330,000. Mukalla, about 300 miles (483 km) east of Aden, with a population of 80,000, is the next largest town and port. The other large towns—Seiyun, Tarim, and Shibam—are all in the Hadhramaut. Tarim is the center of traditional culture.

Until independence in 1967, there was very little sense of national unity in South Yemen. Ethnic links, tribal affiliations and tribal loyalties formed the warp and the woof of Yemeni life, and no doubt still do. In the eastern half of the country, political authority remained in the hands of the local sheikhs until 1967. The British never administered the area directly; their impact was far greater in the Aden area than anywhere else in the country.

All banking, insurance, and commercial activities in Yemen have been nationalized since 1970. The administration has been restructured, and six governorates have been created. The boundaries of the governorates correspond roughly to natural boundaries and deliberately ignore former state territories and ethnic loyalties. Some effort has been made to improve the rudimentary road system, but since the country is both poor and large and the population is relatively small, not much has been accomplished.

As for the economy, the government's record since independence has been poor, because of bad luck and bad management. Before 1967, Aden was a thriving port, servicing 6,000 ships a year, with a network of ancillary services and small industries. The closing of the Suez Canal in 1967 a few months before independence was bad luck. Overnight Aden became largely derelict. Its population fell by one-third. Even when the Canal reopened in 1975, prosperity did not return. Fewer ships use the Canal, and of those that do, some prefer to use the port facilities of Jidda or Djibouti. The one large industry in Aden, the oil refinery owned and operated until 1977 by British Petroleum, is technically obsolete and badly maintained.

Revolutionary attitudes and policies have had effects as economically traumatic as those stemming from bad luck. Nationalization and the compulsory shutting down of "luxury" and "unnecessary" businesses have discouraged the creation of wealth; and many people with modern training and education have left the country.

South Yemen has had large budget deficits since independence, and its plans for development are heavily dependent on foreign aid. More than half the $220 million used in the investment plan in effect from 1974 to 1978 came from foreign sources—from the Soviet Union, China, East Germany, Arab sources, and UN agencies. South Yemen depends on Soviet-bloc countries for trained personnel. It was estimated in 1979 that there were 10,000 foreigners in South Yemen, including 4,000 Russians who gave military and other assistance, 3,500 Cubans who trained and controlled the militia, and 1,100 East Germans who controlled the security police.

According to some sources, the Soviet Union has completed the construction of a base on the island of Socotra, and Soviet naval activity has been very noticeable there. However, there are indications of disenchantment with Soviet aid. There are complaints that the Russians take twice as long as the West Europeans or Americans to finish a project, that their medicine is poor, and that spare parts for equipment are often unavailable.

Recent travelers report that Aden is "shabby" and "listless," that shops are boarded up, and that essential supplies are extremely scarce. The regime has allegedly done much for the countryside and most villages are said to be more prosperous than they were. Since foreigners are not allowed to see for themselves, however, some skepticism is appropriate.

It is claimed that considerable social progress has been made in the areas of health, education, and the emancipation of women. In 1967, there were 15,000 children in school; there are now said to be 250,000. The University of Aden opened in 1970 with 103 students; it now has 2,400 in its schools of education, agriculture, economics, and medicine. A real advance was the virtual elimination of the use of the drug kat (*Catha edulis*), formerly common all over South Arabia, and used a great deal in North Yemen.

Historically, Aden and its surroundings were crossroads of trade routes. The British (through the agency of the East India Company) occupied Aden in 1839 in order to establish coal-bunkering facilities on the route from Britain to India. Aden's importance as a port with good facilities was enhanced by the opening of the Suez Canal in 1869. A loose British protectorate was established, reaching along the coast to the boundary with Oman in the 1870s and 1880s. The centers of British influence and administration were Aden and Mukalla. Until 1937, both were under the direct supervision of the government of India, and only indirectly, of Britain.

Toward the end of British rule—that is, in the early 1960s—the British tried to unify the area so that it might stand on its own after independence. By 1963, a Federation of South Arabia (including Aden) had been formed, but several of the large sultanates in the Hadhramaut refused to join. Two radical organizations fought each other to succeed the British—the Egyptian-backed Front for the Liberation of Occupied South Yemen (FLOSY) and the rival National Liberation Front (NLF). The NLF emerged victorious during the final days of British rule, which were a nightmare of disintegrating authority, and destroyed the old order in South Arabia by overthrowing most of the local rulers.

After independence on November 30, 1967, the new NLF government centralized administration and proclaimed the whole area the People's Republic of Southern Yemen. Renamed the People's Democratic Republic of Yemen in 1970, South Yemen sought to emphasize the desirability of unity with North Yemen. South Yemen has had chronically bad relations with its neighbors—North Yemen (Sana), Saudi

Arabia, and Oman—largely because of its repeated attempts to make trouble for these more conservative regimes. It was at war briefly with North Yemen (Sana) in 1972 and in 1979; the brief wars were followed on both occasions by plans for union of the two Yemens. For many years, South Yemen also supported a rebellion against the sultan of Oman.

In October 1978, the NLF merged with two smaller factions to form the Yemeni Socialist Party (modeled after the Soviet party), which proclaimed as its objectives proletarian dictatorship and "people's democracy." Earlier in 1978, the head of the NLF, Abdel Fattah Ismail, overthrew President Salem Robaye Ali in a power struggle and ordered Ali executed by firing squad for his "reactionary attitude." In October, Ismail made himself President as well as head of the new Yemeni Socialist Party.

South Yemen today is an exception in the Arab world because it embraces Marxist doctrines and attempts to reconcile them with Islam. It would obviously gain from a union with the larger population and better soil and climate of North Yemen; it is less clear what gains the union could possibly offer the North Yemenis. Yet Yemeni nationalism, even if it is a recent phenomenon, seems to have considerable strength, and a genuinely cooperative union might well benefit both partners. This, however, would entail South Yemen's abandonment of doctrinaire policies and fratricidal feuding. Until then, the People's Democratic Republic of Yemen is likely to follow a thorny path, creating problems for its neighbors as well as itself.

Arthur Campbell Turner

South Asia

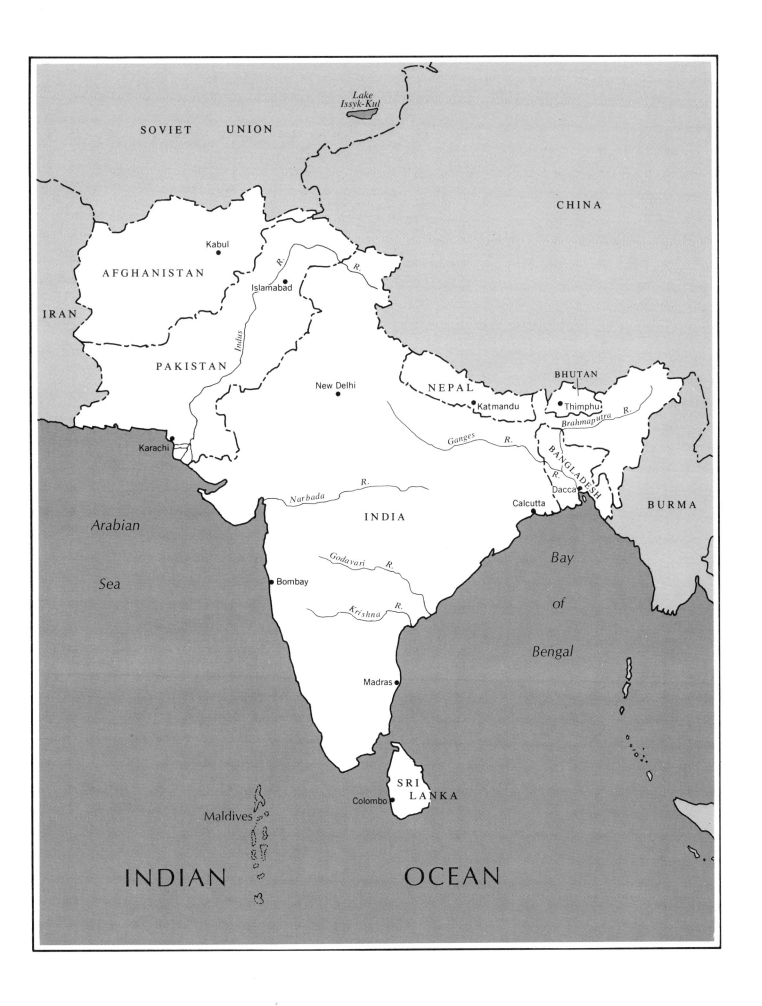

Afghanistan
(Democratic Republic of Afghanistan)

Area: 250,000 sq mi (647,500 sq km)
Population: 14.6 million
  Density: 58 per sq mi (23 per sq km)
  Growth rate: 2.2% (1970–1977)
Percent of population under 14 years of age: 44%
Infant deaths per 1,000 live births: 269
Life expectancy at birth: 42 years
Leading causes of death: not available
Ethnic composition: Uzbek; Turkman; Hazara; Tajik; Pashtan
Languages: 35 languages (including Pashtu and Farsi)
Literacy: under 15%
Religions: Sunni Muslim 99%; Shiite Muslim 1%
Percent population urban: 15%
Percent population rural: 85%
Gross national product: $3.5 billion
  Per capita GNP: $240
  Per capita GNP growth rate: 2.7% (1970–1977)
Inflation rate: 4.1% (1970–1977)

Afghanistan is a land of diversity and contrast; geography and topography are very important to its people and to its economy. The raging rivers of spring wash away roads, bridges, and canals and dwindle to narrow channels or a series of unconnected pools by autumn. In the narrow valleys, every inch of land is cultivated, and the rocky mountainsides are grazed by small flocks of sheep and goats.

For more than 25 years, Afghanistan tried to further economic development and received $2 billion in foreign grants and credits—the highest per capita technical assistance in the world. Under favorable conditions, Afghanistan could support many times its existing population at a far higher standard of living. Yet in 1971–1972, the United Nations classified it among the least-developed of the less-developed countries, and Afghanistan has incurred one of the highest debt-service ratios in the world. The failure of the economy can be traced in part to the failure of foreign economic aid, which in the 1950s took the form of aid rivalry between the United States and the Soviet Union. More important, the Afghan leadership itself was unable to initiate a sound economic strategy that could win mass support.

In this landlocked country of central Asia, 250,000 square miles (647,500 sq km) in area, more than 14 million inhabitants live in a conservative Muslim society. The northern border, following the Amu Darya River, separates the country from the Soviet Union along the plains of Turkestan. The villages and grazing lands of the Uzbek and Turkman lie north of the central mountains. In the northeast, a 180-mile (289.6-km) corridor forms a tiny stretch of border with China. The ancient silk-trade route to China crossed the plains of Turkestan, and the caravan route to India lay across the deserts of the south. In the east, south,

and southwest, Afghanistan borders Pakistan and Iran.

The country is divided into four major geographic zones: the northern plains, the central mountains, the eastern and southeastern mountains and foothills, and the southern and western lowlands. Cold winters with 4 to 6 weeks of freezing temperatures are followed by variable spring weather with thundershowers, and hot dry summers with temperatures up to 104°F (40°C). Annual rainfall seldom exceeds 10 inches (25 cm).

The plains of the north are separated from the rest of the country by great ranges of the snowcapped Hindu Kush mountains. In the east, Jalalabad provides the route to Pakistan and the Indian subcontinent through the famous Khyber Pass. The capital city, Kabul, at an altitude of 9,000 feet (2,745 m), lies in the middle of a string of rich valleys. To the north through the Salang Pass, Kabul is linked to Mazar-i-Sharif and the Soviet Union. All major roads connecting the capital and northern cities to the Soviet Union have been paved, thanks to Soviet technical and economic aid programs. To the south, Kabul is linked to the historic city of Ghazni and further south to the former capital, Kandahar; it is linked to Herat and Iran in the west.

Afghanistan's central location has led to a mingling of different cultures and languages; there is no Afghan racial stereotype. The population of the north and

Workers help build a road to provide access to the Dewagal Forest's timberlands in this landlocked agricultural country. (Photo: United Nations/Ray Witlin.)

193

central regions is largely Tajik, Uzbek, Turkman, Pashtan, and Hazara.

Some 35 languages belonging to the Indo-Iranian, Turkic-Mongolian, and Semitic groups have been identified in Afghanistan, but the dominant spoken languages are Pashtu and Farsi (Dari), the language of Iran. The population is 99 percent Sunni Muslim; the remaining 1 percent are the Hazara, who are Shiites like the Muslims of Iran.

Most Afghans are villagers, living in some 20,000 villages that range in size from 10 to 500 farming families. Some 1.5 million nomads live in moving villages, taking their flocks into the mountains in the summer months.

Agriculture constitutes the major economic resource, providing a livelihood for most of the people and contributing more than 55 percent of the gross national product. In this arid land, water is the key to life; only 12 percent of the land is cultivated, although two-thirds of the countryside provides winter and summer grazing. With U.S. aid, a major river basin development project—the Helmand Valley Development—has revitalized the dusty plains south of Llashkargah. More than 66 percent of the cropland is irrigated. Fifty percent of the irrigated land is under wheat, and 30 percent is under maize, rice, and barley with the balance devoted to fruits, vegetables, cotton, oilseeds, sugar beets, and forage legumes. Average yields are low, because little improved seed is available and chemical fertilizer is applied to only about 12.5 percent of the irrigated land.

Factory laborers prepare wool for washing. Wool is one of Afghanistan's major export commodities. (Photo: United Nations/H. K. Lall.)

About 60 percent of the land is farmed in holdings of 49 acres (20 ha) each; 98 percent of all farms are of this size. Some 3,000 tractors and 1 million oxen provide all draft power on the farms. The livestock population is estimated at 20 million. Only 3 percent of the land is classified as forest.

Agriculture, handicrafts, and rural trade provide employment for 85 percent of the working population. The rest are employed in government administration, industry, urban trade, tourism, and transportation.

Some 130 small- and medium-scale private industrial enterprises employ about 10,000 people, but heavy industry and mining are state-owned and -run. Natural gas, exploited by the Soviet Union, earned the country a total of $70 million per year in the late 1970s (the international market value of the gas was 4 to 6 times higher than the rate the Soviets were paying). There are large deposits of iron ore and copper. Electricity is available to only 5 percent of the population, and hydroelectric power is the least-developed resource. However, the four major power plants in Sarobi, Wardak, Jabul Siraj, and Helmand could make Afghanistan a net exporter of electricity to neighboring Pakistan. There are only 26,000 telephones and 300 post offices in the country.

Traditional values and conservative Muslim attitudes characterize social life. Of the older generation, only the mullahs (priests) read and write, and the overall literacy rate is below 15 percent. Of the children of primary school age, fewer than 30 percent (mostly boys) attend school. Of all children, 50 percent die before they are 5 years old, and those who live have a life expectancy of only 50 years.

Most villages have neither paved roads nor piped water. In contrast, Kabul has paved streets, motels, parks, palaces, department stores, restaurants, television, and many other amenities of urban life. Indeed, Afghanistan is actually two societies—a traditional society for the rural 85 percent of the population and a modern society for the urban 15 percent. There are, however, increasing links between these two sectors as successive governments attempt to expand the modern economy. In the rural areas there has been a rapid expansion of nontraditional education and health facilities; crop production has also improved, thanks to government agencies that distribute seed, fertilizer, and credit, and thanks to improved communications and modern appliances.

International trade constitutes less than 1 percent of the gross national product. Afghanistan has never been a major exporter of cash crops or minerals, and has fairly diversified exports, including fruits and nuts, ginned cotton, karakul pelts and carpets, and handicrafts. Natural gas exports to the Soviet Union constitute 15 percent of all exports.

Afghanistan's major imports are textiles, tea, sugar, and petroleum. Although there is a chronic trade deficit, in practice the Afghan economy has been able to finance trade because of an average of about $65 million a year in aid and substantial remittances from

Afghan workers employed in Iran and the Middle East since 1974. Before 1953, the Afghan economy was in balance; after 1953, Afghanistan invited foreign aid, which created new tensions and imbalances.

Present-day Afghanistan was formed in 1747 by the Saddozai dynasty, whose founder was Ahmed Shah Baba. British influence was established in two Anglo-Afghan wars, between 1839 and 1842 and between 1878 and 1880. In 1835, Amir Dost Muhammad Khan founded the Muhammadzai dynasty, which lasted until 1973, when Sardar Muhammad Daud Khan formed the first Republic of Afghanistan. However, in April 1978, a pro-Soviet military coup engineered the overthrow of the Daud regime and established a Marxist regime, headed by Noor Muhammad Taraki.

Even before Taraki's pro-Soviet coup, the Soviet Union had gained control of most of Afghanistan's mineral resources, gas, fruits, and other raw materials through a series of barter agreements extremely favorable to the Soviet Union. In exchange, the Soviet Union supplied obsolete military equipment and set up technical and economic development projects to produce goods for export to the Soviet Union.

In September 1979, Taraki was eliminated by Prime Minister Hafizullah Amin, who was in turn overthrown by a bloody Soviet-backed coup that ushered in the Soviet takeover of December 1979. On December 27, Babrak Karmal became President and Secretary-General of the ruling People's Democratic Party.

Afghanistan today faces many interrelated problems, in addition to the Soviet incursion. Frequent periods of adverse climatic conditions and the pressures of increasing population and herds have reduced soil fertility. Fallow time has declined, but farming technology, the application of fertilizers, and the development of irrigation schemes have not changed substantially. Instead, resources have been allocated to the cities and to the developing urban centers at the expense of rural areas. And there are indications that the gulf between Kabul and the rest of the country is widening, the result of a development policy that has been geared to the creation of a modern sector.

Low producer prices bear no relation to costs or world prices. Farmers producing cotton, hides, fruits, and carpets have been paid the same prices for decades, although inflation is pervasive. There are no opportunities for saving, credit, investment, or employment in the traditional sector; this has led to seasonal migration of the young and productive labor force to the cities.

Poverty is by no means confined to the rural areas. Income distribution in Kabul is extremely skewed—the bottom 56 percent of all households earn only 15 percent of the income; the top 6 percent earn 49.2 percent. The rate of movement into the modern sector has been much faster than the increase in employment opportunities and the development of social overhead in the modern sector, where only 5 percent of the population have access to a public piped water system; polluted water is a major cause of illness and disease; and inadequate housing, education, health care, and nutrition indicate a failure to meet basic human needs.

Meanwhile, the civil war and the Soviet incursion involve a contest between Soviet military technology and Afghan cultural and religious values. Some 100,000 well-equipped Soviet soldiers control Kabul and other major cities; some 400,000 Afghans have fled into Pakistan; Afghan tribespeople continue to resist but apparently cannot unite against the Soviet threat. In the long run, the Soviet Union may have created a Soviet Vietnam, which may keep Soviet troops occupied for decades.   *Nake M. Kamrany*

Bangladesh
(People's Republic of Bangladesh)

Area: 55,126 sq mi (142,776 sq km)
Population: 83.6 million
   Density: 1,517 per sq mi (585 per sq km)
   Growth rate: 2.1% (1970–1977)
Percent of population under 15 years of age: 45%
Infant deaths per 1,000 live births: 140
Life expectancy at birth: 45 years
Leading causes of death: not available
Ethnic composition: Bengali, Hindu, tribal peoples
Languages: Bengali, rural Bengali dialects, Urdu, other dialects
Literacy: 20%
Religions: Muslim, nearly 90%; Hindu 10%; Buddhist; Christian
Percent population urban: 10%
Percent population rural: 90%
Gross national product: $7.6 billion
   Per capita GNP: $90
   Per capita GNP growth rate: −0.2% (1970–1977)
Inflation rate: not available

When Bangladesh became an independent nation in December 1971, after a devastating civil war, its leaders faced gigantic challenges. An agricultural country with limited land and natural resources, Bangladesh lacks the infrastructure fundamental to economic development. It has a territory of only 55,126 square miles (142,776 sq km), a growing population of more than 80 million, and a per capita income of less than $100 a year.

The population will probably almost double by the end of this century, and such growth may be catastrophic, given the size of the country. It is estimated that about 45 percent of the population is less than 15 years old, and more than 40 percent are in their reproductive years. Marriage is universal, and women often marry in their teens.

Traditional, social, and cultural norms in Bangladesh are not conducive to fertility control. After initial ambivalence, the government is apparently committed to population control; international agencies are helping Bangladesh give top priority to family planning. But even if family-planning projects meet with reasonable success, it will be years before these programs show tangible results. Population control is aggravated by mass illiteracy (80 percent), agricultural backwardness, and the subservience of women; superstition and religion also contribute to social inertia.

Another serious constraint on Bangladesh's development is the nation's resource limitation. About the size of Florida, Bangladesh is bounded by the Bay of Bengal in the south, the Republic of India in the north, northeast, and northwest, and Burma in the southeast. Most of its land mass is low-lying delta, rivers, and marshy areas. For the most part it is a flat, fertile land, severely affected by the monsoons that dump an average of 85 inches (213 cm) of rainfall a year.

Fertile land is the country's only real asset. Except for natural gas, Bangladesh has no other significant natural resources. Although the land can produce several crops a year, Bangladesh's per capita agricultural output is one of the lowest in the world, and it is usually a food-deficit area. Uncertain weather is an enormous handicap; either there is too much water caused by flood and heavy rain or there is drought. The country is crisscrossed by rivers and their trib-

Shanty settlements like this one create health and sanitation problems. (Photo: United Nations/ Philip Teuscher.)

utaries. The main problem during monsoon is how to control the flooding; during the dry season, many rivers dry up, creating transportation problems.

With a tropical monsoon climate, Bangladesh is rich in flora and fauna, and most of its plants and animals are typical of a tropical riverine country. Among the large forest areas are the Sundarbans, the home of the famous Bengal tigers, the Chittagong Hill Tracts, and Madhupur. But many forest areas have been depleted during recent years because of heavy population pressure.

Rice is the staple food, but the rice crop is very much a gamble; yields are disastrously affected by both too much and too little rain. Because the pressure on land is unusually heavy, there is little diversification of agriculture. The government has been trying to encourage people to eat wheat products, but the demand for rice and rice products has not declined significantly.

Tea is one of the main crops. The foothills of the Himalaya in Sylhet district provide the right soil and climate for growing tea, and processed tea is a leading export and earner of foreign exchange.

Bangladesh is also the world's largest producer of jute, a stronger natural fiber used mainly for gunnysacks, carpet backing, and packing materials. There are about 70 jute mills, and Bangladesh's entire economy is at the mercy of the jute crop.

Ethnically, the Bengalis in Bangladesh and in the state of West Bengal in India are a mixture of Aryans and Dravidians. In the Chittagong Hill Tracts, there are Mongoloid peoples; some hill peoples also belong to ethnic minorities. Mogul legions of Turkish and Pathan extraction also settled in Bengal. Among the Hindus, high-caste Brahmins take pride in their Aryan roots; Muslim aristocrats trace their origin to Iran or Turkey or Arabia. There is some mixture of European blood. However, Bangladesh has no serious ethnic or linguistic conflicts; this may make national integration easier.

Ancient Bangladesh was Hindu, and about 10 percent of the citizens today are Hindus. Around the European middle ages, Buddhism flourished; there is still a small group of Buddhists in Bangladesh. Because Muslim rulers established a firm foothold in the thirteenth century, nearly 90 percent of the Bangladeshis are Sunni Muslims. There are also a few Christians, most of whom are Roman Catholics.

Some 98 percent of all Bangladeshis speak Bengali, a derivative of Sanskrit, the classical Indo-Aryan language of South Asia, and one of the world's major language groups. There is a rich Bengali literary tradition. In some urban areas, the refugees who migrated from India after the partition of the subcontinent in 1947 speak Urdu. Ethnic minorities speak a variety of languages; in the Sylhet tea plantations, workers from central and south India speak languages and dialects closer to Tamil and Malayalam.

Only about 20 percent of the Bangladeshis are literate. In the villages, schooling facilities are limited and primary education is not compulsory. Many children help in the fields instead of going to school.

The Bangladeshi social structure is not dominated by any rigid class pattern; after the creation of Pakistan, feudalism was abolished. Even in urban areas, the family system is still strong. The eldest son is usually obliged to educate younger brothers and sisters; and the old parents live with their sons, who support them because there is no old-age pension system or welfare system in the country.

Ninety percent of the people still live in villages in a male-dominated society, where Muslim women usually observe purdah (seclusion). But in many areas women help their husbands in the fields, especially during the harvesting season. Marriages, except in urban areas, are still arranged by the parents.

Although the extended-family system is the rule, pressure on the land, migration to the city, and an increasing population are gradually affecting family patterns. Affluent landholding families exercise substantial economic and political power and control most of the cultivable land. The increasing number of landless villagers (during the last few years, landlessness has increased up to 40 percent) poses a serious economic and political problem, one that is aggravated by inflation.

Since the abolition of feudalism, land-tenure patterns have changed; the landowner now pays an annual tax directly to the government. The Muslim law of inheritance gives equal shares to sons, and daughters inherit a specific proportion of land. The fragmentation of holdings poses an enormous obstacle to modernization.

Mud-walled and thatched houses dominate the rural landscape. Affluent families have brick houses, and well-to-do rural Bangladeshis live in houses made of corrugated iron sheets. Normally, a cluster of houses shared by blood relatives has a common compound and a common source of water, a pond, a well, or a tube well.

The traditional bullock-drawn plow is still the main agricultural tool. Although the use of fertilizers and high-yield varieties of rice is increasing, it is still limited. Productivity remains at a subsistence level, and farmers and peasants do not have much surplus. The government food-procurement program collects surplus food from the farmers at official rates. But the farmers also sell surplus grains, green vegetables, milk, fish, cattle, and poultry at local markets for cash to buy daily necessities. Jute, the farmer's most important cash crop, is usually bought by middlemen and shipped to the jute mills or exported overseas.

During the last decade, agriculture has received serious attention from the national government and from international agencies, which encourage the use of fertilizer and high-yield varieties of rice. But the high cost of fertilizer and the uneconomically small size of landholdings are not conducive to modernization. Although the use of modern agricultural inputs is heavily subsidized, no serious effort has been made to consolidate fragmented landholdings for the purpose of collective farming.

Urban areas are growing. The area which includes Dacca, the capital, together with about 100 square miles (259 sq km) around it constitutes the major urban center. (Dacca was only a district headquarters when it became the capital of East Pakistan in 1947, and its population soared during the next 30 years. Today it has a population of about 1.3 million.) The main port, Chittagong, and its neighboring industrial towns make up the second major urban area. Khulna, the second largest port, is an important industrial area.

The aftermath of civil war brought mass migration to the cities, food scarcity, and unemployment. Bangladesh underwent a demographic change in the 1970s, when hundreds of thousands flocked to the city in search of security and employment, aggravating the housing problem and exhausting municipal resources. The visible manifestation of urban crowding is the increasing number of beggars, destitutes, and squatters in Dacca and other urban areas.

Under increasing population pressure, the urban areas suffer from unplanned growth and inadequate water and power supplies; poor sewage and drainage are chronic. Hospitals and health care facilities cannot sustain the increasing demands for services. No rapid transit system connects suburban areas. Even

Hundreds of workers build an irrigation canal in Bangladesh, where food production has lagged behind population growth despite the fertile soil. (Photo: United Nations/J. O'Brien.)

road transportation to and from the principal cities is barely adequate.

The political and professional elites in Bangladesh are mostly members of the first or second generation of educated and professional people, related by family ties and educated in the same schools and colleges. They are concentrated in the urban areas, predominantly in Dacca, and control most private urban properties. A step below clerical employees in the private and public sector are the manual workers, who cannot afford to bring their families to the city, but send part of their incomes back to their dependents in the villages. Small traders, shopkeepers, and street vendors often live as squatters, and many industrial workers live in their factories. At the bottom of the urban social ladder are the unskilled day laborers who live in the slums and footpaths.

The transformation of Bangladesh into an independent state took place in three well-defined stages. Between 1947 and 1958, while newly independent Pakistan experimented with British-style parliamentary democracy, the Bengalis—moved by grievances against the Pakistani federal government and their desire for autonomy—increasingly espoused separatist nationalism. From 1958 to 1969, the Bengalis were further frustrated by their relations with a military administration in which they had little voice.

The period from 1969 to 1971 was marked by a mass movement for autonomy. Three political leaders emerged after the Pakistani legislative elections of 1970: General Agha Muhammad Yahya Khan, the military head of Pakistan's federal government; Sheikh Mujibur Rahman, the undisputed Bengali leader (later hailed as the "father of Bangladesh"); and Zulfikar Ali Bhutto, leader of the majority party in West Pakistan. After failing to reach a political settlement with East Pakistan's Bengalis, Pakistan's leaders initiated a military crackdown in March 1971. This led to civil war and the merciless killing of civilians in East Pakistan. Bangladesh declared its independence on March 26, 1971, and a mass flight of Bengalis to India followed. India entered the war in support of Bangladesh on December 4, and Pakistan was defeated.

The Bangladeshi administrative structure, weakened by civil war, was strained further by the threat to internal security from the so-called freedom fighters, who often took the law into their own hands. In an effort to restore order, Sheikh Mujibur Rahman banned all freedom fighter organizations, but his orders to surrender arms were disregarded, and most of the guns fell into the hands of antisocial hoodlums who ravaged the countryside.

After the overthrow and murder of Mujibur Rahman in August 1975, the military regime in Bangladesh weakened its ties to India and the Soviet Union; the current leadership has a pro-Western orientation. General Ziaur Rahman's regime has gradually made room for a civilian government. Ziaur Rahman, elected President in June 1978, is the leader of the new Bangladesh Nationalist Party (BNP), which swept the legislative elections in February 1979, winning 206 of the 300 parliamentary seats. The Awami League, the main opposition party, won 40 seats, although it had threatened to boycott the elections.

According to the Bangladesh constitution, the President, directly elected by the people, exercises real executive power; the Prime Minister is responsible to the National Assembly even though both the Prime Minister and the Cabinet are appointed by the President. For all practical purposes, the political system favors the President, who is the country's principal policymaker.

Today, the economy of Bangladesh is neither socialistic nor capitalistic; its economic outlook is bleak. In fact, in the first years after Bangladesh became independent, the economy was sustained by about $3 billion in foreign aid. It was enormously difficult to manage the huge nationalized industries; and poor managerial skills, political patronage, and labor unrest contributed to declining industrial productivity and continuing inflation. After the coup of 1975, Bangladeshi economic policy ceased to favor nationalization and began to encourage private enterprise, although gigantic nationalized industries are still the rule.

Ziaur Rahman's government has received a steady flow of aid from Western countries, the World Bank, and the U.S. Agency for International Development since 1975. In August 1980, France agreed to provide financial and technological aid for the construction of a nuclear power plant.

Although 80 percent of the Bangladeshis are illiterate, the upper- and middle-level leaders are highly educated and neither more inefficient nor more corrupt than those of other developing countries. There is a serious commitment to halting the spiraling population growth. Although there is a strong religious tradition, there is no fanatical opposition to family planning and modernization; the real problem is to motivate the illiterate population. With technological know-how, it might be possible to improve the agricultural system and diversify the economy. Recent advances in agricultural output and in reduction of population growth are encouraging.

Traditionally, Bengali politics has been characterized by agitation, factionalism, and political instability, factors hardly congenial to development; future development depends in part on the political cohesiveness of the new nation. While most political leaders consider foreign aid essential and cultivate the Western powers, an articulate group of politicians, administrators, and intellectuals believe that Bangladesh should depend more on its own resources. They urge a reorientation of development strategy with less reliance on conventional growth-oriented planning and a focus on satisfying the basic needs of the rural population.

Today, Bangladesh suffers from floods and cyclones, malnutrition and famine, political instability, overpopulation, and a stagnant, subsistence economy. Nonetheless, Bangladesh must struggle to meet the basic needs of its people with limited resources and continuing dependence on foreign aid.

M. Rashiduzzaman

Bhutan
(Kingdom of Bhutan)

Area: **18,145 sq mi (47,000 sq km)**
Population: **1.3 million**
  Density: **72 per sq mi (28 per sq km)**
  Growth rate: **2.3% (1970–1977)**
Percent of population under 14 years of age: **42%**
Infant deaths per 1,000 live births: **not available**
Life expectancy at birth: **45 years (1978)**
Leading causes of death: **tuberculosis, cholera**
Ethnic composition: **Tibetan, Nepalese**
Languages: **Dzongkha (official, a Tibetan dialect); Nepali; tribal dialects**
Literacy: **less than 5%**
Religions: **Mahayana Buddhist 75%; Hindu 25%**
Percent population urban: **5%**
Percent population rural: **95%**
Gross national product: **$120 million**
  Per capita GNP: **$100 (est.)**
  Per capita GNP growth rate: **−0.3 (1970–1977)**
Inflation rate: **7–8%**

Bhutan, the second largest landlocked kingdom in the Himalaya, has a potentially adequate economic base, but its resources are underdeveloped. Strategically important, Bhutan is located between the Tibetan plateau and the Assam-Bengal plains of India. In 1960 the late King Wangchuk and his government began the task of transforming Bhutan into a modern nation with economic aid from India. In recent years the development process has gained considerable momentum, yet Bhutan remains one of the poorest of the developing nations.

Bhutan is a land of great diversity. Dense swampy jungles, valleys of rice fields, bleak alpine highlands, and towering snow peaks are found within a few miles of each other. The northern interior has bitterly cold winters; the southern foothills and Duars, less than 100 miles (160 km) away, have a humid tropical climate all year.

The high Himalayan region, with its snowcapped Himalayan ranges, rises more than 14,000 feet (4,300 m) along the Tibetan border. In some places they reach heights of more than 23,950 feet (7,300 m). Northern Bhutan is uninhabited except for a few scattered settlements in the high valleys. Here hardy Bhutanese yaks graze in the high mountain pastures in the summer months.

The inner Himalayan zone contains the mountains radiating southward from the high Himalayan region and enclosing fertile valleys located at elevations varying from 4,920 to 9,185 feet (1,500 to 2,800 m) in the midland of Bhutan. These are relatively broad and flat valleys, with moderate rainfall and a healthy climate, and are well populated and cultivated.

In the thickly populated valley of the Paro River, substantial houses cluster in villages amid lush little fields of wheat or rice, peacefully guarded by rows of tattered Buddhist prayer flags. Typically, a *dzong* ("castle-monastery"), built on an outcrop from the steep side of the valley, looms in the distance, with its vertical series of prayer rooms and temples and richly painted windows soaring above its outer courtyard. Dominated by the new buildings and government offices, the Thimphu Valley surrounding Bhutan's capital, Thimphu, is the political nucleus of the country.

South of the inner Himalayan valleys and the foothills lie the Duars Plain, 5 to 8 miles (8 to 13 km) wide. Here rivers flowing to the south have cut deep gorges into the mountains, which rise sharply from the narrow plains. The rainfall is heavy, and the hillsides are covered with thick vegetation. The climate

A water tower, which is under construction, will store water for irrigation of this terraced farmland. (Photo: Unicef/ Satyan.)

of the Duars tract is unhealthy; the valleys are hot and humid and the forested foothills are wet and misty.

The southern section of the Duars Plain is covered with dense savanna and bamboo jungle for rice cultivation. Clothed in dense vegetation and swarming with deer, tigers, and other wild animals, the northern portion of the Duars, including the adjacent foothills, presents a rugged, irregular, and sloping surface.

The people of Bhutan are as diverse as the topography. There are several distinct ethnic groups with different cultural traditions; topography has hampered population movement and has retarded communication. In the northern and central regions most Bhutanese are of Tibetan extraction. They speak a variety of Tibetan dialects; their written language is identical with Tibetan; they follow Lamaistic Buddhism; and their social, economic, and religious life centers around the monastery. They grow barley and buckwheat, and sheep and yaks are pastured in the mountainous areas. Rice and wheat are grown in low-lying valleys.

In southern and southwestern Bhutan, the people are Hindus of Nepalese origin. A minority group, they belong to the Rai, Gurung, and Limbu ethnic groups of Nepal and speak Nepali. Immigration from Nepal ended in 1959, but Nepalese settlers have not yet been fully assimilated.

The inhabitants of eastern Bhutan are culturally akin to people of the neighboring northeast frontier region of India. They are Buddhists but do not strictly observe religious customs.

Bhutanese in the Duars and adjacent foothills resemble the people of the nearby Indian plains. They are Indo-Aryan-speaking Hindu farmers practicing shifting agriculture. The land, cleared by burning the vegetation, is used for three or four years for dry rice farming and then abandoned when the soil is exhausted.

The population of Bhutan is estimated at 1 million and is dispersed widely across 18,145 square miles (47,000 sq km). Large tracts are virtually empty; others are crowded. The inner Himalayan zone contains nearly half the nation's population, concentrated in the middle portion of the Wong, Sankosh, and Manas river valleys and in the valleys of their tributaries. The southern zone, close to the Indian border, contains approximately 40 percent of the kingdom's population. The Black Mountain Range and associated highland zone extending from east to west across south central Bhutan are thinly populated. The great Himalayan region in the north has sizable tracts that are nearly uninhabited. Bhutan's population, almost entirely rural, is increasing at a rate of about 2 percent annually.

The Bhutanese are directly dependent on the land for a living. Thus, despite the small size of Bhutan's present population, the serious limitations of land suitable for agriculture have generated population pressures on scarce arable land, especially in the intensively cultivated inner Himalayan valleys. Although precise figures are not available, the 1969 census indicates that the total amount of land suitable for agriculture is relatively small. Adverse climate, poor soil, and steep slopes have made it impossible to cultivate large areas of forest, alpine meadows, and grasslands.

Farmers in Bhutan have pushed the limits of cultivation as far as possible with the technological means available to them. Increasing the amount of land under cultivation is not feasible. To meet the needs of the growing population, increases in agricultural production must come from higher yields. Instruction of Bhutanese farmers in the use of improved techniques may increase yields.

Several measures aimed at improving agricultural production have been introduced. In 1961, several land reforms were enacted, including a law that restricts individual ownership of land to 30 acres (12 ha). The system of land taxation has been modernized; payments of tax in kind have been replaced by cash payments in some areas. Eleven state demonstration farms (seven in the temperate zone and four in the subtropical zone) have been in operation since 1964. Four government orchards supply fruit plants (apples, pears, peaches, plums, apricots, and walnuts) to farmers in the temperate zone in a program designed to popularize fruit growing. Livestock-breeding farms, four veterinary dispensaries, and a mobile dispensary unit for livestock have been established. A fish hatchery has been constructed, and rivers and lakes have been stocked with trout. At Kanglung in eastern Bhutan, a silkworm farm supplies raw silk to local weavers.

The development of educational and medical facilities and the expansion of a transportation network are beginning to make significant changes in the social and economic patterns. There are more than 100 schools in Bhutan providing general as well as vocational education. Most of the epidemics and diseases that were formerly fatal are being controlled. There are four general hospitals, 28 dispensaries, and three leprosy hospitals. A network of roads built since 1960 links Thimphu with India, with Tongsa in central Bhutan, and with Tashigang in eastern Bhutan. An east-to-west road across the country is under construction. New roads will connect most of the major settlements in the country. Paro in western Bhutan and Calcutta are linked by a commercial air service. Telephone and telecommunications link principal administrative centers; in 1963, a postal service was inaugurated.

For years the Himalayan Kingdom of Bhutan remained isolated from the outside world, visited only by a few explorers and high government officials. But today cars, jeeps, helicopters, and airplanes make Bhutan easily accessible to visitors, and the tourist trade is steadily increasing.

The quiet revolution that is changing the face of Bhutan did not originate among the people. The dramatic changes were launched by the nation's monarch, the late King Jigme Dorji Wangchuk. During his 20-year reign from 1952 to 1972, the king promulgated many reforms, including the codification of laws and the introduction of modern representative government with a Prime Minister, an advisory council comparable to a Cabinet, and the *Tsongdu*, or National Assembly. Of the Tsongdu members, perhaps a score are lamas from the kingdom's many monasteries.

The present king, Jigme Singye Wangchuk, who succeeded his father in 1972, has stressed the rapid economic, political, and social development of the country but has tried to preserve traditional values and culture. The successful completion of three 5-year development plans has brought about considerable change in Bhutan's economic and social patterns.

For the most part, the development plans were successful because of Indian economic aid and the importation of large numbers of workers and technicians from India. In addition to aid from India, foreign aid has come through the Colombo Plan for Cooperative Economic Development in South and Southeast Asia (established July 1, 1951) and the United Nations.

The development of Bhutan will continue to depend on foreign aid, carefully prepared development plans, and the effective management of the economy. While Bhutan faces the new challenges of economic development, its rulers try to preserve older cultural values. Whatever the long-term effects of economic development, Bhutan will carry into the future a distinctive cultural personality and a national identity formed over centuries.

P. P. Karan

India

(Republic of India)

Area: 1,269,341 sq mi (3,287,588 sq km)
Population: 644 million
  Density: 507 per sq mi (196 per sq km)
  Growth rate: 2.1% (1970–1977)
Percent of population under 14 years of age: 42%
Infant deaths per 1,000 live births: 130
Life expectancy at birth: 52 years
Leading causes of death: not available
Ethnic composition: Indo-Aryan 72%; Dravidian 25%; Mongoloid 3%; others
Languages: Hindi and 14 other official languages; English
Literacy: 34%
Religions: Hindu 83%; Muslim 11%; Christian 2.6%; Sikh 2%; Parsi; Jain; Buddhist; animist
Percent population urban: 20%
Percent population rural: 80%
Gross national product: $112.6 billion
  Per capita GNP: $180
  Per capita GNP growth rate: 1.1% (1970–1977)
Inflation rate: not available

Shaped roughly like a diamond, its long eastern side pushing into the Himalayan forests, India looks big on the map and is big. It is also ancient; its kings and empires of the past flourished and then declined and then were gone. But India, the land and the people, survives, and today this kaleidoscopic nation is standing firmly in the modern world, after some remarkable economic, social, and political achievements since gaining independence from Great Britain in 1947.

But the achievement of India's major development goals still is far off. Plans for progress must overcome harsh constraints: a poverty as profound and deeply rooted as any in the world; a population the largest of any nation except the People's Republic of China, increasing at the rate of 1 million each month; an army of unemployed now more than 20 million

strong; a monsoon-dependent agriculture; an inertia, partly bred by tradition and feudal rule; and a propensity for internal conflict, both political and social.

"It is a cause of legitimate national pride," states

In Bombay climate-controlled luxury apartments stand in sharp contrast to the makeshift shacks of the poor city dwellers. (Photo: United Nations/ J. P. Laffont.)

the *Draft of India's Sixth Five Year Plan* (1978–1983), "that a stagnant and dependent economy has been modernized and made more self-reliant." But, the draft continues, "we must face the fact that the most important objectives have not been achieved, and the most cherished goals seem to be as distant today as when we set out on the road to planned development."

India is a marvelously diverse land, about one-third the size of the United States. This expanse falls easily into four geographic regions: the Himalaya, earth's largest (and youngest) mountains; the fertile Indo-Gangetic plain, thick with the prodigal silt of the Indus, the Ganges (Ganga), the Brahmaputra, and their tributaries; the deserts, including India's part of the Great Thar Desert (Great Indian Desert) and the southern peninsula, girded by the Eastern and Western Ghats and by the Indian Ocean, the Arabian Sea, and the Bay of Bengal.

India has a broadly tropical monsoon climate, except in the snow-draped Himalaya. Temperatures in New Delhi, the capital, in January drop to between 38 and 40°F (3 and 4°C); in May, the thermometer may read 115°F (46°C). The monsoon, or rainy season (from June to September) dominates the weather cycles; storm clouds move in from the Indian Ocean, burst over southwest India, and replenish rivers and ponds throughout the land. Rainfall often is excessive; floods may kill hundreds of people and wash away huts and cattle; yet elsewhere no rain may come. If the monsoon fails or is weak, the soil cracks, crops shrivel, and India may go hungry. No event of the Indian year is of more consequence than the mon-

soon, and all development plans must take grave and attentive account of it.

The Indian land also stores a rich treasury of minerals and forests ripe for development. About 21 percent of the total area, 264,000 square miles (683,760 sq km), is forested, including stands of sal, deodar, spruce, oak, poplar, bamboo (used for huts, furniture, baskets, and paper manufacture), teak, and coconut palm (plentiful in south India and on India's island territories). Coal is abundant [reserves of 80 to 120 million tons (72.6 to 108.8 million t)], as is iron [22 billion tons (19.9 billion t)], and there are large deposits of bauxite, manganese, mica, and thorium (which is used in nuclear technology). There are lesser quantities of lead, copper, zinc, chromite, and other minerals. However, the exhaustion of some Indian minerals is now in sight. Forests too are visibly shrinking as industry and people push back their boundaries. Oil has been struck at Bombay High in the Arabian Sea, and from this suboceanic shelf and wells elsewhere, India produces annually about 9 million tons (8.18 million t) of crude. But it still must import about 65 percent of its oil at continually higher prices. Price rises in 1979–1980 were estimated to have cost India 50 percent extra or $1.5 billion in foreign exchange reserves. (In June 1979 India's foreign exchange reserves stood at a record $7 billion.)

Finally, to India's resources for development should be added its great wealth of water, plentiful for present needs of power, irrigation, and industrial and personal use. But within 30 years India and its vastly increased population will face water scarcity; a national water grid linking the rivers will be a necessity. In April 1979 Morarji Desai, then the Prime Minister of India, proposed to President Ziaur Rahman of Bangladesh (who agreed) that their two nations jointly harness the rivers of the Ganges-Brahmaputra system for the optimum utilization of their waters.

On the Indian land, diverse and well-favored, live 644 million people (up from 361 million in 1951), of wide-ranging ethnic and linguistic diversity. There is no single racial stock; the major strains, some of them millennia old, include peoples of Nordic, Mongoloid, proto-Australoid, and Mediterranean history. Among those of Mediterranean stock are the Dravidians, now dominant in south India, whose wandering ancestors first settled in north India.

There is no single language for all India to help hasten development. Instead there are scores, indeed hundreds, of tongues and dialects, written in many different alphabets and derived from many Indian civilizations of the past. The constitution of India specifies fifteen official languages: Assamese, Bengali, Gujarati, Hindi, Kannada, Kashmiri, Malayalam, Marathi, Oriya, Punjabi, Sanskrit, Sindhi, Tamil, Telugu, and Urdu. In urban India, and in the south particularly, English is widely spoken and is, in fact, India's minor lingua franca. But English is a foreign tongue, and India, denied a national language and needing one, has chosen Hindi and promotes its use.

Indian women pluck tea leaves on a plantation in Conoor, Nilgiri. India is the world's largest producer of tea. (Photo: United Nations/John Isaac.)

Regional languages, however, flourish. Many have a proud literary and historical ancestry and universities in several states now teach in the regional tongue. (There are 105 universities in India and 19 other educational institutions of university level.)

Indeed, the central government has changed its policy and now allows candidates for the Civil Services to answer examination questions in Hindi, English, or any regional language. Loyalty to language runs deep in India. South Indians, for example, protested violently what they took to be the imposition of Hindi a few years ago, and India's leaders must move cautiously on any development plans that touch language.

Other forces shaping the nation's life and developing future include religion, caste, and family. About 83 percent of Indians are Hindu; 11 percent are Muslim; 2.6 percent are Christian; 2 percent are Sikh; and the remainder are Parsi, Jain, Buddhist, and (among India's 40 million tribal peoples) animist. Hinduism places each Hindu by birth in a caste, subcaste, or outside a caste, with the Brahmin priest-scholar at one end of the scale, the "untouchable" scavenger at the other end, and hundreds, if not thousands, of subcastes in between. Here the Hindu arrives, and (with exceptions) here he stays, certain of rights and duties, comfortable in his relationships with others in the caste, and often accepting the compulsions of fate.

Family loyalties, too, are strong; members are less individualistic than in a Western family, and obligations to the family, to sons especially, often will take precedence over other obligations. The joint family, where two or more generations live in one household or, if in separate houses, still share family responsibilities and expenses, is common in India. The number of joint families seems to be decreasing, as sons find employment in cities away from home, but the statistics are not conclusive.

India is predominantly rural; of India's 644 million people (of whom 390 million are 25 years of age or younger) some 80 percent, or about 520 million, live in villages. There are about 575,000 villages dotted across the landscape, some with thatched mud houses clustered together, as if built in a unit, with the fields all outside; or in the south, shaded by coconut trees in a small compound; or in tribal areas, whitewashed mud walls ornamented with paintings of mythological themes; or elsewhere in the south, tiled-roofs, whitened-cement houses with porches, and one of the region's small rivers nearby. Because most Indians are village people, the call of the village is strong, even in those mudholed, dilapidated places which many villages in India unfortunately are, and even the city Indians, long since settled, go back to their "home places" for festivals or to help with the harvest. About 318,000 of the villages have populations of less than 500, and about 6,000 have populations of more than 5,000.

Approximately 45 percent of India is farmland, and perhaps 10 percent of this is planted with two or more crops. Only about 20 percent of the farmland is irrigated, but this produces about half of India's foodgrains. Rice and wheat are the principal grains. India is also the world's largest producer of sugarcane, tea, and groundnuts (peanuts) and a major producer of cotton and tobacco. Crop yields on monsoon-dependent dry-farmed land are among the lowest in the world, but yields on irrigated land and where the farmer uses fertilizer and the Green Revolution's improved seeds often rank with the highest in the world.

Farms are small; 70 percent of the holdings are 5 acres (2 ha) or less; equipment is simple—a wood plough and a bullock (there are 5 million bullock carts in India) or a water buffalo to pull it. But tractors, a record 54,600 produced by India in 1976, now clatter across some of India's farms. In fact, the tractor, the tube well (electric pump), the bicycle, and the transistor radio are working their own revolution in India. Rural life will never be the same.

There are 2,643 cities, towns, and town agglomerates. Some rise on ancient sites—Varanasi (Benares), the holy city on the Ganges, is one of the world's oldest cities. There are more than 40 "new towns"; 34 of these, with a population of 100,000 or more each, were built between 1961 and 1971. Today 148 cities in India have a population of more than 100,000, and 9 have a population of more than 1 million, including Calcutta (and environs), with 7 million; greater Bombay, with 5.9 million; Delhi (and New Delhi), with 3.6 million; and Madras, with 3.1 mil-

Workers assemble tractors in a factory near New Delhi. India's cities are centers of trade and manufacturing. (Photo: United Nations/ J. P. Laffont.)

lion. India's cities are centers of trade and manufacturing; Bombay, for example, is India's largest port. It is also the chief city of the Indian film industry, which produces a record breaking 500 feature films a year.

Lack of housing is common to villages and cities in India, and the inhabitants often live in a condition of utter want, even degradation. (In Calcutta hundreds of thousands of people live on the pavements.) Cities suffer also from a shortage of power for industry, inadequate waste disposal, poor transportation, and that almost-universal defect in India, inefficient maintenance—what is run-down stays run-down. Yet somehow cities survive: Calcutta, though choking, is still alert and argumentative, and Bombay is an impressive and vibrant metropolis. But city and village all make formidable claims on India's planners, and the overcrowding, with all that overcrowding brings with it, will require unceasing efforts for years to come.

India's past, shaped by numberless military and political changes, spans four eras. These are the Hindu era, in earliest times; the Islamic era, from the seventh century through the Mogul conquests until the early part of the eighteenth century; the era of the Europeans, especially the British who came to trade and stayed to rule; and the era of free India, from August 15, 1947, the date of India's triumphant independence, until the present. It is a dramatic history, illumined by great art, architecture, literature, and philosophical thought ("the wonder that was India"), and marked also by the rise and fall of empires, authoritarian rule, and the impact on the Indian people, for good or ill, of invasions.

Today India, free at last, is a sovereign, democratic republic, with a federal, parliamentary form of government. Its constitution pledges to secure for all Indians "social, economic and political justice; liberty of thought, expression and worship; and equality of status and opportunity." The President of India (Neelam Sanjiva Reddy in 1979) is head of state, but real executive power resides in the Prime Minister and her Council of Ministers, chosen by the Prime Minister from among her party members in Parliament.

The first Prime Minister of India was Jawaharlal Nehru, of the Indian National Congress, under whose aegis India won independence. Nehru was chosen to lead the country by Mahatma Gandhi, the frail and idolized father of the nation; for 17 years until his death in 1964 Nehru did just that, setting and keeping his goals of industrial and agricultural advance, encouraging liberty of thought and expression, guided by a firm belief in democracy at home and India's rising importance in the world. Nehru's foreign policy was based on nonalignment, though he leaned sometimes in the direction of the Soviet Union. Nehru was succeeded in 1964 by Shri Lal Bahadur Shastri, also of the Indian National Congress Party; and Shastri was succeeded by Nehru's daughter, Indira Gandhi, in 1966.

In the face of rising economic and political discontent, Gandhi in 1975 declared a national emergency, which the nation found oppressive and dictatorial. She was defeated in the twice-postponed parliamentary elections in March 1977, and a new political force, the coalition of various opposition parties known as the Janata Party, took control of the Union government under the leadership of Morarji Desai, an 83-year-old Gandhian and former stalwart of the Congress Party. In July 1979 the faction-ridden Janata government, headed by Prime Minister Morarji Desai, resigned, knowing that it could not survive a vote of no confidence in Parliament. A new government led by Charan Singh of the dissident Janata (Secular) Party also resigned in August, after 24 days in office; and the President dissolved the Lok Sabha (the lower house of Parliament) and called for midterm elections. In January, 1980, the Congress Party led by Indira Gandhi made a surprising comeback, winning a two-thirds parliamentary majority in national elections, and Mrs. Gandhi was once again sworn in as Prime Minister.

India is a socialist country, although there is debate in India over the precise definition of socialism. In practice Indian socialism involves a mixed economy, the economic development of the nation by both the government and the private sector. The state owns and controls the so-called commanding heights, the steel and petrochemical industries and the railways, while agriculture and village industries, including handicrafts, are privately owned.

But socialism in India also means the welfare state, and there is full agreement on social goals: food, employment, housing, and literacy for all; improved education and health care; a higher income for the poor; and the eventual eradication of poverty.

Girls using sickles reap wheat in Gujarat State. Wheat and rice are India's principal grains. (Photo: United Nations/ J. P. Laffont.)

These goals are to be met through the implementation of India's 5-year plans, the sixth of which was prepared by the Janata government. Financing of planned development has come from taxation and import duties, from foreign loans and grants (the consortium to aid India organized by the World Bank in June 1979 pledged further assistance of $3 billion to be used in implementing India's sixth 5-year plan), and, in large part, from domestic savings.

To recapitulate, India is an Asian nation that can gaze back over a panoramic history of between 4,000 and 5,000 years; it is a land rich in natural resources, with an increasingly productive agriculture that is highly dependent upon the monsoon. The Indians are a people of many races, languages, and religions, and their nation is a poor nation, one of the poorest in the world, its population soaring and unemployment still rising—but with all this, a nation determined to follow a peaceful, planned transition from colonial rule to a modern democratic society.

Where is India now, after more than 30 years of independence and planning? India is still free. The elected rulers govern, however weakly at times, by democratic means. Indians are free to speak, to worship, to assemble, to put their rulers in office, and to remove them from office. Even the "emergency" of Prime Minister Indira Gandhi could not quell India's desire for freedom.

There is now more food available than ever before, with a record crop in 1978–1979 of 130.5 million tons (118.6 million t) of grain, plus a reserve against crop failure of 17 million tons (15.4 million t). Approximately 7 million acres (2.8 million ha) of land were brought under cultivation in 1978–1979, the greatest increase in cultivated land ever achieved in a single year by any country. Against this dramatic growth in food production, however, must be set the low level of food consumption per capita, which has increased only slightly from 15.2 ounces (430.9 g) a day in 1956 to 15.5 ounces (438.7 g) a day in 1977. Millions of India's poor are too poor to buy enough to eat.

India now is a major industrial power, ranking among the world's top 10 countries in aggregate physical output. In 1977–1978 it was the leading world producer of cotton yarn [2.48 billion pounds (1.13 billion kg)]; fifth in coal production [104.7 million tons (94.96 million t)]; ninth in cement, pig iron, manganese, caustic soda, and nitrogenous and phosphate fertilizers; and twelfth in electricity generation. It is self-sufficient in all consumer goods. Its prospects for future growth are brightened by the third largest pool of scientific and technical manpower in the world, a pool of experts developed over the past few decades, and exceeded in number only by those of the United States and the Soviet Union.

A nationwide industrial superstructure now supports India's expanding industry and agriculture: a network of irrigation canals; regional hydroelectric projects; a long-established railway system with a route length of 37,500 miles (60,375 km) and running 11,000 trains a day; an export establishment multiplying world outlets for Indian manufactures; and a road network that has tripled in length [to 750,000 miles (1,200,000 km)] since 1950. (About one-third of these roads are surfaced.)

India is undergoing dramatic social changes. Life expectancy at the time of independence was 32 years; it is now 52 years. Smallpox, responsible for millions of Indian deaths in the past, has been totally eradicated with the help of the World Health Organization. In 1950 there were 50 medical colleges; today there are 106. About 33 percent of India's children age 6 to 11 attended school 25 years ago; today 87 percent do so. In 1950 about 16 percent of Indians could read and write; today the total is 34 percent, and by 1983 it is hoped that it will be 65 percent.

Striking as these and other gains are, they have proven not to be enough; poverty is still a basic fact and literally tens of millions of India's people lack sufficient food, shelter, clothing, and almost every amenity of life. Population growth has slowed, but not enough, though here too India can claim progress. "Five years ago," said the former Indian ambassador to the United Sates, Nani A. Palkivala, in Washington, D.C., in June 1979, "we had increases in population of 2.6 percent per year. Today it is 1.9 percent. We hope that through our programs of economic incentives and various other methods of voluntary birth control we can lower the rate of increase to 1.1 percent by 1985."

Other problems face India. Inflation, under control in early 1979, has risen to 10 percent annually, and is moving steadily higher. Before the 1979 monsoon, eastern India was confronted with what *The Statesman* of Calcutta called "the worst power crisis in living memory"; the city was forced to shut off power

At a plantation in Punjab, workers make sugar from sugarcane. (Photo: United Nations/ J. P. Laffont.)

to offices, homes, factories, trains, and even hospitals. Police in several states agitated for higher wages and improved working conditions, and complained of constant political interference. In the eastern coalfields, violence surged as miners struck and unemployed youths attacked officials, demanding jobs in the mines. Riots, in part politically motivated, flared anew between Hindus and Muslims; and new sources of conflict developed when lower castes, newly conscious of their political power, rioted over the issue of government job reservations. India indeed may be on the threshold of far-reaching political changes, as some observers predict. But whichever party or coalition of parties holds power in India, now or in the foreseeable future, the nation's immense and complex problems will remain.   *John E. Frazer*

Nepal
(Kingdom of Nepal)

Area: 56,136 sq mi (145,392 sq km)
Population: 13.6 million
  Density: 242 per sq mi (94 per sq km)
  Growth rate: 2.2% (1970–1977)
Percent of population under 14 years of age: 42%
Infant deaths per 1,000 live births: 300
Life expectancy at birth: 43.6 years
Leading causes of death: not available
Ethnic composition: Limbu, Rai, Newar, Tamang,
    Gurung, Magar, Brahman, Thakuri, Chetri
Languages: Nepali, more than 12 others
Literacy: 20%
Religions: Hindu 90%; Buddhist; Muslim
Percent population urban: 5%
Percent population rural: 95%
Gross national product: $1.6 billion
  Per capita GNP: $120
  Per capita GNP growth rate: 2.4% (1970–1977)
Inflation rate: not available

The mountain Kingdom of Nepal is one of the poorest countries in the world. Low-yielding subsistence agriculture supports more than 95 percent of the population, but growing population pressure is damaging the rural ecology. Although Nepal has no mining or industrial sector to provide alternative employment, it possesses considerable forest resources, reclaimable lands, surplus-producing agricultural regions, and a tremendous potential for tourism and hydroelectric power. Attempts to exploit these resources are hampered by the continuing conflict between the people of the politically dominant but impoverished midland hills and the people of the prosperous southern plains. Development efforts are further complicated by the rugged terrain, by dependence on the more advanced Indian economy, and by authoritarian political traditions.

Nepal extends for approximately 530 miles (850 km) along the southern slopes of the Greater Himalayas, a formidable mountain barrier that separates the predominantly Hindu and Muslim culture of southern Asia from the Buddhist culture of the Xizang (Tibetan) Region in China. The high Himalayan region in northern Nepal exhibits some of the most spectacular mountain scenery in the world, including Mount Everest and Annapurna Mountain. The countryside descends from these highlands through the midland hills region to the southern sea-level plains in less than 50 miles (80 km). Nepal's rivers, swollen by heavy monsoon rains in the summer and accelerated by the rapid drop in altitude, have scoured deep, north-south canyons in the hills and flood channels in the plains. The topographic complexity provides opportunities for hydroelectric development, but poses serious obstacles for economic development.

Each of the major geographic regions—the northern Himalayan highlands, the midland hills, and the southern plains—extends the entire length of the country, and each has its distinctive ecology and way of life. The northern region lies over 9,835 feet (3,000 m) above sea level and supports less than 10 percent of Nepal's population. Animal husbandry provides the basis of this pastoral economy; most villagers follow the herds of yak and goats to high summer pastures and return to lower altitudes for the winter. Villagers have traditionally supplemented local food production by exchanging animal products and Tibetan goods for grain from the southern plains.

In the rugged midland hills, the endless series of north-south ridges and intervening watersheds creates a diversity of microclimates, ranging from temperate on the hilltops to subtropical in the valleys. Slightly over half of Nepal's population is scattered in small, predominantly self-sufficient agricultural settlements throughout this region. Meticulous cultivation produces two crops a year on most good land, including rice and corn or wheat in rotation on terraced, irrigated fields and millet, buckwheat, and mustard on fields dependent on rainfall.

In areas of food grain shortage, some family members seek temporary employment in the southern plains or in India during the slack winter season. Two small but prosperous valleys, Kathmandu to the east and Pokhara to the west, have developed into urban areas and commercial centers, but other commercial and administrative centers in the hills are little different from the villages surrounding them.

Only a strip of the Gangetic plains 5 to 20 miles (8 to 32 km) wide lies within Nepal's southern border, but the rich, alluvial soil, the subtropical climate, and the plentiful (although seasonal) water for irrigation make this the most productive and fastest-developing region of Nepal. Almost 40 percent of the country's population live in this area, producing large surpluses of rice and jute for export. Crops can be grown throughout the year where water is available, although small-scale irrigation systems supply water to less than 10 percent of the fields during the dry winter season. Tropical forests provide fuel, animal forage, and building materials for villagers, exportable timber for lumber contractors, and rich lands for settlers.

Monsoon-swollen rivers and muddy roads discourage commerce during the summer rice-growing season, but grain merchants and traders caravan in weekly rotation from bazaar to bazaar in the winter and spring, buying the newly harvested grain and selling tobacco, cloth, and Indian consumer goods. Improved roads and trucks have begun to alter the bullock cart trade patterns. New commercial towns in each plains district process agricultural exports and consumer imports. Thus most plains residents are near small modern centers with fancy shops, restaurants, newspapers, and the inevitable Hindi cinema.

Each geographic region in Nepal has distinctive cultural traditions and ethnic characteristics. In the sparsely populated Himalayan region, cultural, linguistic, and ethnic patterns are similar to those of the Tibetan plateau to the north.

Inhabitants of the southern plains, on the other hand, share numerous economic, cultural, linguistic, and ethnic ties with the peoples of the Gangetic plains to the south. Except for the small indigenous tribal groups, most plains groups migrated from India during the past two centuries. They speak Bhojpuri, Maithili, and Awadhi, languages shared with sizable populations in India. Their caste system is similar to that found in the border regions of India. Hinduism in the plains reflects the modern reform movements and secular influences found in India. Only 10 percent of the plains inhabitants belong to hill groups, and most of these are new immigrants who settled close to the foothills. Yet earlier immigrants from the hills dominate many areas of the plains despite their minority status, primarily because hill groups dominate the central government.

In the midland hills, the interaction between indigenous Tibeto-Burman (non-Hindu) ethnic groups and the Indo-Aryans who immigrated from the west and south during the last millennium has created a distinctive Nepali culture. The rugged hill terrain that inhibited central controls, combined with a tolerance for cultural diversity and well-established patterns of interaction among local elites from different groups, preserved considerable autonomy for the non-Hindu groups within the framework of the Hindu state. And despite some cultural differences between Tibeto-Burman and Indo-Aryan hill groups, both have an accepted place in the national society.

Nepal's economic problems are most severe in the northern highlands and midland hills. The Chinese government has gradually imposed restrictions on local trade and access to the highland pastures north of the border traditionally used by villagers, disrupting the delicate balance in the highland economy. In the midland hills, despite elaborate terracing and careful labor-intensive farming, population growth has outstripped food production, and the hills and highlands face annual food grain deficits of over 220,000 tons (200,000 t). Even worse, the depletion of forest resources and the cultivation of increasingly marginal lands near overpopulated hill villages have increased erosion and landslides and may have caused irreversible damage to fragile hill ecosystems. It is unlikely that industrial and commercial activities will provide alternate sources of income for the hill farmers in the near future; the subsistence economy generates little local demand, and the transportation system (human porters in most areas) is too costly and unreliable to attract entrepreneurs.

Nepal has the resources to alleviate these problems, primarily in the southern plains. The plains economy already produces over 60 percent of Nepal's gross domestic product, 75 percent of the government's revenue, and 80 percent of the country's exports. Yet the agricultural potential of this region is even more promising. Population pressure on cultivated land is less than one-third the pressure in the hills, where each cultivated acre supports 4 people (10 people per ha). As a consequence, per capita output in plains agriculture is over twice that of the hills, and yields per acre in the plains could be increased simply through more intensive cultivation of local crops. Although the remaining forests are being cleared and settled at a rapid rate, the plains still contain enough potential agricultural land to expand Nepal's total cultivated area by almost 10 percent.

A pastoral way of life is slow to change in this landlocked mountainous kingdom of Nepal, one of the world's poorest countries. (Photo: United Nations/Ray Witlin.)

The industrial and commercial potential of the plains is also underexploited. Over 85 percent of the nation's industrial investments and 95 percent of its industrial labor force are already located in the plains (the rest are concentrated primarily in the Katmandu valley) primarily because of the proximity to more developed Indian markets and transportation systems. But industry still contributes less than 4 percent of Nepal's gross domestic product.

The Kingdom of Nepal was formed in the late eighteenth century when a minor raja, Prithivi Narayan Shah, conquered many hill principalities and established a unified Hindu monarchy, with its capital in Kathmandu. From the beginning, scattered settlements in the plains were valued as a source of revenue, but they were never an integral part of the mountain kingdom. After the Rana family seized power in 1846 and established an alliance with the British rulers of India, the defense barrier of the forest-covered plains was no longer needed.

During the next century, the Ranas encouraged an expansion of plains agriculture through land grants and tax contracts. Settlements were organized and financed primarily by Brahmin and Chetri hill elites, who contracted to clear, settle, and collect rents or taxes on large designated areas in the plains. Most settlers and the subcontractors who recruited and supervised them, however, came from neighboring areas of India; hill groups disliked the malarial plains, and contractors were not allowed to recruit and possibly

In Nepal, where bare subsistence agriculture supports 95 percent of the people, peasant women winnow the newly harvested mustard seed. (Photo: United Nations/Ray Witlin.)

disrupt the revenue base in existing hill settlements. Thus the Rana policy of exploiting the plains to expand central power encouraged massive immigration from India and, ironically, insured the economic and cultural integration of Nepal's plains area with India.

It was primarily the Brahmins and Chetris with established interests in the plains who, after an apprenticeship in the Indian independence movement, organized the attacks by the Nepali Congress Party that accelerated the collapse of the autocratic Rana regime in 1950. They provided the funds and leadership for most party activities during the 1950s, when the struggle for legitimacy and power weakened state controls.

After King Mahendra seized power from the elected Nepali Congress government in 1960, however, he banned all political parties and set up the panchayat (village assembly) system, based on indirect elections and organized to give the royal regime an elective facade; the new system favored hill areas where party controls were least developed. More important, the regime's interventionist, administratively controlled development programs funded by foreign aid enable central bureaucratic elites to strengthen their control of the wealth of the plains.

Since 1960 the government has tried to harness the plains' economic potential to solve the problems of the hills. In the 1960s development programs, like the successful malaria eradication program and the construction of the East-West Highway through uninhabited areas of the plains forests, attracted a massive wave of new settlers from hill villages. Because of this migration, population in the overpopulated hill region rose only 14 percent during the 1960s, compared to a 42 percent growth in the plains. In addition, the migration increased the percentage of hill settlers from 2.5 percent of the plains population in 1961 to 10 percent in 1971. This percentage has continued to grow, insuring hill groups a greater role in the plains economy.

Both Mahendra and his son Birendra, the current ruler, tried to decrease the economy's dependence on India. The government placed a high tariff on specific Indian imports to encourage domestic production. Government policies also indirectly subsidized overseas trade to reduce Nepal's almost complete dependence on Indian goods and markets; non-Indian trade has risen to 10 percent of Nepal's total (including unofficial) foreign trade. More directly, Nepal has limited Indian investment by prohibiting industrial developments close to the border and by restricting the kinds of business licenses available to noncitizens. And finally, Nepal has attracted considerable foreign aid from all over the world, which financed over half the government's development projects.

But emphasis on an independent national economy has led to two major problems. Despite considerable government and foreign aid expenditures, annual economic growth averaged only 2 percent during the last decade, barely keeping pace with annual population growth. Also, Nepal's trade deficits threaten to become a major limit to future growth. Trade diversification policies have not increased exports enough to pay for the imported consumer goods and supplies needed for development projects, and foreign aid and remittances by Nepalis working in India no longer assure a positive balance of payments.

If national growth becomes more important than economic integration, Nepal could encourage greater private Indian investment and commerce in the plains to develop Nepal's economic potential through fuller integration with Indian markets—a move avoided by previous governments fearful of Indian economic domination. Nepali leaders also fear that a secessionist movement by pro-Indian plains groups might give India a pretext to absorb Nepal, as it has absorbed other princely states in southern Asia.

Beginning in 1978, the government demonstrated some interest in cooperative ventures with public and private sectors in India to establish export industries in the plains able to compete in Indian markets. Nepal's active participation in the international community and the economic controls established by new government institutions have helped allay fears of Indian domination.

Integrating the plains people into the national society remains an acute problem, requiring a solution that would impose fewer restrictions on economic growth opportunities. Instead, government policy in the last three decades has exacerbated conflicts between hill and plains peoples, and government attempts to impose the dominant hill culture and language further alienated plains groups. The problem, however, is not just one of cultural differences; if the central government wishes to harness the plains' economic potential, it must convince all the elites to support its vision of Nepal's future. Hence the problem of integrating the plains depends in part on the solution to a larger problem—how to create participatory institutions of government that can overcome the divisiveness of Nepal's heterogeneous population.

Nepal's authoritarian political tradition is being challenged, particularly by the illegal but still active parties. Many regional and ethnic groups that had little access to central political institutions before 1950 are now represented—at least symbolically—in the National Panchayat, the Cabinet, and, to a lesser extent, in the rapidly expanding bureaucracy. Political parties lost the 1980 referendum that would have legalized their participation in elections, but King Birendra's promised electoral reforms, including direct elections to the National Panchayat, could increase the responsiveness of elected officials to a broader public. Responsive elected officials might gradually reshape Nepal's authoritarian traditions.

John T. Scholz and R. Doss Mabe

Pakistan
(Islamic Republic of Pakistan)

Area: 345,753 sq mi (895,496 sq km)
Population: 77.3 million
    Density: 224 per sq mi (86 per sq km)
    Growth rate: 3.1% (1970–1977)
Percent of population under 14 years of age: 46%
Infant deaths per 1,000 live births: 113
Life expectancy at birth: 49.8 years
Leading causes of death: not available
Ethnic composition: Punjabi, Sindhi, Baluchi, Pushtun
Languages: Urdu, English, Pashto, Hazara, Punjabi, Baluchi, Sindhi, Brauhi
Literacy: 30%
Religions: Muslim, Christian, Parsi, Buddhist
Percent population urban: 20%
Percent population rural: 80%
Gross national product: $17.5 billion
    Per capita GNP: $230
    Per capita GNP growth rate: 0.8% (1970–1977)
Inflation rate: not available

Pakistan, once a showcase for economic development, is suffering a severe shortage of energy resources and must import large quantities of increasingly expensive oil; in 1979, the cost of its oil imports rose to $935 million, some 40 percent of Pakistan's total foreign exchange earnings. Coupled with growing population pressure, the rising price of oil threatens to wipe out all the economic gains of previous decades, already eroded by an annual birthrate of more than 3 percent, which results in a per capita gross national product of only $230 a year.

Situated between the majestic mountain ranges of the Himalaya in the north and the waters of the Indian Ocean in the south, Pakistan is approximately 345,753 square miles (895,496 sq km) in size. The terrain varies from the mountainous areas of the North-West Frontier Province to the flat desert of the southern regions of Sind and Baluchistan.

Because of Pakistan's varied geography, there are climatic changes from cold to hot and humid, and a consequent variation in vegetation. The average annual rainfall is less than 10 inches (25.4 cm) in Baluchistan and Sind and between 30 and 40 inches (76.2 and 101.6 cm) in the Punjab and North-West Frontier Province. Areas of lower Sind are badly affected by waterlogging and salinity, which destroy arable land, and the government is seeking help from international agencies in order to ameliorate this difficulty.

Punjab, the breadbasket of Pakistan and the largest

province in terms of population, is laced by five rivers that supply an intricate system of canals, bringing precious water to irrigate the rich soil. Punjab produces much of the country's cash crops of cotton, wheat, and rice. The fertility of its soil is unmatched by any other province.

Major government efforts have been made to expand agriculture, encouraging the education of farmers, introducing modern farming, and promoting the large-scale use of fertilizers, "miracle seeds," and a network of canals to bring virgin land into cultivation. The Mangla Dam on the Jhelum River was Pakistan's first large hydroelectric project. The Tarbela Dam on the Indus River, the world's largest earth-filled dam, supplies areas up to 700 miles (1,127 km) away with power as well as water.

Agriculture is the most important component of Pakistan's economy. The principal cash exports are cotton, rice, sugar, tobacco, poultry, and fresh fruits. Many of these products are exported to the neighboring oil-rich countries of the Arabian Peninsula and the Persian Gulf, and earnings from these exports help pay for imports of oil. But rising oil prices have led to higher prices for fertilizer, which is cutting into the production of agricultural exports; at the same time, more earnings from agricultural exports are needed to offset the negative balance of payments resulting from the high cost of oil imports. Rice and cotton are also exported to the Far East and the West and are important sources of foreign exchange, which remains critical to industrialization because Pakistan must import both machinery and raw materials.

Food production for domestic consumption is crucial to the government's overall strategy for development. The staple is wheat, supplemented by rice and a variety of vegetables and fruits. Beef and goat meat provide animal protein; and in the coastal areas of Baluchistan and Sind there is an ample supply of fish. In times of normal rainfall, Pakistan is self-sufficient in food.

Pakistan's development strategy relies on a twofold approach: increasing agricultural output while at the same time concentrating on industrial development. The government seeks foreign aid in the form of credits, loans, and technical know-how. The Aid-to-Pakistan consortium, made up of major Western aid donors and Japan, and the World Bank have been supplying expertise as well as credits; credits and grants from the oil producing Muslim countries, especially Saudi Arabia, Kuwait, and the United Arab Emirates, are also a critical source of assistance. Between 1952 and 1977, aid to Pakistan from all sources totaled more than $9 billion.

The search for resources that could provide the indigenous underpinning for economic development is a major concern. There may be valuable mineral deposits, but a systematic geological survey has not yet evaluated known deposits of coal, iron, copper, bauxite, laterite, phosphate, graphite, and chromite. Good-quality iron ore is desperately needed because it is critical to the steel mill complex currently under construction with Soviet aid at Karachi.

Sources of energy are particularly crucial to a developing country like Pakistan, which must spend over $3 million daily on imported oil (domestic oil meets only 14 percent of the present requirements). The recorded annual production of coal ranges between 1.3 and 2.1 million tons (between 1.2 and 1.9 million t), and the coal is generally of poor quality with a high sulphur content that makes its use uneconomical. Pakistan's hydroelectric power generation stands at only 867 MW; another 2,500 MW is

A farm laborer uses a camel to draw water from a well; this water is used to irrigate cultivated fields in Pakistan. (Photo: United Nations/Carl Purcell.)

under construction and should be available by 1986. There is, however, a relative abundance of natural gas, supplied at a fairly low price to industrial and domestic consumers. A program of nuclear energy is under way, but it is limited by its cost and its dependence on external technology.

Pakistan has a mixed economy, with a traditional emphasis on the private sector. A variety of industries have been set up; the main products are textiles, sugar, cement, surgical instruments, and sporting goods (all of which are produced by the private sector). The government is involved in the development of ship-building facilities and heavy machinery and in the steel mill complex, which is scheduled to begin operation by 1981. This is the first industrial project in Pakistan to be built with Soviet help.

Industrialization has brought urbanization, and while only 20 percent of the people live in urban areas, the cities are the dynamic sector of Pakistan. In the cities and the surrounding areas, industry thrives, education is more widely available, and trade and markets prosper, luring people from the village to the city.

With an annual economic growth rate around 11 percent in the 1960s, Pakistan enjoyed considerable economic development, thanks to the special incentives given to the private sector to invest and expand, the availability of foreign sources of economic assistance, and a period of domestic stability under Ayub Khan. But when the post-Ayub regime of Zulfikar Ali Bhutto launched a program to nationalize several key industries, capital was scared away, foreign aid became increasingly difficult to obtain, and political instability made it difficult to attract foreign investments and implement domestic programs. The 1973 hike in oil prices was also devastating.

Most Pakistanis are Muslims; Hindus, Christians, Parsis, and Buddhists form small minorities. Religion, the raison d'être of Pakistan's formation, remains a vital force, helping to unify the various regions of the country. The country is officially designated "Islamic Republic of Pakistan," and the government intends to promulgate and enforce the fundamental laws of Islam, basing civil as well as criminal law on the Koran and the Sharia. Laws dealing with marriage and the division of property must conform to Islamic principles. In sectors like banking, where charging interest on loans is contrary to Islamic law, new rules are being tested.

Although industrialization has advanced substantially since independence, the structure of society has remained largely rural. The family is the primary unit of the community, and family ties and tribal relations are still strong. An individual's life is determined by the wishes of his or her family. Whether and where a child will be educated, what vocation a child will follow, and whom a child will marry are all decided by the family. Women's rights are protected, and the family laws promulgated in 1960 prohibit more than one marriage without either a divorce or the permission of the current wife; yet the society remains male-oriented and polygamy exists, albeit in declining numbers. Only women coming from urban centers with access to education are likely to be career-oriented. For the 80 percent of the women who are rural, life begins and ends with family responsibilities.

The government hopes to provide at least a primary school education for all rural children, although not all parents are convinced that education is essential, especially for girls. The government has not yet built enough schools; the goal of a universally literate population is still out of reach; and the literacy rate is only 30 percent. Nevertheless, the gains have been impressive in terms of numbers, and the growth in universities from 2 in 1947 to 10 in 1960 and in colleges from 12 to 400 in the same period underlines the government's emphasis on education.

The educational structure has helped turn Pakistan's manpower into the country's greatest national asset by training Pakistanis to fill jobs in the lucrative markets of the Persian Gulf and the Middle East. Many technically trained Pakistanis go abroad because overseas jobs pay far better than comparable jobs at home. Others leave Pakistan because they can-

In the capital city of Islamabad, newly constructed apartment buildings provide housing for the urban 20 percent of the population. (Photo: United Nations/Wolff.)

not be absorbed into the domestic market, where there is a surplus of trained people. Unskilled and semiskilled workers also emigrate to work in the construction and service sectors of foreign economies. As a result, the construction trade has suffered, a fact reflected in the poor quality of work in some projects.

Pakistan earns $1.6 billion annually from the remittances sent home by citizens working abroad. Despite these gains, the export of manpower breaks up families and has an adverse effect on the domestic economy, which cannot compete with foreign salaries for the best-trained people.

The export of handicrafts, particularly carpets, provides another source of foreign-exchange earnings. The carpet industry, originally a village and tribal enterprise, has been expanded to meet a growing international demand for quality products and age-old designs. Wool for carpets is produced locally.

Pakistan's road and railway network is extensive, except in the rugged mountain regions, and travel is cheap. Private competition in road transport has greatly reduced the cost for the traveler who is willing to go by bus or minibus. Air travel, although subsidized by the government, is expensive, but the major cities of Pakistan have access to a vast international air network.

Rural life revolves around farming, yet a few absentee landlords almost always own most of the village land. In return for the right to live on and work the land, villagers turn over a specified amount of produce

Pakistanis hold class at an open-air school in Balakot. (Photo: United Nations/Wolff.)

to the landlord. Various Pakistani governments have tried to alter this relationship; land reforms limit the amount of land that can be held by a single family and distribute the rest to the farm workers. Unfortunately, the land-reform program has eroded the landlord's responsibility to his farmers, who are often left at the mercy of moneylenders if crops fail.

The people of Pakistan belong primarily to the Dravidian, Semitic, and Mongolian races. In the fourth century B.C., the Greeks, led by Alexander the Great, invaded the region through the famous Khyber Pass in the Hindu Kush Mountains, marched down the length of the Indus, and eventually returned via Baluchistan and Persia. Contact between the Hellenic civilization and the North-West Frontier Province and the northern regions of Punjab continued long after the invaders left. Finally, the British came as traders, gradually occupied various sections of the subcontinent, and ruled over it directly for more than 100 years.

British rule instilled a long-lasting appreciation of British political, judicial, educational, legal, and military systems. Nonetheless, the history of the subcontinent under British rule was marked by bitterness and conflict between the two major communities, Hindus and Muslims. The Muslims had ruled the subcontinent for hundreds of years before the advent of the British. Although they were outnumbered (300 million Hindus to 100 million Muslims in 1947), they formed a substantial majority in the northwest and northeast zones of the subcontinent. Ever since the unsuccessful war for liberation in 1857 (called "the Indian Mutiny" by Western writers), the Indian Muslims had struggled to preserve their ideological and cultural identity; finally, after 1940, the Muslim League demanded the creation of a separate Muslim state.

Muslim demands for independence, under the leadership of Muhammad Ali Jinnah, were finally accepted by the British rulers and conceded by the Hindu majority after countrywide elections. The subcontinent was divided into India and Pakistan in August 1947 when the British government relinquished control. However, war broke out between the two countries immediately afterward over the state of Kashmir, whose 5 million people were overwhelmingly Muslim. A large part of Kashmir was occupied by India, and since independence there have been three hot wars and a continuous cold war between India and Pakistan over Kashmir. When East Pakistan became the separate state of Bangladesh after Pakistan's war with India in December 1971, the original state of Pakistan was reduced to the former West Pakistan.

Despite more than 33 years of experimenting with different political institutions, Pakistan has yet to develop a viable political system because of internal problems and external threats. Pakistan is not ethnically homogeneous; its ethnic diversity is reflected in the quarrels between the largest and richest province, Punjab, and the smaller provinces, which accuse it of usurping economic and political control.

Periods of representative government have been interspersed with years of martial law; military control has weakened political institutions. On July 5, 1977, the third military takeover since 1958 toppled the five-and-a-half-year-old regime of Prime Minister Zulfikar Ali Bhutto, who came to power at the end of the civil war that led to the creation of Bangladesh. General Zia ul-Haq heads a government committed to strengthening the economy and supporting Islamic values. Zia, who became President in 1978, denationalized some industries.

Pakistan's relations with the United States, the Soviet Union, China, and Muslim nations have been carefully cultivated. Regional stability is important, and Pakistanis worry that turbulence in Iran and Afghanistan will destabilize Pakistan. Iran's economic aid to Pakistan has come to an end. Oil-rich Muslim nations who generously support Pakistan today may not be able to extend aid when their resources are needed elsewhere. Lack of a work force and industrial unrest have scared away capital investment, and the presence of more-lucrative markets in the Persian Gulf countries has reduced the investments of Pakistani industrialists in the domestic economy.

Increases in the cost of oil imports absorb a high proportion of Pakistan's foreign exchange earnings; coupled with this is the growing population (3.1 percent a year), which places a heavy burden on the virtually stagnant economy.

Pakistan's economic future is uncertain because the traditional sources of assistance on which it depended may dry up. Provincial rivalries and external threats from neighboring states add to the challenges that Pakistan must confront if it is to survive.

Shirin Tahir-Kheli

Sri Lanka
(Democratic Socialist Republic of Sri Lanka)

Area: 25,332 sq mi (65,610 sq km)
Population: 14.3 million
  Density: 565 per sq mi (218 per sq km)
  Growth rate: 1.74% (1970–1977)
Percent of population under 14 years of age: 39%
Infant deaths per 1,000 live births: 51
Life expectancy at birth: 67.8 years
Leading causes of death: not available
Ethnic composition: Sinhala, Ceylon Tamil, Indian Tamil, Burgher, and Muslim descendants of Arab traders
Languages: Sinhala (official), Tamil, English
Literacy: 85%
Religions: Buddhist, Hindu, Christian, Muslim
Percent population urban: 24%
Percent population rural: 76%
Gross national product: $2.72 billion
  Per capita GNP: $190
  Per capita GNP growth rate: 1.3% (1970–1977)
Inflation rate: 11.8% (1970–1977)

Sri Lanka, a small island lying off the southern tip of India, was known as Lanka in antiquity and Ceylon in more recent times. Since 1972 it has been called Sri Lanka, literally "the resplendent isle." The nation, comparable to West Virginia in size, has a population of about 14 million, and keeping the population adequately fed and gainfully employed has been Sri Lanka's most pressing problem since independence from British rule in 1948.

Situated only 500 miles (805 km) north of the equator, Sri Lanka has a perennially warm climate. Although variation in temperature is slight, there is considerable variation in rainfall. Most of Sri Lanka's population live in the wet zone, where the population density currently averages more than 1,000 persons per square mile (386 per sq km). In Colombo, the cap-

ital of the island, density exceeds 3,000 per square mile (1,158 per sq km).

Ethnically, Sri Lankans are mostly Sinhala, descendants of early migrants from north India who came to the island around the fifth century B.C. They speak

Silkworm cocoons are mounted on bamboo frames, part of a comprehensive sericulture program to create jobs and foreign exchange earnings from silk exports. (Photo: United Nations/ Saw Lwin.)

a language (also called Sinhala) that is derived from Sanskrit and is related to the Indo-European languages of north India. Sinhala was made the official language in 1961.

The Ceylon Tamils, the largest ethnic minority, are descendants of early Dravidian settlers from south India and speak Tamil. Although they live in all parts of the island, they are found in significant numbers only in the northern and eastern districts and in Colombo. The Ceylon Tamils must be distinguished from the large population of Indian Tamils, whose ancestors were brought in by the British in the nineteenth century to work on the tea estates as indentured laborers. Most Indian Tamils, who live mainly in the tea-growing areas, do not hold Sri Lankan citizenship.

The other major ethnic groups in the island are the Muslims, descendants of early Arab traders, and the Burghers, those of Portuguese and Dutch descent. In recent decades, the Burghers have emigrated from Sri Lanka in large numbers.

The dominant religion of Sri Lanka is Theravada Buddhism. Ever since its introduction in the third century B.C., Buddhism has influenced national affairs and has been the main cultural tradition. The majority of Sri Lankans are Buddhists, but Hinduism, Christianity (90% Roman Catholic), and Islam are well-represented.

Sri Lanka is a kin-oriented society, but there is no joint family system. The basic unit among the Sinhala is the nuclear family; marriage is generally arranged,

and a wife brings a dowry. In urban areas, there has been an erosion of family tradition and an increase in individual choice in marital selection.

Sri Lanka has always been a highly stratified society. Although the British did not deliberately disrupt the caste power structure, subsequent economic and social changes weakened traditional bases of power and prestige. The new economic opportunities offered by British rule, together with English education, led to a secular economic and occupational mobility independent of ritual (caste) status, and class superseded caste as the dominant mode of stratification.

Today the elite includes high-level bureaucrats, politicians, professionals, university dons, mercantile executives, western-type entrepreneurs, and trade union leaders. Members of the elite are mostly English-educated; they speak English and wear Western dress. Thus, they are clearly distinguishable from the masses (90 percent of the population) who are mainly peasants. Lower classes also include urban blue-collar workers, minor government and private-sector employees, and Indian workers in the tea estates. In the last two decades, a rural Sinhala- and Tamil-speaking intelligentsia has appeared. Buddhist monks, Ayurvedic physicians (practitioners of native medicine), and village schoolteachers are traditional members of this group. A newer element in the rural power structure includes entrepreneurs (merchants and moneylenders), officials of cooperative societies, and farmers who have become affluent thanks to the Green Revolution. These rural notables play an important role in maintaining the elite system. The national elites are dependent on the rural power groups, who are skilled as village-level political organizers. Although since 1944 free secondary education has given the peasantry some access to elite positions, the Sri Lankan elite is in fact mainly urban; upward mobility means moving from rural to urban society.

Sri Lanka's economy is largely rural and agricultural. Paddy (rice) is the main agricultural crop and the main source of employment. Since about 1960, peasant farming has been diversified to include subsidiary food crops, like onions, chilies, potatoes, cereals, and pulses. The principal export crops are tea, rubber, and coconuts. Tea and rubber are usually large-estate crops, while coconuts are cultivated in small holdings. These three crops (especially tea) provide the bulk of Sri Lanka's foreign exchange.

There are some manufacturing industries in urban areas, especially in and around Colombo, including textiles, ceramics, plywood, paper, and cement. Sri Lanka is well known for its precious and semiprecious stones, including rubies, sapphires, topazes, tourmalines, alexandrites, and cat's-eyes. The island has only recently begun to develop the export potential of its gems.

The growth of Sri Lanka's economy has been sluggish. During the 1960–1970 period, the increase of per capita real product was about 2 percent; in the 1971–1975 period, it fell to less than 2 percent. Since

Villagers tend the fields on a passion fruit plantation at a cooperative farm. This project is part of a government effort to introduce new cash crops. (Photo: United Nations/Saw Lwin.)

the end of the 1950s, Sri Lanka has experienced a continuous foreign exchange deficit. Heavily dependent on tea, rubber, and coconut for export earnings, Sri Lanka became dangerously vulnerable to price trends in the world market. The problem was compounded by the high cost of imported petroleum, rice, sugar and flour. Sri Lanka's response to the shortage of foreign exchange in the early 1960s was to cut imports drastically. This had the effect of running down the nation's capital stock and causing acute shortages of consumer goods.

The years 1976–1978 brought a much needed respite from further deterioration, due to an increase in the world price of tea. But this boom is likely to be only temporary; Sri Lanka needs to work out long-term strategies to diversify its economy, ending its dependence on a colonial-type plantation economy. Since 1965, the government has increasingly depended on foreign aid from individual nations and bodies like the International Monetary Fund (IMF).

In contrast to the performance of export crops, domestic agriculture has made considerable progress. Paddy is a smallholder's crop, and over 90 percent of the land is owned in units of less than 10 acres (4 ha). Thanks to new seeds and the greater use of fertilizer, rice production has increased significantly in the last two decades to make the nation nearly self-sufficient. The massive Mahaweli River irrigation project is expected to bring over 400,000 acres (161,900 ha) of new land under cultivation by 1983. Self-sufficiency in rice would provide Sri Lanka with significant savings in foreign-exchange payments.

In 1972, the Sri Lanka Freedom Party (SLFP) government introduced the first radical land reform in Sri Lanka, imposing a ceiling of 25 acres (10 ha) for paddy land and 50 acres (20 ha) for other lands per family. In 1975, all estate lands were nationalized, ending foreign ownership of the plantation sector. These reforms are consistent with socialist principles shared by all political parties in Sri Lanka.

The SLFP government followed a more explicitly socialist strategy utilizing land reforms, income ceilings, import and exchange controls, and cooperative undertakings. The focus of the current United National Party government is somewhat different. It has greatly liberalized imports and exchange controls, effecting a consumer boom unparalleled since the 1950s. In 1978, a free-trade zone was established in Greater Colombo. To attract foreign investment, incentives, such as tax holidays, concessionary import duties, and modern infrastructural facilities at low rents, are offered to potential investors to promote export-oriented industrial development and to provide new sources of employment.

When the Portuguese arrived in 1505, there were three independent kingdoms in Sri Lanka: the Sinhala kingdoms of Kotte and Kandy, and the Tamil kingdom of Jaffna in the north. By 1619, the Portuguese ruled all of Sri Lanka, excluding Kandy. Their lasting contribution was the introduction of Catholicism.

In 1658, the Dutch captured Sri Lanka, but the kings of Kandy once more defeated all attempts to capture their kingdom. The Dutch period introduced Roman Dutch Law and Protestant Christianity. Both the Portuguese and the Dutch also contributed to the ethnic mix, and their descendants are today's Burgher community.

The British took over the island in 1796; in 1802 the maritime provinces were declared a Crown Colony; and in 1815, Kandy also fell to the British. Unlike the Portuguese and Dutch, the British introduced fundamental and far-reaching changes. Among the many lasting consequences were the growth of modern education with the establishment of English schools; a unified administrative bureaucracy; constitutional government based on the parliamentary model; the development of a plantation economy; export-import commercial activity and consequent urbanization; and new types of employment and the growth of professions.

On February 4, 1948, Sri Lanka became an independent nation within the Commonwealth after nearly 450 years of Western rule, and on May 22, 1972, Sri Lanka became a republic. The first Prime Minister of independent Sri Lanka was D. S. Senanayake, the leader of the United National Party (UNP). The rule of this conservative, pro-Western, multiethnic coalition was interrupted by S.W.R.D. Bandaranaike's Sinhala nationalist, left-of-center Sri Lanka Freedom Party, which came to power in 1956. After Bandaranaike's assassination in September 1959, his widow, Sirimavo Bandaranaike, took control of the party. Sirimavo Bandaranaike became Prime Minister in July 1960, the world's first woman Prime Minister. The SLFP was defeated by the UNP in March, 1965, but Mrs. Bandaranaike regained

Children and adults pluck tea. Sri Lanka's chief export crops are tea, rubber, and coconuts. (Photo: ILO/J. Mohr/ Distributed by United Nations.)

power in May 1970, and continued as Prime Minister until the UNP's stunning victory in July 1977. Under a new constitution promulgated in 1978, J. R. Jayewardene became the nation's first President, with French-style executive powers.

Sri Lanka's parliamentary record has been impressive. Political power has alternated between the two major parties with regularity and without conflict or disorder, although all governments since independence have had to face difficult social and economic problems. At the political level, the language problem persists. The Tamil minority, demanding parity for the Tamil language, has been opposed by Sinhala nationalist politicians. The conflict led to two major clashes, in 1958 and in 1977. Tamil frustration has been vented in agitation for a separate state and terrorist attacks, and political radicalism has grown among the Sinhala population as well. In April 1971, an armed insurrection of youthful Che Guevarists was stifled only after the government received foreign military assistance. Economic stagnation has exacerbated interethnic tension and has generally promoted radicalism.

Despite an impressive drop in the population growth rate from over 2 percent annually in 1970 to 1.74 in 1975, Sri Lanka's population increases by 1 million every four years. At least half the population is less than 20 years old, and high school and university enrollment has soared in the last two decades. But a stagnant economy has failed to meet the demand for employment; the high unemployment rate is a major source of instability, especially since a significant proportion of those without jobs are young and relatively well-educated.

Although the island is the custodian of a great civilization, in terms of gross national product Sri Lanka is a poor country. Nonetheless, in terms of the physical quality of life, Sri Lanka ranks high in the Asian region and in the developing world as a whole. This is a reflection of Sri Lanka's emphasis on health, education, welfare services, and income redistribution.

Tissa Fernando

East Asia, Southeast Asia, and the Pacific

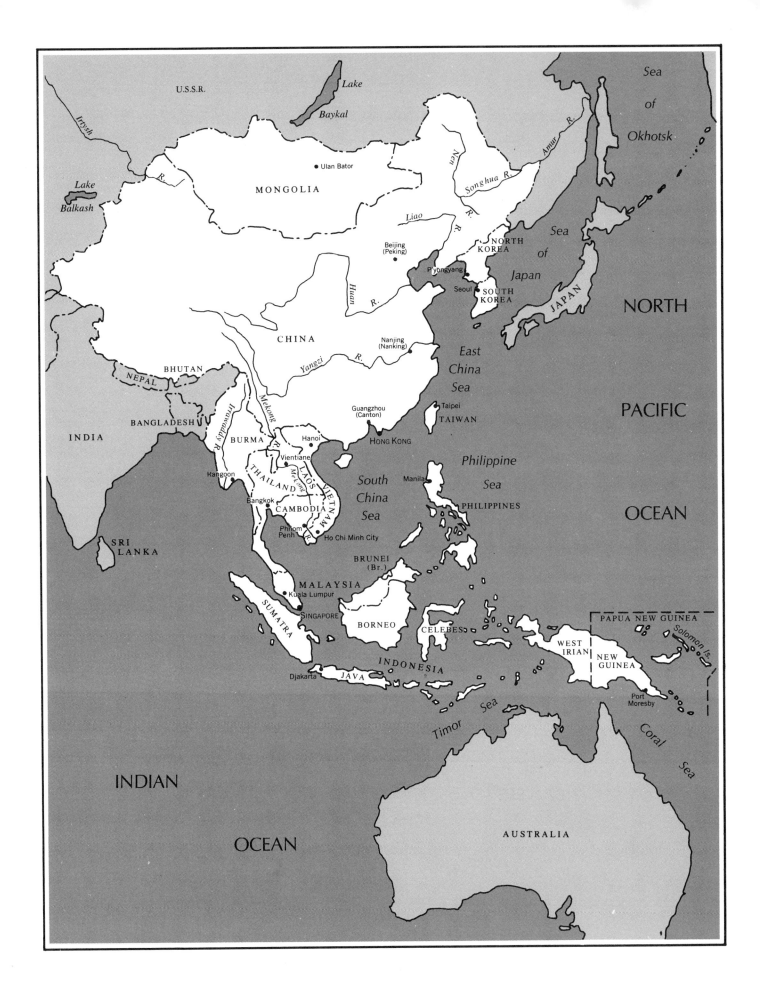

Burma

(Socialist Republic of the Union of Burma)

Area: 261,226 sq mi (676,577 sq km)
Population: 32 million
  Density: 122 per sq mi (47 per sq km)
  Growth rate: 2.2% (1970–1977)
Percent of population under 15 years of age: 40%
Infant deaths per 1,000 live births: 56.3
Life expectancy at birth: males 56.3 years; females 60.2 years
Leading causes of death: not available
Ethnic composition: Burman, Karen, Shan, Kachin, Chin, Arakanese
Languages: Burmese 80%
Literacy: 75%
Religions: Buddhist, Muslim, animist
Percent population urban: 25%
Percent population rural: 75%
Gross national product: $4.9 billion
  Per capita GNP: $150
  Per capita GNP growth rate: 1.3% (1970–1977)
Inflation rate: 15% (1970–1976)

Burma has been the most isolationist of all the Southeast Asian nations since World War II; it has avoided involvement in the major power conflicts, but it has also stagnated. A potentially prosperous country, thanks to its wet rice agriculture, teak, and mineral resources, Burma suffers from ethnic strife, scarcity of capital investment, poor transportation and communications, and autocratic and xenophobic political leadership.

Burma's social remoteness, even from its immediate neighbors, is a consequence of its location and topography. Situated at the head of the Bay of Bengal in the Indian Ocean, Burma has always been far from the major trade routes. Portuguese, Dutch, and Spanish traders and colonial conquerors established territorial presences in Southeast Asia 300 years before Britain's conquest of Burma in the nineteenth century.

Burma's land frontiers in the east, north, and west naturally separate it from its neighbors: Bangladesh, Laos, Thailand, and giant China and India. Not impenetrable, but a major obstacle to commerce and other types of peaceful interaction, most of this border territory is mountainous and forested. The chief exception is the northeast, where Burma and China meet; there the land is fairly flat, and population movement continues.

Although Burma's land and sea frontiers separate it from other peoples, they also give it a natural unity. Self-sufficient in rice and other food products, Burma has been able to satisfy most of its modest economic needs internally. Wet rice agriculture is the dominant economic activity in the hot delta and southern coastal regions, where most of the people live. The Rangoon delta has an average annual rainfall of 100 inches (254 cm), compared with more than 200 inches (508 cm) of rain in the southern coastal regions.

Most of the country has fairly predictable alternating wet and dry seasons, to which the farming system is geared. Rich in teak forests and several other resources (including petroleum, tin, tungsten, lead, and zinc), Burma has not developed its natural wealth to the same degree as other Southeast Asian lands—partly because of several insurrections involving ethnic minorities since independence in 1948. Burma's coastal waters contain a wide variety of fish, but this resource has not been developed.

The civil wars that have marred Burma's independence reflect the ethnic, linguistic, and general cultural diversity of the nation's inhabitants. All nationals of the country are called Burmese, but Burmans, the dominant ethnic grouping, comprise three-quarters of the population estimated at 34 million. The Burmans are concentrated along the central river corridor of the country, between the chief cities of Rangoon and Mandalay (which are linked by the important Irrawaddy River), and in the lower delta and coastal regions. This is about half of the national territory.

Most of Burma's indigenous minorities live in the other half of the country, bordering Bangladesh, India, China, Laos, and Thailand. There are 3.5 million Karen in the eastern part of the country. The Karen were favored by the British, but they (and other minorities) have been victims of discrimination at the hands of the Burman majority since independence.

There are nearly 2 million Shan in northeastern Burma, adjacent to Thailand and Laos. Part of a population movement out of southern China several centuries ago, the Shan are more closely related to the Thai and Lao than to the Burmans. The Kachin, who live in northern Burma, number 500,000 people, many of whom are recent migrants from China; they are indistinguishable from Kachin on the Chinese side of the frontier. The two most important ethnic minority insurrections of the 1970s (continuing into the 1980s) involved the Shan and Kachin.

Other, smaller ethnic groups have tried to avoid assimilation. The most important minorities in western Burma are the 250,000 Chin, who are related linguistically to the Burmans but identify with their ethnic kin in neighboring India, and the Muslim Arakanese, hundreds of thousands of whom fled into Bangladesh in 1978 because of alleged Burman religious persecution.

The economic development of Burma from the late nineteenth century through the Depression of the 1930s was largely the result of the efforts of large Indian and Chinese minorities. After independence, both these groups were the objects of public and private discrimination, and now there may be only 400,000 Chinese and 120,000 Indians in the country.

The Burmans are overwhelmingly Buddhist, though President Ne Win has sought to minimize the importance of Buddhism as an ideological rival to his official socialist doctrine. But Ne Win's anti-Buddhism has not reduced the Burman people's identification with their historic faith. Most Burmans are animists as well as Buddhists, believing, as the vast majority of non-Buddhists do, in a life-force that inhabits inanimate objects. In the west the minorities are Muslim. About 80 percent of the population speak Burmese, the national language, but in each minority group, most people cannot speak Burmese.

The family and Buddhism are the most important instruments of socialization and social control. However, personal morality, weakened by new patterns of acceptable behavior since the ruthless Japanese rule during World War II, declined further after General Ne Win proclaimed the "Burmese way to socialism" in 1962. Economic conditions were so harsh in the 1960s and 1970s that black marketeering, hoarding, and theft sometimes became necessary for survival.

There has been no revolution of the sexes in Burma comparable to the movement for women's liberation in the West, primarily because females have historically been the equals of males, as reflected in the fact that Burmese women do not take their husband's name, nor are Burmese children given family names. The traditional extended kinship system has survived the colonial rule, the wartime Japanese occupation, and the forced march to socialism, but it is sometimes the vehicle for the exploitation of younger and poorer relatives.

A farmer with his buffalo plows a wet rice field. Burma is self-sufficient in rice production, but the amount of rice available for export is declining. (Photo: United Nations.)

Burma's largely rural population is young. More than 40 percent of the population is less than 15 years old, a reflection of a 2.2 percent annual population growth rate and a life expectancy of 56.3 years for males and 60.2 years for females. About 75 percent of the population are literate; this figure is higher for Burmans and lower for various minorities. But many of the graduates of higher educational institutions cannot obtain employment commensurate with the level of education they possess. Socialism in Burma was not a reaction against the unequal distribution of wealth, because Burma has never experienced the dramatic extremes of rich and poor, nor the poverty found in India and China. Instead, Burmese socialism was directed against foreign ownership of the land and foreign control of the economy—particularly by the nonindigenous minorities. The Burmese believed that the Indians and the Chinese had a stranglehold on the economy on the eve of World War II.

Because there was no precolonial concentration of land, Burma traditionally had a classless society. The chief divisions were among the ethnic groups, some of which were not included in Burma until the British conquest of the country was completed in 1885. A gap also existed between a fairly small royal court and the general population. Traditional Burma was almost completely rural; the precolonial capital city of Mandalay was not large, and there were no other cities. Rangoon, the present capital, functioned as a British economic and government center; it did not increase markedly in size in the 1960s and 1970s like other major Southeast Asian cities, largely because of Burma's low rate of development. Rangoon has 2 million inhabitants today.

Following Burma's independence in 1948, the new government terminated all foreign ownership of land, primarily to end the control of the economically powerful Indians. The actual redistribution of land was delayed, however, because of several simultaneous civil wars and lack of preparation on the part of the new and inexperienced leaders of the country. In 1962, army leader General Ne Win, who is still ruling the country, seized control of the government and embarked on a second stage of nationalization. All remaining important economic activities were closed to foreigners, and many new sectors of the economy were taken over by the government.

Burma's economy today is no less socialist than that of the East European countries after which it was modeled. Mining, transportation, banking, manufacturing, and wholesale and retail trade are all government-operated, although there has been some slight modification permitting private activity in small and unimportant sectors of the economy. Rice remains the main agricultural crop, and farmers are required to sell their grain to the government at controlled prices.

Before World War II, Burma was the world's leading exporter of rice. Of all the Southeast Asian lands, it may have been the one most devastated by World War

II. Subsequently, ethnic minority and Communist rebellions impeded the restoration of agricultural production. Population growth, moreover, exceeded the rate of growth of agricultural output; the size of the Burmese population expanded at an annual rate of 2.2 percent between 1965 and 1975, while rice production remained largely stagnant. In 1962, when General Ne Win came to power, Burma had almost 23 million inhabitants; by 1978, it had an estimated 34 million. Domestic rice consumption increased about 50 percent during this 16-year period but was not matched by a comparable growth in production. Moreover, additional rice output resulted from an expansion in acreage and not from increased per acre yields. Rice is still Burma's single most important export, but a steadily declining percentage of the gross national production is available for export.

Inefficient, state-run "peoples' shops" and cooperatives are the main outlets for domestic goods. They have few goods to sell, the quality of their wares is inferior, and prices are too high. Only the ruling military elite can afford luxuries like automobiles; in the 1970s there was a far more extensive exchange of goods on the black market than in government shops. There were even estimates that illegal foreign trade across the borders with Thailand, India, and Bangladesh rivaled the level of legal international commerce. There were apparent improvements in the domestic economy after 1977, but Burmese-manufactured goods remained shoddy, the living standards were far below those of any other non-Communist Southeast Asian state, and economic inequalities between the ruling class and the ruled were greater than ever. The Ne Win government's policy of excluding outsiders, though modified slightly in the late 1970s, denies the country badly needed foreign investment, aid, and advice.

The Ne Win government has tried to improve the well-being of its predominantly rural population, although civil warfare and a persisting sense of Burman racial superiority have limited its efforts in the border regions. There has been progress in rural health and education. However, both the overall death rate and the infant mortality rate remain high: 10.4 per 1,000 per year and 56.3 per 1,000 live births, respectively. There are only 0.18 doctors for each 1,000 Burmese and only 0.71 hospital beds.

Transportation also remains undeveloped. Railroad and highway development is limited, and inland waterways—such as the Irrawaddy River, navigable for 900 miles (1,450 km)—play an important economic role. There are less than 4,000 miles (6,440 km) of all-weather roads and only 2,701 miles (4,350 km) of railroad track in a country with an area of 261,226 square miles (676,577 sq km). Motor vehicles of all kinds number less than 57,000 in a population of 34 million.

The nation's communications system is no better developed. Burma is one of the few countries in the world without television. There is a state radio broadcasting corporation, but programming is not offered throughout the day. There are 1.6 million radio receivers in the country and 32,881 telephones.

Burma's present problems are rooted in historical circumstances. The five centuries up to the mid-eighteenth century were characterized by constant warfare among the Burmans, other Burmese peoples, and the neighboring Thai. British unification was forced, as the years after independence demonstrated. Burma is still not an integrated nation, though colonial rule ended more than three decades ago.

For 50 years Britain ruled Burma as a neglected province of India. Indians, free to migrate to Burma, were the chief beneficiaries of British rule. Burma was usually denied the positive benefits of the British presence and direct access to the world beyond its shores. As a result, the Burmese remained more provincial and unskilled than most other peoples of Southeast Asia. Burma's leaders—U Nu and General Ne Win—feared that a loss of freedom would result from contact with foreign corporations and foreign states. In their view, Burma was not strong enough to deal with foreigners and should limit its contacts with other governments, multinational corporations and banks, and international agencies.

The government of President Ne Win nonetheless supports modernization. In 1974, 12 years after he toppled U Nu, Ne Win proclaimed a Socialist Republic of Burma and became its first President. The new political institutions provided the structure for what the soldier-politician had earlier called "the Burmese way to socialism." But Burma, which became an independent, parliamentary democracy in 1948, has always been ruled autocratically. Pre-British Burma had no indigenous tradition of consultative institutions. Colonial governance came from London, by way of India.

Burmese farmer uses traditional methods to irrigate a rice field to increase crop yields. (Photo: United Nations.)

Ne Win and his soldier-henchmen still rule Burma autocratically, through institutions that include a nominally elected People's Assembly and the single Communist-style Burma Socialist Program Party. New ideas are not encouraged, and criticism is stifled. Perhaps more than anything else, Burma needs open political and economic dialogue. Burma's leaders knew little about economic matters when they came to power, and they know little more today.

Burma is potentially wealthy, but it sorely needs foreign help. Its leadership, however, is xenophobic, and its ruling soldier class realizes that it could lose much of its relative wealth and near-absolute power should foreign aid—private or public—encourage the development of a new managerial and technical class.

There is another element, perhaps the controlling force: Burma is still a bitterly divided land. Most of its minorities are in revolt against the Burman-dom-inated central government; one-third of the national territory is in minority hands. There is no united national effort for development. Indeed, resources are wasted on senseless civil war. The central government is fearful, resistant to change, and politically domineering.

In addition, Burma sits precariously in the shadow of a resurgent China, a large and overpopulated India, an even more crowded and fiercely Muslim Bangladesh, a Vietnamese-dominated Laos, and a Thailand which has aided opponents of the Ne Win regime. Burma's leaders fear the foreign exploitation of their country's internal differences.

Burma is falling further and further behind its neighbors each year—in terms of national unity, economic development, and practical experience.

Richard Butwell

China

(People's Republic of China)

Area: 3,700,000 sq mi (9,583,000 sq km)
Population: 914 million (1978)
  Density: 247 per sq mi (95 per sq km)
  Growth rate: 1.6% (1970–1977)
Percent of population under 14 years of age: 33% (1975)
Infant deaths per 1,000 live births: not available
Life expectancy at birth: 60 years
Leading causes of death: not available
Ethnic composition: Han Chinese 95%
Languages: Mandarin, Cantonese
Literacy: more than 60%
Religions: atheist (official)
Percent population urban: 17%
Percent population rural: 83%
Gross national product: $424.6 billion
  Per capita GNP: $460 (estimate)
  Per capita GNP growth rate: 4.5% (1970–1977)
Inflation rate: not available

China and the United States resemble each other in two respects: they are about the same size [China is 3.7 million square miles (9.58 million sq km), slightly larger than the United States] and they are located in roughly the same latitudes, with approximately the same climatic variations. But there, for all practical purposes, the similarity ends. China's population is close to 1 billion, 4.5 times the population of the United States. Land suitable for agriculture represents at best 12 to 13 percent of China's total land area, compared with 25 percent of the land area of the United States.

Most Chinese farmland requires constant irrigation or drainage, making management of the water supply a matter of compelling importance for any government that intends to retain its legitimacy. An enormous population pressing on limited land resources is China's most intractable problem; at the same time, China's strength lies in its enormous human resources and its efficient government system.

China is ethnically compact; 95 percent of the people are of Chinese, or Han, stock. The population is still overwhelmingly rural; more than 80 percent of the people live and work in the countryside. Despite large strides over the last three decades, China's income level remains modest: the per capita gross national product is currently around $450, compared with $9,600 in the United States (or $6,400 in deflated 1972 dollars). The average industrial wage in China is believed to be $360 a year; in the United States it is nearly $13,500 for workers in manufacturing industries.

Almost one-fourth of all humans are Chinese. Although the rate of natural population increase in China is slower than the rate in many developing countries (probably about 1.5 percent a year, although the Chinese claim 1.2 percent for 1978), there are enormous absolute numbers involved. Every year, China must feed, clothe, and shelter an additional 12 to 15 million people, which means that in just over a decade (assuming current rates of increase), the equivalent of the entire 1980 population of the United States will be added to a limited area in China.

The demographic revolution began after 1949. There was a sharp decline in death rates because of improved disease control and diet, while the fertility rate remained high. As a result, the country's rate of population growth, once around 0.5 percent a year, quadrupled after 1949, and by 1978 the total population was roughly double the 1948 population. After some hesitation, the Chinese have come to recognize that a rapidly swelling population represents an obstacle to economic development in a country that has limited agricultural land and severe shortages of capital equipment. The government planned to bring down the population growth rate to 1 percent or less by 1980 and to 0.5 percent by 1985, through massive birth control education backed by administrative and legal pressures in favor of marriage postponement and family size limitation. The likelihood that the plan will succeed is very slim, given the youthful age structure of the population, the immensity of the undertaking, the vastness of the countryside and the traditional attitudes toward family size.

Besides sheer numbers, there is the problem of population distribution. About 95 percent of China's people live in the eastern half of the country, where there is level, rolling, and hilly terraced agricultural land and where soil and climatic conditions permit intensive farming. The 5 percent of the population that inhabit the topographically and climatically hostile western half of China [the mountains, plateaus, and arid regions of Xizang (Tibet), Xinjiang (Sinkiang), and Nei Monggol (Inner Mongolia)] are largely non-Han, belonging to some 50 national minorities that are ethnically, linguistically, and culturally distinct from the Han. These nationalities live in border areas [including the 4,000-mile (6,440-km long) stretch contiguous to the not-always-friendly Soviet Union] and often share religious beliefs and cultural traditions with similar peoples across the border. For this reason, China has always been sensitive out of all proportion to the nationalities problem. The bloody Tibetan revolt against the Han and against Chinese communism in 1959 sharpened the government's apprehension about minority loyalties and gave renewed impetus to Beijing's (Peking's) policy of settling the lands of minority nationals with people of Han stock. Carefully selected members of various nationalities have been trained in special institutes (the largest of which is located in Beijing), and on completion of their studies—in which political indoctrination plays a major role—they return to their native lands to serve as local officials.

The Han majority speaks several dialects of Chinese; most important is the northern dialect known as Mandarin. A national vernacular based on the Beijing pronunciation of Mandarin has been popularized since 1949 to strengthen the common bonds of culture and written language by establishing a single tongue, intelligible to people in every part of the country. In addition to the Beijing variety of Mandarin, now taught in all Chinese schools, there are several spoken Chinese languages south of the Chang Jiang (Yangtze River), among them Cantonese. The common written language is composed of several thousand characters or ideograms. Since the early 1950s many of the old characters (some of great complexity) have been simplified as part of the government's drive for universal literacy. Illiteracy, which afflicted as much as three-fourths of the population before 1949, has been drastically reduced, but it has not been altogether eliminated among some minority nationalities and the elderly. China's objective is to introduce universal education through the eighth grade by the year 1985.

As in other developing societies, the rising educational level of the population confronts the regime with the difficult task of finding appropriate employment for the educated youth, who prefer blue- and white-collar jobs in the cities to manual work in the still backward countryside. So far the solution has been authoritarian. Nearly 20 million educated young city dwellers have been sent to the countryside for what is intended to be permanent settlement.

The more or less forcible transfer of educated urban youths to often very remote villages (a movement known as *hsia hsiang*) has met with considerable passive and, lately, not so passive resistance from the displaced youngsters. The driving force behind the movement is the regime's desire to prevent the emergence of urban teenage unemployment (even with

Farmers terrace their land in Tachai, a model Chinese commune, to prevent devastation by floods and droughts. (Photo: United Nations/ A. Holcombe.)

migration to towns banned, the cities are not able to produce all the jobs needed to absorb their natural population growth) and to send muscle and talent where they are needed most—to the countryside—where they can be used for badly needed rural capital formation. Despite the policy of transfer, the unemployment rate in China's large and medium-sized cities at the end of 1978 was 7.4 percent of China's industrial labor force. The hsia hsiang movement, currently being reappraised, is part of a more general policy of allocating labor by administrative command rather than in response to wage differentials as is done in other socialist countries.

One of the results of this policy has been the slow growth of urban populations relative to total population, from about 13 percent in 1953 to not more than 17 percent at the present time. This is a phenomenon unique in the annals of economic development. Instead of bringing peasants to urban industry, simplified urban industry has been brought to the peasants under a strategy of labor-intensive, rural industrialization. Since the death of Chairman Mao Zedong (Mao Tse-tung), emphasis has shifted to more orthodox development strategies that involve the promotion of large, urban-based, technologically advanced, skill-intensive industries. A somewhat similar procedure was followed at an earlier stage in Communist China's development, during the Soviet-inspired interlude of 1952–1957.

Of the 170 million or so people who live in China's

Commuters ride home in Beijing during the rush hour, when bicycles and buses dominate the traffic. (Photo: United Nations/ A. Holcombe.)

urban areas, nearly 7 million live in Shanghai, the country's largest port and commercial industrial center, over 4 million live in Beijing, and another 3 million in nearby Tianjin (Tientsin). Of the more than 200 urban centers with populations exceeding 50,000 each, some 90 percent are located in the eastern half of China. Of the 16 cities with populations in excess of 1 million, only one—Guangzhou (Canton)—is situated south of the Chang Jiang. A sizable portion of the grain needed to feed the coastal and near-coastal cities is imported by sea from North America and Australia, but most larger cities are self-sufficient in vegetables, which are grown on specialized suburban farms.

The staple food in the north is wheat; in the south, rice. In the cities, all grains are rationed, as are cooking oil, soy sauce, cotton fabrics, and housing. Other items (e.g., meat) are rationed occasionally as the supply situation requires. Peasants working on cooperative farms known as rural people's communes are guaranteed a minimum annual ration of grain per household.

Peasant earnings, however, are well below those of urban workers. On the poorer communes, which constitute most of the country's communes and on which perhaps as many as 800 million people make their living, the average yearly income from collective work (i.e., excluding earnings from subsidiary activities and work on the rural household's private plot) is probably less than $75 per head, or roughly 20 cents a day. The pooling of household earnings, the addition of income from private plot production (most of the 300 million pigs in China are privately owned and raised by households on small plots allocated to each rural family by the collective), and the low, officially controlled prices for bedrock necessities enable most rural households to make ends meet. While there appears to be little destitution, living standards in China's countryside remain extremely primitive. Because of rapid population expansion, grain availability per head in 1978 was about the same as in 1957, despite a more than 50 percent increase in domestic grain output.

Before the establishment of the People's Republic by the victorious Communist forces in 1949 (following intermittent civil war that raged for more than 20 years), China's spiritual sustenance consisted of a combination of Confucian ethics, Buddhism, and Taoism. Religious observance is de facto not permitted in contemporary China. To conserve land and help uproot ancestor worship practices dating back thousands of years, burial grounds have been plowed up; the officially preferred (and hence followed) method of disposing human remains is cremation.

The family unit remains a significant force as a provider of labor and a milieu within coming generations are reared, but in modern China the family is subject to strong pressures from the state and the Communist Party machines. While the regime acknowledges the usefulness, indeed, the indispensability, of the family as a biological unit, a supplier of labor, and a baby-sitter, it does not view the family as a legitimate basic social organization. Actions not consonant with the interests of the party, the state, and the official ethic of Marxism-Leninism–modified Mao Zedong Thought—the official "line"—cannot be justified on the grounds of having been taken with the private family interests in mind.

Legitimate grass roots social units in contemporary China start at the level of the block or street committee in the cities (directed and supervised by an appropriate organ of the Communist Party) and of the production team in the countryside. (A production team is roughly, although not invariably, equivalent to the old village community.)

At all times, the proletarian class interest, as defined in the currently promulgated line, overrides the family bond. Deviations from this norm are corrected through organized peer group pressure, which may range from educational "heart-to-heart chats" to psychological violence, known as the struggle session (or struggle–public criticism–self-criticism–transformation). Although less prominent than they were in Stalin's Russia, cruder physical means of eliciting compliance have not been unknown in the People's Republic. In today's China, the individual human being is vulnerable and is not allowed to find refuge even in silence.

Much headway has been made in providing basic public health and medical services. Most of the old killer diseases, like cholera, smallpox, and schistosomiasis, have been brought under control, while newer maladies, especially cancer, have moved to the top of the list. A cooperative medical service has been established in the countryside and is staffed by several million public health workers, paramedics (called "barefoot doctors"), practitioners of traditional Chinese medicine, and doctors trained in Western medicine. For a small yearly membership fee (1 yuan, or about 60 cents), everyone—with the exception of those people designated as class enemies—can be insured and, through a system of upward referrals, is cared for in the event of illness. The system's network of paramedics and public health workers has also been used to promote birth planning.

Since 1949, the land has seen the world's largest and most intensive melioration effort. Every year, especially during the slack farming season, hundreds of millions of people are mobilized to dig irrigation channels, drainage ditches, and reservoirs; level and terrace fields; build roads, railroads, and canals; plant millions of trees; drain marshlands; construct rural workshops, factories, storage facilities, and residential housing; and generally transform the face of the earth. To compensate for the niggardliness of nature, double and triple cropping and intercropping are widely practiced on improved land, and manure is increasingly supplemented by chemical fertilizer, much of it produced locally in small and medium-sized factories. Improved strains of rice and other

crops are being introduced; irrigation has been extended to about half the cultivated area, and the destructive effects of flooding have been significantly reduced.

In a remarkable application of abundant manpower, tens of thousands of people are watching the Huang (Yellow) River in its lower reaches, round the clock, for any breaches in the dikes. As soon as signs of damage to the dikes are spotted, hundreds of thousands of people are notified and instantly mobilized by communes and counties along the river's banks and thrown into battle against the mighty river that for centuries was known as "China's Sorrow."

But not every program has been constructive. The one-sided emphasis on growing more food grains and the repeated mass campaigns to which the peasants have been subjected over the years have caused much destruction. While the tree-planting program was going forward, vast areas of forest were hacked down to make way for fields. In Yunnan, for example, over 1,037,400 acres (420,000 ha) of rare tropical forests were burned to create poor cultivable land. In Heilongjiang (Heilungkiang), the forest area has been reduced by 16.55 million acres (6.7 million ha) in the last 20 years, that is, by some 30 to 40 percent, compared with the mid- to late 1950s. In Nei Monggol, plowing up grasslands has turned 9.88 million acres (4 million ha) of good pastureland into desert, while some 19.76 million acres (8 million ha) of pastures have been invaded by sand. An investigation carried out in the Sanjiang (Sankiang) Plain in Heilongjiang

Shoppers examine the fish for sale in a food market in Shanghai. Most vegetables and fruits are sent in to the city from surrounding communes. (Photo: United Nations/A. Holcombe.)

province revealed that the organic content of the soil there is declining at the rate of 4 to 6.6 percent a year because of indiscriminate lumbering and damage done to the ecological balance.

Silting of reservoirs in the Huang River basin continues, despite 30 years of efforts to control it. The antisilting effort has been partly undone by the thoughtless turning of forests into tillage and the consequent enhanced erosion of the soil. Many lakes have been reduced in size or turned into cultivated land. In Hubei (Hupeh) province, there were 1,056 lakes in 1949, each with a surface of 164.5 acres (66.6 ha); today, only 500 of these lakes are left. As a result (according to the *People's Daily*), the quantity of fish now being caught does not reach the level of 20 years ago, and the total amount of aquatic produce from natural sources is about half what it was in 1954. "Cultivating the land on orders from above can be very dangerous," reflects the Beijing paper *Guangming Ribao* (December 30, 1978).

Although the mechanization of agriculture has made some progress, most farm work continues to be done by hand. China's leadership, headed by Communist Party Chairman Hua Guofeng (Hua Kuo-feng) and Deputy Chairman Deng Xiaoping (Teng Hsiao-p'ing) set itself the objective of agricultural modernization through the mechanization of major farm processes and through chemicalization. These modern additions to the production process are integrated into the traditional methods; for example, the increased use of pesticides is combined with biological pest control. Ingenious ways of using all kinds of

Workers in Shanxi Province store a harvest of corn. (Photo: United Nations A. Holcombe.)

wastes for constructive ends are employed in almost every field, and for long the impression was given that very little, if anything, was ever thrown away in China. But things are not always what they seem. In May 1979, *Guangming Ribao* revealed that in Heilongjiang province 70 percent of the night soil was simply thrown away.

The Herculean effort in agriculture has resulted in a growth of agricultural output of more than 2 percent a year over the period 1952–1978, just marginally ahead of the growth of population. The problem of feeding the largest mass of humanity in the history of mankind continues to cast its shadow over China. New trouble is looming: diminishing returns to labor are setting in, yet it takes ever larger additions of labor to produce steady increases in farm output. That is why the current leadership so urgently stresses modernization, the application of up-to-date science and technology.

While China is still an agricultural country, industry has moved ahead rapidly in the last 30 years. Between 1952 and 1978, industrial production grew on the average about 10 percent per year, with machinery output growing fastest and consumer goods production lagging behind. Since the early 1960s, China has pursued a policy of balance between very modern and semitraditional industrial (and other) technology. The policy known as "walking on two legs" consists of upgrading old ways of going about production, transport, construction, and so on, at very little cost. For example, cart wheels are fitted with rubber tires, making the job of pulling the cart easier. Then, perhaps, a small, locally made motor is attached to the cart, making the conveyance self-propelled.

Everywhere in China, there is evidence of this kind of intermediate technology. The vast sector of rural industries that includes the manufacture of cement, chemical fertilizer, and clothing, the generation of electricity, and the mining of coal, iron ore, and other local deposits rests on precisely this sort of comparatively labor-intensive use of rather simple techniques. However, current modernization plans stretching forward to 1985 and the year 2000 shift the emphasis toward ultramodern, capital-intensive technology, since in industry—as in agriculture—the time has apparently come to make the transition from growth through increased application of production factors to growth through increases in factor productivity. The current drive, which involves large and very expensive imports of industrial and other equipment and know-how from the West and Japan, is known as the "four modernizations": modernization of industry, agriculture, science and technology, and the armed forces. The cost of the project runs into tens of billions of dollars, and the Chinese hope to settle at least part of the bill with revenues from oil sales abroad. Significant oil deposits have been found both inland and offshore. To reach offshore oil, large investment in exploration and development equipment and know-how is required, much of which is available only in the United States, Japan, and West Europe.

China has large deposits of coal, especially in Shanxi (Shansi), Shaanxi (Shensi), Henan (Honan), Nei Monggol, and Ningxia (Ningsia), and the coal is of good quality. In the years to come, coal production, which in 1978 stood at 618 million tons (560 million t), is to play a leading role in supplying Chinese industry with sources of primary power. The major problems are raising the efficiency of the country's coal mines and improving the transportation of coal from the coal-rich north to the coal-deficient south. (Transportation remains a bottleneck in the economy.) At present, coal is used wastefully by both the electric power and the steel industries. While in Japan it takes 1,764 pounds (800 kg) of coal to produce 1 ton (0.9 t) of steel, in China it takes 2.6 tons (2.3 t) of coal to turn out 1 ton (0.9 t) of steel. According to the *People's Daily* (May 27, 1979), "Because of improper management, some 200–300 million kwh of electricity and tens of millions of tons of coal are annually wasted."

The social, political, and economic institutions of the People's Republic of China are drawn from Soviet blueprints. However, far-reaching modifications reflect the specific cultural and historical conditions of China and the policy struggles within the Communist leadership. There are two institutional pyramids: the monopolistic Communist Party of China and, overlapping it at every hierarchical level, the structure of government. At the top of the party pyramid is the Politburo; at the bottom, all the party branches of rural production brigades or of city neighborhoods. The topmost government organ is the Council of State; the lowest organ of government in the countryside is the rural people's commune. For farming and water conservation purposes, the commune is subdivided into production brigades and production teams (the teams are actual farming and income-distribution units). The economy is centrally planned, and the plans are mandatory; but there is considerable decentralization at the provincial level.

Since the founding of the People's Republic in October 1949, after the defeat of Nationalist forces led by Jiang Gaishek (Chiang Kai-shek) (whose armies' remnants retreated to the island of Taiwan), the economic history of China went through several phases that reflected, by and large, policy swings in the party and the government. Following a period of reconstruction (1949–1952), during which most industrial and commercial property was socialized, central planning based on the Soviet model—with stress on heavy industry—was inaugurated in 1953. With Soviet assistance, a modern industrial infrastructure was laid between 1953 and 1957 (the first 5-year plan). Then,

in 1958, Mao Zedong launched the "Great Leap Forward," an epic assault on the development problem. Hundreds of millions of people were mobilized to surpass production in Britain and other West European countries in 15 years or less. During this brief interlude (1958–1960), farms that had been collectivized in 1955 were transformed into huge rural organizations called people's communes. During a 3-year economic depression that followed the leap (1960–1962) and until 1966, a series of pragmatic policies were implemented under the leadership of China's head of state Liu Shaoqi (Liu Shao-ch'i) and Premier Zhou Enlai (Chou En-lai).

Under these leaders, the economy progressed solidly if not spectacularly. Then, in 1966, Mao Zedong launched still another frontal assault, this time on what he regarded as Soviet-type revisionism that had taken over China's Communist leadership. The assault known as the Cultural Revolution wreaked havoc with the country's political, social, and economic institutions, inflicting particularly severe damage on higher education, science, and the arts. By 1970, the Cultural Revolution, which had unleashed quasi-anarchic forces in China's society, had been brought under control by the People's Liberation Army. A period of bitter intraparty struggle followed, culminating after the death of Mao Zedong (in September 1976) in the arrest and disgrace of the leftist (or radical) faction within the leadership—the Gang of Four—and the eventual emergence of the leadership under Hua Guofeng, Deng Xiaoping, and Zhao Ziyang, who replaced Deng Xiaoping as First Deputy Prime Minister in 1980.

China is currently engaged in a long-term modernization program that has so far meant discarding much that was central to Mao Zedong's thought and his version of Marxism-Leninism. While still mentioned, the virtues of self-reliance, egalitarianism, moral incentives, and peasant innovation are no longer of pivotal importance. Instead, the accent is on trade, professional expertise, differentiated material incentives, and top-notch scientific talent.

Despite the size and complexity of the problems facing China's long march toward modernization and toward a higher and less precarious standard of living, there is reason for optimism. A positive assessment of China's chances rests on its 30-year record of ministering (with a fair degree of success) to the world's largest population; the demonstrated organization ability of the regime; and the assiduousness, application, and inventiveness of the people, who, perhaps more than any other human beings, are quick to learn from past mistakes and to transform weakness into strength.

Jan Prybyla

Hong Kong

Area: 401 sq mi (1,039 sq km)
Population: 4.6 million
  Density: 11,471 per sq mi (4,428 per sq km)
  Growth rate: 2.0% (1970–1977)
Percent of population under 14 years of age: 31 (1975)
Infant deaths per 1,000 live births: 15 (1975)
Life expectancy at birth: males 67.36 years; females 75.01 years
Leading causes of death: not available
Ethnic composition: Chinese 99%
Languages: English (official); Chinese 99%
Literacy: 92%
Religions: Buddhist, Taoist, Christian (small minority)
Percent population urban: 92%
Percent population rural: 8%
Gross national product: $14.05 billion
  Per capita GNP: $2,620
  Per capita growth rate: 5.8% (1970–1977)
Inflation rate: not available

The British Crown Colony of Hong Kong, a teeming, thriving capitalist enclave on the southern coast of China, is by any standard one of the world's most exotic places. The capital of Hong Kong is Victoria (also called Hong Kong). Formerly a retreat for smugglers and pirates, it has become in modern times one of the world's greatest harbors and entrepôts. Hong Kong's strategic location and excellent natural harbor—the only really good harbor between Shanghai and Singapore—have made the colony a gateway between East and West.

One-tenth the size of Kentucky, the crowded colony holds 4.5 million people. Hong Kong city (Victoria) is the most highly urbanized city in the world.

Workers build junks on the island of Cheung Chau. In Hong Kong harbor, thousands of people live on junks in the harbor because living space is so scarce and expensive. (Photo: Hong Kong Tourist Association.)

People live literally on top of one another, for Hong Kong is a land of high-rise apartments. But there still is not enough room. Many people, forced off the land, live on the water in a variety of houseboats. Some have no homes and live in the streets. Most of the people are Chinese (99 percent), but there are also some Americans, Europeans, and other Asians, all under British rule.

The colony of Hong Kong consists of Hong Kong Island [32 square miles (83 sq km)], Kowloon Peninsula and Stonecutters Island (Ngong Shuen Chau) [3.75 square miles (9.71 sq km)], and the New Territories [365 square miles (945 sq km)], consisting of a mainland area adjoining Kowloon and 235 adjacent islands). Hong Kong Island, located at the mouth of the Canton or Pearl River and some 90 miles (145 km) southeast of Canton, is about 11 miles (18 km) long from east to west and varies in width from 2 to 5 miles (3 to 8 km). The island is separated from the mainland by the Lyemun Pass. Hong Kong city extends for several miles along the north shore of the island.

Hong Kong is located in the tropics but its climate is subtropical. The monsoon that prevails from May to August brings warm moist air from the south and southwest, and the annual temperature range varies from 59°F (15°C) in February to a high of 82°F (28°C) in July. Annual average temperature is 72°F (22°C). Although summer is the rainy season, much of the precipitation accompanies the typhoons, which are usually most severe in the fall.

Hong Kong has many mountains and little level land. Victoria Peak on Hong Kong Island reaches an elevation of 1,817 feet (554 m). Lantau Peak on Lantau Island and Tai Mo Shan (shan is Chinese for "mountain") in the New Territories exceed 3,000 feet (914 m). Another half dozen peaks exceed 1,500 feet (457 m). There is little room for agriculture, although the climate ensures year-round greenery and permits double-cropping. Rice, sugarcane, and vegetables are grown where space permits, primarily in the New Territories. In spite of the abundant rainfall, population pressure on Hong Kong Island creates a shortage of fresh water, much of which must be brought from the mainland. The greenery of the countryside, the blueness of the sea, and the marvelous beaches make Hong Kong one of the world's most scenic locations.

The most impressive aspect of Hong Kong is the variety of people. There are millions of them—Chinese, English, Japanese, Americans, Malays, Indians, other Europeans and other Asians, Muslims, Buddhists, and Christians—all living in harmony and constantly on the move. Hong Kong is a beehive of activity. Ships, planes, and trains are constantly arriving or departing. Factories operate night and day;

some shops never close and housing is so scarce that in poorer sections people sleep in shifts. Near Aberdeen one may see the Shiu Sheung Yan, the "waterborne people," more than 20,000 living on junks and sampans. The figure was once far higher but in recent years manufacturing industries and new housing have lured the people ashore. The official language of Hong Kong is English, but Chinese (Cantonese or Mandarin) is spoken by 99 percent of the population.

The characteristic social structure in Hong Kong is the traditional Chinese family group, with the oldest man the most influential and the new wife of the youngest son the least influential. Some marriages are still arranged by the families, but there is a trend to let young people make their own marital choices. A class structure is recognized, and persons seldom marry outside their class. Children are prized; they play a large role in the Chinese family and in many cases provide the only old-age security for their parents. Women have fewer privileges than they have in Western society.

Immigrants and refugees, many of them illegal, create a continuing problem. In the first 5 months of 1978, it was estimated that 23,500 legal and 6,500 illegal immigrants, excluding those arrested and repatriated, had arrived in Hong Kong. Immigrants add to the problem of overcrowding, increasing the demands on educational and medical facilities and on programs for public assistance.

Demographic statistics show that Hong Kong has one of the most modern societies of Asia. The birthrate is slightly higher than that of the United States but the infant mortality and death rates are lower. The divorce rate among the Chinese residents is low, while life expectancy from the time of birth—probably the best overall indicator of the standard of living—is second only to Japan among Asian countries. Life expectancy for women is 75.01 years in Hong Kong, 76.5 years in the United States, and 72.15 years in Japan. For men, life expectancy is 67.36 years in Hong Kong, 68.7 years in the United States, and 72.15 years in Japan. Because there are many more male than female immigrants (many illegal) coming into Hong Kong, males outnumber females in all age groups below 60 years. This is particularly evident in the 15- to 35-year age group.

A major problem for Hong Kong officials is the daily supply of food, 85 percent of which must be imported, much of it from mainland China. Each day, the people of the colony consume 6,000 pigs, 100,000 chickens, 1,100 tons (1,000 t) of rice, 1,320 tons (1,200 t) of vegetables, and 330 tons (300 t) of fish.

Compared to most Asian countries, Hong Kong has good medical and health care facilities, but they are mediocre by American or European standards. Population per physician is more than twice that of the United States (1,517 versus 622). Population per hospital bed averages 241 in Hong Kong and 152 in the United States. Dentists, nurses, and medical technicians are also in short supply.

Until recently education in Hong Kong was neither compulsory nor free. In spite of this, 92 percent of all adults are literate. The colony has three colleges, two universities, and a technical institute, and all schools are required to register with the Department of Education. Hong Kong has four types of elementary and secondary schools: private schools, government-subsidized schools, grant schools maintained by missionary organizations, and government-staffed and operated schools.

The University of Hong Kong, established in 1912, has colleges of arts, medicine, and engineering. In recent years, the Department of Education has extended aid to schools at all levels. In 1978, college-level students numbered 65,781; secondary, 488,044; and primary, 591,267. Plans have been made for the construction of new school facilities and for expanding the enrollment of the two universities. However, progress has been hampered by scandals in the administration of educational funds.

From the 1840s to the 1950s (except for the Japanese occupation of 1942–1945) Hong Kong was primarily an entrepôt for trade between China and the West. During the Korean war, much of the trade with China was cut off, and Hong Kong turned to manufacturing. Now manufactured goods comprise 93 percent of exports. Manufactured products include textiles and garments, yarn, cement, cigarettes, processed meat, beer, batteries, a variety of electrical products, jewelry, and other consumer goods.

Inflation appears to be under control and the econ-

In crowded Hong Kong, Nathan Road in Kowloon teems with people, traffic, and neon signs. (Photo: Hong Kong Tourist Association/ Ray Cranbourne.)

omy is relatively stable. The labor force includes approximately 2 million persons: 39 percent in commerce and services, 44 percent in manufacturing, 2 percent in agriculture and fishing, 7 percent in construction, 6 percent in government, and 2 percent in other occupations. Hong Kong has small deposits of iron ore and tungsten, but mining produces only 0.1 percent of the gross domestic product while manufacturing accounts for 26 percent, services 59 percent, and agriculture 1 percent.

Tourism plays a large role in the economy, and Hong Kong tourist facilities are among the world's best. The tourist's Hong Kong is Nathan Road in Kowloon and the shopping arcades of Victoria. Hong Kong is a free port, and one can buy watches, cameras, fine silks, pearls, jade, ivory, and woolen cloth cheaper there than anywhere else. The restaurants of Hong Kong boast the best of Chinese dishes, and the hotels provide every possible luxury. A modern airport and harbor, buses, streetcars, and cable cars make travel easy. Hong Kong's most famous tourist ride is the tram ride to the top of Victoria Peak, which takes about 10 minutes and offers a spectacular view of the city.

Before 1840, Hong Kong was a small fishing community, a haven for pirates and smugglers. At the

At the Taipo outdoor market in the rural New Territories of Hong Kong, there is an abundance of fresh vegetables and meats for local consumption. (Photo: Hong Kong Tourist Association/ Ray Cranbourne.)

time of the First Opium War between Great Britain and China, the British used Hong Kong as a naval base. At the end of the war in 1842, the island was ceded to the British by the Treaty of Nanking. After the Second Opium War, 18 years later, the British gained Kowloon and Stonecutters Island. Other islands and the New Territories, all part of the Crown Colony, were obtained later. In 1898, Britain took control of the New Territories under a 99-year lease from China. Thus, most of the land area of the colony is scheduled to revert to China in 1997. The New Territories account for 90 percent of Hong Kong's land, and 25 percent of the population lives there. Hong Kong lives in Peking's political shadow, and the future of the colony is dependent on what happens when the lease expires.

The present governor of Hong Kong is Sir Crawford Murray MacLehose. In office since 1971, he is popular and was the first governor of Hong Kong to be invited to China's national day celebrations. Various pressure groups have intensified their criticism of the government in recent years. The government, like most colonial governments, is not representative. Major decisions are made by the governor with the consent of the Queen of England. Complaints that government officials do not communicate with the common people and that decisions are based on advice from an elite group of businessmen and bureaucrats are not uncommon. This could become a major obstacle to development in the future.

Communist China has an ambivalent relationship with Hong Kong. On the one hand, the Chinese consider British control of the colony illegal and unacceptable; on the other hand, Hong Kong is China's window to the world. Hong Kong plays an important role in China's new drive for economic progress. The colony is a busy financial and manufacturing center. It is a source of hard currency and business expertise for the Chinese, who are learning modern business methods from the colony. Communist China has more than 50 state-controlled corporations in Hong Kong. They serve as training schools for working-level officials who usually stay in Hong Kong for 6 months to 2 years and then return to high-level jobs in mainland China. The Bank of China on Queen's Road Central has huge portraits of Chairman Mao Zedong and Hua Guofeng but most of its activities are indistinguishable from those of capitalist banks. China has invested heavily in capitalistic projects that include apartment houses, shopping centers, department stores, gas stations, and office buildings; Chinese executives are learning every facet of the hotel business, international banking, and containerized shipping.

It seems unlikely that China will want to alter the status quo when the British lease expires in 1997. Hong Kong is dependent on China and China needs Hong Kong. Its colonial status may change, but it is probable that Hong Kong will continue to be China's outlet to the West. Hong Kong can never be a viable independent nation because it lacks the necessary resource base. However, if its population level can be controlled, it will continue to be the easiest place on earth to do business. The U.S. Consulate General on Garden Road is the world's largest consulate: more than 450 U.S. firms are doing business in Hong Kong.

Many Hong Kong natives want Hong Kong to become a free city, controlled by neither the British nor the Chinese. Nonetheless, for the time being Hong Kong is prospering as a British Crown Colony.

W. A. Bladen

Indonesia
(Republic of Indonesia)

Area: 736,000 sq mi (1,906,240 sq km)
Population: 136 million
  Density: 185 per sq mi (71 per sq km)
  Growth rate: 1.8% (1970–1977)
Percent of population under 14 years of age: 44% (1975)
Infant deaths per 1,000 live births: 115 (1975 est.)
Life expectancy at birth: 48 years (1975)
Leading causes of death: not available
Ethnic composition: Javanese, Sundanese, other
Languages: Bahasa Indonesia
Literacy: 62% (1975)
Religions: Muslim 90%
Percent population urban: 17.4%
Percent population rural: 82.6%
Gross national product: $48.8 billion
  Per capita GNP income: $360
  Per capita GNP growth rate: 5.7% (1970–1977)
Inflation rate: 6.69% (1978); 29.5% (Jan.–June, 1979)

Indonesia, the largest by far of the nations of Southeast Asia and one of the world's most populous nations, has long been regarded as a land of vast, untapped wealth. This notion of abundant resources is not altogether false; Indonesia is a major oil exporting state and produces considerable timber, palm oil, rubber, coffee, tin and other metals, spices, and other commodities for world trade. Some of these resources, most notably oil, are exhaustible, however, and all require careful management. Moreover, their exploitation provides employment and income for only a small fraction of the Indonesian population.

The vast majority of the population are small-holding or landless farmers operating on the margin of subsistence. Particularly in Java, the massive agrarian sector is faced with scarce and dwindling supplies of food and employment. Java's population will approach 100 million in the late 1980s; in combination with the region's vulnerability to such natural disasters as drought, earthquake, and volcanic eruption, this population will test severely the legendary adaptability, social stability, and even the national unity of the Indonesian people.

A sense of national unity is noteworthy in view of the nation's geographic diversity. The distance from northern Sumatra to the farthest point in Irian Jaya (West New Guinea) is more than 3,300 miles (5,313 km), an expanse which encompasses more than 3,000

additional islands that comprise the Republic of Indonesia. The Indonesian term for homeland is *Tanah Air*, which translates literally as "earth and water," recognizing the archipelagic character of the nation. Because the seas of the region are relatively shallow and calm, they link as well as separate the islands and foster hundreds of fishing communities, although large-scale commercial fishing and maritime activity in general is far less extensive than the country's geography would indicate.

Indonesia's tropical climate generally provides warm temperatures and substantial rainfall. Straddling the equator and harboring dozens of volcanoes that have deposited fertile ash and lava, Indonesia includes large areas of land well suited to rice cultivation. Indeed, rice farming, both wet and dry, is the most characteristic mode of human adaptation to the country's geography and climate. Other forms of farming are less common and, except for plantations, are generally practiced only where soil quality or water supply are inadequate to sustain rice. Plantation agriculture, including the production of rubber,

Workers dig out and deepen the cut of the Tarum Timor Canal in West Java; Indonesia's expanded irrigation systems make land more productive. (Photo: IDA/Tomas Sennett.)

Far Right: Workers repair a secondary canal that carries irrigation water to the fields in West Java; every inch of ground is needed for growing food. (Photo: IDA/Tomas Sennett.)

coffee, tea, sugar, and palm oil, was established during the long period of Dutch colonialism that ended with World War II; agriculture remains an important sector of the economy. In more recent years, Indonesia has enjoyed a harvest of hardwoods from the forests that cover well over 50 percent of its territory.

The natural resource most vital to Indonesia's national economy is petroleum. The first successful oil well was drilled in Sumatra in 1883; today, oil revenues account for more than half the government's income. In the future, however, it is likely that oil surpluses and earnings will steadily diminish; the consequent economic loss will be offset only partially and temporarily by Indonesia's recently acquired capacity to produce and export liquid natural gas. Other mineral resources are important. Indonesia ranks third among tin producing nations and has significant deposits of nickel, coal, iron ore, bauxite, copper, and manganese; but these resources are supplements to petroleum as earners of foreign exchange.

The nation's human resources are also rich and geographically diverse, with some 140 million people divided into dozens of ethnic groups. The regional, cultural, religious, and linguistic variations of the population are reflected in the national motto, "unity through diversity." Most major ethnic groups are descendants of the same Malay ethnic stock; no single group constitutes a majority of the population (although the Javanese, with over 45 percent of the total,

Women harvest rice in West Java. The fields are irrigated by the Tarum Timor Canal, a project that has expanded Indonesia's irrigated fields. (Photo: IDA/Tomas Sennett.)

have a reputation for imperialism that sets them apart from the other ethnic groups). Islam, the preferred religion of 90 percent of all Indonesians, links all but three or four small ethnic communities, and the Indonesian language, consciously adopted as a vehicle for nationalism in the late 1920s, has been a powerful integrative force. Bahasa Indonesia, as it is called, has not displaced the many dialects specific to various regions; but, like the "market Malay" from which it was derived, it has been readily adopted as a national language.

The Javanese live in the eastern two-thirds of the island of Java, and the western third is the home territory of the Sundanese, the second most populous ethnic group. Java ranks fifth in size among Indonesia's islands and, combined with the small island of Madura, has slightly less area than the state of North Carolina. Yet Java's population is over 80 million, making it one of the mostly densely populated areas in the world. In comparison, the other islands, which comprise 93 percent of Indonesia's territory, are inhabited by no more than 60 million people.

For years, the government of Indonesia has tried to reduce the effects of uneven population distribution by encouraging transmigration of people from Java to other islands. In recent years, as many as 50,000 peo-

*Far Left:
Women pluck tea in
West Java; tea is
one of Indonesia's
main crops.
(Photo: IDA/
Tomas Sennett.)*

ple have been relocated annually. However, authorities responsible for transmigration apparently have conceded that the program can have little direct impact on Java, where the natural population growth amounts to well over 1 million a year. They are nevertheless hopeful that a new emphasis on the development of potentially productive territories, particularly in Sumatra, will yield long-term economic and social benefits.

Transmigration will give the migrants an opportunity to use technologically more advanced agricultural methods than prevail in the intensively farmed countryside of Java and Bali. And assuming that each migrant is given a parcel of land adequate to produce crops that exceed his family's needs, he will be better off than his typical counterpart on Java or Bali, where most rural residents own plots of less than 1.23 acres (0.5 ha) or no land at all.

Even though Indonesia's agricultural land has been divided more equally than land in most Asian nations, the unavailability of new cultivable space in Java and Bali, along with the growing population, makes increased rural landlessness inevitable. The exploitation of the rural landless people by the wealthy landed elite has not been a major problem in the past. But the landless become highly dependent on anyone who offers tenancy, sharecropping arrangements, or temporary employment.

Although the organization of village life varies and rural traditions are heterogeneous, Indonesian rural areas have common features. Communal responsibilities, for example, such as caring for people in trouble

or contributing to the rehabilitation of an irrigation facility, are taken seriously. Social status is clearly defined and respectfully observed. Javanese culture prescribes appropriate behavior, including speech, contingent upon the relative rankings of people interacting socially.

Rural life has been affected by technological change. Most villagers have access to ideas and information conveyed by radio; some read newspapers; and increasing numbers travel to towns and cities. But the cultural traditions of rural Indonesia are resilient. The values of social harmony and the tolerance of diversity are effectively conveyed through puppet shadow plays and other traditional art forms. The relationship between performer and audience is intimate, reaching its quintessential state in Bali, where virtually every villager has been or is a dancer, musician, or other artist. In this setting, ritual and correct deportment are as important as economic advancement.

The Green Revolution, through which international and Indonesian agricultural experts and planners are trying to revolutionize rice farming, has encountered considerable resistance. A farmer whose crop is especially good is likely to spend the profits on quasi-religious ceremonies and cultural performances rather than investing in more expensive strains of seed, fertilizer, and pesticide. Traditional farming techniques, such as harvesting rice with a small curved knife, also have an aesthetic (if not religious) significance that no mechanized device can match. In any case, mechanization in densely populated areas would displace many peasants. Government planners and administrators are therefore giving less emphasis to mechanization than to pesticide and fertilizer utilization. The world's largest fertilizer plant is in production in south Sumatra, and construction of another such facility will soon begin.

*A father's club in
Djakarta meets to
learn about family
planning. Because
of Indonesia's
rapidly expanding
population, the
government is
giving strong
support to a
national family
planning program.
(Photo: United
Nations/
R. W. Witlin.)*

Because it is easier to increase the production of fertilizer than to increase its use, substantial quantities of fertilizer made in Indonesia are exported. There are several obstacles to fuller exploitation of the benefits of such agribusinesses as fertilizer manufacture; they include not only the peasants' unwillingness to adopt new methods—a cultural problem that is probably exaggerated—but also limited transportation facilities and the unavailability of stable and secure sources of credit for small-scale agricultural investment.

Even without the potentially disruptive adoption of new farming techniques, peasants are already being dislocated. The flow of migrants from rural to urban areas is substantial; many young men adopt a pattern of more or less seasonal migration. In the cities, rural youth join a large floating substratum of unskilled and unpropertied citizens. They tend to cluster in neighborhoods that retain some of the social qualities of villages, where services like sanitation, housing, and public health are limited and prospects for economic advancement and security are virtually nil.

In Indonesia's 27 provinces, hospitals are few and poorly equipped. Moreover, there are only about 9,000 doctors. In recent years, the government has increasingly emphasized the establishment of rural health clinics and polyclinics, all of which are staffed largely by nurses, midwives, and paramedics.

Since the earliest days of independence, the government of Indonesia has given education a high priority. Not surprisingly, there are more schools in the cities, and they are better staffed and funded than village schools. At the primary level, there are over 17 million pupils. Most students at all levels are in public schools, but the network of Muslim schools of various types is not insignificant. At the university level, some of the 284,300 students are enrolled in excellent technical and scientific curricula. In general, however, the university system is stronger in social and humanistic studies than in theoretical and applied science. This is true at the secondary level as well.

All Indonesian cities have been affected by rural-urban migration, but none has experienced such a dramatic influx as Jakarta, the capital city. Whereas the 1961 census recorded a population of 2.9 million for Jakarta, its current population is estimated at over 5.9 million. As the administrative and economic center of the nation, Jakarta has a great attraction. Not surprisingly, however, its rapid growth has produced extensive social disorganization, including crime and severe unemployment. Even those fortunate enough to obtain positions in government offices find that their incomes are scarcely adequate. Urban underemployment is commonplace, particularly in the swollen government bureaucracy.

The government has tried to alleviate unemployment by encouraging manufacturing and light industry. In this free market economy, imports of automobiles and appliances have been restricted in order to protect the local manufacture of parts and assembly of vehicles, refrigerators, air conditioners, and sewing machines. Other manufactured items are tires, paper goods, radios, dry-cell batteries, plastics, leather products, textiles, aluminum sheets, cigarettes, and processed and packaged foods and beverages. The latter provide a particularly vital source of jobs: over 600,000 are employed in food processing packaging.

During and since the colonial era, industrial management and major commercial activity have been the domain of nonindigenous people, especially the Chinese. This small minority, comprising no more than 3 percent of the population, were favored by the Dutch, who regarded the Chinese as more likely to be loyal to the colonial government and as possessing an aptitude for commerce. The Chinese community also has overseas connections that are valuable in the importing and exporting activities so important to Indonesia's economy. Recent efforts by the government to reduce the Chinese domination of some economic sectors have probably been offset by the tendency of officials, particularly the military, to establish close working relationships with Chinese businessmen. The role of the Chinese is a long-standing source of

Women clean peppercorns in a pepper factory in Sumatra. Pepper has been a traditional export crop for Indonesia. (Photo: United Nations/ L. Groseclose.)

discontent to indigenous Indonesians and at times has given rise to violence.

Since he relinquished the presidency to General Suharto in 1967, President Sukarno, the dominant political figure during the country's first two decades of independence, has been faulted for his ineffectual response to economic and administrative problems. On the other hand, Sukarno is fondly remembered by many Indonesians as a visionary who devoted his skills to the enhancement of Indonesia's unity and international prestige. One of Sukarno's favorite topics was the glory of precolonial Indonesia. He reminded Indonesians of the power and achievements of the great Hinduized kingdoms; the architectural remains of these and other kingdoms, some with a Buddhist orientation, are objects of pride to Indonesians.

Sukarno emphasized the continuity between the pre-European past and the postindependence present; he also strengthened the nationalist movement, in which he was a central figure. The revolution itself, from 1945 to 1949, involved considerable military combat, and euphoria accompanied the eventual Indonesian victory.

By the 1960s Sukarno had consolidated his system of guided democracy, a more centralized and personalized government than the parliamentary structure that had been attempted earlier. As his health failed, however, the rivalry between the two likely successors to his power, the army and the Communist Party, intensified. The showdown came in late 1965, culminating in widespread violence, a decimated Communist Party (most of its supporters, if not killed, were imprisoned for years), and the advent of a military government that still controls the major government institutions.

In more recent years, President Suharto's regime has been criticized for the same deficiencies that characterized guided democracy: inefficiency, corrup-tion, and the inadequate protection of civil liberties. From the beginning, Suharto stressed his commitment to the resolution of economic problems, in contrast to the symbolic-political style of the previous regime.

The two most impressive accomplishments of Suharto's technocrats have been the relative containment of rampant inflation and the large increase in oil revenues. The third 5-year plan, which began in April 1979, seeks to improve agricultural productivity and capital investment. But since Indonesia continues to be dependent on foreign capital, its massive foreign debt—$19.5 billion in 1979 and likely to double in 7 years—is a serious problem. Agricultural output has shown a slight increase, but much larger increases have been registered in food imports. In 1977, for example, Indonesia imported 2.6 million tons (2.36 million t) of rice, nearly one-third of the rice traded on the world market.

For all the nation's natural beauty and cultural richness, the race between population and food supplies is a central problem. A reasonable estimate places the nation's population at 250 million in the year 2000; current government officials no longer accept the view, once articulated forcefully by Sukarno, that Indonesia's power and prestige increase in direct proportion to its population growth.

Family planning has been promoted by the government; official statistics show a decline in the rate of population increase from 2.9 percent in 1969 to 2.1 percent in 1976. The problem is even more critical than the food and population data reveal, however, because nutritional levels in many areas of the country are substandard. In some rural areas, the average caloric intake is estimated to be 42 percent below minimum standards.

Economic and demographic statistics on Indonesia are difficult to compile. Even the most favorable forecasts, however, envision widespread economic hard-

Farmers harvest a rice field in Java. Rice cultivation, both wet and dry, is the most common form of farming in Indonesia. (Photo: United Nations.)

ship. And a continued reliance on foreign aid will probably be criticized by domestic groups. Development policies may lead to political and social crises, even though the policies appear to be successful when measured by the usual economic indicators. Because of its size and strategic location, any Indonesian instability is sure to affect its neighbors in Southeast Asia.

Stephen Douglas

Kampuchea
(People's Republic of Kampuchea)*

Area: 69,000 sq mi (178,710 sq km)
Population: 5 million (1980 est.)
   Density: 72 per sq mi (28 per sq km)
   Growth rate: not available
Percent of population under 14 years of age: not available
Infant deaths per 1,000 live births: not available
Leading causes of death: famine, civil war, political murder, epidemics
Ethnic composition: Khmer, Chinese, Vietnamese, Cham-Malay, hill tribes
Languages: Khmer
Literacy: 50% (pre-1970)
Religions: Theravada Buddhist, animist, Muslim
Percent population urban: not available
Percent population rural: not available
Gross national product: not available
   Per capita GNP: not available
   Per capita GNP growth rate: not available
Inflation rate: not available

*NOTE: Statistical data is not available and information on what is happening is scant or highly contradictory.

Kampuchea's fertile, sparsely settled land has long served as a magnet to its more powerful aggressive neighbors. Because of their lack of natural defenses, the Cambodian (Khmer) people must struggle just to survive as a nation. Under favorable conditions, Kampuchea (Cambodia) could have a prosperous economy based on rice farming, plantation crops, tourism, and agro-industries. However, today the war-ravaged nation is ruled by a puppet government under the Vietnamese. This regime faces intermittent guerrilla attack by Cambodian Communist forces, which are supplied by China.

Caught between these warring factions are the Cambodian people. During the 1970s, they suffered almost every kind of disaster imaginable. Fighting between well-armed ground and air forces resulted in thousands of civilian casualties. Military prisoners of war were often slaughtered. Racial bigotry led to wholesale pogroms. From 1975 to 1979, a radical Communist government used mass murder to wipe out the educated class and intimidate the peasants. Epidemics of malaria and other diseases swept through the country after virtually all doctors and medical services were destroyed by the Communists. In 1979, famine ruled the land as a result of the grim

struggle between Cambodian and Vietnamese Communists.

Cambodia is bordered by Thailand, Laos, and Vietnam. Somewhat larger in area than the state of Florida, it resembles a shallow-rimmed saucer. The flat, central area, formed by the basin of the Mekong River and the great lake of the Tonle Sap, provides ideal conditions for wet rice cultivation.

A low rim of mountains and uplands forms the western and northern border regions. The Cardomom Mountains on the western border include Phnom Aurel, the highest peak in Cambodia [5,741 feet (1,750 m)]. The Dangrek plateau in the north and the Annamite plateau in the northeast are considerably less rugged. Although much of the northern half of the country is densely forested, some 12 million acres (4.85 million ha) of cleared land can be farmed with irrigation.

The Tonle Sap lake provides a huge catchment basin for flood waters during the annual rainy season. Wet monsoon winds blow from June to September and bring an annual average of 58 inches (147 cm) of rain to Phnom Penh and much of central Cambodia. The dry season lasts from October to May. The northeast region is most subject to drought; it is somewhat higher in altitude and cooler in winter than the rest of Cambodia.

In addition to wet rice farming and freshwater and saltwater fishing, the country has abundant wild fruit and considerable timber. The soil of eastern Cambodia is ideal for rubber trees, and some rubber plantations survived the turmoil of the 1970s. Corn, coffee, sugar cane, cotton, and other tropical crops have also been grown successfully. A mineral survey carried out in the 1960s was disappointing; however, the country has some iron ore, manganese, and phosphate. Small amounts of gold have been mined for many years in Kompong Thom province, and sapphires and other precious stones can be found near Pailin in Battambang province. During the 1970s, some offshore oil is believed to have been discovered by drilling operations that were conducted in the Gulf of Thailand.

Cambodia's 1980 population was estimated at about 5 million. A decade earlier, in 1970, there were about 7 million inhabitants. The unprecedented decline resulted from war, political repression, disease, and the flight of hundreds of thousands of refugees. All reports by observers who entered the country in 1979 stressed the shockingly small number of people and their pathetic condition. The rigors of the 1970s apparently killed almost all the middle-aged and elderly. However, very young children were perhaps more vulnerable than any group to the famine.

Although the Soviet Union claims to have sent substantial food aid to Cambodia during 1979, all non-Soviet bloc visitors to the country spoke of massive problems of malnutrition, and refugees continued to pour across the Thai border at every opportunity. Press reports in late 1979 estimated the number of Cambodians who were starving to be 2.25 million, roughly half of the entire population of the country.

In 1979, most of the Khmer were living in rural villages. A shortage of tools, seeds, and fertilizer, as well as continuing guerrilla warfare, hindered rice planting. Nonetheless, some schools and hospitals were said to be reopening. Several factories, including those that produce textiles, cement, and rubber products, were functioning at partial capacity. The network of paved (mainly lateritic) roads linking most of the old provincial capitals with Phnom Penh was probably maintained by the Vietnamese army, with the aid of Khmer peasants. The main airport at Pochentong and portions of the railroad line—which runs from the Thai border to Phnom Penh and down to the sea at Kompong Som—were also open. But the Vietnamese army sought to prevent any supplies sent from China or Thailand from reaching the Khmer guerrillas.

Over 90 percent of the prewar inhabitants of Cambodia belonged to the Khmer ethnic group, probably descended from early immigrants from China and Indonesia. The Khmer are a sturdy, handsome race, with almond-shaped eyes and wavy black hair, somewhat darker skinned and shorter than their Lao neighbors. In the towns, intermarriage with Chinese and Vietnamese minorities became fairly common in the twentieth century, producing variations in the predominant physical type.

Theravada Buddhism was introduced in Cambodia in the twelfth century; it swept the country and its humane influence may have contributed to the decline of the rigidly autocratic Angkor Empire. Because the Khmer are among the world's most devout Buddhists, they have probably clung tenaciously to their religion throughout the turmoil of the 1970s. However, it is doubtful that many Buddhist monks or temples have survived.

Before the events of the 1970s, the Khmer people's social structure closely resembled that of their Thai and Lao neighbors. Most people lived in small, generally self-sufficient villages. Wet rice cultivation was the basic means of livelihood, and over half the family households owned enough land to feed themselves and produce a small surplus that they sold to Chinese rice millers. Only in Battambang province was land tenancy common.

The *wat* (Buddhist temple) was the center of village (and urban) life. Men customarily spent a few weeks or years of their lives as monks. The temple served as a center of worship, as a place for weddings, funerals, and various social occasions, as a place for refuge for those in need, and as a school (for boys only). During the 1950s and 1960s, the government offered basic education to girls as well as boys. At that time, about half the population was literate, but the rate of literacy may have declined in the 1970s.

Ethnic Chinese and Vietnamese minorities each accounted for about 5 percent of the pre-1970 population, but current numbers are difficult to estimate. The Vietnamese minority suffered a pogrom in 1970, and nearly all the survivors left Cambodia by 1975. The French, Thai, and Lao minorities also left by 1975.

By 1979, most of Cambodia was occupied by the Vietnamese army. As in Vietnam, any remaining Chinese will probably be expelled or mistreated. It is also likely that substantial numbers of Vietnamese settlers will follow the Vietnamese army into Cambodia.

Two other ethnic minorities, each numbering a few tens of thousands, may have survived the 1970s. The Cham-Malay are a Muslim community; many of them trace their ancestry to the ancient kingdom of Champa (located in central Vietnam several hundred years ago). Known collectively to the Khmer people as Upper Cambodians, there are also numerous small groups of hill people in northeastern Cambodia. These people are mainly animists with close ties to the hill people of Vietnam and Laos, and they have

Cambodian refugees sleep at the Ban Mai Rut camp near Klong Yai, Thailand. There were about 5,200 refugees living in this makeshift wooden structure. (Photo: United Nations/J. K. Isaac.)

long migrated freely back and forth across those borders. Both the Cham-Malay and the hill people have, in the past, obeyed their traditional leaders; they have had limited contact with the authorities in Phnom Penh.

Under Khmer Communist rule (from 1975 to 1979), the entire social structure of Cambodia—at the family, village, and national levels—was subjected to drastic change. Families were often separated, and most people were forced to live in rural communes far from their native towns or villages. All forms of religious practice were forbidden, and a highly puritanical social code was enforced by terror and by summary executions. No money circulated, and people were forced to work long hours in return for meager rations of food.

Paradoxically, the Vietnamese conquerers of 1979 apparently allowed a return to some old social norms—like traditional New Year celebrations centering around the village temple—as a means of gaining the approval of the Khmer. Partly to prevent Cambodian guerrillas (mainly Communists) from gaining control, the Vietnamese authorities also encouraged the Khmer people to leave the communes created by the Cambodian Communist regime and return to their native villages. However, it seems unlikely that Communist Vietnam will allow private ownership of land in Cambodia, and it is impossible to predict the social structure that will emerge.

The Khmer people have inhabited their present homeland since the first century. Their culture shows far more Indian than Chinese influence, and their script is related to ancient Indian religious scripts.

Children play in the rubble in the streets of Phnom Penh; some 2 million Cambodians are reported to have died in the civil war there. (Photo. UNICEF/J. Danois.)

From around the year 800 to the year 1200, the Khmer Empire of Angkor ruled much of mainland Southeast Asia. The kings ruled by divine right; the common people were little more than slaves. Throughout this period, an elaborate irrigation system made it possible for the peasants to produce enough surplus rice to support a lavish program of wars and temple building.

Angkor's four centuries of imperial brilliance began to fade around the year 1200, and a long decline followed. Cambodia was nearly dismembered by its Thai and Vietnamese neighbors in the nineteenth century. From 1864 to 1953, French rule arrested this process; it also raised living standards and produced a small cadre of trained administrators. Cambodia's natural rubber was sent to France. Its surplus rice was shipped mainly to French West Africa, but its small population and primitive methods made Cambodia a minor rice exporter compared to Thailand and Burma.

After winning his country's independence from France in 1953, King Norodom Sihanouk attracted large-scale foreign investment and helped to build towns and factories, improve the livelihood of his people, and keep the country out of the Vietnam war through the 1960s.

Early in 1970 Sihanouk was overthrown by his top general, Lon Nol. American and South Vietnamese forces subsequently invaded Cambodia, and it became the main battleground of the Vietnam war for the next three years. At the same time, a civil war developed between Communists and anti-Communist Cambodians. The Communist forces won in April 1975, wiped out all traces of traditional Khmer and foreign culture, and renamed the country Kampuchea. Their main foreign policy objective was to isolate Cambodia politically and economically, but their vicious attacks on bodering Thailand and Vietnam—although meant to restrain their neighbors—helped provoke the 1978 Vietnamese invasion.

In early January 1979, the Vietnamese seized control of the road network and major towns and established a puppet government under Heng Samrin, a former Khmer Communist military officer who defected to Vietnam. This Vietnam-supported regime tried to wipe out remaining pockets of Khmer Communist guerrilla resistance and turn Cambodia into a food-exporting country to help feed Vietnam.

Heng Samrin's regime in Phnom Penh was undoubtedly receiving economic and technical assistance as well as direct military support from Vietnam, which in turn was supplied by the Soviet Union. No assistance could reach areas of Cambodia controlled by Hanoi and Heng Samrin without the full cooperation of the Vietnamese army. During the first half of 1979, Khmer Communist and non-Communist resistance forces reportedly received some economic and military aid from China and possibly from Thailand, though this was denied by Bangkok.

Despite Vietnamese denial, most foreign observers believe that Hanoi intends to seal off Cambodia from non-Vietnamese contacts and to integrate the country into an Indochinese economic and political federation. In doing so, the Vietnamese doubtless believe that they are completing a historic process of expansion that was interrupted by the French colonial period and by Cambodia's brief resumption of its independent status as a nation.

The fate of the Cambodian people depends most of all on Vietnam, their strongest and most ruthless neighbor. The Vietnamese show no sign of giving up their determination to control Cambodia, although they have allowed international relief agencies to provide desperately needed food and medicine to the Cambodian people.

Under Vietnamese tutelage, the economy has made a partial recovery and Kampuchea may well be incorporated into an Indochina federation. How much of Kampuchea's national identity and culture will survive is hard to predict. *Peter Poole*

Korea

Because of Korea's long history as a single nation, the Korean people are racially among the most homogeneous in the world. Korea has no racial or linguistic minorities. Most Koreans share typical Mongoloid physical features, and all speak the Korean language, with slight regional differences in accent. About half of all Korean words are Chinese derivatives, although the Korean language structure is similar to Japanese. One striking linguistic difference between North and South Korea is that in the North the use of Chinese characters has been abolished; phonetics are used exclusively in all forms of publication. South Koreans still mix Chinese characters with Korean phonetics.

Before Japan annexed Korea in 1910, most Koreans were farmers. Their fundamental loyalty was to their families, and this was the principle on which the whole society was built. Many family members lived together in an extended family, and the family was more important than either the individual or the nation.

Korea's traditional religions were Buddhism and Shamanism, with a deep-rooted Confucian influence. The Confucian code of ethics that governed everyday life stressed the people's duties and the respect they owed one another.

Throughout the history of Korea external forces played a strong and persistent role in shaping the course of this ancient nation.

The Chinese ruled part of the northern half of the peninsula for more than 400 years between 108 B.C. and A.D. 313, leaving an indelible imprint on Korean culture. Then came the Mongol invasion in the early 1200s, culminating in the Mongol conquest that lasted until 1368. The Japanese invaded Korea in the 1590s, and the Manchu conquered it in the 1630s.

Korea's xenophobic reaction was to isolate itself for 200 years beginning in the 1600s. The country was closed to all foreigners except the Chinese and was termed the "hermit kingdom." In 1876, Japan forced Korea to open some ports to trade; in the 1880s the United States, Russia, and other European nations signed commercial treaties with Korea. Japan's influence in Korea increased after Japan defeated China in the Sino-Japanese War of 1894–1895, and by 1910, Korea was formally annexed to Japan, remaining a Japanese colony until 1945.

Substantial economic development and modernization took place during the Japanese occupation. The Japanese developed railroads, a communications network, and industry. Few Koreans, however, were allowed to participate in government and industry; for this reason Koreans did not directly benefit from the development experience, nor did they acquire the basic skills essential for modernization. At the same time, growing urbanization weakened traditional Korean family ties. Discrimination against Koreans in education compounded these problems.

After nearly half a century, the Japanese occupation of Korea came to an end in August 1945, when Japan surrendered to the Allied forces at the conclusion of World War II. The fact that American and Soviet troops received the Japanese surrender in the southern and northern parts of Korea, respectively, became the basis for the partition of Korea and the eventual creation of the two opposing politico-economic systems. Thus, a republic with an economic system based more or less on free enterprise evolved in the south, while a Communist state with a Soviet-type economic system developed in the north. The Korean war (1950–1953) was the tragic consequence of these developments.

After the partition, particularly after the Korean war, economic contacts between the two Koreas ceased; both North and South Korea faced the challenge of building viable nations without the other half that complemented it in resource endowments and economic development. Severance from Japan and the destruction caused by the Korean war made the task more difficult. *Joseph Chung*

North Korea
(Democratic People's Republic of Korea)

Area: 47,000 sq mi (122,000 sq km)
Population: 17.0 million
   Density: 362 per sq mi (140 per sq km)
   Growth rate: 2.6% (1970–1977)
Percent of population under 14 years of age: not available
Infant deaths per 1,000 live births: not available
Life expectancy at birth: males 52 years; females 55 years
   (1974 est.)
Leading causes of death: not available
Ethnic composition: Korean
Languages: Korean
Literacy: nearly 100%
Religions: Buddhist, Shamanist, Confucianist, Christian
Percent population urban: 50% (est.)
Percent population rural: 50% (est.)
Gross national product: $12.5 billion
   Per capita GNP: $730 (est.)
   Per capita GNP growth rate: 5.3% (1970–1977 est.)
Inflation rate: not available

Severed from Japan and South Korea after the Korean war (1950–1953), North Korea had to develop a viable nation reoriented toward the Communist countries. The devastation of the war made the task more difficult. North Korea has made substantial gains in its development efforts during the quarter century since the end of the Korean war, but its economy faces monumental problems. Its much publicized goal of a self-sufficient and independent economy based on the constitution-sanctioned ideal of *chuche* (self-reliance) is still far from reality.

Situated in the northern half of the Korean peninsula, North Korea is a small mountainous country, bordered on the north by the People's Republic of China, in the northeast by the U.S.S.R., and in the south by South Korea. Most (80 percent) of North Korea's total area of 47,000 square miles (122,000 sq km) is made up of mountains and uplands; the plains, which are for the most part in the western region, form the major agricultural center. Flowing from Mount Paektu, the tallest mountain in all Korea [9,-000 feet (2,743 m) above sea level], the 500-mile (805-km) Yalu is the longest river. Mountain torrents provide North Korea with hydroelectric potential estimated at 8 million kilowatts. Rivers also provide water for irrigation and for transportation. The main port on the west coast is Nampo, located at the mouth of the Taedong River. On the east coast, several major ports (Unggi, Wonsan, Chongjin, Kimchaek, and Najin) have been expanded and improved to handle rapid industrial development.

North Korea's climate is more continental than marine. The winter is extremely cold, particularly in the northern interior provinces, where temperatures fall below freezing 5 months of the year. Summer temperatures are more uniform, averaging in the 70°sF (20°s C). In the far north, summer lasts only about two months, shortening the growing season considerably, but further south a typical growing season lasts a minimum of four months. There is a wide variation in the amount of precipitation from one area to another and from one year to the next. Rainfall is concentrated in June, July, and August, with 50 to 60 percent of the yearly rainfall, averaged at 22 to 60 inches (56 to 152 cm).

Although North Korea's moist climate is conducive to forest growth, high-quality timber is limited to the northern interior, where extensive stands of larch, spruce, fir, and pine provide the basis of the lumber industry. Elsewhere, excessive cutting before 1945 destroyed most of the original trees. With 80 to 90 percent of the important mineral deposits of the peninsula concentrated in its territory, North Korea is relatively rich in resources. According to official sources, North Korea has about 300 different minerals, some two-thirds of which are of economic value. Most important among these are coal, iron ore [2 billion tons (1.8 billion t)], lead, zinc, tungsten, mica, and fluorite. While coal reserves are substantial at 8 billion tons (7.26 billion t), they are mostly composed of low-quality anthracite, forcing North Korea to import much of its bituminous coal. It has no known reserve of petroleum and hence relies on imports from the Soviet Union and China. The main fishing ground is the Sea of Japan, which attracts pollack, octopus, anchovy, sardine, flatfish, cod, sandfish, herring, and mackerel. Species caught in the Yellow Sea include yellow corbina, hairtail, stingray, sand eel, and shrimp.

The traditions of the Korean people have been overturned by the Communist regime of North Korea. The government teaches that the interests of the nation and the Communist Party supersede the interests of individuals and the family. Despite constitutional guarantees of religious freedom, in practice religious services of any kind are banned.

North Korean women are encouraged to take jobs and to work as equals with men. Day-care centers have been established to take care of children while their mothers work, weakening family ties still further. Traditional living arrangements have changed; most urban North Koreans live in one- or two-room apartments built since the country was partitioned. Despite the pressures for modernization, however, most North Korean women still wear traditional Korean dresses; men's clothing tends to be plain and uniformlike.

North Korea has one of the world's most highly socialized and centrally planned economies. The economy was socialized by 1958, when the private ownership of all means of production was abolished, profoundly affecting everyday life in North Korea. Today, industrial enterprises are either owned by the state or take the form of cooperatives, the former contributing more than 90 percent of the total industrial output. The basic agricultural production units are either collective or state farms. Collective farms are predominant in terms of their output and the amount of land they use for cultivation. State and cooperative ownership extends to all other sectors of the economy.

In 1978, North Korea's GNP was estimated to be about $12.5 billion. With an estimated population of 17 million, the per capita GNP amounts to $730. Per capita GNP has been estimated to have grown at an average annual rate of 5.2 percent during 1960–1976 and 6.8 percent during 1970–1976. The rate of economic development since 1960 is much lower than the phenomenally high growth rate from 1954 to 1960. This reflects a marked slowdown in North Korea's economy, particularly in the industrial sector, since the introduction of the 7-year plan in 1961. The outcome of the plan was an extension of the target year from 1967 to 1970.

There has been a fundamental shift in the composition of North Korea's output, indicating the transformation of the country's economy from a primarily agricultural to an agro-industrial system. Its strategy of economic development has been rapid industrialization via heavy industry, with particular emphasis on the machine-building industry. North Korea's major industrial products are iron and steel, chemicals, machinery, textiles, processed food, graphite, magnesium, and tungsten.

Industrialization and the socialization of the economy fundamentally changed the makeup of the labor force. At the time of the division, individual private farmers made up more than 70 percent of the labor force. In 1970, it was estimated that of the 6 million workers, 54.7 percent were engaged in agriculture, mostly on collective farms, while 27.7 percent were industrial workers. The corresponding figures in 1960 were 62 percent and 23.3 percent, respectively. Urbanization was another consequence of industrialization and the socialization of the economy. After 1970, urban population began to surpass rural population, a dramatic change from 1953, when 82.3 percent of the population lived in rural areas.

The cost of allocating priority to heavy industry has been the slow development of the consumer goods and agricultural sectors. By official admission, North Korean consumer goods lack variety and quality as well as quantity. The coercive nature of the collectivized farm operation is one cause of lagging agricultural productivity. Major agricultural products are corn, barley, millet, wheat, and rice, which is the most important food and export crop.

North Korea has established a fairly well-developed railroad network of 3,000 miles (4,830 km), which handles the bulk of its freight and passenger traffic.

The country also has over 3,000 miles (4,830 km) of roads. Since few North Koreans own automobiles, people rely on buses for short-distance travel, and many ride bicycles in the cities. The airline is principally for government use. Bottlenecks in transportation have been cited by the government as a major cause of the recent economic difficulties that partially nullify progress in extractive industries. For this reason, in recent years the government has placed greater emphasis on the expansion of transportation facilities.

The government controls the country's only radio network; programs are relayed nationally, with local programs provided by local radio committees. Loudspeakers are installed in factories and in open spaces in every town. Limited television broadcasting is in operation in major cities and will eventually serve the entire country. Public telephone service is available only in the cities.

North Korea has instituted a free, 9-year compulsory educational system. Beginning after the fifth year of school, students are required to work 2 summer months for the government. Elementary school consists of grades 1 through 4, and middle school consists of grades 5 through 9. Those who continue may choose between a 2-year high school, a 2-year general vocational school, or a 3- or 4-year technical school.

North Korea has only one university, named after its leader, Kim Il-sung, and more than 100 specialized colleges. The state provides night schools for adults, training schools in factories, and correspondence courses for workers. The whole educational system is geared to the needs of development programs based on a principle of putting theory into practice.

As in overall economic development, North Korea's foreign trade, while growing substantially, has not matched South Korea's spectacular record in this area. North Korea's international trade and balance of payments situation has seriously deteriorated in recent years. Its exports in 1975 were $755 million while imports amounted to $1.075 billion; in 1976, both exports and imports declined markedly to $555 million and $825 million, respectively. Between 1970 and 1976, its exports grew at 9.9 percent per annum. Its two principal trade partners are the Soviet Union and China, in that order. Since the mid-1960s, however, trade with Western and other non-Communist countries has increased. Japan has become North Korea's largest non-Communist trade partner.

North Korea's main export items are manufactured metal products, particularly rolled-steel products, minerals (chiefly iron ore), copper, lead, tungsten, and zinc), rice, and silk. The bulk of its imports are machinery, transport equipment, crude oil, fuels, rubber, and wheat. Since the early 1970s, North Korea has utilized Western capital and technology, including complete plants, breaking away from its traditional dependence on Soviet technology.

North Korea attracted worldwide attention in 1976 by stopping payments on its international debts owed to Japan and several West European nations and requesting a postponement of the payments. This request dramatized North Korea's chronic balance of payments deficit and the depletion of its foreign exchange reserves. At the end of 1977, it was estimated that its total foreign debt amounted to some $2.4 billion, a large sum relative to its export earning capacity.

North Korea is a defense-constrained nation. It maintains the fifth largest army in the world, estimated at having between 500,000 and 600,000 soldiers, and has developed considerable capacity for domestic weapons production. It is estimated that its defense spending as a share of GNP is one of the highest in the world—second only to Israel. Such a heavy defense burden for a small country severely limits its development efforts.

Kim Il-sung, President of North Korea, has been the undisputed leader of the country since partition. Arriving in Korea in 1945 at the tail of the Soviet troops, Kim was pushed to the forefront of North Korean politics by Soviet authorities. A strong personality cult has emerged around Kim to a level unknown in other Communist countries. Kim's son, Kim Chong-il, may assume the presidency after his father's retirement or death. If he does, North Korea will provide the first example of hereditary succession of power in a Communist country.

Tension between North and South Korea has not eased. In 1972, representatives of both sides unexpectedly began a direct dialogue, but little progress has been made so far. The peaceful reunification of Korea is as elusive a goal now as it has been for some 35 years; the prognosis for achieving reunification in the near future appears very dim, in view of the continued tension along the demilitarized zone and the military commitments of both Koreas.

North Korea's future depends on its ability to increase its economic efficiency. However, without the infusion of Western capital and advanced technology, it will be nearly impossible for North Korea in the near future to achieve the degree of industrialization it desires or to catch up with South Korea. North Korea must meet past-due international debts soon to insure the continued flow of Western imports. Unless its exports increase geometrically in the immediate future, it is doubtful that North Korea will earn sufficient foreign exchange to meet all its debt obligations within several years. Faced with severe balance of payments and debt problems, North Korea will probably draw closer to the Communist orbit in an effort to obtain more assistance.

North Korea could raise efficiency through more rational and creative reforms in its economic system. Such reforms seem improbable in the foreseeable future, given the country's rigid and Stalinist economic structure. North Korean authorities face a dilemma. Economic liberalization may raise incentives and productivity significantly, but it may also threaten the highly centralized power structure. In the controversy between getting "red" assistance and getting "expert" assistance, North Korea seems to have opted for the former, which has resulted in adverse effects on its economic performance.   *Joseph Chung*

South Korea
(Republic of Korea)

Area: **38,000 sq mi (98,000 sq km)**
Population: **36.6 million**
  Density: **963 per sq mi (372 per sq km)**
  Growth rate: **2% (1970–1977)**
Percent of population under 14 years of age: **38% (1975)**
Infant deaths per 1,000 live births: **38 (1975)**
Life expectancy at birth: **68 years (1975)**
Leading causes of death: **not available**
Ethnic composition: **Korean**
Languages: **Korean**
Literacy: **90% (est.)**
Religions: **Buddhist, Shamanist, Confucianist, Christian**
Percent population urban: **50% (est.)**
Percent population rural: **50% (est.)**
Gross national product: **42.5 billion**
  Per capita GNP: **$1,160**
  Per capita GNP growth rate: **7.6% (1970–1977)**
Inflation rate: **14.4% (1978)**

After a disappointing initial performance during the 1950s, South Korea began to develop rapidly, becoming a country with one of the fastest growing economies in the world. However, the economic miracle was not achieved without serious problems, such as persistent inflation, inequality of income between rural and urban dwellers, the sacrifice of political freedom and human rights, overdependence on international markets and capital, and a constant military threat (real or perceived) from North Korea. The goal of Korean unification seems as distant now as it was during the Korean war.

Situated in the southern half of the Korean peninsula, which extends south from northeastern China, South Korea is a small country of 38,000 square miles (98,000 sq km) bordered on the north by North Korea. Japan lies about 120 miles (195 km) to the east across the Sea of Japan. Like North Korea, South Korea is a mountainous country; only about 23 percent of the total area is cultivated. The Taebaek Range, the watershed of the peninsula, runs in a north-south direction along the eastern coastline and forms the backbone of the country. The Taebaek Mountains are also the source of South Korea's principal rivers (the Han,

Nakdong, and Kum). Several lower mountain ranges extend in a northeast-southwest direction, leaving plains in the western and southern regions that form South Korea's agricultural centers. Pusan, South Korea's second largest city, located on the southern tip of the peninsula, is the principal port of South Korea.

South Korea's climate is more continental than marine. As a result, the summer is hot and humid and the winter is cold and dry. The average monthly temperature in January drops below freezing and rises to about 78°F (25°C) in July. The annual precipitation varies from 30 to 50 inches (76 to 130 cm); about half the rain falls during the monsoon months from June through August. The growing season varies from 170 to 226 days. Although South Korea's moist climate is conducive to forest development, excessive cutting before 1945 destroyed most of the original trees, and lumbering, mainly of coniferous trees, is limited to the mountains of the Kangwon and Kyongsang provinces.

With only 10 to 20 percent of the peninsula's mineral deposits, South Korea is relatively poor in resources. Its principal mineral resources are graphite, anthracite coal, fluorite, salt, gold, silver, tungsten, and some iron ore. Most mountain torrents capable of generating hydroelectric power also are located in North Korea. For this reason, in South Korea, thermal electric power is far more important than hydroelectric power; the ratio has been 6 to 1 in recent years.

Marine resources are important sources of the South Korean diet and are valuable exports. Principal catches are pollack, codfish, flatfish, sharks, stingray, pomfrets, butterfish, hairtail, perch, sole, porgies, and shrimp; seaweed is also collected. Recently, South Korea has become one of the largest ocean-fishing nations in the world, with tuna as its chief catch.

Almost all of South Korea's 2.5 million farms, averaging about 2.25 acres (0.9 ha) each, are owned privately. Rice is the principal crop and the basic food item. Other farm products include barley, beans, potatoes, and wheat. In spite of progress in mechanization, farmers rely heavily on bullocks and on manual labor.

Most of South Korea's more than 24,000 manufacturing firms, mainly concentrated in the Pusan and Seoul areas, are also privately owned. The chief manufactured products are chemicals, machinery, processed foods, and textiles. In 1976 textiles provided about one-third of manufacturing employment and made up one-fourth of national output and one-third of exports.

In recent years, the government has begun to develop the expressways connecting major cities. As a result, the road network of more than 23,000 miles (37,000 km) has recently caught up with the railroad both in terms of the number of passengers and the amount of freight traffic. Although some South Koreans own automobiles, buses remain the major means of transportation within and between cities, and bicycles are used widely for short trips. The gov-

ernment-run Korean National Railroad controls more than 3,200 miles (5,510 km) of railroad track. The privately owned Korean Air Lines provides an air link between major South Korean cities and Japan, other Asian countries, the United States, and Europe. Public telephone service is available in major cities, and an increasing number of South Koreans have become private telephone subscribers.

Most South Korean families own at least one radio, and about 1 in every 40 persons owns a television set; television broadcasts reach most parts of the country. Newspapers are widely circulated and about 40 dailies are published. But the news media is subject to strict censorship.

South Korea maintains a 6-year compulsory educational system; all children are required to finish elementary school. Although parents must pay some educational expenses, more than 90 percent of the children complete sixth grade. After completing grade school, a student may go on to middle school (grades 7 through 9) and high school (grades 10 through 12). High school graduates, after passing the entrance examinations, may enter one of the country's more than 200 colleges.

Buddhism and Shamanism, are the traditional religions of Korea, and Confucianism is very important in Korean everyday life. Christianity has also made a significant inroad. Today there are about 7.1 million Buddhists, 3.2 million Protestants, and 0.8 million Roman Catholics. Some of the best-known universities in the country, such as the Yonsei University, the Ewha Woman's University, and the Sogang University, were founded by various Christian missions from the United States.

The South Korean population, estimated to be about 37.5 million in 1979, is divided about equally between the urban and rural areas. South Korea is one of the most densely populated countries in the world; in 1978 the population density was 963 per square mile (372 per sq km). There are 19 cities in South Korea with populations of more than 100,000. Seoul, the capital, is the largest city, with a population of 6.9 million (1975 census).

Before Japan annexed Korea in 1910, most people in Korea (both North and South) were farmers in small villages. Their fundamental loyalty was to their families, and this was the principle on which the whole society was built. Many family members lived together in an extended family, and the family was more important than either the individual or the nation. The Confucian code of ethics that governed everyday life stressed the people's duties and the respect they owe one another. As Japan introduced industry and modernization into Korea, many Koreans began to move to the cities, a move that weakened traditional family ties.

After the partition, South Korean life was Westernized considerably because of its close ties with the United States and other Western nations. In the cities, Western clothing has become the norm for both men and women, in sharp contrast to North Korea. Continued industrialization and urbanization have some-what weakened family ties, although Confucianism and other traditions remain strong, and most families in South Korea still follow the practice of honoring their ancestors in special ceremonies.

Although many high-rise apartment buildings and modern houses have been built in big cities, most houses in South Korea are traditional one-story structures. They are heated by the ancient method of *ondol* in which pipes under the floor carry hot air from the kitchen fireplace.

South Korea has a mixed economy. The basic tenets of private enterprise and a market economy are practiced, but the government plays a crucial role in economic decision making and resource allocation, using the devices of direct and indirect government ownership and control of enterprises and financial institutions, government spending, control of foreign exchange, and monetary and fiscal policies. Although reliance on the market, private initiatives, and pecuniary incentives remain the basis of the system, government influence changes the parameters and incentives of the market to achieve desired economic, social, political, and cultural goals.

Post-Korean War economic development can be divided into three periods: the reconstruction period of 1953–1958, a period of stagnation and political unrest (1959–1962), and a period of rapid growth starting in 1963. During the first period, a large-scale infusion of foreign aid made it possible to rebuild the war-damaged productive facilities. This period was also characterized by moderate growth, but a high annual average inflation rate of 30.1 percent continued to plague the economy.

The second period saw the rate of inflation reduced to an annual average of 10.4 percent. However, the pace of economic development slowed down somewhat from 5.5 percent per annum during the first period to 3.6 percent. The growth rate of per capita national income declined to nearly zero, and dwindling foreign aid and import levels acted as a brake on production and investment. Economic stagnation was matched by political unrest and revolution. The dictatorial government of Syngman Rhee, the first President of South Korea, was overthrown in April 1960. The Chang Myun government that took over from the Rhee government, was, in turn, overthrown in May 1961 by a military coup that ushered in the government of Chung Hee Park.

South Korea's phenomenal economic growth had its beginning in 1963, one year after the Park government introduced its first 5-year plan. The economy subsequently achieved a very high rate of growth in output, income, and employment. At the same time, there were rapid structural changes in the form of rising absolute amounts and in their ratio to GNP of investment, saving, exports and imports, and industrial output.

South Korea transformed itself from an agricultural to a semi-industrial economy in the process. The GNP in 1970 constant prices registered an annual average growth rate of 10.3 percent for the years between 1964 and 1977. The South Korean economy in 1978 handled $44.5 billion worth of business. The per capita GNP rose from $98 in 1963 to $1,200 in 1978 (assuming an estimated population of 36.8 million). The share of primary products (agriculture, forestry, and fisheries) in the GNP rose from 40.3 percent in 1954 to 42.4 percent in 1963, but declined sharply to 21.2 percent in 1978. In contrast, the share contributed to the GNP by mining and manufacturing increased from 12.4 percent in 1954, to 16.6 percent in 1963, and to 28.2 percent in 1978.

The most dramatic indicator of South Korean growth was the spectacular expansion in exports, which rose from $39.6 million in 1953, to $86.8 million in 1963, and to $10.0 billion in 1977. In terms of annual average growth, exports increased at an astonishing rate of 40.4 percent during the 14 years between 1964 and 1977. Such a record reflected not only quantitative change but also impressive improvement in the quality of South Korean products and their acceptance in international markets.

Although South Korea was plagued by chronic trade deficits, the faster growth of exports over imports between 1975 and 1977 began gradually to rectify the unfavorable balance of trade. After 1977, however, largely because of the rising cost of oil imports, the trade deficit again increased. South Korea's principal trade partners are the United States, Japan, and other Asian nations. Its chief exports include electronic products, textiles, clothing, fish, raw silk, and tungsten, and its imports include mostly crude oil, industrial raw materials, chemicals, machinery, and motor vehicles.

Since the mid-1960s, South Korea's growth has outpaced North Korea's; in the mid-1970s South Korea's GNP reached a level more than double that of North Korea—enough to compensate for South Korea's larger population. As a result, for the first time South Korea surpassed the North in per capita national income, an area in which the North formerly had an edge. Major factors contributing to faster economic growth in South Korea include the North's heavier defense burden relative to its GNP and population; larger and better educated and trained manpower in the South—particularly in the areas of economic planning, managerial know-how, and marketing; a larger number of workers receiving middle- or higher-level technical education in the South and more Western-trained engineers and scientists; South Korea's efficient use of Western capital and technology; the South's success in expanding foreign markets and the foreign exchange earning capacity needed to finance imported capital; and the South's disciplined and pragmatic economic planning.

Rapid growth, however, has caused serious problems that may continue to challenge the economy. Severe inflation has been a fixed factor, although the rate was brought down to a more or less manageable level in the late 1960s and the early 1970s. Many factors exert continued pressure on prices, including the maintenance of a large army, the government's developmental financing, bank lending to finance investment, a reduced supply of goods sold domestically so that exports can be increased, pressures from foreign exchange inflows arising from expanded exports and remittances from abroad, and worsening world-wide shortages and high prices of raw materials, particularly oil.

In recent years, there has been a resurgence of inflation; in 1978, the consumer price index rose by 14.4 percent. Its dependence on exports and foreign capital for growth and the high proportion of imports needed to produce its exports are factors that leave South Korea susceptible to external developments and introduce high risk and instability. Industrialization accompanied by urbanization and growing output-per-worker differentials have widened the inequality that characterizes the distribution of the benefits of development.

Political stability has exerted a favorable influence on economic growth. The beginning of South Korea's rapid development coincided with the military revolution and Chung Hee Park's assumption of power. The discipline of a military government introduced the aggressive economic plans that imposed austerity. Such stability made the climate conducive to foreign investment.

However, stability was achieved through measures that severely curtailed democratic political processes and human rights. The Park government was also charged with widespread corruption and political favoritism. The expulsion of the leader of the opposition Shimmin (New Democratic) Party from the National Assembly and the subsequent mass resignation of all opposition assemblymen in October 1979, were followed by student demonstrations in several major cities and large-scale arrests. The cities of Pusan and Masan were placed under martial law. On October 26, President Park was assassinated and martial law was extended to the entire country. On December 6, Choi Kyu Hah was elected President by the electoral college; he took office on December 21, 1979.

Dissidents continued to call for an end to martial law and for constitutional change and new elections. A massive anti-government riot in the city of Kwangju in May 1980 led to military intervention. In the aftermath of the Kwangju incident, General Chun Doo Hwan, commander of the Defense Security Command, continued to consolidate his power. He became President on Sepatember 1, 1980, after President Choi resigned.

Democratic political processes and human rights are still severely curtailed; since his inauguration President Chun has launched nationwide "anticorruption and purification" campaigns. The future of his government, and hence South Korea's stability, may depend on Chun's ability to deliver economic progress.   *Joseph Chung*

Laos
(Lao People's Democratic Republic)

> *Area:* 91,430 sq mi (236,803 sq km)
> *Population:* 3.3 million
>   *Density:* 36 per sq mi (14 per sq km)
>   *Growth rate:* 2.2% (1970–1977)
> *Percent of population under 14 years of age:* 42% (1975)
> *Infant deaths per 1,000 live births:* not available
> *Life expectancy at birth:* 40.4 years (1978)
> *Leading causes of death:* not available
> *Ethnic composition:* Lao, less than 50%; Thai tribes; Yao;
>   Meo; Chinese; Vietnamese
> *Languages:* Lao
> *Literacy:* 12% (1976)
> *Religions:* Theravada Buddhist, animist
> *Percent population urban:* not available
> *Percent population rural:* not available
> *Gross national product:* $300 million (1976)
>   *Per capita GNP:* $90 (1976 est.)
>   *Per capita GNP growth rate:* not available
> *Inflation rate:* not available

Laos, the only landlocked nation in Indochina, is also in many ways the least developed. Throughout its history, Laos has been a prey of foreign powers who coveted supposed mineral riches, including gold, which were never there in abundance; its territory was repeatedly violated by far more populous neighbors in quest of secure lines of communication. Unlike Switzerland, with which Laos's natural situation has sometimes been compared, Laos had no urban population base from which to recruit an army to defend its territory and its neutrality. Vientiane, the country's capital and largest city, was a sleepy village nestled on the left bank of the Mekong River until the political upheaval of the 1950s set in motion the process of urban sprawl; the city was modernized with wide, treeless boulevards, huge concrete monuments, and a jet-age airport. Sparsely populated and still largely agricultural, Laos faces an uncertain future in a world where the competition for scarce resources grows ever more acute.

The geography of Laos is dominated by the long serpentine shape of the Annam Cordillera, which forms a physical and ethnographic boundary of fundamental importance, and the complex mountain and plateau forms that descend gradually to the Mekong Valley, the country's other major border. Covered by dense rain forest, the mountain slopes are often so steep and the intervening valleys so confined that there is little room for the cultivation of crops. However, in tiny upland clearings and along streams men have cleared away the forest by burning, and have established their villages of thatched-roof huts on stilts; and here they grow food for themselves and for their animals.

Laos lies in the path of the southwesterly monsoon. For 6 months of the year, mist and clouds hang low over the mountains and drenching rains turn footpaths into soggy, muddy rivulets. The tropical rain forest is dark green the year round and forms a canopy festooned with giant lianas and scattered with orchids, ferns, and wild figs. Here and there the rain forest gives way to less dense stands of softwoods where various grasses, wild ginger, tropical rhododendron, and other flowers and bamboo thickets find sufficient sunlight to grow. In areas that have been subjected to burning, a secondary cover of wild bananas and coconut and areca palms is growing. These forests are the home of tiger, buffalo, elephant, deer, and other wild animals.

Some significant geophysical features of Laos stand out. One is the Plain of Jars, a wide area of rolling green hills resembling the dairy land of southern Wisconsin. Situated at an average elevation of 3,600 feet (1,097 m), the Plain of Jars, named after the large prehistoric sculptured stone jars found there, is surrounded by high mountains. One of these, Phou Bia,

Workers in an experimental cooperative in the small village of Pak Cheng pick cabbages. Better utilization of farmland is a goal of the government. (Photo: United Nations/Saw Lwin.)

with an elevation of 9,246 feet (2,818 m), is the highest summit in Indochina south of the latitude of Hanoi. Another significant feature is a region of abrupt karst (limestone) hills in south central Laos. Yet another is the Bolovens Plateau in southern Laos, where the French tried to grow coffee for export.

The great Mekong River, which rises in Tibet and courses south through the gorges of China's Yunnan province, forms Laos's western border, first with Burma and then with Thailand. In April, just before the first monsoon rains, the Mekong at Savannakhet is a narrow stream hiding among sheets of gray and black rock, its exposed bed presenting little obstacle to the foot traveler. In September, on the other hand, the river, which becomes 1 mile (1.61 km) wide and 30 feet (9 m) deep, is a chocolate-colored giant carrying a heavy load of mud, tree trunks, and lesser debris on a long voyage to the sea.

Aside from paddy land, Laos has few valuable natural resources. The French, who arrived in the latter part of the nineteenth century, thought there was gold near Attopeu; they ended up extracting hardwood timber and tin ore where access was not too difficult. Initially, they regarded the Mekong as a gateway to southern China; this also proved to be an illusion because the river is obstructed by rapids that make navigation impossible. While some small steamer services were instituted to link the riverside towns of Luang Prabang, Vientiane, Paksane, Thakhek, Savannakhet, and Pakse, plans to build a railway across the waist of the country, linking the heartland with France's protectorate of Annam on the east, never materialized for lack of funds.

The original inhabitants of Indochina, according to recent research, were most probably people who inhabited the Phou Loi massif north of the Plain of Jars and were settled there long before the first migrants from the north eventually peopled Laos. Their descendants came to be known as Kha, a Lao term meaning "slave."

The ethnic Lao, who today constitute somewhat less than one-half the population, are the descendants of the Thai peoples who entered during the great migration from southern China between the sixth and thirteenth centuries. Like the inhabitants of modern Thailand, the Lao are Theravada Buddhists, and the languages of the two peoples (Lao and Thai) are closely related. The Lao, like the Thai and the Khmer, were subjected to the influence of Indian Buddhism from the west, while the Vietnamese, another people who migrated from China, were Sinicized; thus, the Annam Cordillera forms an ethnographic as well as a political border.

Another group from the same migration, made up of the Black Thai, White Thai, and Red Thai tribes, very early settled in the upper valleys in the mountainous areas around Muong Sing and Dien Bien Phu, between the Red River and the Mekong. They remain distinct from the Lao; like them, they are rice cultivators, but they are not Buddhists. Subsequent arrivals were the Yao, who settled on the lower mountain slopes, followed by the Meo, who occupied the highest crests and ridges. They came from southern China during the last major migration, which was in the middle of the nineteenth century.

Two other minorities, the Chinese and the Vietnamese, are also inhabitants of present-day Laos. The Chinese are settled mainly in the larger towns and are merchants and traders. The Vietnamese are also primarily townspeople, but they have a tradition of civil service under the French, who found the Vietnamese more energetic and possibly more disciplined than the Lao and therefore encouraged their emigration to Laos.

For the Lao, family and clan are still very important, even now when a new and radically different government is attempting to inculcate egalitarian ways of thinking. For Laotian tribesmen, it is the tribe that is important. This is not to say that the nation is not an important concept, nor that the monarchy did not provide a symbol of unity, but that the concept of nationhood is relatively recent and is unfamiliar to people who are mainly illiterate and who are separated by many physical and ethnic barriers.

Laos is still a land half Buddhist, half animist. For the mountain people, and even for many Lao today, the jungle is full of powerful spirits, called *phi*, which must be propitiated with sacrifices, exorcised by complicated rites, and never wantonly abused or angered.

Rural life in Laos follows the annual cycle of paddy cultivation, with the planting at the onset of the monsoon in May and the harvest at the start of the dry season in October–November. Irrigation for rice production is still rare. Rural life allows a large measure of equality between the sexes; men and women share the burden of physical labor. As in all Southeast Asian cultures, children quickly find a useful place in the household; their allotted task is watching the family's water buffalo.

The market economy has only recently begun to impinge on rural life, although commerce flourished in the towns before the Communist takeover. The government is attempting to tackle the literacy problem; by 1971, there were more than 3,000 primary schools in Laos. The Lao People's Democratic Republic stresses the importance of education and literacy, but what progress, if any, has been made is not known.

The population of Laotian towns, which swelled during the long war, has begun to decrease as the new government encourages people to move back to the countryside to lessen the country's dependence on imported rice. In this sense, at least, the new government may be attempting to revert to an older tradition of self-sufficiency.

Laos emerged as a unified state in the fourteenth century, because of the efforts of a Thai prince, Fa Ngoun, a convert to Buddhism who had spent his youth in exile at Angkor. He established his court at Muong Swa, later Luang Prabang. Fa Ngoun's domain,

consolidated in 1353 under the name Lan Xang (Kingdom of the Million Elephants), extended from the crest of the Annam Cordillera on the east to the watershed division between the Mekong and Menam rivers on the west, and from China in the north almost as far as Angkor in the south.

The reign of Fa Ngoun's son, Sam Sen Thai, was peaceful and constructive. Many *wats* (pagodas) were built and a unified civil service was established. But Sam Sen Thai's successors were not so fortunate, and Laos became prey to foreign aggression. An invasion from Annam (Vietnam) threatened Lan Xang with extinction in 1478 when Luang Prabang was captured and the king was deposed. The king's son, however, rallied his subjects and drove out the invaders. A sequence of civil wars, secessions, and intrigues involving Vietnam, Siam (Thailand), and Burma followed. A Siamese army captured Vientiane in 1827 after Laotian King Anourouth had rashly attempted to march on Bangkok.

In 1885, Siam launched a military expedition into Laos, avowedly to put down armed bands from China who had been marauding there, but actually to forestall any move by the French (who had established protectorates in Annam and Tonkin in the previous year) to enforce Annamese claims to sovereignty beyond the cordillera. Thus began a period of intense rivalry between Siam and France. By 1893, Siam had been compelled to sign a treaty with France renouncing all claims to territory on the left bank of the Me-

These Laotian refugees are among the 10,000 inhabitants of the Sobtuang camp in Thailand. Most of the Laotian refugees in the camp are from the Meo, Yao, Phai, Lao, and Khmu ethnic groups. (Photo: United Nations/ J. K. Isaac.)

kong. The French subsequently won control of additional right-bank territories in Luang Prabang and Champassak. The court of Luang Prabang accepted a French protectorate, which was to last until 1945.

The administration was French, although there were only 600 French residents in Laos in 1940. It put an end to piecemeal depredations by other foreign powers and brought some benefits, in terms of fiscal control, education, and judicial organization. However, in view of Laos's lack of economic attraction (Laos's exports never accounted for more than 1 percent of the total French export trade from Indochina), the country remained a backwater compared to Vietnam and Cambodia.

In the wake of the imprisonment of all French civil servants by the Japanese in March 1945, an independence movement led by Prince Souphanouvong (a member of the Luang Prabang royal family) and several part-Vietnamese associates allied itself with the Viet Minh and attempted to oppose by force of arms the reestablishment of French control over Laos. The French overcame these efforts in the towns, but found themselves involved in a protracted war against Souphanouvong's guerrillas and their Viet Minh backers on Laotian territory.

Under pressure to win American support for their war effort in Indochina, the French governments of the Fourth Republic accorded increasing measures of independence to Laos. By the terms of the 1954 Geneva Conference that put an end to the French Indochina War, Laos was accepted as a fully independent nation, but with a proviso that temporary control over two provinces strategically situated on the China

Children study in a primary school in the village of Non Nong Khoey. (Photo: United Nations/Saw Lwin.)

and Vietnam borders go to the pro-Viet Minh rebel movement, known as the Pathet Lao, pending an internal settlement and unification.

In the post-1954 period, the United States came to play a larger role in Laos. With the creation of an anti-Communist state in South Vietnam, the United States felt that support for a non-Communist government in Laos was vital to its interests. In these circumstances, the projected reunification of Laos encountered serious problems. A first coalition attempt in 1957 and a second in 1962 failed. By then the nationalist Prime Minister of the Vientiane government, Prince Souvanna Phouma, a half brother of Souphanouvong, was closely identified with the United States. The Pathet Lao were regarded as the pawns of North Vietnam, whose principal interest in Laos was to ensure the security of the Ho Chi Minh Trail, its line of infiltration of men and arms to South Vietnam.

A third attempt to set up a coalition government and bring about a cease-fire in Laos was made in 1973. By this time the Pathet Lao and North Vietnamese already controlled two-thirds of Laos, although they ruled only a minority of the population, which now included hundreds of thousands of refugees. Renewed fighting in 1975, however, led to the flight from Vientiane of many rightist members of the coalition, leaving the Pathet Lao in virtually uncontested control of the government. On December 2, 1975, in a carefully arranged scenario, the Pathet Lao announced the dissolution of the coalition, the abdication of King Savang Vatthana, and the establishment of a Lao Peoples Democratic Republic. Souphanouvong was named President, and Kaysone Phomvihan, a key figure of the Pathet Lao movement since 1945 and the secretary-general of the small Communist Party of Laos, was named Prime Minister. Souvanna Phouma and the former king were relegated to the positions of advisers. This government has ruled Laos ever since.

The new government of Laos proclaimed a planned national economy during 1978. However, bad harvests and popular resistance to new agricultural measures, including an agricultural tax (introduced in 1976), made the achievement of planned targets of output in the agricultural field difficult. In June 1978, the government announced another important step in the direction of state takeover of the agricultural economy; agricultural cooperatives were to be formed throughout the country. By the end of June 1979, a total of 1,819 such agricultural cooperatives had been formed, encompassing 325,819 members and including 189,605 acres (76,790 ha) of tilled land, according to the official news agency, the Pathet Lao News Agency (KPL).

Rice production, which accounts for a major share of Laos's gross national product, was hard hit by drought in 1977 and floods in 1978. The government has largely failed in its efforts to procure rice for distribution in the towns by buying from producers at a fixed price, and undoubedly the regime looks on the formation of agricultural cooperatives as a means to facilitate rice procurement. It is unfortunately possible that by collectivizing agriculture the government will induce a sharp drop in rice production; it is not profitable for farmers to produce more rice than they need themselves when the official procurement price is low.

It is clear from the information available that at the present time the rice grown in Laos is usually kept by the grower or is distributed privately within the village (government procurement averaged only 8 percent in 1977 in the major rice producing regions), while imported rice and rice donated to Laos as foreign aid is used to feed the urban population, the army, and the civil servants. Government employees and soldiers are paid mainly in rice rations. Farmers also demand payment for their rice in hard goods rather than cash, and until now they have been getting their way.

Laos produces few consumer goods, and these are now imported at the free market exchange rate, some four times the official exchange rate. With salaries averaging little more than $3 a month at the free market rate, consumer goods are available mainly to those Laotians who still have household possessions, jewels, or gold they can sell, and to foreigners (primarily Russians, East Europeans, and UN officials). In the towns, nationalized hotels, restaurants, and the state airline accept only hard currencies, not the kip.

The government's economic problems are compounded by the poor condition of the rice mills, the difficulties of rice transportation, and improper rice storage. These are all connected with the mass exodus of skilled workers and managers after the 1975 Communist takeover, and the failure to acquire replacement parts and to maintain equipment. About one-fourth of all trucks in the government's truck fleet are out of order. Rice warehouses are heavily pest-infested.

If Laos's economy can be put in order by the kind of centralized planning the government is trying to introduce in the face of great obstacles (the first official economic plan was established for 1978–1980, and a full 5-year plan is to follow), the country will be able to develop its considerable economic potential. It has been reported that there is mineral wealth to be tapped. Hydroelectric power generation and the export of this power to Thailand may also bolster the economy.

As a member of the socialist camp, Laos can be expected to receive some aid from countries like the Soviet Union and socialist Vietnam. However, this aid is still relatively little, and the Vientiane government will have to develop the Laotian economy largely on its own for the time being. The government is aware of this situation and is willing to move slowly toward greater cooperativeness and collectivism. The future depends to a great extent on the success of the government in mobilizing popular acceptance of the need for self-reliance and, therefore, austerity in living style.   *Arthur J. Dommen*

Malaysia

Area: 128,553 sq mi (332,952 sq km)
Population: 13.3 million (1980 est., State)
   Density: 103 per sq mi (40 per sq km)
   Growth rate: 2.7% (1970–1977)
Percent of population under 15 years of age: 35%
Infant deaths per 1,000 live births: 30.7
Life expectancy at birth: 64 years
Leading causes of death: not available
Ethnic composition: Malay 45%; Chinese 35%; Indian 10%; Bornean 8%; other 2%
Languages: Malay, Chinese dialects, English, Tamil, Hindu
Literacy: 60%
Religions: Muslim, Buddhist, Confucian, Taoist, Hindu
Percent population urban: 35%
Percent population rural: 65%
Gross national product: $14.5 billion
   Per capita GNP: $1,090
   Per capita GNP growth rate: 4.9% (1970–1977); 8.5% (1976–1980)
Inflation rate: 5.2% (1979)

Beautiful and friendly Malaysia is prosperous, well endowed with natural resources, and law-abiding, with an efficient bureaucracy and a parliamentary form of government that preserves respect for both individual and organized interests. But potentially disintegrating forces of communism, communalism, traditionalism, and regionalism have affected Malaysia's development ever since Malaya became independent in 1957, and perhaps even more after the creation of Malaysia in 1963. Nonetheless, a strong free market economy, affluence and democracy have minimized the problems of nation building.

Many of Malaysia's development difficulties stem from its geography. From the Isthmus of Kra, the country extends in a 1,600-mile (2,575-km) arc through the South China Sea, with an almost 3,000-mile (4,830-km) coastline and a 900-mile (1,450-km) land border with Indonesia in Kalimantan (Borneo). West Malaysia, with 50,840 square miles (131,675 sq km), is about the size of New York State, and is separated by hundreds of sea miles from East Malaysia, which is one and one-half the size of its western counterpart. Although West Malaysia constitutes only 39.7 percent of the entire land mass, it contains over 85 percent of the total population; it is also the seat of government and the center of political, cultural, and economic activity.

As the southernmost projection of the Asian mainland, Malaysia lies athwart the historic sea-lane approaches from the Indian and Pacific Oceans and was the cultural repository of the seafaring nations of the world: nations of the Middle East, India, China, Japan, Spain, Portugal, the Netherlands, and Great Britain. The success of trading centers in Tumasek (later Singapore), Malacca, and Penang, the increase in tin mining, and the acceptance of rubber as an estate product in the late nineteenth century resulted in a large influx of foreign labor, which is reflected today in Malaysia's multiracial society.

Almost 70 percent of the country is made up of tropical rain forest. There are few natural harbors, and human settlements are concentrated along the coastal plains. There is a rapidly expanding network of excellent roads, an efficient but structurally minimal rail service, and frequent domestic service by a national airline. The availability of transportation and communication stimulated economic expansion.

The economy is still largely export-oriented, fed by sales of rubber, petroleum, timber, tin, and palm oil. To ensure a steady annual growth rate of 8.5 percent, the government seeks to preserve nonrenewable resources, to achieve price stabilization in agricultural export commodities, and to stimulate industrial development through increased domestic consumption. Careful economic planning and the industriousness of its people have made Malaysia the most prosperous country in Southeast Asia, second only to the city-state of Singapore.

In 1978, the per capita real gross national income (based on 1970 purchasing power) was $763, and it showed an annual growth rate of more than 8 percent in 1976–1980. While this rate is phenomenal compared to the rate in most other Asian countries, Malaysia must try to ensure that this income is equitably distributed. The objectives of the New Economic Policy (1971–1990), particularly the accomplishments of the Third Malaysia Plan (1976–1980), have been directed toward the eradication of poverty and the equalization of income levels.

By 1978, the incidence of poverty in peninsular Malaysia had declined to 36.6 percent, but poverty still prevails. Rubber smallholders, paddy farmers, tenant farmers, and estate workers are usually poor, earning a mean monthly income of $46.60. Because of insufficient drainage or irrigation and a lack of fertilizers and insecticides, productivity is low. Government projects seek to correct these inadequacies and to improve the rural infrastructure, education, medical services, and electricity. In urban areas, the median household income amounts to $157, but escalating prices of essential commodities affect city dwellers. Urban migration is exacerbating the problem.

Structurally, and by ethnic composition, income distribution in Malaysia leaves much to be desired. The mean monthly income (in 1976 current prices) for Malay households was $166, for Indians, $256, and for the Chinese, $414. The mean urban income was $435; the mean rural income, $194. Unemployment was greatest among Indians (8.1 percent) and lowest among Eurasians (5.8 percent).

During 1978, in peninsular Malaysia, 66.1 percent of the agricultural work force consisted of Malays. The main share (49.9 percent) of jobs in mining, construction, and manufacturing was held by the Chinese. In trade, banking, and public service employment, manpower was almost equally divided between the Malays and Chinese. The trend, however, was in favor of hiring Malays for higher-paid administrative and managerial jobs. The income gap among the major racial groups still persists; but with increasing employment opportunities in the commercial and industrial sectors, inequities should diminish without adversely affecting any ethnic group.

Despite its relative material wealth, the country's

In a land where the trade union movement is very strong, a union meeting is well attended. (Photo: United Nations/ UNESCO/D. Roger.)

primary uncertainty is its demographic diversity. Large ethnic blocs retain their cultural, religious, and linguistic identities, with almost no intermarriage; the people are communally compartmentalized in living habits and working conditions. Political power is vested in one racial group and economic power in another. Such divisions have led to violent conflicts, and the government's major objective is to reduce them by redistributing wealth, educational skills, and settlement patterns. Nation-building has been retarded until the integrative forces of nationalism can assert themselves.

In a multiracial country in which each ethnic group aspires to perpetuate its cultural heritage, education remains the most emotionally divisive issue. Ideally, the educational system promotes national integration by emphasizing the unifying factors of Malaysian life. Inevitably, this approach challenges communal sensitivities and stimulates demands for culturally independent institutions.

Despite these problems, Malaysia has had some success in providing a broad and qualitative education. Today, 90.9 percent of all children 6 to 11 years of age are attending primary schools, and 86.4 percent of children up to the age of 16 are going on to lower secondary schools. Close to 11 percent will receive upper and postsecondary education, and about 2 percent will eventually reach the tertiary level. By 1980, more than 3.3 million students will be enrolled in Malaysian educational institutions.

Still, problems persist. Bahasa Malaysia (the national language, Malay) is to be the primary medium of instruction at the university level. This has led to a shortage of Malay textbooks at Malaysia's five universities and difficulties in the precision of scientific terminology. Consequently, many professional non-Malays have left the country, decimating the teaching ranks. Despite the 19 teacher-training colleges in operation, teacher shortages are also evident at lower levels.

Malays are being given preferential access to universities to redress racial imbalances in various occupations. Admissions to tertiary institutions in 1978 consisted of 70.7 percent Malays and 24.7 percent Chinese, a ratio which was at variance with the respective national percentages of the two communities. Of the 36,000 Malaysians who went overseas in 1978 obtaining a foreign education, some 60.8 percent were Chinese.

Since primary education is compulsory in Malaysia, the statistical assertion that about 40 percent of the population is illiterate may be misleading. In most cases, this figure refers to functional illiteracy, covering those who do not speak the national language. This will change; today 130 million people in Southeast Asia converse in Malay. In the meantime, English is widely used as a lingua franca.

A developing tropical country has special health problems. The preservation of food and clean water, the eradication of mosquitoes and flies, and the improvement of sanitary facilities all seem to pose greater problems in tropical climates than in temperate climates. Yet, despite these inherent difficulties, Malaysia has attained a level of performance in public health standards, hygiene, and preventive medicine that may surprise a Western visitor.

Today, 62 percent of the population live in malaria-free areas. Typhoid and infectious hepatitis are under control, water is being chlorinated, and environmental sanitation is improving. But there is still a high incidence of waterborne diseases, primarily in rural areas, and some malnutrition as a result of an imbalanced food intake and an absence of a nutritious diet. During 1978 there were 1,635 cases of cholera, 450 cases of dengue haemorrhagic fever, and 1 person in 1,000 was infected with malaria. In 1979, the hospital bed–population ratio stood at 1.6 per 1,000 persons, and the ratio of doctors to the population at 4 per 1,000.

Two health problems are directly related to Malaysia's development. One problem is that regulations governing occupational hazards have been outpaced because of accelerating progress in industrialization. Consequently, industrial accidents have increased by 14 percent since 1975, and came to about 48,000 in 1978. The other problem is population control. Religious considerations (e.g., the Islamic practice of polygamy) and customs (e.g., the perceived need for a son) have sharply restricted family planning, which has been largely confined to the urban sector. For this reason, the government is expanding the number of rural health clinics and trained midwives and is subsidizing the production and sale of contraceptive de-

Students watch while an instructor shows how to tap a rubber tree. Rubber is a major export crop in Malaysia. (Photo: United Nations/FAO/ J. Ling.)

vices. The birthrate is expected to decline to 28.2 per 1,000 in 1980.

Nonetheless, Malaysia's population of 13.3 million people is expected to double in number within 28 years. But the ethnic ratio will remain virtually unchanged, with about 45 percent Malay, 35 percent Chinese, 10 percent Indian, 8 percent Bornean, and 2 percent of other racial origins. Thirty-five percent of the population are less than 15 years old, and life expectancy has reached 64 years.

The Malay community lays claim to native status, with its attendant political rights and privileges. More than 500 years of Islamic influence before the Christian era (A.D. 1500) unified Malay culture. But the unity was soon shattered by small feuding sultanates, which were later perpetuated for the advancement of European colonial interests. Most Malays still live in rural areas, usually on their own land, but an increasing number are migrating to urban areas and entering business activities. Antedating the Malays on the peninsula were Negritos, Senois, and Mongoloid Indonesians. There are still about 45,000 of these aborigines, mostly in less accessible parts of the jungle. Many are hunters and gatherers, using blowpipes and poisoned darts on monkeys, large birds, and the mouse deer. Others are more sedentary, cultivating rice and sago, collecting wild fruits and chicle, or producing intricate wood carvings. In number and impact, aborigines are of greater interest to the anthropologist than to the politician or economist.

The sizable immigration of Chinese into Malaysia began in the sixteenth century, when European settlements in the area offered trading possibilities and a greater measure of security. Even after independence, the Chinese ignored integration in favor of Chinese-language schools, Chinese secret societies, clan associations, and communally oriented political parties. As a group, they dominate in capital formation, business, banking, and trade, as well as tin mining and vegetable farming. Because of their economic preferences, the Chinese in Malaysia are primarily city dwellers.

Beginning in the nineteenth century, the British demand for labor in mining, urbanized trade, and the developing rubber industry increased Indian immigration. Politically agile but numerically of little consequence, Indians eventually became the most unionized community. In Sabah and Sarawak, the two East Malaysian states, indigenous people form the majority group: only 24 percent in Sabah and 38 percent in Sarawak are Malay Muslims, with 23 percent and 31 percent the respective figures for the Chinese community in those states.

Yet the divisions in this plural society are not unbridgeable; there are relations among ethnic groups. It is not an uncommon sight to see a Tamil (South Indian) medic accompanied by a Chinese nurse distributing medicine in a Malay village from an ambulance driven by a Sikh (North Indian). Communities are neither politically nor economically autonomous. Some interracial affinity is based upon English-language education as well as economic and political interdependence. Cultural assimilation is minimal, but the near balance of indigenous and nonindigenous groups produces accommodation. There is still no Malaysian culture.

Islam is the declared state religion of the Malays, with the king supreme in matters of faith and the sultans ruling on such diverse subjects as Muslim law, education, and custom. Muslim courts adjudicate religious offenses, such as unfaithfulness, nonattendance at Friday prayers, and consumption of intoxicating liquor. Muslims are also forbidden to accept interest or dividends, a law that can affect Malay participation in industrial progress.

Traditions and religious customs are most evident at the village level; about 70 percent of Malaysia's population live in villages. Forty-four percent of the total work force of 4.5 million are engaged in agriculture. A Malay village community is economically comfortable; overwhelming problems of debt are absent, but many villagers have neither electricity nor piped water. Paddy culture predominates; kerbaus (water buffalo) are used for heavy duties; and, if need be, the villagers call on a *bomoh* (mystic healer).

Villages of Chinese composition differ in architecture, social relationships, and even function, remaining ethnically inward-directed. They are often mere transitional units, before growing into small townships. Rubber production resulted in the new social dimension of estate living, almost exclusively for Indian laborers, who occupy long row houses under the paternal tutelage of the estate management.

Both increasing mobility and growth in the manufacturing and services sectors contribute to a rapid rate of urbanization. By 1981, it is expected that 35 percent of the population will live in towns, and that the largest influx will be of Malay people. In a communally divided country like Malaysia, the integrating habits of urban living can have a revolutionary effect on the structural base of politics.

But there are other problems. The migration from rural areas outpaces urban employment opportunities, and unemployment and underemployment in the cities have risen to nearly 20 percent. This results in high labor mobility, the development of slum and squatter areas, and, ultimately, urban instability. Malaysia has had its share of domestic conflict, but, compared with neighboring countries, it has been fortunate in experiencing continuity in leadership and policy.

Much of what happens in Malaysia today has its origins in institutions, attitudes, and societal factors rooted in the British colonial period that began in the late eighteenth century with the Straits Settlements in Penang, Malacca, and Singapore. The English traders found separate sultanates in the coastal regions, but no unified country. The term "Malaya" is British, and Malaya itself is a political accident of British rule. British residents were attached to the sultanates to improve administrative practices, tax collection, and transportation; in the process, good government was substituted for self-government, and advice was superseded by control.

The first Federation of the Protected Malay States, consisting of four states, was created by British Governor-General Swettenham in 1896. Over the next two decades, another five "unfederated states" were added which, with the Straits Settlements, brought British Malaya 15 loosely coordinated units. The establishment of a political and economic infrastructure was interrupted by 4 years of Japanese occupation during World War II. Subsequently, a communist guerrilla war plagued the country until the defeat of the guerrillas in 1960.

Communist subversion continues, although it is limited geographically to the northern states bordering Thailand and to Sarawak, adjoining Indonesia. The situation is aggravated by more than 100,000 Filipino refugees in Sabah and an equal number of refugees from the Indochinese states living along the east coast of West Malaysia.

Eleven peninsular states, except Singapore, formed an independent Federation of Malaya in 1957. With the accretion of Singapore, Sabah, and Sarawak in 1963, Malaya became Malaysia. However, only 2 years later, in August 1965, Singapore left the federation because of ethnic incompatibility. Ever since, Malaysia has been a parliamentary democracy with a multiparty system, regular elections, and a competitive, free-enterprise system. The path toward modernization has been followed successfully, but some inherent obstacles remain.

Fundamental sociocultural cleavages make Malaysia's viability questionable. The ethnic cleavage is the most serious because the communities are divided along parallel lines, reinforced by religion, language, cultural traditions, wealth accumulation, and geographic separation. The economic cleavage is also causing concern. The income differential works to the disadvantage of the rural areas, and the urban rich get richer. Chronic unemployment among the young is particularly dangerous to the government, because 58 percent of Malaysia's electorate are between the ages of 21 and 35. Finally, there is a territorial cleavage between West and East Malaysia, between urban and rural, and between the need for centralization and the parochial desire to maintain a regional identity.

Cleavages can nonetheless produce a productive pluralism, and the Malaysian government is encouraging a new nationalism to overcome ethnic loyalties. Rapid industrialization will stimulate integration and wealth accumulation. Government emphasis on aid to *bumiputras*, "the sons of the soil" (Malays), may rectify economic imbalances. Coercive forms of federalism are being replaced by greater regional cooperation and consensus building. Despite its weaknesses, Malaysia may well become a model country in the area of national development.

Hans Indorf

Mongolia
(Mongolian People's Republic)

Area: 600,000 sq mi (1.554 million sq km)
Population: 1.6 million
   Density: 2.67 per sq mi (1.03 per sq km)
   Growth rate: not available
Percent of population under 14 years of age: not available
Infant deaths per 1,000 live births: not available
Life expectancy at birth: 63 years
Leading causes of death: not available
Ethnic composition: Mongol 90%; Kazak; very few Chinese and Russian
Languages: Mongolian, Russian
Literacy: almost 100%
Religions: Buddhist
Percent population urban: 48%
Percent population rural: 52%
Gross national product: $1.5 billion (est.)
   Per capita GNP: $940 (est.)
   Per capita GNP growth rate: 1.6% (1970–1977, est.)
Inflation rate: not available

Mongolia's very small population and its vast area, low level of productivity, and shortage of manpower block its development as a modern nation. The government's continuing failure to increase its livestock herds and to meet plan goals indicates a lack of commitment to modernization and change. Development in Mongolia comes from outside and is urged by foreigners, for the most part. Many Mongols leave the encouragement and management of change to the Soviet Union.

There has been no economic miracle, and economic self-sufficiency has not been attained. The herds of livestock have not increased in 40 years; repeated shortfalls have marked grain harvests; industrialization has been limited; the attempt to drill for and refine oil failed; hundreds of thousands of Mongols still live in *yurts* (tents with wooden latticework frames), and even Ulan Bator, the capital, includes many clusters of tent dwellings. Foot-dragging and passive resistance delay the fulfillment of the government's ambitious goals.

In addition, Mongols are not being readied for independence and self-sufficiency; instead, the Soviet Union's economic and military infiltration increasingly dominates and absorbs the vulnerable infrastructure. What results is not oppression or exploitation, but a spurious and artificial kind of independence.

Mongolia's 600,000-square-mile (1.554-million-sq-km) territory is cold, high, and dry. Rainfall is generally light, but it is heavier in the northern third of the country, which can better sustain people, animals, and economic endeavors than the southern two-thirds of Mongolia. The forest and steppes of the north contrast markedly with sparse and scrubby vegetation of the Gobi Desert in the south. Lack of water, a problem almost everywhere in Mongolia, reaches critical proportions in the Gobi. The U.S.S.R. in the north and west and China in the east and south completely surround Mongolia, which thus lacks direct access to any other country or to the sea.

Its natural resources are limited. Copper and molybdenum are now being mined for export in addition to the small-scale traditional mining of coal for domestic use. In the Gobi, oil production and refining were attempted in the 1960s, but were abandoned after only a few years because of mediocre results.

The very small population of 1.6 million is growing rapidly because of a high birthrate and an infant mortality rate reported to be "favorable" by the government. Life expectancy is steadily increasing, but underpopulation remains a serious problem.

The Mongols are a Turkic people, distinct from the Chinese or other Asians. Their language is unrelated to either Chinese or Russian, although today it employs the Cyrillic (Slavic) alphabet. Most Mongols were traditionally *arats* (livestock-herding nomads)

who practiced Lamaist Buddhism of the Tibetan variety.

Khalkha Mongols constitute about 75 percent of the total population, and western, Oirat Mongols another 10 percent. Buryat Mongols, 5 percent of the total, have migrated across the border from the Soviet Union in the Lake Baikal area. Other groups include the Kazaks in the extreme western part of the country, and smaller groups related to ethnic minorities in Sinkiang Uighur (in China) and Soviet Central Asia.

The once large Chinese population (at least 150,000) was greatly reduced by forced expulsion in the 1920s, and only a small Chinese colony remains. There are a few thousand Russians in Mongolia, most of them on temporary assignment, who do not become permanent residents.

Many Mongols continue to lead a nomadic life, herding livestock and living in yurts. But the pattern of nomadism is changing, and so is the yurt; almost always this kind of tent now includes a wooden floor and an iron stove, plus a stovepipe to draw out the smoke. The establishment of the livestock collective has meant the construction of permanent buildings, a fixed headquarters, and a regular operational base. A school and sometimes even some fixed, permanent dwellings are included in the collective. At the headquarters of the collective, the presence of electricity encourages Mongols to settle there for longer periods. Trucks are often used to help Mongols with their moves, so that more and heavier household possessions can be brought to these collectives than could be carried by camels.

While most rural Mongols continue the traditional nomadic pattern, today many Mongols grow wheat on state farms. An increasing number of them are radically changing their lifestyles, opting for apartment living in the big city. Ulan Bator's population has been rapidly increasing for decades, and now totals nearly 400,000 (one-fourth of the total population of the country). The city of Darkhan, established in 1961, and Erdenet, established in 1974, account for tens of thousands of city dwellers. Rural manpower is becoming increasingly scarce.

The urban areas have developed dramatically. The original core of a traditional Mongolian city—a Buddhist monastery surrounded by a community of Chinese shopkeepers—no longer exists. Cities are now centers of government bureaucracy and industrial development. Government offices, factories, and blocks of apartment buildings are gradually displacing clusters of yurts. Unquestionably revolutionary change has occurred, including a psychological and motivational revolution for many Mongols. Many Mongols in government offices manage their careers to include considerable travel in the Soviet Union and elsewhere. Little support exists for a return to the old days and old ways, even though many problems and some resistance continue.

Soviet-style bureaucracy has mushroomed; govern-

Almost everyone tended livestock for many years until alternative job opportunities became available. Operations at a sheep-dipping tank control infectious diseases. (Photo: FAO/ N. G. Ipatenko.)

ment employees constitute a "new class" and a major new factor in Mongolian society. The ruling elite is dominated by economists and planners who consult with Soviet advisers. Other elite groups include journalists and educational administrators, who propagate and defend ideology and assure conformity through indoctrination and propaganda. While egalitarianism has not developed, the substantially increased career opportunities available to Mongols suggest that the many years of Communist domination have had some important positive effects.

The more than 20 million head of livestock in Mongolia are a major economic asset. Over half the herds are sheep; there are also horses, cattle (including many yaks), goats, and camels (the two-humped Bactrian variety). Modern veterinary practice and some improvements in breeding have enhanced the economic value of the herds. Limited and small-scale industry mostly deals with the processing of animal products. The Soviet Union established the factories and supplied the machinery. Wool is washed and meat is canned or otherwise processed before being sent to the Soviet Union. The collectivization of the herds effectively imposed political and bureaucratic control, circumscribing the freedom of the arats without improving their living standards.

Mongols began grain farming on a significant scale when the so-called "new lands" were organized. The first stage of organization began in 1959, and the second, which substantially increased the area under cultivation, was started in 1976. Thus, settled agriculture became an integral part of the indigenous economy. Today, some Mongols drive Russian tractors and mechanical harvesters, and often Russian teams assigned to the harvest in Eastern Siberia continue across the border and join the Mongols. The Soviet Union has established flour mills and bakeries, whose products have already modified the Mongolian diet.

Mining has been limited. A new project in 1979 was a large copper and molybdenum mining and smelter operation at the new town of Erdenet. The products are destined for export to the U.S.S.R. and are expected to go a long way toward balancing trade between Mongolia and the U.S.S.R. For many years, the Soviet Union has sent far more to Mongolia than it has received in return, and it is hoped that the copper and molybdenum will substantially reduce that imbalance. The Soviet Union planned the project, and Soviet architects and planners laid out the new town there.

The isolated and peripatetic existence of many Mongols has been significantly altered by improved communications and transport facilities. Trucks, cars, jeeps, and motorcycles, supplied to Mongolia from the U.S.S.R. and the East European countries, all weaken Mongolia's former near-total dependence on the horse. The north-south Trans-Mongolian Railroad, with spurs to coal mines and to the Erdenet mining complex, links Mongolia to the Trans-Siberian Railroad. Local airline operations serve the various regional centers and the U.S.S.R.'s Aeroflot line provides regular service to Ulan Bator from Moscow and Irkutsk. Buses serve most major points in the country.

Telephone, radio, television, and newspapers are in operation on a scale sufficient to maintain social intercourse in a manner never envisioned in pre-Communist Mongolia. Television reaches large parts of northern Mongolia and radio operates everywhere. Electricity is available in many places, but often only from inefficient and unreliable small generators. The northern part of the country adjoining East Siberia is being tied into the massive power grid being built in the U.S.S.R.

Education is the major positive accomplishment of the Communist regime in Mongolia. The population, formerly almost totally illiterate, have become practically 100 percent literate in the Mongolian language, and tens of thousands of Mongols also speak Russian with some fluency. University and specialized technical education is provided in Mongolia, and thousands go every year to the Soviet Union for part or all of their education.

Mongolian access to Soviet facilities, education, and training opens up a far larger world of opportunity and makes possible all sorts of specialization. Consultation, direction, and advice from the Russians provide Mongolia with a range of experience and knowledge far beyond its autonomous capability.

At a modern poultry farm, women workers feed the animals. Rural labor has become scarce because of the exodus to the urban areas. (Photo: FAO/ N. G. Ipatenko.)

Thus, Mongols are often apprentices or protégés of Russian intellectual and/or political patrons.

Education emphasizes economics, vocational training, science, and technology, all practical matters of production and efficiency. Economics and planning are an important part of Mongolian education; these fields are important routes to political power. Trained economists dominate the political elite and the government bureaucracy. Six of the eight full members of the Mongolian Politburo and both of its candidate members have a background, education, and experience predominantly in economics. Four Politburo members served previously as chairmen of the State Planning Commission. The two top political leaders, Yumjaagiin Tsedenbal and Jambyn Batmunkh, have served as directors of the Economic Institute in Ulan Bator. At least two Politburo members received advanced degrees in economics from universities in the U.S.S.R.

Women have been fully included in the process of education at all levels of instruction. Though Mongolian women were never sequestered or veiled, their literacy rate was formerly much lower than that of their male counterparts, and educational opportunities for them were nonexistent.

Three factors that have affected the economic development of Mongolia are closely interrelated. Mongolia is to some extent an appendage of East Siberia and major developments in the area affect Mongolia's economy, particularly the development of a permanent population settlement in East Siberia. Mongolia is also an extension of the East Siberian military district, a strategic buffer between the Soviet Union and China. Soviet army troops operate in Mongolia essentially without restriction. Finally, Mongolia's economic development is supported by the U.S.S.R. in response to the Chinese challenge and threat. Thus, to a great extent China determines the rate of development supported by the Soviet Union in Mongolia. Russia's presence in Mongolia is necessarily anti-Chinese in character. Soviet-Chinese competition accelerates Mongolian development and is a crucial factor in Mongolia's modernization.

The Mongols traditionally fear absorption by the Chinese, who are so many and so close; they do not fear the Russians, fewer in number and for the most part much farther away. Many Mongols are indifferent or even hostile to the Communist system the Russians introduced. But that is not so important to them as maintaining a defense against permanent Chinese settlement.

The underlying ideological pattern of economic development in Mongolia is officially described as a transition from feudalism to socialism, bypassing capitalism. Soviet experience and Soviet technology and economic assistance are said to have made possible this leap forward. Substantial improvements in public health, sanitation, and medical care has reversed the population decline of earlier years. The Mongolian medical and public health system follows the Soviet pattern; Russians established the first medical-training facilities and hospitals in Mongolia. The Soviet model has improved Mongolian education and health, multiplied career opportunities, and raised the standard of living. This model has meant the collectivization of most of the livestock and tight restriction on private ownership, and has led to the establishment of state farms for raising wheat. Factories are all state-owned, and the factory workers are considered a proletariat in the Marxist sense. The miners at Erdenet and in the coal mines are similarly classified.

A State Planning Commission (Gosplan) prepares the successive 5-year plans that promulgate the goals of economic development. The goal of education, training, and indoctrination is the creation of the "new Mongolian," who will be entirely devoted to the interests of the collective group. Socialized medicine prevails. Nomadism tends to be scorned as a remnant of feudalism, and permanent settlement of the population is encouraged by the regime. Living in an apartment building in the city is ideologically preferable to living in a yurt.

The most important factor in Mongolia's modern history is the traditional triple role played by Russia. Both before and after 1921—the date when Communism took root in Mongolia—Russia represented the

A mounted herdsman tends sheep in the northern Gobi province. The country's more than 20 million head of cattle are a major economic asset; over half are sheep. (Photo: FAO/ N. G. Ipatenko.)

main agent of change, modernization, and progress. Before and after 1921, Russia protected Mongolia from its foreign enemies, China and Japan. And, for the most part since 1921, the Soviet Union has attacked and very nearly destroyed Mongolia's culture, history, and unique identity. The Soviet Union has attempted to force Mongolia to identify its national interest with the Soviet Union's national interest. Mongolia is to be a nondeviant satellite.

Modernization and Westernization entered Mongolia when the Russians established their first consulate in the capital city of Urga (now Ulan Bator) in the mid-nineteenth century. In Mongolia, the Russians have been the "Westernizers," bringing the twentieth-century methods to a backward and remote land. The Russians introduced almost everything new to the Mongols, and the Russian version of Western civilization has been the model for Mongolians.

One shared interest of Mongolia and Russia is their mutual fear of China. Mongolia wanted to evade Chinese domination, and requested Russian help. The Russians responded in 1911. In the 1920s the Soviet Union helped the Mongols to expel the Chinese. The amount of Russian aid increased considerably when the Sino-Soviet dispute began to develop seriously after 1957. Until an energized and industrializing China challenged and threatened the Soviet position, it had suited the U.S.S.R. to let Mongolia stagnate. Fearing China, the Soviet Union responded with accelerated investment and development. The continuing Sino-Soviet dispute keeps alive the Soviet fear of a Chinese threat to Siberia, which increases its interest in Mongolia.

Mongolia has traditionally been a Russian buffer state. When a militarized and aggressive Japan defeated China in 1895 and Russia in 1905, and then three decades later developed Manchuria and built up a serious military threat there, the Russians used Mongolia as a buffer. In 1939, in the Battle of Nomonkhan, on Mongolian soil, the Russians decisively defeated the Japanese. The 1945 Japanese surrender ended an important chapter in Asia and in Mongolia.

The essence of traditional Mongolian culture was the Buddhist Church, with its tens of thousands of lamas, hundreds of monasteries, and its revered religious leader, the Jebtsun Damba Khutukhtu. In the 1930s the Soviet-dominated Communist regime first restricted and then interdicted the assumption of lama status, physically destroyed many of the monasteries and converted others to secular use (e.g., as warehouses), and forbade the search for a successor to the Jebtsun Damba Khutukhtu after the eighth and last one died in 1924.

Use of the Tibetan language, which had been common in church circles, was discouraged, and the old traditional vertical Mongolian script was replaced by Cyrillic. Both moves had the effect of making access to religious texts difficult. Because Communist bureaucrats believed that progress required settled existence rather than nomadic life, livestock herding and living in yurts were patronized as primitive and backward.

Khorloin Choibalsan, the most important of the Soviet-oriented Mongols, occupied top leadership positions from 1940 until his death in 1952, and he copied Stalin in his actions and even in dress and style. Choibalsan had long been important in the Mongolian secret police organization before he became leader of the party and the government, carrying out directives from the U.S.S.R. and the Communist International (Comintern).

An officially promulgated propaganda version of Mongolian history attempts to bolster the legitimacy of the Communist regime, and to supply ammunition against China in the Sino-Soviet dispute. Genghis Khan is manipulated as a symbol by the U.S.S.R., China, and Mongolia, without much regard for historical accuracy. The Soviet Union usually condemns him as a tyrant and oppressor, while China often defends him as a unifier and nation builder. Mongols in Mongolia have several times tried to honor the Great Khan, but have been forced to bow to Soviet anti-Genghis pressure. China usually honors Genghis Khan, some Mongols attempt to honor him, and the ruling Mongols go along with Soviet policy prohibiting such attention.

Although the Soviet Union and China as well as the Communist regime in Mongolia have condemned Buddhism, destroyed many of its temples and much of its property, and harassed and killed many of the lamas, they all try to exploit Buddhism. In 1979 the Dalai Lama, for many years a refugee from his native Tibet, was invited by Mongolia to a World Buddhist Congress in Ulan Bator, which he attended. China has also been trying to attract the Dalai Lama back to Tibet. Recently, the Russians, Mongols, and Chinese have been cleaning up religious buildings and restoring them as museums and (in a few special cases) as functioning monasteries. All three regimes now support a small number of "official" lamas.

The U.S.S.R. and the regime it supports in Ulan Bator build up to heroic proportions a Mongol named Sukhe Bator, who is presented as Mongolia's Lenin, and the meeting of Sukhe Bator with Lenin (which did in fact occur in November 1921) is memorialized in paintings, songs, books, and manifold paraphernalia.

The Battle of Nomonkhan of 1939, in which Soviet forces commanded by General Zhukov, plus some Mongolian military units, defeated Japan, is the subject of exceptional attention. There is not only a memorial at the site, but a museum is scheduled to open there. The symbolism encourages the conception of the Soviet role as protector of the Mongols and of military collaboration between Russia and Mongolia. It also serves to warn China of the Soviet Union's tough defense of Mongolia from an invader threatening from Manchuria.

The future development of Mongolia will be determined by the course of Sino-Soviet relations and by

Soviet and Chinese economic development; in other words, both by the interaction of these two giant countries and the separate paths they take. Mongolia's control of its fate is minimal. The Soviet Union's control of Mongolia's fate is near total, and China's direct influence is slight.

The U.S.S.R. has responded to what it perceives as a Chinese threat by consolidating its control of Mongolia and increasing its presence there. Sino-Soviet détente might slow Mongolian development, but vigorous Chinese development of Manchuria and Inner Mongolia would probably appear threatening to the Soviet Union and would accelerate the development of Mongolia. The successful development of East Siberia and the Soviet Far East and success in populating those areas would also lead to the further development of Mongolia.

The Soviet Union's military response to the Chinese threat includes maintaining regular Red Army units in Mongolia, on the border with China.

Mongolia is treated strategically as part of the Soviet Union, territory not to be yielded to an enemy. It is not a buffer state but serves as a line of defense. Mongolia is not negotiable; Russia's economic tentacles from Eastern Siberia enter directly into Mongolia and so do the military tentacles of the Soviet Red Army.

Mongolia's Russian orientation and the cultural Russification of its society will continue, but the high birthrate of the Mongols and the scarcity of Russians in East Siberia will ensure the physical survival of the Mongolian ethnic group, even if Mongolian cultural identity is eroded or lost entirely. Today, the border separating Mongolia from the Soviet Union is in effect being erased and absorption is occurring. Progress is defined not in terms of self-sufficiency but rather in terms of closer integration with the U.S.S.R. Ultimately, Mongolia may be fully incorporated into the U.S.S.R., though international political considerations may prevent the realization of this Soviet goal.

Robert A. Rupen

Papua New Guinea

Area: 178,260 sq mi (461,691 sq km)
Population: 2.9 million
  Density: 16 per sq mi (6 per sq km)
  Growth rate: 2.4% (1970–1977)
Percent of population under 15 years of age: 46%
Infant deaths per 1,000 live births: rural 170; urban 100
Life expectancy at birth: rural 50 years; urban 60 years
Leading causes of death: pneumonia, malaria, diarrhea, tuberculosis, leprosy, and malnutrition
Ethnic composition: Papua New Guineans, Australians, Chinese, others
Languages: Hiri Motu, English, Melanesian Pidgin
Literacy: 32% (1975)
Religions: traditional, Christian
Percent population urban: 13% (1975)
Percent population rural: 87% (1975)
Gross national product: $1.64 billion
  Per capita GNP income: $560
  Per capita GNP growth rate: 2.5% (1970–1977)
Inflation rate: 7.2% (1970–1977)

Long isolated by seas and mountains, Papua New Guinea's people were plunged into intensive contact with the outside world during World War II. Independence came in 1975, only 30 years later. This fascinating country is affected by three dominant influences: the rugged geography and cultural diversity of the country, the tremendous influence of Australia on development patterns, and the search by Papua New Guineans for ways of life reflecting truly national values.

Papua New Guinea (PNG) has an area of 178,260 square miles (461,691 sq km) and comprises the eastern half of the island of New Guinea plus smaller islands off the main coast, including New Britain,

New Ireland, Bougainville, Buka, Manus, and Trobriand Islands. High central mountain ranges dominate the interior highlands, isolating scores of mountain valleys inaccessible except by air; thus, PNG is said to have the largest number of bush airstrips per capita in the world. At lower altitudes, swamps, rain forests, and broad rivers provide additional barriers to transport and communication. In such a country, it is difficult to establish national networks of production and distribution.

Rainfall is abundant and soils are good; rural farmers have been described as living in "subsistence affluence" because it is relatively easy to produce staple food crops in this fertile and well-watered tropical country. Other important natural resources include forests, fish, and minerals. The huge copper mines in the North Solomons Province (formerly Bougainville) provide almost half of PNG's export totals, and 20 to 30 percent of its gross domestic product. There are energy potentials under study, such as petroleum and hydroelectric power.

The population of PNG is just under 3 million; Papua New Guineans are Melanesians, but the country also includes some Chinese and Caucasian (mainly Australian) expatriates. Port Moresby is the national capital, and the country contains 20 provinces, which are self-governing to a large degree. The population is overwhelmingly rural. Between 60 and 70 percent of PNG's people are subsistence farmers, many of whom are involved only marginally, if at all, with the cash economy. Most of the population are Christian; heavy mission activity in earlier years has virtually eliminated traditional religions.

Papua New Guinea's population is young (in 1971, 46 percent of the population were less than 15 years old) and is increasing rapidly; the 1970–1977 growth rate of 2.4 percent is expected to rise to 3.1 percent by 1981. Pneumonia, malaria, diarrhea, tuberculosis, leprosy, and malnutrition are prevalent. Health services are good, however, in comparison with many other developing countries. In 1976, rural infant mortality was put at 170 per 1,000 live births, while in urban areas it was 100 per 1,000 live births. Life expectancy also showed rural-urban differences, from 50 years (rural) to 60 years (urban).

There are hundreds of diverse ethnic groups, each with its own language and distinctive customs. In this linguistically complex environment, there are three lingua francas: Hiri Motu, English, and Melanesian Pidgin. Of these, Pidgin is the most widely understood. Traditional PNG societies are small-scale, with no large centralized political groupings. Most ethnic groups have nonascriptive leadership systems structured through clan and subclan groupings. Kinship, expressed through the clan, is of major importance; the Pidgin term *wantok* (literally "one talk/language") refers to members of the same clan, language group, or geographical area.

In rural society, leadership is generally achieved rather than ascribed, with leaders—or "big men," as they are called in Pidgin—rising up through a combination of personality, ability, and kin support. The prestige of big men is enhanced by the various forms of exchange that they organize. These take place within or between clan groups, often involving pigs, shells, food, and, increasingly, money, alcohol, and manufactured goods. Such exchanges are often complex and lengthy, establishing or reaffirming special relationships between groups. Geographic and linguistic barriers have made ethnic groups generally suspicious of each other until relatively recently, and even now regionalism is an extremely strong force in PNG, with the wantok system manifesting itself in patterns of national politics, economic activity, and urban settlement patterns.

Overall population density is low—15.7 per sq mi (5.2 per sq km), but some rural areas are becoming crowded. Little land is alienated—97 percent of PNG's land is communally owned, usually through clan groups. Rural villages rarely have more than 300 to 400 inhabitants, although settlement patterns vary. Typical of parts of the highlands is a dispersed pattern of individual families or clusters of descendant groups, often over a large area. Ground is cultivated with simple tools; gardens are cut from bush and eventually returned to fallow. Lowland staples include yams and taro; in the highlands, sweet potato is the staple; in the river deltas, the people eat sago. In addition to agriculture, people engage in fishing, hunting, and trading and producing some cash crops, including tea, coffee, cocoa, copra, and pyrethrum. While many rural people do not deal with cash crops at all, there is a general trend toward a combined sub-

sistence agricultural–cash agricultural system where possible.

Urbanization, while not a traditional pattern in PNG, has proceeded especially rapidly since the 1960s. Although in 1976 there were only seven towns with populations larger than 10,000, they grew at a rate of 16 percent per year between 1966 and 1971. This rate is expected to fall to between 8 and 12 percent in the future. In 1971, the urban population was 9.5 percent of the total; this is expected to rise to approximately 27 percent by 1991.

Until recently, Papua New Guineans have been virtual strangers in their own towns and cities, which were the creations of an Australian colonial administration. Their design and functions reflected Australian needs and values; there are few sidewalks in Port Moresby, for example, since it was assumed that everyone owned a car.

Rapid urbanization has brought the usual problems of unemployment, housing shortages, and crime. Unemployment in particular is growing. Out of a labor force of approximately 1.25 million, only about 12 to 14 percent have wage jobs; at the same time, almost 40,000 people enter the work force annually. Unemployment among young school-leavers is of special concern. Informal sector employment has been of negligible importance until recently, mainly because of Australian-based restrictive legislation. Most of the urban work force are unskilled or semiskilled, and few local businesses are run by nationals. Chinese

In the central highlands, workers harvest coffee and carry it to the village. Farming is primitive, and roads are very poor. (Photo: United Nations/C. Chigi.)

dominate middle-level commerce, while big business is almost wholly Australian.

The National Housing Commission has successfully introduced new housing schemes to enable urban migrants to construct their own dwellings, originally restricted by high-standard Australian building codes. Housing continues to be a problem, however; the National Planning Office estimates that there would have to be a fivefold increase in house construction to keep pace with urban growth.

Although urban migrants often retain strong links with home or replicate aspects of the rural social network through the wantok system in town, the comprehensive interlocking support systems typical of rural village life usually disappear in the towns. As a result, urbanites depend more and more on Western-style welfare organizations, some of which seem poorly suited to local needs. Urban crime is a persistent problem and is also expected to worsen as the urban population rises. For housing, welfare, and crime prevention, urban dwellers and government officials are attempting to find and apply indigenous solutions that reflect local rather than imported values.

Present problems are, of course, rooted in a past largely dominated by Australia. Until well in the 1960s, PNG was controlled from Canberra, and a policy of "uniform development" placed emphasis on primary education for all, with less emphasis on developing technical skills, leadership, or an entrepreneurial class. Under the Australians, primary education was well-developed, even in the most remote parts of the country. Christian missions provided much of the educational input in these areas. There is now an extensive network of secondary schools, high schools, vocational schools, and teachers colleges spread throughout the country. But the literacy rate is still a low 32 percent.

Marchers celebrate independence day in Port Moresby. The country became independent on September 16, 1975, after 90 years of foreign rule and 2 years of self-government. (Photo: United Nations/NJ.)

In the late 1960s, the University of Papua New Guinea was created to provide tertiary training across a broad spectrum of disciplines both classical and development-related. Essentially based on an Anglo-Saxon model and heavily staffed by expatriates, the university system includes three campuses: at Waigani near Port Moresby, at Lae, and at Goroka in the highlands. Papua New Guineans have increasingly attempted to make their university system more responsive to the country's development needs, so far with only mixed success.

Before the 1960s, Papua New Guinea was one of the last great unknown areas of the world, at least as far as Westerners were concerned. Prehistorians have established the fact that man lived in the territory 10,000 years ago, and probably longer. European and Asian seafarers knew of the island centuries ago, probably long before the first recorded European sighting by a Portuguese mariner in the early 1500s. Spanish, Dutch, English, French, and German explorers followed.

In 1884, Britain proclaimed a protectorate over southern New Guinea, and in 1888 it annexed the territory. As the Territory of Papua, it was placed under Australian control in 1906. Germany claimed possession of northern New Guinea in 1884, and the area came under the direct control of the German government in 1899. Shortly after the outbreak of World War I, the Australians forced the Germans to surrender German New Guinea, and in 1920 Australian control of the area became complete, when the League of Nations gave it a mandate to govern the former German colony.

Exploration and development of the country continued at a slow pace until 1942, when the Japanese invaded Rabaul and subsequently occupied large areas of the mainland. By 1944, the territory had come under Allied control; after World War II, the United Nations granted Australia the right to continue governing New Guinea. The Australians administered Papua and New Guinea as a single unit. The war had stimulated the development of the territory, and large areas of the hitherto unexplored highlands were opened to Western planters, missionaries, explorers, and administrators.

In the 1950s, the first steps toward eventual self-rule were taken, with the establishment of a combined Papua and New Guinea Legislative Council. In the early 1960s, Australia realized that Papua New Guinea would eventually become independent. A national House of Assembly was set up in 1964, and elections were held. By 1968, local political parties had emerged, and in 1972, the Pangu Pati Party succeeded in forming a coalition government under Michael Somare, which pressed for early independence. Papua New Guinea became self-governing in 1973 and fully independent in 1975. Given the fact that before 1973 a large percentage of the population did not actually favor independence, and given the frequently expressed fears of both nationals and expatriates about the likelihood of interethnic and interracial violence, the transition to independence was exceptionally smooth and peaceful. Somare became Prime Minister in a Westminster-type government.

Internal regionalism emerged as a full-blown political force after independence, with the appearance of separatist groups in many regions, incuding Papua, East New Britain, Bougainville, and Trobriand Islands. Some of these—notably Papua and copper-rich Bougainville—threatened secession, and Bougainville actually broke away briefly in 1976, to be quickly reunited with PNG as the North Solomons Province. By mid-1977, the threat of regionalism had faded considerably, mainly because of the success of provincial self-government and other national efforts at decentralization and redistribution of government resources.

Papua New Guinea seeks development that encourages growth and the quality of life. Increasing financial viability should be accompanied by an equitable redistribution of benefits. A national development philosophy was first articulated in 1972, with the publication of the Somare coalition government's "Eight Aims." These, while largely programmatic, have become the general basis for development planning. The eight aims include: a larger proportion of the economy in local hands; more equitable distribution of benefits; greater government decentralization; more small-scale artisan activity; increased self-reliance; more revenue from local sources; more participation by women in development; and government control, where necessary, of portions of the economy. Subsequently, the government outlined further guidelines and priorities for foreign investment and instituted a budget priorities system. A recent World Bank report stated that PNG had an "unusually clear" set of development aims.

The greatest problem facing PNG is its continuing dependence on Australia. This takes several forms, chief among them financial. As much as 40 to 50 percent of the national budget comes from an Australian grant-in-aid, without which many government services would cease to function. This grant amounts to about A$200 million yearly, or US$80 per capita in PNG—one of the highest aid levels in the world. Although analysts are optimistic that the country will eventually end its dependence on Australian money, they expect this to take a decade or more.

Another aspect of dependence is the lack of skilled manpower. Australian policy did not produce more than a handful of experienced Papua New Guinean politicians, administrators, or trained technicians before independence and even today, with 90 percent localization of the public service, PNG depends heavily on expatriate skilled labor. There are approximately 35,000 expatriates in PNG, several thousand of whom work in the public service. About 30 percent of them are teachers. An increasing number of graduates from the recently created national university system, plus a steady buildup of other trained nation-

als, will in time end PNG's dependence on expatriates, if the country can prevent its brainpower from emigrating to Australia.

Finally, PNG has been heavily dependent on outside—mainly Australian—institutions and values. Until PNG's independence, virtually all national structures came from Australia. As the main modernizing force, the government imported nearly everything it needed from Australia, from building materials to social institutions. As a result, in addition to an infrastructure far superior to that of many other developing countries, PNG has a government that is far too costly and complex for the country it serves, an overlarge and highly organized public service whose high salaries constitute a major drain on government funds, and a nationwide wage and price structure based on Australian standards rather than on local realities.

The years since independence have been auspicious; Papua New Guineans have shown their resourcefulness and skill in building a new nation and in applying national values and approaches in a variety of areas—education, the arts, government, and urban development, to name a few. The problems of regionalism, self-reliance, and national identity will not be solved quickly. But Papua New Guineans have demonstrated their willingness and determination to confront these problems; in their first years as a nation, they have made an impressive beginning.

Riall W. Nolan

In a country where 85 percent of the land area is covered with tropical forest, modern tractors are used to collect the logs for the developing timber industry. (Photo: United Nations.)

Philippines
(Republic of the Philippines)

Area: 115,600 sq mi (299,404 sq km)
Population: 45.6 million
  Density: 394 per sq mi (152 per sq km) (1975)
  Growth rate: 2.78% (1970–1977)
Percent of population under 15 years of age: 44% (1975)
Infant deaths per 1,000 live births: 80 (1979)
Life expectancy at birth: 58 years (1975)
Leading causes of death: tuberculosis, pneumonia
Ethnic composition: Malay, indigenous minorities, Chinese
Languages: Pilipino, English, more than 100 other languages
Literacy: Manila 90%; elsewhere 83%
Religions: Christian, Muslim, animist
Percent population urban: 32% (1975)
Percent population rural: 68% (1975)
Gross national product: $23.2 billion
  Per capita GNP: $510
  Per capita GNP growth rate: 3.7% (1970–1977)
Inflation rate: 40% (1974)

The Philippine island nation is rich in human and material resources. Its more than 45 million people are hardworking and resourceful; mineral resources are extensive; and the potential for economic development is great. The country's liabilities include a high birthrate, grinding poverty, chronic unemployment, and political repression. The average annual increase in per capita income has been 3.7 percent, but the increase has not provided a basis for self-sustained, long-term development; the distribution of the benefits of growth has been unequal, and it is unlikely that the rate of growth can be maintained.

Located 500 miles (805 km) off the coast of southern China, the Philippines stretches over 7,100 islands, covering a land area of 115,600 square miles (299,404 sq km), about the size of Italy or the state of Arizona. Luzon in the north and Mindanao in the south are the two largest islands, which account for nearly 65 percent of the Philippine territory. The other major islands—Samar, Negros, Palawan, Panay, Mindoro, Leyte, Cebu, Bohol, Masbate, and Sulu—make up most of the archipelago's land surface. The Philippines shares three larger physical and cultural worlds: Asia, the Pacific, and the West.

The Philippines has twice as much coastland as the United States, and marine life is abundant. It also ranks as one of the most mineral-rich areas in the world, with extensive deposits of gold, silver, copper, zinc, chromite, platinum, lead, nickel, iron ore, gypsum, salt, lime, marble, and coral rocks. With a contribution of 1 percent to the world's total gold production, the Philippines is the eighth leading gold producer in the world.

For a country with a relatively small land area, the Philippines is heavily populated, with a 1978 population of 46.3 million. The annual rate of population growth for the 1960–1970 decade was 3 percent, and it is estimated that by the year 2000 there will be close to 100 million Filipinos. Today, some 44 percent of the population are less than 15 years old.

The Philippines has 73 provinces, which divide into 1,445 municipalities (similar to counties), 21 municipal districts, 60 cities, and 42,000 barrios (now called "barangays" under martial law). The premier region, Manila, the nation's capital, is a bustling metropolis of more than 5 million people which offers extremes of affluence and poverty. Manila's elite reside here, along with millions of squatters and slum dwellers.

There are at least 116 languages in the country, mostly belonging to the Malayo-Polynesian family. Pilipino, based on Tagalog, is the national language, and English is spoken widely, particularly in the schools.

Culturally, Filipinos may be divided into three major groups: Christians, Muslims, and indigenous cultural minorities, neither Christian nor Muslim, who retain the lifestyle of precolonial Filipinos. The Christians, 85 percent Roman Catholic, inhabit most of the lowland areas and constitute more than 90 percent of the population.

The Muslims are found in Mindanao and Sulu and are estimated to comprise about 5 percent of the total population. Long before the Spaniards set foot on Philippine soil, Islam had taken root in Mindanao and Sulu and would have spread northward had it not been for the Spanish conquest. This Muslim area therefore underwent a different historical evolution. Muslims were derogatorily called Moros by the colonizers and other Filipinos. Over the years, the Manila-based Philippine government has tried to impose majority standards of education, justice, politics, and economic development that are alien to them. Muslim lands have also been grabbed by outsiders. As a result, there has been continuing Muslim unrest; a significant Muslim movement led by the Moro National Liberation Front (MNLF) wants Mindanao to secede from the Philippines.

The animists live in the rugged interior areas of the country. There are more than thirty mountain peoples. These groups, who are often called pagans (a Christian terminology), are the true Filipinos, since they were descended from the earliest settlers on the land and were least exposed to and corrupted by foreign influences.

More than two-thirds of the Philippine population still live in rural areas, and the economy is rooted in agriculture, which accounts for 56 percent of the total labor force. Rice, corn, and coconut are the major crops, and about 16 million Filipinos depend on them as their main source of income. Other significant products are sugar and abaca (Manila hemp). The non-farm population, estimated at 2 million, is directly dependent on fishing and forestry.

In 1972, 94 percent of all Philippine rice farms were smaller than 9.8 acres (4 ha) and almost 70 percent were smaller than 4.9 acres (2 ha). The large estates, or haciendas, are devoted to sugar production, particularly in the Visayan region. In 1960, farms larger than 247 acres (100 ha) accounted for 50 percent of the total sugar area under cultivation. Since 1960, there has been an increase in the number of medium-size [between 24.7 and 246.7 acres (between 10 and 99.9 ha)], probably as a result of the conversion of rice and corn farms to sugar. Some of the wealthiest Filipinos, the hacenderos, own sugar farms and plants. Conversely, some of the poorest Filipinos, the *sakadas* (migrant workers), are in the industry's work force.

Philippine agriculture has one of the highest rates of tenancy in Asia. Tenancy is highest in the central Luzon and southern Tagalog areas, both leading rice producing regions: by 1972, the number of tenant-operated rice and corn farms had increased to 1 million, but the rate of tenancy—about 45 percent of all rice and corn farms—stayed about the same as in 1960. Data is not available on tenancy in the sugar industry, but it is safe to assume that it is low compared with the rice, corn, and coconut industries.

The Philippine economic system is a legacy from the colonial era, which favored the development of agriculture and extractive industries, such as logging and mining. The United States insistence on free trade geared the Philippine economy to the production of exports like sugar, abaca, copra, coconut oil, lumber and other primary products in exchange for American imports like consumer goods and machinery. Philippine industrialization was never encouraged because it would compete with American products that were entering the local market tax-free.

The American colonial policy of promoting export agriculture had profound long-term effects on Philippine society. It led to a dependent type of economic development that tied the Philippines to the U.S. as a basic supplier of raw materials. Moreover, this colonial-type economy developed a character of its own, with a system of conservative values. The overall result was the classic dual economic structure, with a small wealthy elite concentrated in Manila and the big cities, and a very large group of peasants, farmers, and other lower-class Filipinos, who suffer varying degrees of deprivation and poverty.

Even after independence in 1946, the Philippines continued to depend on a neocolonial economy, and Americans continued to exploit Philippine natural resources and engaged in a wide range of economic activities, particularly mining, public utilities, power development, and agricultural industries. Philippine postwar economic policy set a high premium on industrialization; nonetheless, the economy remained primarily agrarian, although the country's productive agricultural potential remained largely untapped. Recently, the introduction of high-yielding varieties of rice has increased production. The growth of manufacturing has been sluggish, and manufacturing absorbs only 11 percent of the total work force. This is not enough to absorb a rapidly multiplying labor force, in which 800,000 young Filipinos become available for employment every year.

In spite of difficult economic conditions, education is a priority, and the number of highly educated and highly skilled Filipinos is impressive. Literacy is currently estimated to be 90 percent in Manila and 83 percent elsewhere. In 1975, the total enrollment at all educational levels was 11,314,000, of whom nearly 700,000 were in college. Each province has a public school system under the Ministry of Education and Culture. There are 44 state colleges and universities, including the University of Philippines, a leading institution of higher learning in Asia. There are also 3,027 private schools and colleges including 38 universities, and 281 vocational schools offering various training in trade, agriculture, fisheries, and home industries.

However, while education is one of the strongest Philippine assets, unemployment among the educated is high, hence the migration of Filipino profes-

Using a carabao distributed by the government's Animal Husbandry Bureau, a Muslim farmer plows his paddy. The government is encouraging the breeding of high-quality livestock. (Photo: FAO/ F. Mattioli.)

sionals to the United States and other countries. During 1967–1973, for instance, about 66,100 Filipino women—mostly doctors, nurses, dentists, workers in other medical and related fields, teachers, scientists, and engineers—emigrated to the United States, and 15,700 more left for other countries. If one adds the number of male migrants, the overall figure is much higher.

The basic unit of Philippine society is the family, which consists of the nuclear circle of father, mother, and children, and also their relatives. The nature of the Filipino family makes for an extensive kinship system. The relationships in this network are a powerful cohesive force, and the individual is expected to adhere to its norms and expectations. Older siblings, for instance, are responsible for younger ones, and children are expected to take care of their parents and elders. There are no old-age homes or welfare systems in the Philippines.

In rural areas, the family functions as a close productive unit. The father does the heavy work in the fields; the mother takes care of household tasks; children have a variety of responsibilities, such as running errands, pasturing work animals, and cleaning the yard; and other relatives help in various ways.

In urban areas, the family is more dispersed, and members pursue a variety of jobs, since there are more work opportunities in the cities. Consequently, there is greater chance for upward mobility in the cities

than in the barrios. It is estimated that 10 percent of the urban population is composed of a middle class of entrepreneurs, civil servants, writers, teachers, merchants, clerical workers, and small property owners. The great majority of the urban population, however, belongs to the lower class and are peddlers, domestics, drivers, stevedores, and laborers.

There is no strong evidence to suggest that urbanization has diminished family ties. Filipino elite families control most of the big businesses in the urban areas, particularly in Manila. Even longtime residents in the cities retain their provincial ties and loyalties. The squatter communities that make up almost 30 percent of the Manila population are recent arrivals from the provinces and show strong family solidarity.

Thus, the solidarity of the family is the essential ingredient of Filipino life. Philippine law, in the constitution and the civil code, upholds the "paramountcy of family relations" through the "indissolubility of marriage bonds, the legitimacy of children, the community of property during the marriage, the authority of parents over their children, and the validity of defense for any member of the family in case of unlawful aggression." There is no provision for divorce in the Philippines. However, changes like equal rights for women, if adopted, will radically affect the conservative nature of the Filipino family.

Recent archaeological discoveries in Tabon Cave in Palawan indicate that man existed in the Philippines as far back as 22,000 years ago. Islam gained a foothold in Sulu in the south as early as the year 1450, but its northward spread was arrested by the Spanish conquest in 1565, which imposed Christianity on the native population.

Spanish colonial rule in the next 333 years was highly repressive, and some 200 revolts broke out against the Spaniards. Following the Spanish-American War, Spain ceded the Philippines to the United States in 1898, and American colonial rule lasted for 50 years. The Americans introduced a public school system and various public health programs and improved transportation, communication, and civil service training. Concepts like consent of the governed, due process of law, and political participation became part of the Philippine vocabulary. But the Americans governed through the Filipino elite class and did not try to democratize the feudal social structure left by Spain. They regarded the Philippine economy as a supplier of raw materials for American industrial needs. When the Philippines became independent in 1946, it had some preparation for self-government, but the economy was underdeveloped and controlled by American interests.

From 1946 to 1972, the Philippines operated under a presidential type of government inherited from American colonial rule. Although the political system was based on the principle of checks and balances among the executive, legislative, and judicial branches, a strong presidency was favored in theory and in practice. A unitary rather than a federal system

This fishing village of Dumagok was completely destroyed in the earthquake and tidal wave of August 1976, and it was rebuilt with aid from the government and from Australia. (Photo: FAO/Mattioli.)

was established, and a high degree of centralization has given every Philippine President from Manuel L. Quezon to Ferdinand Marcos a tremendous amount of power. Postwar politics revolved around the presidency and the elections held every 2 years for national and local offices. Electoral activity, in turn, was based on the Filipino adaptation of the two-party system, a contest between competing political elites drawn from the country's most affluent families. Politics was considered a national pastime, lively, dynamic, personalistic, violent, and corrupt. A free and freewheeling press that was like a fourth branch of government continuously exposed political scandal, graft, and corruption in high places. Elections were costly and marred by violence, and only bourgeois elite groups could afford to participate. The interests of the great voting public were neither articulated nor advocated by the major parties, and a broad antisubversion law banned the existence of radical groups.

Political corruption and ineptness led to the deterioration of the economy, particularly in the 1960s. In 1970, the peso was devalued, an economically disastrous move. Emerging political forces, including student activists, intellectuals, economic nationalists, labor leaders, and mass organizations, began to protest in the streets. The American stranglehold on the economy, the presence of U.S. military bases, the antinationalist policies of Philippine postwar administrations, and the escalating official graft were the major issues that caused violent demonstrations in the so-called first quarter storm period of 1970. Marcos' two terms as President were almost overwhelmed by a rising tide of new radical nationalism that was supported even by conservative institutions like the courts. There were riots, marches, and demonstrations at Malacanan Palace, the U.S. embassy, and other bastions of the establishment. In August 1971, a Manila bombing incident killed 10 people and injured several others during a Liberal Party political rally. Marcos suspended the writ of habeas corpus, a prelude to the martial law that he imposed on the whole country a year later.

In declaring martial law, Marcos said two grave dangers threatened the state. One was a rebellion mounted by "a strange conspiracy of leftist and rightist radicals," obviously referring to the Maoist New People's Army (NPA) and the powerful oligarchs that have traditionally dominated Philippine society. The other was a "secessionist movement supported by foreign groups," referring to the Muslim movement in Mindanao, which was reportedly supported by Islamic countries, particularly Libya. Marcos abolished the Philippine Congress and elections, suspended all civil liberties, imposed a curfew, took over the mass media, and arrested thousands of students, journalists, professors, intellectuals, labor organizers, and others suspected of being subversive.

Marcos has ruled by presidential decree and has given the military a leading institutional role that includes (in addition to arresting people) intensified campaigns against NPA and Muslim guerrillas, civic action programs, building infrastructure facilities, and administering government institutions and some local governments. Military tribunals were also created to try cases involving crimes against the state. The size of the military and their fringe benefits were enormously expanded for martial law purposes. It is estimated that the Armed Forces of the Philippines number around 193,000 (not including paramilitary forces), almost three times the pre-martial law number of 70,000.

To downplay the military aspects of his administration, Marcos has used euphemisms to describe the current order such as New Society, "constitutional authoritarianism," and "revolution from the center." According to Marcos, the main goal of the New Society is not only to restore civil order but to bring about needed reforms, aimed at democratizing wealth, reducing inequality, and conquering mass poverty.

Marcos declared martial law when he was no longer eligible to run for a third presidential term in accord with the 1935 constitution. His second term would have ended in December 1973, and at 56, he decided that he was too young to retire from public life. Martial law was the only way he could retain the helm of Philippine politics; he apparently intends to remain in power at least until 1984.

After 8 years, what did martial law mean for Filipinos? Order, tourism, and economic growth are claimed as major achievements, but the New Society has fallen short of the lofty goals Marcos set.

Land reform is in fact a failing program, opposed by landlords and tenants alike. There has been no fun-

Farmers watch the demonstration of a modern harvesting machine. To increase agricultural production, modern machinery, fertilizer, irrigation, better seed, and land reform will be needed. (Photo: United Nations/ UNESCO/D. Roger.)

damental reform of Philippine society under martial law. Marcos may have eliminated some old elites, but he has not significantly altered the feudal cast of society; the upper class still dominate. The new power holders are mostly relatives and close associates of the Marcos family. Top military leaders are also relatives and close friends of Marcos, and they control the mass media, government corporations, financial institutions, and other sensitive areas of the economy.

The Philippines has had to contend with double-digit inflation, unemployment, a worsening balance of payments, the skyrocketing costs of food and other prime commodities, and a growing income inequality. In June 1978, outstanding foreign loan obligations hit an all-time high of $7.2 billion, an increase of $650 million over the December 1977 figure, which makes the Philippines one of the most indebted countries in Southeast Asia. Philippine Central Bank statistics show that as of August 1978, the country suffered a huge deficit of $879 million in its export earnings.

Runaway inflation is exacerbated by the First Lady's extravagance and the regime's penchant for nonproductive projects, such as the multimillion dollar Philippine International Convention Center, the Philippine Heart Center, and other showcase edifices. The regime has also spent millions of dollars hosting international events like the Miss Universe contest, the Ali-Frazier fight, the Karpov-Korchnoi chess match, and the World Peace Through Law and International Monetary Fund Conferences. The 1979 United Nations Conference on Trade and Development meeting cost the Philippine government $9.8 million.

In the meantime, the majority of Filipinos are far more impoverished and malnourished than they were before the imposition of martial law. Of the world's 800 million people who belong to "the poorest of the poor," 35 million are said to be Filipinos. They constitute 80 percent of the total population of the Philippines, earning a daily income of 2.25 pesos (30 cents) or less. Even in metropolitan Manila, which is relatively more developed than the rest of the country, 62 percent of the families lack proper housing and shelter. The degree of malnutrition, particularly among children, is alarming; an Asian Development Bank report shows that the average daily caloric intake for the Philippines is lower than that for Bangladesh.

Political opposition to martial law has escalated. The continuing NPA and MNLF guerrilla movements remain the major threats to Marcos. Another formidable center of resistance has crystalized among church-related groups like the Association of Major Religious Superiors and influential bishops. Even the normally moderate Jaime Cardinal Sin, the spiritual head of the country's large Catholic population, has asked Marcos to step down. Several labor, professional, student, and mass organizations have led demonstrations and rallies, in spite of severe government restrictions on freedoms of speech and assembly. Former political figures continuously criticize the repressive and illegal nature of the regime. Opposition has also grown among the Kalinga, Apayao, and other cultural minorities whose lands and homes are being threatened by the government's development programs. Finally, international bodies like Amnesty International, the International Commission of Jurists, and the British Broadcasting Corporation have released extensive documentation of torture of Filipino political prisoners and serious violations of human rights.

Two questions can be asked about the political future of the Philippines: how long can Marcos remain in power? and what will happen afterward? He seems firmly entrenched at the moment because the military, his main power base, is still behind him, in spite of reported factionalism in the ranks. The United States also keeps his regime alive with massive doses of military, economic, and other aid.

However, he shows signs of weakening in the face of worsening economic conditions and expanding opposition. This double bind of economic depression and political repression may lead to an explosive situation that could hurt Marcos. The pendulum could swing further to the right in a military takeover, or it could swing left under the leadership of the National Democratic Front. Other major groups that are more or less centrist in their political orientation will opt for a nonmilitary and non-Communist alternative similar to (but not the same as) the pre-martial law system.

Future development depends on the government's ability to redress long-standing inequalities and to solve the severe problems of urban and rural poverty. However, economic change will not be possible without the political will to redirect the country's development. Otherwise, poverty of the nation's masses will be perpetuated.   *B.A. Aquino*

Singapore

(Republic of Singapore)

Area: 225 sq mi (583 sq km)
Population: 2.35 million
  Density: 1044 per sq mi (403 per sq km)
  Growth rate: 1.6% (1970–1977)
Percent of population under 24 years of age: **60%**
Infant deaths per 1,000 live births: **11 (1977)**
Life expectancy at birth: **70 years (1977)**
Leading causes of death: not available
Ethnic composition: **Chinese 75%; Malays 15%; Indians
  7%**
Languages: **English, Chinese**
Literacy: **75% (1975)**
Religions: **Buddhist, Hindu, Christian**
Percent population urban: **100% (1975)**
Percent population rural: **0% (1975)**
Gross national product: **$7.7 billion**
  Per capita GNP: **$3,260 (including the expatriate com-
  munity)**
  Per capita GNP growth rate: **6.6% (1970–1977)**
Inflation rate: **7% (1970–1977)**

The tiny island republic of Singapore lies astride the Strait of Malacca, one of the world's busiest sea passages, and at the center of Southeast Asia, one of the world's richest and most important regions. Singapore's future is thus a matter of vital interest to all of the major nations of the world. With only 225 square miles (585 sq km) of land territory, a population of 2.3 million, and no natural resources, this tropical island depends heavily on the talent and wits of its leadership and the intelligence and industry of its people. Singapore once had a tradition of political turmoil and social upheaval. But for nearly three decades, political stability and steady economic and social progress have been hallmarks of this republic.

The population is intelligent, increasingly well educated, healthy, and young. Approximately 60 percent of Singapore's population is under the age of 24. The pressing need to provide a satisfactory outlet for the energies of its intelligent, young population challenges Singapore's leadership. The promotion of peace and free trade are equally vital to this small country, whose prosperity is dependent on the economic activity of its neighbors and trading partners.

Singapore has a pluralistic society in which the Chinese constitute approximately 76 percent of the total population, Malays 15 percent, and Indians 7 percent. The Chinese are Buddhists and spirit worshipers, the Malaysians are Muslim, and the Indians are Hindu. Christianity is much in evidence and is growing, particularly among the Chinese. Divided by education and language as well as by wealth, occupation, and even religion, the Chinese are not a homogeneous community.

Singapore lies 70 miles above the equator and experiences no seasons and little climatic change. Its average annual temperatures range from a low of approximately 75°F (24°C) to a high of about 88°F (31°C). Warm sunshine, cloudy days, frequent rainfall, and high humidity make Singapore a perennially green and lush garden whose landscape is broken by broad boulevards, high-rise apartment buildings, luxurious hotels, public markets, food stalls, Chinese "shophouses", tall office buildings, factories, wharves, warehouses, and dry docks—evidences of a dynamic and expanding economy.

For nearly 150 years after the founding of Singapore by British Empire visionary Thomas Raffles in 1819, Singapore's economy depended upon its entrepôt trade. As a free port with few taxes, many services, and much security, Singapore was the middleman where Southeast Asian minerals and produce were exchanged for European manufactures. With its natural deepwater harbor, abundance of inexpensive but intelligent Chinese labor, enlightened authoritarian rule, and few popular demands, Singapore prospered mightily, becoming and remaining one of the three or four busiest ports in the world. Singapore was also a bastion of British Empire defense in South and East Asia for many decades. The military establishment provided stable and significant employment.

Manufacturing began modestly in the 1930s, based on the skills acquired through processing raw materials and repairing ships and machinery. Industrialization, which began seriously in the 1950s, has proved highly successful; today Singapore has plants producing steel, textiles, chemicals, electronics, pharmaceuticals, ships, and many other products of a

Because Singapore's rising population makes economic development difficult, the government has established a Family Planning Board to educate the people and provide family planning facilities. Members of the Family Planning Board meet to discuss the program. (Photo: United Nations/ R. Witlin.)

modern industrial economy. The manufacturing sector grew 17.3 percent during the first half of 1979. Singapore's continued economic growth will depend not on inexpensive labor but on its technology and its ability to recruit skilled workers from abroad.

In recent years, Singapore's trade and manufacturing have been supplemented by a large and growing tourist industry. The beauty of the city, its political stability, its superb hotels and restaurants, and its convenient access attract visitors. Singapore emerged as a world financial center in the 1970s, second in Asia only to Tokyo and often reported to be the headquarters of the Asian dollar.

Singapore had one of the world's fastest growing economies in the late 1960s and early 1970s with an average annual growth rate of 14 percent between 1968 and 1972. In the late 1970s, the gross national product was still growing, at a rate of 7 to 8 percent annually in real terms. This figure is complemented most favorably by a low population growth rate of 1.7 percent. Only a few years ago Singapore's birthrate was one of the highest in the world. But family planning has been highly successful, and immigration has almost stopped. An expanding economy and minimal population increases have brought rising incomes to nearly everyone. Singapore's per capita income of more than $3,000 is the second highest in Asia (after Japan). Nonetheless, it does not appear that any basic redistribution of wealth has occurred.

Singapore's urban renewal program is replacing dilapidated housing with modern high-rise apartment complexes. (Photo: United Nations/ Philip Teuscher.)

Economic success has brought many social benefits, particularly for the lowest income groups, without significantly increasing government debt. Singapore is a model for the rest of Asia in the construction of modern low-cost housing. It is estimated that over 60 percent of the population live in government-built or government-sponsored apartment complexes. Those familiar with the crowded, substandard housing of Singapore's population in the 1950s are amazed at the transformation. The move to modern high-rise single-family housing required difficult cultural adjustments for Singaporeans.

Gains in education are no less remarkable. Since the 1950s, the goal of the government has been to provide elementary, secondary, and postsecondary education for all of its people according to their abilities. Today, virtually every elementary and secondary school-age child is in school. At one time, the medium of instruction in secondary schools was equally divided between English and Mandarin Chinese; multilingualism remains official, but in fact English has become the more prominent language.

The cornerstone of postsecondary education is the University of Singapore, a comprehensive institution with undergraduate, graduate, and professional curricula. Its faculty and facilities are very good, and Singapore is not dependent upon foreign universities for the advanced education of its people. The curriculum of Nanyang University, formally a Chinese-language university, is gradually conforming to the curriculum of the University of Singapore, and English is becoming the medium of instruction. A polytechnic institute provides vocational training, and adult education, which witnessed an explosive growth in the 1960s, continues to attract a high level of citizen participation.

Virtually all education is directed and financed by the state, because education is one means by which the government intends to achieve its economic and social goals. The overwhelming emphasis of the curriculum is on essential vocational and professional skills.

Singapore's politics has been dominated since the late 1950s by the People's Action Party (PAP) and its leader, Lee Kuan Yew. Lee and his associates are lawyers, doctors, engineers, economists, and teachers, who constitute intellectual as well as political leadership for Singapore. The PAP rose to power by a vigorous espousal of socialism. Once in power, the ever-pragmatic PAP became economically and socially conservative, candidly declaring that geography and economic reality take precedence over ideology. But the PAP has not embraced unbridled laissez-faire. PAP leadership has harnessed the financial system, trade unions, employers, education, military services, and social policy to serve Singapore's economy. Eloquent testimony to the safety of capital are the billions of dollars of foreign investment in Singapore and the strength of its banks. Singapore has often been called the "Zurich of Asia."

From 1867 until 1959, Britain ruled Singapore as a Crown Colony headed by a governor and executive and legislative councils. Elections with a very limited electorate were introduced in 1948. The first elections with a broad electorate were held in 1955, and internal self-rule was achieved in 1959. As a further step of constitutional evolution, in 1963 Singapore became a state within the Federation of Malaysia. Failure to define clearly the relationship before the merger, different goals and values, and conflicting ambitions of the leaders made Singapore's association with Malaysia short-lived. Full independence for Singapore came in 1965 when Malaysia's Prime Minister ousted Singapore from the Malaysian Federation. At the time, Lee Kuan Yew expressed anxiety about Singapore's ability to manage alone in the world. But the struggle for survival has proved manifestly successful.

In recent years, PAP's very success has been a major challenge to the People's Action Party and perhaps to the Singapore political system. The rationality, efficiency, honesty, effectiveness, and near monopoly of administrative talent of the PAP government have considerably reduced opportunities for opposition parties in Singapore. The PAP's passionate desire for political stability and economic growth has helped create an atmosphere in which criticism is not much articulated in the media or other public forums. The PAP's treatment of Singapore's newspapers has invoked criticism abroad and has led to charges of authoritarianism and of a garrison-state mentality. In 1976, Singapore resigned from the Socialist International because of criticism of the government's treatment of the press and the detention of persons for political reasons. From time to time efforts have been made to encourage opposition and criticism but have met with only moderate success at best.

The younger middle class and intelligentsia want more variety and diversity in their politics, finding modern Singapore with its comprehensive social services, political stability and always-positive press politically bland. Lectures by the aging PAP leadership on the fragility of success fall on deaf ears. The new generation, no less able than its elders, is not much concerned about past accomplishments. It seeks personal and collective goals toward which young people can work. Outlets for their energies and ambitions are increasingly difficult to find in Singapore.

Dissatisfaction with politics is paralleled in cultural matters. Singaporeans have been described as having an obsession with money and materialism. In an effort to overcome materialism and provide cultural diversion and growth, the government in the late 1970s began to promote culture among its citizens. A large cultural center is being constructed, an arts festival was launched as an annual event, and a national symphony has made its debut.

The PAP leadership's concerns about the fragility of success are not without validity. Singapore's gains in politics, economics, social policies, and now cultural enhancements are vulnerable to developments over which it has little control. Singapore is dependent on agricultural imports, and its economy is dependent on the level of economic activity in other nations, on peace in Southeast Asia and in the world, and on the curtailment of economic nationalism, especially in neighboring countries. Singapore's leaders thus pay close attention to regional and world affairs and seek effective foreign policies.

The determinants of Singapore's foreign policy are the island's small physical size, its location in an Indonesian-Malaysian world of perhaps 200 million people, its need to encourage investment and maintain good trading relationships, and its Chinese population. Singapore's leaders advocate peace and stability in Asia and in the world and favor as few restrictions on trade as possible.

Southeast Asia has for centuries been a stage for international rivalries. Until the mid-1970s, Singapore espoused nonalignment and was nevertheless comfortable with a large American military presence. The subsequent withdrawal of U.S. forces from Vietnam and the low American profile in the region have influenced Singapore's leaders increasingly to put their faith in the Association for Southeast Asian Nations (ASEAN), formed by Malaysia, Indonesia, the Philippines, Thailand, and Singapore in 1967. ASEAN leaders usually confer with one another and exchange information on cultural subjects. By the close of the

Two youngsters stand on a porch outside a modern apartment complex in Singapore. The move to high-rise housing was a difficult cultural adjustment for many Singaporeans. (Photo: United Nations/UNESCO.)

1970s, ASEAN had become more cohesive, and the objective of establishing a "zone of peace, freedom, and neutrality" in Southeast Asia seemed possibly within their grasp. Regional cooperation, long encouraged by the United States, seemed almost a reality. ASEAN was being courted by most of the major nations of the world. ASEAN took its first important political position in early 1979, when the five governments condemned Vietnam's invasion of Cambodia. By participating in ASEAN, Singapore has helped to overcome earlier frictions with Malaysia and Indonesia.

There is no doubt that Singapore and its ASEAN partners view China as the long-term threat to their peace and independence. Singapore's large Chinese population has caused its leaders to go slow in formal diplomatic recognition of the People's Republic of China although economic relations have been important for many years. Deng Xiaoping, the Chinese First Deputy Prime Minister, visited Singapore in November 1978, and Lee Kuan Yew has traveled to China.

While pursuing a policy of peace and friendship, Singapore has looked to its own defense. Eclectically borrowing concepts from Switzerland, and Israel, a military force has been created that is likely to prove effective if it is ever tested. Military service is compulsory; every Singaporean is a soldier. Training and equipment emphasize urban street fighting. The objective is to make Singapore an expensive military prize.

Modern, affluent, well-educated, pragmatic, socially responsible, increasingly cohesive Singapore looks to the future with a confidence founded on personal and collective achievement. Its optimism appears justified provided no large-scale political or economic rivalries threaten the area and provided Singapore's leadership learns to tolerate political opposition.

J. Norman Parmer

Taiwan
(Republic of China)

Area: 13,893 sq mi (35,981 sq km)
Population: 17.1 million
  Density: 1,221 per sq mi (471 per sq km)
  Growth rate: 2.0% (1970–1977)
Percent of population under 20 years of age: 45%
Infant deaths per 1,000 live births: 14 (1975)
Life expectancy at birth: 68.6 years (1975)
Leading causes of death: not available
Ethnic composition: Chinese 98%; aboriginal people (Malay-Polynesian linguistic and genealogical groups) 2%
Languages: Mandarin Chinese, Taiwanese
Literacy: 89% (1978)
Religions: Confucianist, Taoist, Buddhist, Motist, Christian
Percent population urban: 67% (1979)
Percent population rural: 33% (1979)
Gross national product: $23.9 billion
  Per capita GNP: $1,400
  Per capita GNP growth rate: 5.5% (1970–1976)
Inflation rate: 5%

Early Portuguese navigators labeled Taiwan "Ihla Formosa," the beautiful island. Taiwan's intelligent, skilled, and highly motivated people have fostered its rapid industrialization and modernization. The endemic Chinese work ethic and traditional family-centered capitalism are carefully nurtured by the dedicated and disciplined leadership of the Kuomintang (Nationalist Party, KMT), which exerts strict central planning and controls. This leadership has been massively assisted by U.S. aid (drastically reduced in volume since 1965) and by other foreign sources of investment capital. Income distribution has been increasingly egalitarian, which fosters a stable developmental climate. Detracting from these assets are Taiwan's increasing dependence on foreign trade; especially for its energy needs, its severely structured, ominously brittle political system, and the ever-present uncertainty of its relationship to mainland China.

Dramatically volcanic in origin, Taiwan has arable plains that face westward, with isolated pockets of cultivation on the narrow rim of the east coast. The rugged mountainous backbone of the island is crossed only by roads around the northern and southern tips of the island and in mid-island by a spectacular road system. Over the centuries, migrating Chinese have pushed the indigenous proto-Malay peoples into the mountains. Today, there are no more than 200,000 aborigines, and few of them lack Chinese genes. Between Taiwan and the mainland are the Pescadores (Penghu Islands) and several small fortress islands that are held by the government of Taiwan.

Most Taiwanese live and work on the western plains, moving uphill as communications and public services become available in order to shift from rice (60 percent of the cultivated land), sugar, sweet potatoes, and tea to fruits, nuts, vegetables, and animal husbandry.

Taiwan has a population density of 1,221 persons per square mile (471 per sq km). Although the population growth rate has decreased markedly, from 3.9 percent a year in 1952 to 1.8 percent in 1978, there is continuous pressure from the expanding population to produce more food, clothing, and amenities. Good agricultural land is being eroded by spreading industry and infrastructure, and rampant urbanization. The mechanization of agriculture, new seeds, crops, and fertilizer are also changing old ways.

Water is abundant, and Taiwan enjoys comprehensive water control: dams, power generation, distribution systems, reforestation, and increasingly sophisticated land management. But most of the silt-burdened rivers are seriously polluted and air pollution is a problem, especially in Kiaohsiung and Taipei.

Approximately 55 percent of the land area is forest, including a wide variety of temperate and tropical broadleaf stands, and forest planning is extensive and well conceived. But timber is giving way to rice, vegetable, and orchard culture, much of it terraced.

Coal is mined in northern and central Taiwan, copper in the north, and phosphorus in the Pescadores in the strait. There are modest reserves of zinc, lead, silver, and gold. State monopolies produce aluminum from imported bauxite. The Taiwan Sugar Corporation, another state monopoly, makes sugar from cane, three-fourths of which is exported, mostly to Japan, Korea, the United States, and the Middle East. Petroleum exploration continues off the western shores of the island, but Taiwan's oil is not yet a significant factor in Taiwan's energy resource planning.

Taiwan's successful "Big Ten" construction projects, the heart of the first 3 years of the 1976–1981 6-year plan, include new superhighways, a massive international airport at Taoyuan, increased rural and urban electrification, dams, railways, new harbors, shipyards, steel mills, and nuclear power plants. Twelve additional major projects, scheduled to begin operation in the early 1980s, include the construction of three new cities to relieve the pressure of urbanization—in the Greater Taipei, in the Taiching area in mid-island, and in metropolitan Kiaohsiung. Communications in Taiwan are efficient, inexpensive (for Asia), and improving.

The island community is an economic success story, with a high and consistently improving level of prosperity. Unemployment in 1978 was no more than 2 percent, and there is a chronic shortage of agricultural labor. Per capita income soared from $168 in 1964 to $1,304 in 1978. The benefits from Taiwan's phenomenal production levels and economic diversification have been spread broadly among the population and are not confined to the urban middle and upper classes.

Rapid diversification has been the pattern in light industry, especially in electronics, plastics, textiles, shoes, clothing, tools, sporting gear, and scores of products for both local and foreign consumption. The output of heavy industry, notably steel, has risen. Industry provided slightly more than 40 percent of the net domestic product in 1978, services and bureaucracy 48 percent, while agriculture had declined to 12 percent from the 1952 level of 36 percent.

Trade volume in 1978 was nearly $24 billion, almost twice that of the People's Republic of China. Taiwan's agricultural purchases from the United States, including corn, soybeans, and soybean oil, doubled between 1976 and 1978. Taiwan ranks twentieth in world trade, and its economy, like those of Japan and Korea, depends on the importing and upgrading of raw materials, and its industry is totally dependent on petroleum imports.

Life in Taiwan is rooted in family capitalism; the senior head of the extended family is very influential. Villages are still collections of extended families who worship at shrines dedicated to the respected dead. Taoism, Motism, Buddhism, and Confucianism are the traditional religions, and there are some 800,000 Christians in Taiwan (two-thirds are Protestant and one-third are Catholic), but ancestor worship prevails. Chinese filial piety has its roots in early history, before the third millenium B.C.

Rapid industrialization has disrupted placid village family life. Today, women are employed in factories, providing semiskilled work on the production lines and frequently living in dormitories until they marry. After military service, young men do not always return to the farms; instead, they are sometimes stimulated by the newly found glamor of urban life and urban jobs. This pattern seems irreversible, yet filial respect for the elders has not been forgotten. Traditional allegiance patterns and social attitudes are changing, but T-shirts and blue jeans clothe young people who are proud of their ancestral heritage.

The energetic people of Taiwan include more than 13 million Taiwanese and more than 3 million mainlanders and their children. The two segments of

Farmers prepare a terraced field for planting, working without machinery. Population pressure has forced the Taiwanese to terrace their hillsides to use all available space for farming. (Photo: United Nations/Chen.)

Taiwan society try to alleviate or endure mutual alienation. The Taiwanese did not welcome the mainlander soldiers who went to Taiwan on troopships after 1945. For their part, the mainlanders were suspicious of the Taiwanese and equated them with the traitors in China who had labored and fought for the Japanese. Tension between the mainlanders and the Taiwanese has dissipated very slowly.

With the aim of replacing Taiwanese and other local dialects with Mandarin Chinese as the common language, Taiwan's educational system has been conducted in Mandarin for the last 30 years. The Taiwanese receive equal treatment in the perennial examinations that lead to educational promotion, government advancement, and status in the armed services. Unless they are disqualified for medical reasons, all young men serve in the armed forces for 6 months to 3 years after their 9 years of required school, upper middle school, technical school, or undergraduate or graduate school.

The Taiwanese have gradually moved into the national bureaucracy and now occupy major positions of authority in local and provincial government. The provincial government of Taiwan, set up in Nantou near the attractive mid-island city of Taichung, is ensconced in new buildings, with ample housing and other advantages. Economic discrimination favors the Taiwanese, who enjoy the advantages generated by Taiwan's average annual GNP growth rate of more than 8 percent, which has prevailed for some 20 years. In 1979, Taiwan's gross national product growth rate was 10 percent. Soaring real estate values and rapidly

Young men study diagrams of a television set. Electronics is one of the specialties offered by the government's National Vocational Training Service for Industry. (Photo: United Nations/ Chen.)

increasing industrialization have also helped to assuage the Taiwanese dislike of mainlanders' advantages.

According to U.S. estimates, of the top 100 companies on the island, 79 are controlled and/or owned by Taiwanese, including 8 out of the top 10. Except for the commitment of previously unused or little-used mountain land to rehabilitation programs, real estate development is largely in the hands of Taiwanese. Nevertheless, the fact that Taiwanese dominate private capitalism while mainlanders monopolize public policy is potentially unsettling in this highly complex, sensitive, politically fragile economy.

Taiwan has been a refuge for centuries for Chinese fleeing mainland political disorders. Early centuries were marked by sporadic Chinese inroads that established Chinese-controlled outposts but little or no formal control over the island. In early modern times, the Spanish, Portuguese, and Dutch also established trading bases and lasting cities.

With the fall of the Ming dynasty to the Manchu in the 1660s, a significant short-term migration, largely from Fujian (Fukien), Guangdong (Kwangtung), and other southeastern Chinese areas, was led by Ming dynasty mandarins and military leaders. The best known of these refugee-invaders was Cheng Ch'eng Kung, who expelled the Westerners in the late seventeenth century. Thus began an era during which Chinese religions, languages, and familial groupings were established in Taiwan, leading to a distinctive "Taiwanese" pattern of behavior and social organization. After its defeat in the Sino-Japanese War, China ceded its interest in Taiwan to the Japanese in 1895, and Japan ruled the island until after World War II.

The largest single Chinese migration to Taiwan occurred between 1945 and 1949, as the defeated forces of Chinese Generalissimo Chiang Kai-shek's KMT, driven from the mainland by the victorious Chinese Communists, swelled the Taiwan population by 600,000 military men and an additional 1.5 million civilians, mostly bureaucrats and their families. Taiwan, regarded by Chiang as a bastion for regroupment, became a laboratory for socioeconomic change.

Economic development in Taiwan had already begun during the Japanese occupation (1895–1945). The Japanese brought industrialization, better public health, more education, and diversified creature comforts. The Chinese anti-Maoists who took control of the island after World War II soon dominated the military, educational system, communications media, and state economic monopolies of essential goods and service, including economic planning. Chiang Kai-shek's arrival was unwelcome to the mass of Taiwanese, but it did not significantly disturb their economic position, and a well-devised land-reform program introduced in the 1950s improved the lot of rural Taiwanese.

Economic development has always been high on

the KMT priority list, aided by direct U.S. assistance between 1952 and 1965, and since then by American military aid. During the Vietnam war, sales in goods and services to the United States approximated about 2 percent of Taiwan's gross national product.

Political power in Taiwan is centralized in Taipei, under the leadership of the KMT, whose control has not been validated in any electoral process. Although party membership exceeds 1 million, a large central committee and a carefully selected central executive committee control the party and the government. Because all the provinces on the Chinese mainland are represented within the political machinery, the mainlander-dominated bureaucracy is overbearing. Some superficial political opposition is permitted, but censorship remains a factor in political life. Leaders of the KMT and the armed forces hold power by seniority. The party leadership is carefully trained, and public-information devices are widely used. All private associations are monitored by the KMT under ongoing martial law. There is no organized labor movement in Taiwan comparable to labor organization in a developed and free economy. Labor organizations are social clubs and are not allowed to harass the gov-

ernment or to burden the economy, which is devoted to the inexpensive servicing of overseas markets.

Taiwan's future is mortgaged to its strategic location and the obsessive ideology of its government. Like his father, President Chiang Ching-kuo passionately refuses to deal with Marxists anywhere and lives for the day when his government takes over mainland China.

Taiwan's existence as an entity independent of Beijing (Peking) depends upon relations between the People's Republic of China and the United States. No sophistries can change this fundamental. Union, which would almost surely benefit the mainland Chinese, would threaten the continuing economic development of Taiwan. Eventually, institutions and systems in China and Taiwan may alter enough to permit mutually acceptable unification. Less likely, the evolution of representative government on Taiwan may bring proponents of an independent republic to power. Meanwhile, the people of Taiwan continue to concentrate on economic prosperity and efficiency. Determined to maintain a rising level of living and tempo of economic activity, they seem inclined to let the future take care of itself.   *L. Edward Shuck*

Thailand
(Kingdom of Thailand)

Area: 198,445 sq mi (513,970 sq km)
Population: 44.3 million
   Density: 223 per sq mi (73 per sq km)
   Growth rate: 2.8% (1970–1977)
Percent of population under 14 years of age: 46% (1975)
Infant deaths per 1,000 live births: 68 (1975)
Life expectancy at birth: 61 years (1978)
Leading causes of death: not available
Ethnic composition: Thai more than 75%; Chinese 15%; Malays; tribal groups
Languages: Thai, English
Literacy: 82%
Religions: Theravada (Hinayana) Buddhist 94%; Muslim; Christian (less than 1%)
Percent population urban: 14%
Percent population rural: 86%
Gross national product: $21.8 billion (1977)
   Per capita GNP: $490
   Per capita GNP growth rate: 4.1% (1970–1977)
Inflation rate: 9.3% (1960–1977)

Thailand is the most populous non-Communist nation on the mainland of Southeast Asia. Its 45 million people have been increasing at a rate of about 1 million people each year since the late 1950s, and by 1985 the population is expected to reach more than 50 million, surpassing the population of a large European country like France. Population pressure and grossly inequitable income distribution challenge efforts to modernize the economy. At the same time,

Thai development has been furthered by Thailand's strategic location, its abundance of valuable natural resources, and the absence of Western colonial rule. These characteristics, combined with the unique pragmatism of the Thai people, have aided greatly in the modernization and advancement of the kingdom.

Continued progress toward modernization appears hampered by recent developments. For the time being Thailand is entirely dependent on imported oil. The rapid increase in oil prices, along with lower agricultural productivity and higher prices for manufactured goods, caused the rate of inflation to increase from about 10 percent in 1978 to approximately 18 percent in 1980. Inflation has led to labor unrest and the demand for higher minimum wages.

Thailand is approximately 14 percent urban; almost 5 million people live in Bangkok, the capital city. The society is relatively homogeneous; more than 75 percent of the people are ethnically Thai. About 15 percent are of Chinese descent, although this minority has been largely assimilated into Thai society. The only distinct minorities are the 1 million Malays, who live in the four southern provinces which adjoin Malaysia, and several ethnic groups (Karen, Meo, Yao, Lahu, and Lisu), numbering about 75,000, who inhabit mountain communities in the northern region.

Thailand is shaped like the head of an elephant. Its area of 198,445 square miles (513,970 sq km) is about three-fourths the size of the state of Texas. The northern provinces bordering Burma and Laos are covered with dense forests, which produce valuable teak, now embargoed to protect the forests. The large northeastern plateau consists mostly of semiarid soil that can provide only limited food for the people of this impoverished region. The central area comprises the fertile alluvial valley of the Chao Phya River, which has produced large rice surpluses for over a century. Much of the narrow southern peninsula adjoining Malaysia is covered with dense rain forests and is the site of productive tin and rubber plantations.

The warm and humid climate affects both the people and the vegetation. Tropical monsoons bring heavy rainfall from May to October followed by a cool season from November to February. The months of March and April are extremely hot and dry.

The Thai people enjoy one of the highest standards of living in Southeast Asia. The country has a modern transportation system with regular railroad service to the northern, northeastern, and southern regions as well as hard-surfaced roads to most of the rural provinces. The Don Muang Airport at Bangkok is used by 28 international airlines, and a domestic airline serves 20 smaller airports throughout the kingdom. There are approximately 20 newspapers in Bangkok in the Thai, Chinese, and English languages, and about 50 newspapers in the provinces. Thailand has a modern television system, and 30 government radio stations provide daily broadcasts to most of the country. Modern public health facilities are maintained in Bangkok and provincial cities, and, with the help of international organizations, like the World Health Organization, many communicable diseases have been greatly reduced during the past two decades.

Thailand's gross national product was $21.8 billion

Villagers pump water at the communal pump. In poor rural areas, there is no piped running water. (Photo: United Nations/Carl Purcell.)

in 1977, with a per capita GNP of more than $490 a year, and the annual growth rate of the economy is 5 to 6 percent. Since the mid-nineteenth century, the economy has been oriented toward the export of food and raw materials; major exports are rice, tapioca, sugar, rubber, and maize. Thailand's chief trading partners are Japan, the United States, West Germany, Singapore, and the Netherlands.

Industry and tourism have bolstered the modernization of the national economy. Since the early 1960s, an expanding manufacturing sector has elevated economic and social living standards. Aided by modest government planning and extensive domestic and foreign investment, the industrial sector has applied new technology to a variety of manufactured products. Most industries in Thailand consist of small enterprises employing less than sixty workers, but an increasing number of manufacturing firms are engaged in large-scale operations, including steel mills, textile mills, tire factories, glass factories, and motor vehicle assembly plants. Most manufactured goods are sold in domestic markets, although an increasing number of products, like bicycles, cement, and canned foods, are exported.

Thailand may be moving away from the policy of economic nationalism that has influenced the development of the economy for several decades. In May, 1980, a new policy for development modeled after development plans in Singapore, South Korea and Japan was proposed. Basically, the plan calls for a massive influx of capital from both local and foreign investors to construct transportation facilities and other developmental enterprises. Large Western multinational corporations have already committed sizeable capital investments in the country.

Tourism continues to be a growing factor in the Thai economy; at present, it is the fifth largest source of foreign exchange. In 1977, 1.2 million tourists visited Thailand (mostly Americans, Germans, Japanese, Malaysians, and Australians) and produced $220 million in revenue. The tourist industry has successfully utilized the beautiful beaches on the Gulf of Siam, the attractive mountain communities in the northern provinces, and the colorful Buddhist temples in Bangkok and other areas. By 1981, tourism will probably be the largest single producer of foreign exchange, with 2 million visitors each year generating $600 million in the national economy.

Modern education is a significant influence in the rapid economic and social development of the country. Almost every village has an elementary school that provides 4 years of basic education for most of the nation's young people. This widespread public elementary school system has produced a literacy rate of 82 percent for the entire country. Only a small fraction of young people, however, go on to secondary schools, most of which are located in Bangkok and the large provincial cities. Secondary schools provide students with vocational training, and few students continue to the university level.

The most prestigious universities are located in Bangkok. Chulalongkorn University was founded in 1917 and is named after one of Thailand's most renowned kings. Thammasat University was founded in 1933 by Pridi Phanomyong, who led the bloodless revolt that toppled the absolute monarchy. Other universities in the capital city are the Agricultural University, the University of Medical Sciences, the University of Fine Arts, and Ramakhamhaeng University. Provincial universities constructed during the 1960s play an increasing role in the national educational system. These include Chiengmai University in the north, Khonkaen University in the northeast, and Prince of Songkhla University in the south.

Some Thai students obtain advanced education at foreign universities, and approximately 12,000 Thai are enrolled in universities abroad.

Approximately 94 percent of the Thai people follow the teachings of Theravada, or Hinayana, Buddhism, which encourages its followers to seek detachment from worldly influences. In practice, this religion contributes a sense of gentleness, patience, and tolerance to Thai culture and behavior.

Most Thai males join the sangha (a Buddhist religious community) for brief periods to study religious writings and to meditate on sacred teachings. Thai women have a subordinate status in Theravada Buddhism, because they cannot enter the sangha. A few Buddhist temples in Thailand have women devotees, or *chi* (sometimes translated as "nuns"); yet, they number only a few thousand. Most Thai women express their religious devotion by offering rice and fruit to the monks who come to their homes each morning and by adhering to the teachings of Buddhism.

In Thailand, Buddhists of almost all social and economic classes combine their religion with varying degrees of astrology and animism. Almost all important occasions, including weddings, cremations, and military coups, are conducted at a propitious time—determined by consulting an astrologer who is usually a learned Buddhist monk at a nearby temple. Animism promotes a vast array of beliefs, from spirit worship to amulets adorning various parts of the body to ward off adverse happenings.

The only sizable religious minority in the kingdom is made up of the 1 million Malays in the four southern provinces, who adhere to the teachings of Islam and desperately try to preserve their own language and customs. Their strong religious and ethnic loyalty has contributed in recent years to a violent separatist organization seeking to transfer the four southern provinces from Thai to Malaysian sovereignty.

The Thai people have a rich and varied history. Early records depict them as a small nomadic race moving southward from the Altai Mountains in Mongolia. They established a sedentary kingdom at Nanchao in southern China around A.D. 650, and many Thai people emigrated further south into the territories that today comprise Laos, northern Thailand, and the Shan State in Burma. The defeat of the kingdom at Nanchao by the famous Mongol emperor, Kublai Khan, caused a mass migration into the Chao Phya River valley, where the Thai quickly overwhelmed several small Khmer (Cambodian) feudal states and established their first kingdom at Sukhothai.

The kingdom at Sukhothai, which lasted from 1253 to 1350, has been labeled by many historians "the cradle of Thai culture." During this period, the Thai adopted their own written script by borrowing from the Khmer alphabet and copied Khmer forms of art and architecture.

The second kingdom at Ayudhya lasted from 1350 to 1767; the monarchy assumed absolute power and enshrined itself with an aura of divinity and sacred ceremonies. Thai society became highly stratified,

Poor urban families live along the canals of Bangkok. Canal water is used for bathing, drinking, and washing, and canals provide the transportation waterway for the wooden punts. (Photo: United Nations/Marvin Bolotsky.)

and many people in the lower classes were reduced to slavery.

The Burmese sacked the Thai kingdom at Ayudhya in 1767, and a new Thai kingdom was founded by a military leader, Phraya Chakkri, in 1782 at Bangkok. Absolute dynastic rule remained intact until the middle of the nineteenth century, when King Mongkut opened the country to extensive Western influences. Early steps toward modernization were modest, but they started the process of development and change. Mongkut's son, Chulalongkorn, was the most successful Chakri absolute monarch in promoting new national advancements. During his long reign (1868 to 1910), he reorganized the administrative structure and established the first unified control over the entire kingdom by constructing modern railroads and communications. Chulalongkorn also abolished slavery, protected religious freedom, and established a modern educational system. His successors, King Wachirawut and King Prajadhipok, continued to promote administrative and technological progress until the absolute monarchy was overthrown in a bloodless revolt in June 1932.

The Western-educated military and civilian leaders of the new ruling regime hastened the political, economic, and social modernization of the kingdom and established a constitutional monarchy. Yet the government was soon dominated by authoritarian military leaders, and in spite of a new constitution and occasional national elections, political power remained highly centralized. The military leadership brought Thailand into World War II on the side of the Japanese, who occupied the country for 4 years.

After the war, an attempt was made to establish a civilian-based democratic system, but this effort soon failed because of the fragmentation and bitter infighting among political parties, factions, and groups. Authoritarian military rule was firmly established by 1948, and the new Thai government began receiving economic and military aid from the United States to oppose the spread of communism in Southeast Asia. Thereafter, the bulk of the Thai people devoted their major efforts to rapid economic and social modernization; the desire to establish a genuine democracy received less attention and a lower priority.

Since the early 1950s, Thailand has made enormous progress. Bangkok has become one of the most modern cities in Asia, and its increasingly sophisticated population has become deeply involved in the mainstream of international politics and foreign trade. Many streets in the capital city are lined with modern office buildings utilizing some of the most recent computers and electronic devices. Domestic and foreign corporations with highly trained management personnel are engaged in financial and commercial transactions with countries all over the world.

In spite of these impressive advancements, there are still enormous differences in the income of different classes of Thai people. It has been estimated that approximately 90 percent of the wealth of the country is owned by less than 10 percent of the Thai people. Income gaps have actually widened as certain elements of the Thai economy have become increasingly centralized. The Thai peasants, who constitute 85 percent of the total population, have made some notable advances, yet they have not received a fair share of the national income.

An encouraging sign for the future economic picture is the discovery of untapped natural resources. An estimated 8.5 trillion cubic feet of natural gas has been located in the Gulf of Siam, oil deposits have been discovered near the old capital of Sukhothai, and uranium deposits have been found in the north.

There are also encouraging signs in recent political trends. Since the violent overthrow of the unpopular military regime in 1973, there have been several attempts to establish a form of democratic government. While the military still exerts considerable power, the political parties in parliament have also developed an effective voice. Early in 1980 the Prime Minister Kriangsak resigned in response to parliamentary criticism of his economic policies and was succeeded by General Prem Tinsulanond. For his Cabinet the new Prime Minister chose members of five different parties in the parliament and prominent civilians, including the well-known banker, Boonchu Rajanasathien, who is serving as Deputy Prime Minister.

Thailand's future economic and social development is very promising. It will be far more difficult to make progress in the political field, and success will depend on the ability of the Thai people to combine some of their traditional values and behavior with modern democracy. Thailand's future also depends on peace and stability in Southeast Asia and on cooperation among the major international powers.

Frank C. Darling

Vietnam
(Socialist Republic of Vietnam)

Area: 127,300 sq mi (329,705 sq km)
Population: 52.1 million
  Density: 409 per sq mi (158 per sq km)
  Growth rate: 3.1% (1970–1977)
Percent of population under 14 years of age: not available
Infant deaths per 1,000 live births: not available
Life expectancy at birth: 40.5 years (1975)
Leading causes of death: not available
Ethnic composition: Vietnamese 90%; Chinese; Cambodian; tribal groups
Languages: Vietnamese (official); French; Chinese; English; Khmer, tribal languages
Literacy: not available
Religions: Buddhist, Confucianist, Taoist, Catholic, animist, Hoa Hoa, Caodaist
Percent population urban: not available
Percent population rural: not available
Gross national product: $8.9 billion
  Per capita GNP: $170
  Per capita GNP growth rate: not available
Inflation rate: not available

The Socialist Republic of Vietnam—the world's third largest Communist state—has set itself ambitious targets for economic growth. Since peace returned in 1975, much of the war-related damage in the northern region has been repaired. However, in the southern half of the country, the market-oriented and largely agricultural economy was severely disrupted in the final months of war. Urban unemployment 4 years later was still high, and agricultural production remained very low. The southern region has not been fully integrated into a Communist system. Major obstacles to economic recovery and growth are Vietnam's hostile relationship with China and its effort to conquer Cambodia, which have caused great internal disruption and forced Vietnam into a position of political and economic dependence on the Soviet Union.

Vietnam is bordered by China, Laos, Cambodia, the Gulf of Thailand and the South China Sea. It is an S-shaped country, somewhat larger in total area than Virginia, North Carolina, and South Carolina combined. The immensely fertile deltas of the Red River in the north and the Mekong River in the south are often compared to two rice baskets, with the Annam Mountains running down the country's narrow midsection forming the carrying pole. Most of Vietnam's population is compresed into these and several smaller coastal plains and deltas.

The Red River delta was settled by the Vietnamese over 2,000 years ago, and the population density of this area averages 1,200 persons per square mile (463 per sq km). In the most crowded rural districts of this delta, the density is one of the highest for any farming area of the world—over 2,500 people per square mile (965 per sq km). The coastal plain around Danang is almost equally crowded. Over the centuries, high birthrates have forced a steady flow of immigrants down the coastal plains and into the large Mekong delta, which was entirely under Cambodian rule until the early 1600s. The population in the Mekong delta is only about 300 per square mile (116 per sq km). In recent decades, there has been a steady trickle of Vietnamese settlers into Cambodia and Laos and even further west into Thailand.

The Red River and its two major tributaries arise in China and merge to form a single channel before reaching Hanoi. There the river divides into many channels defined by natural silting and by man-made dikes. Since this delta region is only a few feet above sea level, the dikes must be high enough to carry the water above the land in the flood season.

If the dikes should break, thousands of human beings would almost certainly drown and many thousands more would see their crops ruined. It is hardly surprising that traditionally the Vietnamese have gauged the competence of their rulers by their success in strengthening the dikes and warding off overwhelming disasters. When one of the worst floods in recent history occurred at the end of World War II, the so-called national rulers who had been installed by Japan were irreparably disgraced because they were unable to cope with this emergency.

Workers dig an irrigation canal with hand tools. (Photo: United Nations/ G. Cohen.)

Vietnam has two seasons: wet and dry. From November to April, a northeast winter monsoon blows dry, cool air from China. During these months, the mean temperature in most of Vietnam is about 70°F (21°C), and it occasionally drops as low as 50°F (10°C). The southwest summer monsoon blows from late April to September or October, the rainy season. Rainfall reaches a high of 16 inches (41 cm) a month in Hanoi, where mean temperatures hover in the upper 80s°F (about 30°C). In Ho Chi Minh City (formerly Saigon) the mean temperature stays close to 82°F (28°C) all year.

Besides rich delta farmland, Vietnam's natural wealth includes tropical hardwood forests, abundant freshwater and ocean fish, and many minerals. There are large deposits of coal in north Vietnam and some evidence of offshore oil in the south. However, Vietnam's industrious population is plainly its greatest asset for development.

Ethnic Vietnamese make up at least 90 percent of the population of Vietnam, which reached 50 million in 1978. Until recent decades, intermarriage between Vietnamese of the northern, central, and southern regions was comparatively rare. Northerners were considered the most industrious and most puritanical. Southerners were sometimes regarded as lazy and pleasure-loving, while central Vietnam had a reputation for cultural elitism and revolutionary political activity. Distinctive regional accents reinforced these stereotypes. With the upheavals in recent years, the people of the three regions have mingled somewhat more freely, but mutual antagonisms remain.

Large minorities of Chinese and Cambodians—more than 1 million each—live in the towns and lowland areas. They have been the helpless pawns of

Vietnam's often tense relations with China and Cambodia. Thai, Lao, Meo, Mung, and other groups inhabit the upland regions. (The ethnic Vietnamese have never settled willingly in the mountain and plateau areas, which comprise four-fifths of their country and are difficult to farm. The Vietnamese regard these areas as cold, unhealthy, and even dangerous, since there are many species of snakes and wild animals.) The Vietnamese and the hill people, who are scattered through this region, share a strong mutual antipathy.

The Thai, distantly related to the lowland people of Thailand, may number as many as 1 million. The Lao and Meo, who are linked to the largest ethnic groups in Laos, probably number about 300,000. The Muong, who seem to be related to the ethnic Vietnamese, number around 400,000. Many other peoples in the uplands of central and southern Vietnam are probably descendants of early immigrants from Indonesia.

Since the early 1950s, Hanoi has allowed ethnic groups under its control a fair degree of cultural autonomy while denying them any real political self-determination. This device seems to have worked in the north. However, in pre-1975 South Vietnam, there was serious friction between the tribal groups and the ethnic Vietnamese, and the tribal people of the south may not be easily integrated into a Communist society. Nonetheless, the Hanoi regime should be able to govern the relatively few and militarily weak tribal people.

Vietnam's Chinese minority has been active in mining, stevedoring, and a variety of urban occupations in the north, and the ethnic Chinese have traditionally been the most active entrepreneurs and tradesmen in the south. Millions of Chinese refugees and immigrants have been absorbed by Vietnam over the centuries; but racial animosity between the two peoples has always been strong.

In 1975, the Vietnamese government evidently decided to force the Chinese in both the northern and southern regions either to leave Vietnam altogether or to move into the infamous "new economic zones." In these rural communes in frontier regions life is said to be extremely harsh. Little shelter is provided except what the people build with their own hands; tools, seeds, and fertilizer for farming are inadequate, and few schools or clinics are provided. Some of the new economic zones lie in areas of military operations against Cambodia, and many have had to be abandoned.

During 1978 and 1979, over 200,000 Chinese residents were forced to flee across the border into China. Thousands more were sold exit permits at exorbitant sums by the Vietnamese government and were allowed to escape in unseaworthy boats; many drowned at sea before reaching the coast of increasingly hostile and apprehensive neighboring countries. Many thousands of ethnic Vietnamese who had ties with the anti-Communist government have been given the same brutal treatment.

Trucks and pedestrians crowd the Long Bien Bridge over the Red River in Hanoi. (Photo: United Nations/G. Cohen.)

According to estimates of foreign diplomats in Hanoi, the Vietnamese government was earning several billion dollars a year selling exit permits; indeed, the revenue generated by emigrating boatloads of its best-educated people exceeded revenues from any export commodity. Hanoi was reportedly using some of these earnings to pay the Soviet Union for arms. The Hanoi government is apparently determined to rid itself of all its urban Chinese residents and to concentrate most of the southern Chinese population in rural communes.

Little is known of the Cambodian minority (the Khmer) in Vietnam. These people probably numbered about 1 million in 1979. The Khmer community was swollen by hundreds of thousands of new refugees from Cambodia during the decade of war and the Communist oppression in the 1970s. Some Khmer may have returned to Cambodia (voluntarily or otherwise) in 1979 after the Vietnamese invasion, and a few have undoubtedly found places in the Hanoi-sponsored regime there.

Racial antagonism between the Khmer and Vietnamese is deeply engrained. Their cultures are distinct; Khmer and Vietnamese Buddhists even belong to different sects. In the past, however, the Khmer in Vietnam have had less friction with their hosts than Vietnamese residents in Cambodia.

Despite the unification of Vietnam in 1975, sharp differences persist between the northern and southern regions in both rural and urban areas. The forced collectivization of agriculture in the 1950s in North Vietnam added to an already sharp contrast between the two regions. Most of the country's industry is located in the north, where a great deal of destruction was caused by U.S. bombing during the war; since 1975, however, prewar production has been restored in many sectors. The main industries are textiles, food-processing, cement, paper, metallurgy, and chemicals. The Hanoi government has recognized that foreign aid is essential to achieving the goals established in its 1976–1980 5-year plan. Most of the aid has come from the Soviet Union and Soviet-bloc countries.

The overcrowded north, despite highly intensive labor and double-cropping, has a deficit of food; about 10 percent of its food must be imported. In the south, the land is far less densely settled, and the average holding is larger and can be worked more efficiently. As a result, the southerners do not work as hard and often plant only a single crop; yet, they manage to harvest more than enough to feed themselves.

The 1976–1980 5-year plan hoped to raise food production by nearly 50 percent to 21 million tons (19 million t) of rice. The main industrial goals were to raise textile output to 493 million yards (450 million m) of fabrics and to produce 130,000 tons (118,200 t) of paper pulp, 1.3 million tons (1.18 million t) of chemical fertilizers, and 2 million tons (1.8 million t) of cement.

The road and rail network has been almost completely rebuilt since 1975. Hanoi and Ho Chi Minh City are now connected by railroad, air, and long-distance bus service. There are also air links between Vietnam's capital, Hanoi, and Beijing (Peking), Vientiane and Phnom Penh.

The country's medical system includes over a thousand hospitals, dispensaries, and sanatoriums, and mobile medical teams circulate in rural areas. In 1977, there were some 12 million students in school (out of a population of 50 million). There is one university and one polytechnic school in Hanoi, and it is reported that three universities have reopened in the south.

The south is now undergoing collectivization, but the process has been disrupted by the war with Cambodia. Many urban dwellers are being forced to move to new economic zones, and thousands of former officers and officials of the old Saigon government are also undergoing indefinite periods of forced labor in reeducation centers in remote areas away from their families. Only the Vietnamese leadership knows how many Vietnamese are living under these conditions.

By 1979, most aspects of the free market economy in the south had been brought under some form of state control, and the currencies of the northern and southern regions had been made uniform. Private property has not been entirely abolished, but large holdings of any kind have been or are being confiscated. Some of the old Saigon regime administrators

Vietnamese boat people at the Pulan Bidong refugee camp in Malaysia receive food and relief supplies. (Photo: United Nations/J. K. Isaac.)

of public and private enterprises were initially retained by the Hanoi government, but they have been replaced by Communists.

Many Western journalists and other visitors to Ho Chi Minh City report that the South Vietnamese openly express resentment against their northern rulers, probably not only because they are Communist but also because they are northern. In the towns and cities of the south, a more puritanical social code has been imposed, along with a network of spies to root out potential dissidents.

Vietnam's long history can be read as a series of maneuvers to avoid Chinese domination. The ethnic Vietnamese moved from southern China into the Red River delta around Hanoi in the fourth century B.C. Before long, the Chinese established a system of indirect rule against which the Vietnamese rebelled. Partly because of this, the Chinese incorporated Vietnam directly into their empire between 111 B.C. and A.D. 939. In that year, the Vietnamese took advantage of China's dynastic weakness to regain their independence. Since then, many aspects of Chinese culture have found their way into the national amalgam, as have millions of Chinese refugees and immigrants. But resisting Chinese imperialism has been the country's proudest tradition; the Vietnamese do not forget that their ancestors defeated the Mongols who swept over much of the rest of Asia in the thirteenth century.

The century of French colonial rule in Vietnam and three decades of American involvement (ending in 1975) gave urban Vietnamese a long exposure to Western ideas and values. Catholicism, Western science, Marxism, and the French language, culture, and administrative system all made deep inroads in the major cities. And yet, just a few years after winning two prolonged wars with the West, Vietnam's leaders are almost totally absorbed by their traditional obsessions—asserting their independence of China and asserting full control over Laos and Cambodia.

Vietnam is one of the most overpopulated countries in Southeast Asia, and it has the strongest, best-trained army in the region. However, the leaders of Vietnam have yet to prove that they can succeed in economic development as brilliantly as they have on the battlefield. The country's foreign exchange reserves are exhausted; by exiling the Chinese minority and many of the most talented Vietnamese, the Communist regime has deprived itself of a vital resource. It has also sacrificed much of the goodwill that was felt toward it by third world and other nations. Coping with the enormous exodus of refugees from Vietnam has placed a huge strain on the resources of many Asian countries and on the United Nations. Vietnam joined the World Bank and the International Monetary Fund in 1976 (and the United Nations in 1977). But in 1979, the outlook for further economic aid from these sources—or from the major Western powers—seemed dim.

Thus, the Vietnamese government has placed itself in a position of close dependence on the Soviet Union, whose main interest may lie in trying to keep the Chinese government off-balance. Vietnam has joined the Council for Mutual Economic Assistance (COMECON, or CEMA), the Soviet economic bloc. However, no one can be certain how much more aid the Soviets will supply to Vietnam—or for how long or for what purposes. If the Soviet Union is willing to meet the deficit in Vietnam's economic development budget until the mid-1980s—when Vietnam may be self-supporting—Moscow will be providing a useful service. However, if Soviet and Vietnamese aims coincide only in provoking continuing tension in the region, Southeast Asia's steady economic growth may be seriously disrupted.

Peter A. Poole

Central America
and
the
Caribbean

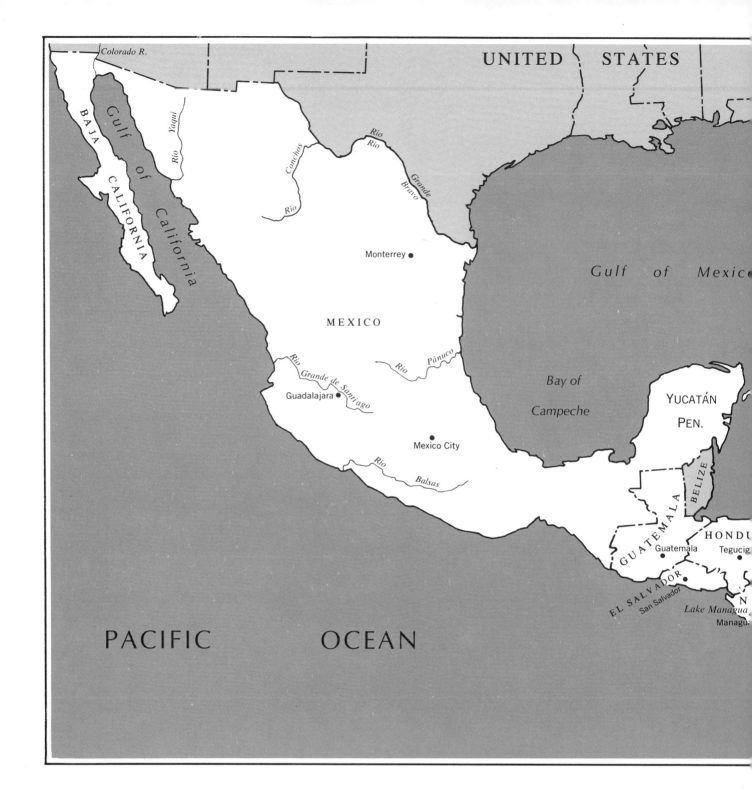

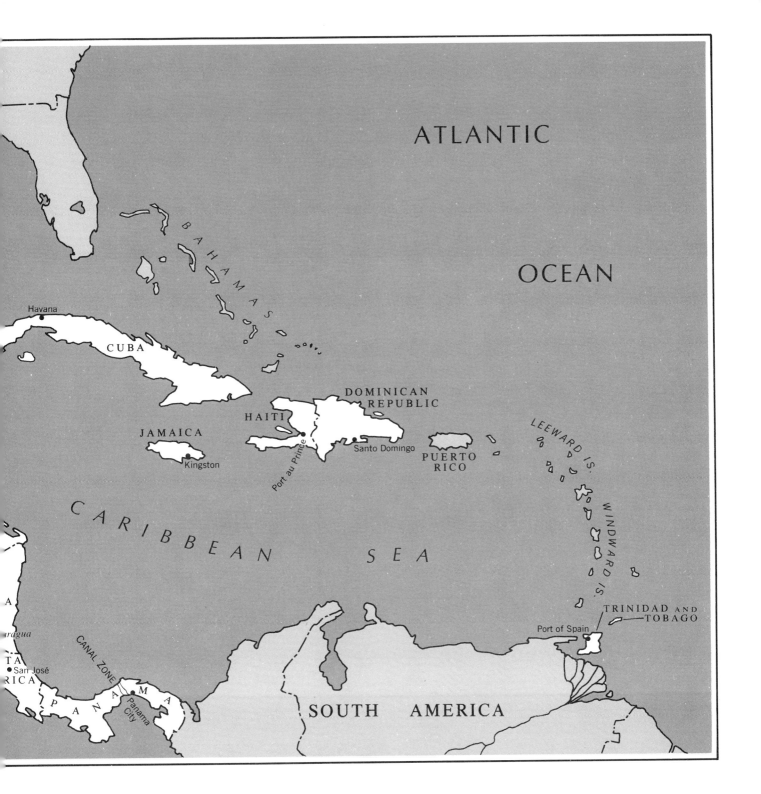

Costa Rica
(Republic of Costa Rica)

Area: 19,700 sq mi (51,022 sq km)
Population: 2.1 million
   Density: 107 per sq mi (41 per sq km)
   Growth rate: 2.5% (1970–1977)
Percent of population under 14 years of age: 42%
Infant deaths per 1,000 live births: 38
Life expectancy at birth: 70.3 years
Leading causes of death: not available
Ethnic composition: white, mestizo, black, Indian
Languages: Spanish, English, Boruca, Talamanca
Literacy: 88% (1976 est.)
Religions: Roman Catholic (majority)
Percent population urban: 41% (1975)
Percent population rural: 59% (1975)
Gross national product: 3.3 billion
   Per capita GNP: $1,540
   Per capita GNP growth rate: 3.2% (1970–1977)
Inflation rate: 15.6% (1970–1977)

Often called the Switzerland of Central America, Costa Rica is recognized as an exceptional Latin American country. Because Costa Rica has enjoyed political tranquility, its leaders are often credited with a measure of humanitarian statesmanship. "Ticos," as Costa Ricans call themselves, claim that their cherished political and economic characteristics are traditional and attribute them to their allegedly white, well-educated, and middle-class population.

In fact, Costa Rica's population is far from homogeneous and far from white, disproving this claim, and racial tensions within the country present a challenge to Costa Rica's myths about its society. At the same time, the widening gaps between rich and poor Costa Ricans cannot be ignored.

Although the country occupies less than 20,000 square miles (51,800 sq km), it is well situated. Four principal areas differ in terms of cultural and natural ecology: the Caribbean lowlands, the Pacific lowlands, the central plateau, and the southern highlands. The Caribbean coast is hot and humid, peopled largely by English-speaking blacks whose forebears were brought from Caribbean islands in the late nineteenth century to build a port and a railroad and to establish vast banana plantations.

Except for the seaport, Limón, and scattered settlements along the rail line that services banana plantations, the area east of the mountains is virtually unsettled, including virgin jungles that have only recently been invaded by lumbering crews. By contrast, the Pacific coast tends to be hot and dry, peopled by Spanish-speaking descendants of native Indians and mestizos, with large-scale cattle ranching in the northwest and little development to the south. The two ports on the Pacific are Puntarenas, which is linked with the capital by rail, and Golfito, primarily involved in the export of bananas.

Volcanoes have erupted from time to time in recent years, causing considerable damage, and minor earthquakes are commonplace. The terrain is well suited to the development of hydroelectric power, but faulty installations have forced the country to adopt extremely austere patterns of systematic weekly brownouts.

Most Ticos live on the central plateau (Meseta Central) which has a temperate climate at elevations of about 3,000 to 5,000 feet (915 to 1525 m). In fact, because more than half the population and most of the major cities are concentrated within a 20-mile (32-km) radius, the Costa Rican 95 percent who are considered white or mestizo in the census may perhaps forget the 4 percent who are black or the 1 percent who are Indian. The densely populated area around San José, Heredia, Alajuela, Cartago, and neighboring towns is remarkably homogeneous, in terms of physical characteristics and in terms of those social and cultural features that are sometimes confused with racial differences. Blacks (culturally as well as physically distinctive) live mainly on the east coast. Not more than 8,000 Indians survive, most of them as subsistence farmers in the rugged Cordillera de Talamanca, southeast of the Meseta Central. Other settlers in the southern highlands are largely peasants who moved from the Meseta Central to the General Valley when free land became available in a homesteading program a few decades ago.

The country has a young population, and had one of the highest birthrates in the world until a recent, little-discussed but remarkably effective campaign of sterilization was implemented. This campaign is not officially sponsored by the government (although it evidently enjoys tacit approval, including payment of physicians' fees and hospitalization costs). It is not widely publicized, and often patients are sterilized without being consulted or even informed. The preponderance of people less than 15 years old has become a major burden in terms of increasing costs for education (on which Costa Ricans pride themselves), as well as the other services and benefits required for so large an unproductive segment. They also represent the specter of increasing numbers soon to enter the ranks of the unemployed.

Agriculture is still the principal economic activity in terms of employment and in terms of national income. Enormous quantities of bananas and coffee are produced, although they are subject to the limitations that all primary products suffer in a world market. They always command prices that are proportionately lower than those of processed and manufactured goods, and prices are often set by foreigners over whom there is no control and to whom there is little personal recourse. In recent years, beef has also become an export commodity. Bauxite is said to be abundant in the southern mountains, but the enthusiastic promises that were held out for mining in the late 1960s have been quietly ignored by subsequent administrations. There is more manufacturing in Costa Rica than in most Central American countries, but it is still inconsequential in worldwide perspective, and it comprises mostly nondurable consumer goods, like clothing, bottled drinks, housewares, and tires.

Compared with other countries in Latin America, Costa Rica has a sizable class of small-scale farmers. The quasi-feudal hacienda system that dominated many areas never developed in Costa Rica, largely because there were so few native people and because little was produced of sufficient value to repay transportation costs to distant markets. In the mid-nineteenth century, a distinctive land-tenure pattern developed. As coffee cultivation spread throughout the Meseta Central, small holdings were often bought up and consolidated into plantations larger than those of the colonial period.

Similarly, late in the nineteenth century, vast tracts of the hot Caribbean lowlands were bought up by the United Fruit Company (now United Brands), a U.S. company that turned this land into an enormous banana plantation. After a blight damaged many of the trees, they bought land in the southern lowlands, and then replanted bananas on the Caribbean side. Despite these exceptions and the more recent pattern of large-scale cattle ranching in the northwestern

Cars are assembled at a government-operated plant in San José. The plant assembles several models of American, German, and Japanese cars. (Photo: United Nations/Jerry Frank.)

lowlands, more than 75 percent of the farms in Costa Rica are operated by their owners. When Costa Rica initiated a land-reform program, it was not with the usual aim of expropriating and reallocating large estates but to open new lands for homesteading (generally jungles in the north, or the temperate General Valley in the south).

Coffee is a long-term crop that, with minimal care, continues to produce for several years, once it grows to maturity. Because the berries fall so soon after they ripen, harvesting must be prompt. This results in an intensive demand for labor during short periods and little demand throughout the rest of the year. In fact, school vacations coincide with the coffee harvest, and entire peasant families often work together, paid on the basis of how much they pick. Small coffee processing plants are scattered throughout the area, and the plants buy from small-scale farmers as well as handle the coffee grown on their own property. With regard to the banana industry, by contrast, there is a virtual monopoly; company towns and, historically, even the major railroad and most seaports are closely managed by a foreign corporation.

During recent years, some of the best coffee land has been given over to construction, and it is not clear what the long-range prospects for coffee production will be. There is a housing boom on the Meseta Central. For many years, Costa Rica had an exceptionally high rate of indigenous population growth, over 3 percent. At the same time, the country was attracting retirees from the United States who enjoyed its scenic beauty, benign climate, cheap labor, and tax advantages. The foreign acquisition of land has led to the closing of beaches that were traditionally open to anyone, a development resented by many Costa Ricans.

Another cost of development has been the rapid diminution of the few remaining unspoiled rainforest areas in the world. This has led to the virtual extinction of some of Costa Rica's incredibly rich flora and fauna; it has also initiated the familiar cycle of erosion, the silting of rivers, and the other irreparable ecological damage that has occurred wherever shortsighted steps for the sake of progress are taken.

There is a special aura of self-righteousness about the people of Costa Rica. Contrasting themselves with other populations in Latin America, they invariably point to their supposed racial purity and to their high level of literacy, their lack of an army, and widespread social security. Virtually all school-age children attend school, at least during the first two or three grades. Education is highly esteemed, but many peasants cannot afford to have their children spend many years in school, where clothing, books and supplies are costly and the children are not earning anything. According to official figures, 95 percent of the adult population are literate—but the criterion is simply having attended school at some time, and many remain functionally illiterate. True, there is no standing army, but there is a paramilitary and ubiquitous national police force. An unusually high percentage of thc population are covered by social security, and clinics are scattered throughout the country. Compared with neighboring countries, health services in general are good, as reflected in extensive medical facilities, low infant mortality, and greater life expectancy.

Costa Ricans also claim—and the claim is rarely challenged—that they are a beacon of political stability and pacific democracy, surrounded by countries habitually torn by revolution or civil war and dominated by ruthless dictators. But Costa Rica's highly touted stability and democracy are relative. There have usually been regular elections, without intervening military coups, since 1889. But universal suffrage and a variety of other social and welfare benefits were enacted only after the Party of National Liberation (PLN) came to power through a violent revolution in 1948. Even the peaceful image of the nation can be challenged, in view of the fact that there continue to be periodic skirmishes along both borders with Nicaragua and Panama, and that Costa Rica was an important staging area for the Sandinista rebels who drove President Somoza out of Nicaragua in 1979.

There is a widespread belief in Costa Rica that everyone knows everyone else. Although that is not nearly true in any literal sense, it is true that, over the years, leaders in politics and in the professions have not only known each other but are often related. The popular image of an open class system is not wholly accurate, although education and wealth offer mobility for many who do not have traditional family connections.

Women not only have the vote, but hold many positions of responsibility in professional and administrative fields. At higher social levels, marriage is highly valued, whereas common-law cohabitation is commonplace among the poor. However, kinship is considered important at all levels. Nuclear families are large, and people are attentive to a wide range of relatives in their extended families; the Catholic system of *compadrazgo* (coparenthood, based on a godparent's informal obligation to the parent of the godchild) both extends and reinforces these bonds.

Extended-family ties do not climinate the need for institutions that provide social welfare and support. Costa Rica's immense social security system provides for retirement pensions and comes close to combining what the United States would call a national health program, an unemployment program, and welfare benefits. An impressive range of services is available to an enormous number of people, often in remote areas. Some observers fear that the increasing population and the consequential expansion of benefits may mean that Costa Ricans may not long be able to finance the program; others point proudly to its advantages and seem confident that the program will continue somehow. This latter viewpoint reflects the Costa Rican fatalism, shared with many other Latin Americans.

Similarly, *machismo* is a dominant attitude, in the sense that there is a striking double standard of expectations for the sexes; women are expected to be subservient or at least less than equal to men. The ideal is not destroyed by exceptions to the pattern nor by the reality that women often control the purse strings and make major family decisions. *Personalismo* is another characteristic value Costa Ricans share with other Spanish-speaking people throughout the world. This is the view that individuals who are acquainted owe a wide range of special treatment to one another, and is, in a sense, the antithesis of the bureaucratic attitude.

The name of the country itself, meaning "rich coast," sets the tone for the traditional and continuing ambiguity in Costa Rica. When Columbus reached the Caribbean coast in 1502, he misnamed the area on the basis of some gold jewelry, presumably traded from some Indians from Panama. However, the conquistadores found no easily exploitable mineral deposits there, and the native populations were small and scattered. There was little to attract European settlers, and the area languished as the poorest and most remote section of the enormous administrative entity of Guatemala.

During the Spanish colonial period, neither cities nor churches of any consequence developed. Independence was more nearly granted than won in 1821, and the local population, hopeful of gaining from a wealthy and powerful ally, promptly joined the newly established Mexican Empire. When it fell apart in 1823, the Costa Ricans joined the new United Provinces of Central America. That loose federation broke

Students from the National Institute of Apprenticeship in San José build low-income houses. (Photo: United Nations/Jerry Frank.)

up in 1836, and the Republic of Costa Rica continued to languish for several decades, until coffee and bananas brought wealth and some social innovations brought unusual prestige.

Today, Costa Rica has much in common with wealthier and more highly industrialized nations. But it also shares many of the traditions of other developing nations. Among the developing nations, Costa Rica has already accomplished much of what other nations hope to achieve. Nonetheless, the persistence of traditional patterns of belief and behavior may be an obstacle to its further progress.

Mounting malaise became visible in mid-1979, when a general strike shut down the principal port,

Limón, for several weeks. Widening gaps between the image and reality of Costa Rican life—like the widening gaps between the richest and the poorest of its people—can no longer be ignored. In recent years, Costa Rica's boast that it has no military has had an increasingly hollow ring to it, as the police force has been trained and equipped like armed forces elsewhere. This seems an unlikely country for another armed revolution, but mounting popular pressures will probably, at the least, restrict foreign investment and may even lead to some major reforms in taxation and other distributive mechanisms.

Dwight B. Heath

Cuba
(Republic of Cuba)

Area: 42,827 sq mi (110,922 sq km)
Population: 9.7 million
  Density: 226 per sq mi (87 sq km)
  Growth rate: 1.6% (1970-1977)
Percent of population under 14 years of age: 38% (1975)
Infant deaths per 1,000 live births: 29 (1975)
Life expectancy at birth: 69.8 years (1975)
Leading causes of death: not available
Ethnic composition: not available
Languages: Spanish
Literacy: over 96%
Religions: nominally Roman Catholic (majority)
Percent population urban: 60% (est.)
Percent population rural: 40% (est.)
Gross national product: $7.9 billion
  Per capita GNP: $810 (est.)
  Per capita GNP growth rate: −1.2% estimate (1970–1977)
Inflation rate: not available

Cuba is a potentially rich and relatively advanced agricultural country. For well over 100 years, sugar has been the dominant product in its economy and is expected to remain so until at least the end of this century. Large areas of Cuba's fertile land are also dedicated to cattle breeding and to a variety of crops harvested on a year-round basis. The light and medium industries of the island country are well developed, as is its infrastructure. The education level and skills of Cuba's 10 million people far outpace those of most nations of the world. There is virtually no illiteracy, and a high proportion of young people attend vocational schools and universities.

Yet Cuba is beset by perennial shortages of food, manufactured goods, and housing. Even its traditional products, such as sugar, coffee, cigars, and cigarettes, and the staples, rice and beans, are rationed. A socialist state, Cuba suffers the economic malaise affecting most Communist countries: very low labor productivity, government waste, inefficient bureau-

cracy, and haphazard planning. Moreover, Cuba lacks petroleum and other fuels, which it cannot afford to buy on the world market at current prices. This makes it almost totally dependent on its main oil supplier and creditor, the Soviet Union. Short of a technological breakthrough in the field of energy, this dependence is bound to continue indefinitely, thwarting Cuba's plans to terminate the present economic stagnation, and its aspirations to attain real political independence.

About the size of Pennsylvania, Cuba is the largest [42,827 square miles (110,922 sq km)] and the most populous (10 million) nation in the Caribbean. It lies less than 100 miles (160 km) from the Florida Keys, stretching approximately 750 miles (1,207 km), from Cape San Antonio in the western part to Cape Maisí in the east. It is a narrow island; at a point just west of Havana, it is barely 25 miles (40 km) from the Straits of Florida to the Gulf of Batabanó. Cuba commands the approaches from the Atlantic to the Gulf of Mexico, as well as to the Caribbean Sea and the Panama Canal. It is surrounded by numerous islands and keys, the largest being the Isle of Pines, about 80 miles (130 km) south of Havana. Approximately 40 percent of the island is covered by hills and low mountains. The highest peak of Cuba is Pico Turquino [6,389 feet (1,947 m)], located in Sierra Maestra, in the southeastern part of the island.

Cuba has one of the best soils in the world and a moderate and stable subtropical climate, with a mean temperature of about 70°F (20°C) in winter and 85°F (30°C) in summer. The fertility of the land, even without optimum fertilization and irrigation, is astonishing; on the island there are some 8,000 different species of plants and trees. The westernmost part of Cuba, Pinar del Río, is the area where the famous tobacco, Habano, is grown. A fortuitous combination of soil, moisture, temperature, and sunlight provides an inimitable climate for tobacco cultivation in Pinar del Río's Vuelta Abajo district. Cuba is regarded as the best place in the world for cigar manufacture.

Large cattle farms and rice plantations are located in the generally flat country of central Cuba. Besides sugarcane, fruits and vegetables are grown all over the island. The eastern part of the country, called Oriente, is the most mountainous and economically the richest region, with large sugarcane mills, nickel and cobalt mines and processing installations, and manganese and copper mines. Cuba's mineral output represents less than 15 percent of all its exports, and is shipped primarily to the Soviet-bloc countries.

Because the country depends on agriculture, the shortage of water hinders Cuban development. The island has few wide and deep rivers; many rivers and streams that appear on the map are dry most of the year. But when torrential tropical rains engulf the country, as they frequently do during the July–October hurricane season, the rivers swell, overflow their low banks, and cause widespread flooding. The government has made progress in water conservation and, where possible, dam construction; the country needs an average amount of rainfall to sustain a modest growth of agricultural production.

While the country's fishing industry is expanding, its production is destined mainly for export. Fish, like beef, milk, and even citrus fruits, is rationed. The revolution intended to increase agricultural production to enable Cuba to become self-sufficient in food. But today much more food is imported than before the revolution.

Under Cuban socialist rule there has been a shift of population. Drawn by job opportunities, young people from small towns and rural districts have flocked to the cities. Havana, east of Pinar del Río, is the country's industrial center and its administrative capital. With a population of about 2 million people, Greater Havana accounts for 20 percent of the country's total population. Still, at harvest time, hundreds of thousands of city volunteers are ordered to work the fields for weeks, sometimes months.

This migration notwithstanding, the Cuban family structure has changed little under socialism. Women are rapidly increasing their participation in the labor force and gaining economic independence. Yet the Cuban family continues to be male-dominated, a dominance upheld by the government's conservative attitude toward divorce. Thus the Cuban woman bears the main burden in the family unit, even if she is also a breadwinner. She not only works, but also stands in line for the rationed products, cooks, takes care of the children, and performs other domestic chores, which Cuban men regard as demeaning.

The role of the church—the overwhelming majority of Cubans are nominally Roman Catholic—has not changed either. The church has always—both before the revolution and after 1959—been a minor element in the nation's life, except for its role in educating the elite. Many of Cuba's church-educated leaders were

and are agnostics. José Martí, the nineteenth-century national hero, became a Freemason. Educated in Jesuit schools, Fidel Castro and his brother Raúl, became the top leaders of Communist Cuba.

Rhetoric is very much part of Cuban life. Whatever is said, or written, is regarded as true. Parsimony of the spoken and written word is not regarded as a virtue in Cuba, as Fidel Castro's (and his subordinates') endless speeches indicate.

After 1959, the revolutionary government tried to change the Cubans' attitude toward work and their insistence on materialistic rewards. The author of the plan to create a new *homo Cubanus* was Ernesto Guevara, the Argentine revolutionary who was Castro's top aide during the struggle against Batista and in the first years of the revolutionary regime. Guevara wanted to create a pure socialist society that would do away with money, where the "new men" would work selflessly and where all workers would be rewarded equally according to their needs. The experiment with the egalitarian society was an unmitigated failure in terms of its stifling regimentation and the pervasive lack of initiative. Nonetheless, the revolutionary government did succeed in establishing in Cuba an egalitarian society, albeit at a considerable cost in terms of human rights. The government succeeded only because of a massive infusion of aid from the Soviet Union, which totaled almost $10 billion by 1979.

Although Cuba is mainly agricultural, it is one of the most urbanized countries in Latin America. Historically, there were a few basic differences in lifestyles between the great majority of rural dwellers, now about 40 percent of the population, and the inhabitants of large and small towns. Even these differences diminished after 1959, as the revolutionary government improved communications with the remote areas of the island, which were connected to the national electric grid. The eradication of rural (and urban) illiteracy, the implementation of a uniform wage-salary structure, and allocations of more funds for social services to the rural areas diminished lifestyle differences even more, and so did the national system of rationing that guarantees every citizen the same small amounts of basic foods and consumer goods.

Most rationed goods are subsidized, because salaries, unchanged for years, are relatively low. Both an urban and a rural laborer make a basic monthly salary of about $110. An experienced engineer makes about $500 a month and a Cabinet minister earns about $1,000. But the salaries of high government and Communist Party officials are augmented by substantial perquisites.

Since Castro came to power, about 800,000 Cubans have left the island for political and economic reasons, including some 120,000 between April and June 1980. Initially, the Havana government was glad to get rid of many enemies, and potential saboteurs of the country's new socialist system, even though it realized the nation was losing many experienced technicians and managers. While exiles can now visit the island, so far Havana has made no effort to seek their advice in the economic field.

Before the oil crisis of the 1970s, Cuba was a developing country with great expectations. Charging that the capitalist system had condemned Cuba to an almost complete economic dependence on sugar, Castro launched a program of rapid industrialization and agricultural diversification in 1961. With Soviet aid, Castro hoped to find petroleum, which American companies (according to Havana) had allegedly discovered and kept secret. But the Soviet method of industrialization produced few tangible results, and despite extensive drilling, no new oil deposits were found either on the island or offshore.

Prosperity has not come to Cuba, which needs increasing annual subsidies from the Soviet Union. Agricultural diversification has also faltered. Grandiose plans for huge cattle ranches and coffee plantations were revised drastically downward and were later forgotten. The government planned to produce 10 million tons (99.1 million t) of sugar in 1970, and between 8 and 10 million tons (7.3 and 9.1 million t) in the following 5 years, to finance the country's development. While Cuba's 1970 sugar output was 8.5 million tons (7.7 million t)—a respectable total—the effort, including the mobilization of a million so-called volunteers (among them students and office workers), proved disastrous in other economic sectors. The year 1970 marked a major economic watershed for the revolution. Recognizing a defeat, Castro pledged to rely on more conventional, less ambitious economic methods to overcome underdevelopment.

As a result, Cuba abandoned its unique economic theory, including the policy of moral incentives, and adopted the Soviet system of economic management. In 1972, Cuba formally joined the Moscow-led Council for Mutual Economic Assistance (CMEA), tying its economy to that of the Soviet bloc, and becoming the group's principal supplier of sugar.

Cuba has had a racially mixed society for centuries, and the Castro government is trying to eradicate any latent racial prejudices. When the island was discovered, about 150,000 peaceful and hospitable Indians inhabited Cuba, but they were quickly exterminated by the aggressive colonizers. Because slavery existed in sixteenth-century Spain, the early conquistadores brought with them black slaves, who soon replaced the Indians.

Large-scale importation of African slaves followed in the eighteenth century, when the Spanish colonizers, like their North American counterparts, faced a growing demand for agricultural labor. The slave trade ended in 1820, after Spain and Great Britain agreed to prohibit the practice.

According to the 1827 population census, Cuba had 311,000 whites, 287,000 black slaves, and 106,000 free colored inhabitants. The freedman segment of the colonial society increased rapidly because manumission was relatively easy during periods when export crops were low-priced; emancipation was regulated by law, and slaves were able to buy their freedom on installment. Because of the rapid disappearance of the Indians, today Cubans have no indigenous roots; their national characteristic is Spanish with a strong African influence and the country is ethnically Afro-Cuban.

The Spanish, unlike the Anglo-Saxons, had fewer inhibitions about sexual contact with blacks. Because few Spanish colonizers took families to the New World, white male–black female sexual union was common in the colonial period, and since independence there has never been any legal prohibition against interracial cohabitation or marriage. Well into the twentieth century, many Spaniards and white Cubans, even if they were married, had mulatto mistresses. In time, blacks and mulattoes attained positions of prominence in the country's political life. The two Presidents who preceded Fidel Castro, Carlos Prío Socarrás and Fulgencio Batista, were quadroons.

Whatever the extent of African physical and cultural influence, the principal influence on the Cuban character and mores was Spanish. Spain was regarded as the *madre patria* (native country) even by Cubans who fought against colonial rule. Class distinctions in prerevolutionary Cuba were patterned after Spanish society. But Cuba offered lower-middle-class Spaniards the social upward mobility that was denied them in their own land. Wealth and education, not birth, were the principal ingredients for social advancement.

In prerevolutionary times, Cubans were fatalistic, individualistic, and materialistic. Their attitude toward work was inherited from immigrants from Andalusia, who (unlike other Spaniards) believed that one had to rely on a lucky break, rather than hard work, to succeed. "God created work as a punishment," says one popular Cuban song.

For most of the five centuries since its discovery, Cuba was isolated from the center of world developments. But in the last 20 years it has moved out of the world's political backwater. On January 1, 1959, Cuba's dictator, General Fulgencio Batista, fled the island and Fidel Castro, a 33-year-old guerrilla leader, assumed power. The change of leadership marked the beginning of the most profound social upheaval in the Americas since the 1917 Mexican revolution. On May 1, 1961, the country became a socialist state and the first member of the Soviet bloc in the Western Hemisphere.

Under Castro's direction, Cuba underwent deep political, social, and economic transformations. In the process, the country shed the popular image of a pleasure island that it had acquired after independence from Spain in 1902, and particularly during the 1930s and 1940s.

Emerging from relative obscurity and suddenly plunged into the maelstrom of international politics, socialist Cuba has made an indelible impact on contemporary history. Because of the country's strategic location and the ideological orientation of its government, Cuba was the focus of a momentous confrontation between the United States and the Soviet Union. In October 1962, the two countries were brought to the brink of war over the placement of Soviet nuclear missiles on the island.

Cuba's close ties with the Soviet bloc and CMEA will have positive and negative effects on Cuba's national development in the 1980s. Continuing Soviet economic aid, estimated in 1979 at $5 million a day, guarantees that whatever the country's output, its standard of living will not appreciably diminish. But this means that Cuba's dependence on Soviet assistance will continue to grow, limiting Havana's economic options. In 1979, the Soviet Union supplied Cuba with 10 million tons (9.07 million t) of oil and petroleum products, about 95 percent of Cuba's consumption. At 1979 Soviet prices—below those of the Organization of Petroleum Exporting Countries (OPEC)—the cost of petroleum consumed by Cuba practically equaled the value of the country's annual sugar output. Any increase in world oil prices makes Cuba a more expensive ally of the Soviet Union, which already buys petroleum from OPEC with Western currency. Consequently, Cuba has had to scale-down its long-range development plans. According to

all indications, the 1981–1985 plan will be more modest than the 1976–1980 plan, which was unfulfilled and adversely affected by worldwide inflation.

Thus after two decades of revolutionary rule, Cuba's economy has traveled a full circle: the country is again a sugar monoculture, and sugar, whose prices fluctuate unpredictably, accounts for over 80 percent of all exports. The state owns all industry, commerce, services, and transportation and about 75 percent of all arable land. No new sources of foreign exchange have been developed except, ironically, tourism. The exiles, who were once much criticized, are now welcome because they provide a source of American dollars.

Because Havana does not publish meaningful data, it is difficult to verify the country's economic performance and to forecast its long-range outlook. But all indicators point toward a long period of austerity and economic stagnation. In the foreseeable future, Cubans will have to resort to greater belt tightening because the country has few untapped resources. Thus, the principal task of the Castro government in the coming years will be to learn how to manage an economy during a time of growing scarcities and how to distribute Cuba's limited resources to avoid aggravating potentially dangerous social and political tensions.

George Volsky

Dominican Republic

Area: 19,000 sq mi (49,000 sq km)
Population: 5 million
   Density: 263 per sq mi (102 per sq km)
   Growth rate: 3% (1970–1977)
Percent of population under 14 years of age: 49%
Infant deaths per 1,000 live births: 104 (1975)
Life expectancy at birth: 57.8 years (1975)
Leading causes of death: Enteritis and other diarrheas, perinatal causes, pneumonia
Ethnic composition: mulatto 73%; white 16%; black 11%
Languages: Spanish; minor pockets of Creole and English
Literacy: 60% (est.)
Religions: Roman Catholic; small percentages of Protestants and folk Vodun
Percent population urban: 48%
Percent population rural: 52%
Gross national product: $3.8 billion
   Per capita GNP: $910
   Per capita GNP growth rate: 4.6% (1970–1977)
Inflation rate: 12.5% (1960–1976)

The Dominican Republic is in the midst of rapid social, economic, technological, political, and cultural transition. Its main assets are its hardworking, resourceful, and young people and its rich land, which—if properly exploited—could feed the whole Caribbean basin. Its major liabilities include high illiteracy rates, uneven distribution of wealth, and a history of polit-

ical instability. This country's promising development strategy must aim at the obliteration of its social, economic, and political difficulties.

Lying between Cuba to the west and Puerto Rico to the east, the Dominican Republic occupies the eastern two-thirds of the island of Hispaniola—the second largest island of the Greater Antilles. (The remaining third of the island is the Republic of Haiti.) Hispaniola (or Quisqueya) occupies a strategic position on major sea routes leading from Europe to North, Central, and South America. The Dominican side of the island covers some 19,000 square miles (49,000 sq km). Slightly larger than Denmark or Switzerland, it is subdivided into 26 provinces and the National District (comprising the capital city of Santo Domingo). The provinces contain 77 municipalities and 20 municipal districts.

The island is predominantly mountainous. The Pico Duarte in the Cordillera Central (the central mountain range) is the highest point in the West Indies, reaching 10,417 feet (3,175 m). In contrast to Haiti, the Dominican plains and valleys are fertile, save for the extreme west, which is drying up. The north central Cibao Valley–Vega Real area, the main agricultural region, is one of the most fertile in the Western Hemisphere. Sugarcane (introduced by Columbus) has traditionally been the major crop; most of the cane plantations are in the southern coastal lowlands. Except in the highest mountains and the dry zones, where the temperatures are extreme, the rest of the country's climate is pleasantly moderate, subtropical, and stable.

The native flora is diverse because of variation in elevation and rainfall. (It was in Hispaniola that the Spaniards were introduced to tobacco by the Indians.) Animal life is also varied. Fish and shellfish resources are abundant on the coasts, though not well exploited. Although cattle-breeding utilizes increasingly sophisticated methods, land erosion and forest depletion are permanent problems. Minerals mined include bauxite, nickel, clay, gold, gypsum, iron ore, and marble. Other less-developed mineral resources include coal, cobalt, zinc, sulfur, and molybdenum. Salt Mountain is possibly the world's largest national salt deposit.

By the time the Spaniards arrived in 1492, Hispaniola had been populated by Amerinds for several hundred years. The Taino Arawak had established an elaborate ceremonial center there. However, most of the original population disappeared very quickly. The most important cause of death was from European epidemics, to which the indigenous people were especially susceptible. Others were killed during the war of conquest or by excessive slave work. Intermarriages (of male Spaniards with natives) also led to the disappearance of the original population. Toward the end of the 1520s, African slaves were introduced

to work in the incipient sugar industry, replacing the depleted indigenes. Miscegenation between Europeans and Africans has been common ever since.

In 1960, some 73% of the population were mulattoes. Dominicans range from black (about 11 percent) to white (presumably 16 percent), with every likely intermixture. Negritude is undesirable for sociocultural reasons and is popularly identified with Haiti. For the 1970 census, it was decided to omit a racial classification. In 1978, the country's population was estimated to be 5 million, among the fastest growing in the Americas (about 3 percent per year). More than half the Dominican population is under the age of 20, and the proportion of women is slightly larger than that of men. Except for minor pockets of distinct language subgroups, Spanish is the language of the country.

The country has traditionally welcomed immigrants from all over the world. Under the Rafael Leonidas Trujillo Molina dictatorship in particular (1930–1961), European, Near Eastern, and Japanese immigrations were encouraged and persecuted European Jews were welcomed. In addition, thousands of Puerto Ricans and people from the non-Hispanic Lesser Antilles migrated as workers and managers in the sugar industry. Political unrest in Cuba has spurred emigration to the Dominican Republic.

Thousands of illegal and seasonal migrant Haitian workers also find their way to Dominican cane plantations every year, despite the protests of locally powerful ultranationalists. The question of Haitian migrants is extremely complicated. Haitian troops have invaded the Dominican Republic twice (in the late 1700s and the early 1800s). In 1937, dictator Trujillo ordered a massacre that cost the lives of probably as many as 30,000 Haitians, including many Dominicans of Haitian descent or Dominicans that looked Haitian.

In addition to immigration, the population has increased because of improved health care and a decline in infant and adult mortality rates. Although the existence of small groups of political exiles may persist, a new kind of economic expatriate emerged after Trujillo's downfall. Perhaps as many as half a million Dominicans live overseas, mostly in the United States. The economic impact of their monetary remittances to relatives at home has not fully been explored yet.

Ethnic composition is closely related to the social structure. Generally the wealthier, traditional upper class looks white, and most (though not all) white-looking Dominicans are well-to-do. The Dominican Republic does not have a landed oligarchy. Frequent political upheavals have forced the aristocracy to emigrate. Nonetheless, contemporary upper-class groups (mostly urban-based industrialists, business people, and professionals) command a great deal of power and influence. However, this power is shared—if reluctantly—with the dynamic rising middle-class sectors. The elite participate actively in all political groups,

Ramshackle dwellings of the poor lie just beyond a modern apartment complex in Santo Domingo. (Photo: United Nations/ M. Guthrie.)

from the extreme conservative (usually promilitary) to the most radical. Since the elite have the education, administrative skills, and know-how, they fill many leadership positions, creating an establishment that guarantees some continuity. The seat of the national oligarchy is the city of Santiago in the Cibao area.

Traditionally most Dominicans have been at least nominal Roman Catholics. However, Protestant sects are spreading quickly, especially among the rural and urban poor. Dominican versions of African Catholic syncretic cults, like vodun (voodoo), are also pervasive. Freedom of religion has been guaranteed by the laws, though under Trujillo, Jehovah's Witnesses were persecuted. Significantly, Pope John Paul II visited Santo Domingo late in 1978 and received a warm welcome.

The major social unit in the Dominican Republic is the nuclear family. The joint family including several generations and the extended family are also strong, although these units are weakening. Illegitimacy and mother-centered, fatherless homes are common. Ritual kinship in the form of *compadrazgo* (co-godparenthood), fosterage, and informal adoption of children is also characteristic. The average number of people per household is about 5.5. Sexism and dual standards are part of the cultural ideology, although lower-class working women enjoy some degree of freedom. But the reported proportion of women in the labor force, one-third, is one of the lowest in the Americas.

Almost 50 percent of the population remains illiterate, despite various literacy campaigns. Elementary schools are found throughout the country; however, many of these offer schooling only to fourth grade (particularly in the distant rural zones). Many students travel long distances for higher elementary and secondary schooling. Teachers are generally illtrained and ill-paid. About 18.5 percent of the national budget is allocated for education. Economic necessity discourages many poor youngsters from completing their education. Yet about 90 percent of the student-age population, 20 percent of all Dominicans, receive some kind of schooling. Despite its educational limitations, the country produces fine artists and intellectuals. There are half a dozen state and private universities, four of which are in the capital. All of them attract thousands of medical students from Puerto Rico and the United States.

Some 18 percent of the national budget is allocated for health services, which serve only 60 percent of the population. Health conditions are substantially improved, and common epidemics have been brought under control, though parasites still plague the infant population. Family planning is becoming more sophisticated and acceptable (despite religious opposition). A poor, high-starch diet is the usual fare.

Despite increasing urbanization and industralization, the Dominican Republic is a predominantly rural, agricultural society. Approximately 60 percent of the labor force are employed in agriculture; sugar production is the main industry. Slightly over 10 percent are engaged in nonagricultural industrial activities (especially rum and other beverages, and construction); most others work as service providers. The country is self-sufficient in major food staples, like rice; with proper technology production could be increased to multiply agricultural exports. Major exports include sugar (of which the Dominican Republic is one of the world's largest exporters), tobacco, cacao, tropical fruits and vegetables, and hides. Most manufactured and capital goods and some processed foodstuffs are imported. The United States, Western Europe, Japan, Venezuela (for needed oil), and other Latin American countries are major trading partners.

There are a few large landholdings (*latifundia*), mostly state-owned or foreign-owned, and many uneconomical small holdings (*minifundia*). However, land-reform legislation and recently established cooperatives are slowly changing land-tenure patterns.

The GNP for 1976 was estimated at almost $4 billion with a growth rate of 13.2 percent, and a per capita income of some $800 (although the figures are lower at constant prices, they are still higher than comparable nations). However, these figures do not reveal income distribution; in the mid-1970s, the trend toward a more equitable distribution of wealth and income was in fact being reversed.

Although foreign national private investments are encouraged (and various multinationals take advantage of this), many of the industries and services are

Youngsters work on a road-building project. Many children of poor families have to work instead of attending school. (Photo: United Nations/ P. Teuscher.)

controlled by the state because of a historical accident. During the dictatorship of Rafael L. Trujillo, his family amassed a great fortune, and most of the family's belongings passed to the state after Trujillo's assassination. The all-important sugar industry, for example, is composed of 16 sugar mill–plantation compounds; 12 of these once belonged to the Trujillos and are now administered by the state. Many public services (such as electricity) are government monopolies. Unfortunately, the state enterprises are generally the most inefficient and most subject to nepotism and corruption.

Although no real organized labor existed before Trujillo, he encouraged a union system to serve his interests exclusively. In the post-Trujillo period, unionism has expanded rapidly, but it has not yet been centralized. Its influence is still limited, and unions do not include the most exploited groups, seasonal agricultural workers and household servants. The country's labor force is estimated at 1.2 to 1.5 million (a small proportion of the overall population relative to other developing nations). The sugar industry employs over 100,000 workers, but for only 9 months each year. Total unemployment is estimated at 20 percent, as is underemployment.

The urban population increased from close to 25 percent in 1950 to some 40 percent in 1970. Reliable projections estimate that in the 1980s the population will be evenly distributed. A movement from rural to urban areas and the return migration from overseas of formerly rural dwellers (who now prefer cities) are partially responsible for this urban boom. With a population of some 1 million people, the capital city of Santo Domingo has grown fivefold. Concurrent with this expansion, however, are the increasing numbers of improvised poor shanty towns in otherwise prosperous Santo Domingo and Santiago.

The country possess a network of roads and highways (though upkeep has been a problem), as well as airports and seaports, radio stations and newspapers, and telecommunications, but many rural areas still lack electricity and/or telephones. And yet, the beautiful beaches, the unspoiled natural scenery, the unpolluted environment, the characteristic Dominican cleanliness, and the popular merengue ballad music lure thousands of tourists from all over the world.

Although the Dominican side of Hispaniola was the site of the first European settlement in the Americas, by the mid-sixteenth century, the colony was virtually abandoned because of rapid exploitation and the availability of new continental lands.

The colony remained desolate for the next three centuries, although it suffered occasional attacks and raids from competing British, French, and Dutch imperial powers. The French eventually succeeded in establishing a sugar producing, slave-based colony in the western part of the island, which lasted until 1804, when a slave revolt resulted in the establishment of Haiti.

Between 1795 and 1821, both Spain and France ruled the island intermittently. In 1821, the first Creole-fostered independence from Spain was achieved, only to be frustrated by Haitian occupation, which lasted until 1844, when Juan Pablo Duarte led the Dominicans to independence. The last half of the nineteenth century and the early twentieth century were characterized by political instability.

The United States took over the administration of the customs revenues in 1905 (presumably to avoid direct intervention of competing European creditors) and in 1916 occupied the country. Following eight years of U.S. occupation and six years of democratic experimentation, a once low-ranking mulatto army officer of humble origins, Rafael Trujillo, took power with the backing of a now unified military. Trujillo ruled for 31 years as if the whole country were his private, personal domain. In 1961, he was assassinated.

From 1961 to 1966, instability again plagued the nation. In 1963, Juan Bosch, a renowned exiled intellectual, was elected President with the backing of the populist Dominican Revolutionary Party (PRD), in the first free national elections since the 1920s. The democratic experiment, however, only lasted half a year; a military coup d'etat subsequently deposed Bosch. A succession of temporary governments followed until civil war broke out in the capital in April 1965. Critics argue that American military intervention resulted in Bosch's return to power. In the new elections that were held in 1966, Joaquín Balaguer overwhelmingly defeated Bosch. Balaguer succeeded in reelecting himself in 1970 and again in 1974.

The Dominican Republic has had some 25 constitutions since the nineteenth century. The Balaguer-sponsored 1966 constitution, now in force, established a tripartite government, consisting of an elected Executive, a bicameral Congress, and an appointed, independent judiciary. In 1978, when Balaguer was already over 70 years old, in ill health, and semiblind, his electoral bid for a fourth consecutive term failed, despite the military's blatant attempt to reverse his defeat. The challenging PRD won the election with the explicit sanction of the United States. The composition of the PRD has changed since the 1960s; it is now ostensibly guided by center-liberal, social-democratic ideals and is a well-regarded member of the already heterogeneous (non-Marxist) Socialist International.

The new President, Don Antonio Guzmán, is a businessman from Santiago. The fragmented opposition consists of a series of groups whose philosophies range from the right to the extreme left. Human rights are now more respected, and an amnesty has freed most political prisoners, including former guerrilla fighters. The new government has inherited many problems that cannot be solved overnight. The administration has neutralized the power-hungry military sector. Yet it will probably continue to maintain a costly military force, because it shares a small island with a dissimilar country. In reality, Haiti is no longer a threat, but the military finds in this myth—coupled with the existence of a neo-imperialist Cuba—its main raison d'etre.

Despite many reforms, including land redistribution and an expanding economy, corruption is rampant. Modernization is not improving the living standards of rural people. Worldwide inflation also contributes to decreasing the real income of the poorest sectors. Some experts believe that this pattern of rapid development and growth in certain indexes and stagnation in others is a sign of faults in the development process, rather than of gross underdevelopment. The country's history shows that relative techno-economic progress was achieved mostly under the dictatorships, semidictatorships, or even foreign dominations that fostered stability. Political unrest has been very costly in economic and human terms.

But except for these words of caution, the future for development in the Dominican Republic looks very hopeful. The country is blessed with an extremely rich, self-supporting land, populated by a homogeneous, very young, and hardworking people. If political democracy is to succeed, it must solve the most pressing problems of increasing the literacy rate, providing health care, adequate housing, employment, a more equitable distribution of wealth, honesty in public administration, industrial and agricultural diversification, and a fair solution of the Haitian question.

Rolando Alum

El Salvador
(Republic of El Salvador)

Area: 8,260 sq mi (21,393 sq km)
Population: 4.4 million
  Density: 533 per sq mi (206 per sq km)
  Growth rate: 3.1% (1970–1977)
Percent of population under 14 years of age: 46% (1975)
Infant deaths per 1,000 births: 58 (1975)
Life expectancy at birth: 65 years (1975)
Leading causes of death: not available
Ethnic composition: mestizo 90%; Indian, less than 10%; white, less than 5%
Languages: Spanish
Literacy: 50% of persons over age 10
Religions: Roman Catholic (majority)
Percent population urban: less than 50%
Percent population rural: more than 50%
Gross national product: $2.8 billion
  Per capita GNP: $600
  Per capita GNP growth rate: 2.1% (1970–1977)
Inflation rate: not available

El Salvador has the largest population and the smallest land area in Central America. The pressures resulting from that discrepancy are acute, despite the varied and successful steps that have been taken to foster economic development. The crowding of over 4 million people in an area of 8,260 square miles (21,393 sq km), resulting in one of the highest population densities in the world, is aggravated by the concentration of people on the central plateau. Less than half the people are urban; agriculture is not only the principal occupation, employing 60 percent of the labor force, but this sector is also the principal source of goods for export, earning nearly 90 percent of the foreign exchange.

The country is roughly rectangular, with a chain of volcanic mountains along the northern and southern boundaries and a high plain between them. This narrow plain between the southern mountains and the Pacific coast is hot and humid, with cotton farms, cattle ranches, and the few ports. The northern mountains are temperate in climate, but have been so completely deforested that the land is virtually useless. The central plateau with its 2,000-foot (610-m) elevation has a fertile volcanic soil and a temperate climate; most cities and towns and the coffee farming and burgeoning industries are located here.

There are three cities that have over 100,000 people each: San Salvador (the national capital), Santa Ana, and San Miguel, all in the central highlands. Smaller cities are the commercial and administrative centers

Woman work in the spinning section of a textile factory. El Salvador's textile mills process the cotton grown in the southeast region of the country. (Photo: United Nations/ UNESCO/D. Roger.)

of other regions, although most of the population are scattered in small towns or even in isolated homesteads.

The soil is generally rich, except in the northern mountains. The hot and humid southwestern plain supports cattle ranches; large cotton farms dominate the southeast, and their fibers are generally processed in the country's excellent textile mills. The coffee that is so important for export is grown on both small and large farms on the central plateau.

Many Salvadorans are basically subsistence farmers, who produce little more than they need to support their families at a low level and who participate only marginally in the market economy. There was a pioneering venture in land reform shortly after World War II. It did not involve the expropriation and reallocation of large estates but allowed homesteaders to claim and work small holdings on land that had been national reserves in the north. Unfortunately, the supply of unclaimed land was soon exhausted, and pressures increased as a decreasing death rate, combined with a high birthrate, led to a population explosion.

One of the safety valves that kept the pressure of increasing population on limited land from erupting in revolutionary violence was the ease with which Salvadorans could, during most of this century, emigrate to Honduras. In Honduras, land was abundant, and industrious newcomers could gain a degree of security. Uneasy relations between the two countries were aggravated by the relative success of Salvadoran immigrants, many of whom entered Honduras illegally and who were stereotyped as aggressive and opportunistic.

The oligarchy that manages most large-scale business (including plantation agriculture) and industry belongs to the less than 5 percent of the population who call themselves "white." According to the 1971 census, less than 10 percent of El Salvador's people are Indian and about 90 percent are identified as mestizo. The census categories have more to do with social attributes than they do with genetics or biology, although racial terminology is commonplace.

Educational facilities in El Salvador are neither widespread nor very effective. Elementary schooling is supposedly free and compulsory, but many families send their children to school for only a few years or not at all, because of the cost of clothing and supplies and because they cannot afford the loss of the children's contribution to the family's work.

Health is generally poor, with very limited services available except in the capital city. Gastrointestinal infections, parasitosis, malnutrition, and respiratory diseases are widespread, and infant mortality is high. Water and sewage systems are being built in cities, and clinics are being established in some towns, but rural areas remain neglected.

Although there is little variety and not much protein in their diet, peasants work hard, subsisting on small quantities of rice, beans, and manioc, and black coffee. Tropical fruits and sugarcane are enjoyed in season.

In many respects, Salvadoran workaday life is not significantly different from that of people at similar levels of society anywhere. Many Salvadoran values and attitudes persist from the colonial period. Among these legacies are *machismo* and *marianismo*, the two sides of the coin of sexual discrimination; men are expected to be forceful, egoistic, and aggressive in sexual and other terms, while women are expected to be submissive and long-suffering. *Personalismo* is another feature of the culture: an individual's contacts and influence are often more important than the individual's other capabilities.

In El Salvador, industry is rapidly increasing in importance; special incentives in the form of loans and tax breaks have stimulated new developments in food processing and the production of textiles and clothing, furniture, leather goods, and even small electrical appliances. The modest but early reforms in labor conditions and social welfare were unusual among developing nations. Relatively efficient modes of transportation and communication link the country, partly because of its small size. There is an adequate network of roads and highways, so that few settlements are truly isolated.

El Salvador's economic dependence on primary products leads to fundamental problems. Raw materials and unprocessed foodstuffs command prices that are relatively low in comparison with the manufactured products that these same countries must import. And even a small change in demand, price, or production can shake the national economy, especially when coffee exports amount to nearly 65 percent of the foreign exchange.

In pre-Columbian times, El Salvador was occupied

A rehabilitated squatter settlement is located at Tutunichapa near San Salvador. Housing is a serious problem in this densely populated country. (Photo: United Nations/ Jerry Frank.)

by Pipil Indians who were related to the Aztecs, they left some impressive ceremonial centers and fine ceramic and carved stone artifacts. They were strong enough to hold back the Spanish conquerors until 1525, but during the subsequent quarter of a century, their way of life was virtually destroyed, as was much of their population.

Throughout most of the colonial period, the region was a backwater. There was no easily accessible mineral wealth, and most of the Indians were shipped as slaves to South America, rather than being used to work the large local haciendas. The area played virtually no role during the successful wars of independence, and the Spanish withdrawal in 1821 left a people ill prepared for self-government. El Salvador declined to ally itself with the Mexican Empire at that time, instead, it affiliated with the United Provinces of Central America in 1823 and even managed to have the capital moved from Guatemala City to San Salvador in 1835. When the confederation was dissolved in 1838, El Salvador became an independent republic.

Intermittent fighting between so-called liberals and conservatives has been endemic. However, the labels do not reflect significant differences in political or social philosophy; most national leaders are members of a small wealthy elite, cooperating with the army. Political parties have often been little more than personal constituencies based on patronage and clientage relations between an individual and his supporters, instead of being organs of popular support for coherent platforms. The persisting image of oligarchial rule is reflected in habitual reference, by people in all walks of life, to the 14 families, who are said to control most of the land, wealth, and power in the country even today.

El Salvador has enjoyed relative political stability, discounting the quick succession of Presidents during the nineteenth century (including several dictators). Throughout several successive constitutions, the government has generally been structured as a nominally representative democracy with an elected President heading the executive branch, and with a separate judicial branch and a unicameral legislature. But since 1932, the government has been controlled by the military with the support of the elite and with all opposition fiercely suppressed.

In 1969, the so-called Soccer War, a full-scale war between Honduras and El Salvador, erupted. It is a reflection of the generally low prestige of Central American nations that this violent international conflict was virtually dismissed by much of the world's press as a sort of comic-opera overreaction about who won a soccer game. But the conflict had deep roots. Salvadorans resented the series of laws that had been passed by a xenophobic Honduran legislature, presumably aimed at protecting local interests from the increasing competition of some 300,000 Salvadoran immigrants. Fierce fighting raged along the border for about a month, before the arrival of a peacekeeping commission sent by the Organization of American States. There have been no further armed clashes, but diplomatic relations were only restored in 1979, a full decade later.

Although little of the country suffered actual physical devastation during the war of 1969, its effects will probably hamper further Salvadoran development for some time to come. Trade with Honduras was completely cut off; the closing of the major international highway also severely curtailed commerce with Nicaragua, Costa Rica, and Panama. Perhaps even more debilitating in the long run was the return (as refugees) of tens of thousands of Salvadorans who had emigrated to Honduras and had been sending remittances to relatives.

In a significant sense, a major victim of the war between El Salvador and Honduras was the Central American Common Market. It had been initiated in 1961, after much discussion, as a means of stimulating and rationalizing economic development throughout the region. Under the Common Market, customs duties and other barriers to trade were lessened, and there was some cooperative decision making about the distribution and allocation of new industrial enterprises so as to lessen overlap and competition. But real achievements lagged far behind goals, and the organization was never strong. Following the war both Honduras and Costa Rica withdrew from the Common Market.

The pressure of a large and rapidly increasing population on limited resources—both in terms of land for farming and in terms of opportunities for employment—continues to mount. Resentment over the high concentration of land ownership in the hands of a few led to protests by the peasants, whose efforts at unionization, partisan political organization, and other activism had been met with repression. Labor unrest was widespread and increasingly violent. The vicious cycle of civil disturbance and brutal repression has gained momentum. In October 1979, a military junta seized control of the government. But the junta's reforms, nationalization of large private banks, and a land redistribution program, which aims to expropriate 60 percent of the private land of large landholders, did not stem the violence.

Although the guerrillas have not yet been unified, except in their opposition to the government, they may eventually coalesce and effect a populist revolution. If that occurred, a major redistribution of wealth and power would probably follow. In the meantime, the violence is threatening vital agricultural production, causing the flight of capital and creating more hardships for the impoverished masses. Whatever leadership may emerge, it seems unlikely that El Salvador's political, economic, and social institutions will survive without major change.

Dwight B. Heath

Guatemala
(Republic of Guatemala)

Area: 42,000 sq km (108,780 sq km)
Population: 6.6 million
  Density: 157 per sq mi (61 per sq km)
  Growth rate: 2.9% (1970–1977)
Percent of population under 14 years of age: 44% (1975)
Infant deaths per 1,000 live births: 74 (1979)
Life expectancy at birth: 54.1 years (1975)
Leading causes of death: not available
Ethnic composition: Indian, Ladino
Languages: Indian languages more than 50%; Spanish
Literacy: 38% (1979)
Religions: Roman Catholic, pre-Columbian religions
Percent population urban: 37% (1977)
Percent population rural: 63% (1977)
Gross national product: $6.04 billion
  Per capita GNP: $910
  Per capita GNP growth rate: 3.3% (1970–1977)
Inflation rate: 10.4% (1970–1976)

Guatemala's ecological diversity offers a wide range of opportunities, but diversity imposes difficulties in terms of transportation, communication, and national governance. Traditionalism, a dominant theme among the Indian groups that constitute a majority of the population, is also deplored as an obstacle to

At a public laundry in Antigua, women wash the family clothes. (Photo: United Nations/ A. Jongen.)

economic progress and other kinds of development. This simplistic interpretation ignores fundamental problems in the political and social structure of the nation, including population pressures, a highly stratified society, inequities in the distribution of wealth, unemployment and underemployment, a high rate of inflation, and widespread illiteracy.

With more than 6 million people in about 42,000 square miles (108,780 sq km), Guatemala is mostly rural, and large areas are still virtually undeveloped. There is an adequate network of roads in the densely populated highlands, but access is difficult elsewhere. The Petén area, a sparsely populated limestone tableland covered with jungle and grass, occupies almost the entire northern third of the national territory. The central highlands include two ranges of mountains that run east and west and a plateau that lies between them, rich with volcanic soils and temperate in climate because of the elevation. The vast majority of the population is concentrated in this area. The Caribbean coast is a hot wet plain, with few, mostly black, occupants. The southern (Pacific) coast is also a hot moist plain where mestizos predominate. Along the northeast border lies Belize (former British Honduras); although it was recently given its independence by Great Britain, it is still claimed as a province by Guatemalans, whose episodic "saber-rattling" has always been met by shows of British force rather than open fighting.

In the jungles of the Petén, chicle, a naturally occurring tree crop, is collected for a world market. On the Pacific coast, rubber, coffee, sugar, cotton, and cattle are raised in commercial quantities. In some highland areas, coffee also grows well, as do sheep, grains, and vegetables for domestic consumption. Few minerals have been exploited, but recently large nickel deposits have been discovered; lumbering has not yet done much damage to the vast forests.

Although the entire country lies within the tropical latitudes, small differences in elevation result in significantly different microclimates within short distances in steeply mountainous terrain. Local specialization in crops, crafts, and other economic activities is efficient because it is combined with a system of cyclical markets. Traveling vendors convene in different communities on different days, collecting and distributing locally produced goods without any need for national-level freighting, wholesaling, or brokerage. This cyclical market system, in which both cash and barter are used, is often viewed as an archaic remnant of pre-Columbian patterns even though it interacts closely with the nation's modern economic system, providing a way to sell manufactured goods and buy important produce and raw materials.

More than half the population still speak aboriginal languages; more than 20 survive and are mutually unintelligible. In addition, in some areas—especially the mountainous northwest—each village has its distinctive style of clothing, pottery, and ceremonial observances.

Many upper-class Guatemalans blame "the Indian problem" for the lack of economic development in their country; a strain of racism pervades the national consciousness. There is much talk of "race" in terms of biological determinism, even though the criteria of "race" are generally social and cultural rather than genetic.

The Indians are not united, but they tend to have strong loyalties to their local communities. Most of them are farmers or herders, either independent peasants or tenant farmers in the employ of hacienda owners. They generally share a strong commitment to folk-Catholicism that combines elements of the Roman Catholic religion with vital vestiges of pre-Columbian beliefs and practices.

The Indian majority have been relatively neglected in terms of schooling. Their many languages make teaching difficult, and rural areas have few schools. In addition, there is a clear policy to keep Indians repressed. The situation is further complicated by the fact that peasant children go to work at an early age, so that parents are often reluctant to let them go, apart from the fact that clothing, supplies, and other costs add up quickly even in the public schools that are nominally free.

Almost the same lack of opportunities characterizes the life of Ladinos, the next largest component of the population. Ladinos in Guatemala resemble the mestizos in most other Latin American countries, they are Spanish speakers whose physical and cultural traits reflect the combination of their Indian and European ancestry. Their access to jobs, education, health services, and other aspects of social welfare are distinctly limited, except in Guatemala City, Quezaltenango, and Escuintla. The Ladinos share with most other Latin American peasants the combined values of *machismo* (assertive masculinity) and *marianismo* (long-suffering deference as the feminine ideal).

The blacks are an enclave population descended from runaway slaves and Indians. Some of them retain the Carib language and other traits from both African and West Indian cultures, but they are so few in numbers and so isolated on the Caribbean coast that they play no role on the national scene. Most of them are subsistence farmers on isolated homesteads or agricultural laborers on banana plantations.

A small stratum of so-called whites dominates Guatemala's administrative, artistic, commercial, and international activities. The heirs of a commanding position in a highly stratified society, they are reluctant to give up their virtual monoploy on wealth and power.

Population pressure is a problem in Guatemala; even though medical facilities are rare, the death rate does not balance the high birthrate. Thus there is pressure on the land that has been intensively cultivated in the highlands for centuries, and both unemployment and underemployment are endemic. One safety valve for population pressure is migration into frontier areas; this is happening in the Petén and is one reason for the continuing friction with Belize.

Homesteaders who have moved into the sparsely populated forests in the north and east are generally subsistence farmers, cultivating small plots by the slash-and-burn system that is widespread in the tropics. Indians in the highlands produce most of the maize and vegetables that feed themselves and the urban population.

About 27 percent of the nation's GNP comes from agriculture, and in 1977, coffee accounted for almost half Guatemala's export earnings. Today, the high price of coffee helps Guatemala's balance-of-payments position. It is hoped that nickel mining will strengthen Guatemala's export earnings in the 1980s.

Currently, coffee and tourism dominate the foreign-exchange economy, with the usual problems that beset those industries: prices tend to be set by outsiders, and profits accrue to outsiders. There is little prospect of the trickle-down benefits that are regarded as an advantage of big business in other countries. On coffee, sugar, banana, or rubber plantations, wealthy corporate or individual landlords often exploit those who are competing for the few available jobs.

Many elements of the Indian cultures persist from pre-Columbian times, when the Maya were already

Maya Quiche Indians display their handicrafts at a Sunday market in the town of Chichicastenango. (Photo: United Nations/Jerry Frank.)

building large cities, crafting fine ceramic and stone sculptures, and making mathematical and astronomical discoveries that Europeans only achieved centuries later. After easily conquering the Aztecs in Mexico, the Spanish conquistadores were not prepared for the stiff opposition that Quiche and Cakchiquel Indians gave them in what is now highland Guatemala. But Spanish arms prevailed, and Antigua became the seat of colonial administration for all of what is now Central America; when that opulent city was devastated by an earthquake in 1773, Guatemala City became the capital, and it remains so.

The wars for independence during the first two decades of the nineteenth century had little immediate impact on any Central American nation, and freedom from Spain in 1821 was more nearly given than won. With experience in administration, the people of Guatemala were in an advantageous position and dominated the United Provinces of Central America. When that federation fell apart in 1838, Guatemala became an independent republic.

The country is nominally a representative democracy, with an executive branch headed by an elected President, an independent legislature, and a judicial branch. The widespread pattern of infighting among political factions that characterizes the rest of Central America has been less marked here. Instead of so-called liberals opposing so-called conservatives in quick succession, a series of fairly stable military dictatorships has prevailed.

Wealth and power are concentrated in the hands of a very few, and the vast majority of the population are engaged in subsistence activities or live as virtual serfs in a quasi-feudal system. Their access to small plots of farmland was granted in exchange for their work on the large holdings that belonged to the haciendas. As coffee increasingly dominated the economy, the communal ownership of land was abolished, and Indians who had been self-sufficient were forced into wage labor or debt peonage.

In the middle of this century, Guatemala undertook a pioneering program of land reform, expropriating a few large holdings and reallocating portions of them to the peasants. Although the principle was subsequently championed by both the United States and the United Nations, at the time it was interpreted as a "Communist threat"; one of the earliest-known large-scale interventions of the U.S. Central Intelligence Agency (CIA) in another country's politics was the CIA organization and support of a counterrevolution in Guatemala in 1954. Since then violence has been chronic and has claimed tens of thousands of lives.

During the past two decades, there have been increasing efforts to break the domination of the oligarchy. A major aim is land reform, but progressive taxation and other means of narrowing the gap between the extremely rich and the extremely poor are also discussed, as is the appropriateness of providing more public services throughout the country. Inflation is a continuing problem.

Various antigovernment groups representing a broad political spectrum have been summarily lumped together as "Castroite Communists" by the successive regimes that consider this gross misrepresentation an easy way to discredit populist opposition. For their part, antigovernment forces have increasingly engaged in both rural guerrilla warfare and urban terrorism in order to harass, discredit, and draw attention to the military oppression under which they live.

There is little hope that Guatemala will regain the splendor that characterized the area in the centuries before the Europeans arrived. Nor is it likely soon to regain the wealth and power that it had during the Spanish colonial period. But Guatemala has adequate resources, both ecological and human, to support a variety of lifestyles that would be congenial to the diverse ethnic populations of the country. Unfortunately, more violence will probably occur before those who enjoy a virtual monopoly will relinquish any significant portion of their wealth and power.

Dwight B. Heath

Haiti
(Republic of Haiti)

Area: 10,714 sq mi (27,749 sq km)
Population: 4.8 million
    Density: 448 per sq mi (174 per sq km)
    Growth rate: 1.7% (1970–1977)
Percent of population under 14 years of age: 40% (1975)
Infant deaths per 1,000 live births: 149 (1975)
Life expectancy at birth: 51 years (1977)
Leading causes of death: not available
Ethnic composition: black; mulatto (5%)
Languages: French (official), Creole
Literacy: 23% (1975)
Religions: syncretic African; Catholic, Protestant
Percent population urban: 10%
Percent population rural: 90%
Gross national product: $1,240 billion
    Per capita GNP: $260
    Per capita GNP growth rate: 2.1% (1970–1977)
Inflation rate: 13.3% (1970–1977)

During nearly two centuries, independent Haiti has a history marked by chronic political instability, massive injustice, and tragic and all-pervasive poverty. But Haitians have learned to survive in poverty with dignity; they enjoy a vibrant national culture and find a world of meaning in their art, religion, dance, and other rituals despite their chronic misgovernment.

Haiti is the poorest country in the Caribbean and Latin America (even the per capita income figure of $120 per year is deceptive because much of the population has no monetary income). Its economic prospects are dismal; its current government, somewhat less repressive than its predecessor, is still a family dictatorship for life; and its military and police are the pillars of power. Somehow Haitians must learn to mobilize their singular and vital human resources to make inroads on the poverty, injustice, and oppression that characterize Haiti's past and present.

Haiti occupies the most-eroded, mountainous, and least-fertile western third of the island of Hispaniola, dominated by the neighboring Dominican Republic in the east. Its 10,714 square miles (27,749 sq km), including several small offshore islands, is about the size of the state of Maryland, and it supports a population close to 5 million. Approximately 80 percent of the population live in the lowland, tropical plains, where a hot and humid climate is relieved by Caribbean breezes. Two-thirds of Haiti consists of steep, denuded mountains and is mostly unsuitable for cultivation.

Natural resources are scarce, and mineral deposits are confined to meager deposits of bauxite, copper, and lignite. All energy except firewood is imported, and human labor prevails in the production of cash crops of coffee, sugar, and sisal, and in basic foodstuffs. The tourism industry relies more on Haitian color and style than on the few unattractive beaches.

Haiti and Haitians are a riot of color: women in swathes of orange, red, and yellow bandannas and scarves, blue skies and green fields (where irrigation exists), the rainbow spectrum of roadside markets, and the extraordinary vivacity of Haitian muralists and primitive painters. Never has poverty been so ugly, open, striking, alive, and overcome as far as possible by sheer human exhilaration.

The Haitian population is almost exclusively descended from the slaves who fought their French masters to a standstill between 1791 and 1804. A handful of mostly Lebanese and Syrian merchants has had a major influence on wholesale trade. The mulattoes, proudly tracing their ancestry to the house slaves and miscegenation of the colonial period, comprise about 5 percent of the population but have a disproportionate influence in the professions. The elites, defined by formal education and fluency in French (still the official but hardly the popular language), number about 5 percent of the total population and are concentrated in the capital of Port-au-Prince and in a few provincial towns. The population remains nearly 90 percent rural, fluent in a lively French-derived Creole language, profoundly faithful to a syncretic blend of African, Catholic, and Protestant beliefs, and able to eke out a subsistence living from a tortured, fragmented, eroded, and overpopulated terrain.

Haiti has never had a reliable national census, and all available information is subject to considerable doubt. Birthrates are estimated at 40 to 1,000 and may actually be higher in some areas. Infant mortality

Youngsters hitch a ride with a farmer taking his produce to market in the town of Petionville. Poor transportation is one of Haiti's pressing problems. (Photo: United Nations/ J. F. Viesti.)

303

runs anywhere between 125 and 200 deaths per 1,000 live births and constitutes the principal check on population increase. Private and voluntary family planning efforts begun in the 1960s received considerable external assistance and some government support in the 1970s. Private and government health services are largely confined to the urban population and will probably not have a fertility-reducing effect for many years. Instead, any improvements in general health in a population where malnutrition is endemic and many tropical diseases like malaria are pervasive may save infant lives and increase a population growth rate now estimated at around 2 percent per year.

Haiti is the only society in the Western hemisphere where population pressures on limited arable land and other scarce resources could lead to large-scale famine. Added to this risk are the annual dangers of the Caribbean hurricane season and periodic droughts.

Since the 1920s, the Haitian response to a frightening demographic situation has usually been emigration. Lured by sugar-plantation jobs, several hundred thousand Haitians migrated to Cuba before the Great Depression. Since 1950, approximately 500,000 Haitians have left the country, emigrating for the most part to the United States, Canada, the Bahamas, and the Dominican Republic. The emigrants have included intellectuals, political exiles, urban skilled and semiskilled workers, and fishermen and peasants seeking jobs, economic opportunities, and personal and political freedoms unavailable at home.

People crowd a street in downtown Port-au-Prince. Population pressure continues to force Haitians off the farms and into the densely populated capital. (Photo: United Nations/ J. F. Viesti.)

The Haitian economy has clearly demarcated subsistence and external-trade sectors. There is very little domestic manufacturing or food processing. Most Haitians rely on their tiny and fragmented plots to feed themselves, trading with their neighbors for eggs, chickens, fish, and other high-protein luxuries. The rugged terrain and lack of transport have resulted in a plethora of West African–style local rural markets dominated by market women who are keen, if illiterate, traders. The lack of storage facilities, the danger of failed harvests, and poor transportation make hunger a constant and starvation a credible fear in most Haitian's lives.

Efforts to improve subsistence production have focused on transport, fertilizers, irrigation, and the organization of cooperatives, with an emphasis on rice, beans, peas, and other vegetables. Results have been sporadic, but not because of peasants' lack of interest. Maladministration in a poorly motivated agricultural-extension service has left most Haitian farmers to rely on their own wits and to distrust government schemes.

Lacking other sources of energy and faced with chilly evenings at heights of 2,000 feet (610 m) or more, rural Haitians depend on brambles, bushes, and other forms of vegetation for firewood. Deforestation has been a vital national problem for more than 40 years, but more and more land continues to be lost. Coercive government schemes to compel replanting and deny firewood to peasants are unpopular and mostly unenforceable. Soil erosion combines with land fragmentation and population pressure to force young Haitians off the soil, either for the appalling slums of Port-au-Prince, the bleak life of migrant workers on Dominican sugar estates, or the hardship and struggle of Montreal, Miami, or New York City.

The export economy still revolves around the staples of coffee, grown by small farmers on hillside plots, and plantation sugar and sisal. The marketing of these cash crops is in the hands of foreign merchants and the black and brown urban business elites. The Haitian gourde and the United States dollar remain the official currencies as they have been since the United States marines occupied Haiti (1915–1934).

Tourism faltered during the harsh regime of François Duvalier. Perhaps more significant, Haiti has few outstanding beaches. It competes with its sun-and-sand–endowed Caribbean neighbors by offering a distinctive culture, flourishing crafts (especially woodwork and sculpture), and an overwhelming history exemplified in the Citadelle and Sans Souci palaces of the nineteenth century Emperor Henri Christophe, symbols of Haitian victory over the French.

The principal growth factor in the Haitian economy in recent years has been the development of assembly or subassembly manufacturing for export. Since the 1960s, when U.S. firms found that wages were rising too quickly in their Puerto Rican outlets, Haiti has become a tax haven and a source of cheap, trainable labor. Nearly 40,000 Haitians are now employed in factories at wages considered low by North American standards but princely in local terms, manufacturing everything from baseballs and baseball gloves to electronics for export. Many newly employed skilled and semiskilled workers are women. Mostly located in Port-au-Prince, the new factories import most of their components, contribute little to the Haitian economy (except wages), and enjoy generous long-term tax incentives. Nonetheless, they improve the life of thousands of urban families.

Development proposals for Haiti have focused on agricultural diversification for export and domestic markets. It has been estimated that along the river valleys and in the remaining uneroded fertile hillsides there is a maximum potential of 3.71 to 5.43 million acres (1.5 to 2.2 million hectares) of arable land. At present, only 172,900 acres (70,000 hectares) of a potential 419,900 (170,000 hectares) are irrigated. Rainfall in the mountains is irregular, and much of Haiti is semiarid; but the humid tropical lowlands have potential, although they are exposed to Caribbean hurricanes and cyclones. One major hydroelectric and irrigation project for the Artibonite River valley has dragged on for years, plagued by corruption, maladministration, land-tenure disputes, and other conflicts. When given a chance, Haitian peasants have been responsive to the use of fertilizers, cash-cropping vegetables for local urban markets, and other innovations. Nevertheless, the elites and the government rely on their control of marketing, transport and occasionally land tenure to extract income and taxes. Few peasants are willing or able to invest in their own scattered pieces of land.

The vision of Haiti as an agricultural breadbasket that could feed itself and export to the substantial Puerto Rican market and even to the Dominican Republic is not a fantasy. However, this would require major structural changes in the relations between the farmer and the government and a considerable external investment. Experience selling rice, vegetables, and a few other crops to tourist hotels proves that commercial farming outside the traditional export crops can be profitable in Haiti. Most such ventures so far have excluded the peasants.

Barring a systemic increase in domestic agricultural production, Haiti will be unable to import both the fuels and the foodstuffs that it needs. The peasants are already living as close as they can to a subsistence level. The urban elites are capable entrepreneurs with a flair for investment in real estate, hotels, and residential construction, but they have little desire to invest their money and skills to increase food output. External aid from the World Bank, the Inter-American Development Bank, and bilateral donors has focused on infrastructure projects like the paving of the north-south highway from Port-au-Prince to Cap Haitien and in efforts to improve the Haitian bureaucracy. But more and more foreign donors will be drawn into rural development projects, seeking a direct impact on rural life.

Haiti imports processed fish, while its coastal fishermen, using canoes, sailboats, and a handful of small motorized craft, venture into Caribbean waters. This translucent deep sea is not a fisherman's haven, and its depths can be plumbed only with the most modern and expensive equipment. Haiti should be able to increase its catch of fish substantially, but it cannot rely on the ocean to feed its growing population.

The population of the capital, a squalid, environmentally filthy eyesore, is increasing at a rate of at least 6 percent a year. No secondary cities or towns are growing nearly so rapidly, a testimony to the concentration of services and wealth in Port-au-Prince. External aid has launched a series of sewage, water, hillside-erosion-control, and other projects, but Port-au-Prince is environmentally out of control. Tropical rains have a devastating effect on its services, and its layers of hills defy easy rationalization. Paved roads have made it easier for the ubiquitous open buses and trucks to circulate between the towns and the villages. While the donkey remains the principal mode of transport between the farm and the village on village and secondary roads, the government paves the highways between the capital and provincial towns, creating the conditions for even more rapid urbanization.

External air- and sea-transport services link Haiti to the rest of the world. The 120-mile (192 km) trip between Santo Domingo (capital of the Dominican Republic) and Port-au-Prince on the same island is a day's trip by road, and there is still very little trade. However, the capitals are linked by daily flights, and even Dominicans come to Haiti as tourists. Kingston, Miami, San Juan, Montreal, and New York City are all part of the Haitian transport orbit and are far more easily reached than many parts of the interior of this small nation. Air and shipping services are almost entirely foreign-owned and -controlled, and free-enterprising Haiti lacks a national carrier.

Culturally, there are several Haitis, with one predominating. The elites often send their children to private French-language schools in Haiti, and to Paris or Quebec for higher education. While lapsing into Creole at home or with friends, the pride of the elite is their mastery of the French language and culture. Haiti retains French as its official language, although it is doubtful that French is spoken by more than 10 percent of the population.

Yet for all Haitians, no matter what their amount or kind of education, the basic Haitian culture is a unique syncretism of their mostly Dahomeyan roots and their slave, colonial, and Haitian experience. In spite of years of official discouragement, the Creole language, with its own grammar, vocabulary, radio programs, and literature, has enriched Haitian culture, and Haitian forms of kinship, marriage, popular religious worship, folk arts and crafts, foods, and rituals are all part of the culture of all social classes.

Haiti is the first authentically black culture anywhere in the world outside Africa. Yet the slaves and their masters were not the first humans on the island of Hispaniola. In 1494, Columbus, on his second voyage, found in Hispaniola a metal-working, cotton-growing and -weaving Carib people with a complex social organization. Within 50 years they were decimated by plagues and forced labor in the mines, and were subsequently replaced by slaves.

A French colony from 1697 to 1791, Saint-Domingue on the western end of the island quickly outdistanced its Spanish rival to the east. Sugar grown on estates by slaves imported from West Africa generated enormous wealth and a plantocracy addicted to Parisian tastes. A small but significant class of freed slaves served as overseers for absentee owners. The spontaneous revolt that began in 1791 produced a united people, burned and destroyed an economy that was never to recover, and created a society in the very name of the French Revolution.

An independent, impoverished, isolated Haiti subsequently floundered throughout the nineteenth century. Revolutionary leaders like Toussaint L'Ouverture, who died in a French prison, were replaced by megalomaniac tyrants like ex-slave Henri Christophe, who established his own kingdom and court.

A combination of bad debts, internal political squabbling, and U.S. imperialism brought about the American occupation (1915 to 1934). The occupiers improved roads and public health, brought some U.S. investment, and were thoroughly disliked by most Haitians. Perhaps the most important effect of the American occupation was the stimulation of a nationalist and cultural revival among the elites. A series of civilian governments dependent on military rule (the U.S.–trained National Guard) followed the American occupation. After World War II, a new generation of socially conscious intellectuals, mostly black, challenged the establishment.

François Duvalier, a rural public health physician with an extraordinary flair for crowd psychology, was quick to take advantage of these new tendencies. He emerged as President in 1958 after a fierce and complicated political struggle and established a brutal family dynasty. The economy languished; the number of political exiles reached unprecedented totals; and Haiti's reputation for injustice grew.

As self-designated "President for Life," Duvalier (known as "Papa Doc") acted to curb internal dissent and external risks. Haiti rejected many forms of external aid, and the doctrine of negritude was used to eulogize a poverty-perpetuating self-reliance. Ostentatious wealth and open family quarrels did not help the Duvalier image. The succession was personally passed from the dying father to his 19-year-old son in April, 1971.

Sharply criticized abroad, Jean-Claude Duvalier (known as "Baby Doc") loosened the repressive apparatus, encouraged external aid and private investment, and permitted a minimum amount of dissent. The economy, especially the export sectors, grew initially, but it was hard hit by the post-1973 energy crisis. Baby Doc has brought many technocrats into the administration, but a still greater number of skilled Haitians remain abroad. His business- and international-oriented administration has restored some of Haiti's tarnished image, without making any major internal changes.

Haiti's political and economic prospects are poor, but a vibrant culture thriving in a chronically sick society seems to be the hallmark of its future. Emigration is important, because it drains off potential dissent and provides needed remittances for those who remain behind. A slowdown in the North American economy would have drastic consequences for the urban Haitian middle and working classes now so closely tied to New York and Miami. The exiles are fragmented, apparently incapable of uniting to overthrow a family dynasty in its second generation. There is more risk of instability because of renewed family feuds and dissension, which may divide the military. Today, Haiti lacks the political institutions to base a government on anything but coercion.

Aaron Segal

Honduras
(Republic of Honduras)

Area: 43,000 sq mi (111,370 sq km)
Population: 3.5 million
  Density: 81 per sq mi (31 per sq km)
  Growth rate: 3.3% (1970–1977)
Percent of population under 14 years of age: 47% (1975)
Infant deaths per 1,000 live births: 34 (1975)
Life expectancy at birth: 53.5 years (1975)
Leading causes of death: not available
Ethnic composition: Ladino 90%; Indians 10%
Languages: Spanish
Literacy: 47%
Religions: Roman Catholic
Percent population urban: Less than 20%
Percent population rural: More than 80%
Gross national product: $1.6 billion (1976)
  Per capita GNP: $480
  Per capita GNP growth rate: 0.0% (1970–1977)
Inflation rate: not available

Because of its long history of political instability, its few natural resources, its poor soils, and its sparse population, Honduras is one of the poorest nations in the Western Hemisphere, despite its size [over 43,000 square miles (111,370 sq km)], its favorable location (with ports on two oceans and a wide range of climates), and its relatively progressive system of land tenure.

The entire national territory lies in the tropical latitudes, but variations in altitude are linked to differences in climate, flora, and fauna. The Caribbean coast, the long northern boundary, is a hot, humid, lowland plain, where dense forest and swamp alternate with vast banana plantations. The shorter coast on the Pacific, between El Salvador and Nicaragua, is also low, hot and humid, but it features plantations of cotton rather than bananas. Two major mountain ranges transect the country from northwest to southeast, and the relatively temperate valleys and plateaus between the mountains remain the areas of greatest population density.

Fully 45 percent of Honduras is still covered with forests and there are less than 2,500 miles (4,000 km) of roads, only a small portion of which are paved. Of the country's three railroads, two are privately owned and are used almost exclusively for the benefit of the U.S. banana companies. The irregular lay of the land has led to a complex network of small valleys, many of which have arable soil and contain small groups of Indians who have only occasional contact with others outside their immediate vicinity.

The few cities have tended to dominate national affairs out of all proportion to their economic or demographic contributions. In Honduras, less than 20 percent of the population live in cities, and urbanization is progressing slowly.

The Honduran census suggests far more uniformity of population than is the case. An unusual category, Ladino, embraces that 90 percent of the people who might elsewhere be called white, mestizo, black, or acculturated Indian.

Within the blanket term Ladino, there are blacks who were brought from the West Indies to build the railroads and stayed to work on banana plantations along the north coast in this century. Many of them are English-speaking Protestants whose lifestyle and interests are closer to those of other Caribbean islanders than they are to Spanish-speaking Catholics.

Black Carib are even older residents of the area, descendants of black slaves and Carib Indians, who were brought by the English from St. Vincent in the Windward Islands almost two centuries ago. Similarly, the Isles de la Bahía (Bay Islands), off the north coast, are peopled largely by another group of Protestant English-speakers, both black and white, brought by the English from British Honduras and the Cayman Islands in the 1830s. Like the similar population on the nearby Swan Islands, they live by a combination of fishing and copra production.

Although they comprise less than 10 percent of the population, various nonacculturated Indian groups in different parts of the country cling to their languages, to some crafts, and to aspects of their traditional religion and social organization. The Lenca of the mountainous southwest is the largest group; like the Jicaque of the northern lowlands, the Lenca combine subsistence farming with seasonal migration to earn wages harvesting coffee or bananas. The Chorti and Pipil are smaller enclaves of small-scale farmers who raise food for themselves and their families on communally held land, but who participate only on the fringes of the money economy. Similarly, the Miskito, Sumo, and Paya on the northeast coast combine hunting, fishing, and slash-and-burn horticulture in ways that seemed quaintly isolated, until it was recognized that their turtle-fishing was directly linked to the world market in tortoiseshell cosmetics.

The overwhelming majority of Honduras are mestizos, whose cultural and physical traits reflect a combination of their Spanish and Indian heritage. The mestizos put special emphasis on ties of kinship and ritual kinship, even including the bonds of common-law marriage, which predominates among the poor. The family is ostensibly authoritarian, although the *machismo* theme of male dominance and its feminine counterpart, long-suffering *marianismo*, may not always be manifest to the degree that males would like outsiders to believe. Although most people profess to be Roman Catholics, their beliefs and practices attest more folklore than doctrine, and the clergy rarely serve remote communities.

Central America and the Caribbean

A sense of the propriety of hierarchy does not conflict with an emphasis on *personalismo*, because the latter refers to one's uniqueness rather then to equality. A degree of fatalism is a realistic adaptation on the part of poor peasants, but the peasants are not always bound by tradition or blind to opportunities. On the contrary, they will adopt and even struggle for changes that they see as improvements. In the 1950s and 1960s, when some of the large-plantation interests illegally began to fence in ejidal lands, the peasants aggressively defended their rights.

Minor improvements in medical and other social-welfare benefits have lowered the death rate, despite widespread malnutrition and other endemic health problems. The high population growth rate of 3.3 percent resulted in sharply increasing population pressure even before there was a large influx of enterprising Salvadorans.

Scarcity of good farmland is a problem even with the ejidual system of common lands. In contrast with other Central American nations, which have rich volcanic soils, Honduras has soil that is generally lacking in nutrients, even in areas that are intensively cultivated. Careless lumbering practices have set into motion a vicious cycle of erosion, silting, flooding, and soil depletion. The opening of new lands in the sparsely populated northern lowlands has served as a temporary safety valve for land hunger, but confrontation between homesteaders and Indians will probably increase as the frontiers of mestizo settlement expand.

Most crops are cultivated on a subsistence basis. Freeholders who cultivate coffee for the world market tend to be caught in a cycle of seasonal indebtedness to the companies that own the processing plants, so that it is difficult for them to change their lifestyles. The few who go to the city discover that there are not many opportunities for those without skills or education. On the banana plantations, managed by the U.S. companies Standard Fruit and United Brands, the workers enjoy fringe benefits that independent peasants do not have, but they know that they will probably never be anything other than manual laborers.

Lead, zinc, and antimony mining employ only a small fraction of the labor force and produce few mineral or nonmineral goods, but mining is important as one of the few sources of foreign exchange. There is a little incipient industry involving simply expendable consumer goods. Logging is a short-term economic venture; although resources are abundant, the methods of exploitation are ecologically disastrous, and there has been no attempt at reforestation. Agriculture dominates the economy; most people are engaged only in subsistence farming, often using ancient techniques and working on a small scale. The other kinds of agricultural enterprise are the market-oriented cotton plantations or cattle ranches and the multinational "factory-in-the-field" banana plantations that are rarely a sound basis for national development.

Among developing nations in Latin America, Honduras is unusual; it has no readily identifiable oligarchy of wealthy landlords who control a mass of landless peasants. This is not to say that Honduras is an idyllic egalitarian participatory democracy. A striking difference between Honduras and most of its neighbors is the system of *ejidos*, whereby each municipality holds some common lands in perpetuity (some 17 percent of the total national area). Periodic allocation of use rights allows small-scale farmers to raise food for their families without entering into the quasi-feudal peonage dependency on a landlord that is more typical.

Private ownership is also commonplace, and much of the coffee that is an important export crop is raised on small private holdings in the mountainous central portion of the country. In contrast, most of the tropical lowland in the north is held by United Brands and Standard Fruit in the form of banana plantations.

Members of a poor rural family stand in the doorway of their home in the village of Santa Rita. The swollen stomachs of the young boys are symptoms of malnutrition. (Photo: United Nations/Jerry Frank.)

In fact, nearly half the country's foreign exchange comes from bananas. As is usual in economies that are dependent on raw produce, the prices they command are much lower than the prices they pay for manufactured and otherwise processed goods. The problem is even more severe in the case of banana monoculture, where fluctuations in price on the world market (remote and unresponsive to local interests) have a disproportionate impact on countries that do not have diversified exports.

The banana companies are often seen as exploitive, practicing a "siphon economy" that drains off profits and returns little in the way of development investment. Nonetheless, the commerce in bananas has fostered the development of most of the railroads and seaports and has supported San Pedro Sula, which has become the major commercial and industrial city in recent years, eclipsing the older cities in the interior. Similarly, although the plantations can hardly be viewed as utopian communities, they provide generally better housing, schooling, medical facilities, and other social and welfare benefits than are available elsewhere in the country.

Although elementary schooling is officially free and compulsory, only about half the population are literate; many children never go to school. In some rural areas, there are not enough schools, and children are needed to help with the family's work. Even when tuition is free, the cost of clothing, books, and supplies is more than many peasant families can invest in their children's future.

Rice, beans, and manioc are staples; black coffee is the usual beverage. Malnutrition, undernutrition, and endemic parasitic infection are reflected in a generally poor health level and relatively short life expectancy. There is almost no health service available except in the two major cities, Tegucigalpa (the capital), and San Pedro Sula. Gastrointestinal disturbances, parasitosis, malnutrition, and undernutrition as well as respiratory diseases are widespread. Few communities have water or sewage systems, and even clinics are rare in rural areas.

A high degree of centralization in Honduras does not necessarily mean continuity and stability in terms of administration. Honduras is nominally a representative democracy, in which an elected President heads the executive branch; there is an independent judicial branch and a unicameral legislature. But few Presidents have ever completed their term of office; elected for 6 years, they have averaged about 15 months. Provincial governors are appointed from the capital rather than elected by local constituencies; civil servants below the highest levels have little autonomy or even opportunity to recommend priorities; and political parties tend to be more concerned with individual leaders than with platforms or social philosophies. In such a situation, it is normal that political leadership tends to emphasize personalistic relations of patronage and clientage rather than broadly conceived policies, general social welfare, or even

large-scale development. Since 1963, Honduras has been ruled by the military, except for a brief 12 months. In a step toward restoring civilian government, in April 1979 Honduras elected a constituent assembly, charged with writing a new constitution and scheduling direct elections for 1981. The constituent assembly voted to retain President Policarpo Paz García, former head of the three-man military junta, as interim head of state.

In prehistoric times, what is now Honduras was the seat of a rich and exceptionally advanced civilization. Major cities and ceremonial centers of the Maya attest to a lavish way of life, including spectacular architecture, fine ceramics, and mathematical and astronomical sophistication that surpassed that of European contemporaries. Unfortunately, that culture had virtually disappeared by the time that Spaniards arrived in the 1520s.

In this area, the conquistadores encountered little opposition from native peoples. An Indian uprising occurred in 1537, but it was squelched a few years later, and the native population rapidly decreased in numbers from a combination of causes: warfare, the introduction of new diseases, and exportation to South America as slaves. Several isolated Indian groups remain, small in numbers but retaining some cultural integrity.

The area was under Spanish colonial jurisdiction until 1821; unlike most other Latin American countries, however, it was not a single administrative unit

Men construct a water tower in rural Honduras. Few rural communities have water supplies. (Photo: United Nations/Jerry Frank.)

under the Crown. When Spain capitulated, Honduras was annexed to the Mexican Empire, and when the Empire fell apart in 1823, Honduras became part of the United Provinces of Central America. That federation was dissolved in 1838; Honduras then became an independent republic.

Foreign intervention was a sporadic factor throughout much of Honduran history. Guatemala is a relatively powerful neighbor that had the machinery and experience of a large-scale administration during both the colonial and the United Provinces periods; frequent Guatemalan interventions throughout the 1800s were usually abandoned. When the North American filibusterer William Walker was driven out of Nicaragua, he invaded Honduras, but he and his mercenaries were eventually defeated there. Honduras and Nicaragua are not in agreement on the demarcation of their borders in the densely forested and sparsely populated Mosquito Coast region.

The boundary with El Salvador on the southwest also was never clearly settled; apart from the boundary dispute, Hondurans resented the immigration (often illegal) of nearly 300,000 Salvadorans in the preceding two decades, and skirmishes erupted into large-scale open warfare in 1969. This bloody war was for a long time dismissed by the world's press as a sort of comic opera fiasco and was dubbed the Soccer War. Coverage about events in the banana republics focused more on the fact that the opponents had met on the field of sport that weekend than on the war's underlying demographic, economic, and other causes. Although fighting did not last long before the Organization of American States was able to arrange an uneasy cease-fire, full diplomatic relations were not restored for a decade, and a peace treaty was concluded only in late 1980.

Honduras is fortunate in having a diverse and industrious population that has not yet encountered the problems of urban sprawl or the isolation of peasants from access to land. On the other hand, its traditional regionalism is an obstacle to meaningful national integration. Although it has no obvious source of great wealth, Honduras has adequate resources and has tried to avoid the excessive concentration of wealth and power in the hands of a few. For these reasons, the country may have more promise for equitable economic development than it has yet demonstrated.

Dwight B. Heath

Jamaica

Area: 4,411 sq mi (11,424 sq km)
Population: 2.1 million
   Density: 476 per sq mi (184 per sq km)
   Growth rate: 1.7% (1970–1977)
Percent of population under 14 years of age: 46% (1975)
Infant deaths per 1,000 live births: 26 (1975)
Life expectancy at birth: 69.5 years (1975)
Leading causes of death: cardiovascular diseases, accidents
Ethnic composition: black 80%; colored 15%; Asian 4%; white 1%
Languages: English (official), Creole
Literacy: 65%
Religions: Roman Catholic 30% (est.), Anglican; other Protestant; Jewish; Afro-Christian sects
Percent population urban: 38%
Percent population rural: 62%
Gross national product: $2.4 billion
Gross national product growth rate: 0.4% (1975)
   Per capita GNP: $1,110
   Per capita GNP growth rate: −2.0% (1970–1977)
Inflation rate: 20–25% (1974–1977)

The small Caribbean island-state of Jamaica relies on the hard work and dedication of its people, on the fertility of its soils, on its great natural beauty (which has attracted visitors for many years), and on its deposits of bauxite ore that are needed by industrial nations. Jamaica also faces major problems. It depends heavily on other nations—mostly on the industrial Western nations—for fossil-fuel supplies, capital investment, markets for its products, and places of emigration for its crowded population. Chronic problems of unemployment (about 25 percent) and the need for foreign-exchange earnings hamper development. The island's three largest sources of income have severe limitations. Bauxite does not employ enough people and is a nonrenewable resource. The sugar industry is increasingly beset by foreign competition and severe fluctuation in world prices. Tourism depends on changes in world economic and political conditions that are largely beyond Jamaica's control.

Jamaica has long beaches, broad coastal plains, deep river valleys, a central-western plateau, and steep eastern mountains rising to over 7,400 feet (2,256 m) at Blue Mountain Peak. In the northeast, rainfall can reach 180 inches (457 cm) a year, falling mostly between October and January. Rainfall lessens to the south and west, often not exceeding 25 to 30 inches (64 to 76 cm) annually on the dry, south-central coast. Extreme concentration of heavy rains in short periods contributes to erosion in hilly areas, flooding in ill-drained coastal plains, and rapid runoff of topsoils and silt at the mouths of the larger rivers.

English is the official language of Jamaica, and everyone can at least understand standard English. In addition, almost all lower- and middle-class Jamaicans speak Creole, which developed from elements of West African languages brought by slaves and elements of seventeeth-century lower-class English dialects. Today, the former disdain of the upper classes for Creole is being replaced by its increased use in the arts in Jamaica.

Although some 65 percent of the Jamaicans can read and write, illiteracy is still an obstacle to development. Several literacy programs have been undertaken during the past few decades, but these are usually hampered by lack of trained personnel, difficulty in finding and recruiting illiterates, and lack of incentive. JAMAL, the current literacy program, is relatively well staffed and seems to be meeting with some success.

Health services in Jamaica are hampered by shortages of equipment and trained personnel. The University of the West Indies includes a nursing school and a general hospital that serves people from many parts of the island. Most physicians are trained abroad, especially in England, Canada, and the United States. Doctors are in short supply, as are qualified dentists, especially in rural areas and towns. High cost, lack of transportation, ignorance and other problems—including the concentration of medical personnel in Kingston—hinder adequate health care.

Major health problems include malnutrition and related conditions, diabetes, hypertension and cardiovascular problems, and complications related to pregnancy.

Religion has played an important part in Jamaica's development. The Anglican Church was the church of the early English planters. Methodist and Baptist missionaries played prominent roles in assisting the development of free villages of former or runaway slaves in the hills of the interior during the eighteenth and nineteenth centuries.

The Roman Catholic Church (which currently claims the adherence of nearly one-third of the churchgoing population) was established in Jamaica by the Spaniards and was reintroduced about 1790 by the whites who fled to Jamaica after the Haitian revolution. Various Pentecostal groups claim many adherents, while older, African-based syncretic religious traditions, such as Kumina, Myal, and Convince, seem to be waning in numbers and influence.

In contrast, the Rastafarian brethren, who trace their origins to the teachings of Marcus Garvey, the coronation of Haile Selassie, and other roots, form a political-cultural-religious force of growing numbers and powerful influence.

Religious organizations run most of the older established educational facilities on the island, including both primary and secondary schools. Jamaica followed the British system of education, but in recent years efforts have been made to introduce locally relevant materials into the general curriculum. Education is plagued by lack of trained teachers (there are teacher-training facilities on the island), by lack of money and supplies, and by crowded conditions. Regular school attendance is hampered by poor transportation, especially during the rainy season, and by the fact that children often work in the fields.

In recent years, the government has tried to widen opportunities for attendance among poorer Jamaicans and to reduce the formerly closed, private structure of basic and secondary education; yet facilities for higher education remain inadequate (a campus of the University of the West Indies, located near Kingston, is the only university or institution of higher education on the island).

The peasants, small farmers, and rural and urban workers of modern Jamaica are descended from slaves. In general, class and occupation cleavages tend to follow racial lines. The upper-class elite remains largely white or light-skinned, and urban-based or expatriate. The middle classes, including a preponderance of "colored" Jamaicans, tend to remain in Kingston or in the towns, while the lower classes are largely black and form the bulk of the rural population and the poor sections of urban areas. Over 80 percent of the Jamaican population is racially classified as "black," while another 10 to 12 percent is considered "colored." Despite the national motto, "out of many, one people," race remains a factor in Jamaican life, in treatment, in access to resources, and in the forms of internalized oppression.

The peasant and small-farming population in the rural areas has declined, and there has been a massive movement toward Kingston, especially during the past 30 years. Traditional peasant-landholding patterns that postpone or deprive youth of landholding, the hard work, low return, and drudgery of rural farm life, the lack of supportive services, good transportation, and social amenities, and the rising expectations of the young all contribute to the urban movement.

Men cut sugarcane by hand. Sugar has played a major role in shaping Jamaica's economic and social life. (Photo: United Nations/R. King.)

In addition, land speculation and development schemes put increased land pressure on rural people near towns and Kingston. The city—the only one in the island—has also grown as a result of its importance as the seat of national government and commerce. A commercial, nonindustrial city, Kingston today contains over 700,000 people—about one-third of the nation's total population. Squatter settlements, crowding, crime, and pollution plague the urban area. Its population reflects every sector of Jamaica, from fishermen to university professors, from old-time elite families to newly arrived rural peasants.

Kingston is also a center for those seeking to emigrate. Emigration has been massive during the 17 years of independence from Britain and has been a mixed blessing for Jamaica's development. Poorer Jamaicans and workers emigrate to the United States, England, or Canada for steady, well-paying employment, either temporary (cutting cane in Florida or picking apples in New York) or permanent. Professionals often emigrate because there are few professional opportunities. The Jamaican upper classes, in particular the business elite, have emigrated because they feared the economic and political positions of the Manley administration and wanted to protect private assets and investments.

Emigration of poor Jamaicans has acted as a safety valve for the excess labor and population of Jamaica over the past two decades. The exodus of professionals poses problems, however, for social and other serv-

A dragline excavator loads bauxite ore into tractor scrapers. Bauxite is Jamaica's largest foreign exchange earner. (Photo: United Nations/ YN/MH.)

ices in Jamaica. And the emigration of the business elite over the past few years has meant the departure of over $200 million in private assets.

For the past two decades, bauxite has been the most important foreign-exchange earner for Jamaica, outstripping by far the value of the second earner, agriculture. Large-scale mining for bauxite, the raw material from which aluminum is made, began in the 1950s. During the first decade of independence (1962–1972), the Jamaica Labor Party government invited large-scale investment by U.S. aluminum companies and kept down taxes and levies, while making a few stipulations about land restoration after mining operations were finished. By 1972, the major U.S. and Canadian aluminum companies owned or controlled nearly one-third of the total land area of the island, and the United States derived well over half of its total bauxite imports from Jamaica. During the late 1960s and throughout much of the 1970s, Jamaica remained the largest or second-largest exporter of bauxite in the world. In 1972, bauxite reserves still in the ground in Jamaica were estimated to be enough to last about another 25 to 30 years at the current rates of extraction. A portion of the mined bauxite is reduced to alumina in the island, but most of it is shipped directly to the United States to be processed. This is due in part to the lack of energy sources in Jamaica, and in part to politico-economic considerations in the United States, where processing creates additional jobs.

In 1974, the government of Prime Minister Michael Manley (People's National Party) increased the tax rate on the bauxite companies in Jamaica. Within 2 years, revenue from this source had increased nearly fivefold. The government then began to use the additional income to finance a few capital-improvement projects and especially to fund social- and economic-development programs, including literacy training, land reform, and employment on public works projects for chronically unemployed persons.

In addition, Manley's government began to repurchase some of the lands held by the companies, leasing the lands back to the companies for continued operations or using them for land-reform programs and distribution to small farmers or state farms. The government also entered into negotiations with the aluminum companies to obtain a 51 percent interest in the Jamaican operations of the companies. Jamaica also took the lead, in 1975, in forming the International Bauxite Association (IBA) with the major producer nations thereby increasing bargaining power vis-à-vis the aluminum companies and the industrial consuming nations and protecting the interests of the producing nations.

Sugar, Jamaica's second-largest income earner, has played a major role in shaping the economic and social structures of the nation ever since slaves worked the plantations in the late seventeeth century. Jamaica was once one of the world's major sugar producers, and much of the wealth extracted from the slave-worked sugar plantations of the eighteenth century by the English and Jamaican planter families helped in the capital formation that financed the industrial revolution in England. Today, while sugar exporting remains an important source of income and employment for Jamaica, the island has long since ceased to be a major world producer of the commodity.

Two problems in particular plague the sugar industry in Jamaica: the monocrop syndrome and the legacy of the traditional plantation structure. Sugar is an increasingly unprofitable export; yet, shifting away from sugar production is (or seems to be) risky. Prices fluctuate over a wide range, making planning more difficult. Severe world competition from major producers, including other Commonwealth nations and the beet-sugar market of the European Economic Community, has added to the burden of production costs in Jamaica (among the highest in the world). The island can no longer successfully compete in the international sugar markets.

Since 1972, the Jamaican government has been purchasing sugar plantations as they have become available. Most of the plantations have been owned either by Jamaican families or by foreign corporations, such as United Brands and Tate and Lyle. Currently, there are fewer than a dozen major sugar plantations in operation in Jamaica (at one time there were several hundred), but they are very large. The government has also supported the leasing of plantations to sugar workers who own and operate sugar-producing cooperatives. The first and largest of these was the Sugar Workers Cooperative Council, which began cooperatives on three plantations in 1974–1975, and it has maintained a relatively successful worker-owned and -managed business.

In the tourist industry, the Jamaican government has also promoted the idea of worker-run cooperative ventures. Since independence in 1962, tourism has become the third major income earner in the nation, but for years much of the development of tourist centers rested with foreign investors or with local private Jamaican entrepreneurs. Recently, the government has begun to purchase privately owned beach and hotel complexes and has entered into ventures to build several others. Jamaica has also offered assistance to several other nations in developing their tourist industries in return for other kinds of technical assistance for Jamaica. Still, tourism in Jamaica remains dependent upon external conditions in the tourist nations, primarily the United States, Canada, and England. Economic recessions in these countries have a dampening effect on the volume of tourism in Jamaica, as do alarming press stories of incidents of crime, violence, or political events in Jamaica. During the period of violence and the state of emergency in Jamaica in 1976, tourist-hotel bookings fell significantly, if temporarily, on the island.

Jamaica's historical development has given rise to race and class distinctions and varied lifestyles. The small, family farms of the late seventeenth century were consolidated by successful sugar- and coffee-planter families into the large slave-worked estates of the eighteenth century. The nineteenth century saw the end of slavery, the institution of wage labor on the plantations, the movement of former slaves into the mountainous interior to form villages and engage in peasant subsistence farming, and the rise of Kingston and the larger towns as commercial centers.

The twentieth century has seen the flourishing and decline of the peasants, who almost until World War I made the island nearly self-sufficient in food production. Recent years have seen a few new industrial investments, especially in bauxite, and large-scale emigration by Jamaicans in search of work elsewhere. Major political and unionization movements have taken place as well.

The planter families and the elite of the traditional plantations either left Jamaica or have become the modern commercial and business elite, moving into ventures like construction or media. The managers and attorneys who ran the old estates produced the modern middle class of businessmen, civil servants, and professionals.

The prospects for Jamaica's future development are mixed. The expatriation of private assets, the rise in oil prices, the slowdown of the aluminum companies' operations, and other events caused a crisis in the economy (in balance of payments and foreign exchange) in early 1977. Since then Jamaica has been deeply influenced by the demands placed on it by the International Monetary Fund (IMF) as conditions for loans in recent years. These conditions have meant the curtailment of inflationary social services, a freeze on wage hikes, the removal of subsidies on basic food items (allowing prices to rise over 100 percent), and other measures that have caused hardship for the poor and middle class; the conditions have had questionable impact in reversing Jamaica's weakened economic position.

A divisive political debate followed the IMF loan agreements. The Manley administration continued to pursue a strategy of pressure for a new economic order—diversifying and expanding trade with new, non-Western partners, increasing self-reliance in food production (for example, state farms, assistance to small farmers), venturing into regional economic integration, and exploring solar and other sources of energy (except nuclear energy).

In 1980 after a bitterly contested election punctuated by violent incidents, Manley was defeated by a considerable margin by the Jamaica Labor Party under the leadership of Edward P. G. Seaga. Jamaica's future will depend on the success of the Seaga government in luring back to the island expatriated talent and money, in dealing with the serious balance of payments problem and with inadequate domestic food supplies and job opportunities.

James Phillips

Mexico
(United Mexican States)

Area: 764,000 sq mi (1,978,750 sq km)
Population: 65.5 million
   Density: 86 per sq mi (33 per sq km)
   Growth rate: 3.3% (1970–1977)
Percent of population under 14 years of age: 46% (1975)
Infant deaths per 1,000 live births: 52 (1975)
Life expectancy at birth: 63 years
Leading causes of death: heart diseases
Ethnic composition: mestizo, Indian
Languages: Spanish
Literacy: 70%
Religion: Roman Catholic (95%)
Percent population urban: 55% (1979)
Percent population rural: 45% (1979)
Gross national product: $84.1 billion
   Per capita GNP: $1,290
   Per capita GNP growth rate: 1.2% (1970–1977)
Inflation rate: 26% (1979)

The republic of Mexico has been modernizing since the 1930s. An institutionalized social Revolution with a capital "R" indicates ongoing government direction. The constitution of 1917 gave the rights to subsoil mineral riches to the nation, mandated land reform, and guaranteed union rights to urban workers. Mexico's assets include 60 billion barrels of oil reserves and expanding industry and tourism, which fueled a gross national product increase of 5 percent

during 1978 and a per capita income of $985. Its liabilities include a sluggish agricultural sector which grew only 1.6 percent a year from 1970 to 1978, although 40 percent of the work force are engaged in agriculture, and a population increasing at a faster rate than the job market.

Mexico's territory resembles a funnel, with the wide end adjacent to the United States along a 1,900-mile (3,058-km) border from Tijuana to Matamoros. The long western Baja California peninsula encloses the Gulf of California. In the far south at the narrow end of the funnel, which is called the Isthmus of Tehuantepec, tropical forest lands cover the Chiapas highlands, which border Guatemala. A dry desert in the southeast corner turns into the flat Yucatán peninsula.

Mexico's area of 764,000 square miles (1,978,750 sq km) is one-fourth the size of the continental United States. More than half of mountainous Mexico rises over 3,200 feet (975 m) above sea level, with the terrain ranging from desert to swamp. Dry northern states flourish with irrigated farming made possible by hydroelectric projects, but flood control still cannot subdue Gulf Coast inundations in the southeastern states.

The central plateau lies between the eastern and western Sierra Madre mountain ranges. In Veracruz state, above the Gulf of Mexico's coastal plain, Orizaba, the highest mountain in Mexico, rises to 18,700 feet (5,700 m). Forming the eastern rim of the Valley of Mexico that surrounds Mexico City are the spectacular mountains Iztaccíhuatl at 17,887 feet (5,452 m) and Popocatépetl at 17,780 feet (5,419 m). In the Pacific and Gulf of Mexico coastal lowlands, annual rainfall averages 80 inches (203 cm), with summer temperatures above 85°F (29°C). In the temperate highland zones, up to 5,000 feet (1,524 m) in altitude, year-round temperatures stabilize at 60 to 75°F (15 to 24°C). In the southeast lowlands, the one Mexican region with consistently dependable rain, annual rainfall totals 120 inches (305 cm).

About 7 percent of Mexican territory can be cultivated, and because of hydroelectric dam projects and irrigated farming methods, another 7 percent of the land is under cultivation.

Corn, beans, wheat, sugarcane, and alfalfa grow in several regions. Rice grows in the tropical regions and wheat in the northern climes. Potatoes are a highlands crop, along with coffee, watermelons, and tomatoes. In the states of Sonora and Tamaulipas, cotton is the major crop. Livestock includes large cattle herds, goats, sheep, and burros. The tropics furnish henequen, fruits, lumber, and rubber. Shrimp fishing flourishes along the Pacific Coast, which also has the

A young girl washes her clothes with water supplied by government trucks in a squatter development on the outskirts of Mexico City. (Photo: United Nations/Jerry Frank.)

resort cities of Acapulco, Guaymas, Mazatlán, Puerto Vallarta, and Zihuatanejo. The government-built resort of Cancún lies on the Yucatán peninsula coast. The most important rivers—the Lerma, Balsas, and Pánuco—have headwaters in the high basins of the central highlands.

Copper, sulphur, zinc, silver, and graphite are mined. Oil fields are concentrated in the Gulf Coast states of Veracruz, Campeche, and Tabasco, with 60 billion barrels of proven oil reserves administered by the government's oil agency, Pemex. A natural gas pipeline runs from the state of Chiapas along the Gulf Coast for 774 miles (1,246 km) to just south of the tip of Texas. Funded by Nacional Financiera, the government development bank, the pipeline can deliver 1.2 trillion cubic feet (33.9 billion cu m) of natural gas a year to Mexican industries. Pemex, with 1978 oil sales of $5.5 billion, is Latin America's largest corporation. In 1978, Mexico exported $1.57 billion worth of crude oil. In 1980, it planned to export 1.1 million barrels of oil a day.

The vast majority of Mexicans are mestizos, Spanish-Indian hybrids. But 4 million Indians, illiterate and non-Spanish-speaking or only marginally bilingual, cluster in hundreds of villages. The Maya people concentrate in the Yucatán peninsula; in the southern state of Oaxaca, the Zapotec and Mixtec; in the northern state of Sonora, Yaqui and Seri; in the northern state of Chihuahua, the Tarahumara; and in central Mexico, the Huichol.

Of the 1979 population of 69 million, 45 percent are rural or small-town residents. Of the urban majority, 20 percent crowd the metropolitan areas of Mexico City, Guadalajara, and Monterrey, with 12 million living within 50 miles (80 km) of downtown Mexico City.

From 1917 through 1976, through the revolution's ongoing land reform, some 188 million acres (76 million hectares) of land were given to landless peasants and, as communal farms, or ejidos, to villages. Yet 7 percent of private landowners, with the largest holdings, receive 35 percent of Mexico's total agricultural income. Only 1.3 percent of all landowners control 20 percent of all land. Economically, 5 percent of all Mexicans belong to the upper class, 30 percent to the middle class, and 65 percent to the working class.

Some 26 percent of the government's 1978 budget of $40 billion went for health and education, yet rural Mexicans had only token access to hospitals and schools, and three out of four were served by neither.

Approximately seven out of ten Mexicans are literate, but there are twice as many rural illiterates as urban illiterates. Both rural and urban Mexicans stress extended-family relations and the godfather-godmother system of friendships, with godparents serving at the christening of children of close friends.

Some 95 percent of all Mexicans are Roman Catholic, but in small towns and villages, pre-Hispanic customs and beliefs are intertwined with Christian practices. Every village or small town celebrates its annual fiesta on its patron saint's day. Holy Week, from Palm Sunday to Easter, is the time for vacations. Pilgrims walk to the Shrine of Guadalupe in Mexico City or to shrines throughout the republic.

Rural Mexicans use barter to trade homegrown livestock or crops for tools, textiles, and transistor radios. Rural families have on the average less than one-fourth the income of urban families. Rural Mexicans tend to wear sandals or go barefooted; whereas, a majority of urban Mexicans wear shoes.

In both rural and urban families, the father remains the authority figure, and the social liberation of women is cosmetic rather than substantive. The role of homemaker is exalted. More than the papal encyclical against birth control, Mexican social psychology works against family planning. *Machismo*, the cult of male virility, prompts men to prove themselves by fathering as many children as possible, not only with their wives but with any consenting female.

The government began to open Family Planning Centers in 1973. Today comic books, television talk shows, and slogans for "Responsible Parenthood" in newspapers and magazines and on billboards challenge *machismo*, as do soap operas on radio sponsored by the government. Yet only 1 woman in 4 of childbearing age uses the free services of the thousands of Family Planning Centers across the nation, and few men ever contact the centers.

Fatal diseases that once kept the population growth rate stable have been eradicated. With a declining death rate and a high birthrate, life expectancy has risen from 46 years in 1940 to 63 years in 1978. More than half the population is 15 years or younger, giving Mexico a dangerous fertility potential that pressures its resources and job market. The population increases annually by 3.6 percent.

Massive underemployment and unemployment

A mother and her child stand outside their poor dwelling in a village in the state of Hidalgo. New housing is being built by the villagers under a government sponsored self-help program. (Photo: United Nations/Jerry Frank.)

plague this developing nation; 1 out of every 4 Mexicans is jobless, and the annual inflation rate of the late 1970s ranged from 16 to 26 percent. The unemployment rate remains twice as high in the countryside as in urban areas, encouraging the peasant farmers, or campesinos, to migrate to the cities and northward into the United States. Only 2 percent of rural workers belong to labor unions, contrasted with 80 percent of industrial workers.

Campesinos are represented by the National Campesino Federation, which lobbies on behalf of rural workers with the Ministry of Agrarian Reform and with the Ministry of Agriculture and Hydraulic Resources.

Credits and loans from the government's agricultural and ejido banks have helped modernize farming by supplying fertilizers, chemicals, and machinery to increase production. The government's Basic Commodities Corporation (CONASUPO) subsidizes farmers by purchasing and storing the following basic crops: corn, beans, rice, coffee, and sugar. CONASUPO retail stores sell food at cost throughout the republic, but they account for only 4 percent of the total food sales. Middle-class Mexicans shop at supermarkets, but working-class Mexicans shop at smaller grocery stores where the cost per unit may be higher, because their lack of cash limits them to small purchases. Manufactured clothing is sold mostly to urban residents.

Urban workers are employed in textile factories, the building construction industry, and in the manufacture of appliances, clothing, beverages, typewriters, bicycles, shoes, cement, petrochemicals, automobiles and trucks, steel and iron, and many other goods and services in a vastly diversified economy.

The government operates the railroads, one of Mexico's two major airlines, Aeromexico, the retail automotive service stations of Pemex, and DINA, one of the truck and automobile manufacturers. In partnership with private industry, the government expanded the steel and iron industry in Monterrey and in the states of Veracruz, Coahuila, and Michoacán. Since 1977 its goal has been to double production every 7 years.

With the government's development of industry, the number of skilled and semiskilled jobs has expanded, but not rapidly enough to absorb 800,000 young Mexicans trying to enter the job market annually.

Urban Mexicans want mass market consumer goods, and, since 1946, a credit card culture has helped the growth of United States–style merchandising through department stores and discount stores. But less than 20 percent of urban Mexicans are able to participate. Some 29 percent of all Mexican families receive only 6 percent of the total national income, whereas the top 2 percent of the families receive as much as 16 percent.

In rural Chiapas, boys enjoy their schoolbooks. Rural Mexicans have only token access to schools. (Photo: United Nations/ D. Mangurlan.)

With regard to diet, urban residents are twice as likely as rural Mexicans to eat wheat bread, vegetables, and meat. In slums and poor city neighborhoods, however, corn, beans, and rice are the staples for 8 out of 10 Mexicans, like their rural counterparts. Poor city dwellers also eat the flat corn pancake, or tortilla, which is the staff of life in rural Mexico. The National Nutrition Institute reported in 1978 that 18 percent of the population consume 88 percent of the available food; 8 out of 10 Mexicans are classified as undernourished.

Urban Mexicans utilize most hospital facilities in the republic and have access to 87 percent of the social security clinics.

Twice as many Mexican children need schooling as there are classroom vacancies, and most children do not complete the sixth grade. A vast majority of those attending secondary schools are urban children, and middle-class children predominate. Because they must contribute to family earnings, many children leave school after a few years. The dropout rate reaches 70 percent at the sixth-grade level and is even higher at the secondary level. The federal government funds national universities and participates with state governments in funding state universities, which accommodate a fraction of 1 percent of the population of people ages 18 to 30.

Ignoring housing and job shortages, migrants from the countryside continue to pour into the cities, giving Mexico an urban population growth rate of 6 percent a year. Despite government efforts to decentralize industry, half the population crowd into only 14 percent of the national territory, the central Valley of Mexico.

Hernán Cortés and his Spanish conquistadores subdued the Aztec Empire in 1520. For the next three centuries, Spanish viceroys solidified centralized authoritarian government. Then, from 1810 to 1821, mestizos, led by the defrocked priests Miguel Hidalgo and José Morelos, fought for Mexican independence from Spain. Crown and cross were entwined and the Church supported the king of Spain. Thus after independence Mexico had a political legacy of church-state conflicts that did not end until the 1930s.

Most of Mexico's nineteenth-century leaders were as arbitrary as the Spanish viceroys they replaced. An exception was Benito Juárez, an Indian who rose from self-taught attorney to President of the republic in 1857, and tried to institute land reforms and representative government.

General Porfirio Díaz came to power in 1876 and ruled as a repressive dictator until 1911. He gave lands that were stolen from villages and political opponents to a small elite, using his army and police to maintain order through torture and killings. His granting of mining concessions to foreign investors engendered a strong antiforeign sentiment that erupted with the revolution in November 1910.

In 1920, after a decade of civil war, the social reforms of the constitution of 1917 were begun by President Alvaro Obregón. In 1929, President Elías Calles established the dominant political party, the Institutional Revolutionary Party (PRI). For half a century the PRI has monopolized the presidency, the governorships, all Senate seats but one, and most of the seats in the lower chamber of the federal Congress. The conservative National Action Party (PAN), the Popular Socialist Party (PPS), and the Authentic Revolutionary Party (PARM), were joined on the 1979 ballot by the Communist Party of Mexico (PCM), legalized in 1978.

Since the revolution strong Presidents have governed Mexico, reducing the legislative and judicial branches to mere collaborators. The republic is federal in form, but states' rights are meager. The President and the President's Cabinet have control over the governors of the states and the mayors of the municipal governments, even though the officials at each level are popularly elected. The federal government appropriates 80 percent of all public revenues and collects a similar percentage of the taxes.

During 1934–1940, President Lázaro Cárdenas gave full meaning to the revolution by organizing unions into the Mexican Federation of Labor (CTM) and expropriating the oil industry in 1938. He also organized the National Campesino Federation and distributed more land to peasants than any other President before or since, land totaling some 90 million acres (36.4 million hectares).

The revolution was launched in the name of the campesino and land reform. But in recent decades,

Children relax in the compound of a middle-income housing project in a suburb of Mexico City. (Photo: United Nations/Jerry Frank.)

beginning with the presidency of Miguel Alemán during 1946–1952, governmental priorities have been focused on the development of industries and the diversification of the economy. Once dependent on silver and copper mining, Mexico has developed diversified manufacturing and, more recently, oil production. In Mexico's mixed public-private economy, the government owns the telephone, telegraph, and electric power companies, and sugar refineries, the motion picture theaters and studios, tobacco production, two of the five television networks, and the largest insurance company.

Government investments and loans have expanded electronics, petrochemicals, steel products, and vehicles. The government manufactures locomotives and freight cars and Mexico City's subway cars. Mexican law limits foreign investors to minority ownership of corporations; only Mexican public or private owners can hold majority control. The government encourages the development of technology in Mexico.

To decentralize industry, now concentrated in the three largest metropolitan centers, the government has created 11 development zones where tax rebates are linked to levels of increased employment. Thus, shoe factories in Guanajuato state, fiber and plastics plants in Chihuahua, and automobile parts factories in Querétaro are expanding.

Mexican President José López Portillo's National Development Plan covering 1979 to 1990, contemplates economic growth rates of 8 percent a year, with industry expanding 12 percent a year. The plan set as a goal the use of oil earnings to finance industrial expansion and decentralization, and the creation of at least 600,000 new jobs a year. The government wants to turn nonrenewable oil resources into renewable industrial wealth through industries with products that can continue to be manufactured.

In each development zone, new industries receive a first-year 25 percent tax credit and an additional 20 percent tax rebate for up to 10 years for maintaining high levels of employment. In the port cities of Tampico and Coatzacoalcos on the Gulf Coast and Las Truchas and Salina Cruz on the Pacific, new industries receive for 10 years a 30 percent discount on the price of electricity, natural gas, and fuel oil.

The government's 11-year development plan looks for facilities and incentives to create enough new jobs to reduce unemployment drastically and to establish more industries based on renewable resources. In order to keep oil export revenues from causing inflation, they will be limited to $5 billion a year through 1982. If the annual population increment can be reduced, Mexico will have a viable development strategy.

Marvin Alisky

Nicaragua
(Republic of Nicaragua)

Area: 57,100 sq mi (147,888 sq km)
Population: 2.5 million
  Density: 44 per sq mi (17 per sq km)
  Growth rate: 3.3% (1970–1977)
Percent of population under 14 years of age: 48% (1975)
Infant deaths per 1,000 live births: 36 (1975)
Life expectancy at birth: 52.9 years (1975), 54 years (1977)
Leading causes of death: not available
Ethnic composition: mestizo 70%; white 17% black 9% Indian 4%
Languages: Spanish, English
Literacy: 52%
Religions: Roman Catholic 95%
Percent population urban: 50% (1975)
Percent population rural: 50% (1975)
Gross national product: 2.1 billion
  Per capita GNP: $840
  Per capita GNP growth rate: 2.5% (1970–1977)
Inflation rate: 11% (1970–1977 est.)

Nicaragua, largest of the Central American countries, seemed until recently to be the prototypical example of economic and political oligarchy in the guise of democracy. In mid-1979, however, the single family that had dominated the nation for half a century was ousted. The loose coalition of populists who took over after a devastating civil war face exciting opportunities—and enormous obstacles—as they attempt to reunite and strengthen their country.

With only about 2.5 million people in its roughly 50,000 square miles (129,000 sq km), Nicaragua has a low average population density. But regional imbalance is a striking feature of this diverse country, in ecological as well as demographic terms. The eastern two-thirds of the country is virtually unsettled, hot, humid, and heavily forested. In sharp contrast, a narrow strip of alternating mountains and valleys in the west is densely populated, temperate, and intensively cultivated. Most of the towns, roads, industries, and commercial enterprises are concentrated on the temperate plateau formed between low parallel chains of mountains, whereas the tropical plains to the east remain a frontier region, undeveloped except for vast banana plantations along the Caribbean coast. The San Juan River is navigable by big boats all the way from the Caribbean to Lake Nicaragua, which is only about 30 miles (49 km) from the Pacific Ocean. (Although the United States still holds the option to build a sea-level canal there, construction of the Panama Canal made it seem moot for many years.)

The volcanic soil of the well-watered highlands supports coffee and cereal crops and cattle, most of which were grown on large haciendas for export until the revolution. Similarly, the sugar and bananas grown in the lowlands were often sold abroad, making Nicaragua a rich agricultural country that did not produce enough basic foodstuffs for its population. For decades, large farms had been established at the expense of small farms, with homesteaders and small-scale peasant farmers displaced in large numbers—alienated from the means of production in the most direct and literal sense. As production became increasingly concentrated in the hands of a few landlords, they used their enormous profits to invest in other sectors of the economy, leading to virtual domination of the nation's trade by a favored few. At the same time, the vast majority of the population suffered not only unemployment but also abject poverty, and were subject to other kinds of exploitation.

The other kinds of exploitation resulted from the fact that the Somoza family ran the country as a virtual fiefdom. Anastasio Somoza, third in a familial succession that monopolized the presidency, used the National Guard as his personal army and usurped most of the profitable ventures in the country. For this reason, statistics on economic growth are misleading if the degree to which wealth was concentrated is not taken into account.

Unlike many other developing countries, Nicaragua has a fairly uniform population in terms of language and culture. Most of the people are mestizos who speak Spanish and whose physical and cultural traits reflect both their Spanish and their Indian ancestry. Although nearly one-fourth of the labor force are engaged in manufacturing, they are often people whose view of the world does not differ substantially from that of peasants in other Latin American areas. Folk Catholicism is practiced by women in a way that bespeaks faith and resignation, with little concern for doctrine; men have little to do with religion. A double standard is expressed in the contrasting ideals of *machismo* (assertive and even aggressive masculinity) and *marianismo* (feminine subservience).

Personalismo is another important factor in social relations; that is, who you know tends to be more important than what you know. This is not so difficult as an outsider might expect, because few Nicaraguans have much schooling, or few travel far from the community in which they and their parents grew up. Although education is supposedly free and compulsory at the elementary level, not many poor families can afford to let their children spend time in school, or provide the clothing, supplies, and other costs that are associated with schooling.

Poor health is linked with poverty in Nicaragua. Malnutrition and undernutrition, respiratory diseases, and parasitic infestation are endemic. Despite a high infant mortality rate, however, the even higher birthrate results in a rapidly expanding population; this has aggravated pressure on the land and has set in motion a vicious cycle of underemployment and unemployment that offers little hope to unskilled peasants when they lose their subsistence base.

A small group of Nicaraguans consider themselves white, and generally attribute their greater wealth and social standing to intelligence and culture, which, in turn, they consider to be inherited from their pure European ancestry. They are relatively well educated and cosmopolitan, if only in comparison with most of their compatriots.

Along the Caribbean coast, there are still small enclaves of Indians who live by desultory farming or by hunting sea turtles that are valuable for their oil and their shells. The Indians are relatively isolated, and some still speak indigenous languages; they have little to do with the national government, and vice versa.

Another enclave group is made up of relatively few blacks who also live along the Caribbean coast. Most of them are descendants of slaves who were brought from Africa or from the West Indies to work as loggers or as laborers on banana plantations. In contrast to the dominant population, they are English-speaking Protestants, whose music, food, and lifestyles are Afro-American rather than Hispanic.

In the late 1800s, the introduction of coffee into the temperate uplands became a basis for limited international trade, and the development of banana plantations in the lowlands had a similar effect. Although these export crops are valuable, they fit the pattern familiarly known as "economic imperialism," a facet of underdevelopment. This is true because unproc-

Bananas, one of the country's cash crops, are loaded on a ship in Corinto, the only deep-water port on the Pacific coast of Nicaragua. (Photo: United Nations/YN/MH.)

essed produce and raw materials always command prices that are low in comparison with the prices of goods that are purchased after value has been added through processing or manufacturing. In addition, the prices of coffee, bananas, and similar goods are set by a world market over which producers normally have little control, so that most of the profits go abroad and there is no hope of the trickle-down economic benefits that are widely touted as deriving from big business in other contexts.

Before the revolution, the degree to which commercial competition was squelched was extraordinary. A thriving cattle industry, which used select stock and modern methods of production and processing, developed in recent decades, but the benefits accrued only to the Somozas. Similarly, the profitable fishing fleet and national airline were owned by the Somozas, as was 30 percent of the commercially cultivated land, including nearly all land on which large-scale modern techniques, like heavy machinery, herbicides, insecticides, and chemical fertilizers were employed. Although production was high in these ventures, they employed few workers, much of the capital invested was spent abroad, and there was little local economic development as a result. The distributorships for cement, bricks, hardware, trucks, and automobiles were also virtually monopolized by the Somozas and a few friends, assuring a further concentration of commercial profits.

The degree of centralization of business interests in Nicaragua became evident to outsiders in 1972, when relief supplies sent from around the world in response to an earthquake that devastated the capital, Mana-

Workers tend machinery in this automated textile mill, which produces cotton and polyester blend fabrics. (Photo: United Nations/ Y. Nagata.)

gua, were diverted on a massive scale and resold by Somozan interests. The country never fully recovered from that natural disaster, because civil strife became a continuing sporadic feature of life in the densely populated western region. The antecedents of Nicaragua's popular revolution were not exclusively economic, however; a combination of historical and cultural factors contributed to it.

In pre-Columbian times, a variety of Indian populations occupied the area, including simple nomadic hunters and the agriculturalists who built cities and developed great technical skill and aesthetic sensitivity in making pottery, carving stone, and other crafts. The Spanish conquistadores were disappointed at finding neither gold nor silver, so they shipped most of the Indians to South America for sale as slaves, and had little interest in colonizing the region.

The Caribbean coast played an important and unorthodox role in the complex economy of the eighteenth century. The dense forests were good for logging, and shipbuilding flourished. The coast also became a prime area for smuggling by Dutch, English, and French privateers and buccaneers, who prospered by flouting the strict controls on trade that Spain tried to maintain throughout its empire. African slaves were brought to work in the hot humid lowlands, and runaways seem to have been welcome among the Indians, resulting in a racially and culturally pluralistic society that eventually became the Miskito Kingdom and enjoyed a special protectorate relationship with Great Britain until 1859.

The administrative center during the colonial period was far removed in Guatemala, so that there was little government machinery or experience, or any other basis for stability when the wars of independence (which had little local impact) were concluded in 1821. A brief affiliation with the federated United Provinces of Central America provided little more preparation for effective government when Nicaragua became an independent republic in 1838.

Throughout the nineteenth century, political instability was normal as local leaders jockeyed for power. Changes in government were frequent, but they rarely had much effect outside of the capital city. Several caudillos took turns being President—some called themselves "liberal" and others "conservative," but such labels had little to do with political or social philosophy and made virtually no impact on the narrow distribution of wealth and power.

The active involvement of American citizens in the internal affairs of Nicaragua dates from 1855, when William Walker led a small group of American mercenaries to oust the incumbents; having done so, he routed the opposition who had hired him and set up a short-lived filibuster government. Early in this century, when long-term dictator José Zelaya seemed on the verge of annexing nearby countries, U.S. Marines were sent to occupy Nicaragua, ostensibly in the interest of regional economic and political stability, but also in part to defend the Panama Canal. When they left 30 years later, United States–educated Anastasio Somoza, father of the recently ousted President, became the leader of the newly constituted National Guard, which he used as his personal army to consolidate control of the country. A nationalistic opposition force existed for several years, until its leader, Augusto Sandino, was murdered during negotiations with Somoza. His name endures among those "Sandinistas" who recently overthrew Somoza's son after almost five decades of the Somozas' virtually uninterrupted monopoly of power.

For several years, there were occasional guerrilla forays in various parts of the country, underscoring Somoza's inability to suppress opposition even with ruthless measures. Although the administration attempted to discredit all opposition as "Castroite Communist," when rebel forces coalesced in a broadly based civil war following a general strike in 1979, even the historically conservative Catholic hierarchy supported them as champions of human rights. Although the Sandinista opposition was still a part-time force in civilian clothes, a qualitative change occurred at that time, and episodic skirmishes gave way to unrelenting antigovernment combat. By mid-1979, various Latin American countries were increasingly open about aiding the rebels, and the United States finally withdrew its support of Somoza.

A civilian five-member junta, organized in exile in Costa Rica, represented a wide range of political and economic viewpoints, and was recognized by some countries even before the leaders returned in triumph to Nicaragua. The war took a heavy toll on all the major cities before Somoza fled. (Somoza was killed on September 17, 1980 in Asunción, Paraguay.)

Insofar as Somoza was able to convert his immense wealth into liquid assets, he took most of the nation's capital with him into exile. But one principal resource remained and was promptly nationalized—his farms and ranches that made up a significant portion of the country's productive land. On August 9, 1980, the junta decreed that all of Somoza's property would be turned over to the people in the form of public facilities, and that the Nicaraguan Institute of Internal and External Commerce would be the sole buying agent for exports of coffee, cotton, sugar, and fish. Banks, insurance companies, and mines were nationalized and the government negotiated an agreement with thirteen foreign commercial banks to reschedule payments on those debts incurred by the Somoza government.

Nicaragua is experiencing the first genuine revolution that has occurred in Latin America in more than a decade. Reconstruction will be slow. But in their ouster of the harsh old regime, the Nicaraguan people have already effected a significant change in the distribution of wealth and power.

Dwight B. Heath

Panama
(Republic of Panama)

Area: 29,209 sq mi (75,650 sq km)
Population: 1.8 million
  Density: 62 per sq mi (24 per sq km)
  Growth rate: 3.1% (1970–1977)
Percent of population under 14 years of age: 43% (1975)
Infant deaths per 1,000 live births: 33 (1975)
Life expectancy at birth: 66.5 years (1975); 59 years (1978)
Leading causes of death: not available
Ethnic composition: mestizo 70%; black 13%; white 10%; Indian 6%; Oriental or Levantine 1%
Languages: Spanish (official); English
Literacy: 82% (1978)
Religions: Roman Catholic 95%; Protestant 5% (1978)
Percent population urban: not available
Percent population rural: not available
Gross national product: $2.4 billion
  Per capita GNP: $1,290
  Per capita GNP growth rate: −0.1% (1970–1977)
Inflation rate: not available

In Panama, geography has played a continuing and dominant role, and the country's small size has been a distinct asset. Forming the narrowest isthmus in the hemisphere, Panama has been an avenue for transshipment of goods from ports on the Atlantic ever since Vasco Nuñez de Balboa discovered the South Sea (Pacific Ocean) in 1513. To this day, Panama's strategic location is its greatest asset, and it is a center for large-scale commercial activity even though its people produce few goods that enter the world markets.

Comprising only 29,209 square miles (75,650 sq km), Panama lies in an approximate S shape between Costa Rica on the west and Colombia on the east. A chain of mountains runs the entire length of the country, but the elevations decrease toward the center, so that there is almost a basin at that strategic midpoint, only 38 miles (60.8 km) from coast to coast, where the Panama Canal has become a major avenue of world commerce.

The climate is hot and humid during most of the year, and the rainy season brings daily cloudbursts to most of the country. The eastern third of the nation, called Darién, remains virgin jungle and swamp. The alternating rugged mountains and boggy lowlands are sparsely populated by Indians, largely Choco-speaking. This is the site of the only remaining gap in the

Pan American Highway that runs from Alaska to Cape Horn, Chile. This relatively unpopulated area is still a frontier. It is not likely to become economically important except as an escape valve for those hardy peasants who are willing to live in relative isolation, farming on a subsistence basis.

Central Panama includes the low saddle of the isthmus, the traditional channel for transportation, and an area of rolling hills to the southwest of the Canal where there are several small towns and where farming is concentrated. The people of Chiriquí, the westernmost province bordering Costa Rica, have a strong sense of regional pride in their frontier life; the northwestern quadrant contains a series of banana plantations oriented toward external markets.

The two major cities are located on the Canal: Panama City, the capital, is near the Pacific end, and Colón is near the Caribbean. Both are predominantly commercial centers, with almost no manufacturing. They are both growing rapidly as peasants stream in from rural areas expecting—but not finding—work.

The population is under 2 million, with a population growth rate of 2.7 percent. Although medical facilities and personnel are highly concentrated in the cities, some rural clinics are being established, and the spread of public works has helped somewhat to diminish the prevalence of parasitosis and gastrointestinal and pulmonary diseases.

As is the case in many developing countries, population pressures are mounting as improved nutrition and health care significantly lower the death rate. However, Panama has not yet suffered severe population pressures on limited land; vast tracts of virgin forest are still available to squatters and homesteaders.

But nearly half the people live in the cities where jobs, housing, water, schooling, and other facilities are inadequate. In recent years, there has been a major

effort to increase services and expenditures for education and other kinds of social welfare. The impact has been impressive, especially in rural areas, but it becomes increasingly difficult to sustain these gains as the numbers of unemployed young people increase. Panama's census of 1970 listed 70 percent of the population as mestizo, 13 percent black, 10 percent white, 6 percent Indian, and 1 percent Oriental or Levantine. The last group are mostly storekeepers and entrepreneurs, concentrated in the cities and major towns. By contrast, the several small groups of Indians are largely rural, and live by hunting, fishing, and horticulture. Tourism has become a boon to the Cuna of the northeast, whose brightly colored cloth *molas* stitched in imaginative reverse-appliqué patterns are popular among tourists as a distinctive handicraft. The white population manage the few cattle ranches and banana plantations, and also exercise a virtual monopoly on key administrative, financial, and commercial positions.

Blacks are largely English speakers whose parents or grandparents were brought from the West Indies less than a century ago to work on the construction of the Panama Canal. They are predominantly an urban proletariat, employed either in miscellaneous blue-collar jobs or on the banana plantations, where they comprise most of the workers. Mestizo is a sort of residual category, applied to Spanish speakers whose ancestry includes European and Indian strains. There are mestizos throughout the country, but they predominate among small-scale farmers, artisans in towns and cities, and workers on cattle ranches.

Panamanians pride themselves on showing less racial prejudice than do people of other countries. However, Panamanians may be overstating the case. The economy has always been dominated by the small white elite. Despite this they have succeeded in avoiding the quasi-feudal pattern of direct exploitation.

In terms of basic values and attitudes, the people of Panama share many Iberian traditions with their neighbors. With respect to government and interpersonal relations, there is the combined concern for hierarchy and *personalismo*, the emphasis on each individual's uniqueness. The double standard between the sexes is expressed in *machismo*, the ideal of male dominance, and its counterpart, *marianismo*, the ideal of female submissiveness and forbearance. Kin ties are important, and links of interpersonal loyalty and reciprocity are both intensified and extended through the Roman Catholic institution of *compadrazgo* (coparenthood, or ritual kinship based on the godparent-godchild bond).

In a sense, Panama's economy is based more on services than on goods. Although agriculture employs 40 percent of the labor force, it does not yield nearly so high a proportion of the gross national product. Transit and commerce dominate, with fully 20 percent of the national income derived from the Canal Zone even in years before the United States agreed to

A ship passes through the Pedro Miguel locks in the Panama Canal; income from the Canal tolls is important to Panama. (Photo: United Nations/ Jerry Frank.)

adjust tolls and begin to turn over control of the Canal to Panama. Construction, food processing, and petroleum refining are other secondary activities that play a major role in the economy. The tradition of brokerage as a business has long been recognized in relation to the country's merchant marine fleet, which is one of the largest in the world if only as a "flag of convenience."

In recent years, valuable minerals have been discovered and exploited, especially manganese and bauxite, and copper may soon become another important export. These extractive industries are highly mechanized, intensive in terms of capital rather than labor. So there are few jobs created for local people, and what wealth is generated in the form of royalties goes to the national government.

Mining will probably never surpass banking and commerce. Already flourishing out of all proportion to the wealth of the local people, financial services will undoubtedly boom as the government experiments with tax shelters, confidential banking, and free-trade zones. In Panama, as in few other developing countries, ingenuity and geography have already paid high dividends, although natural resources have not yet been grossly exploited. The recent and accelerating expansion in the provision of educational, health, and other social welfare services, as Panama's share of the Canal revenues increases, will raise living standards.

The Panama Canal, completed in 1914, was only the most recent of a long series of commercial ventures that brought fame and fortune to this relatively unproductive and sparsely populated region. In the sixteenth century, the Nombre de Dios trail across the narrow part of the isthmus, paved with cobblestones and including several bridges, was the point of transshipment of goods en route from Spain to the west coast of South America and, for many years, of goods to and from the Philippine Islands. Portobelo on the Caribbean coast became the site of an annual trade fair that dazzled all who saw it.

By the early eighteenth century, the importance of Portobelo and of the trail across the isthmus declined when new ports were developed in South America and Spain lost control of the Caribbean. By the end of the century, Panama was a backwater.

Panama played no role in the war of liberation from Spain. In 1821, it became a province of Simón Bolívar's Republic of Gran Colombia (now Colombia, Venezuela, and Ecuador). By 1830, Venezuela and Ecuador broke away, but Panama remained part of Colombia.

In 1529, Hernán Cortés had recommended that a canal be built across the isthmus. Three centuries later, in 1834, the United States obtained little support when it suggested building a canal. Instead, the accession of California prompted North Americans to invest in a railway across the isthmus, which carried heavy traffic during the California gold rush.

After an abortive French effort, the United States finally elected to dig an interocean canal and negotiated a series of treaties, at the same time that it sponsored—and supported with naval forces—Panama's declaration of independence from Colombia in 1903. The treaty that remained in force during most of the ensuing years, with periodic renewal, contained a provision that made the Canal Zone a focus of contention. It set aside a strip of land 10 miles (16 km) wide bordering the canal " in perpetuity," and with ". . . all the rights, powers and authority . . . which the United States would possess and exercise if it were the sovereign. . . ." New treaties concluded in 1978 provide for the gradual transfer of the Canal Zone as well as the Canal to Panama.

Panama profited enormously from the Canal, although Panamanians resented their treatment as colonials. Black laborers were originally brought from the West Indies in large numbers to help in the construction of the Canal, with the understanding that they were to be repatriated when the job was done, but they were never repatriated. For many years, U.S. citizens who worked on the Canal were paid in gold, while Panamanians were paid in silver and there were very different pay scales and fringe benefits. Racial and ethnic prejudice, striking differences in standards of living between the privileged enclave of the Canal Zone and the surrounding national territory of Panama, the prevalence of foreign troops and the showing of a foreign flag, combined with a complex combination of other slights and aspirations culminated in riots against the United States by Panamanian students in 1964. In the ensuing years, there has been progressive and accelerating diminution of U.S. control and increasing Panamanian involvement.

Indian women of the Cuna tribe display their knitted hats and scarves. (Photo: United Nations/Jerry Frank.)

The Panamanian constitution provides for representative democracy, but the legislative branch was dissolved in 1968 when a military coup occurred and political parties were banned. General Omar Torrijos lifted the ban on parties a decade later, and renounced the title of Head of State, suggesting that the presidency, held by Aristides Royo, might become more than the figurehead position it had been for so long. Torrijos remains Commander in Chief of the National Guard, which is stronger and more pervasive than most armies, and he is still obviously a powerful leader. Panamanians admire his successful negotiation of a favorable settlement of the Canal treaty with the United States and they also know that he did more than any previous politician to provide marketplaces, schools, clinics, water systems, and other improvements to small communities throughout the country.

Although the U.S. Congress first dragged its heels with respect to the enabling legislation and funding for the new treaties, it is evident that increasing fees and royalties from the Canal will significantly increase Panama's income without further depleting its resources. Panamanians will undoubtedly be able to manage the Canal effectively. Assuming political stability, prospects for real development seem unusually bright in Panama.

Dwight B. Heath

Trinidad and Tobago
(Republic of Trinidad and Tobago)

Area: 1,980 sq mi (5,128 sq km)
Population: 1.1 million
   Density: 556 per sq mi (215 per sq km)
   Growth rate: 1.1% (1970–1977)
Percent of population under 14 years of age: 39% (1975)
Infant deaths per 1,000 live births: 31 (1975)
Life expectancy at birth: 69.5 years (1975)
Leading causes of death: same as U.S.
Ethnic composition: African (known locally as Creoles); Muslim and Hindu of Indian origin; Chinese; Lebanese; Portuguese
Languages: English
Literacy: 78% (1977)
Religions: Hindu, Muslim, Catholic, Protestant
Percent population urban: 80%
Percent population rural: 20%
Gross national product: $3.3 billion
   Per capita GNP: $2,910
   Per capita GNP growth rate: 1.5% (1970–1977)
Inflation rate: not available

The Caribbean island republic of Trinidad and Tobago faces two overriding problems: how to use its oil wealth to prepare for a twenty-first century in which it may run out of oil, and how to maintain and strengthen the common bonds among its extraordinarily mixed multiethnic and multiracial population. Its prosperity and its survival depend on its ability to respond to these two issues. Neither its past nor its present provide definitive answers or even direction.

The larger island of Trinidad is 1,864 square miles (4,828 sq km), an area slightly larger than Rhode Island. It is 7 miles (11.3 km) north of the South American mainland and the coast of Venezuela, and 2,000-plus miles (3,220-plus km) from the Bahama Islands and Miami, at the bottom of the Caribbean archipelago and the Leeward Islands chain. Strategically, Trinidad is a crossroads for shipping traffic between Europe and North Africa and the New World, especially northern South America and the Caribbean. Its climate is hot and humid, graced by cool ocean breezes. Its highest elevation is less than 2,000 feet (3,220 km), yet its tropical location includes mangrove swamps, rain forests, and markedly rugged terrain. Its beaches are few and the sand is mostly coarse. Its oil deposits are located offshore, and its natural gas is found in the tar pits and deposits at the south side of the island.

The island of Tobago is a little "sister." Located nearly 100 miles (161 km) to the north, it is merely a green speck of 116 square miles (300 sq km) with a population of 50,000. Lacking the natural resources of Trinidad and its distinctive rugged topography, Tobago is devoted to agriculture and tourism. It is green, hilly, and verdant, with dazzling aquarmarine beaches, bays, and coral reefs. It is a quiet, peaceful island compared to noisy, rambunctious Trinidad.

Because it is a geographic crossroads, Trinidad (but not predominantly African Tobago), has acquired a crossroads population, one that is racially and religiously mixed. The various groups include descendants of African slaves, nineteenth-century indentured laborers brought from China, India, and Pakistan, the offspring of French settlers expelled from Haiti in the uprising of 1798, Venezuelans, Lebanese, Syrians, Jews, and all possible mixtures. This is as dazzling a display of races and peoples, all packed on one little island, as one could hope to see anywhere. Since Trinidad and Tobago's independence in 1960, no statistics based on race or ethnicity have been kept for a population that has been growing at 2 percent a year, and in 1979 numbered 1.2 million. It is crudely estimated that people of African origin (known locally as Creoles) comprise about 35 percent; of the people of Indian origin, Hindus may make up 30 percent and Muslims, 15 percent; and Europeans, Chinese, Lebanese, and Venezuelans comprise 20 percent. These are only guesses; what matters is that a coalition of Creoles, Muslims, Europeans, and Chinese has run the island for more than 20 years and shows few signs of relinquishing power. The Hindu minority, defeated at the ballot box and fragmented by its own leadership, has yet to see its growing economic strength reflected politically, although individual Hindus have done well by cooperating with the government.

Population growth has been recognized as a national problem since 1967, and an aggressive government and private campaign helped to reduce fertility sharply, from 38.3 births per 1,000 people in 1955 to 25.3 per 1,000 in 1975, projected to drop to 17.0 per 1,000 by 2000. Given the strong emigration, mostly of professionals, to Canada, the United States, and England, Trinidad may be a candidate for zero population growth by the year 2000. However, large numbers of young people under age 20 continue to place severe demands on job markets, education, and other social services.

Since the 1930s, Trinidad's economy has been dominated by petroleum, which comprises 80 percent or more of its exports, is the principal source of all government revenue, and the motor of the society. Originally selected as a safe transshipment point for the storage and refining of Venezuelan crude by Shell and Caltex, Trinidad's south coast was soon crowded by refineries. As Venezuelan oil exploration extended into the Orinoco Basin and Lake Maracaibo, Trinidad shared some of the offshore fields. Similarly, as Venezuela began to process its own heavy sulphur crude, Trinidad switched to Middle Eastern crude for its refineries.

The petroleum-based economy generated a boom in residential and commercial construction, in government public works, and in the light consumer goods industry. Unfortunately, agriculture suffered when production stagnated; sugar prices wavered and foodstuffs, especially rice, had to be imported. Once dependent on its exports of coffee, cacao, citrus fruits, sugar, and other tropical foods, Trinidad now finds itself a substantial net food importer, while its exports lag. Fishing remains small-scale and cannot meet domestic demand. High wages for the few jobs in the petroleum industry have skewed the entire economy and constituted disincentives for agricultural and fishing investment. Tobago, in contrast, has few other options than agriculture and fishing.

Petroleum revenues have also made it possible for Trinidad to remain lukewarm about tourism. The government fears the racism and social unrest that might come in its wake. Venezuelans taking advantage of Trinidad as a free port are welcome, but Caribbean-style luxury package tourism is frowned on, except again for Tobago, a favorite resort for Trinidadians.

The government's development strategy is to use oil money to establish major capital-intensive petrochemical and steel industries with a government majority share, and to expand an islandwide welfare state. Trinidad is a minor oil producer, not a member of the Organization of Petroleum Exporting Countries (OPEC), but its pricing policies have followed world levels in recent years.

The moderate government of Eric Williams, Prime Minister since 1956, has established a development fund to assist the poorer Caribbean islands, including Jamaica, and has lent funds to the World Bank and the Inter-American Development Bank. Trinidad has also borrowed heavily in the Eurodollar market to finance its new industries. The opposition has argued that new industries will not create jobs for the unskilled unemployed, and that the multinational corporations have had the best of the negotiations.

Persistent unemployment—especially among the young—and skewed income distribution are continuing problems. Fortunately, income distribution inequities apparently occur in each major racial group rather than in favor of any one group.

Urbanization as a concept has a special meaning on small islands. The largest town on Tobago is Scarborough, with a population of 5,000, but the entire island consists of a series of closely related villages. Similarly Trinidad's capital, Port of Spain, has been losing population in recent years (the population remains near 50,000). However, people have moved to the nearby new suburbs and growing villages, and the metropolitan area is growing very rapidly. A similar phenomenon is occurring at San Fernando, the commercial center of the south coast petroleum refineries.

Approximately 60 percent of Trinidad's total population now live in an urban or peri-urban setting, with paved roads, telephones, running water, elec-

A worker tends gauges at a valve station of a thermal power plant for Port of Spain. (Photo: World Bank/Hilda Bijur.)

Far Right: Workers prepare a path through a sugarcane field to lay a pipeline that will bring natural gas from the oil fields to power a sugar refinery. (Photo: World Bank/ Flip Schulke of Black Star.)

tricity, and other amenities. Much of the rural population live on housing adjacent to sugar estates. The government intends to quickly improve rural and suburban amenities to discourage a rural exodus. Since a 2- to 3-hour drive takes one around Trinidad, this may be feasible.

Land-use planning is essential but new to the republic. The environmental impact statements of new industries have just begun to be introduced. National parks have been created, but good beaches and other recreational areas are in jeopardy. Cheap gas and easy credit for cars have produced an automobile civilization on a small island where space is precious. Public collective taxis help reduce excess traffic between cities, but public transportation is generally poor and the private car rules the road.

Transport usually refers to shipping in Trinidad. Small freighters and schooners ply between the islands, but trade is dependent on giant oil tankers and other major vessels. The government shares in the rather inefficient inter-island West Indian Shipping Corporation, but ocean transport is generally left to the private sector.

Instead, government has concentrated its efforts on air transport. Various subsidies have maintained an air shuttle service between Port of Spain and Tobago. A major investment established British West Indian Airways, serving the Caribbean and North America, though it operates generally at a loss. The thousands

A worker examines the coconut harvest at a coconut fiber plant in Tobago. (Photo: United Nations/Hilda Bijur.)

of Trinidadians living abroad keep in close touch with their homeland and are constant travelers.

The Republic of Trinidad and Tobago belongs to several worlds, geographically and culturally. Since 1800, its roots have been British colonial and West Indian. A founding member of the Caribbean Community (CARICOM) and the Caribbean Development Bank, Trinidad has advocated closer ties with its fellow islanders. But because Trinidad's per capita income is two to three times greater than that of other CARICOM members, there is considerable concern in the smaller islands about Trinidad's possible domination. Another pole consists of Latin American countries, especially Colombia and Venezuela, as markets for Trinidad's goods and as competitors. Trinidad is an active member of the Organization of American States and the Inter-American Development Bank. Personal and ethnic loyalties tie some Trinidadians to India, Pakistan, the United Kingdom, Canada, and the United States. The American military presence on Trinidad during World War II left a mixed but permanent impact as reflected by Trinidad novelist V. S. Naipaul in *A Flag on the Island*. Because of these multiple loyalties, Trinidad has a far more active diplomacy than one would expect from a small, if oil-rich, island.

Trinidad's cultural and social life has both national and ethnic aspects. The stirring rhythms of the calypso, steel bands (invented during World War II, using petroleum drums), the glorious annual carnival, the costumes, the dancing, the quick, acerbic wit, the distinctive accent, the distinctive style in cricket (the national sport), and many other characteristics are shared by all Trinidadians.

At the same time Hindus, Muslims, Catholics, Chinese, Protestants, and all the other members of the panoply of peoples and cults that make up this society have their own clubs, rituals, and social lives. Mixing is generally limited (Hindus do not usually take part in carnival although they may watch). Intermarriage is rare and is generally frowned on. Trinidad is not a melting pot, and its several cultures coexist, sometimes comfortably and sometimes uneasily, each preserving its own folkway.

Education is free and compulsory for children of both sexes up to age 14, and parents encourage children to go on to technical, commercial, and academic senior secondary schools. The Trinidad campus of the University of the West Indies, with its colleges of agriculture, engineering, science, and social sciences, is one of several campuses that serve 2.5 million West Indians from 11 countries, including Trinidad. A surprising number of those who cannot gain admission to the University of the West Indies go to Canada, the United States, or the United Kingdom for further study.

A highly urbanized form of village life continues in Trinidad. In most households, tradition prevails, several generations may share the same roof, and religion is taken seriously. Casual and boisterous Trinidad is still a Catholic, Hindu, and Muslim society, where instruction in virtue is pervasive, if not effective.

Archaeologists date the first settlements in the Caribbean at 3000 B.C. Trinidad was an early stop as waves of Arawak and then Carib Indians paddled northward from the Orinoco Basin up the Caribbean chain.

The period 1500–1800 was marked by rivalry among English, French, and Spanish forces for the two highly valued islands. Buccaneers and settlers, slaves and runaways, all fought, loved, and perished. It was not until 1800 that Britain definitively established its authority over the two islands, but the French and Spanish influences persisted.

From 1800 to 1830 Trinidad was a sleepy British colony whose people spoke a French patois brought from Haiti. The abolition of slavery was followed by the importation of thousands of Hindu, Muslim, and Chinese indentured laborers, whose presence would eventually change the entire social structure.

World War I and its aftermath saw the introduction of political parties and trade unions and the beginning of a nationalist movement. The Great Depression and the oil boom triggered the mass movements and riots of the late 1930s. World War II further stimulated the economy, while exposing Trinidadians to American ways, including racism and segregation.

The drive for independence first united and then divided the society. Eric Williams championed the

People's National Movement (PNM), garnered trade union support, including the powerful oil workers, and swept the 1956 elections. He has been victorious in all elections since, although by far smaller margins. Radical intellectuals, dissident unionists, and much of the Hindu community remain disaffected, but they lack any effective leadership of their own. Tiny Tobago, too, chafes under PNM rule and seeks greater autonomy, although not independence.

A major uprising and minor army coup were crushed in 1970, although sporadic violence has continued. Economic development has been prodigious but grossly uneven. The ostentatious nouveau riche are resented; the poor remain poor, their laments captured by calypso. Corruption and the gross misallocation of resources have been widespread. The government has cautiously courted foreign investment and has encouraged local private savings; in doing so, it has alienated many radicals.

The future depends on the intelligent use of present oil wealth (at present rates Trinidad reserves may run out by 2000, and it is risky to depend on imported crude for refining). The agriculture sector needs a boost, and the restless young need jobs. The stake in heavy industry seems too high in relation to possible social returns.

The polity also needs a shake-up. The PNM has grown old and stale in power. Were the opposition not so narrowly based ethnically, a democratic change might be welcome. Perhaps, instead, a new coalition could form, cutting across racial and ethnic lines, on the basis of issues and policies. Personality is so important in the politics of face-to-face societies like

A farmer tends his pigs in their sty. Trinidad and Tobago suffers from inadequate food production. (Photo: United Nations/ Hilda Bijur.)

Trinidad that it is difficult to envisage a major re-shuffle. One fears not so much racial unrest (as in more conflict-prone Guyana), but a persistent failure to bring certain groups into national politics, thus casting doubts on the legitimacy of the entire system. Some renovation is badly needed.

Trinidad's multiple international axes will continue, since no one orientation can satisfy its needs. Its opportunities for CARICOM leadership are great, if it refrains from trying to dominate the other countries and is willing to share its resources.

Aaron Segal

South America

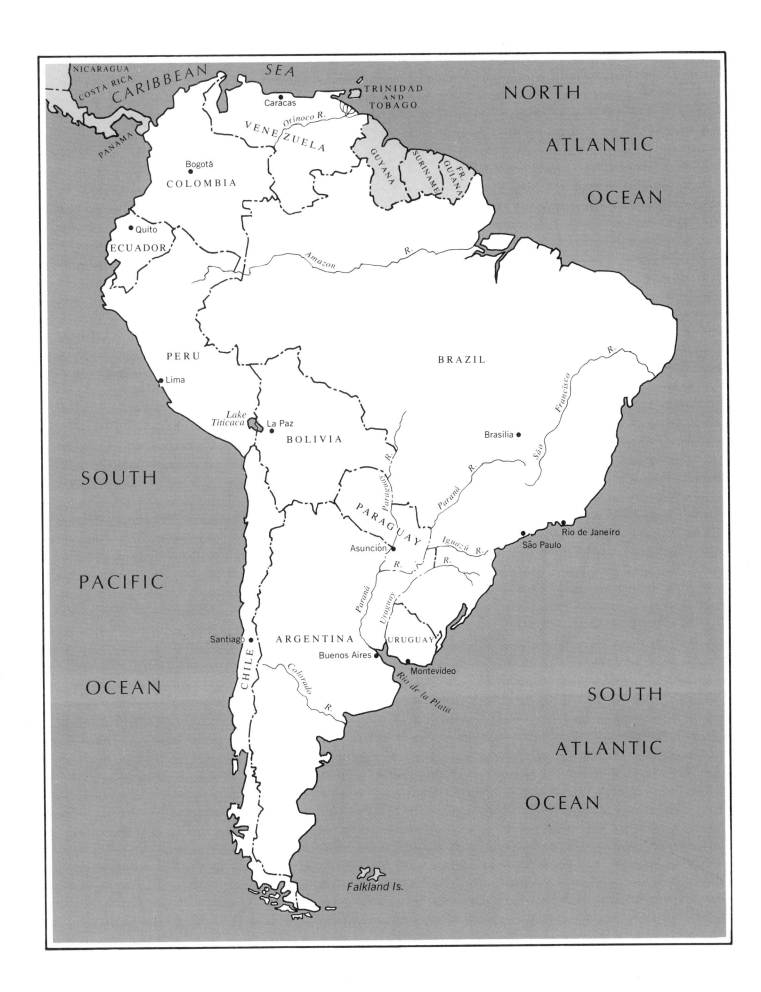

Argentina

(Argentine Republic)

Area: 1,070,000 sq mi (2,771,300 sq km)
Population: 26.4 million
  Density: 25 sq mi (10 per sq km)
  Growth rate: 1.3% (1970–1977)
Percent of population under 14 years of age: 28% (1975)
Infant deaths per 1,000 live births: 51
Life expectancy at birth: 68 years
Leading causes of death: not available
Ethnic composition: European 97% (mostly Italian and Spanish)
Languages: Spanish (official); English; Italian; German; French
Literacy: over 90% (1977)
Religions: Roman Catholic 94%; Protestant 2%; Jewish
Percent population urban: 80%
Percent population rural: 20%
Gross national product: $50.3 billion
  Per capita GNP: $1,910
  Per capita GNP growth rate: 1.8% (1970–1977)
Inflation rate: 125% (1978)

A richly endowed nation with a highly educated population, Argentina enjoys continuing economic growth and is free of many of the shortcomings that plague other developing nations. Its demographic, literacy, urbanization, health, educational, and other vital statistics rival those of developed nations. Based on agricultural and livestock exports, the economy expanded rapidly before World War I, while a small but growing industrial base took hold. Since the 1930s, however, despite significant industrialization, the country has suffered from periodic stagnation and social and political unrest, and it has frustratingly failed to fulfill the dreams of an earlier age.

Within Argentina's 1,070,000 square miles (2,771,300 sq km) of impressively diversified terrain, nature and man have combined forces to produce sometimes bleak and sometimes wondrous beauty. In the south, the windswept mostly arid plateaus of Patagonia stretch in elongated steps toward the Andes Mountains from the cliffs of the Atlantic seaboard. Here, in the late nineteenth century Welsh immigrants established many of the ranches that feed millions of sheep and cattle today. The natural gas and oil fields on the coast at Comodoro Rivadavia provide 90 percent of Argentina's oil needs. High in the Andes near the Chilean border, the ski resort of San Carlos de Bariloche overlooks the deep blue waters of Lake Nahuel Huapí. Several hundred miles to the northeast, rivers descending from the mountains irrigate the lush orchards of Río Negro Province and power the hydroelectric stations at Chocón.

Farther to the north the Andes, which define the country's western border for 2,300 miles (3,700 km), rise to surround Mount Aconcagua; at 22,830 feet (6,959 m) it is the highest peak in the Western Hemisphere. As the Andes descend to the east, the often snowcapped lower ranges stand in startling contrast to the emerald green vineyards of Mendoza and San Juan provinces. This arid western region taps the melting snows and instant rivers of the cordillera to produce wine, fruit, and a wide variety of cereals and vegetables. In southern Mendoza, a vast hydroelectric complex will soon be linked with Chocón and several other facilities to supply 90 percent of the nation's electricity needs by the early 1980s. The remaining demand will be filled by nuclear generators powered with uranium, also from southern Mendoza, while oil fields in the northern part of the province complement Comodoro Rivadavia's production.

As they stretch into northwestern Argentina, the Andes broaden to a complex of mountains and plateaus from 7,000 to 18,000 feet (2,100 to 5,500 km) high and 250 miles (400 km) wide. The intermountain valleys in the east support agricultural production for local consumption, while the region looks to its copper, iron, oil, and other minerals to restore the prosperity of the colonial period, when it supplied food and mules to the Bolivian silver mines. Once the southern frontier of the ancient Peruvian Empire of the Incas, the northwest is the *cuna* (cradle) of an important part of the country's folklore. While Argentina lies almost entirely within the temperate zone, it approaches the semitropical zone beyond the eastern rim of the plateaus, where sugarcane fields contribute to the vivid green of the Tucumán Province.

Throughout the country, rainfall levels increase from west to east, while in the central and northern regions the terrain slopes gently toward the coast. Across the country's northern perimeter and along its northeastern limits an arc of lowlands receives 35 to 50 inches (90–130 cm) of rain annually. Except for the cotton plantations near the Paraguayan border, the precipitation falls on scrub forests, savannas, and swamps. In the southern portion of a mesopotamian corridor straddled by the Paraná and Uruguay rivers, the rain supports horse farms, cattle and sheep ranches, orange groves, and rice plantations. The lowlands then finger out into the extreme northeastern province of Misiones, where red soil and dense semitropical forests open to the tea, yerba maté, lemon, and rice crops that point the way to the thunderous falls of Iguazú on the Brazilian border.

At the confluence of the Paraná and Uruguay rivers, the wide Río de la Plata begins its southeasterly flow into the Atlantic Ocean and signals the eastern terminus of the humid pampa, one of the world's three richest agricultural zones. Unbroken by major rivers, these almost treeless plains fan out from the coast to the limits of the lowlands, Andean, and Patagonian regions. They encompass less than one-fifth of the country's surface area, but support the economic, demographic, and political core of the nation. The fertile soil, watered by 36 to 39 inches (91–99 cm) of rain yearly, produces wheat, corn, oats, alfalfa, flax, vegetables, and peanuts, and feeds cattle, hogs, and sheep for both the domestic and international markets. With more than four-fifths of Argentina's industrial capacity along key areas of its perimeter, the pampa supplies almost 90 percent of the nation's exports and crops, and 50 percent of the nation's cattle and horses and 80 percent of its hogs are raised in this area.

Just 100 years ago, Argentine soldiers drove the nomadic Araucanians off the pampa and deep into Patagonia. In their stead came iron rails, steam locomotives, purebred stock, selected grains, European capital, and immigrants, primarily from Spain and Italy. The immigrants, who totaled 4.5 million by 1914, blended easily into Argentine society and buttressed the religious (Catholic), ethnic (south European), and linguistic (Spanish) homogeneity of the country's vastly expanded population. The Tupí-Guaraní people in the northern forests, whose ancestors lived on Jesuit communes, and the Quechua-speaking groups of the northwest are the only remnants of the country's pre-Columbian past.

Beginning in the 1880s, an agricultural revolution on the pampa displaced the gauchos—mestizo (Spanish-Indian) frontier people—who became range hands, while the tight control exercised by landed elites foreclosed rural settlement to most immigrants.

Instead, Italians, Spaniards, and other Europeans found employment in the rapidly growing port city of Buenos Aires, nicknamed the Paris of South America. Under the impact of the pampa-based agricultural export economy supported by a complex rail system that focused on the city, Buenos Aires quickly came to dominate this highly urbanized nation. Today, 40 percent of the country's 25 million inhabitants live in metropolitan Buenos Aires, and an additional 30 percent live on the pampa, mostly in a few key cities.

Rural families on the pampa enjoy a moderate standard of living, while the migrant farm laborers, plantation workers, and peasants of the interior suffer from low wages, lack of education, inadequate health facilities, and periodic unemployment. Such problems are in stark contrast to the dynamism of the cities in a country that is 80 percent urban and more than 90 percent literate. Argentina has traditionally emphasized free public education; 500,000 students (excluding education majors) are enrolled in 14 major universities.

In the interior, lifestyles are as diversified as the local and national economies. The wide, tiled sidewalks of Mendoza City, washed daily with a kerosine solution, reflect the middle-class prosperity of the province. Peasant families work the sugar plantations of Tucumán Province, where poverty, poor health, and illiteracy are endemic. Maté-sipping peasants exchange folktales at the local markets of Misiones, where women from the countryside, carrying baskets on their heads laden with vegetables, eggs, lace, and hand-rolled cigars, conduct their business. In many areas, folk religions and herbal medicine have blended with Catholicism and modern medicine. Everywhere in the interior, in busy provincial capitals and in tranquil rural areas, the afternoon siesta is a time-honored, almost sacred tradition.

While in cosmopolitan, European-oriented Buenos Aires, modernization and economic development have stripped away traditions like the siesta, the asado is a tradition that remains as strong in the city as elsewhere in the nation. A kind of beef and sausage barbecue, the asado symbolizes the gaucho past, mirrors the opulence of the pampa, and approximates an individualized philosophy of life. There are elaborate, personalized styles of preparing the asado. However, during the week, construction workers, road crews, railroad gangs, and other laborers with outdoor jobs often eat a mini-asado for lunch.

The ranks of the unskilled and semiskilled workers have been filled in the last few decades by migrants from the interior and from the border countries, drawn to Buenos Aires by its promises of employment and a better standard of living. A rapid, efficient, and

Gauchos drive cattle to pasture on a large ranch on the pampas. Agricultural and meat products earn most of Argentina's foreign exchange. (Photo: United Nations/V. Bibic.)

cheap system of mass transportation combining sub-ways, buses, and suburban trains gives these immi-grants maximum access to job opportunities.

The unions, among the strongest in Latin America, are backed by progressive legislation and provide the workers with organized social activities, often through private recreational clubs. The largest unions own hotels in the country's main summer resort, Mar del Plata, where members can rent inexpensive rooms. Medical care for everyone is free through pub-lic hospitals; private consultations are paid for by gov-ernment- and union-sponsored health plans.

In a country with one car for every eight inhabit-ants, the city's streets are clogged at rush hour as white-collar workers head for their jobs in govern-ment, commerce, and industry. Manufactured in the highly industrialized city of Córdoba in the north-central pampa, automobiles are expensive, and many middle-class people travel to work on the mass transit system. Also unionized, white-collar workers enjoy the same benefits as blue-collar workers, while both groups suffer from a housing shortage because con-struction has failed to keep pace with demand. Often, finding a home in one of the new subdivisions spon-sored by a particular union and business depends on the luck of a lottery, in which the names of prospec-tive owners are drawn.

While union benefits, free health care and educa-tion, and mass transit facilities are available through-out the country, the dynamism of Buenos Aires and the diversity of its social life remain distinctive in a society that places a premium on the extended family and interpersonal relations. In the evenings people crowd into movie houses, the Colón opera house, res-taurants, cafés, and tango houses. The barrio, or neighborhood, with its small bread, vegetable, peri-odical, and butcher stands, continues to be the center of everyday life where transactions often seem less important than animated conversation.

The Italian immigrants who crowded into the slums of a booming city worked on the docks and the railroads, in the granaries, slaughterhouses, and meat-packing plants that funneled the produce of the pampa to European—especially British—markets. These workers had come to get rich during the two major economic booms between 1880 and 1914 that seemed to propel the nation firmly in the direction of sustained economic development.

The exchange of raw materials for finished goods worked well as the gross domestic product expanded between 1860 and 1914 at an impressive average an-nual rate of 5 percent. Two world wars and the Depression of the 1930s, however, created severe dis-locations that convinced a broad spectrum of Argen-tine society of the need to industrialize. Moreover, the years of rapid growth and high rates of urbaniza-tion had created severe tensions that lay just beneath the surface of national politics. Workers, for example, tried repeatedly to form unions and struck for better wages and improved working conditions but with lit-

tle success. By 1940, only 473,000 of the country's 3.5 million urban laborers were unionized. The middle-class Radical Party had swept into power in 1916 on a reformist platform, but failed to produce a coherent economic program or to address labor's problems be-fore it was overthrown in 1930 by a military coup. The country's traditional dependence on English mar-kets, capital, and technology contributed to a growing sense of antiforeign nationalism while the economy suffered.

In 1943, a military coup brought Colonel Juan Domingo Perón, a highly charismatic and astute pol-itician, and his flamboyant wife Evita into national politics. Through the power of his position as Min-ister of Labor he systematically facilitated unioniza-tion and improved benefits for workers as he built a solid political following among unskilled and semi-skilled workers. A combination of newly organized laborers and small- to medium-level national entre-preneurs elected him President in 1946 on a populist, antiforeign platform. With $1.7 billion in foreign ex-change revenues available from the export boom dur-ing World War II, his administration adopted stri-dently antiforeign investment laws, promoted selective industrialization, and passed numerous pro-gressive social justice laws. The latter significantly raised real wages, improved working conditions, pro-vided for social security, educational, recreational, and health benefits and job security.

By the end of the decade, it was painfully obvious that the success of the attempt radically to transform the economy of the country depended on the huge exchange surplus and favorable foreign market con-ditions for traditional exports. As market conditions slumped and reserves rapidly dwindled, Perón's deli-

A technician uses an end meter interference comparator to calibrate a measuring instrument at the National Institute of Industrial Technology in Buenos Aires. (Photo: United Nations/INTI.)

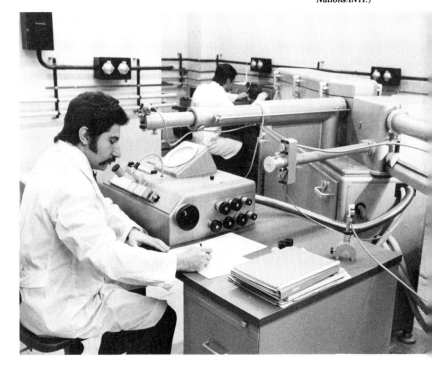

cate balancing of urban labor and urban entrepreneur interests eroded. The adoption of more conservative policies aggravated this trend; the national debt, which had been retired soon after Perón's election, expanded again, and political discontent increased markedly. Tensions rose and violations of civil and human rights intensified as the government resorted to political oppression to maintain its control. Critics mysteriously disappeared, opposition newspapers were shut down, and a neighborhood spy system made free speech dangerous. Real wages declined, a drought crippled the rural sector, and the economy fell into disarray, opening the door to a popular military coup that sent Perón into exile and proscribed the Peronist Party.

Between 1955 and 1973, a succession of civilian and military governments failed repeatedly to produce sustained economic growth or political stability. Their difficulties stemmed in part from the prohibition on Peronist involvement in politics enforced by the military, and from the attempt to restore conservative principles to economic policies. The latter led to a reversal of incomes policies, new pro-foreign investment regulations, sharp reductions in the government bureaucracy, and the return of many enterprises taken over by the state under Perón's administration to private ownership. By the 1960s, leftist guerrillas and radical university students had launched a serious challenge to institutional order. By 1973, fears of a revolution, coupled with the recognition that only Perón could harness sufficient popular support to end the unrest, led to his return after 18 years of exile and to his election by nearly two-thirds of the popular vote to a third presidential term.

While he drove radical leftists underground, Perón attempted to recreate the populist, antiforeign programs of his earlier years through a renewal of the old alliance of urban laborers and national entrepreneurs. Aged and suffering from poor health when he returned to office, Perón died in July 1974, leaving the presidency to his Vice-president and third wife, María Estela Martínez de Peron (Isabelita). Without the charisma or political talent of her husband, Isabelita proved incapable of handling the escalating political violence between extreme left- and extreme right-wing factions, or the economic disarray that once again characterized Peronist government. In response to the kidnappings, extortion, murders, and armed attacks perpetrated by the guerrillas, the President declared a state of siege, while paramilitary groups like the Argentine Anticommunist Alliance (widely rumored to have government support) carried out a systematic campaign of political violence and repression. There were violations of civil and human rights by both political extremes. By mid-1975, gross domestic product was declining at over 4 percent a year and foreign investment had all but ceased. At the same time, the national debt had risen alarmingly, and the nation was on the verge of declaring bankruptcy. When the rate of hyperinflation spiraled to a

high of 56 percent in March 1976, in that month, the military once again took over through a nonviolent and popularly supported coup.

The military junta immediately prohibited all civilian political activities. An all-out campaign to eradicate the guerrillas only added to the already serious violations of human rights. General of the Army Jorge Videla, head of the three-man ruling junta, proved as incapable of controlling extreme right factions (especially among the armed forces) as his civilian predecessor. Despite protests from international agencies and foreign governments, the pattern of arbitrary arrests and civil rights violations, mysterious kidnappings, torture, and murder altered only moderately. Although his government announced the successful completion of its antiguerrilla campaign, President Videla was unable to restore traditional civil liberties or to end human rights violations. He had to maintain a delicate balance between his programs to restore the country to democratic rule (begun when he resigned his commission to assume the presidency as a civilian) and pressure from military extremists. In October 1980, the military junta designated one of its former members, retired commander in chief of the army, General Roberto Eduardo Viola to succeed General Videla as President for a three-year term beginning in March 1981.

In the meantime, the shock treatment policy for the economy that Minister of Economy José Martínez de Hoz has pursued since 1976 produced some significant gains. By 1978, annual inflation was reduced to 125 percent, but it rose to 160 percent in late 1979. Foreign reserves are once again on the rise, investment has climbed, business and industry are expanding, and the public debt has fallen significantly. These gains, however, have come at the expense of labor and the middle class which has had to endure frozen wages and rapidly increasing costs of consumer goods. Peronist social legislation and income policies have been dismantled.

Since the 1930s the industrial sector has consistently accounted for a larger share of the gross domestic product than the rural sector. The rural sector, however, still earns most of the foreign exchange necessary for both industrialization and an optimum rate of growth. Given the nature of the global economy since World War II, the relative positions of foreign and national firms in both the industrial and rural sectors will persist. In this sense, the nation will continue to depend to an important degree on foreign capital, technology, and markets. This does not make it impossible to achieve a greater degree of economic independence. The nuclear power industry, for example, is wholly independent of foreign influence; it was created, developed, and sustained by local initiative.

That Argentina will achieve full-scale development has never been in doubt. Instead, the social, economic, and political tensions that have plagued Argentina since the 1930s represent an all too frequently violent debate over the conditions and the nature of that development. The question is not simply whether the many groups loosely categorized as Peronists and anti-Peronists can compromise, but whether the inevitable return to electoral politics will bring the institutionalized means to reconcile politi-cal and social realities with technical economic problems. Given the country's vast natural and human resources and its historical, social, and cultural heritage, Argentina will inevitably resolve its current difficulties and become a major developed nation.

William J. Fleming

Bolivia
(Republic of Bolivia)

Area: 424,162 sq mi (1,098,579 sq km)
Population: 5.3 million
　Density: 12 per sq mi (5 per sq km)
　Growth rate: 2.7% (1970–1977)
Percent of population under 14 years of age: 43%
Infant deaths per 1,000 live births: 154 (1970)
Life expectancy at birth: 47 years
Leading causes of death: not available
Ethnic composition: Aymara 25%; Quechua 30%; mestizo (cholo) 25–30%; European 5–15%; other 5%
Languages: Spanish; Aymara; Quechua
Literacy: 40%
Religions: Roman Catholic 95%
Percent population urban: not available
Percent population rural: not available
Gross national product: $2.7 billion
　Per capita GNP: $510
　Per capita GNP growth rate: 2.9% (1970–1977)
Inflation rate: not available

For many years, Bolivia has been described as "a beggar sitting on a golden throne." This image highlights the irony that a land so rich in natural resources has a population that lives at a level of poverty extreme even in worldwide perspective. Bolivia is a landlocked land of many contrasts, torn by a heritage of conflict.

The country's ecological diversity is reflected in the irregular distribution of the population. About 70 percent of the roughly 5.8 million people live in the 30 percent of the territory that has an elevation of over 4,000 feet (1,220 m), while the rest of the people are scattered throughout the vast lowland plain that constitutes the rest of the country. Like most Andean countries, Bolivia comprises three very different kinds of territory; the altiplano, the valleys, and the lowlands.

The altiplano (literally high plain) is the basin [about 12,500 feet (3,810 m) high] between the two rugged chains of the Andes Mountains that cut diagonally across the southwestern corner of the country. Many visitors characterize the altiplano as bleak and forbidding, but it has supported simple agriculture and herding for centuries. Wheat, barley, quinoa, and many varieties of potatoes give adequate yields when cultivated by traditional methods, including shallow plowing and strict rotation of crops.

Although the rugged mountainous regions above the plateau do not always fit the label, these regions are generally regarded as part of the altiplano. It is in this broader sense that the altiplano can accurately be called the focus of Bolivian development throughout most of the country's history. The elaborate Tiahuanaco culture flourished there even before the Incas made it part of their expanding empire. The mountains were so rich in silver that the amount of silver extracted from the mines in a single peak is credited with having upset the currencies of Europe, while Potosí, the boomtown at its base, flourished briefly as the largest and richest city in the Western Hemisphere. During the past 100 years, tin and tungsten have become major mineral exports, and they dominate the national economy, out of all proportion to the few employed in mining.

An even more densely populated zone is the narrow band of valleys along the eastern slopes of the Andes. Some of them are broad and flat, with a Mediterranean climate at 5,000 to 6,000 feet (1,525–1,830 m) elevation, like Cochabamba, Sucre, and Tarija. Wheat, maize, alfalfa, and a spectacular variety of fruits and vegetables can be grown in abundance in these relatively fertile, warm, and well-watered regions. More specialized are the yungas, distinctive rugged subtropical valleys that, when cleared of montane rain forest, provide a rich and spectacular setting for cocoa, coffee, and citrus cultivation.

To the east of the Andean escarpment sprawl the vast lowlands that, until recent years, were virtually neglected, except episodically when specific natural resources become the focus of international exploitation. Locally called llanos (plains) or Oriente (the eastern area), the lowlands include large areas of dense tropical rain forest, grassy prairie, and scrub desert, in roughly that sequence from north to south. There is little development in the far north, although rubber, timber, Brazil nuts, and cinchona bark are valuable natural exports. In the middle, grasslands support vast herds of cattle and are being rapidly brought under cultivation for rice, cotton, and sugarcane, especially in the flourishing region around Santa Cruz, where thousands of migrants from the highlands have pushed back the frontiers of settlement in recent decades. In the southeast, oil and natural gas flow out of a generally desolate area.

The Bolivian people are even more diversified than the landscape. Fewer than half the people can even speak Spanish, the official language. Nationality has little meaning for many native peoples who are remote from the government and who sometimes know and care little about the world beyond their own communities. In the tropical lowlands, there are probably close to 100 small tribes that have never even been studied, each with its distinctive language, customs, and other cultural patterns. In the valleys, the Quechua language is a reminder of Inca occupation from the fourteenth century until the Spanish conquest; Quechua and Aymara are the largest native groups in the altiplano, and music, dress, religion, and other aspects of their lives reflect the fact that four centuries of acculturation have not really obscured many vigorous pre-Columbian traditions.

The jungle dwellers are largely hunters, fishers, and collectors of wild foods; their small numbers are rapidly diminishing, as outsiders encroach on areas that were previously ignored. Most of the Quechua and Aymara are peasant farmers or herders of sheep, llamas, and alpacas.

It is perhaps ironic that the word "indio" has been virtually outlawed as a racial epithet in a country where so large a portion of the population were previously called Indian. It reflects the fact that in Bolivia race is considered a sociological and not a biological concept. Social categorization is based on a combination of factors, including (but not limited to) dress, occupation, style of house, as well as ancestry or physical features.

Thus a rapidly growing portion of the population are mestizos, Spanish speakers, whose possessions and wants follow the mainstream of Western culture, even if a few of their beliefs and behavior patterns may be more traditional. Many mestizos are peasant farmers, but others are cowboys, factory workers, commercial and administrative personnel, and the people who provide myriad services in all the cities and towns.

A small upper stratum that prides itself on being white tends to dominate the professions and large-scale agriculture and industry. Although the 1952 revolution undercut the traditional oligarchy, a new Bolivian elite emerged, itself subject to foreign influences, in terms of foreign aid, technical assistance, or international commerce.

A variety of immigrants who have come at different times and for different reasons are statistically insignificant but sociologically important in some areas. A few black slaves stayed in the yungas after emancipation; their communities have remained remarkably intact as endogamous enclaves. Many so-called Turcos who came from the Levant early in this century have prospered, often as merchants. Germans who entered in the 1930s and 1940s run many urban shops, hotels, and restaurants. Immigrants invited from Japan to help expand the agricultural frontier into the jungle, together with Mennonites from Paraguay and several other groups, live on the lowland farms that they made commercially successful.

Although regional variation is enormous, some general features recur. There are few cities, but each dominates a large outlying area, in terms of administration and commerce, and each has become a focus of large-scale migration. As in most developing countries, the cities have insufficient housing; they are lacking in water and other utilities; and, perhaps even more important, they cannot provide the jobs that newcomers expect to find.

Manufacturing continues to be small scale and does not figure significantly in the national economy. Most manufactured products are nondurable con-

Women collect potatoes in a field near Lake Titicaca on the altiplano, where wheat, barley, and quinoa are also grown. (Photo: United Nations/J. Foxx.)

sumer goods, like textiles, clothing, cooking utensils, and bottled beverages.

Bolivia is one of the world's poorest countries in terms of infrastructure. Means of transportation and communication continue to be crude; there are few railroads or paved highways, and the combination of rugged terrain and a torrential rainy season takes a heavy toll on other roads. Virtually the entire northern half of the country lacks overland links with the capital or other cities, and an enormously rich iron deposit near the eastern frontier with Brazil remains unexploited because of inadequate transportation facilities.

Regional pride and even narrower concern with ethnic group or community are factors that stand in the way of any strong sense of national unity. Even among those who take an active role in electoral politics, allegiance to individuals in the expectation of special benefits—a personalistic patronage-clientage relationship—is more important than party platforms or ideological factors.

Pre-Columbian patterns of population distribution have had a lasting impact on development. Many areas of dense native population retain much of their ancient heritage, whereas other areas of sparse native population have, in many instances, become loci of an undifferentiated mestizo cultural pattern like that found in many other areas that were once colonies of Spain. Throughout the densely settled Inca Empire, Spaniards were able to take over preexisting bureaucratic structures like taxation and labor conscription; although the overlords were different, this did not have much impact on the workaday life of a peasant in the altiplano and valley areas. In general, the peasants continued farming and herding much as before, although those groups who were not fortunate enough to gain and retain recognition as free communities became tenant farmers on large estates. The quasi-feudal character of such haciendas remained intact until the revolution of 1952. Landlords enjoyed virtually complete autarchy even in instances where the production did not make them wealthy in any absolute terms. The landed elite in the highlands tended to pride themselves, whether realistically or not, on their pure white heritage and to look down on the native population as somewhat less than human. The 5 percent of landowners that controlled over 90 percent of the cultivable land—in a country where agriculture was the overwhelmingly predominant occupation—also obviously enjoyed considerable wealth and power, even if only in a relative and local sense.

There was a similarly striking contrast between the dominant few and the subordinate majority in the eastern lowlands, although the population there tended to be more nearly homogeneous in physical terms. During pre-Columbian times, the sparse population of the eastern lowlands were scattered in small autonomous bands, with no political integration. Even the famous Jesuit experiment in founding communal republics did not endure, and an unknown number of groups managed to survive by retreating deeper into the forests, where they are only now being exterminated or absorbed as market-oriented farmers and cattle ranchers steadily expand the frontiers of settlement. A racially mixed population has flourished in those frontier areas where only a few Europeans lived in close and sustained proximity with native peoples.

There are few countries in the world that have had a more consistent heritage of conflict than Bolivia. The Inca Empire itself was polarized by contenders to the throne when a small band of conquistadores invaded from the north in 1532. Shortly after their victory over the Incas, the Spanish leaders began to disagree, and fights between factions were commonplace. In the eighteenth century, a series of native leaders rallied the Indians to fight for restoration of the glorious Inca past. Although such revolts recurred throughout the highlands, they tended to be short-lived and uncoordinated. The war of independence from Spain involved episodic and sometimes fierce fighting from 1806 through 1815, and resulted in greater autonomy for the local Spanish-speaking elite but little change in the lives of the native population.

Throughout the turbulent republican era, Bolivia has been racked by internal conflicts, and it has had protracted boundary disputes with Chile, Argentina, Brazil, and Paraguay. In each instance Bolivia has lost territory, until it is now landlocked and only half as large as it was at independence.

Bolivia's internal political history has been similarly tempestuous. The Presidents, officially elected for 4 years, have averaged less than half that time in office, not even counting the many occasions in which a military junta intervened. However, many of

The unpaved roadway and open sewage are in sharp contrast to the modern appearance of the buildings in a slum district in La Paz. (Photo: United Nations/Rothstein.)

the shifts of chief executives were not revolutionary, in the sense of involving major change. Many of them might be characterized as palace revolts, involving little more than a change in the composition of the guard and the passing of the presidential sash from one crony to another, with virtually no impact on the people outside the small ruling circle.

Beginning in 1952, there was a different kind of revolution. A few days of bloody fighting toppled a military junta and brought the Nationalist Revolutionary Movement (MNR) to power. But the event was not so important as the process that followed; this was a revolution that changed the social order by instituting significant shifts in the distribution of wealth and power. The MNR was a loose coalition of vaguely populist interests, but it quickly implemented a series of important changes that were nationalistic and revolutionary.

Universal suffrage was enacted, broadening the electorate from less than 10 percent to the entire adult population. At the same time, the MNR set out to undercut the opposition and to consolidate its own position in the countryside. The armed forces were virtually stripped, and their weapons given to peasants "for the defense of the revolution." Significant discounts on staples were given to friends of the party, and efforts to organize local groups of peasants as *sindicatos* were effective, as a means of implementing land reform and as channels for political patronage and support.

Agrarian reform resulted in the expropriation of many large estates, and the land was reallocated among peasants who had been virtual serfs. Although there were exceptions to the rules and occasional abuses, the land reform was important. In a very real sense, it broke the back of the old social order by dispossessing those landlords who had kept quasi-feudal haciendas and by freeing peasants from the virtually total domination of their landlords. Many peasants wound up with no more land than they had been able to use before. But the psychological impact of having title has been cumulatively significant. Peasants were no longer subject to the supervision and myriad nonagricultural duties that landlords previously exacted; they were able to participate freely in the market, both with their labor and with their produce.

Nationalization of the major tin mines was symbolically important in dispossessing the tin barons, three corporate giants that had long dominated the national economy. After nationalization, however, profits did not accrue to the people; the mines were in poor condition, the world market fell abruptly, mismanagement was rife, and the mines became a sort of white elephant. Runaway inflation consumed whatever savings may have been held by the middle or upper classes; the exchange rate went from 90 bolivianos per US$1 in April 1952 to 18,500 bolivianos per US$1 in December 1956 before a stringent program of monetary stabilization was effected in December 1956 under pressure from the United States.

Educational reform was intended to bring schooling and to open new opportunities for the rural masses. Although it has accomplished far less than was originally hoped, it is a significant improvement over pre-revolutionary education. Schooling is normally free and compulsory for grades 1 through 6, but many children do not attend.

The MNR maintained power for more than 12 years—a record in Bolivian history—and brought some kinds of development that had long been anticipated. With large-scale economic and technical aid from other countries, the eastern lowlands, a promising frontier area for agricultural development, have been partially settled by migrants from the overpopulated highlands and by immigrants. Instead of spending precious foreign exchange on the importation of such basic foodstuffs as rice and sugar, the country is now not only self-sufficient but is also an exporter of foodstuffs. The same is true of petroleum and natural gas. With improved technology and changing world prices, it is now economically feasible to work tin, tungsten, and silver deposits that had been marginal or worse.

It would be wrong to attribute all these changes to the MNR (nor did the MNR introduce a period of widespread affluence, participant democracy, and ethnic equality). A succession of anti-MNR governments, few of them elected and most dominated by the military, have exercised uneasy control over the country since the MNR was ousted in 1964. Despite dire predictions, reactionary politicians did not undo the populist programs.

Presidential elections, which had been periodically scheduled and postponed during the years of military domination, were finally held in mid-1979. When no candidate won the requisite majority, Congress chose Walter Guevara Arze of the MNR to serve as President for a year. He was subsequently overthrown by a military contingent, and on November 16, 1979, Congress elected Lidia Gueiler Tejada as acting President until elections could be held. After the election of 1980, a military junta again took over and named General Luis Garcia Meza as President. All opposition was quickly suppressed.

During this one hundredth anniversary of the War of the Pacific, Bolivian saber rattling appeared to be trying to persuade Chile to return the "corridor to the sea" that left Bolivia landlocked; the two countries have not yet resumed diplomatic relations more than a decade after they broke them, ostensibly over diversion of the Lauca River.

Although Bolivia's standard of living has improved greatly, it remains one of the least developed and poorest countries in the Western hemisphere. The totalitarian suppression of dissent, the electoral manipulation, and other abuses make life difficult for the opposition at the same time that many supporters are making small but important gains. And economic and ethnic inequality continues, with many old prejudices still alive.

But progress is inherently relative. Thus a few old

Bolivian hands, who remember when the per capita annual income was less than $100 (1964) and when Indian serfs could be sold or rented as part of the realty, marvel at how rapidly development has occurred, while newcomers are equally impressed by the abysmal poverty and the workaday difficulties in the lives of most Bolivians.

Although highland Indians are increasingly involved in political and economic systems that link their interests with those of the nation, lowland tribes have been increasingly displaced or exterminated. Improved means of transportation and communication have brought innovations to remote areas, so that the equivalent of two or three centuries of material progress have been experienced within the span of one lifetime. Nevertheless, a pervasive attitude of distrust of outsiders is persistent and often, in fact, realistic. Participant democracy on a broad basis cannot thrive in this context. The organizational and administrative skills necessary for economic growth are in short supply, and political and social insecurity create a climate that is inimical to many kinds of investments.

It appears likely that a small group of cosmopolitan Bolivians (less than 5 percent)—different from those of the pre-1952 landed gentry—will continue to monopolize wealth and power, while the peasant majority (more than 70 percent) savor gains that are minimal in worldwide perspective.   *Dwight B. Heath*

Brazil

(Federative Republic of Brazil)

Area: 3,290,000 sq mi (8,521,100 sq km)
Population: 119.4 million
   Density: 36 per sq mi (14 per sq km)
   Growth rate: 2.9% (1970–1977)
Percent of population under 14 years of age: 42% (1975)
Infant deaths per 1,000 live births: not available
Life expectancy at birth: 61.4 years (1975)
Leading causes of death: cardiovascular ailments, cancer, parasitic diseases, malnutrition
Ethnic composition: white (European); African; mixed; Indian; Japanese
Languages: Portuguese (official)
Literacy: 70% (1977)
Religions: predominantly Roman Catholic
Percent population urban: 56% (1970 census)
Percent population rural: 44% (1970 census)
Gross national product: $187.1 billion
   Per capita GNP: $1,570
   Per capita GNP growth rate: 6.7% (1970–1977)
Inflation rate: 40.8% (1978)

Brazil is the fifth largest nation in the world, and its diversity is almost as great as its resources. In recent years, Brazil's economic growth has pushed it to potential superpower status in the third world. Yet that development has also resulted in severe problems in politics, social conditions, and domestic and international economies. Brazil's continued dependence on foreign oil will limit its rate of economic growth for some time, and its industrial growth cannot continue without the transnational subsidiaries. It may become less dependent on foreign technology, but it still needs foreign markets for manufactures, since local markets are limited by the low income level of most of the populace.

Brazil is a land of considerable contrast in physical and human geography. Its nearly 3.3 million square miles (8.5 million sq km) include rain forests and deserts, cool mountains and steamy lowlands, lush prairies and near-sterile savannas. Soil types range from extremely fertile, as in the coffee and sugar lands, to lateritic clays, which yield little once they have been stripped of vegetation. Landforms are relatively low-relief, with no high mountains, many rolling hills, vast floodplains, and many tablelands. The climate ranges from extremely humid and warm in the Amazon Basin, to dry and hot in the northeast, to temperate in the south. As a result, virtually all types of vegetation zones, except alpine, are found.

Natural resources are plentiful. The Amazonian forests have yielded vast amounts of lumber and extensive mineral deposits, including bauxite, manganese, and iron. Elsewhere there are huge pine forests, now largely felled, coal deposits, and other industrial minerals, as well as the many varieties of precious stones for which Brazil has long been famous. Oil reserves have not been discovered in any quantity, although exploration is constantly encouraged. Hydroelectric power is being developed, and the Paraná River dams under construction will greatly increase electrical output.

One of the problems facing economic planners is resource distribution and ownership. Exploitation of the huge deposits of iron, oil, and manganese is handled through foreign companies in cooperation with the federal government, which doubles bureaucratic red tape and lowers efficiency. Water, which is overabundant in the north, is scarce in many parts of the country, and in some areas, land control is realistically reckoned in terms of control of water rather than control of the land itself.

Land ownership is grossly unbalanced. A few families or individuals own most of the arable lands, while the great majority of farmers own less than 10 hectares (24.7 acres) apiece. There is a serious problem of contested titles because of the parallel registration of titles at the state and national level; thus ownership, especially of small holdings in densely populated areas, is often in jeopardy. As a result, there is some reluctance to improve property because of the possibility of eviction. Inheritance patterns also pose a problem because of the tendency to fragment holdings that are already uneconomically small.

A rich mixture of cultures, Brazil is a multiethnic country with every possible combination of Indian, European, and African peoples. In the north and west the mix is predominantly European and Indian, while the northeast coast, where slavery was most common, is primarily African. The southeast and south are predominantly European, with strong elements of Italian and German as well as Portuguese and Spanish.

Diversity is evident in language, dress, food, social custom, and religion. Although Brazil is basically a Roman Catholic country, all religions are practiced freely, and a substantial body of popular Indian beliefs and lore exist side by side with the Catholic observances. The growing influence of the African religions, or *umbanda* cults, have long enjoyed a limited popularity in the coastal northeast, but their acceptance is now spreading. Many Brazilians practice both Catholicism and one of the African cults with little apparent contradiction.

Portuguese, the official language, is thoroughly interlaced with many African and Indian words, and African and Indian influences are also visible in food and its preparation, and in costume.

Family ties are strong, with relatively little alienation of youth or isolation of elders. The extended

These slum dwellings have been constructed on a garbage dump outside the city of Bahia. Because of overcrowding in the cities, many urban poor live in shantytown slums. (Photo: United Nations/ T. Teuscher.)

family still exists, particularly in rural areas, but the nuclear family is more common. Families are patriarchal, and women are expected to play a subservient role. There is a strong sense of community in the rural village or town or the urban district. At the national level, flag-waving patriotism and national pride are unabashedly visible.

Brazil is almost two countries: rural and underdeveloped (44 percent); and urban and developed (56 percent), and rural existence is dramatically different from the urban experience. Rural environments range from isolated homesteads along rivers and roads to rural towns with populations of 500 to 2,000. In the family, the sexual division of labor is traditional; women work in the household, tend gardens and family, and do some marketing and selling of surpluses. Men work in the fields, in the transportation and selling of the cash crop, and as day laborers. Illiteracy is high (26 percent) in rural areas because of the shortage and understaffing of schools. Religion and tradition play strong roles in the rural family.

There is a clear gulf between the rich and poor in rural areas. Rural farmers range from sharecroppers, day laborers, and tenant farmers to small independent farmers and members of agricultural cooperatives. Most small farmers have a cash crop or outside activity to provide cash income beyond the subsistence level.

Among the rural elite (the large landowners) there is a strong tradition of political bossism, *coronelismo*, with roots in patron-peon relationships. Closely intermarried and bound by ties of kinship and common interest, the elite families control the rural vote; in return for this the state and federal governments (with which they have strong connections) allow them to run local affairs as they wish. The elites are conservative in values, religion, and attitudes toward land, labor, and social class.

Both traditional and modernized agriculture exist; 38 percent of the land is devoted to agriculture. Most subsistence farmers rely on traditional slash-and-burn methods and casual pasturage of animals. Because of infertile soil and poverty, modern methods are too costly and complex in most of the rural sector. In the south, however, large ranchers and farmers who can afford change are interested in improved breeds of cattle, new high-yield crops, and better fertilizers, although there is little interest in agricultural mechanization because of the low cost of rural labor.

Modernization through the market economy has made little headway against traditional institutions. Rural areas remain poor, with an increasingly large gap between large landholders and small farmers. Government attempts to open new areas to colonization, primarily in Amazonia, have been resounding failures because of faulty infrastructure and inadequate budgets. Irrigation has not solved problems of droughts in the northeast. Producer cooperatives have enjoyed only modest success except where they are controlled by large landowners, as in the case of coffee. Subsistence agriculture with cash cropping on a small scale remains the dominant form of tenure, existing alongside extensive grazing and large holdings of export crops such as coffee, sugar, soya, and rice. Most rural workers live in a credit economy in which they constantly mortgage next year's crop for this year's expenses, a practice which keeps the rural sector underdeveloped and poverty-stricken.

Rural health care is marginal at best, and there are very few doctors in the interior. The government-operated social security system usually has offices in the municipio seats, but they are rarely properly equipped. Medication is relatively easy to obtain, but it is expensive. Malaria and worm infestations exist everywhere, and tuberculosis and respiratory, skin, and gastrointestinal ailments are endemic. The birth rate is high in rural areas, but because of unhealthy conditions, the death rate is also high, which limits population growth.

Rural areas are closely linked to each other and to the cities. The highway system has had high priority in government budgets, and most major highways are now paved, with good interconnections. Bus transportation is plentiful and relatively cheap, although the energy crunch is pushing up prices. Because of limited track mileage and different gauges, the little used railroads remain the least-developed sector in transportation. Along the Amazon, most travel is by boat, and most people live along various rivers or along the Trans-Amazon and Belém-Brasilia highways. Air travel is well developed but is financially out of reach of most rural people.

In terms of society, economy, and politics, Brazilian urban existence differs markedly from that in the agrarian sector. The distribution of urban population is still uneven. Most Brazilians live in the south and southeast, where the cities of Rio de Janeiro and São Paulo contain approximately 4.9 and 7.2 million people respectively. With the exception of Brasilia, located in the arid interior, with a population of some 241,000, and Belo Horizonte, with a population of about 1 million, Brazil's larger cities are located along the coast; Salvador (1.2 million), Recife (1.2 million), Fortaleza (1.1 million), Porto Alegre (1 million), Belém (771,000), and Santos (345,000). The coastal settlement in Brazil is a heritage of the colonial era, when little attempt was made to develop and populate the interior.

In the cities, the nuclear family predominates, particularly among the middle class; although there are extended family ties, they are not so strong as they are in rural areas in the interior. Working-class women nearly always work outside the home in menial occupations, and women also fill many white-collar jobs, particularly in the lower ranks of the government bureaucracy. In general, however, males control decision-making jobs in all sectors.

The observance of religion is much more complex in the city than in the countryside, because many non-Catholic religions, ranging from the umbanda cults to many Protestant sects, have attracted large followings. Umbanda has become fashionable among the middle and upper classes, and many people practice both Christian and non-Christian religions.

Economic opportunities vary considerably in the city. The individual is generally locked into a particular socioeconomic class at birth, and except among the higher social ranks there is relatively little social or economic mobility. Underemployment is common, especially among manual laborers and petty bureaucrats. Minimum wages are low, forcing women and children to work for subsistence wages. Middle-class youths, who can afford a technical education in private schools and universities, have good job opportunities. Government-controlled education produces a small technocratic elite and a large semi-skilled and unskilled labor force.

Urban class divisions are complex and highly visible. The middle class is fragmented, with the lower levels closely associated with the workers and the upper echelons aspiring to elite status. The urban poor and working class live in shantytown slums, where lighting, sanitation, and housing are inadequate, while upper-middle-class people live in high-rent districts and spend ostentatiously. Such wide disparities are caused by the unequal distribution of wealth.

The military government has exerted strong pressure for industrialization, often couched in terms of national pride. Industries range from steel production to the manufacture of consumer durables to other light industries. Brazil is a growing exporter of manufactures, as well as processed raw materials, with an annual growth rate of from 3 to 10 percent. Since most oil is imported, the major limiting factor is en-

A huge container holds liquefied steel at a government-owned steel mill at Cubatão. (Photo: United Nations/ T. Sennett.)

ergy, and so there is active involvement in a series of nuclear power projects and hydroelectric plants. Some industries are dominated by a few "founding families," such as the Hering family in textiles. Most factories, large businesses, and other investments are controlled by the educated, upper middle class, through outright ownership, kinship, or shareholding. Many small businesses are run by individual middle-class families, but these frequently lead a precarious economic life. Labor relations are strained but are usually quiet because of the ban on strikes and labor activity.

Health care and medical facilities are generally better in urban areas than in the countryside. Water is potable in large cities, although sanitation quality is uneven. Intestinal and respiratory diseases, caused by overcrowding and poor sanitation, are widespread, and in recent years there have been epidemics of measles and meningitis. There are many private clinics and doctors, but most are beyond the reach of the working class, which depends on public health facilities. The social security service maintains clinics, pharmacies, and hospitals, but is underbudgeted, overbureaucratized, and inefficiently cumbersome.

The urban death rate, especially among young children, is somewhat lower than it is in rural areas, and the birthrate remains very high, causing slow but steady growth. The great boost to the urban population comes from the flood of rural immigrants, especially young working-class people, that swells the urban population, straining transportation, marketing, health care, and housing. The urban population grew 14 percent in the period 1960 to 1970, and there is no sign that this explosive population growth will soon come to an end.

Brazilian responses to the pressures of moderniza-

tion and industrialization will continue to be influenced by Brazil's long history as a colony and by the domination of her politics by a small plutocracy. As a colony of Portugal for 300 years, Brazil's primary function was to produce sugar, gold, and diamonds for the European market. Coastal Brazil was oriented toward Europe, with an export crop economy and a society that tried to copy everything European. Interior Brazil was based on subsistence agriculture, oriented around a frontier existence; society in the interior was based on the extended family, and those who lived in the interior did not concern themselves with outside matters. Thus, from the very beginning, there have been "two Brazils;" both continue to exist, although their composition has changed.

After obtaining political independence from Portugal in 1822, Brazil changed economic masters. British investment dominated and tightly controlled the Brazilian economy until World War I. Brazil's colonial status meant that it was forced to continue in the role of an exporter of raw materials, while remaining a lucrative field for foreign investment; this retarded Brazil's ability to develop an independent economy. Following World War I the government promoted an economic philosophy that encouraged import substitution industries, and at present Brazil is making headway in the development of heavy industry, local industries, and domestic marketing networks. However, promises of total economic independence are unrealistic.

Since World War II, United States investment has dominated the Brazilian economy, primarily through transnational corporations. Thus, once again, Brazil has changed foreign masters. At the same time, it has embarked on a form of colonialism inside the nation. Brazilian capital from São Paulo and other industrial centers is being channeled into investment in the less-developed parts of the country. These areas, most notably the Amazon Basin and the central west, now serve as the economic colonies of the developed south. Vast sums of money are invested in various agricultural and industrial projects, and profits return to the south.

Since independence, Brazilian politics continues to be dominated by a plutocracy, which has changed in composition since independence but has not relinquished control. Nineteenth-century politics were dominated by the rural bosses in a two-party system, and there was little substantive disagreement over most issues. The great majority of people were denied the vote because of literacy or property restrictions, or their preferences were predetermined for them by local political bosses. Even the military coup in 1898 that ended the empire and set up a republic did nothing to change the basic political structure, which was controlled by economic elites, most notably the coffee planters of the south. The brief existence of the old republic from 1898 to 1930 saw only semantic changes in politics.

The populist Getúlio Vargas, who took power in

Farm laborers pack peanuts. Brazil aims to reduce its dependence on coffee exports and food imports. (Photo: United Nations/J. Frank.)

1930 and ruled as dictator until 1945, recognized some of the aspirations of the lower and middle classes. During the Vargas years, there was considerable government interest in labor and social welfare legislation, but most tangible benefits went to the middle class. In an atmosphere of economic expansion, the middle class began the first strong push for industrialization which finally wrested economic and political control from the rural sector and deposited it firmly in the cities.

In the decade after Vargas's death in 1954, a new economic elite emerged: the upper middle class. As its economic power grew, it exerted an increasingly powerful influence on politics. When the military decided to seize the government in 1964 most of the new elite supported the move. The military desired to stem the growing pressures for social and economic change, such as land reform. The coup brought to an end to all progress in the areas of labor and land reform and social legislation, and marked the end of the recognition of Brazil's huge working class as a legitimate interest group.

Since 1964, the political framework has remained intact, with a President, a bicameral Congress, and a two-party system; however these structures are superficial because the military holds all political power. Both government parties are approved by the military, and attempts to create a meaningful opposition party have been crushed. The President is a military man, chosen by his predecessors with the approval of the Chiefs of Staff and then by plebiscite. The Congress is controlled, silenced, and rigged. It is subject to strong censorship, purges, and occasional closures, so that open opposition to government policies is impossible.

The military has systematically eliminated dissidents, labor leaders, professors, and others who dare to oppose the regime. There is considerable evidence of gross violations of human rights, and dissenters are still imprisoned for political viewpoints. Active civilian participation is confined to the upper middle class; although everyone is supposed to vote, elections are notable for their tight control and lack of issues. In general, business has supported most government policies, since they keep labor costs low, production high, and inflation nearly under control. There is little promise of extensive change in government policies in the near future. The hard-line generals apparently remain in the political front lines, and, although the current government is slowly and cautiously moving toward greater civilian participation in politics, there is no sign that the military intends to relinquish any substantial control to civilians.

The economic and social philosophy of the current regime centers on development, to which all else is sacrificed. The Brazilian military is determined to make Brazil the next world economic superpower. In the meantime, little attention is paid to critical domestic issues, like overpopulation, low-income housing, minimum wages, improved health care, labor relations, or land reform. The military will continue to emphasize corporate development at the expense of personal liberties. Government policy will continue to benefit industrialists, bankers, and exporters, but will do little or nothing for workers, small farmers, and white-collar personnel.

The government is making a conscious effort to reduce dependence on foreign technology. Brazil has traditionally depended heavily on foreign aid, technology, and outright investment, and the move to reduce that dependence has grown in strength and popularity since World War I. British and American capital and know-how, which provided the basis for development in Brazil, now competes directly with expertise and investment from countries such as West Germany and Japan, and with local entrepreneurs. Direct foreign aid from the United States has been generous, but has lessened somewhat since the 1977 cutoff of military aid in response to violations of human rights, an action that reinforced the military's insistence on economic independence.

Efforts to block foreign goods by extremely high import duties, forcing all but the most wealthy to purchase Brazilian-made goods, have had considerable success. Restrictions on outward capital flow through tourism or the direct export of profits have also helped to channel money into the economy. Brazil does not want to cut itself off from all foreign technology, but is searching for it more broadly, using competition between countries to secure the best deal.

Political, social, and, above all, economic development in Brazil has been uneven. Industry is booming, road building and colonization plans abound, investment opportunities are limitless, and military strength is increasing. Yet between 65 and 70 percent of the population exist at subsistence level, and the real income of workers has dropped 35 percent since 1960. If achievement is to be measured in terms of the popular desire for a living wage, decent housing and working conditions, and human rights and dignity, then Brazil has a very long road ahead.

Robin L. Anderson

Chile
(Republic of Chile)

Area: 292,258 sq mi (756,945 sq km)
Population: 10.7 million
  Density: 37 per sq mi (14 per sq km)
  Growth rate: 1.7% (1970–1977)
Percent of population under 14 years of age: 36% (1975)
Infant deaths per 1,000 live births: 56
Life expectancy at birth: 62.6 years (1978)
Leading causes of death: same as U.S.
Ethnic composition: mixed European and Indian 66%
  (est.); European; Indian
Languages: Spanish
Literacy: 89%
Religions: Roman Catholic 80%
Percent population urban: 83% (1978)
Percent population rural: 17% (1977)
Gross national product: $15.2 billion
  Per capita GNP: $1,410
  Per capita GNP growth rate: −1.8% (1970–1977)
Inflation rate: 70% (1978 est.)

Chile, one of the smaller countries of Latin America, has a long and honorable history of freedom. For more than four decades Chile provided its neighbors with a rare example of a working democracy. But small countries do not necessarily have small problems, nor is their influence limited by their size. A land of earthquakes, Chile has given its inhabitants an ironic sense of impending cataclysm. They experienced cataclysm in their recent political past, when, with a sudden upheaval, everything was changed.

Since the military coup d'etat of September 11, 1973, put an end to Chile's constitutional democracy, Chileans have suffered acute social, economic, and political crises. Their main discontent revolves around political violence and economic policy, both of which have drastically affected huge segments of the population. A profound unease has gripped Chileans, both rulers and ruled, in recent years.

Often referred to as an island, this long and narrow ribbon of land, stretching 2,630 miles (4,233 km) from Arica to Cape Horn, is surrounded by formidable natural boundaries that make communication with the outside world difficult by land or sea. A deep and cold Pacific Ocean lies to the west; in contrast on the east are the towering Andes, which reach altitudes of 22,516 feet (6,863 m) near the capital city of Santiago. Isolating Chile from world centers of commerce, culture, and power, these imposing natural boundaries give Chileans a sense of isolation that intensifies their personal and political introspection and conflict.

Of Chile's total area, 7.6 percent is arable, and 6 percent is actually cultivated. The country is bordered on the north by Peru; on the east by Bolivia and Argentina [with the latter it shares an often disputed boundary 2,000 miles (3,220 km) long]; on the south by the Drake Passage, including a small Atlantic seaboard; and on the west by the ocean.

This long stretch of territory, which, if laid across the map of the United States, would run from New York almost to San Francisco, is divided latitudinally by climate into three main regions. The northern third is one of the driest deserts on earth. Chile's desert is rugged, parched, and forbidding, but is rich in mineral resources, the backbone of the Chilean economy. At the far south are the wet southlands, with dense forests, snowcapped peaks, and beautiful lakes; this terrain is broken by the invading sea that forms a lacework of fjords and islands. Chile's forests are too cold and damp even for the hardiest humans, but the forests' resources of lumber and coal are beginning to bolster the Chilean economy significantly. Central Chile is a beautiful area, made up of a narrow strip that does not exceed 45 miles (72 km) in width, and carved by many small rivers and by two large Andean rivers, the Bío-Bío and the Maule. This densely populated area is covered with green pastures and growing crops, and is bordered by graceful rows of pines, poplars, eucalypti, and weeping willows.

All three regions contribute to the country's development. Northern Chile has valuable nitrates and copper. From the second half of the nineteenth century to World War I, when synthetic nitrate was first introduced, the exploitation of the nitrate beds was the prime source of Chilean wealth. Subsequently, Chile was forced to find a substitute export, and copper became—and still is—its most important form of export wealth.

Southern Chile supports a sheep-raising industry in its northerly reaches and in the city of Punta Arenas, the southernmost city in the world. The most important economic development of the land is lumbering, but little of the commercially usable timber is accessible because of Chile's limited road network. The forests also contain considerable deposits of coal, though not of the highest grade. The major problem is the long distance from the coalfields to the nation's industrial centers.

Central Chile, with a climate and topography similar to that of northern California, is the heart of the country. Like California, this area is occasionally plagued by long droughts, but natural precipitation and water from the Andes usually provide an abundant water supply.

The agricultural economy that the conquerors and their successors established in this region changed little until recent years. With time, the list of products lengthened, as vegetable, fruits, and wine grapes joined the older staples of meat and grain. The inefficient system of *latifundia*, or mammoth estates, owned by absentee landlords, run by unambitious overseers, and worked by poor tenant farmers lasted until 1970, when socialist President Salvador Allende

Gossens (1970–1973), continuing the agrarian reform begun by his predecessor, Eduardo Frei Montalva (1964–1970), upset this structure of land tenure.

Before World War I, Chile imported sugar, cotton, tea, coffee, and edible fats, but produced almost all its own food. After World War I, industrialization and urbanization reduced Chilean agrarian activity, and today it is a net importer of foodstuff. Among Chile's principal imports are crude petroleum, machinery, motor vehicles, wheat, and coffee. Its principal exports are copper, which accounts for two-thirds of all exports and constitutes about 78 percent of Chile's foreign exchange; wine, which accounts for 12 percent of the foreign exchange; and, in order of importance, iron ore, fish meal, nitrate, beans, and iodine.

Unlike most Latin American countries, Chile has a predominantly industrial economy. Since World War II, the iron and steel industry at Huachipato, near Concepción, has developed rapidly, and the country is almost self-sufficient in coal production. Petroleum production has developed chiefly since 1945 in Tierra del Fuego, and today Chile produces 25 percent of its oil needs. The increased use of hydroelectric power has helped to expand manufacturing in leather, textiles, and rubber.

In 1979, the labor force numbered 3 million, including more than half a million women. Of those 3 million, 19 percent were employed in agriculture, 20 percent in manufacturing, 9 percent in transportation, and 7 percent in mining. Approximately half a million were white-collar workers.

Chileans are remarkably homogeneous. An estimated two-thirds of Chile's population are of mixed European and Indian (predominantly Araucanian) blood. The slow, consistent amalgamation of diverse European groups with Amerindians has produced a highly uniform culture. Since the last century, only a trickle of new people have moved across mountains, desert, and sea into the central region. Today, less than 2 percent of the population is foreign-born.

The highly patriarchal family life in Chile is similar to that of other Latin countries. Among the lower segments of society, poverty exerts an overriding influence on family structure. Some 8 out of 10 workers do not earn enough to support a family. Poverty leads to broken homes, illegitimate births, and abandoned children.

Women always enjoyed a high degree of independence in Chile, and during the Allende government they became highly organized. Today, they participate in public life, trade, and professions. Lower-class women usually have clerical jobs, while middle- or upper-class women attend universities and pursue teaching and other professional careers.

Illiteracy is relatively low in Chile and is estimated to be 11 percent. Until the 1973 coup, education was quite adequate, especially in institutions of higher learning, but today the universities are controlled by the military and have become subservient.

Of all Chileans, 80 percent are nominally Roman Catholic. Because all political parties have been dissolved, the Catholic church is Chile's strongest institutional bridge to social progress.

Since 1920, the transformation of Chilean life has been reflected in the growth of urban centers. When the tenant farmer is jarred loose from the estate on which his ancestors worked, he comes to the city looking for work. If he does not find it (which is often the case), he looks around for a place where he and his family can live. He becomes a *roto*—literally "broken," "torn," or "tattered"—and he goes to live in the *poblaciones callampas,* the urban slums, referred to as mushroom communities because of the rapidity with which they grow. Other urban poor live in tenements called *conventillos,* "little convents," whose rooms are strung together under one roof. It is estimated that about one-fifth of all Chileans live in the urban slums.

The rural poor are called *inquilinos,* or tenant farmers. They perform menial farm tasks for an average wage of $1 a day, and, in spite of their poverty, they are reluctant to leave. There are also migrant farmers, *afuerinos,* or outsiders. They are paid higher wages than the tenant farmers, but their lot is no better. In Chile, one out of every four workers is employed on a farm.

About one-fifth of all Chilean workers have white-collar or professional occupations and work in Chile's principal industrial cities: Santiago (population 3 million); Valparaíso, the country's largest port (600,000);

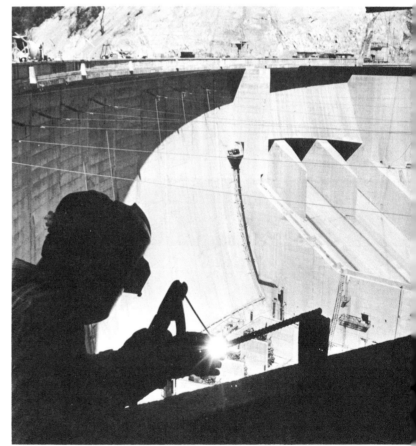

The Rapel Dam built in the 1970s on the Rapel River about 75 miles (121 km) southwest of Santiago, provides hydroelectric power. (Photo: International Bank for Reconstruction and Development/ Paul Conklin.)

Concepción, Chile's most industrial city (300,000); and Valdivia, the site of new manufacturing industry (100,000). The rest are farmers, fishermen, miners, skilled and unskilled workers, and servants.

There is very little social movement from lower-class to middle-class status, and even though some skilled workers (*obreros*) earn more money than some white-collar employees (*empleados*), they regard their status and their lifestyles to be inferior. No such sharp division separates upper-middle-class professionals from aristocratic landowners or wealthy industrialists and merchants.

In 1964, and again more emphatically in 1970, Chile began political processes to change the economic structure of the country and to bring social justice to the nation. The Christian Democratic government of Eduardo Frei, and, later, the Socialist government of Salvador Allende embarked on a program of reforms that attempted to undo a system in which 5 percent of the families controlled 35 percent of the agricultural land; 90 percent of Chilean copper was owned mainly by two U.S. firms (Kennecott and Anaconda); the banks worked for the established rich; and industry underproduced products that were overpriced.

Allende's transition to socialism angered the oligarchy, the coalition of big business and big landowners that also had opposed Frei. Subsequently, the army abandoned its neutrality and decided to intervene. The result was a violent coup d'etat, with the force of an earthquake, which toppled Chile's social, political, and economic structures.

Laborers work in a field on a modern truck farm in Valparaíso Province. (Photo: FAO/Peyton Johnson.)

The intensity of the military coup astonished most Chileans, who had believed in the neutrality of the armed forces. Traditionally, the military had always seemed institutionally loyal; it overthrew the government only twice in its history. In 1891, the military overthrew reformist President José Manuel Balmaceda, and in 1973, it overthrew Allende. Both times the military sided with the oligarchy. Balmaceda was driven to suicide for refusing to deliver the nitrate riches to foreign companies. Allende was murdered after he nationalized the copper mines. There is evidence that in both cases the oligarchy incited the army to intervene, and that in both cases foreign interests (the English companies in Balmaceda's time, U.S. companies in Allende's time), played decisive roles.

The death of Balmaceda rescued the landed aristocracy and the nitrate barons, and opened the way to foreign exploitation of Chilean copper; thus Kennecott was allowed to work its El Teniente mine from 1906 to 1930 without paying taxes. When Allende took office, U.S. corporations had $1 billion invested in Chile's three largest mines located at Chuquicamata, in the Atacama desert; Sewell, near Rancagua; and Potrerillos, near Chañaral. Their annual profits were estimated at about $500 million, of which $200 million was repatriated.

Allende's economic policies sought to establish national control over the basic means of production, to increase industrial and agricultural activities, and to redistribute Chile's wealth more equitably. These policies threatened not only a small privileged class, but most of the middle class and even some working-class groups that were relatively comfortable in an economy of scarce resources. Food shortages, economic sabotage from abroad, the failure to win the support of the peasantry, and crippling strikes in transportation and in the mines undermined Allende's programs and contributed to his downfall.

The junta led by General Augusto Pinochet Ugarte followed economic policies designed to reverse the direction taken by the Allende regime. By freeing prices while holding down wages, the junta almost completely eliminated the benefits won by the workers.

The government claims that its monetary policies are successful, citing an increase in the cost of living of 37.7 percent for the 12-month period ending in August 1978, compared to 79.9 percent for the previous 12 months; a decrease in the unemployment rate from 16 to 12 percent; and a decrease in the inflation rate from 70 percent to around 25 percent. Agricultural production for the period from 1973 to 1976 was up 6.7 percent, compared with a rise of 4.6 percent during the 3-year (1970–1973) experiment with Marxism.

The government also asserts that by 1983 the economy will be sound, and makes the following predictions: (1) the gross domestic product (GDP) will grow at an annual rate of 7 percent while internal savings will reach 15 percent of the GDP, which will mean a return to pre-1970 interest rates; (2) inflation will probably be kept at 15 percent a year; (3) the unemployment rate should be no higher than 7 percent; (4) the private sector share in total investment should rise from the present 45 percent to 55 percent; and (5) cuts will continue to be made in state spending, which should fall from 27 percent of the current GDP to 22 percent in 1983.

However, neither skillful manipulation of statistics nor optimistic predictions can hide the fact that the government's policies have benefited only a small segment of society. The extent to which its economic objectives can be reached will depend, in large measure, on whether political variables remain constant. President Pinochet's promise that the military will run the country until 1991 has elicited critical statements by political leaders, trade unionists, and church figures. More than 5 years of harsh military rule have failed to eliminate the traditional democratic idealism that has molded Chilean political life since independence.

Chile's economic development must be correlated with political freedom. With 11 out of 25 heads of families jobless, and more than 400,000 unemployed, there have been powerful demonstrations of worker discontent. The regime's violations of human rights have isolated it and have led the international community to reject the government. Unless the government gains a significant degree of popular support, it is difficult to see how its monetarist policies can help it on the road to development.

Salvatore Bizzarro

Colombia

(Republic of Colombia)

Area: 440,000 sq mi (1,139,594 sq km)
Population: 25.1 million
   Density: 57 per sq mi (22 per sq km)
   Growth rate: 2.1% (1970–1977)
Percent of population under 14 years of age: 46% (1975)
Infant deaths per 1,000 live births: 97 (1975)
Life expectancy at birth: 60.9 years (1975)
Leading causes of death: not available
Ethnic composition: mestizo 75%; European 20%; African 3%; Indian 2%
Languages: Spanish
Literacy: 73%
Religions: Roman Catholic
Percent population urban: 65%
Percent population rural: 35%
Gross national product: $21.8 billion
   Per capita GNP: $870
   Per capita GNP growth rate: 3.8% (1970–1977)
Inflation rate: 15–30%

The chief determinants of Colombian development are the Spanish cultural heritage that shaped institutions and attitudes for more than 300 years, the international economic system through which Colombia traditionally exchanged its raw materials for costly manufactured goods produced by more industrially advanced nations, and the mountainous terrain that made communication difficult and economic development slow. This trinity of cultural, economic, and geographic factors combined to shape Colombia's present-day reality.

The mountains that have so hindered economic development and national integration also make Colombia one of Latin America's most beautiful nations. From its southern border with Ecuador, three emerald green, forested cordilleras branch from the Andean massif and run northward in parallel ranges that comprise nearly 40 percent of the national territory. More than half the population live in and among these mountain regions. The Central Cordillera is the loftiest of the three cordilleras, with numerous peaks above 19,685 feet (6,000 m), many of them snow-capped year-round. Both the Central and Western Cordilleras end in marshy lowlands on the side of the Caribbean coast, while the Eastern range extends on into Venezuela.

High in the Eastern Cordillera lie several fertile, densely populated intermountain valleys. These were

Coffee beans are picked on a coffee plantation in Colombia. Colombia is the second largest exporter of coffee in the world. (Photo: United Nations/ J. Frank.)

centers of the Chibcha Indian civilization in pre-Columbian times, and are heavily populated today. Bogotá, the national capital, is located in one of these highland valleys. Colombia's two most important rivers, the Cauca and the Magdalena, flow through valleys lying on either side of the Central Cordillera. The Cauca and Magdalena valleys are significant population areas where mechanized commercial farming methods prevail.

Surrounding the mountainous heartland of Colombia are four other geographic regions. Beyond the Western Cordillera are the humid, marshy Pacific lowlands. In the north are the more extensive Atlantic lowlands. East of the mountains is a vast but sparsely populated region made up of rolling grasslands in the north and jungles of the Amazon Basin in the south. Only one in ten Colombians live in these grassland-jungle territories that together occupy more than half the national domain.

Colombia's rugged terrain has not been an entirely negative force in national development. Of Latin America's coal reserves, 64 percent, are found in mountains of the Eastern and Central Cordilleras, and the mountains hold great hydroelectric potential. In the first 7 years of the 1970s, Colombia doubled its hydroelectric generating capacity through an extensive dam-building program. Nickel and natural gas are also present in sizable amounts, and it is believed that Colombia possesses significant untapped oil reserves.

Climate in Colombia is also determined by the mountains. As one moves into cordilleras from tropical lowlands, the temperature decreases, giving highland towns and cities eternally springlike, even chilly, weather year-round. Because of its proximity to the equator, there is very little seasonal variation in Colombia.

Most Colombians are of mixed ancestry. Some 75 percent of the population are considered mestizo, the descendants of European-Indian unions, although there are also admixtures of blacks, particularly in lowland Colombia. Another 20 percent are of European descent, 3 percent are of African ancestry, and 2 percent are Indians. These proportions are only approximate, because Colombia's racial composition continues to change and the mestizo component tends to increase. The mestizo and white populations are evenly distributed throughout the nation except along the Caribbean and Pacific coasts, where blacks and mulattoes are in the majority. Indian tribes are settled on government-protected reservation lands.

Colombia's social structure is broadly determined by the Mediterranean ethos brought by the Spanish conquistadores who settled the land in the seventeenth century. The society they established was Roman Catholic. It was characterized by hierarchy and sharp caste distinctions, as exemplified by the family, Colombia's elemental social institution. The typical family is extended and male-dominated. The wife controls matters of the home but stands below her husband in the hierarchy that extends down through younger family members and thence to servants and others dependent on the family. Important families have traditionally wielded great influence both regionally and nationally. Colombians who combined leadership ability with high social status and landed or other wealth formed the nation's political elite. Underneath them all others were bound into a complex system of dependence. The society that emerged was inegalitarian, hierarchical, and paternalistic, with corporate overtones.

While this social system was constantly modified, its basic structure was retained. When European liberal ideals of individual freedom and egalitarianism

These children in Cartagena are suffering from malnutrition. Most Colombians suffer from the effects of poor diet. (Photo: United Nations/ P. Griffing.)

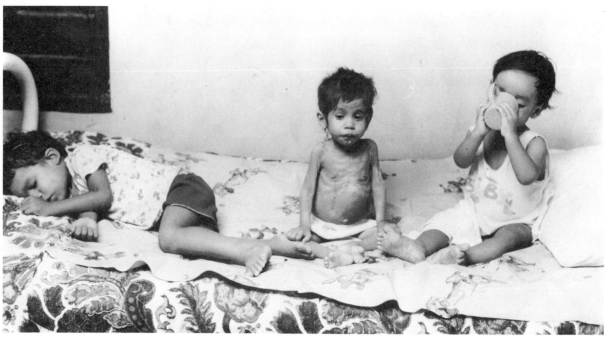

under constitutional government swept Colombia in the nineteenth century, they were adopted by the elite, but in a way that the underlying structure of society remained unchanged. Likewise, although modernization brought social inequities into sharper relief during the twentieth century, the sociopolitical system maintained its traditional inegalitarianism without serious challenge.

Until very recent times Colombia was a predominantly rural nation known chiefly for the production and export of coffee, of which it remains the world's second greatest supplier. While rapid urbanization and economic diversification are changing its one-crop, rural image, the agrarian past and present are very important in national life. More than half the work force are engaged in agricultural and livestock production. In addition to coffee, Colombia produces cotton, rice, sugarcane, corn, beef, dairy products, fruits, and vegetables. Foreign exchange earned through the sale of nontraditional agricultural exports fluctuates between 10 and 15 percent of the total, while coffee accounts for about 50 percent of all exports.

Although it is not recognized in official economic data, marijuana rivals coffee as an earner of foreign exchange. An estimated 10,000 Colombians furtively cultivate and market marijuana, and some 150,000 are said to be economically dependent upon its trade. Annual revenue from the smuggled commodity surpassed $1 billion in the late 1970s, compared with $1.5 billion earned by coffee in 1977.

Whether a Colombian farmer uses traditional or modern agricultural methods depends in large part on his economic resources. Poor farmers typically employ animal power and primitive implements, while the operators of large, often corporately owned, commercial farms use the most modern techniques and machinery.

Landownership is uneven in Colombia; between 20 and 30 percent of the agricultural population own no land whatsoever. Of those who own land, 10 percent possess 80 percent of the total. The poorest 50 percent own only 3 percent of the total. This image of inequality is modified somewhat by the fact that 8 acres (3.2 ha) planted in coffee may be sufficient to support a rural family. More than 25 percent (300, 000) of all Colombian farmers are coffee growers, and a substantial majority own farms in the small to intermediate category. In many of the largest landholdings the soil is of poor quality and therefore productivity is limited.

Nonetheless, in Colombia agricultural property is concentrated in relatively few hands, and many small and landless farmers live in poverty. Inequities in land tenure appear to be growing. The number of farms in Colombia decreased from 1.21 million in 1960 to 1.18 million in 1970. A much-heralded agrarian reform program launched in the 1960s has not met with notable success. This is reflected in heavy migration out of rural areas, particularly by the marginal population. More women migrate than men; many of them find domestic employment in towns and cities. Thus, there are slightly more males than females in rural Colombia. The rural population is also younger on average than the population of urban areas, because many heads of households travel to the cities in search of more remunerative work, leaving their families in the countryside.

At least half the rural Colombians—one-fourth of the total population—live in subhuman conditions. In the countryside 4 out of 10 people are chronically ill, a condition aggravated by inadequate caloric intake and poor dietary habits. In some areas, 1,600 or fewer calories are consumed daily, far below the national daily average of 2,200 calories. Dietary insufficiencies are aggravated by the traditional Colombian preference for starches instead of fruits and vegetables. Although an estimated 73 percent of the population over age 15 are literate, educational opportunities are limited for the less affluent. In the 1970s, 40 percent of rural and 20 percent of urban primary-school-age children did not attend school.

The disadvantaged rural class becomes urbanized through a process of "step migration," called so because rural migrants tend to move from rural areas to nearby towns, then to provincial cities, and, finally, to the nation's largest urban centers. Colombia has no great city that overshadows all others. Rather, it is a nation of cities with 3—Bogotá, Medellín, and Cali—that surpass 1 million in population; 8 others with more than 200,000 residents; and 10 more with populations greater than 100,000.

By the end of the 1970s more than 65 percent of Colombia's 25 million people lived in urban areas;

A young girl studies by candlelight in the village of Taguales which, like many villages in Colombia, lacks electricity. (Photo: United Nations/ D. Mangurian.)

this is an approximate reversal of the urban-rural ratio prevailing 20 years earlier, when the population totaled only 11 million. Many who flooded into towns and cities arrived without funds and with little training for the work they hoped to find. They contributed to the persistent, high unemployment rate. Unemployment coupled with inflation, which fluctuates between 15 and 30 percent annually, were Colombia's greatest producers of social tension. Never under 10 percent, unemployment has run at times to 20 percent of the work force.

These problems have been aggravated by a very high rate of population growth founded in high birthrates and a steady increase in the life expectancy of Colombians. The birthrate was 41 per 1,000 in the 1960s, a time when more than 50 percent of the population were under the age of 20. However, this trend changed during the following decade. It is estimated that the birthrate fell to 31 per 1,000 during the 1970s. Another factor easing population pressure has been a heavy, usually clandestine migration to neighboring Venezuela.

Rapid urbanization has had a profound impact on all sectors of Colombian society. The pressures of city life have weakened the traditional family, although the extended family continues to be the norm. Related families frequently live in close proximity in urban neighborhoods, and employment is often secured through family contacts. The slums surrounding towns and cities are extensive, and one-fourth of all urban housing is substandard. Colombian slums are not static, however, but are often stopping places for upwardly mobile migrants from the countryside.

The mushrooming of urban Colombia had led to the growth of a large, vocal proletariat. Populist political movements have swept the nation twice since the mid-twentieth century, the first in the late 1940s and the second in the late 1960s and early 1970s. Neither succeeded in toppling the government, but they seriously troubled the nation's leadership elite. These movements called attention to the plight of the disadvantaged and pressured for reform of a system that allocates 60 percent of the national income to 20 percent of the population and only 9 percent to the bottom 40 percent.

Thanks in part to the pressure brought to bear by the urban masses, the state has expanded welfare services. A majority of the urban population are covered by a social security system funded in large part by government and industry. Although the network of social welfare programs is continually expanding, it tends to bypass the rural population.

This ever-expanding welfare function of the Colombian state is supplanting many of the services traditionally provided by the Roman Catholic church. However, the church is still an important adjunct in the area of public welfare. In addition to attending the spiritual needs of the people, it keeps parish records and administers its own social programs. Increasing secularism and the rationalization of society have hardly lessened the attachment of Colombians to the Catholic church. Protestant sects have long proselytized, but have only succeeded in converting less than 1 percent of the people.

Expansion in the mining, construction, and manufacturing industries may relieve the strain created by Colombia's long-standing social problems. Gross domestic product increased at an annual rate of 7 percent during the late 1970s, and government policy stresses the regional diversification of industry to lessen overcrowding in the nation's largest cities. Today, Colombia produces most of its own nondurable goods and is increasing its manufacture of durable and capital goods. However, the production and processing of foods and beverages continues to make up the larger part of manufacturing.

Industrial exports are increasing and diversifying. Textiles, refined petroleum products, machinery, chemicals, animal hides, and leather goods are important nontraditional exports. Colombia has a large, modern textile industry, and nearly one-third of its production is exported. Most Colombian exports are sold in West Europe and in North America, and a majority of imports come from the same regions.

Colombian industry is heavily monopolized, a trend that has increased in recent years. The rapid growth of conglomerates in the late 1970s has been hotly debated in government circles and elsewhere, leading to demands for closer regulation of transactions on the national stock exchange. Sources of credit, both public and private, are closely controlled by the government. Colombia's persistent and high inflation (more than 30 percent annually at the end of the 1970s) makes credit difficult to secure.

Recent government policy has stimulated economic development, but has also increased the concentration of wealth in a few hands and widened the gap between rich and poor. While economic growth has resulted in the expansion of the middle class (now estimated at around one-fourth of the total population), the middle class is beleaguered by the high inflation that is part of the overall development process.

Colombia's history has had a strong influence on its social and economic structures. It inherited an inegalitarian society and a capitalistic economic system that tended to aid the privileged at the expense of the less fortunate. Until the development of the interventionist state of modern times, the only mechanisms that softened economic and social disparities were the traditional paternalism and the benefits accruing to membership in the corporately constituted groups in society. Social and economic inequalities are doubly hard to change because of Colombia's unfavorable position in the world economic system. That is, Colombia has traditionally been an exporter of raw materials and an importer of manufactured goods. Much of its recent economic progress—for example the striking increase in hydroelectric generating capacity—has led to growing indebtedness to foreign lending institutions. Mitigating Colombia's ongoing economic dependence upon other nations, is the fact that foreign investment has never been great in Colombia and the fact the import substitution has moved apace in recent years.

Since the mid-nineteenth century, constitutional democracy and a two-party system have prevailed in Colombia. Colombians traditionally claimed allegiance to one or the other multiclass parties that replicate in their structure the hierarchial nature of society at large. Colombian's allegiance to their parties runs so deep that national history has been repeatedly marred by partisan conflict. The most recent breakdown of two-party government led to the Violencia, an undeclared civil war that claimed 200,000 lives over a 20-year period beginning in 1948. In spite of periodic partisan feuding, the political system has continued with little change. For good or ill it has lent stability to Colombian society.

Though it is slow and imperfect, the developmentalist strategy of the Colombian state has kept revolutionary social protest to a minimum. The predominantly rural Violencia played an oddly conservatizing role in setting Colombia on its present course. That conflict, lasting until the mid-1960s, quickened the pace of state-directed social reform; at the same time it dampened popular desire for radical social action. Still, popular malaise runs at high levels; there are periodic strikes by industrial and agricultural workers, and sporadic terrorist acts on the part of small guerrilla groups.

Colombia is a traditional but dynamic society that will probably maintain the status quo. Its stability is rooted in popular acceptance of a traditional social system that is regarded as preferable to other ways of organizing national life, although the system's flaws are noted. Barring unforeseen catastrophic social dislocation at the international or domestic levels, the process of development should continue to move ahead in Colombia.

James D. Henderson

Ecuador

(Republic of Ecuador)

Area: 104,506 sq mi (270,669 sq km)
Population: 7.6 million
  Density: 72 per sq mi (28 per sq km)
  Growth rate: 3.0% (1970–1977)
Percent of population under 14 years of age: 46%
Infant deaths per 1,000 live births: 70 (1975)
Life expectancy at birth: 59.6 years (1975), (WB)
Leading causes of death: not available
Ethnic composition: Indian 40%; mixed Indian-Spanish
  (mestizo) 40%; Spanish (white) 10%; black 10%
Languages: Spanish (official); Quechua; Shuar; other
Literacy: 68%
Religions: Roman Catholic, Protestant, other
Percent population urban: not available
Percent population rural: not available
Gross national product: $6.9 billion
  Per capita GNP: $910
  Per capita GNP growth rate: 6.1% (1970–1977)
Inflation rate: 15%

Ecuador enjoys both the divergence and blend of Native American, African, and European cultural traditions. Within the past decade it has changed drastically from a country relying on an agrarian economy to an oil-rich, industrializing nation. Dependency on foreign capital, imports, and economic demands characterizes Ecuador's development. With a growth rate of 3.5 percent, its population will double in 22 years. As this expansion of mostly poor people presses extant resources, national dependency on oil revenues will increase greatly. Yet the nation's output of oil is relatively small, and it may have to import petroleum in the 1980s.

Ecuador's territory, which is about the size of Oregon, encompasses extraordinarily diverse maritime, Andean, and upper Amazonian ecosystems. A popular political slogan often emblazoned on government stationery proclaims that "Ecuador has been, is and will be, the Amazonian Country!" The cry follows from the loss of Amazonian territory to foreign nations, which has reduced Ecuador by nearly 75 percent over the past two centuries. It lost half its remaining Amazonian territory, including navigable rivers entering the Amazon River, after Peru's invasion of 1941. Although Brazil took the side of Ecuador, Peru prevailed with the aid of the United States.

Peru lies to Ecuador's southeast, and Colombia to the north. The country is bisected from north to south by two cordilleras of the Andes, where habitable zones from 6,000 to 12,000 feet (1,800 to 3,600 m) high are punctuated by majestic volcanic peaks 15,000 to 20,000 feet (4,500 to 6,000 m) high, eight of them perpetually snowcapped. This is the Sierra; its population of about 3.36 million constitutes 48 percent of the nation's 7 million people, only about 40 percent of whom live in urban sectors.

East of the Sierra is the Oriente, the Amazonian lowlands, and to the Sierra's west is the Litoral, or coast. The Galápagos Islands are 600 miles (965.4 km) away in the Pacific, and Ecuador reckons its sovereign 200-mile (321.8-km) fishing territory from these Pacific islands, as well as from the mainland. Much of the topography of the Oriente resembles the Great Smoky Mountains, and the Litoral is, in many areas, reminiscent in terrain of the Sierra Nevada of California. Some 3.43 million people, 49 percent of Ecuador's population, live west of the Sierra—about 43 percent in urban zones; and 3 percent live in the Oriente.

Sparse in population and low in its agricultural and industrial contribution to the gross national product, the Oriente is the wellspring for Ecuadorian economic development. Oil was discovered there in the 1930s, reexploration took place in the 1960s, and pumping from the Oriente across the Andes to the coastal port of Esmeraldas began in 1972. In 1973, Ecuador became the twelfth member of the Organization of Petroleum Exporting Countries (OPEC).

Ecuador's capital, Quito, situated in a green valley 9,000 feet (2,700 km) high between the cordilleras, is a city of well over 600,000 people. Once a pre-Incaic coordinating hub of trade and agriculture, Quito became the northern capital of the Inca Empire; it had a central *audiencia* (court) under Spanish colonial rule. Since 1830, it has been the national capital. Historically, Quito derived its power from access to Oriente and Litoral resources and from control over rich, varied foodstuffs and other Sierran resources.

Until the mid-1960s, Quito was a town with a charming blend of colonial and modern architecture washed in a perpetually springlike climate. Today, the colonial center is in the throes of urban renewal; the periphery is undergoing massive expansion and construction, and the atmosphere is often shrouded in dust and diesel fumes. But despite modernization, Quito remains a bastion of conservatism and Catholicism.

Guayaquil, the sprawling Pacific port on the turbid Guayas River, contrasts sharply with Quito. The largest city in Ecuador, with a population of around 1 million, Guayaquil is the locus of commerce, bank-ing, industry, and agribusiness. Guayaquil is an open, secular, boisterous, and achievement-oriented city. Its pre-Columbian maritime economy was transformed in response to colonial shipping requirements, making its economy dependent upon international demand for raw materials, such as balsa, kapok, quinine, cotton, and rubber; and foodstuffs, such as cacao, coffee, rice, and bananas. As the metropolitan basis for coastal power, Guayaquil serves as an ecological and economic counterpoint to Quito and as a challenge to Quito's conservatism and Catholicism.

Until the undulating oil pipeline, 318 miles (512 km) long, fueled its nation's economy, Quito's economic power was dependent upon coastal shipping and agribusiness, which, in turn, were partially dependent upon world demand for a few tropical products. Now Quito's economic power, derived from Amazonian sources, equals or exceeds that of Guayaquil. But this new Quiteño power depends largely on the high energy consumption and industrial demands of the most developed nations. Dependency is as visible in the major towns of the Litoral (Esmeraldas, Santo Domingo, Quevedo, Manta, Machala), as it is in the Sierra (Ibarra, Latacunga, Ambato, Riobamba, Cuenca and Loja) or the Oriente (Puyo, Coca).

Ecuador is determined to channel soaring petroleum revenues into the development of roads, air transportation, and hydroelectric projects, in order to provide a base for the foreign development of products, like pharmaceuticals, refined petroleum products, and petrochemicals. Although the government took strong nationalist measures to protect its oil deposits and territorial waters, it has been reluctant to exclude foreigners from industry and agribusiness. In reaction to increased dependency on products produced outside of Ecuador, even the strictures on oil exploration and exploitation and on tuna fishing have been recently eased.

In Ecuador, European, African, and Native American people mingled genetically over four centuries to produce a mestizo nation. But much of Ecuador's population is still characterized by three primary "races"—white, black, and Indian. Today, whites, the bearers of "civilization, urbanism, and Christianity," rule the national, regional, and local hierarchies. Other "mixed" and "pure" races constitute the ethnic segments from the middle of the hierarchy (white and mestizo) to the bottom of the hierarchy (Indians, blacks, and other mixed groups). Yet there is an increasing number of fairly well-to-do, well-educated native peoples who maintain their customs of dress and speech.

Among the republic's major ethnic groups, blacks inhabit some lowland and highland settings; Quechua-speaking indigenous peoples live throughout the Sierra; native peoples speaking Quechua, Shuar, and other languages live in the eastern rain forests; and Chibchan-speaking peoples live in the western rain forests. Other so-called mixed racial groups are characterized according to the regions from which they

Passengers crowd on a bus in a small village between Esmeraldas and La Tola. (Photo: United Nations/A. Jongen.)

come, the Spanish dialect spoken, phenotypic features, family relations, and economic standing.

Spanish, the national language, is spoken very differently in different regions, ethnic groups, and socioeconomic classes. Quechua is also spoken by indigenous groups and by some mixed racial groups throughout the Sierra, in much of the Oriente, and in some areas of the Litoral. But the Ministry of Education does not recognize Quechua as a second language, even though it supports bilingual schools. There is also a creole language that comprises a Spanish vocabulary and a Quechua grammar. The Cayapa, Tsatchela (Colorado), and Coaiquer of western Pichincha and Esmeraldas speak dialects of the Barbacoan division of Chibchan languages, as well as Spanish; some of these peoples also speak other indigenous languages. In the Oriente, the spread of Quechua is nearly matched by the Shuar language, to which it is not related. Other languages are spoken there, including Cofán, Waorani Auca, Zaparoan, and Siona-Secoya. Bilingualism and multilingualism are also fairly common. Indigenous people have no term in their own language even remotely resembling "Indian" or "indio."

The prehistory of Ecuador has been completely rewritten thanks to the discovery of pre-Incaic archaeological art in the Litoral, Sierra, and Oriente. Intensive farming, permanent villages, and ceramics date back over 5,000 years in the Guayas Basin of coastal Ecuador and constitute a formative culture spanning Sierra and Oriente. This formative phase of indigenous development occurred in coastal Ecuador over 1,000 years earlier than similar manifestations in Mexico and Guatemala and in Peru and Bolivia. Indigenous Ecuadorian culture apparently stimulated the growth of high civilizations in Ecuador's north and south. Thousands of years later in the fifteenth century, Ecuador became part of the Inca Empire. In the early sixteenth century, the Spaniards took over the Incaic bureaucracy and assumed tenuous control.

Rebellious Afro-American peoples began their own conquest of the rain forest of the Esmeraldas province in the sixteenth century. The Kingdom of Quito became a royal *audiencia* of the Spanish Crown in 1563, and was forced to become an ally of the rulers of the Zambo (black-Indian) Republic. To the Amazonian east, sovereign territory was maintained by Shuar and other Native American peoples. The 300-year colonial era imposed a caste system and introduced new crops and animals (especially sheep) from the Old World. Through it all there were uprisings and revolutions.

In 1822, Ecuador joined the confederation of Gran Colombia (with Colombia and Venezuela) and became an independent nation 7 years later. Its political pendulum swung first to a conservative-Catholic alliance linked to the Sierra, so that the power of the white elite would be protected against the more liberal army. But as conservatism reigned, liberalism strengthened. Civil war broke out in the late nineteenth century, and the political pendulum swung to the left. Meanwhile capital from North America, Britain, and France aided economic development. A rightist swing in the early twentieth century caused yet another civil war, and around 1912 Esmeraldas reentered the national political arena when the former Zambo Republic became the bastion of liberalism, supported by military guerrilla resistance forces.

The great haciendas, or landed estates, have exerted tremendous political force throughout Ecuador's history. The landholding role and the concomitant power of the Catholic church were seriously undermined in the early twentieth century by state expropriation; thereafter church domination was mostly at the parish level. The redistribution of private and state haciendas began after 1964, with the formation of the Institute of Agrarian Reform and Colonization. In this reorganization, the state for the most part changed state haciendas into cooperatives, where previously "bound" peasants were allowed to lay claim to unused or underutilized land. On the private haciendas, such bound peasants were often given no more than formal title to their traditional meager holdings.

Massive colonization into the Oriente (often onto lands of indigenous people) and some coastal sectors (onto lands of indigenous and black people in the north) was encouraged; agribusiness and cattle ranching were promoted through new systems of bank loans and business incentives. But colonization became little more than an escape valve for landless peasants, and the oligarchy maintained economic control.

A man inspects a newly dug irrigation ditch in Milagro. This is part of a development project that will provide irrigation for 825 farms and will benefit 6,000 farmers and their families. (Photo: World Bank/Edwin G. Huffman.)

Today, Ecuador is ruled by a wealthy, powerful, Christian, white, and generally conservative oligarchy, including many who have economic interests outside the country. The oligarchy's ability to control activities that direct the flow of industry, agribusiness, and commercial fishing exceeds the power or the leverage of any political party or coalition of parties. Economic transformations brought about by the petroleum boom are producing tremendous class, status, and lifestyle cleavages between rich and poor. The present and potential role of the largely white and mestizo middle sector remains problematic. The political economy is extending and recreating great social and economic schisms.

In the recent past Ecuadorian politics oscillated between elections that featured several parties (with great internal dissension) and military takeovers. Within this oscillation, Presidents are usually deposed by military coups before they complete an elected term. With military rule, dictators may be ousted by a junta's coup, or a junta may be forced out of office by a dictator before free elections are restored. The caudillo, a charismatic leader with the ability to gain the support of opposing factions, is the acknowledged antithesis of the corporate military figure. On August 10, 1979, after 9 years of military rule the pendulum swung back to elected-civilian rule with the election to the presidency of populist Jaime Roldós Aguilera.

Political fluctuations at national, regional, or local levels may produce changes in personnel in provincial, canton, and parish structures; political parties are involved in these changes even when no election is held or when the country is under military rule. The structure of local and regional political economy appears to depend on networks of individuals who manipulate economic, social, ethnic, family, and kinship ties to maintain strong footholds in contending political groups. There are also cooperatives formed for colonization, and *comunas* (communes) that are ostensibly self-governing units under either de jure or de facto control of a parish or canton. Periodically, the military may also take over control of any of these systems.

Students and their political movements sometimes seem to trigger a coup or countercoup. Truckers' unions provide the ultimate power potential for radical military intervention because of their ability to paralyze the country during a general or regional transportation strike.

Despite endemic unrest, the ruling oligarchy maintains and profits from Ecuador's dependency on the industrial demands of other nations. Developers and planners struggling to effect rapid economic growth are unable to harmonize international industrial requirements with regional and local ecologies. In regions where resources like oil, land for agribusiness, and timber, are sought by foreign and national interests, strategies of development are based on the ideology of North American industry rather than on the ecological needs of Ecuador. In the tropical forest ecosystems, the arid coastal monsoon ecosystems, and the various Andean ecosystems, indigenous ways of ecosystem maintenance are more successful than the techniques recommended by specialists from industrial nations who train Ecuadorian planners. These indigenous systems, which include mixed-multicrop-shifting horticulture, ridged field cultivation, terracing transhumance, and the vertical exploitation of different ecosystems, irrigation, and crop rotation, are generally and erroneously viewed as archaic remnants of the colonial era.

The boom-and-bust quality of Ecuador's economy was based on cacao and then bananas, until the petroleum boom of the 1960s. Between 1972 and 1976 the gross national product rose 400 percent; and per capita income a little more than doubled during that period. Current inflation is 15 percent per year. Despite imported luxury and consumer goods for the rich, subsistence agriculture is as important now for the poor as it was in the recent past. While they are drawn into the vortex of dependency on cash for minimal well-being, poor people often have difficulty purchasing basic foodstuffs.

Today, although the oligarchy stays strong, dependence increases, and the poor remain poor. But a new ideology of development is being expressed by President Roldós, who has made public promises of respect for the various cultures and countercultures in this nation. These cultures are becoming increasingly visible as they cope with dependency processes imposed by a world where high levels of energy are consumed. Whether or not the promise is fulfilled remains to be seen. In the meanwhile oil is running out.

Norman E. Whitten, Jr.

Paraguay
(Republic of Paraguay)

Area: 157,047 sq mi (406,750 sq km)
Population: 2.9 million
  Density: 18 per sq mi (7 per sq km)
  Growth rate: 2.9% (1970–1977)
Percent of population under 14 years of age: 45% (1975)
Infant deaths per 1,000 live births: 84 (1975)
Life expectancy at birth: 62 years (1975)
Leading causes of death: not available
Ethnic composition: mixed Spanish and Indian 95%
Languages: Spanish, Guaraní
Literacy: 66–80% (est.)
Religions: Roman Catholic
Percent population urban: not available
Percent population rural: not available
Gross national product: $2.5 billion
  Per capita GNP: $850
  Per capita GNP growth rate: 4.3% (1970–1977)
Inflation rate: 12.8% (1970–1977)

Paraguay remains distinctive among South American nations; its landlocked isolation, lack of important, exportable natural resources, and huge losses of wealth and workers in two wars have combined to block economic progress and maintain a rural way of life reminiscent of the eighteenth century.

The semitropical country is divided by the Rio Paraguay (Paraguay River) into two strikingly different physiographic provinces. The little-developed, sparsely populated western portion of the country is known as the Gran Chaco, a giant basin rising from the littoral of the Paraguay River, past the Bolivian border, to the foothills of the Andes. The Paraguayan portion of the Chaco encompasses 95,338 square miles (246,925 sq km), or 60 percent of Paraguay's total land area, but has a population of only 94,111 (1970 census), 3.9 percent of the nation's total. The area is marked by extremes of temperature and rainfall. In winter it can be characterized as a huge swamp; in summer, as a scrubby desert with temperatures of 110°F (43°C). The low population density of the Chaco [about 2 square miles (5 sq km) per person] is attributable to frequent and severe droughts, poor drainage, and lack of potable water, which combine to make agriculture and cattle raising difficult or impossible.

Eastern Paraguay, the most important part of Paraguay, has 96.1 percent of the population, greater economic resources, and a preeminent place in the nation's history. Encompassing an area of 61,709 square miles (159,827 sq km), it has an environment that ranges from semihumid to tropical, many large rivers, great expanses of forest, extensive grasslands suitable for cattle raising, and rich agricultural land.

Eastern Paraguay is divided into three zones. The Paraguay River valley is the most densely populated area, including more than 60 percent of the nation's population; the capital, Asunción (population 420,165), is also located there. Its rich land and abundant water sources make this area the most agriculturally productive region of the nation. The Central Plateau is the second most populous subregion of Paraguay, with 22.2 percent of the population. Because of its elevation, the climate is moderate, favoring the production of coffee, rubber, vanilla, and cacao. Its natural forests contain many valuable plants, such as the famous yerba maté used for making a tealike drink, hardwoods for logging, and various species of palm that are exploited for fiber and oil. Extensive deposits of kaolin clay used in making brick and ceramics are found along the banks of the Rio Tobatiry.

The Alto Paraná River valley, comprising 9 percent of the national territory and 11 percent of its population, is subject to fewer seasonal climatic changes than other parts of the nation and has abundant rainfall and dense forests. Despite the vast agricultural potential of the area, it is little-developed. The completion of the Itaipú dam near the Guaitá Falls on the Paraná River for the production of hydroelectric power, in collaboration with neighboring Brazil, will transform the nation in the next few years.

Paraguay is the only truly bilingual nation in South America; Spanish and the Guaraní Indian language are both official languages. Some 45 percent of the population speak only Guaraní, 49 percent are bilingual in Spanish and Guaraní, and 6 percent speak Spanish only.

Because Guaraní is used extensively in everyday life, especially in rural areas, some observers assume that Guaraní Indian culture pervades the national character. In reality, the Paraguayans are typical South American mestizo peasants and retain very little of their aboriginal character; only about 3 percent of the population are Indian. However, the Guaraní language and nation have implications that are exploited by the government to maintain Paraguay's distinctiveness. (The President frequently addresses the nation in Guaraní).

The pure Indian population is almost entirely concentrated in the vast Gran Chaco, isolating it from the rest of the population. Many Indian societies, like the Moro (Ayoreo), Mbya, Aché-Guayakí, and Chamakoko, are among the most primitive people in the world and make their living primarily by hunting and gathering. They are visited only infrequently by missionaries or other Paraguayans; thus, some of these people flee or react hostilely to strangers, remembering incidents of murder or maltreatment. The only Indians outside the Gran Chaco are the Aché-Guayakí of the Alto Paraná; and they are rapidly being exterminated or enslaved by the local non-Indian population.

Roman Catholicism is Paraguay's official religion, but religious freedom is guaranteed. In the colonial period, Catholicism was more influential. Today, it plays a minor role, especially in the larger cities and among the upper classes. Church attendance is low by Catholic standards, and nearly all churchgoers are women. The peasants view the church and the priests with much more respect than do urban people, but the peasants are primarily interested in religion as magic to cure illness and bring luck.

Aside from the capital, Asunción, with approximately 36 percent of the nation's population, only three cities (Encarnación, Concepción, and Villarrica) have population in excess of 18,000. Asunción, which was established in 1637, is the center of the governmental, economic, and social life of the nation. Of all freight entering and leaving the country, 75 percent is handled through Asunción's harbor on the Paraguay River. About 75 percent of the nation's industrial production is centered in Asunción or in the Greater Asunción area.

The heavily centralized government is dictatorial. Administratively, Paraguay is organized into a series of departments of varying sizes that function like states in a federal union. The larger towns and villages serve as centers for smaller rural villages (compañías), where the bulk of the nation's population live, having only infrequent and sporadic contact with the towns.

A typical rural Paraguayan family lives in a small house with a thatched roof of palm fronds, mud or wood-stake walls, and an earthen floor. Most families are nuclear; extended-family groupings are infrequent. Peasant farms are usually 17 to 37 acres (7 to 15 hectares) in size with no more than 5 to 10 acres (2 to 4 hectares) under cultivation at any one time.

Most rural Paraguayans are subsistence farmers, practicing a primitive form of pre-Columbian horticulture known as shifting cultivation. Plots are cre-

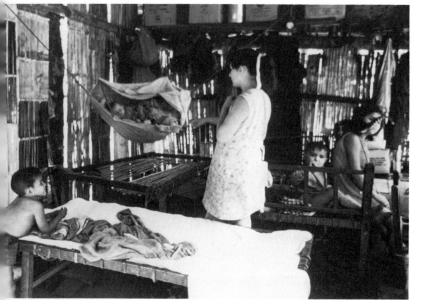

A mother tends the youngest of her eight children in their crowded living quarters. (Photo: United Nations/ Karen Kerschen.)

ated by clearing an area of forest or scrubland with an ax and a machete and then burning the debris during the dry season. Crops, like manioc, maize, peanuts, and cowpeas, are planted in the soil that has been enriched by the ashes. After 3 to 5 years of continuous cropping, yields diminish and weeds become increasingly difficult to eradicate. When this occurs new land is cleared, the original garden is abandoned, and the process begins again.

Peasants who own oxen or can afford to rent them for plowing can crop continuously for longer periods of time, but eventually they, too, must abandon their plots. It is difficult for the rural farmer to abandon this extensive farming, because he owns only a machete, ax, and hoe for working the land; and the current economic situation provides no incentive to intensify production or to widen holdings.

Peasants market excess farm produce or grow crops like cotton, tobacco, or citrus to secure cash for buying manufactured necessities. Occasionally, a peasant is paid in cash for making tannin, logging, brickmaking, or working in other extractive or small industries. Very few Paraguayans work on large haciendas, both because the haciendas need little labor and the wages paid on them are very low, and because there is no shortage of land in Paraguay. Thus Paraguayans work outside their own farms only for specific short-term periods.

Although population density is low and the land is rich, 75 percent of all Paraguayan subsistence farmers are technically landless; they do not have title to the land they farm. Officially, all land in compañía settlements is owned by the government, and the inhabitants may buy it cheaply. In practice, however, most farmers on government land make no attempt to purchase it; government officials seldom visit the compañías and generally do not enforce the law. Even many of the largest landowners do not have title to their land and have to tolerate squatters. In reality, there is no economic incentive to gain title to land; if squatters were forced to move, they could easily find new land.

All Paraguayans are reasonably well fed, although the poorest rural populace may lack calcium, vitamin A, and riboflavin in their diets. The low consumption of milk, paradoxical in a country where cattle outnumber people by three to one, accounts for the calcium and vitamin A deficiencies. These deficiencies could also be overcome by educational programs to encourage diversification of cropping practices, particularly the production of more green leafy vegetables. The government has recently taken steps to increase milk production.

Paraguay suffers from high infant mortality and morbidity, the result of unhygienic practices, ignorance, and the lack of rural health facilities. (In rural areas there is only 1 doctor per 6,000 people.) The government must educate the rural populace in the basics of nutrition and sanitation, and should extend medical services to both rural and urban poor.

Education is compulsory and free for all children between the ages of 7 and 14. Estimates of illiteracy rates range from 20 to 34 percent. The actual rate is probably higher because 43 percent of the people have had less than 3 years of education, and in some areas 25 to 35 percent of all local government officials are functional illiterates.

Paraguay is one of the poorest nations in Latin America, with a gross national product of $2.5 billion and a per capita GNP of approximately $850. Per capita income is about $300 and in rural areas the figure is $80 or less, which indicates an insufficient commercial market for agricultural products.

Paraguay's landlocked position between Argentina and Brazil and its lack of important natural resources have been strong influences throughout its history. In 1524, the Spaniard Alex García entered Paraguay after his ship was wrecked off the Santa Catarina Island near the Brazilian coast. He explored the interiors of Brazil and Paraguay after hearing stories of Inca silver possessed by the inhabitants. Soon afterward explorers like the famous Sebastian Cabot explored the interior of Paraguay. In 1535, a full-scale expedition under Pedro de Mendoza went to the La Plata, and in 1537 a group of about 70 men pushed on to found Asunción.

The Spanish Crown soon realized that Paraguay offered little to exploit and that its landlocked position made commerce difficult; thereafter it languished as an isolated outpost of the Spanish Empire. Because of the shortage of Spanish women, soldiers and administrators freely married or held Guaraní women in concubinage (often polygynously). These unions created a mestizo people, who inherited their father's Spanish culture and their mother's Guaraní language, household customs, and dietary habits.

In 1811, Paraguay became independent, and in 1814, José Gaspar Rodríguez de Francia, known as El Supremo, assumed dictatorial powers. He expelled foreigners, closed the borders, stopping international commerce, and ended relations with the Vatican. His ruthless reign lasted until 1840.

When Carlos Antonio López succeeded Francia, the policy of self-imposed isolation was reversed. Trade and railroad communication (the first in South America) was established, roads were built, and the army was enlarged and modernized. López died in 1862, and 3 years later his son Francisco Solano López plunged the nation into war against Brazil, Argentina, and Uruguay. The War of the Triple Alliance dragged on for 5 years, taking a huge toll in lives (two-thirds of the population died or fled) and devastating farms and industry. Paraguay is still feeling the effects of that war.

For the next 60 years, Paraguay struggled to rebuild its devastated economy. In 1932, a long fermenting feud between Bolivia and Paraguay over the Gran Chaco broke into open warfare. Neither country had the resources to afford a protracted war and both were on the brink of economic collapse when a treaty was signed in 1935. Considerable political instability followed the war. Order was finally established, albeit dictatorially and repressively, in 1954, when General Alfredo Stroessner seized control of the country in a bloodless coup and had himself proclaimed President in an uncontested election.

Under President Stroessner, the Colorado Party has ruled for 25 years and the Liberal Party's political activity has been heavily restricted. The Colorado Party brooks no opposition and deals with outspoken opponents by seizing their property and by torture, imprisonment, and exile.

Autonomy for local government bodies is restricted by the centralized power structure. All local administrative officials are appointed by the Department of the Interior. The powerful autocratic regime maintains peace and political stability at the cost of political freedom.

The lack of a seaport, the absence of important natural resources, and devastating wars have hindered Paraguay's economic development. Although Paraguay is a rich agricultural land that is potentially able to export large quantities of food, its landlocked situation makes the exporting costly because large oceangoing ships cannot reach Asunción. Foreign ownership of most of the export agriculture and cattle industry is exploitative and drains the economy of the profits that should be reinvested locally. Both the economic disparity between large landowners and small-scale subsistence farmers and the absence of credit facilities for improving agricultural methods also work against the modernization of agriculture.

Workers clear land for a tobacco plantation in the San Estanislao region of Paraguay. (Photo: United Nations/Karen Kerschen.)

Approximately 43 percent of all farmland and ranchland is owned by 25 landowners; 1,526 landowners own 50.2 percent of the land; 98 percent of the population own only 6.7 percent of the land. Very little of the land owned by the largest landowners is used. Over 66 percent of the farms range from 2.5 to 18.5 acres (1 to 7.49 hectares), but a family needs 62 to 74 acres (25 to 30 hectares) to make a decent living. Because of a lack of modern methods and techniques and the high costs of imported technology (for example, there is a 50 percent tax on imported seed and insecticide), Paraguayan farmers earn about one-fifth of what the average Latin American farmer earns with the same amount of land.

With one of the lowest gross national products in Latin America, Paraguay must increase its research and development efforts, especially in its national technical schools; develop its infrastructure; and make greater efforts to process its raw export products so that it can gain higher rates of return. These efforts require large expenditures of capital, which Paraguay currently lacks. But there is a bright spot on Paraguay's horizon: the construction of the Itaipú dam on the Alto Paraná, in collaboration with Brazil. This dam will generate between 10 and 15 million kilowatt hours, more power than any other dam in the world. This has obvious implications for industrial development and rural electrification. More important, the Itaipú dam will enable Paraguay to sell power to Argentina and Brazil; this source of capital will fund internal development to move Paraguay into the twentieth century.

Elman R. Service
Raymond Hames

Peru
(Republic of Peru)

Area: **496,222 sq mi (1,285,209 sq km)**
  Population: **16.9 million**
  Density: **34 per sq mi (13 per sq km)**
Growth rate: **2.8% (1970–1977)**
Percent of population under 14 years of age: **44% (1975)**
Infant deaths per 1,000 live births: **58.2 (1970–1975)**
Life expectancy at birth: **58 years (1972)**
Leading causes of death: **not available**
Ethnic composition: **mestizo 75%; white 10–15%; Indian 10–15%**
Languages: **Spanish and Quechua (official); Aymara**
Literacy: **77% (71.6% of those over 15 years) (1972 Peruvian census)**
Religions: **Roman Catholic 96%**
Percent population urban: **60%**
Percent population rural: **40%**
Gross national product: **$12.4 billion (1976)**
  Per capita GNP: **$740**
  Per capita GNP growth rate: **1.8% (1970–1977)**
Inflation rate: **74% (1978)**

Peru is a country of dramatic contrasts: great extremes of topography and climate, an ethnically diverse population, and, unfortunately, tremendous inequities in wealth and well-being among its almost 17 million citizens. Once the heart of the ancient Inca Empire, Peru in recent years gained renown for its innovative efforts to build a modern nation.

For farmers, who comprise more than 40 percent of the labor force, Peru is a difficult place to make a living. Although Peru is nearly twice the size of Texas, less than 3 percent of the land is suitable for agriculture. Over half the population, including most farmers, live in the Andean highlands, the rugged north to south backbone that accounts for one-fourth of the nation's territory. Here, most of the land is too high or too steep for cultivation, and the sparse natural vegetation provides poor pasturage for the region's cattle, sheep, llamas, and alpacas. Many Andean croplands have inferior soils and are plagued by an austere and unpredictable climate. Flash floods punctuate long droughts, and, at the high elevation of the Andes, crop-killing frosts can strike at any time of the year. Often employing a primitive technology, most Andean farmers produce potatoes, cereals, and other vegetables for their own use or for a limited local market.

Almost 66 percent of Peru lies east of the Andes in the Amazon Basin. Because this area provides a home for only 12 percent of the country's people, Peruvian governments have long sought to colonize this zone with the surplus farmers of the Andes. However, the lush vegetation of the rain forest obscures the fact that soils in most of the region cannot support permanent cultivation.

A narrow strand of lowland separates the Andes from the Pacific Ocean to the west. This region has only 11 percent of the nation's surface, but 33 percent of the population. Although most coast dwellers earn a livelihood in urban pursuits, the region also has many farmers. The coastal lowland receives little precipitation—only 1 to 2 inches (2.5 to 3 cm) per year in most places. But some 50 streams flowing from the Andes provide water to irrigate about 2 million acres (808,000 ha) of land. Most irrigated land is controlled by large, heavily capitalized plantations that produce sugar and cotton for export and rice for domestic consumption.

In contrast to its meager agricultural resources, Peru is relatively well endowed with minerals, the nation's principal exports. The Andes yield large amounts of copper and significant quantities of iron, lead, zinc, silver, bismuth, vanadium, and gold. Oil from the north coast, adjacent offshore wells, and newly discovered deposits in the northern Amazon supply the country's modest domestic needs, leaving a small but growing surplus for export. Before ecological changes that began in 1972, Peru's cold coastal waters teemed with marine life. Tuna and other food fish were plentiful, but Peruvians specialized in harvesting tiny anchovies from which they manufactured protein-rich fish meal. In terms of the tonnage of its catch, Peru was the world's foremost fishing nation, and fish meal provided more than one-third of the country's foreign exchange.

Most of the nation's resources are concentrated in small pockets isolated from one another by great expanses of nearly lifeless desert, barren mountains, and dense jungle. At great cost, the state has provided a basic network of roads and railroads. But the country's frequent earthquakes and resulting avalanches often block these arteries.

Four major families of mankind—American Indians, whites, blacks, and Asians—have contributed to Peru's population. Today, however, most Peruvians are of mixed ancestry. The racial terms employed in Peru (except for the small groups of blacks and Asiatics) are social and cultural designations rather than biological categories. Between 10 and 15 percent of the population are classified as white—the label applied to lighter-skinned members of the upper and middle classes—but they often, in fact, have some non-European ancestors. An equal percentage of the population are monolingual Indians. Most of these generally impoverished and exploited people speak Quechua, the language of the Inca Empire, while a minority speak the Aymara tongue. Indians are often unfairly stereotyped as tradition-bound farmers who retard the nation's progress.

Mestizos, comprising 75 percent of the population, are Spanish-speaking persons of varying degrees of Indian ancestry who are accepted as participants in the dominant Hispanic culture. Peru's Iberian heritage can be seen in the Roman Catholicism of 96 percent of the population; close-knit, male-dominated families; and a constellation of values apparently inimical to the establishment of stable democratic government.

Peru's population has grown dramatically during the last four decades. Primarily because of a sharp drop in the death rate, notably among infants, average life expectancy increased from 37 to 58 years between the census of 1940 and the census of 1972. In 1972, almost half of all Peruvians were under 17 years of age. At its present rate of growth, the country's population will double by the end of the century. In 1972, less than one-third of the people lived in centers of more than 20,000 persons, but urbanization is occurring at a rapid rate. Peru's 13 cities of over 50,000 residents quadrupled in size between 1940 and 1972, a rate of increase 4 times the growth rate of the nation as a whole during that time. Internal migration ac-

counts for much of this growth. Some migrants are farmers forced from the countryside by the scarcity of land, but most of the migrants are young adults from small towns lured to the city by the hope of a better life. Many migrants have provided themselves with makeshift housing in the squatter shantytowns that ring Peru's larger cities. In 1972, almost half of Lima's 3 million people lived in these squalid settlements.

The Peruvian economy is characterized by uneven development and a high degree of external dependence. In every branch of the economy—agriculture, industry, commerce, and services—a few modern, relatively productive enterprises exist alongside many traditional, inefficient units. The modern sector employs about one-third of the labor force, but accounts for about two-thirds of the gross national product. This sector of the economy has grown rapidly in recent years, primarily through the application of an advanced technology that means that few good jobs await the 200,000 persons who enter the labor force each year. Many Peruvians, moreover, lack the skills required by modern industry.

Foreign trade is the dynamic force in the Peruvian economy. The nation obtains about one-fourth of its income directly from exports. The money earned by overseas sales enables the country to purchase many items required by Peru's modern industries, which obtain about half of their raw materials from foreign suppliers. The government derives most of its revenues from the export-led, modern sector of the economy. Unlike some of its neighbors, who rely precariously on a single commodity for their foreign

Workers clean fish in the harbor of Parachique in northern Peru. Fishing has been an important segment of Peru's economy. (Photo: United Nations/Martin Pendl.)

exchange, Peru has diversified exports: copper and other nonferrous metals, iron ore, petroleum, fish products, sugar, cotton, coffee, and wool. However, a significant, uncompensated decline in the earnings of a few key exports—as occurred in the mid-1970s—can bring severe economic and political problems.

Before 1969, overseas investors (primarily North Americans) owned most of Peru's railroads, public utilities, and mining companies; the bulk of the oil industry; and a majority of the large factories. Foreigners also had significant investments in fishing, export agriculture, and banking. Peruvians believed that their external dependency compromised the nation's sovereignty and created a distorted pattern of development that benefited only a small minority of their compatriots.

Wealth and the amenities of life are very unevenly distributed in Peru. The richest 10 percent of the population enjoy more than 50 percent of the national income, while the poorest 50 percent of Peru's citizens share only about 10 percent of the national income. Similar disparities in health, education, political power, and human dignity divide the society, like the economy, into modern and archaic sectors. This pattern of inequity is found in all regions of the country and in the cities as well as the rural areas. In general, however, the good life of modern Peru is concentrated in the urban centers, especially Lima. One-third of the population live in centers of 20,000 or more. Peru's poorest citizens are found most often in the rural areas, notably in the heavily Indian southern highlands.

In Iquitos, children play near their floating houses on the Amazon. Unsanitary conditions in these settlements threaten the residents' health. (Photo: United Nations/Martin Pendl.)

For Peru's peasants, land is of primary importance, and the uneven distribution of this scarce resource has been the keystone in an arch of socioeconomic woes. According to the 1961 agrarian census, more than 83 percent of the nation's farms were smaller than 12.5 acres (5.1 ha) and occupied only 5.5 percent of the land. Conversely, 1.3 percent of the agricultural units held 93 percent of the land. Some 1,100 estates, exceeding 42,000 acres (16,970 ha), controlled 60 percent of the land. In the Andes, most farmers owned small parcels as freeholders or members of 4,500 indigenous communities. They frequently supplemented their income by working on nearby haciendas, generally archaic estates which usually had a permanent labor force—the poorest of Peru's peasants. In return for the use of a small plot and a token cash wage, they labored as many as 5 days a week for the landowner. A master-servant relationship characterized this undemocratic society.

Many of Peru's contemporary problems are rooted in the distant past. In ancient, pre-Columbian times, succeeding waves of conquerors usurped lands from the small, relatively egalitarian farm communities that once characterized Peruvian society. The common people worked these properties for the benefit of their rulers—paying taxes in the form of labor. In the 1430s, the Incas—the last of the native conquerors—began to create their empire. Within a century this empire extended along the Andes from northern Ecuador to central Chile and included perhaps 18 million people.

Francisco Pizarro won Peru for Spain in 1532. The Spaniards built upon the exploitative apparatus fashioned by their Andean predecessors, and added a new element of oppression: an alien people who denigrated the native culture, stamping the stigma of inferiority on the Indian. Peru's independence from Spain, proclaimed in 1821, did not change the basic pattern of exploitation. The nation's heritage of conquest—its undemocratic society—prevented the development of the democratic political system prescribed by Peru's many constitutions.

During Peru's first century of independence, new avenues for social mobility were opened to some Peruvians. A series of foreign wars and endemic civil strife afforded mestizo military men opportunities to improve their status. The development of the export economy in the mid-1800s, and the onset of industrialization in the early twentieth century provided new sources of wealth and new motives for the domination of the weak by the powerful. Over the years the Peruvian elite was flexible enough to admit the new rich into its own ranks, and to accommodate some of the demands of the industrial proletariat and the salaried middle class, groups that emerged with economic diversification.

In the 1920s, reformers and revolutionaries began the struggle for fundamental change. But neither ballots nor bullets produced the basic reforms needed to create a democratic society. Peru's privileged groups tenaciously defended the old order that permitted the minority to exploit the majority.

Leaders of the developing world closely observed events in Peru during the years from 1968 to 1975. A nationalistic, reform-minded military regime under General Juan Velasco Alvarado attempted to lead the nation by force on a difficult journey toward social justice, economic development, and greater independence. The Revolutionary Government of the Armed Forces nationalized public utilities, banks, and many foreign businesses. The state assumed control over nearly all the exports and about half of the imports. A series of broad, general laws regulated major economic activities, imposed strict rules on foreign capital, and reserved key industries for development under government auspices. A system of labor communities gave workers a share of the profits and a voice in the management of the state-dominated fishing and mining industries, and provided for the gradual transformation of modern factories into cooperatives. Most important, the regime accomplished a bold agrarian reform that converted all large estates into cooperatives or distributed them among peasant communities and small freeholders.

The military regime also attacked the country's social problems. It reformed the educational system, provided low-cost medicines to the poor, and improved the national pension program. It promised women essential equality with men and, to emphasize the government's desire to uplift the Indian, proclaimed Quechua the second national language.

The regime's avowed goal was the creation of a social democracy that would be neither communist nor capitalist. The government in Lima vigorously pursued an independent foreign policy. It became a major advocate of third world interests, broadened its relations with socialist countries, and became embroiled in disputes with the United States over Peru's 200-mile (322-km) fisheries limit and over U.S. demand for compensation from Peru for expropriated businesses.

A combination of bad luck, ill-conceived and mismanaged programs, and the intractability of Peru's fundamental problems halted the revolution short of its ambitious goals. Beginning in 1972, ecological changes in Peru's coastal waters brought near collapse to the state-owned fishing industry. The regime invested heavily to expand production at the nationalized copper mines, only to suffer a sharp decline in the world price for the metal. Overly optimistic reports of vast petroleum deposits in the Amazon prompted the state to spend $1 billion on a pipeline to carry the "liquid gold" to the Pacific Coast. By 1976, when this project was completed, Peru had discovered much less oil than it had anticipated. The regime spent millions of dollars on new weapons and on office buildings for its bloated bureaucracy.

The Velasco government boasted that Peru's new plural economy eliminated the evils of both communism and capitalism. Unfortunately, the system also lacked the advantages of either the command or free market economies. The regime continued to rely on the private sector for much of the nation's capital; but, burdened by government regulations and fearful of reforms that threatened the existence of private enterprise, Peruvian and foreign businessmen sharply reduced their investments. Although the government attempted to fill this void, its domestic revenues were insufficient. Because of frosty relations with the United States, Peru was unable to obtain low-cost loans from international lending agencies dominated by Washington. Instead, Lima borrowed large sums at less favorable terms from commercial banks.

The Velasco regime made many important enemies, while gaining few sufficiently powerful or reliable friends. The ownership reforms, in the main, redistributed income within the two sectors of the nation's dual economy. The principal beneficiaries were workers in the modern enterprises, persons who already ranked among the upper quarter of Peru's income earners. Thus, the labor communities did not include the vast majority of the urban poor who earned their livelihood from small-scale commerce, handicrafts, and menial service occupations.

The transformation of the coast's modern plantations into cooperatives brought significant gains to the already privileged workers in these enterprises. But the archaic haciendas of the Andes merely became impoverished peasant cooperatives. Because of the scarcity of land, less than one-third of Peru's farmers received any benefits from the agrarian reform. The regime failed to adopt taxing, spending, and pricing policies that could have shifted income from the modern to the traditional sector of the economy.

Young boys carry maize from the fields to their home in a rural village. (Photo: United Nations/A. Jongen.)

The Velasco administration encountered the following major economic problems in 1975: a huge deficit in the nation's foreign trade, a towering international debt, and rapidly escalating unemployment and inflation. The resulting popular unrest was met by harsh repression. In August of that year, the armed forces ousted Velasco Alvarado and placed the more moderate General Francisco Morales Bermúdez in the presidency.

To gain the confidence of private investors, the new President dismantled some of Velasco's industrial reforms. The adoption of a severe austerity program enabled the government to renegotiate the foreign debt. But massive popular protests and growing dissension within the armed forces convinced the President that the time had come for a retreat to the barracks. A constituent assembly elected in July 1978 began work on a new constitution which, according to the military government, would preserve the major reforms of the Velasco years. About one-third of the assem-blymen represented parties of Peru's badly fragmented radical left, while rightist candidates won almost as many seats. The centrist American Popular Revolutionary Alliance (APRA) had 35 votes in the 100-member assembly. In the elections held in May 1980 Fernando Belaúnde Terry, founder of the Popular Action Party (AP), won 43 percent of the vote and returned to the presidency.

For several years to come, questions will be asked about the Peruvian revolution of the 1970s. What changed and how much? What remained the same and why? What were the costs? The benefits? The answers to these questions have great significance for other developing nations. Peru's future leaders face difficult tasks: the utilization of scarce resources to achieve true economic development, and the distribution of the resulting benefits among a rapidly growing population whose impoverished majority is increasingly unwilling to tolerate the gross inequities of the past.

David P. Werlich

Uruguay
(Oriental Republic of Uruguay)

Area: 72,200 sq mi (186,926 sq km)
Population: 2.9 million
  Density: 40 per sq mi (16 per sq km)
  Growth rate: 0.2% (1970–1977)
Percent of population under 14 years of age: 28% (1975)
Infant deaths per 1,000 live births: 48 (1975)
Life expectancy at birth: 69.8 years (1975)
Leading causes of death: same as U.S.
Ethnic composition: white 85–90%; mestizo 5–10%; mulatto or black 3–5% (1978)
Languages: Spanish
Literacy: 94.9% (1977)
Religions: Catholic
Percent population urban: 80.8% (1977)
Percent population rural: 19.2% (1977)
Gross national product: $4.7 billion
  Per capita GNP: $1,610
  Per capita GNP growth rate: 1.3% (1970–1977)
Inflation rate: 40% (1976)

Uruguay has had an almost unique experience with modernization; it reached a relatively high level of prosperity in the context of stable, democratic institutions and advanced public programs, only to suffer an extended period of economic stagnation and decline lasting almost 30 years. With economic decline and severe inflation came political instability, terrorism, military intervention, and ultimately military control of national, political, and governmental institutions. Uruguay's experience is unsettling for anyone who believes that modernization is irreversible, that long-established democratic traditions cannot be destroyed, and that a free-enterprise economy will respond to changing market demand.

Uruguay is small in area, not much larger than the states of North Dakota or Oklahoma, situated between Argentina and Brazil in the temperate zone of South America. It is a land of gently rolling plains with no high mountains, bordered by rivers and the Atlantic Ocean. The percentage of its arable land is one of the highest in the world. Much of the land is in pasture for sheep and cattle. The hospitable land and the available water resources help balance what Uruguay lacks in mineral resources; virtually all minerals and energy must be imported.

Most Uruguayans trace their roots to Europe; their ancestors migrated in the nineteenth and twentieth centuries. They represent virtually all European nations, but particularly southern Europe. Their language is Spanish, their religion nominally Catholic. Culturally, Uruguay is divided between rural and urban societies; one large city, Montevideo (Uruguay's capital), contains almost 40 percent of the 2.8 million people in the country. The remainder live in rural areas and small cities; only two cities, Paysandu and Salto, which have a population of a little more than 60,000 people. The contrasts between Montevideo and the rest of the country have been of great importance, economically, politically, and culturally.

In Uruguay, as in all of Latin America, there are profound differences in classes and their standards of living, but even the Uruguayan poor have lived relatively well. And today, after several decades of economic stagnation and decline, Uruguay has one of the highest standards of health and nutrition in the world, and its daily consumption of meat protein is one of the highest worldwide.

Uruguay's geographical position as a small nation between two large ones has created a cosmopolitan atmosphere and a tolerance for different cultures. One of the major businesses of the country is tourism, and hundreds of thousands of Argentines and Brazilians flock to the attractive beaches and resorts during the summer months. Because of its size, this small nation could never defend itself against either of its more powerful neighbors. Therefore, Uruguay has needed wit and tolerance in order to survive. At the same time, to avoid being overwhelmed by Argentine or Brazilian culture, Uruguay has developed a strong sense of national pride, which helps sustain its independence and spirit.

The family in Uruguay, as in most Latin cultures, is the center of individual identity and preoccupation, but roles for men and women are less rigid and less stereotyped in Uruguay than in many other Latin American nations. Since Uruguay is one of the three Latin American nations that established a viable system of free public education early in the nineteenth century, the country has a high literacy rate (about 95 percent), and there are relatively equal opportunities for men and women from similar backgrounds to receive higher education. Despite the diverse origins of its people, Uruguay has evolved a distinctive national culture and a sense of national identity ever since its independence from Spain in 1828. Its folk music and legends reflect a romantic identification with the rural, pastoral life; but in growing proportions, its people have chosen to live in the capital city and pursue the assumed benefits of modernization. The relatively harsh rural life has created a sense of individual independence that permeates the entire society.

The rural economy of Uruguay is primarily pastoral, not agricultural, although the land is equally suitable for both purposes. The pastoral economy—based primarily on sheep and cattle—provides important export products; the agricultural economy, on the other hand, is unable to meet the food requirements of the population, and food must be imported. Rural land is primarily used for large sheep and cattle ranches. Landholdings of over 1,235 acres (500 ha) in size contain more than 75 percent of the rural land. Most people who live in rural areas either work on the large ranches tending the animals or live on small plots that yield a subsistence or only slightly better living. Those employed on the ranches have traditionally been paid only partially in salary, receiving some of their income in kind (e.g., animals for fresh meat, usually sheep) and in small plots of land on which to grow their own food. While modern technologies, economic growth, and highly advanced ideologies have influenced the capital city, the rural areas remain traditional, and the differences between the two have widened.

The dominance of powerful, landowning families in rural areas established a patrimonial relationship between the landowners and the workers that has affected most areas of life, including politics. In rural areas, those who control the land have controlled the wealth, and those who have controlled the wealth have controlled political and government institutions. With the strong family ties that persist in rural Uruguay, family dynasties have developed extensive power bases in rural areas.

Because of the need for increased production of food, modern agricultural techniques are slowly replacing less efficient, traditional methods. But the change has been slow. Uruguayan workers and landowners alike retain their traditional commitment to the rural, pastoral life. Worldwide demand for sheep-related products—fresh meat, wool, skins—began to diminish after World War II. Income from exported sales of meat and its by-products declined, but landowners failed to use their land to produce other products. In so small a country and so small an economy, the consequences ultimately bred disaster.

By contrast with the rural areas, the urban area of Montevideo at the peak of its prosperity—during the 1940s—was an affluent, sophisticated, urbane city. Montevideo is a relatively small city whose central area can be easily crossed on foot. It is filled with theaters and sidewalk cafés where people congregate during the late summer afternoon hours. Until they were banned, foreign newspapers, especially from Ar-

Sides of beef hang in a storage room in a refrigerated plant in Melo. Beef is an important export product of Uruguay. (Photo: Inter-American Development Bank.)

gentina, could be purchased as easily from local news-stands as domestic papers.

During the first quarter of the twentieth century, through a combination of state-subsidized and state-owned industries and private enterprise, Uruguay industrialized as far as its small market would permit. Standards of living were relatively high, education was free, and an advanced system of social welfare relieved many of the anxieties of daily life. From about 1945, many residents of Montevideo could retire at age 55 on full salary, but chronic, disastrous inflation over the past two decades has eroded retirement benefits to all but nothing.

Montevideo's factories produce countless consumer goods, generally inefficiently. The levels of demand and the economies of scale are so limited that prices are high. As industrial investments became unprofitable, the government took over plants; however, until the current military regime came into power, political sensitivity to union demands further escalated the costs of production and decreased the levels of productivity.

Because of the small size of Uruguay's economy and its problems of foreign trade, Uruguay's currency has always been at a disadvantage compared with that of stronger, larger economies. For the foreigner with relatively hard currency, investment in the country is a bargain; for an Uruguayan, survival has become increasingly more difficult and more challenging.

Uruguay's economic decay in the post-World War II period, most noticeable in Montevideo, was so incremental that it could almost be ignored. Buildings came to look a bit shabbier, buses broke down more often, scarcities sometimes occurred, and even the

Two gauchos lean on a cattle fence. The rural economy of Uruguay is primarily pastoral, with large cattle and sheep herds. (Photo: Inter-American Development Bank.)

lights went out now and again, but these signs could be ignored, and most Uruguayans chose to do so. However, opposition groups from both ends of the political spectrum began to dramatize the nation's plight.

The twentieth-century model for Uruguayan modernization and economic growth was created in response to the conflicts of the previous century. The nineteenth century was turbulent for Uruguay. At the time of independence, it was unclear whether Uruguay would be a province of Argentina, would be totally absorbed by Brazil, or would remain independent. Independence was largely a result of British intervention. In the nineteenth century, a series of civil wars and conflicts broke out between competing regional armies. The armies, supported by wealthy landowners, eventually merged into two groups that came to be known by the colors they wore; Blancos (Whites) and Colorados (Reds). By the end of the nineteenth century, the Blancos and Colorados had become political parties with paramilitary capabilities. At the same time, the nation had begun to experience considerable economic growth and prosperity through increased exports of fresh meat to Europe, made possible by the invention of refrigerated ships.

The advantages of political stability became increasingly obvious. One of those who was committed to economic development was José Batlle y Ordóñez, publisher of the influential Montevideo newspaper *El Día*, and a member of a wealthy family. Without question Batlle had more impact on his country than any other twentieth-century leader. He served twice as President, 1903–1907 and 1911–1915, and was responsible for ending the violence between the Blancos and the Colorados. Batlle was a skillful politician and an effective leader, and had remarkably innovative ideas.

Batlle saw two basic causes for Uruguay's instability: the political leaders' avaricious greed for power, and the inequality of well-being among the people. To control the former he advocated the elimination of a single national executive and the substitution of a collegial executive. To eliminate the latter, he advocated a vast system of state-supported projects that would provide social welfare, guaranteed retirement, free public education, and many other benefits. These proposals were highly visionary, predating the plans that would later be introduced in Europe and the United States. All Batlle's programs were based on the assumption that economic growth would provide the continuing revenues to the state that would be required to pay for the programs. Many of his reforms, with the notable exception of the collegial executive, were soon instituted.

During the first half of the twentieth century, Montevideo gained an increasing percentage of Uruguay's total population, as economic development created opportunities for jobs, and Europeans, fleeing the dislocations of their turbulent continent, migrated to Montevideo to take advantage of the numerous opportunities it offered. The paradox, of course, was that economic development and political stability were a result of the strong export economy of the rural areas, while the benefits from economic development and most of the Batlle policies accrued to the urban dwellers of Montevideo.

After World War II, the demand for the traditional Uruguayan exports—mutton, lamb, and wool—sharply declined. Supplies to Europe increased from other sources, as renewed European prosperity produced a greater demand for beef than for mutton, and synthetic fibers dramatically reduced the worldwide demand for wool. Uruguay failed to respond to these economic trends. It also had an overextended, inefficiently constituted industrial economy, whose growth was constrained by a very limited market for its products. As a result, Uruguay entered into a prolonged phase of economic stagnation and, ultimately, decline.

The visionary policies of Batlle placed a substantial burden on national expenditures at a time when economic growth could not generate the revenues required to support these expenditures. The ultimate result was a spiraling inflation rate that by the late 1960s exceeded 100 percent annually. The effects of the economic decline were profound. Increases in government spending for social and welfare programs failed to keep pace with inflation, and standards of living slowly declined. There was little incentive for capital investment in business, and economic growth slowed. Strikes became more common, and radical political movements emerged to breed upon the slowly rising discontent.

In 1950, as a result of a constitutional referendum, Uruguayans finally instituted a collegial executive that remained until it was replaced in 1966 by a presidential system. The collegial executive came at a critical time in Uruguayan economic history, and the result was a government that could not provide the strong leadership that was required, further exacerbating an already serious national dilemma.

In the early 1960s a group of radical university students in Montevideo formed a clandestine movement called the Tupamaros. Their aim was to discredit existing political institutions and to work toward a new social order. They robbed banks to finance their activities, they seized theaters and radio stations to propagate their message, and they abducted prominent leaders for both profit and publicity. At first they developed a kind of benign Robin Hood image among Uruguayans, taking from the rich and giving to the poor; but increasingly their actions became more violent and the government's response to them equally more violent, until by the early 1970s there was a virtual state of civil war.

The Uruguayan military, historically few in number, professional in training, and nonpolitical in orientation, became increasingly concerned about national security. Slowly and incrementally the military began to pressure the civilian government into stronger and stronger responses to the Tupamaros. While many terrorists were apprehended, questioned, and tortured, many more went undetected, and many who had been picked up by the police or the military escaped from custody.

In mid-1975, the military formally removed the constitutionally elected President, and took power. The act was almost unprecedented for Uruguay. But in effect, the coup changed little. The military was already controlling the decisions of the constitutional government; it was in charge of pursuing the Tupamaros; and the civilian institutions were broadly discredited in the public eye for their failure to solve the economic problems of the country and for not controlling a relatively few urban guerrillas. The military coup in Uruguay followed by less than 2 years the military coup in Chile, South America's other long-standing democracy.

Uruguay never reached the level of modernization achieved by the United States or most of Europe; given its small size and lack of resources, it might never do so. However, by third world standards, it attained a remarkable level of economic development and political stability, and a reasonable level of social equality. Yet it went through an extended period of economic and political decay, producing ultimately a military seizure of power and the elimination of individual freedoms.

Torrents of water cascade over the floodgates of the recently completed Salto Grande Hydroelectric Dam on the Rio Uruguay. (Photo: Inter-American Development Bank.)

The Uruguayan model of modernization was based on an unreliable assumption of continuing economic growth. The failure to adjust the rural economy to the exigencies of worldwide market demand and technology produced a long-term pattern of decline. Uruguay failed to balance the economic necessities of the rural areas—the basis of its critical export economy—with the political leverage of its urban area.

The Uruguayan experience also underscores the vulnerability of urban areas to organized terrorism and the difficulty of maintaining democratic procedures and processes in a context of terrorist violence. Finally, it suggests the possibility that well-estab-

lished commitments to democratic processes can become a low priority in an atmosphere of terrorist violence.

The military government has achieved at least partial success in reversing the trend of economic decay, but at a very high price—the loss of individual freedom and democratic institutions and growing economic inequality. If the country is to continue to enjoy economic development, the cost will probably remain high. The visionary Batlle experiment is over, but its failure will continue to reverberate throughout the modern democratic world.

Ronald H. McDonald

Venezuela
(Republic of Venezuela)

Area: 352,143 sq mi (912,050 sq km)
Population: 13.9 million
  Density: 39 per sq mi. (15 per sq km)
  Growth rate: 3.4% (1970–1977)
Percent of population under 14 years of age: 44% (1975)
Infant deaths per 1,000 live births: 46 (1975)
Life expectancy at birth: 66.4 years (1975)
Leading causes of death: not available
Ethnic composition: mestizo, Indian
Languages: Spanish
Literacy: 80% school-age Venezuelans
Religions: Catholic
Percent population urban: 80%
Percent population rural: 20%
Gross national product: $40.7 billion
  Per capita GNP: $2,910
  Per capita GNP growth rate: 3.2% (1970–1977)
Inflation rate: 10% (1977)

Lying on the northern coast of the South American continental landmass, Venezuela is bountifully endowed with natural resources. Rich and varied mineral deposits lie beneath its soil and waters; a wide range of agricultural products are grown on its fertile soil. Of foremost importance, however, is its petroleum, which for a half century has been the primary source of strength for the economy and has reshaped Venezuelan life, society, and politics. The successes and failures of development and the prospects for the future have been inextricably linked to the production of oil and the use of its earnings.

Venezuela's first major oil strike came near Lake Maracaibo on the western coast in 1922. In the intervening years Venezuela dramatically changed from a poor, pastoral country that exported and imported very little to the richest country of South America. Venezuela enjoys the highest per capita income and the highest standard of living in South America; its high level of affluence has resulted in the characteristic problems of consumerism. At the same time, a

wide gap separates the impoverished citizens from the expanding middle class and from the wealthy.

Approximately the size of Texas and Oklahoma with a territory of 352,143 square miles (912,050 sq km), Venezuela is the seventh largest country of Latin America. While its boundaries resemble an inverted triangle, the rapidly growing population of some 13 million are located predominantly along the 2,000 miles (3,220 km) of Caribbean coast and spread toward the southwest in the Andean mountain range. The land is bisected from west to east by the Orinoco River and its tributaries, which together drain four-fifths of the country and comprise the second largest river system on the continent. Navigable for some 700 miles (1,125 km), it is approximately 1,700 miles (2,735 km) in length and at the widest point is 13.5 miles (22 km).

Bordered by Guyana to the east, Colombia to the west, and Brazil to the south, Venezuela is divided geographically into four major regions: the coastal zone; the Andean chain; the central plains extending south to the Orinoco; and the Guyana highlands beyond the river, which make up over half the country. The highlands are sparsely inhabited and largely unexplored; thus the potential of natural resources is little known. Reserves of oil are found especially in the Maracaibo region and the eastern plains, which also contain extensive deposits of iron ore, bauxite, manganese, and copper. The major city of the region, Ciudad Guayana (Santo Tomé de Guayana), has become the center for heavy industrial growth in the country, enjoying major hydroelectric resources along with the presence of mineral wealth.

The population of Venezuela is predominantly mestizo; more than two-thirds of the people are racially mixed. The Indian strain is somewhat more prevalent in the Andes, and the African strain in the coastal regions, but ethnic heterogeneity is prevalent throughout the country. Only a very few relatively primitive and isolated Amazonian Indians live far in the interior. While racial discrimination is not unknown, it is not a social factor of major importance. Color of skin is not a serious bar to mobility in business, commerce, or politics. Substantial immigration since World War II has contributed further to the democratization of Venezuelan society. Spanish is the common language and Catholicism the predominant religion.

Dominant features in recent years have been the slowing but still rapid population growth rate, the youth of the population, and the high level of urbanization. Over 50 percent of all Venezuelans are 18 years of age or younger. Moreover, although in 1950 the population was 70 percent rural, today nearly 80 percent of all Venezuelans are urban. As a result, the population of the metropolitan zone of Caracas, the national capital, is nearing 3 million. Maracaibo has passed the 1 million mark and nearly a dozen other cities have populations of at least 100,000. The oil-based economy has produced a highly mobile population, always moving from rural areas to the cities. This has meant a heavy burden on municipal and national governments to provide basic services and facilities for meeting the daily needs of the urban masses.

The rapid rate of urbanization has brought a significant expansion in the middle sectors of society. Business, commerce, government employment, and the service sectors have nourished the middle class. At the same time, Caracas and the other urban centers are dotted by slum areas known as barrios. About one-third of the city dwellers live in shacks in conditions of poverty and hardship. Venezuelan development, despite the genuine efforts of the past 20 years, has not yet succeeded in redistributing income in order to meet the needs of these citizens.

Much of the individual wealth in the country has been stimulated by the impact of the oil-based economy. Unlike many Latin American countries, Venezuela has a nouveau riche class. Most of the economically influential families and business empires have acquired their wealth within the last half century. There are relatively few members of the traditional socioeconomic aristocracy, which traces its prestige and prominence to colonial times and to the early Spanish colonizers. In contemporary Venezuela there are many rags-to-riches stories, and opportunities still abound in today's vigorous and thriving economy.

Social and class relationships are more traditional in rural areas. Classic problems of the *latifundia*—the large landholdings—still exist. In the last 20 years, an agrarian reform program has extensively redistributed the ownership of land, creating a large mass of small farmers with their own property. Unfortunately, Venezuela has been less successful in providing the technical aid, irrigation, rural transport, and bank loans necessary to make agriculture productive. Despite massive infusions of money from the central government, agriculture remains a chronically depressed sector of the economy. Most of the advances have come from large, mechanized agro-industrial enterprises; the government continues to import basic commodities that could readily be produced inside Venezuela.

The wealth of the petroleum era, while falling far short of meeting many urban and rural development needs, has, nonetheless, produced progress in health and education. While medical facilities still leave much to be desired, the availability of health care and services is superior to that in much of Latin America. Many tropical diseases have been virtually eliminated, including malaria. Major problems today revolve about the crowded urban slums, where malnutrition, dietary imbalances, and a shortage of hospital facilities remain serious problems. Educational services have grown at a rapid rate, and literacy for school-age Venezuelans is about 80 percent. The dropout rate is still high, although the increase in university enrollments has overtaxed available resources. At the same time, the government consistently provides more funds for education than for any other sector, including the military.

Modern Venezuela is dramatically different from the region discovered in 1498 on Columbus's third voyage. Predominantly rural and agricultural through the 300 years of Spanish colonial rule, it was long a colonial backwater. With the outbreak of wars of independence early in the nineteenth century, Venezuela's social order was near collapse. The conflict involved not only native-born *criollos* and Spanish *peninsulares*, but also slaves and mixed-bloods (*par-*

Slums and squatter settlements cling to the hills outside Caracas. Substandard housing and inadequate services in the cities is the result of rapid urbanization. (Photo: United Nations/M.Guthrie.)

dos). The defeat of Spanish forces led to the establishment of the Gran Colombian federation (Venezuela, Colombia, and Ecuador) by the liberator Simón Bolívar, but in 1830, the year of his death, the three countries went their separate ways.

During the 100 years that followed, the country lacked effective national government. Caracas was little more than one of several provincial market centers. There were 39 major uprisings and many more minor revolts. A decline in cacao production had been followed by a boom in coffee production in the 1880s. By the twentieth century, however, Venezuela remained a poor and backward country characterized politically by violence, regionalism, and instability. This changed when General Juan Vicente Gómez took power in 1908. A shrewd and ruthless dictator, he dominated the country until his death in 1935.

Although arbitrary and repressive, the so-called Tyrant of the Andes also built the foundations of the modern state. He created Venezuela's first effective central government, developed a bureaucratic structure, integrated the domestic market, and capitalized on the emergence of oil wealth. Foreign investment was encouraged, international corporations were attracted to Venezuela, and commercial activities shifted from domestic agriculture to world trade. Although political opposition was suppressed, there developed a group of young democratically oriented political leaders—known as the Generation of '28—who later initiated democratic processes and mass-based parties. Perhaps the most prominent was Romulo Be-

A family purchases meat in a rural market. Because of inadequate domestic production, Venezuela imports many basic foods that are sold at subsidized prices. (Photo: United Nations/J. Frank.)

tancourt, who in 1941 founded Democratic Action (AD), Venezuela's first modern political movement.

The party first came to power in 1945, and the next 3 years marked a political watershed. In Venezuela's first experience with a democratic, electoral, and party-based government, under the leadership of Betancourt, far-reaching reforms were introduced into major sectors of the economy and society. After the failure of these reforms, however, the military seized power and exiled civilian political leaders. A full decade of dictatorial repression and corruption followed, the last 8 years under the leadership of General Marcos Pérez Jiménez.

Government revenue more than doubled as the result of booming oil production, but social welfare and human needs were ignored in the rush for massive public works. Economic mismanagement, political persecution, and unparalleled graft eventually ended with a popular uprising in January 1958.

The overthrow of the military dictatorship introduced the democratic political system which has continued to the present. Leaders of the major parties agreed to the constant consultation and cooperation necessary for building effective political democracy. Romulo Betancourt won election to a 5-year term in December 1958. Harassed by right-wing military revolts and by a major insurrectional campaign by pro-Cuban revolutionaries, he survived an assassination attempt and completed his term in office.

From 1959 to the present, leadership has been in the hands of either Democratic Action (AD) or the Christian Socialist Party (COPEI), which was founded by Rafael Caldera. Although there are a number of small parties, only those representing the left are vigorously active. The several Marxist parties together comprise less than 20 percent of the electorate, and national policy remains in the hands of the two major movements.

Future development problems are well illustrated by the experience of the Pérez administration (1974–1979). Carlos Andrés Pérez took office when the price of petroleum was over $14 per barrel, 4 times higher than 1 year earlier, and followed his predecessors in using oil profits to diversify the economy, create an industrial base, and reverse agricultural stagnation. The government undertook a massive program designed to create permanent foundations for a modern industrialized society. Revenues increased by 150 percent between 1973 and 1974 alone, providing the funds for grandiose government investments. The nation's influence within the Organization of Petroleum Exporting Countries (OPEC) has always been substantial, given the innovative role it played in founding that organization and its long years of pioneering in the industry.

The bulk of public investment was made in industry, especially steel, petrochemicals, aluminum, and electricity. High priority was also assigned to an expanded manufacturing sector. Health, education, and social needs were similarly financed by the post-1974 oil bonanza. A new 5-year plan for balanced development was overly optimistic, calling for faster rates of growth than were possible. In addition, a slackening of oil income by late 1976 reduced the financial base available to the government. Unprecedented domestic demand for oil added to the difficulties. At the same time, the effective work of the new state-operated Petróleos de Venezuela, created by the historic 1976 nationalization of oil, enabled the country to stretch out its existing reserves. These included huge deposits of heavy, viscous oil lying along the Orinoco.

The agricultural sector has been most resistant to government stimulus. Pérez promised to improve the situation, and some $700 million was invested in 1975 and 1976 to increase productivity and reduce imports. Yet by the close of Pérez's term the problems of agriculture remained unresolved. Venezuela still imported many basic foodstuffs at subsidized prices. Overall, Pérez's economic record was mixed. Inefficiency, waste, and an increasing level of corruption were apparent. Popular expectations had been unrealistically high, and disappointment over the government record was a major factor in the loss of power to the Christian Socialists (COPEI) in 1978. It remains to be seen whether the current administration of Luis Herrera Campins (1979–1984) will be more successful in meeting the socioeconomic challenges of development.

With its growing economic power, Venezuela played an increasingly important role in international affairs during the 1970s. Having the most dynamic and vigorously democratic system in the area also provided Venezuela with prestige and influence, especially in light of the many military regimes which existed in the Americas. Rafael Caldera had been among the most prominent leaders in the southern hemisphere, with Venezuela assuming a position of leadership. This was continued and extended under Pérez. He traveled widely throughout Latin America and was a major spokesman for the third world. With the Mexican President he helped to found the Latin American Economic System (SELA) as a focus for regional economic development policies.

Pérez's administration also made wide use of petrodollars in foreign affairs. Major contributions were extended to regional and international developmental agencies. Loans and assistance were also extended to many countries, especially in Central America and the Caribbean. Although a few countries criticized Venezuelan imperialism, the Pérez government continued to emphasize its presence in hemispheric politics. At the same time, long-standing border disputes with Colombia and Guyana were not settled, and Venezuela's border with Brazil was not satisfactorily defined. By the close of the decade, there was widespread agreement that Venezuela should reduce its activities abroad and channel its major efforts toward domestic problems.

Venezuela still has many development obstacles to overcome. Even with efficient and energetic leadership, its programs to diversify the economy and build an industrial society cannot be achieved swiftly. Agricultural problems continue to persist despite the best efforts of national leaders. Relations with the United States are cordial, and the energy crisis assures the importance of Venezuela to Washington. Nonetheless, Venezuelan policy must place its highest priority on the resolution of internal problems. The commitment of the people and their political leadership to democratic government is clear, but the latter must provide more lasting solutions to the inequities of wealth and opportunity.

The domination of COPEI and AD means that the party elites must respond effectively if the democratic system is to survive. After nearly a quarter century of progress, this system still needs to provide more balanced economic opportunities with social justice for all Venezuelans. Until it does so, long-range prospects are uncertain. At the least, the availability of natural resources plus talented political leadership provides Venezuela with an opportunity that is far superior to the opportunities of the vast majority of today's developing nations.

John Martz

Name Index

Subject Index

Abaca exports from Philippines, 265
Abadan, Iran, 146
Aberdare Mountains, Kenya, 45
Abidjan, Ivory Coast, 41
Abiya, Nigeria, 79
Ablode (emancipation) in Togo, 107
Abomey, Benin, 9–10
Aborigines in Malaysia, 254
Acapulco, Mexico, 315
Accra, Ghana, 33
Aché-Guayaki people in Paraguay, 357
Aconcagua, Mount, Argentina, 333
Action Party in Nigeria, 79
Adamawa Plateau, Cameroon 15
Addis Ababa, Ethiopia, 30
Aden (South Yemen), 184–187
Afghanistan, 193–195
African Development Bank, 40, 50
African Financial Community, 19, 27
African and Malagasy Union (UAM), 21, 71
African National Council, 127
African Riviera, Ivory Coast, 4
African Socialist Movement, 27
Agency for International Development, 50
Aghlabite dynasty in Tunisia, 175
Agriculture:
  in Afghanistan, 194–195
  agrarian reform, 35, 363
  agribusiness, 42, 142, 301, 369
  aid for, 255
  in Angola, 6
  in Argentina, 334
  in Bangladesh, 196–198
  in Benin, 9
  in Bhutan, 200
  in Bolivia, 340
  in Brazil, 342
  in Cameroon, 16
  in China, 227–228
  collectivized, 75, 243
  in Colombia, 350–351
  communal, 125, 261
  in Congo, 27
  cooperative, 172, 250
  credits, 236
  in Cuba, 292
  development of, 50–51, 340, 365
  diversification of, 42, 292
  in El Salvador, 298
  exports, 84
  in Ghana, 34
  in Guatemala, 301
  in Honduras, 307–308
  in India, 203
  in Indonesia, 233–236
  industrialization, 42, 243, 369
  in Iran, 142–143

Agriculture (*Cont.*):
  in Ivory Coast, 41–42, 44
  in Korea, North, 243
  labor, 254
  in Laos, 250
  in Lesotho, 50–51
  in Liberia, 53
  in Madagascar, 56
  in Malaysia, 254–255
  in Mali, 65
  mechanization, 100, 143, 257, 342
  methods, 351, 358, 360
  in Mexico, 316
  modernization of, 81, 197–198, 210, 228, 235–236, 316
  in Mongolia, 257
  in Mozambique, 73, 75
  in Nepal, 207–208
  in Nigeria, 81
  in Pakistan, 210, 212
  in Papua New Guinea, 260–261
  in Paraguay, 358, 360
  in Peru, 363
  in Rwanda, 84
  shifting, 200
  in Sierra Leone, 92–93
  slash-and-burn, 56, 73, 119, 301, 307, 358
  in Somalia, 95
  in Sri Lanka, 214–215
  stagnation of, 369–371
  in Sudan, 100
  in Syria, 171–172
  in Togo, 106
  in Trinidad and Tobago, 324–325
  in Turkey, 178–179
  in Uruguay, 365
  in Venezuela, 369–371
  in Yemen, South, 185
  in Zaire, 116–117
  in Zambia, 119–120
  in Zimbabwe, 125
  (*See also* Animal husbandry; Livestock; Tenant farmers; *specific crops and livestock*)
Aid (*see specific agencies and countries*)
Aid-to-Pakistan consortium, 210
Air service:
  in Bhutan, 200
  in Lesotho, 52
  in Pakistan, 212
  in Trinidad and Tobago, 326
Akan people in Ghana, 33
Akim people in Ghana, 33
Akosombo Dam, Ghana, 33
Akuta mine in Niger, 77
Akwapim people in Ghana, 33
Akyem people in Ghana, 33
Alawi, Syria, 171, 173–174

Alawite dynasty in Morocco, 164
Alcoholism in Zambia, 121
Aleppo, Syria, 170, 172–173
Alexandrite deposits in Sri Lanka, 214
Alfalfa farming:
  in Bolivia, 337
  in Mexico, 314
Algeria, 133–136, 164
Algerian War, 24
Algiers, Algeria, 133
All People's Congress in Sierra Leone, 94
Alpacas:
  in Bolivia, 338
  in Peru, 360
Altiplano, Bolivia, 337
Aluminum companies in Jamaica, 312
Aluminum industry:
  in Cameroon, 16–17
  in Guinea, 38
  in Taiwan, 273
  in Venezuela, 370
  (*See also* Bauxite production)
Amazon River system:
  in Brazil, 341–343
  in Ecuador, 353
  in Peru, 360
American Colonization Society, Liberia, 55
American Gulf Oil Corporation, Kuwait, 154
American Popular Revolutionary Alliance, Peru, 364
American residents:
  in Costa Rica, 288
  in Hong Kong, 230
  in Philippines, 266
Amerinds in Dominican Republic, 294
Amhara people in Ethiopia, 30–31
Amharic language, Ethiopia, 31
Amman, Jordan, 151
Amu Darya River, Afghanistan, 193
Anaconda Copper Company in Chile, 348
Anatolia, Syria, 170
Anatolian Plain, Turkey, 178
Ancestor worship:
  in China, 226
  in Taiwan, 273
Andes Mountains:
  in Argentina, 333
  in Bolivia, 337
  in Chile, 346
  in Colombia, 349
  in Ecuador, 353
  in Peru, 360
  in Venezuela, 368
Anécho, Togo, 107

Angkor Empire in Kampuchea, 239
Anglican Church in Jamaica, 311
Anglo-Afghan wars, 195
Anglo-Ethiopian Treaty of 1948, 97
Angola, 5–8
Angolan National Liberation Front, 5–6
Angolan Popular Liberation Movement, 5–6, 8
Animal hide exports from Colombia, 352
Animal husbandry:
  in Nepal, 206
  in Somalia, 95–96
  in Sudan, 97
  in Syria, 171
  in Yemen, South, 185
  (*See also* Cattle; Livestock)
Animism:
  in Angola, 5
  in Burma, 222
  in Cameroon, 16
  in Haiti, 303
  in India, 203
  in Ivory Coast, 41
  in Kampuchea, 239
  in Laos, 249
  in Mozambique, 72–73
  in Philippines, 264
  in Sierra Leone, 91
  in Sudan, 99
  in Thailand, 277
  in Togo, 106
  in Upper Volta, 113
  in Zaire, 116
  in Zambia, 119
Ankara, Turkey, 178–179
Ankole kingdom in Uganda, 111
Annam Cordillera, 247, 279
Annapurna, Nepal, 206
Ansar in Sudan, 99–100
Ansongo, Mali, 65
Antananarivo, Madagascar, 57
Antigua, Guatemala, 302
Antimony mining in Honduras, 308
Anyanya Rebellion in Chad, 25
Aouzou strip, Chad, 22
Aqaba, Jordan, 152
Arab Bank for African Development in Guinea, 40
Arab Fund for Economic and Social Development in Sudan, 100
Arab League:
  in Mauritania, 71
  Pact of 1945, 159
  in Sudan, 99
  in Tunisia, 177
Arable land:
  in Bhutan, 200
  in China, 224
  in Pakistan, 209

375

Index